DATE DUE

OCT 1 04			

DEMCO 38-296

NOTABLE WOMEN
IN WORLD HISTORY

NOTABLE WOMEN IN WORLD HISTORY

A Guide to Recommended Biographies and Autobiographies

LYNDA G. ADAMSON

GREENWOOD PRESS

Westport, Connecticut • London

Library of Congress Cataloging-in-Publication Data

Adamson, Lynda G.
    Notable women in world history : a guide to recommended
biographies and autobiographies / Lynda G. Adamson.
        p.   cm.
    Includes bibliographical references and index.
    ISBN 0–313–29818–1 (alk. paper)
    1. Women—Biography—Bibliography.   2. Autobiography—Women
authors—Bibliography.   3. Diaries—Women authors—Bibliography.
4. Women—Correspondence—Bibliography.   I. Title.
Z7963.B6A28   1998
[CT3230]
016.92072—dc21   97–33136

British Library Cataloguing in Publication Data is available.

Library of Congress Catalog Card Number: 97–33136
ISBN: 0–313–29818–1

First published in 1998

Greenwood Press, 88 Post Road West, Westport, CT 06881
An imprint of Greenwood Publishing Group, Inc.

Printed in the United States of America

The paper used in this book complies with the
Permanent Paper Standard issued by the National
Information Standards Organization (Z39.48–1984).

10 9 8 7 6 5 4 3 2 1

For Frank, Frank III, and Gregory

CONTENTS

ACKNOWLEDGMENTS

Several people deserve credit for helping this idea become a reality. Barbara Rader at Greenwood Publishing Group has offered excellent suggestions and proffered understanding of manuscript delay, and Wendi Schnaufer has carefully led me through production. The interlibrary loan facilitator at my college, Veronica Coleman, has been extremely patient and polite while finding biographies mysteriously missing from Library of Congress shelves. Lastly, my husband, with his editing skills, clarifying questions, and understanding of my late hours at the computer, has supported my completion of this project. Almost but not quite an antithesis of male stereotype, he has tempered some of my rage toward other males during this project for their treatment of women throughout history by having my dinner waiting on the table.

Lynda G. Adamson

INTRODUCTION

> The slightest living thing answers a deeper need than all the works
> of man because it is *transitory*. It has an evanescence of life, or
> growth, or change: it passes, as we do, from one stage to the an-
> other, from darkness to darkness, into a distance where we, too,
> vanish out of sight.
>
> —Freya Stark
> *Perseus in the Wind*

> Thus when I come to shape here at this table between my hands the
> story of my life and set it before you as a complete thing, I have to
> recall things gone far, gone deep, sunk into this life or that and be-
> come part of it; dreams, too, things surrounding me, and the in-
> mates, those old half-articulate ghosts who keep up their hauntings
> by day and night . . . shadows of people one might have been; un-
> born selves.
>
> —Virginia Woolf
> *The Waves*

Carolyn G. Heilbrun in *Writing a Woman's Life* (Norton, 1988) defines how a woman may share her life:

The woman herself may tell it, in what she chooses to call an autobiography; she may tell it in what she chooses to call fiction; a biographer, woman or man, may write the woman's life in what is called a biography; or the woman may write her own life in ad-vance of living it, unconsciously and without recognizing or naming the process. (11)

A disturbing conclusion to Heilbrun's assertion is that many women's lives have not been written at all. Because they have not, many very worthy women will not find exposure within these pages. One of the definitions in the *Oxford English Dictionary* of "notable" is a woman efficient or capable in performance of housewifely duties, who manages and bustles with "no-ta-ble-ness." The women in this work have refused to limit themselves to their homes and this denotation of a female "notable." They have distinguished themselves through noteworthy achievements in their local, often global, communities. Included here are entries on five hundred international women. Each features a brief biography and an annotated list of no more than five biographies, autobiographies, letter collections, or journals concerning their lives. The appendixes list the women according to year of birth; country where born; and acquired title, occupation, or main areas of interest. The work, aimed at high school and college students, will also serve as a general reference for interested adults.

When Barbara Rader at Greenwood suggested this book of notable international women, I thought that research for it would be a simple process. All I had to do was identify five hundred worthy women from around the world who had lived at any time in history and about whom at least five biographies and autobiographies had been published in English since 1970. I thought that the difficult part would be choosing which five works to include. I was wrong.

What I found from a variety of sources such as *The Larousse Biographical Dictionary*, *Webster's New Biographical Dictionary*, and Olsen's *Chronology of Women's History* (Greenwood, 1994) was a list of over one thousand international women who have made a noteworthy achievement. After searching the Library of Congress catalog, I found that approximately 250 women on my list had three or more biographical works available in English. Another 150 had two works available. Of the other six hundred, some had only one biography or autobiography in translation, and the rest had none. My research rapidly changed from which five works to annotate to deciding which of the women with only one source should be included, and although my measures evolved during the research process, I identified several main criteria. The four main criteria for inclusion in this collection are that a woman must have been born outside the United States, that she must have made a noteworthy achievement, that a full-length biography be available about her life published since 1970, and that the biography be listed in the Library of Congress catalog. A fifth criterion for a twentieth-century woman writing in English is that she must have won at least one award.

I have made several exceptions to my criteria. Maria Goeppert-Mayer, Rita Levi-Montalcini, and Nelly Sachs have all won Nobel Prizes but have no full biographies in English. A collective biography features Goeppert-Mayer and Levi-Montalcini, with only Levi-Montalcini having written an autobiography. Sachs has a collection of published correspondence and a lecture about her and her co-Nobel winner. I have also included several women for whom only autobiographies are available. When no biography exists in English about a notable woman who was born outside the United States and made a noteworthy achievement; and she has written an autobiography in her native language now available in translation, I have included her. Isabel Allende, Violeta Chamorro, Melina Mercouri, Halide Edib Adivar, Mary Seacole, Luisa Gonzáles, Nidia Díaz, and Huda Sha'rawi constitute this group.

The heading of each entry contains the woman's name, dates of birth and death, field of endeavor, and place of birth. The short biographical sketch of each woman discusses her general achievement, parental heritage, education, occupation or interests, and recognition or specific awards won. I use the family, married name, or pseudonym by which each woman was known because using the given name implies an informality of tone and lack of respect unacceptable in contemporary educated society. Since current psychological and physiological studies show that the first three years of life are the most important in forming the adult, I have included each woman's father's name and known employment, since his economic or social status indicates the circumstance in which she was raised. If marriage aided a woman's achievements, I have mentioned it. In many cases, marriage, especially an arranged one, was no more than financial support. Finally, I have summarized some of her accomplishments and awards or recognition that she received. Cross-references in entries to other subjects in the guide appear in bold print.

The appendixes list each woman according to date of birth, country of birth, and occupation or area of interest. Some women have several major areas of interest, and their names appear in each category. Because women who have been activists often exhibited concerns in several different areas, I have grouped them into one category. A political activist might have also been an advocate of woman suffrage or a champion of workers. Women who wrote often published in a variety of genres, including novels, short stories, poetry, and essay. They all appear in the category for writers.

In the annotated bibliography, I have broadened the traditional concept of biography. I include not only authentic biography (researched and documented), fictional biography (invented dialogue), and autobiography as a crafted work with a beginning, middle, and end but also correspondence, journals, and interviews as autobiographical, primary sources that biographers use, because they offer the immediacy of an autobiography, although rarely shaped into a cohesive whole. Notable female writers often have biographical information commingled with critical analyses of their work, some, as Heilburn says, writing their lives as fiction or in advance of living it. For this reason, I have included critical analyses when they are one of the few sources of biographical background. Notable female artists often are subjects of exhibition catalogs that focus on biography but contain photographs and analyses of their work rather than traditional biographies. I have included those works as well. An international woman with only one biography in English in no way indicates that her status is lower than one with five. Women from non–English-speaking countries may have several biographies in their native language, but only one in English translation. No biographies or autobiographies in translation eliminated some accomplished women. I selected for inclusion carefully researched biographies or works written by persons who knew their subjects well. With more than five acceptable choices available, I selected the most stylistically aesthetic works. Generally, those biographies published most recently satisfied all the criteria.

Some of the sources are reprints published after 1970 but originally written before. I have also included a few appropriate works written earlier, if later sources are also available. All works are appropriate for the general reader unless otherwise noted in the annotation. Scholarly or critical biographies are usually more abstract than popular biographies, and therefore, require additional attention. If the biographies have won literary prizes, I have named the prize(s) at the end of the annotation.

During my reading, I have made some conclusions, none of which will surprise feminist scholars. Through the centuries, women have been limited as to how they can achieve success. Many have been writers of fiction and nonfiction because most could write in privacy without permission from males controlling their lives. Some have been rulers because no male survived to keep the family in command. Several were the wives or mistresses of a monarch or statesman, "the power behind the throne," making decisions that affected many thousands of people. Some have been actors, activists, saints, or musicians. A few such as Hatshepsut and Cleopatra usurped their positions from younger or weaker men. Very few have been scientists or physicians because males long denied them access to necessary education and research facilities. Women from other cultures may have had different criteria for success, but they have generally had choices similar to those of Western women. However, too few biographies of women in other cultures have been written, much less translated.

I cannot assume, because historians refer to a woman as "courtesan," that she is unworthy of inclusion in this collection, since the person who originally described her would have almost certainly been a male who propagated the biases of his sex, of his culture, and of his times. I have been especially dubious of biographies written by men about women in an earlier century. Many of them are condescending toward their subjects and written in a conversational style that implies gossip rather than fact. They use the subject's first name and sometimes refuse to recognize real individual achievements. A loose definition of "courtesan" could include notable women who have compromised themselves to others in small ways so that they could proceed less encumbered in their pursuits.

Too few biographies about noteworthy international women exist in English. All women, as Heilbrun says, "have historically been deprived of the narratives, texts, plots, or examples with which to assume power over their lives." Women who have achieved "notableness" in the modern sense have had to counter expectations of society and culture, often with males (and other females) maligning them and refusing to see previous wrongs or to accept change. But what these women have achieved has changed the world, and they deserve much more recognition than they have so far received. Women appear in this book because someone has appreciated their worth and taken time to either translate or write about their lives. Many other noteworthy women deserve that attention as well. Readers wondering about the exclusion of a particular woman from these pages should look for biographies about her, find that none exist in English, and then amend the omission by either translating an existing biography or researching her life and writing afresh in English. If enough researchers endeavor in these fertile fields, the next collection of international women will have to expand to a thousand.

ABAKANOWICZ, MAGDALENA (1930–)
Sculptor   Poland

An artist working most of her life behind the Iron Curtain in Poland, Magdalena Abakanowicz pioneered the use of woven fabrics in sculptures. Born into an aristocratic Polish family on June 20, 1930, her life changed when the Germans arrived in 1939 and drove her family from their home. After attending school in Gdansk, she pretended her father was a clerk instead of an aristocrat to gain admission to the university in Warsaw. She supported herself by giving blood, cleaning streets, working construction, and coaching sports. At twenty, she changed her name from Marta to Magdalena, toured Italy with the Artists' Union, and met other artists and intellectuals. The government censored her work, but she entered the first Biennale Internationale de la Tapisserie in Lausanne, Switzerland, in 1962. She won awards at the Bienal de São Paulo in Brazil in 1965 and in Paris and was the first Polish woman to have her own Paris exhibit. Her subjects have included brains, human backs, and eggs. Among the surfaces she now uses, in addition to fabric, are bronze, stone, and wood.

BIBLIOGRAPHY
Abakanowicz, Magdalena. *Magdalena Abakanowicz: Museum of Contemporary Art, Chicago*. New York: Abbeville, 1982. Paper, 0-89659-323-1, 188p. In this autobiographical sketch, Abakanowicz shares incidents about her life with brief critical essays about her work, with photographs following.

Rose, Barbara. *Magdalena Abakanowicz*. New York: Harry N. Abrams, 1994. 0-8109-1947-8, 224p. Rose catalogs Abakanowicz's difficulties as an artist in a socialist country trying to obtain materials and getting the appropriate acknowledgment. The readable text has accompanying photographs.

ADAMSON, JOY (1910–1980)
Writer, Naturalist, and Artist   Austria

Joy Adamson's experiment with Elsa, a lion from the wild, showed that animals, after being tamed, can return to the wild and mate. She was born Friederike Victoria Gessner in Troppau, Silesia, on January 20, 1910; her father had wanted a son, so he called her "Fritz" and encouraged her to wear boy's clothes. Trying to get attention from her unhappy parents, she became an accomplished pianist and artist. After her mother served Adamson's pet rabbit in a stew, and Adamson killed a buck for sport, she decided never to kill another defenseless animal. Adamson married three times, moving to Kenya after the first marriage, staying there, and marrying George Adamson last. Adamson painted Kenyan wildflowers, and after Elsa returned to introduce her litter of cubs to Adamson and her husband, Adamson wrote several books about her naturalist experiments, including *Born Free* and *The Story of Elsa*. Her paintings have been exhibited in the National Museum and Nairobi's State House.

BIBLIOGRAPHY
Adamson, Joy. *The Searching Spirit: An Autobiography*. New York: Harcourt Brace Jovanovich, 1979. 0-15-179919-9, 244p. Unlike her biographers, Adamson recalls her early life in Austria as happy but mentions only her grandparents, and she focuses on later pleasant memories as well.

Cass, Caroline. *Joy Adamson: Behind the Mask*. London: Weidenfeld and Nicolson, 1992. 0-2978-1141-X, 236p. In her psychological study appropriate for young adults, Cass thinks that Adamson's failed marriages mirrored her need for parental approval, but George Adamson was the only male who could match her energy.

House, Adrian. *The Great Safari: The Lives of George and Joy Adamson*. New York: William Morrow, 1993. 0-688-10141-0, 465p. House, Adamson's editor, used the pocket diaries that Joy kept from 1945 to 1975 as his sources for his readable and balanced biography. House thinks that Adamson's informally diagnosed histrionic personality disorder may have been the result of the childhood traumas in her family.

ADIVAR, HALIDE EDIB (1883–1964)
Writer, Activist, and Politician   Turkey

Halide Edib Adivar, also called Halide Salih, was a novelist as well as an important force in the emancipation of Turkish women. From a wealthy family, she was educated privately and at the American College for Girls in Istanbul. She divorced her first husband when he decided to take a second wife. She believed in educational opportunities for women and advocated public lectures that men and women could attend together. An ardent patriot, she and her second husband participated in the Turkish War of Liberation in Anatolia. After traveling extensively throughout Europe, India, and the United States before World War II, she became professor of English literature at Istanbul University and a member of Parliament. Her most famous novels are *Handan* (Family) and *Atesten gömlek* (The Daughter of Smyrna).

BIBLIOGRAPHY
Adivar, Halide Edib. *The Turkish Ordeal: Being the Further Memoirs of Halide Edib*. 1928. Westport, CT: Hyperion Press, 1981. 0-8305-0057-X, 407p.

Adivar describes her experiences as a militant participant in Turkey's Nationalist movement from 1918 through 1922.

AGUILAR, GRACE (1816–1847)
Writer   England

Grace Aguilar's writing profoundly affected Jewish women with its ability to help them understand their role in contemporary Judaism. The daughter of Spanish-Jewish parents, she was born in London on June 2, 1816, and educated at home. When she was twelve, her family moved to Devon. She began writing while still a child, publishing her first poems, *Magic Wreath*, in 1835. She was ill throughout her life, and writing was a suitable profession for her. After her father died, she wrote *The Spirit of Judaism* (1842), in which she attacked the formality of contemporary Jewish beliefs. She followed it with *The Jewish Faith* (1845) and *Women in Israel*. She also wrote sentimental novels with domestic settings which her mother published after her death at thirty-one.

BIBLIOGRAPHY
Galchinsky, Michael. *The Origin of the Modern Jewish Woman Writer Romance and Reform in Victorian England*. Detroit: Wayne State University Press, 1996. 0-8143-2613-7, 275p. Galinsky designates Aguilar as the "moral governess" in his scholarly and critical collective biography of Jewish women writers. He sees her as the writer who best defined the Anglo-Jewish woman's response to culture in the modern world with her themes of selfless ambition and appropriate rewards or punishments.

AGUSTINI, DELMIRA (1890–1914)
Poet   Uruguay

Delmira Agustini was the first notable female poet in Latin America. She was born on October 24, 1890, in Montevideo into a scholarly family. She had a difficult life and marriage, separating from her husband after two months and beginning a relationship, most likely unconsummated, with another man. She won fame throughout the Spanish-speaking world with her two collections of poetry titled *El Libro Blanco* (1907) and *Cantos de Mañana* (1910). Her poetry explored the intensity of sexual relationships, a subject unexpressed elsewhere before or during the time she wrote, and the connection between the themes of love and death. Poetry became an outlet for her sheltered and lonely life. She turned to dreams, to love, and to death, feelings revealed in the posthumous publication of her letters, *Corespondencia intima*, in 1969. In 1914, her former husband killed her and then committed suicide.

BIBLIOGRAPHY
Stephens, Doris T. *Delmira Agustini and the Quest for Transcendence*. Montevideo, Uruguay: Ediciones Geminis, 1975. No ISBN, 220p. In a combination biography and critical study, Stephens discusses Agustini as the first significant modern woman poet in Latin America and thinks that Agustini might have participated in the murder-suicide because she continued to communicate with her husband after their divorce.

AIDOO, AMA ATA (1942–)
Writer   Ghana

Ama Ata Aidoo may be the finest living African woman author. After her birth
on March 23, 1942, in Ghana's central region, Aidoo attended Wesley Girls
School, Cape Coast, and graduated from the University of Ghana in 1964. She
became a research fellow at the Institute of African Studies; attended Stanford
University in California, studying creative writing; and began to publish short
stories in magazines such as the Nigerian *Black Orpheus* and the Ghanaian
Okyeame. Her play, *Dilemma of a Ghost*, was first performed in 1964 at the
University of Ghana. After a visit to Germany, she published her novel, *Our
Sister Killjoy: Reflections from a Black-Eyed Squint* (1977), expressing an African woman's cultural shock in that country. Although Ghana accepts women
with economic autonomy, the feminist Aidoo became secretary of education for
Ghana in 1982. She has taught at the University of Cape Coast and lectured in-
ternationally.

BIBLIOGRAPHY
Odamtten, Vincent O. *The Art of Ama Ata Aidoo: Polylectics and Reading
    against Neocolonialism.* Gainesville: University of Florida Press, 1994. 0-
    8130-1276-7, 202p. Odamtten examines colonial writers in this well-
    documented critical biography and admonishes the West for its neglect of
    Aidoo's works.

A'ISHA (614?–678)
Consort   Arabia

The vivacious A'isha (Ayeshah) became the favorite young wife of the Prophet
Muhammad after the death of his first wife, Khadija, although Muhammad had
originally married A'isha when she was nine to strengthen ties with his chief
advisor, her father Abu Bakr. and Muslims know her as the At Muhammad's
death in 632, she became a widow of eighteen, forbidden to remarry. With no
children to mother, she helped her father become the first caliph of the Muslims and used her energies for social and family activities during his caliphate
(632–34) and that of Umar I, which followed. When Uthman ascended, A'isha
became aware of his weaknesses and led opposition to his administration. Uthman was murdered in 656, and three rivals tried to take over—Ali, Talhah, and
Zubair. A'isha hoped to regain the caliphate for her family, but Ali, who A'isha
thought had killed Uthman, won the succession. After A'isha took a pilgrimage
to Mecca in her early forties, she returned to Medina and began the civil war
against Ali. She led a battle from atop her camel, but her army lost near Bashra
in 656. Ali captured her, but when she promised to keep away from politics, he
released her. She kept her pledge; however, followers recorded her oral statements and public speeches, and Muslims credit her with 2,010 traditions,
1,210 of them that Mohammed supposedly related to her directly. Large
crowds attended her funeral, and most Muslims still admire her as "Mother of
the Believers." However, Ali's supporters, the Shi'ahs, still show her hostility.

BIBLIOGRAPHY
Abbott, Nabia. *A'ishah, the Beloved of Mohammed.* 1942. New York: Arno
    Press, 1973. 0-4050-5318-5, 230p. Using A'ishah's writings and those of
    the men after her, the interesting but exhaustive text tells of A'ishah's per-
    sonal ambition, her practical knowledge of medicine and astronomy, her

great political energy, and her ability to organize and to perpetrate propaganda.

Spellberg, D. A. *Politics, Gender, and the Islamic Past: The Legacy of A'isha Bint Abi Bakr.* New York: Columbia University Press, 1994. 0-231-07998-2, 243p. In a scholarly discussion of A'isha's life and achievements, Spellberg suggests that her story is a composite of what Muslim men thought of themselves rather than the facts. The earliest source about her life, based on oral tradition, was written 150 years after her death.

AKHMATOVA, ANNA (1888–1966)
Poet   Russia

When Anna Akhmatova died in 1966, after publication of her collected verses in 1965, people recognized her as the greatest woman poet in Russian literature. Born near Odessa on June 11, 1888, Anna Andreyevna Gorenko and her family soon moved to St. Petersburg. She started writing poetry at eleven and connected it to being ill and delirious for a week during which she became temporarily deaf. As a young woman of seventeen, she took the pseudonym of Anna Akhmatova to quell her father's fear that her poetry would ruin his name. At twenty-one, she joined the Acmeists who included Boris Pasternak and Nikolai Gumilëv, her husband for a short time. Lenin put her first husband to death in 1921, and another husband, the art historian Nikolay Punin, went to prison in 1953. Her only child was imprisoned for eighteen years. She first published *Vecher* (Evening) in 1912 and gained fame with her second collection of published poems in 1914, *Chetki* (The Rosary). Other collections include *Anno Domini MXMXXI* and *Iva* (Willow). She revealed three images of herself as poet in her poems—the one using the facts of her biography, the one created by Russo-Soviet criticism, and the one she created of herself.

BIBLIOGRAPHY
Davies, J. *Anna of All the Russias: The Life of Anna Akhmatova (1889–1966).* Liverpool: Lincoln Davies, 1988. 0-569-09086-5, 148p. This brief biography overviews Akhmatova with excerpts from her poetry and letters applicable to both her life and the historical period.

Height, Amanda. *Anna Akhmatova: A Poetic Pilgrimage.* 1976. New York: Oxford University Press, 1990. 0-19-282749-9, 213p. In Height's interview with Akhmatova and in her adulatory biography, she reveals that poetry was Akhmatova's only true source of strength and happiness. In it, she could be herself, deeply religious and close to nature and God.

Naiman, Anatolii. *Remembering Anna Akhmatova.* Trans. Wendy Rosslyn. New York: Henry Holt, 1991. 0-8050-1408-X, 240p. Naiman recounts Akhmatova's life from his conversations with her and discusses her succinct and witty work, banished for decades in the Soviet Union. He says that she often exaggerated reality, presenting it as the truth.

Polivanov, Konstantin, comp. *Anna Akhmatova and Her Circle.* Trans. Patricia Beriozkina. Fayetteville: University of Arkansas Press, 1994. 1-55728-308-7; paper, 1-55728-309-5, 281p. After presenting Akhmatova's autobiographical prose of sketches, notes, diary entries, and letters, the text turns to the words of persons who reveal unexpected facets of Akhmatova in various periods of her life.

Reeder, Roberta. *Anna Akhmatova: Poet and Prophet.* New York: St. Martin's, 1994. 0-312-11241-6, 619p. This exhaustive biography places Akhmatova in her time and helps to explain how she related to those around her. Samples of her poetry during the revolutionary years, the Great Terror, the Great War years, the Cold War, and the thaw show her development.

ALBANI, EMMA (1847–1930)
Opera Singer   Canada

Opera and concert lovers admired Dame Emma Albani for the warmth and beauty of her voice. Born Marie Louise Cecilie Emma Lajeunesse on November 1, 1847, she took her professional name from Albany, New York, where she spent her early life. In Canada, she attended school in a French Canadian convent before she became Canada's first international celebrity, rising to heights in a field dominated by Europeans. She studied in Paris and Milan and made her debut in Messina during 1870 and in London during 1872. She debuted in New York in 1891 as Gilda in *Rigoletto*. Among her roles, she was the first Senta in *The Flying Dutchman* at Covent Garden in 1877 and the first Desdemona in *Otello* in 1894 at the New York Met before winning a gold medal from the Royal Philharmonic Society. She made several tours to Russia as well as other areas of the world. She knew forty opera roles as well as forty-three oratorios, cantatas, and other major vocal works. She retired to teach and write her autobiography in 1911. In 1925, she became a Dame of the British Empire.

BIBLIOGRAPHY
Albani, Emma. *Forty Years of Song*. New York: Arno Press, 1977. 0-4050-9667-4, 285p. Albani says that good health blessed her career, and she includes anecdotes about her debuts at Messina and Covent Garden, her first performance for royalty, her first American tour, learning German to sing *Lohengrin* in Berlin, and her most memorable concerts.

MacDonald, Cheryl Emily. *Emma Albani: Victorian Diva*. Toronto: Dundurn, 1984. 0-919670-75-X, 205p. MacDonald asserts that Albani's hard work and belief in her own ability helped her become a gracious professional. Since fans treated nineteenth-century opera stars the way they do rock stars today, they wanted to know everything about Albani, with France, Canada, and the United States all vying to claim her as a native.

ALEGRIA, CLARIBEL (1924–)
Poet   Nicaragua

Claribel Alegria is an acclaimed poet. Born May 12, 1924, in Estelí, she lived in exile with her family in Santa Ana, El Salvador, before immigrating to the United States in 1943 and attending George Washington University. For her poetry, novels, and essays, which she began publishing in 1948, she has been praised for her ability to speak about political reality with passionate objectivity. In her work, she often blends the past and the present through dreams and reality. The awards she has garnered include a finalist position for *Cenizas de Izalco* in the Seix Barral competition in Barcelona, Spain, and the Casa de las Américas poetry award for *Sobrevivo*. She lived in Mexico, Chile, Uruguay, and Spain before the victory of the Sandinista Front for National Liberation (FSLN) allowed her to return to her home in 1979.

BIBLIOGRAPHY
Boschetto-Sandoval, Sandra M., and Marcia Phillips McGowen, eds. *Claribel Alegria and Central American Literature: Critical Essays*. Athens: Ohio University Center for International Studies, 1994. Paper, 0-8968-0179-9, 263p. These scholarly essays about Alegria's life and writing stress the importance of the poor and oppressed to her. She said that she wrote her poems "under obsession's spur," and the essays support this statement by examining the obsessions of her life as they appear in her work.

ALEXANDRA of DENMARK (1844–1925)

Consort   Denmark

Alexandra was a modern thinker who supported variety in education, disapproved of the mass slaughter of game, and worked for better conditions in the military during World War I. Daughter of Christian IX and Louise of Hesse, she was born on December 1, 1844, and in 1863, Alexandra Caroline Marie Charlotte Louise Julia, or "Alix," left Denmark and her five siblings to become the wife of Queen Victoria's son Edward, Prince of Wales. Although Alix disliked Germans, she helped her German-descent mother-in-law, Queen Victoria, reunite with her subjects after Albert's death. In 1867, Alexandra had a severe illness that left her slightly lame and began the deafness that became total in her later years. After she became queen, she supported the poor and the suffering by founding the Imperial Military Nursing service in 1902 and the Alexandra Rose Day for British hospitals.

BIBLIOGRAPHY
Battiscombe, Georgina. *Queen Alexandra*. Boston: Houghton Mifflin, 1969. 0-09-456560-0, 336p. Battiscombe is sympathetic to Alexandra in this well-written, lively biography.
Duff, David. *Alexandra, Princess and Queen*. London: Collins, 1980. 0-0021-6667-4, 327p. Duff thinks the importance of Alexandra's dignity and courage to the British has been underestimated.
Hough, Richard Alexander. *Edward and Alexandra: Their Private and Public Lives*. New York: St. Martin's, 1992. 0-312-09793-X, 369p. This dual biography, an account of Alix and her husband, Edward (Bertie), shows that Bertie's sheer joy in Alix's beauty and their understanding of each other lasted throughout their marriage.

ALEXANDRA of RUSSIA (1872–1918)

Empress of Russia   Germany

When Alix Victoria Helene Luise Beatrix married Nicholas II, emperor of Russia, four weeks after his accession, she converted to the Russian Orthodox Church and became "the truly believing Aleksandra Fyodorovna" and the empress of Russia, the ruler who helped destroy it. Born on June 6, 1872, she was the daughter of the grand duke Louis IV of Hesse-Darmstadt and Queen Victoria's daughter Alice. Alix's mother died when Alix was six, and her childish belief in God's love grew into a burning faith during her mourning. Her German intensity led to a lack of sensitivity that offended others, but she was unaware of their feelings. When Alexandra's reserved temperament made her unpopular in the Russian court society, she began to seek comfort in her family and in religion. She flirted with mysticism and believed in the medieval doctrine of divine right of kings. She thought that supporting Nicholas was sacred and worked to help him retain his power while zealously protecting Aleksei, her hemophiliac son, for his rightful place on the Russian throne. She dismissed capable ministers and began listening to the advice of a "holy man," Rasputin, whom she thought God had sent as to help her protect "holy Russia." She destroyed what she had tried to preserve, and the Bolsheviks executed all her family on the night of July 16–17, 1918.

BIBLIOGRAPHY

Cowles, Virginia. *The Last Tsar and Tsarina*. London: Weidenfeld and Nicolson, 1977. 0-29777-366-6, 232p. The rather cumbersome but informative biography starts with Nicholas's life, covers the marriage of Nicholas and Alexandra, the birth of the child Alexis, Rasputin, World War I, the revolution, and the end of their lives after the monarchy failed.

King, Greg. *The Last Empress: The Life and Times of Alexandra Feodorovna, Tsarina of Russia*. Secaucus, NJ: Carol Publishing Group, 1994. 1-55972-211-8, 431p. In an accessible biography, King gives an overview of Alexandra's childhood, discussing her belief in the divine right of kings. He explains why Russians disliked her and why she and Nicholas were unfit to rule.

Massie, Robert K. *Nicholas and Alexandra*. New York: Atheneum, 1967. 0-689-10177-5, 584p. After discovering that his own son was hemophiliac, Massie investigated the effect of having a hemophiliac son on the Romanovs, Nicholas and Alexandra. Letters, diaries, and memoirs interpreted through modern medicine, psychiatry, and the common experience of all families who have hemophiliacs help him arrive at his thesis.

McLees, Nectaria. *A Gathered Radiance: The Life of Alexandra Romanov, Russia's Last Empress*. Chico, CA: Valaam Society of America, 1992. 0-938635-90-5, 140p. In this accessible biography, McLees sees Alexandra as a faithful and generous woman who had a fierce love for her God, her countrymen, and her family. She was generous to those in need, and she was also courageous because she refused to leave Russia in the moment of defeat.

ALLENDE, ISABEL (1942–)
Writer   Peru

Isabel Allende is an award-winning novelist who has set her early works in Chile. On August 2, 1942, she was born in Lima to a Chilean diplomat, the first cousin of the president of Chile. When she was two, after her parents divorced, she and her mother lived with her maternal grandparents until her mother married another diplomat. They moved to Bolivia, the Middle East, and Europe, with Allende returning to Chile at fifteen. She worked as a secretary after high school and began writing, influenced by her grandmother's storytelling ability. She became a print and media journalist, writing a column for the radical women's magazine *Paula*, and hosting a television show. In 1973, a military coup led to the assassination of President Allende in Chile, and Isabel Allende began providing food and aid for victims of the coup, helping many escape. She began to see the connection between her personal life and writing, beginning to incorporate both the history of her family and of Chile in her work. Interviews with many different people helped her collect material that she used after settling in Venezuela with her family. Her concern for her grandfather, dying in Chile, led to her first major work, the expansion of a letter to him about her memories of her childhood with him. In it she incorporated the device of magical realism, which became part of her style. This novel, *La casa de los espíritus*, won the Grand Roman d'Evasion Prize and a nomination for the Quality Paperback Book Club New Voice. With her second husband, she settled in California, where she has continued to create exotic stories.

BIBLIOGRAPHY

Allende, Isabel. *Paula*. New York: HarperCollins, 1995. 0-06-017252-5, 368p. When Allende's daughter Paula went into a coma in 1991, Allende began writing the story of her family as a present for Paula when she awoke. Paula never recovered, but Allende's letter recalls the phases of her childhood, adolescence, and adult life, and the effect on them of the many places she lived. It also recounts the political upheaval in Chile and what she knows of her parents and grandparents. She comments in this work that "magical realism" is not merely a literary device but the essence of how she lives.

ALLINGHAM, MARGERY (1904–1966)

Writer   **England**

Margery Allingham created a fictional detective, Albert Campion, who solved crimes in detective novels of great wit and ingenuity. Born on May 20, 1904, in London, she was the daughter of an editor of, and contributor to, various boys' papers specializing in adventure stories, including detective tales. Her own first thrillers were for youngsters of her own age, but she found that thirty years later, a new generation was reading those early novels. She began writing when young because she "had to" and spent the rest of her life "experimenting" with the detective genre. She said that her adventures were both "mental and moral," and she presented unique notions of time and varied levels of reality in her work. She saw her own life as tame—a woman living in a village who suffered from ill health, had financial and domestic problems, loved her husband, and enjoyed her house and garden. Her stories gave people a way to escape from the cynicism of the 1920s, the economic woes of the 1930s, World War II, reconstruction, and the British welfare state. Few knew any of the details of her personal life, but her friends remembered her sense of fun, generosity, affection, companionship, ability to laugh at herself, happiness, integrity, loyalty, and understanding. The titles of the over 3 million books that she has sold range from *Crime at Black Dudley* in 1928 to *The Mind Readers* in 1965.

BIBLIOGRAPHY

Martin, Richard. *Ink in Her Blood: The Life and Crime Fiction of Margery Allingham*. Ann Arbor, MI: UMI Research, 1988. 0-8357-1923-5, 255p. Martin has long been a fan of Allingham's books, and he wanted to know about the life of a woman who often had as many as twenty-seven books in print at the same time. He uses diaries, notes, manuscripts, and letters from relatives and friends to find the person who developed the contemporary sophisticated mystery story.

Thorogood, Julia. *Margery Allingham: A Biography*. London: Heinemann, 1991. 0-434-77906-7, 423p. Thorogood uses Allingham's diaries to cover her life. Allingham thought that "having to write" led to better work than writing for either money or popularity. She said that the whole of life was about escape; therefore, temporarily eluding reality through detective fiction could not be wrong.

ALONSO, ALICIA (1917–)

Ballerina   **Cuba**

Alicia Alonzo is internationally recognized for her achievement as a ballerina. She was born on December 21, 1917, as Alicia de la Caridad del Cobre Martinez Hoyo and married at sixteen to Ferdnando Alonso. They moved to New York soon after, and she began her career in Broadway musicals when someone showed her how to tap-dance. She subsequently danced with the Ballets Russes and became one of the principal stars of the American Ballet Theatre between 1941 and 1960, well known for her role of Giselle. Most amazing is that detached retinas kept her bedridden for one and one-half years when she was nineteen and twenty. While Alonso's eyes were covered for six months, and she lay immobile, she learned the role of Giselle by dancing it with her fingers. After her eyes stabilized, she rehabilitated herself and began to dance again. Her eyesight was always a problem, and in mid-life, she was almost completely blind. In 1948, after returning to Cuba, she formed the Ballet Alicia Alonso, renaming it the Ballet de Cuba in 1955, and after the Cuban Revolution of 1959, the Ballet Nacional de Cuba. After being refused reentry to the United States for fifteen years, she danced in New York again in 1975, with her troupe debuting in 1978. Alonso has continued to dance and study and believes that staying in Cuba helped her gain the love of her people.

BIBLIOGRAPHY

Arnold, Sandra Martin. *Alicia Alonso: First Lady of the Ballet.* New York: Walker, 1993. 0-8027-8242-6, 100p. Arnold begins the story of Alicia Alonso when Alonso lay in bed with her eyes bandaged at the age of twenty. She then covers Alonso's earlier life when she met Fernando Alonso and coped with her eye problems after the birth of a child as well as her later life in which she continued to perform in her seventies.

De Gamez, Tana. *Alicia Alonso at Home and Abroad.* New York: Citadel, 1971. 0-8065-0218-5, 189p. Half of the book is text about Alonso's life and personality; the other is photographs of Alonso's European performances through 1969. The first Western ballerina to be invited to dance *Giselle* and *Swan Lake* in the Soviet Union, Alonso earned one of ballet's highest salaries but abandoned the money and returned to Cuba.

Siegel, Beatrice. *Alicia Alonso, the Story of a Ballerina.* New York: F. Warne, 1979. 0-7232-6157-1, 182p. In a thorough, recommended biography, Siegel recounts Alonso's life from her youth and middle age as she continued to dance when she could barely see a pinpoint of light. Alonso verbally admired the great dancers and gave them credit for their influence on her life, especially **Pavlova**.

Terry, Walter. *Alicia and Her Ballet Nacional De Cuba: An Illustrated Biography of Alicia.* Garden City, NY: Anchor, 1981. 0-385-14956-5, 146p. Terry's biography traces Alonso's career from Broadway to ballet, her triumphs over adversity, her return to Havana and subsequent exile from the United States, and her place as the Cuban-American prima ballerina *Assoluta*.

ANDERSON, ELIZABETH GARRETT (1836–1917)
Physician   England

Elizabeth Garrett founded a hospital for women and became dean of the first women's medical school, the London School of Medicine. As the daughter of Newson Garrett, born on June 9, 1836, she was educated at home and in private school. Initially refused admission to medical school, in 1865 she became licensed, and in 1866, she worked as a general medical attendant at St. Mary's Dispensary, London, later known as New Hospital. There she instituted medical courses for women. When she became a doctor, baby clinics and prenatal care were unavailable for mothers. Married with a family, Anderson had no desire to undermine homemaking, but she wanted women to use their talents and intelligence outside the home. Since women from lower economic classes worked twelve-hour days successfully, she thought that women from upper classes could work without health problems, contrary to Victorian belief, and eventually, upper-class women came to Anderson for medical treatment. In 1908, she became the first English woman to be elected mayor in her hometown of Aldeburgh, Suffolk. After her death, New Hospital was renamed Elizabeth Garrett Anderson Hospital.

BIBLIOGRAPHY
Fancourt, Mary St. J. *They Dared to Be Doctors: Elizabeth Blackwell and Elizabeth Garrett Anderson.* London: Longman, 1965. No ISBN, 148p. Fancourt relates that when Anderson began her training in 1859, surgeons still operated in old, dirty, black coats, unaware that mortality rates related directly to germ infection in wounds. Anderson begged friends not to introduce her as "doctor" because people were immediately revulsed, and she refused to treat men, including one with gout who requested her services. Fancourt emphasizes Anderson's earlier years in this juvenile biography.
Manton, Jo. *Elizabeth Garrett Anderson.* New York: Dutton, 1965. No ISBN, 382p. Anderson requested that no biography be written of her, and for many years, none was. Manton thought that Anderson faced problems that all working mothers face, and her thorough biography examines Anderson's handling of her roles as wife, mother, and physician.

ANDREAS-SALOMÉ, LOU (1861–1937)
Writer and Psychoanalyst   Russia

Lou Andreas-Salomé analyzed the major philosophical and psychological works of her time and wrote fiction. Her father was an army officer of French Huguenot origin when Lou Salomé was born in St. Petersburg on February 12, 1861. At seventeen, after the death of her father, she studied comparative religion at the University of Zurich and began friendships placing her at the center of European intellectual life. She was close to Paul Rée and Friedrich Nietzsche, whom she refused to marry. She instead chose Frederick Andreas, a professor of philology, but the two supposedly did not consummate the marriage, and Andreas sanctioned his wife's subsequent love affairs with such men as the poet Rainer Maria Rilke. Andreas-Salomé wrote about Nietzsche's ideas (1899) and Ibsen's characters (1892) as well as other essays and novels. In 1910, she attended a conference on psychoanalysis and began espousing Alfred Adler's theories, but later, she followed Sigmund Freud. In 1913, she began seeing her own patients. After her husband died, his daughter by a maid nursed Andreas-Salomé through diabetes and cancer.

BIBLIOGRAPHY

Andreas-Salomé, Lou. *Looking Back: Memoirs.* Trans. Breon Mitchell. New York: Paragon House, 1991. 1-55778-260-1, 226p. Among the titles of chapters in this accessible autobiography are the names of people important to Andreas-Salomé—Rée, Rainer, Freud, and Andreas. In additional chapters, Andreas-Salomé recounts other experiences.

Livingstone, Angela. *Salomé, Her Life and Work.* Mt. Kisco, NY: M. Bell, 1984. 0-918825-04-0, 255p. According to Livingstone's scholarly biography, Salomé had no cause, joined no movement, and was unpolitical. She never thought being female was a disadvantage and linked herself to no man exclusively.

Martin, Biddy. *Woman and Modernity: The (Life)styles of Lou Andreas-Salomé.* Ithaca, NY: Cornell University Press, 1991. 0-8014-2591-3; paper, 0-8014-9907-0, 250p. The scholarly text examines Salomé as a writer, thinker, and lay analyst in her own times and traces her thought through historical, political, and intellectual contexts. Martin wants to show how Salomé's work and life intermesh.

Peters, H. F. *My Sister, My Spouse; a Biography of Lou Andreas-Salomé.* 1962. New York: Norton, 1974. 0-393-00748-0, 320p. Peters has written a loving portrait of Andreas-Salomé, from her life in czarist Russia to her death in Nazi Germany, showing her talent and courage. Peters thinks Andreas-Salomé suffered the fate of women known for their relationships to brilliant men rather than for themselves because Andreas-Salomé never received appropriate recognition for her feminist study of Ibsen's women (the first) or her major work about Nietzsche.

Sorell, Walter. *Three Women: Lives of Sex and Genius.* Indianapolis: Bobbs-Merrill, 1975. 0-672-51750-7, 234p. The women whom Sorell discusses in short, readable biographies—**Alma Mahler-Werfel**, Gertrude Stein, and Andreas-Salomé—inspired some of the greatest artists of the century. He sees them as intimately involved in their own creativity, atypical of their times, and true to themselves. Andreas-Salomé had willpower and was a respected writer and analyst. Men easily succumbed to her charming personality as did Sorell, although he never met her.

ANDREWS, JULIE (1935–)

Actor   England

Julie Andrews has had a long and successful career on stage and in film. When Julia Elizabeth Wells, born on October 1, 1935, in Walton-on-Thames to a metal- and woodworking teacher and a music-hall pianist, was four, her parents divorced, and she lived with her mother and her new stepfather. Although she appeared on the stage at three, no one recognized her talent until her stepfather heard her sing in an air-raid shelter during World War II while he was leading the group seeking refuge there in a morale-building songfest. He took her to a throat specialist, who noted her well-developed larynx, and she amazed others with her astounding, four-octave range. At thirteen, she became the youngest person to give a command performance before the royal princesses. At nineteen, she opened on Broadway to critical acclaim in *The Boyfriend*. She then starred in *My Fair Lady* in 1956 and won the New York

Critics' Award for best actress in a musical. A movie role in *Mary Poppins* during 1964 won her an Oscar for best actress. *The Sound of Music* followed this success. Several failures followed, during which she divorced and remarried. Her new husband, Blake Edwards, redirected her career. As well as being a mother to five children, Andrews has also been a volunteer, working as an ambassador for the United Nations Development Fund for Women and as a spokesperson and board member with Operation USA, a nonprofit relief organization.

BIBLIOGRAPHY

Arntz, James, and Thomas S. Wilson. *Julie Andrews*. Chicago: Contemporary Books, 1995. Paper, 0-8092-3267-7, 240p. This pictorial biography presents a positive view of Andrews' life and career, emphasizing her performances. It also provides a minihistory of theater and film styles in the second half of the twentieth century.

Spindle, Les. *Julie Andrews: A Bio-Bibliography*. New York: Greenwood Press, 1989. 0-313-26223-3, 151p. Spindle professes to be an admirer of Andrews, as he catalogs her excessive fame in the 1960s and her dignity during Hollywood's hostility toward her. He sees her as a graceful presence who has worked hard and used her talent properly. The somewhat scholarly text combines data with her biography and covers all the major aspects of her career—film, theater, personal appearances, television, recordings, and children's fiction.

Windeler, Robert. *Julie Andrews: A Biography*. New York: St. Martin's, 1983. 0-312-44848-1, 223p. Windeler admired Andrews, and he asked her about her writing an autobiography, but she wanted to do only a series of conversations. Since he thought her to be an original talent and was interested in her public persona and her private personality, he decided to go ahead and write a popular biography.

ÁNGELES, VICTORIA de los   (1923–)

Opera Singer   **Spain**

Victoria de los Ángeles is an opera star who has sung in major houses throughout the world. She was born in Catalonia on November 1, 1923, as the second daughter in her family. As a young girl, she sang for Red Cross concerts and aspired for little more until she won a competition and sang Puccini on the radio. The money she earned singing before she finished studying at the Barcelona Conservatory helped her family escape its poverty. She made her debut in 1945 as the Countess in Mozart's *Le Nozze di Figaro*. After singing Mimi in *La Bohème* at Covent Garden, she began to sing Puccini, Wagner, and Verdi roles regularly. She appeared at the Metropolitan in New York, La Scala in Milan, Bayreuth in Germany, and in Buenos Aires. In 1969, she left opera to concentrate on recitals, and her spirited interpretations of Spanish songs have enhanced her reputation.

BIBLIOGRAPHY

Roberts, Peter. *Victoria de los Ángeles*. London: Weidenfeld and Nicolson, 1982. 0-297-78099-9, 184p. This readable, popular biography tells about de los Ángeles' childhood and career, emphasizing the struggle for success and her enjoyment of her life.

ANNE of AUSTRIA (1601–1666)
Queen of France   **Spain**

When Anne married Louis XIII of France, she became queen. Born in Valladolid on September 22, 1601, she was the daughter of Philip III, king of Spain from the house of Austria and the Habsburgs. She lived separately from Louis XIII for most of her unhappy marriage. During the Thirty Years' War, she could not see her family, and the king's chief minister, Cardinal Richelieu, accused her of conspiring treason against Louis, although no one ever proved this charge. After Louis died, Anne acted as sole regent, relying on Jules Mazarin to advise her, until her five-year-old son, King Louis XIV, became of age. Together, Anne and Mazarin upheld the crown during the civil wars of the Fronde (1648–53). In 1660, Louis XIV married Anne's niece, and in 1661, when he assumed power, Anne retired to a convent. When Alexandre Dumas featured Anne in *The Three Musketeers*, her unhappy marriage and Cardinal Richelieu's attempt to assassinate her character captured French imagination.

BIBLIOGRAPHY
Kleinman, Ruth. *Anne of Austria: Queen of France*. Columbus: Ohio State University Press, 1985. 0-8142-0389-2, 350p. Kleinman sees Anne as a woman with faults who survived difficult circumstances to preserve the monarchy for her son.

ANNE of ENGLAND (1665–1714)
Queen of Great Britain and Ireland   **England**

Anne was the last British sovereign from the house of Stuart. Born in London on February 6, 1665, she was the second daughter of King James II and his first wife, Anne. In 1683, she married Prince George of Denmark, and they remained happy, although few were pleased with the politics of their union. Anne came to the throne at William's death in 1702, but because of her low position in the line of succession, she had never trained to become queen. John Churchill, duke of Marlborough and captain-general of the army, and his wife, Sarah, Anne's closest friend, had great influence over the queen in the early years of her reign. Anne eventually disapproved of the Marlboroughs' actions and took advantage of popular dissatisfaction with the Whigs to remove him and another minister, Godolphin, in favor of the Tories. In 1707, she united England and Scotland. With little natural leadership or intelligence, Anne used her obstinacy to rule. She was neither intelligent nor a particularly good queen but was deeply religious and attached to the Church of England. Her crown revenues for the poor to the Church of England, Queen Anne's Bounty, still remain. After seventeen pregnancies in seventeen years, none of her children survived to succeed her; and because her German cousin, George, elector of Hannover, was Protestant, she chose him to succeed her.

BIBLIOGRAPHY
Curtis, Gila. *The Life and Times of Queen Anne*. London: Weidenfeld and Nicolson, 1972. 0-29799-571-5, 223p. In an accessible text with many illustrations, Curtis emphasizes that Anne never expected to reign but had no choice when she was thirty-seven. Because she was queen when England was triumphant at the Battle of Blenheim, some of her achievements seem grandiose and heroic.

Green, David Bronte. *Queen Anne*. New York: Scribner's, 1971. 0-00-211693-6, 399p. Green thinks that Anne had courage but no resolution. He believes that she could have had a great reign if she had not dismissed the duke of Marlborough and Godolphin from her cabinet. Although a good picture of Anne, the biography tells more about her times than about her life.

Gregg, Edward. *Queen Anne*. 1980. New York: Routledge and Kegan Paul, 1984. Paper, 0-7448-0018-8, 483p. This readable and recommended biography uses quotes as chapter titles from Anne's correspondence opened at Blenheim after World War II. Gregg attempts to integrate the public and private aspects of the queen's life in order to present a balanced picture of her as both a ruler and a private individual. He thinks that the vindictive duchess of Marlborough perpetrated the myth of Anne's weakness, but Gregg believes that Anne never forgot her position in their relationship.

AQUINO, CORAZON (1933–)
Politician   The Philippines

Corazon (Cory) Cojuanco became the first woman president of the Philippines, a nation of 54 million on seven thousand islands, after defeating the government of Ferdinand Marcos. Born on January 25, 1933, she was educated in Manila and at Roman Catholic convent schools in the United States. She graduated from Mount St. Vincent College in New York City and studied law at Far Eastern University in Manila. In 1954, she married Benigno (Ninoy) Simeon Aquino, Jr., who soon entered politics and subsequently became the youngest mayor, governor, and senator to serve in the Philippines. President Ferdinand Marcos imprisoned him, and Aquino waited eight years for her husband's release before they moved to Boston in 1980. In 1983, he flew back to Manila to work in the legislative election while Aquino stayed in the United States. But after agents assassinated her husband as he deplaned, Aquino returned to the Philippines for his funeral and remained to work in the legislative election campaign, helping the opposition win one-third of the seats in 1984. Aquino became the opposition candidate for president, but Marcos declared himself victor in the February 7 election and had himself inaugurated on February 25. An army revolt undermined Marcos, and Aquino formed a provisional government. She implemented a new constitution and held legislative elections in 1987, but opposition within the military, a continuing communist insurgency, and severe economic problems plagued her so that she declined to run for a second term. Her commitment to nonviolence was an anomaly in her society.

BIBLIOGRAPHY
Crisostomo, Isabelo T. *Cory—Profile of a President*. Brookline Village, MA: Branden, 1987. 0-8283-1913-8, 323p. The time frame of this biography covers three historical phases—the death of Aquino's husband; the descent and fall of Marcos; and Aquino's rise and the first one hundred days of her government.

Gullas, Cecilia K. *Corazon Aquino: The Miracle of a President: A Biography*. New York: Cultural House, 1987. Paper, 0-943949-00-9, 124p. Gullas sees the story of Aquino as the transformation of a housewife into a courageous woman after her husband was murdered. Gullas says that the story is typically Filipino but that it is also universal. The text is not a definitive biography but a readable attempt to review Aquino's life.

Komisar, Lucy. *Corazon Aquino: The Story of a Revolution.* New York: G. Braziller, 1987. 0-8076-1171-9, 290p. Komisar says that her book is an unauthorized biography because Aquino, expecting to write her own book, refused to grant interviews and instructed the family not to participate. In this accessible biography, Komisar interviewed Aquino's brother, a politician; the archbishop of Manila, Cardinal Sin; her former minister of defense, Juan Ponce Enrile; people who knew her husband; oppositionists who made the revolution and helped her establish her presidency; military men on both sides; leaders of the Left and the Right; all economic strata of society; and Komisar's journalistic colleagues.

White, Mel. *Aquino.* Dallas, TX: Word, 1989. 0-8499-0670-9, 262p. In this popular and well-researched biography and history, White re-creates the story of Aquino from her childhood to her marriage and her experience when catapulted into international politics at the death of her husband, Nino.

Yap, Miguela G. *The Making of Cory.* Quezon City, Philippines: New Day, 1987. 9-7110-0334-1, 268p. Yap calls Aquino a modern "Joan of Arc" who cast out the "legendary dragon." In this biography, Yap focuses on Aquino's background; her courtship and marriage; her role as a politician's wife and as a prisoner's wife; her life in Boston; and her life as a widow, as a presidential candidate, and as president, with her official visits to the United States and to Japan.

AQUITAINE, ELEANOR of. *See* ELEANOR of AQUITAINE.

ARAGON, CATHERINE. *See* CATHERINE of ARAGON.

ARC, JOAN of. *See* JOAN of ARC.

ARDEN, ELIZABETH (1884?–1966)
Businesswoman   Canada

Elizabeth Arden created a cosmetic business through her ingenuity and her will. She was born Florence Nightingale Graham on December 31, 1884?, in Woodbridge, Ontario, the youngest of five children. Her father had immigrated from Scotland. Her mother died when she was six, and the family had difficulty supporting itself. Graham discovered her aptitude for selling when very young because she accompanied her father to the market and found that her small size would influence women to buy whatever she was selling without trying to bargain. After several false starts, Arden went to New York to work in a cosmetics shop. Her further experience as partner in a beauty salon led her to open her own business and change her name to Elizabeth Arden in 1909. She eventually increased her holdings to more than one hundred exclusive salons and over three hundred cosmetics products, keeping her upper-class image alive with high prices and careful practices.

BIBLIOGRAPHY
Lewis, Alfred Allan, and Constance Woodworth. *Miss Elizabeth Arden.* New York: Coward, McCann, and Geoghegan, 1972. 0-698-10479-X, 320p. The text shows that Arden got what she wanted from places and things but had trouble with people. This balanced biography catalogs her life and the troubles that occurred with her business after her death because she had not

stipulated its future in her will. Her legacy was not what she would have expected or wanted.

Shuker, Nancy. *Elizabeth Arden.* Englewood Cliffs, NJ: Silver Burdett, 1989.
0-382-09587-1, 112p.   This fictional biography for young adults tells how
Florence Nightingale Graham became Elizabeth Arden. Her hard work,
youthful appearance, and independence helped advance her career.

ARENDT, HANNAH (1906–1975)
Writer and Philosopher   Germany

Hannah Arendt asked, "what is politics?," and while searching for the answer,
she gained international renown and a place of preeminence among political
theorists of her generation. She was born in Hanover, Germany, on October
14, 1906. Her father died when she was six, and her mother encouraged her
education. After studies at the universities of Marburg and Freiburg, she received her doctoral degree from the University of Heidelberg at the age of
twenty-two. In 1933, she went to France to escape the Nazis. In 1941, she fled
to the United States, where in New York City, she worked as an editor, Jewish
relief organizer, and political writer for the New York German-Jewish newspaper *Aufbau.* She published her acclaimed and controversial *Origins of Totalitarianism* in 1951, the same year she changed her citizenship. Arendt seemed
to remain aloof from all group sympathies or affiliations, even Jewish ones,
and this independence helped her to reinterpret history and to identify with
society's outsiders, like **Rosa Luxemburg.** Arendt tried to write so that she
would be understood and always assumed that her readers comprehended the
points she was making. Among her many other writings are *The Human Condition* (1958), *Eichmann in Jerusalem* (1963), *On Revolution* (1963), *On Violence* (1970), *Crises of the Republic* (1972), and *The Life of the Mind* (1977).
Her memoirs, *Correspondence, 1926–1969,* were published in 1992.

BIBLIOGRAPHY

Barnouw, Dagmar. *Visible Spaces: Hannah Arendt and the German-Jewish Experience.* Baltimore: Johns Hopkins University Press, 1990. 0-8018-3923-8,
319p.   Barnouw's historical account of Arendt's political philosophy and
historiography is a scholarly biography of her thinking as a Jew in the modern world.   Barnouw tries to point out both the errors and the merits of her
arguments, which some of her other critics have been unwilling to examine.
Brightman, Carol, ed. *Between Friends: The Correspondence of Hannah Arendt
and Mary McCarthy, 1949–1975.* New York: Harcourt Brace, 1995. 0-15-
100112-X, 412p.   Although this collection of letters, which McCarthy requested that Brightman edit in 1989 before her death, is not traditional biography, it gives good insight into Arendt's thoughts and opinions as she
expressed them in her correspondence with McCarthy beginning in March
1949 and ending with Arendt's death.
Ettinger, Elzbieta. *Hannah Arendt/Martin Heidegger.* New Haven, CT: Yale
University Press, 1995. 0-300-06407-1, 139p.   When Arendt was eighteen
and studying at the University of Marburg, she fell in love with Martin Heidegger, married and thirty-five. Their affair lasted for four years until she
went into exile in 1930, a Jew escaping Hitler, and he became a Nazi. After
the war, she believed Heidegger's claims of Nazi persecution, revived correspondence with him, and visited him in Germany, forgetting his association
with her enemy.

Young-Bruehl, Elisabeth. *Hannah Arendt, for Love of the World.* New Haven,
    CT: Yale University Press, 1982. 0-300-02660-9, 563p. Young-Bruehl, one
    of Arendt's graduate students, bases this philosophical and well-researched,
    scholarly biography on reports from those who knew Arendt, her mother's
    album of her childhood called "Our Child," Arendt's only autobiographical
    piece covering her freshman year in college, and other writings. Young-
    Bruehl attempts to show what led Arendt to her concerns and her subjects,
    how she went about making and remaking her books, and how she thought
    her way from one book to the next.

ARMAND, INESSE (1874–1920)
Revolutionary   France

Inesse Steffane Armand supported revolutionaries in Russia and served in major positions of the early Bolshevik government. She was born in Paris, but her
father died when she was very young, and she moved to Moscow to live in the
home of the manufacturer Armand. She later married his son. Before she joined
the Social Democrats and the Bolshevik Party in 1904, she helped a group that
was aiding prostitutes in Moscow. In 1905, after the uprising, she was arrested.
In exile in Europe, she lectured at Longjumeau's Party School near Paris and
wrote for the *Rabotnitsa (Woman Worker)* from 1910. She went underground
and returned to St. Petersburg in 1912, where in 1915, she represented the
Bolshevik party at the International Women's Socialist Conferences in Zim-
menwald and Kienthal. Back in Paris, during 1916, she translated Lenin's
works and his letters to her into French. After the revolution in 1917, she returned to Russia to prepare for the October uprising. As a member of the Moscow Bolshevik Party Committee, she chaired the regional economic council
and founded the Women's Bureau Zhenotdel. In 1918, she organized the first
All Russian Conference of Women Workers and Peasants but died of cholera
soon after and was buried in Red Square.

BIBLIOGRAPHY
Elwood, Ralph Carter. *Inessa Armand: Revolutionary and Feminist.* New York:
    Cambridge University Press, 1992. 0-521-41486-5, 304p. This political bi-
    ography of Armand, based on unpublished police reports, memoirs, and let-
    ters to five children and two husbands, as well as Lenin's 118 published
    letters to her, tells of the woman who was the first director of the Women's
    Section of the Russian Communist Party, second ony to Aleksandra Kollon-
    tai in the ranks of early Soviet feminists but unmentioned in Western litera-
    ture except as Lenin's mistress. Elwood sees Armand as an accomplished
    revolutionary propagandist and Bolshevik organizer before the revolution
    in 1917 and as a feminist who devoted much of her life to defending
    women's interests in the home, the workplace, and society.

ARNIM, BETTINA von (1785–1859)
Writer   Germany

Bettina von Arnim was a writer during German literature's Romantic period.
Born in Frankfurt-am-Main on August 31, 1785, she was the daughter of a
wealthy Italian merchant and a mother who had once been in love with Johann
Wolfgang von Goethe. Her mother died when von Arnim was eight, and she
went to a convent in Fritzlar for her schooling. She met Goethe when she was

young, and he and his mother remained her friends all of her life. She married Achim von Arnim in 1811, a physicist, raised seven children, and began her writing career after his death in 1831, with her wealthy family supporting her artistic endeavors. Her first book, *Correspondence between Goethe and a Young Girl,* in 1835 and her second reminisce about time spent with the Goethe family. In 1844, she wrote biographies of her brother and of her friend, Karoline von Gunderode, a nun who committed suicide in 1806. Von Arnim then stated in other books her concerns about the underclass, treatment of the Jews, and capital punishment.

BIBLIOGRAPHY

Waldstein, Edith. *Bettine von Arnim and the Politics of Romantic Conversation.* Columbia, SC: Camden House, 1988. 0-938100-54-8, 150p. Waldstein calls von Arnim "Bettine," as von Arnim preferred, in a carefully documented, critical biography. She places von Arnim in her times, assessing her contribution to Romanticism and showing how her life intersected with her fiction. Waldstein also looks at the political content of her novels, an aspect only recently acknowledged, and says that *Geselligkeit,* the romantic concept of synthesizing art with life, and a concern with preserving romantic conversation were another two of von Arnim's contributions.

ASHCROFT, PEGGY (1907–1991)

Actor   England

Edith Margaret Emily Ashcroft performed both classical and contemporary drama, creating more complex and difficult roles as the stages of her personal life progressed and always working to solve the mystery of acting. She was born on December 22, 1907, to an amateur female actor and a father who died during World War I. Ashcroft's mother allowed her to attend drama school after she promised not to become an actor, but Ashcroft did not keep her word, making her professional debut in 1926. Two of her leading men were Ralph Richardson and Laurence Olivier. At twenty-four, she became the leading lady at the Old Vic, playing ten roles in nine months. During her stage career, lasting from the 1920s through the 1980s, she played Desdemona to Paul Robeson's Othello (1930) and nineteen other major female roles in the Shakespearean canon. Other playwrights she performed included Ibsen, Chekhov, Shaw, Bulgakov, Wilde, Brecht, Grass, Duras, Albee, Pinter, Webster, and Beckett. She married several times and had children. She spoke for human rights, organized petitions, and raised money by giving poetry recitals on behalf of Amnesty International. Among her awards were becoming a Dame of the British Empire in 1956, an Academy Award for the film *A Passage to India* (1984), and the Olivier Award for lifetime achievement in the theater.

BIBLIOGRAPHY

Billington, Michael. *Peggy Ashcroft.* London: J. Murray, 1988. 0-7195-4436-X, 312p. Billington's life of Peggy Ashcroft concludes with a report of her eightieth birthday celebration, in which she gave a short performance. Billington emphasizes her aid in creating theater companies, with her excellent performances ensuring their continuity and permanence. She proved her acting to be an integral part of society.

Findlater, Richard. *These Our Actors: A Celebration of the Theatre Acting of Peggy Ashcroft, John Gielgud, Laurence Olivier, Ralph Richardson.* London: Elm Tree Books, 1983. 0-241-11060-2, 191p. This collective biography covers four actors in twentieth-century England. The first section reviews Ashcroft's life, tracing her career through the roles she played. Findlater notes that experiences from her private life helped her to develop the depth necessary to play older female characters more fully.

Tanitch, Robert. *Ashcroft*. London: Hutchinson, 1987. 0-09-171030-8, 160p. Tanitch's biography examines each decade in Ashcroft's life from the 1920s when Shakespeare was her greatest influence to the 1970s when she acted in the National Theater. In between, she was a member of John Gielgud's companies and helped begin the English Stage Company and the Royal Shakespeare Company. Her power of interpretation allowed her to play a wide range of roles.

ASHTON-WARNER, SYLVIA (1905–1984)
Educator and Writer   **New Zealand**

Sylvia Ashton-Warner was an innovative educator who developed a method of teaching that effectively helped children learn. She was born on December 17, 1905, and eventually attended Auckland Teachers' Training College in Stratford. There she met her husband, and they started a two-teacher Maori school in a remote area of the North Island. While raising her family of three children, she was the "infant mistress" in the school and developed her revolutionary method of "organic teaching" by creating a unique series of reading books. Later, she wrote for the general public. The protagonist in her first novel, *Spinster* (1958), was a strong but frustrated woman who taught in an isolated school and became an alcoholic. Other novels include *Incense to Idols* (1960), *Bell Call* (1963), *Greenstone* (1967), and *Three* (1970). After her husband died, she traveled for ten years in India, Israel, England, the United States, and Canada. In 1982, she was made a Member of the Order of the British Empire, the first official recognition of her position as one of the world's most influential educators.

BIBLIOGRAPHY

Ashton-Warner, Sylvia. *I Passed This Way*. New York: Knopf, 1979. 0-394-42612-6, 499p. In her autobiography, Ashton-Warner relates anecdotes from her life in New Zealand beginning in 1908 and ending in 1978. She comments that even if a person is not in the home country, the country is still in the person. New Zealand Literary Fund of Queen Elizabeth II Arts Council.

Ashton-Warner, Sylvia. *Spearpoint; Teacher in America*. New York: Knopf, 1972. 0-394-47971-8, 223p. In this autobiographical work, Ashton-Warner writes about the frustrations and rewards of her year of teaching in America.

Ashton-Warner, Sylvia. *Teacher*. New York: Simon and Schuster, 1986. Paper, 0-671-61768-0, 224p. Ashton-Warner discusses her experiments and her belief that teaching is an organic process. She defines the attitude a teacher needs to have to set a creative pattern and gives a practical demonstration of her effective method of teaching.

Hood, Lynley. *Sylvia: The Biography of Sylvia Ashton-Warner*. New York: Viking, 1988. 0-670-81937-9, 264p. Hood says that Ashton-Warner never wanted to be a teacher and claimed that she was never good at it, although she wrote books about teaching and gained recognition as one of the great educators of the world. In this readable biography, Hood sees her as saint and martyr as well as a fraud and a poseur.

ASPASIA (470?–410 B.C.)

Consort   Greece

Noted for her beauty, genius, and political influence, Aspasia married Pericles, the Athenian statesman, after he secured a divorce from his first wife. Since she was not an Athenian citizen, their son, considered illegitimate, was not allowed citizenship. Aspasia was interested in many things; subsequently, her home became a gathering place for the learned and distinguished people of Athens. Associates of the young Socrates knew her well, and she has the reputation of being the teacher of Sophocles. She was one of the two women (Diotima is the other) whom Plato mentioned in his writing. Aspasia influenced many of the decisions that Pericles made, and some historians have held her responsible for the Samian revolt and the Peloponnesian War. She is a character in the play *Menexenus*, and comedies often attacked her private life and her public influence on Pericles.

BIBLIOGRAPHY
Henry, Madeleine Mary. *Prisoner of History: Aspasia of Miletus and Her Biographical Tradition*. New York: Oxford University Press, 1995. 0-19-508712-7, 201p. Although this biography cannot be traditional because much conjecture has been made about the life of Aspasia with little contemporary supporting evidence available, it suggests a range of historical possibilities for Aspasia's life that differ from descriptions and references found in extant Attic comedy. Henry traces Aspasia's *bios* in Greek history and in the comedies; as part of the Socratic tradition and the legacy of prostitutes in the Hellenistic, Roman, and Late Antique Periods; and in the postclassical West. Aspasia's biographical tradition follows those of Sappho and Cleopatra.

ASSISI, CLARE of. *See* CLARE of ASSISI.

ASTELL, MARY (1668–1731)

Writer and Scholar   England

Mary Astell, a serious scholar and supporter of the Anglican faith, espoused the importance of thinking for oneself, became the first Englishwoman of letters, and was probably the first systematic feminist theoretician in the West. A clergyman uncle supposedly educated Astell, daughter of a Newcastle upon Tyne merchant in a Royalist gentry family. After her mother died in 1684, she moved to London, where she sometimes lived alone. She remained single although she had wanted to marry a certain clergyman. She anonymously published *A Serious Proposal to Ladies for the Advancement of their True and Greatest Interest* (1694), proposing an academic community where women could devote themselves to intellectual and religious study while engaging in charitable work. The school or academy, like a monastery, could serve as a refuge for unmarried women of wealth so that they would not have to live with family or undesirable husbands. Her project gained support, but ridicule in newspapers such as the *Tatler* stopped it. In a second tract, *Some Reflections upon Marriage* (1700), she said that marriage should be based on mutual kindness and esteem, with its most important aspect being friendship. She thought that educated women should arrange their own marriages so that they would have more fulfilled lives. Another notable contribution to the intellectual, theological, and philosophical debates of her day was her treatise on *The Christian Religion, as Professed by a Daughter of the Church of England, 1705.*

BIBLIOGRAPHY

Neuburger, Verena E. *Margery Kempe: A Study in Early English Feminism.* New York: P. Lang, 1994. 3-906752-65-8, 219p. Neuburger examines three Englishwomen from the Middle Ages to 1700 using **Virginia Woolf's** commentary in *A Room of One's Own* as a basis. After studying Julian of Norwich and Margery Kempe, Neuburger concludes that Astell was not the first feminist. She thinks, however, that Astell embodies the aspects of both earlier women because she enjoyed the benefits of living alone while simultaneously suffering from her intellectual questioning.

Perry, Ruth. *The Celebrated Mary Astell: An Early English Feminist.* Chicago: University of Chicago Press, 1986. 0-226-66093-1, 549p. Perry demonstrates that Astell deserved her contemporary positive reputation and that historians' judgments of her have been perverse. Perry also posits in this scholarly biography that Astell's ideological convictions may have been detrimental to contemporary women because her separation of mind from body might make them think that only an unmarried woman can be a successful intellectual.

Perry, Ruth. "Mary Astell." *Women and the Enlightenment.* Ed. Margaret Hunt. New York: Haworth, 1984. 0-86656-190-0, 93p. Perry traces Astell's refutation of male arguments with reason, her defense of the Church of England against "progressive" values of English deists, her support of the Stuart monarchy against democratic representation, and her insistence that women should have equal opportunities.

ATHOLL, KATHERINE (1874–1960)

Politician   Scotland

Katherine Marjory Stewart-Murray, duchess of Atholl, became Scotland's first woman member of Parliament in 1923, after being coerced to stand, and was the first Conservative woman to hold a ministerial office on the Board of Education. Born on November 6, 1874, into an old upper-class Scottish family dating from 1232, the Lairds of Banff, and as the daughter of a historian, Kitty Ramsay attended the Royal College of Music, planning to become a composer and performer. In 1899, she married the future duke of Atholl and began her public service by helping in hospitals, organizing concerts to entertain the troops, and investigating medical services. She refused to compromise in her position while working for women, children, and the educational services, although she did not support woman suffrage, opposing **Emmeline Pankhurst's** appeal for a Woman's Party. After becoming a member of Parliament, she opposed international issues such as the enforced circumcision of Kikuyu girls, totalitarianism, and fascism. She read *Mein Kampf* in German and arranged for its translation into English. She went to Spain during the civil war and was in Madrid when Franco bombed and besieged it. She wanted to organize humanitarian relief work, but her party would not support her, so she resigned the party whip to speak against appeasement. In 1938, she tried to warn the country about the buildup of the German air force, knowledge gathered from a private report that the Soviet ambassador sent to her. After losing a by-election during World War II, she kept evacuee children. After the war, she opposed Soviet Russia. She received honorary doctorates from Oxford, Manchester, Durham, McGill, Columbia, Leeds, and Glasgow and published books, including *Working Partnerships* (1958).

BIBLIOGRAPHY

Hetherington, S. J. *Katharine Atholl: Against the Tide.* Aberdeen, Scotland: Aberdeen University Press, 1989. 0-08-036592-2, 234p. In this readable biography, Hetherington reveals a woman of integrity, compassion, and courage. Atholl thought her life was "for the burning" rather than for the wick or the candle, and, as Hetherington documents, Atholl proved it.

Stobaugh, Beverly Parker. *Women and Parliament, 1918–1970.* Hicksville, NY: Exposition, 1978. 0-682-49056-3, 152p. Stobaugh studies women who served in Parliament and includes brief biographies especially successful ones such as Katharine Atholl, who served fifteen years. Stobaugh concludes that the parties discriminated against women, although elected women were better educated and had more experience within their parties and in the local government.

ATWOOD, MARGARET (1939–)

Writer   Canada

Margaret Atwood is an eminent writer adept at irony and satire who has earned international recognition for her novels about contemporary women's lives. Born on November 18, 1939, in Ottawa, Ontario, Canada, she moved to Toronto with her family. She says that she was five when she started writing but that she endured a "dark period" between the ages of eight and sixteen. When she was sixteen, she decided that she must write, expecting to sacrifice family for career, as so many female writers had done before. She attended Victoria College, University of Toronto, and received a Woodrow Wilson Fellowship to begin graduate work at Radcliffe. She unexpectedly married and, later, became a mother. She has taught in Canada and the United States and won many prizes including the Centennial Commission Poetry Competition, the Union Poetry Award, the Bess Hopkins Prize, the St. Lawrence Award for fiction, a Guggenheim Fellowship, and several honorary degrees for works in which she explores role reversals and new beginnings for women seeking to understand their relationships to other individuals and to the world. Novels include *The Circle Game* (1964; rev. ed. 1966), *Surfacing* (1972), *Survival* (1972), *The Handmaid's Tale* (1986), *Cat's Eye* (1989), *The Robber Bride* (1993), and *Alias Grace* (1996).

BIBLIOGRAPHY

Howells, Coral Ann. *Margaret Atwood.* New York: St. Martin's, 1996. 0-312-12891-6, 190p. Howells examines the themes and concerns in Atwood's eight novels, short stories, and analysis of Canadian literature since the publication of *The Edible Woman* in 1969. Howells also looks at the feminist issues, the literary genres, and Atwood's identity as a Canadian writer and woman in this critical and accessible biography.

Ingersoll, Earl G., ed. *Margaret Atwood: Conversations.* Princeton, NJ: Ontario Review, 1990. 0-86538-070-8, 251p. This "biography" is actually a series of twenty-one interviews with Atwood. Atwood disapproves of authorized biographies of boring writers, but the interviews reveal her personal responses to life and, sometimes, to her work.

Rosenberg, Jerome H. *Margaret Atwood*. Boston: Twayne, 1984. 0-8057-6586-7, 184p. Basically a critical study of Atwood's works through 1982, Rosenberg also includes a brief biographical profile. Atwood did not want Rosenberg to write a biography because she was not yet dead. He agreed, and, in addition to the biographical first chapter, he has included incidents from her life in his analyses when they clarify influences on her fiction.

AUNG SAN SUU KYI (1946–)
Activist   Burma

Aung San Suu Kyi (awng san sue chee) won the 1991 Nobel Peace Prize for her campaign of nonviolence to bring democracy to Burma. She was born June 19, 1946, to Aung San, Burma's independence leader and national hero, but he was assassinated when she was two. Her mother became an ambassador to India, and Aung San Suu Kyi went there with her to study before attending Oxford where she met her husband, a Tibet scholar. They lived in Oxford with their two sons until she returned to Burma in 1989 to nurse her ill mother. The government placed her under house arrest in her family home in Myanmar in May 1990, when her party, the National League for Democracy, won a landslide victory. The military government refused to recognize the results and arrested most of the party's leaders but never tried them. She learned about her Nobel Prize on a BBC radio broadcast, one of her few connections to the outside world. She coped with confinement by rising at 4:30 A.M., exercising, and reading voraciously. She was released from house arrest in July 1995. The government says that Aung San Suu Kyi can go free if she leaves the country, but she does not think that anyone should ever have to leave a country with no promise of return.

BIBLIOGRAPHY

Stewart, Whitney. *Aung San Suu Kyi: Fearless Voice of Burma*. Minneapolis: Lerner, 1997. 0-8225-4931-X, 128p. The documented text, based on personal interviews with Aung San Suu Kyi and those around her, relates her story, including her current condition. It reveals the dangers and triumphs that Aung San Suu Kyi has faced in this trying ordeal.

Win, Kanbawza. *Daw Aung San Suu Kyi, the Nobel Laureate: A Burmese Perspective*. Bangkok, Thailand: CPDSK Publications, 1992. No ISBN, 177p. Win notes the difficulties of writing about a living person who cannot be interviewed. The biography gives the Burmese perspective on Aung San Suu Kyi and the indignities to which she has been subjected. She wanted unity, discipline, patience, self-sacrifice, and human rights to become part of the political arena. As Win knows that the Burmese Opposition will speak ill of her, he dwells on the good.

AUSTEN, JANE (1775–1817)
Writer   England

Jane Austen was the preeminent woman novelist of early nineteenth-century England, and her novels reflect the social world of this era. Born on December 16, 1775, into a rector's family of eight children in Steventon, Hampshire, Jane Austen began writing as a child for her own entertainment. She drew her characters from the people she met in her society and through her family, observing with great detail their comments and actions. From her two brothers who became naval officers, she heard about the rituals and realities of life aboard ship. Although pursued, neither she nor her sister Cassandra married; they lived in the family home as best friends. When twenty-five, Austen moved from her childhood home first to Bath (which she hated), then to Southampton, Chawton, and Winchester, where she died from what was diagnosed as Addison's disease. Not until her obituary appeared was her name associated with her novels, four published anonymously and two posthumously. Published before her death to good reviews were *Sense and Sensibility* (begun in 1797, published in 1811), *Pride and Prejudice* (1813), *Mansfield Park* (1814), and *Emma* (1815). Austen finished *Persuasion* in 1815, before she became too ill to write. *Persuasion* and *Northhanger Abbey* (begun in 1797 and sold in 1803 to a publisher who forgot it until 1816) were published in 1818.

BIBLIOGRAPHY

Fergus, Jan S. *Jane Austen: A Literary Life.* New York: St. Martin's, 1991. 0-312-05712-1, 201p. Fergus looks at Austen's life and the situation in which she wrote, including her dealings with publishers, her writing techniques, and her social satire. Fergus thinks that the heroines in Austen's later novels may have had less freedom because Austen became more interested in the constrictions on women in her society.

Honan, Park. *Jane Austen: Her Life.* New York: St. Martin's, 1987. 0-312-01451-1, 452p. Honan used information from diaries, memoirs, letters, and recently disclosed manuscripts to give insight to the kinds of details and ideas that Jane Austen would have observed and heard discussed in her family's home and in the homes of persons in her social class. Chapter titles name the national events that would have affected her and her naval officer brothers.

Nokes, David. *Jane Austen: A Life.* New York: Farrar, Straus, and Giroux, 1997. 0-374-11326-2, 578p. Nokes reveals the Austen family's attitude towards an older mute brother, whom they boarded elsewhere, and posits that Austen's cousin Eliza Hancock influenced her literary development more than sister Cassandra. Although thoroughly researched, the biography approaches fiction when Nokes speculates what people were thinking.

Tomalin, Claire. *Jane Austen: A Life.* New York: Knopf, 1997. 0-679-44628-1, 352p. This carefully researched and recommended biography examines not only the various facets of Austen's life as daughter, aunt, sister, flirt, and author, but also the social customs to which she and her family were subject. Tomalin includes a family tree to clarify relationships among the six branches closely associated with the family.

Tucker, George Holbert. *Jane Austen: The Woman: Some Biographical Insights.* New York: St. Martin's, 1994. 0-312-12049-4, 268p. Tucker discusses topics such as Austen's homes, environments, friends, beaux and blighted romance, timely events, amenities, reading, travel, and religion. He posits that Austen was much more complex than her family biographers wanted people to know and that she revealed the scandals and revolutions through her characters.

ÁVILA, TERESA of. *See* TERESA of ÁVILA.

AYLWARD, GLADYS (1902–1970)
Missionary   England

Gladys Aylward served as a missionary in China and protected the children of the area during wartime. Born on February 24, 1902, in London's Edmonton, Aylward, relatively uneducated and visually impaired, worked first in a shop and then as a parlor maid. Her family of Nonconformists influenced her religious belief, and she became convinced that God had called her to missionary work in China. She went alone to Tientsin via the Trans-Siberian railway. China's ruler, Chaing Kai-Shek, was Christian, but the hostility toward Christians in general forced her to disguise the mission she established as an inn called the Inn of the Sixth Happiness. She worked in Shansi province and became a naturalized citizen, a move that cost her British protection. In 1940, she led over one hundred children from Shansi to Sian, where they would be safe. She returned to London in 1949, but in 1957, she went back to China and started an orphanage in Taiwan. She is buried near Taipei.

BIBLIOGRAPHY
Cowie, Vera. *Girl Friday to Gladys Aylward.* London: Lakeland, 1976. 0-551-00763-X, 156p. Aylward's secretary tells the story of Aylward's Inn of Sixth Happiness in China. People called Aylward "the Small Woman" and admired her work, always selfless, with children of the area.

Swift, Catherine M. *Gladys Aylward.* Minneapolis: Bethany House, 1989. 1-55661-090-4, 128p. Although the China Inland Mission considered Aylward too old to learn the Chinese language, Aylward went to China anyway, proved them wrong, and stayed for twenty years. Swift relates Aylward's tireless efforts to help Chinese children that made royalty and heads of state want to meet her in the later years of her life. Either this biography or Thompson's is a good choice for background on Aylward.

Thompson, Phyllis. *A Transparent Woman; the Compelling Story of Gladys Aylward.* Grand Rapids, MI: Zondervan, 1972. No ISBN, 190p. Thompson tells Aylward's story as she moved from England to China, back to England, and to Taiwan in her career as a missionary. This popular biography reveals a strong woman who fulfilled her beliefs.

B

BADEN-POWELL, OLAVE (1889–1977)
Philanthropist   **England**

Olave St. Claire Baden-Powell established the first Girl Guides and made the organization an international movement through her philanthropy. After her February 22, 1889, birth, she grew up in a family wealthy from the sale of her father's brewery. She disliked society parties, and when she met Lieutenant General Sir Robert Baden-Powell in 1912 while cruising to the West Indies with her father, he was a hero and fifty-five; she married him. She broadened the scouting movement that her husband had begun in 1908, and the Girl Guides (also Girl Scouts) flourished under Lady Baden-Powell's leadership. She slowly extended her responsibility for the organization and modernized its activities. For forty years, she flew nearly five hundred thousand miles helping other countries develop and establish their programs, increasing membership to nearly 7 million. In 1932, she received the Dame of the British Empire. Awards from other countries included the Order of the White Rose from Finland and the Order of the Sun from Peru.

BIBLIOGRAPHY

Baden-Powell, Olave. *Window on My Heart: The Autobiography of Olave, Lady Baden-Powell*. London: Hodder and Stoughton, 1973. 0-340-15944-8, 256p. Baden-Powell's autobiography gives an interesting and reasonably complete overview of her life and her service to Girl Guiding. It contains a list of countries she visited and anecdotes from some of those journeys.

Wade, Eileen Kirkpatrick. *The World Chief Guide—Olave, Lady Baden-Powell: The Story of Her Life*. 2nd rev. ed. London: Hutchinson, 1972. 0-09-110390-8, 174p. This laudatory look at Baden-Powell employs a somewhat condescending tone for the young adult reader. It discusses her achievements and sees her actions as all positive.

BAILLIE, JOANNA (1762–1851)
Playwright   Scotland

Joanna Baillie was the leading Scottish dramatist of her time. Born on September 11, 1762, as the daughter of a clergyman, Baillie lived in Bothwell, Lanark, and Glasgow when her father became professor of divinity. When he died in 1778, the family returned to the country, and Baillie began to write. Five years later, her brother inherited a house in London, and the family joined him. She published her first poems, *Fugitive Verses* (1790), anonymously, and in 1798, her first plays appeared, followed by volumes in 1802 and 1812. Sarah Siddons appeared in Baillie's play *De Montfort* at Drury Lane. Sir Walter Scott liked her work, and she and her sister visited him when they toured Scotland. In Hampstead, Baillie became a society hostess, and the Scotts visited them in return. She traveled in Britain and on the Continent while continuing to write. Even though religion was always an important aspect of her life, she questioned all aspects of doctrine. Her moral beliefs, however, caused her to show women in her plays who were basically virtuous but who were victims of evil men. Wordsworth liked her poetry, and her theory of poetry, written in 1798, was similar to that of the Lake poets and their view of Romanticism.

BIBLIOGRAPHY
Carhart, Margaret Sprague. *The Life and Work of Joanna Baillie*. 1923. Hamden, CT: Archon, 1970. 0-208-00917-5, 215p. This academic biography presents Baillie's life and describes her dramas and their performances. Carhart lauds Baillie as Scotland's greatest dramatist.

BAKER, JANET (1933–)
Opera Singer   England

Janet Abbott Baker has sung leading roles throughout the world and won many prizes for her work as a recitalist, concert performer, and opera singer. When Baker was born on August 21, 1933, her parents neither performed nor listened to classical music, but when Baker's father took her to Gilbert and Sullivan at the D'Orly Carte Theatre, she intuitively knew that it was not "real" music. As a young girl, she decided that she would be an opera singer, and she credits her parents with supporting her decision. She made her opera debut in 1956 as Roza in Smetana's *The Secret* with the Oxford University Opera Club. During her career, she sang at such places as Glyndebourne, the Edinburgh Festival, Royal Albert Hall in London, San Francisco, and New York. She has sung a range of classical works, modern opera, and Bach cantatas for which she received a Royal Philharmonic Society gold medal and the Dame Commander of the British Empire in 1976.

BIBLIOGRAPHY
Baker, Janet. *Full Circle: An Autobiographical Journal*. New York: Franklin Watts, 1982. 0-531-09876-1, 269p. Baker says in her autobiography that after years of fear, she finally learned that she was the channel through which music would reach an audience, and if she prepared musically, physically, and psychologically, the audience would respond to the music.
Blyth, Alan. *Janet Baker*. New York: Drake, 1973. 0-87749-528-9, 64p. Blyth presents Baker's career and shows her conviction and integrity. He thinks that her hard work is what has made her successful because she has always

practiced her belief that every attempt to make music must have meaning for both the artist and the audience.

BARNARD, MARJORIE (1897–1987)
Writer   Australia

Marjorie Barnard, under the pen name M. Barnard Eldershaw, cowrote five novels and three history books with Flora Eldershaw while also publishing award-winning work under her own name. Born August 16, 1897, in Ashfield, Marjorie Barnard studied at the Sydney Girls' High School and Sydney University. Her father made her decline a scholarship to Oxford in England, where she wanted to pursue history; instead she became a librarian at the Sydney Technical College. Her first co-authored novel, *A House Is Built*, reached a large readership, but the co-authored histories have generally received wider acclaim. Although M. Barnard Eldershaw's fiction may be uneven, critics never saw it as mediocre. Other titles co-authored include *Green Memory*, *The Glasshouse*, and *Plaque with Laurel*, all works attempting to present Australia through literature. Barnard published children's stories as well as historical and critical works under her own name, such as *A History of Australia* (1959) and *Miles Franklin* (1965). In 1983, she won the Patrick White Award. During the same year, an uncensored version of *Tomorrow and Tomorrow*, the last novel she wrote with Eldershaw, was published with its original full title, *Tomorrow and Tomorrow and Tomorrow*.

BIBLIOGRAPHY
Rorabacher, Louise Elizabeth. *Marjorie Barnard and M. Barnard Eldershaw*. New York: Twayne, 1973. No ISBN, 211p. This biography looks at the collaboration of Barnard with Flora Eldershaw in their novels and histories as well as their individual writings. Rorabacher emphasizes that Barnard was the better writer of the two, but Eldershaw never revealed whether she liked to write or merely needed the money.

BATES, DAISY (1861–1951)
Writer and Anthropologist   Ireland

Dame Daisy Bates lived with Australian aborigines and documented their languages and customs in anthropological studies. Born in Tipperary, Ireland, on October 16, 1861, Daisy O'Dwyer moved with her family to England. In 1884, she migrated to Australia, where she met and married Edwin Murrant, known as "Breaker" Morant (with the spelling changed). The next year, she married again, probably as a bigamist, Jack Bates, a cattleman. She left for England in 1894 and became a journalist but returned to Australia five years later to investigate alleged ill treatment of the aborigines. Her adoption of the black community at her arrival in Perth seems to have been, at first, intellectual rather than emotional. But by 1910, she had learned enough about the aborigine life to join an anthropological expedition. She became an honorary protector of the aborigines, and, from 1919 to 1935, she lived in a tent at Ooldea, helping the people around her. During that time, in 1933, she was made a Dame Commander of the British Empire. She moved next to the Murray River and wrote *The Passing of the Aborigines* (1939). She also lived in Koolaarrabulloo, Nullarbor Plain, and Adelaide. Reports note that the aborigines often laughed at

other whites, but never at Bates. Her papers on the aborigines, now held by the
National Library at Canberra, are an important historical record. She wrote
her autobiography in 1938.

BIBLIOGRAPHY
Blackburn, Julia. *Daisy Bates in the Desert*. New York: Pantheon Books, 1994.
0-679-42001-0, 232p. Since Daisy Bates gave contradictory accounts of
her life and work, Blackburn has used letters and diaries for her biography.
Blackburn also traveled to places where Bates worked and interviewed the
natives.

Hill, Ernestine. *Kabbarli: A Personal Memoir of Daisy Bates*. Sydney, Australia:
Angus and Robertson, 1973. 0-207-12478-7, 173p. This lively, interesting,
accessible, and recommended view of Bates, called "Kabbarli" or "Grandmother" by the natives, written by a close friend, is biased but informative.
Hill gives the reader a sense of knowing Bates and her devotion to preserving the legacy of the aborgines.

Salter, Elizabeth. *Daisy Bates*. New York: Coward, McCann and Geoghegan,
1972. No ISBN, 266p. Salter relates Bates' complete life story from her
Irish childhood to her days with the aborigines. Since some thought Bates
was a fraud, Salter went into the outback to verify where Bates lived and
describes this journey. After examining Bates' papers, Salter notes that
Bates accomplished much, even though Bates thought her life a failure.

BATTEN, JEAN (1909–1982)
Aviator   New Zealand

Jean Batten established aviation records, and her record in 1937 of flying her
Percival Gull monoplane from London to New Zealand lasted for forty-four
years. She was born on September 15, 1909, in New Zealand. In 1929, Batten
went from New Zealand to England to join the London Areoplane Club in
hopes of fulfilling her dream to fly solo from England to New Zealand. She
earned both her private and her commercial licenses by 1932 and, after two
failures, successfully flew solo to Australia in 1934. In 1935, she flew from
England to Brazil and established a new speed record. She made her last record
flight when she flew from Australia to England in 1937. In 1978, she received
the Freedom of the City of London and the Chevalier, Légion d'honneur in
recognition of her early achievements. During the second half of her life, she
lived in Portugal with her mother, out of the limelight, with few people knowing anything about her past. When she died, failed communications in Lisbon
kept her from being buried as she had requested.

BIBLIOGRAPHY
Mackersey, Ian. *Jean Batten: The Garbo of the Skies*. Auckland, New Zealand:
Macdonald, 1990. 0-908875-11-8, 465p. Mackersey once saw Batten,
alone and beautiful, on a train when she rudely ignored his mother. After
reading her self-absorbed autobiography, he discovered that no one had
written a biography about the woman who had brought honor to New Zealand. His research shows a lonely perfectionist, an organizer, and a professional who never exposed her private life to anyone.

BAUM, VICKI (1888–1960)
Writer   Austria

Vicki Hedvig Baum wrote *The Grand Hotel*, which became a best-seller throughout the world before becoming a play and a film starring Greta Garbo and Joan Crawford. Born on January 27, 1888, in Austria, she trained as a musician but did not perform as a harpist or teach music until after she separated from the man she married when she was eighteen. She moved to Germany and served as a nurse during World War I. She married a conductor in 1916 and ended her brief musical career to begin writing. A friend discovered her manuscripts in 1920 and published *Der Eingang zur Bühnel* (Falling Star). Baum did not publish again until 1929 with *Helene Willfuer* (Helene Willfur) and *Menschen im Hotel* (The Grand Hotel). When Baum came to New York to see a performance of *The Grand Hotel*, she decided to stay. Her family joined her, and after they settled in California, Baum became a naturalized citizen in 1938. She continued to write in German, but the works were translated into many languages. She also wrote *Weeping Wood* (1943), *Headless Angel* (1948), *Hotel Shanghai* (1953), *The Mustard Seed* (1953), and *Ballerina* (1958).

BIBLIOGRAPHY
King, Lynda J. *Best-Sellers by Design: Vicki Baum and The House of Ullstein*. Detroit: Wayne State University Press, 1988. 0-8143-2000-7, 252p. In exploring Baum's Weimar Republic career, King thinks that modern Germanists have ignored Baum because The House of Ullstein aggressively marketed her best-seller *Grand Hotel* between 1926 and 1932, rather than because she lacked literary quality. King documents her case that Baum is an important writer in German literary tradition.

BAYLIS, LILIAN (1874–1937)
Theater Manager   England

Lilian Baylis created a national repertory theater and superb acting school at London's Old Vic Theater. After her birth on May 9, 1874, her musician parents early trained her to be a violinist. Her family emigrated to South Africa when Baylis was six, and, as an adult, she had begun training a Johannesburg ladies' orchestra when her influential aunt summoned her to London for help with managing the Royal Victoria Coffee Music Hall. She had created this place in the Old Vic in 1880 to offer non-alcoholic working class entertainment. Baylis's aunt died in 1912, and Baylis became the sole manager, providing drama, opera, and ballet. Baylis thought God had destined her work, and she devoted her life to provide entertainment for large audiences at prices they could afford. Although she did not particularly like Shakespeare, she felt obligated to present all of his plays, and she did so between 1914 and 1923. Drama became the Old Vic's mainstay, so Baylis used Sadler's Wells Theatre for opera and ballet productions, with **Ninette de Valois** helping Baylis make ballet as popular as opera. When Oxford gave Baylis an honorary master's degree in 1924, she was only the second woman to receive this distinction.

BIBLIOGRAPHY
Findlater, Richard. *Lilian Baylis: The Lady of the Old Vic*. London: Allen Lane, 1975. 0-7139-0902-1, 320p. Because Baylis's work was her life, she wrote few letters other than business correspondence, and those were brisk and impersonal. Findlater says that telling about her life is especially difficult

since she did not direct, design, or present new work. Additionally, she told contradictory anecdotes, which he had difficulty verifying, but he attempts to present her life through the history of the Old Vic beginning in 1880.

BEALE, DOROTHEA (1831–1906)
Educator   England

Dorothea Beale knew as a young child that she wanted to teach, and she became a pioneer in women's education. Her parents, an open-minded surgeon and a feminist, encouraged their children to learn as much as they could and to follow the professions they wanted. Beale attended school in Paris until the revolution began in 1848 and graduated from Queen's College. She then became the college's first woman faculty member as a mathematics tutor, then as Latin tutor, and finally as the head teacher in the school connected to the college. In 1857, she began teaching at the Clergy Daughters School in Casterton. Its rigid educational philosophy disturbed Beale, and she left the next year to become the principal of Cheltenham Ladies' College in 1858, selected over fifty other candidates. She stayed for fifty years, doubling enrollment and improving the school's finances. She encouraged strong academic courses during the morning hours, arguing that well-educated females with a hunger for learning would make better wives and mothers, and freed the afternoon for needlework, drawing, and music. By 1900, the school had over one thousand students with boardinghouses, a secondary school, and teacher training at St. Hilda's College. In 1902, Beale received an honorary doctorate from the University of Edinburgh.

BIBLIOGRAPHY
Steadman, F. Cecily. *In the Days of Miss Beale: A Study of Her Work and Influence.* London: E. J. Burrow, 1931. No ISBN, 194p. Beale hoped that no one would write her life because she thought it was between her and God. Steadman recounts the memories of Beale's friends and those who observed her within the college while she lived.

Raikes, Elizabeth. *Dorothea Beale of Cheltenham.* London: A. Constable, 1908. No ISBN, 432p. Raikes presents Beale's life as inseparable from the life of Ladies' College, Cheltenham, and Beale's work (she called the school her "husband") as more important than her life. Raikes uses letters, diaries, and autobiographical fragments to disclose Beale's personality.

Gathorne-Hardy, John. *The Old School Tie.* New York: Viking, 1978. 0-670-52316-X, 480p. The text relates the history of schools in England through their progression and change. Gathorne-Hardy also discusses Beale's invaluable contribution to the development of schools and women's education.

BEAUFORT, MARGARET (1443–1509)
Activist and Patron   England

The mother of Henry VII, Margaret Beaufort was an aristocrat who helped to stop the Wars of the Roses. Born on May 31, 1443, as the only daughter and heir of John Beaufort, duke of Somerset, Beaufort married four times, the first an arranged marriage to the son of her guardian. Her second husband, Edmund Tudor, earl of Richmond, died when they had been married a year, and three months later, when Beaufort was fourteen, she had a son, who was to become

Henry VII in 1485 at the end of the Wars of the Roses. Her third husband died in 1471, and she left her fourth husband to lead a life of piety. As a prominent member of the English royal house of Lancaster, she was instrumental in uniting the two warring houses of Lancaster and York by helping to arrange a marriage between Henry VII and Elizabeth of York (1465–1503), the eldest surviving daughter of King Edward IV. She was a patron of learning, with such people as William Caxton, the first English printer, in her largesse. She established divinity professorships at the universities of Oxford and Cambridge, with the Lady Margaret professorship at Cambridge being the oldest in the university. In 1505, she founded Christ's College from the former God's House, and in 1508, she changed the tainted hospital of Saint John the Evangelist into Saint John's College, both at Cambridge.

BIBLIOGRAPHY

Jones, Michael K., and Malcolm G. Underwood. *The King's Mother: Lady Margaret Beaufort, Countess of Richmond and Derby.* New York: Cambridge University Press, 1992. 0-521-34512-X, 322p. This readable biography shows complementary but simultaneously conflicting aspects of Beaufort's personality—pious, politic, and businesslike—while carefully placing her in her times. Beaufort was essentially admirable and generous with her wealth, but she was also involved in local and national intrigues as she prepared the way for her son to become king. Of all the biographies, this one focuses most closely on Lady Beaufort herself.

Seward, Desmond. *The Wars of the Roses: Through the Lives of Five Men and Women of the Fifteenth Century.* New York: Viking, 1995. 0-670-84258-3, 379p. Seward observes Beaufort, one of five persons in this collective biography, against a background of real people enduring a difficult war. The biography helps modern readers to understand Beaufort's times, using both modern scholarship and fifteenth-century sources.

Simon, Linda. *Of Virtue Rare: Margaret Beaufort, Matriarch of the House of Tudor.* Boston: Houghton Mifflin, 1982. 0-395-31563-8, 164p. Simon's biography is more a history of the fifteenth century than a re-creation of Beaufort's life. With much extraneous information filling the text, the book will satisfy few readers interested in either Beaufort or the Wars of the Roses.

BEAUVOIR, SIMONE de (1908–1986)

Writer and Philosopher   France

Simone de Beauvoir studied and taught philosophy and then wrote that humans should be responsible for themselves and that women should have rights. Born in Paris on January 9, 1908, as the daughter of a lawyer, Simone de Beauvoir's parents were obsessed with social class. She studied philosophy at the Sorbonne, taking a second to Jean-Paul Sartre, and taught it in Marseilles, Rouen, and Paris. She stayed in Paris during the German Occupation of World War II and published her first novel, *She Came to Stay* (1943), in which she explored the existentialist dilemma of finding meaning in an absurd world. Later novels with the same theme include *The Blood of Others* (1944) and *The Mandarins* (1954), a Prix Goncourt winner. In her autobiographical works, notably *Memoirs of a Dutiful Daughter* (1958) and *All Said and Done* (1972), she continued to express the belief that one is responsible for oneself. One of de Beauvoir's most important nonfiction works is *The Second Sex* (1949), an analysis of women's role in society through mythology, political theory, history, and psychology. Other nonfiction includes *Adieux: A Farewell to Sartre* (1981), a memoir about her lover and longtime colleague, whom she refused to marry. She became sympathetic to the Communist Party during the 1940s and visited the USSR and China with Sartre in 1956 and Vietnam in 1967. A strong advocate for women's rights, she was president of the League for the Rights of Women, helping battered wives, working women, and single parents.

BIBLIOGRAPHY

Bair, Deirdre. *Simone de Beauvoir: A Biography.* New York: Summit, 1990. 0-671-60681-6, 718p. Bair's biography is a readable and balanced view of de Beauvoir's life based on six years of discussion with de Beauvoir. Bair thinks de Beauvoir lived life on her own terms.

Beauvoir, Simone de. *Adieux: A Farewell to Sartre.* Trans. Patrick O'Brian. New York: Pantheon, 1984. 0-394-53035-7, 453p. In this biography, Beauvoir includes the diary of her life with Sartre from 1970 to 1980 and a series of conversations that she recorded in 1974.

Evans, Mary. *Simone de Beauvoir.* London: Sage, 1996. 0-8039-8866-4, 144p. Evans says that the text is not a full biography or discussion of de Beauvoir's work but an account of de Beauvoir's life and some suggestions about the themes and tensions that she projected, including the mother concept and dependence on men.

Fullbrook, Kate, and Edward Fullbrook. *Simone de Beauvoir and Jean-Paul Sartre: The Remaking of a Twentieth-Century Legend.* New York: Basic Books, 1994. 0-465-07827-3, 214p. The authors, in their reexamination of de Beauvoir and Sartre through their letters and diaries, attempt to demonstrate that Beauvoir was the primary impetus to the ideas espoused by the two, having already written the seminal study on which Sartre based *Being and Nothingness* in her *She Came to Stay* two years earlier.

Moi, Toril. *Simone de Beauvoir: The Making of an Intellectual Woman.* New York: Blackwell, 1994. 0-631-14673-3, 324p. In a balanced and readable biography, Moi analyzes de Beauvoir's life, philosophy, and art from sociological and feminist perspectives and finds that de Beauvoir thought that masculinity represented privilege.

BEETON, ISABEL (1836–1865)
Writer   England

Isabel Beeton wrote books that influenced the social life of England for years after her death. Born in London on March 14, 1836, Isabella Mayson became the eldest in a large family when her widowed mother remarried a man with children. Educated at private schools in Islington and Heidelberg, she became a pianist, but after her marriage in 1856 to Samuel Orchart Beeton, a journalist and publisher, she began a professional partnership with him. She published her first articles in his magazine, *The Englishwomen's Domestic Magazine*, in April 1857, the same year of her first child's death. She began planning a household encyclopedia, and by 1860, when she had become the fashion correspondent and editor of her husband's magazine, she began publishing parts of her book. *Mrs. Beeton's Book of Household Management* appeared as a complete book in 1861, and, at one thousand pages, it was the most comprehensive guide to domestic affairs ever published. It addressed household matters encompassing such topics as the management of servants and properly polishing silver. Although she was only twenty-five, her four years of work revealed nineteenth-century social history. Sixty thousand copies sold the first year, and new editions followed, along with two cookbooks. During the birth of her fourth son, she contracted puerperal fever and died.

BIBLIOGRAPHY

Nown, Graham. *Mrs. Beeton: 150 Years of Cookery and Household Management*. London: Ward Lock, 1986. 0-7063-6459-7, 136p. By the time Beeton died at twenty-eight, she had perpetrated the myth of what the Victorian woman should do. Nown shows that Beeton did not "practice" what she "preached," because she and her husband worked together, the opposite of what she proposed in her book. The biography attempts to reconcile who Beeton was with what she said by inserting Beeton's commentary from *Household Management*.

Freeman, Sarah. *Isabella and Sam: The Story of Mrs. Beeton*. New York: Coward, McCann and Geoghegan, 1978. 0-698-10711-X, 336p. While Isabella Beeton compiled her major work on cookery, psychology, etiquette, and management, she and her husband were partners in a happy marriage and in a successful business. Freeman shows the mundane details in their lives as she looks at each of them separately, then together, and finally Sam alone, barely coping after Isabella's early death.

BEHN, APHRA (1640?–1689)
Writer and Playwright   **England**

Aphra Behn was England's most famous writer before the nineteenth century. Almost nothing appears about the first twenty years of Aphra Behn's life except her birth date of July 10, 1640, but facts indicate that she went to live in Surinam as a child, presumably with her parents. In 1664, she returned to England and married Behn, a Dutch merchant who died the next year from the plague. Verifiable facts about her life begin with her service to Charles II, king of England, who employed her as a spy in Antwerp during the war years of 1665 to 1667. Near the end of 1668, after her return, she was briefly jailed for debt. Her need to survive led her to write, and in 1670, she became the first known professional female writer in England. In her one tragedy and fourteen comedies, she attacked mercenary marriages, encouraged James II to become her patron, and deprecated the Whigs (causing a second arrest). She wrote thirteen "novels" before Defoe published *Robinson Crusoe* (which critics have long considered the first novel) and seventeen plays in seventeen years. Toward the end of her life, her novel *Oroonoko*, the story of an African prince sold into slavery in Surinam, influenced content in the English novel by introducing the "noble savage," developing the anticolonial theme, and depicting a realistic background. Her contemporaries hesitated to acknowledge her abilities since her content was often bawdy, but she asserted that women should be able to write anything allowed men.

BIBLIOGRAPHY

Duffy, Maureen. *The Passionate Shepherdess: Aphra Behn, 1640–89*. London: Cape, 1977. 0-224-01349-1, 324p. Since only twenty or so documents exist containing information about Behn's life, Duffy claims that Behn's life was difficult to re-create. Although Duffy wants to introduce Behn to a new generation, her biography is neither carefully documented nor clearly organized.

Goreau, Angeline. *Reconstructing Aphra: A Social Biography of Aphra Behn.* New York: Dial, 1980. 0-8037-7478-8, 339p. In a scholarly biography, Goreau focuses on Behn's position as the first professional woman writer in English. She follows Behn's political activism, abolitionist views, belief in sexual equality, and reputation for bawdy plays, which excluded her burial in Westminster Abbey's Poets' Corner, and presents Restoration politics, drama, and sexual mores.

Mendelson, Sara Heller. *The Mental World of Stuart Women: Three Studies.* Amherst: University of Massachusetts Press, 1987. 0-87023-591-5, 235p. In a collective biography, Mendelson examines the seventeenth-century patriarchal society in which females had to function, control of female sexuality, limitations of their conventional roles, and the male reactions of irritation when women such as Behn did not follow their advice. Mendelson surveys Behn's life before she moved to London, her experience in London as a playwright, and her life after she won fame as a dramatist.

Sackville-West, V. *Aphra Behn, the Incomparable Astrea.* 1927. New York: Russell and Russell, 1970. No ISBN, 92p. This brief study introduces Behn by covering what is generally known about her life in Surinam, Antwerp, and London, with a concluding presentation of her works.

BELL, GERTRUDE (1868–1926)
Writer and Scholar   **England**

Gertrude Margaret Lothian Bell became an expert on Middle Eastern cultures by learning the language and living there. She was born in Durham County on 14 July, 1868, and educated at Lady Margaret Hall, Oxford University, the first woman to earn a first-class degree in modern history. She began traveling after college, socializing in diplomatic circles, and in 1899, visited friends in Jerusalem, where she learned Arabic. In March 1900, she made her first journey into the desert. She returned to England and founded the women's Anti-Suffrage League in 1908, having little regard for the intelligence of other women. During the next six years, she made several archaeological expeditions in Asia Minor and on the Arabian Peninsula. Her knowledge of the Mesopotamian tribes helped British intelligence forces needing information on the Middle East during World War I. After serving the Military Intelligence in Cairo, she went to Baghdad in 1917 to serve as the assistant political officer, and Iraqis called her al-Khatun, "the Lady." She helped to determine the British terms for Iraqi independence and was instrumental in the election of Faisal I as the first king of Iraq. Works about her travel include *Poems from the Divan of Hafiz* (1897), *The Desert and the Sown* (1907), *Amurath to Amurath* (1911), and *the Palace and the Mosque of Ukhaidir* (1914).

BIBLIOGRAPHY
Bell, Gertrude Lowthian. *The Desert and the Sown.* 1907. Boston: Beacon, 1987. Paper, 0-86068-496-2, 347p. In this retelling of her trip through the Ottoman provinces of Lebanon, Syria, and Palestine in 1905, Bell reveals her own habits as well as those of people she met. She searches her own preconceptions as she relates them to the actual social and political situations as well as the history of the area.

Ffrench, Yvonne. *Six Great Englishwomen: Queen Elizabeth I, Sarah Siddons, Charlotte Brontë, Florence Nightingale, Queen Victoria, Gertrude Bell.* Folcroft, PA: Folcroft Library Editions, 1976. 0-8414-4219-3, 246p. In a collective biography, Ffrench looks at Englishwomen with strong reputations. She asserts that they all had a largesse of spirit and a strength of character, with Bell also being brilliant and intrepid. Ffrench concludes that Bell was not "good" or philanthropic but that she was courageous when faced with danger and tried to overcome her difficulties.

Goodman, Susan. *Gertrude Bell.* Dover, NH: Berg, 1985. Paper, 0-90758-268-0, 122p. Goodman gives a brief and pedestrian but viable overview of Bell's life. Goodman posits that Bell's death in Baghdad could have been caused by her taking a drug overdose because Bell did not think she could survive the summer, and she did not want to return to the emptiness of England.

Wallach, Janet. *Desert Queen: The Extraordinary Life of Gertrude Bell—Adventurer, Adviser to Kings, Ally of Lawrence of Arabia.* New York: Nan Talese, Doubleday, 1996. 0-385-47408-3, 400p. Relying on Bell's correspondence and her diaries, Wallach's recommended biography gives a daily account of Bell's life from her childhood in Northumbria until her alleged suicide. Among the pictures of Bell that emerge are traveler, British spy, antisuffragist, and occasional sufferer. The accompanying photographs, previously unpublished, also unveil Bell and her passion for the Middle East.

BERENICE (28?–83)
Consort   Palestine

Berenice is one of the remarkable women of the first-century Christian era who grew up in its political unrest and intrigue and made their influence felt through the men around them. She was the daughter of the first king of Judaea, Agrippa I, and the great granddaughter of Herod the Great in an aristocratic family that regarded power and wealth as its due. A century later than Cleopatra, she also used her charms to further political aims, but she was never queen in her own right. Because of her influence, people accused her of incest and depravity with her brother and being a bigot. She had two kings as husbands and, afterward, lived with her brother, Agrippa II, king of the territories across the Jordan and in Lebanon. She was also the mistress of Titus, son of the Roman emperor Vespasian. She moved between Judaism and Hellenism and was at home in the Court of Women or in the temple of Jerusalem. She sat on a tribunal before which St. Paul appeared around A.D. 60, and during the Jewish Rebellion of A.D. 66, she supported the Romans. Her contemporaries wrote no independent accounts of her life because her part in history was secondary to that of the men around her. No statue has survived, so no one knows what she looked like. All that is known is that she was a woman of charm and beauty, and that in her middle age, she was attractive enough that Titus, twelve years younger than she, probably wanted to marry her, but public outrage quelled the liaison.

BIBLIOGRAPHY
Jordan, Ruth. *Berenice.* New York: Barnes and Noble, 1974. 0-06-493402-0, 248p. The biography shows Berenice as a woman with both faults and virtues and places her against the background of her times. Jordan additionally documents Berenice's appearances in both verbal and visual art.

BERGMAN, INGRID (1915–1982)

Actor   Sweden

Ingrid Bergman received acclaim for her acting in film and on stage. She was born on August 29, 1915, in Stockholm to a painter who became a photography shop owner in order to support his wife and family. Bergman's mother died when she was three, and a spinster aunt who rejected all unsanitary things raised her. Bergman enjoyed singing, playing the piano, and acting for her father while attending Palmgrenska Samskolan, Stockholm's most prestigious girls' school. After going to the theater with her father when she was eleven, she decided to become an actress. When she auditioned for the Royal Dramatic Theater, she won one of eight available places from a field of seventy-five people. In her career, she performed in sixty-two different productions—forty-six films, eleven stage plays, and five television dramas. Her "immoral" extramarital affair with Roberto Rossellini kept her temporarily out of work but did not harm Rossellini. For her performance in *Autumn Sonata,* she won both the New York Film Critic's and Italy's Donatello Awards.

BIBLIOGRAPHY

Bergman, Ingrid, and Alan Burgess. *Ingrid Bergman, My Story.* New York: Delacorte, 1980. 0-440-03299-7, 504p. Bergman says that she wrote her autobiography because her son told her that gossip columnists would recreate her life, and her children would remain unable to defend her without knowing the truth. She shares some of her superficial thoughts, acknowledges contributions from others to her career, and sometimes tries to justify her choices between family and work. Alan Burgess, her writer, adds commentary.

Brown, Curtis F. *Ingrid Bergman.* New York: Galahad, 1974. 0-88365-164-0, 157p. Brown thinks that Bergman embodied the qualities associated with strong but vulnerable women and asserts that Bergman performed best when she played roles illustrating the ideals of womanhood. He ranks her as a superstar in this biography, a best choice for reading.

Leamer, Laurence. *As Time Goes By: The Life of Ingrid Bergman.* New York: Harper and Row, 1986. 0-06-015485-3, 423p. Leamer uses Bergman's autobiography, interviews, letters, diaries, and movie contracts as his sources. A chatty tone controls the balanced and thorough content, but Leamer fails to capture the "real" Bergman.

Quirk, Lawrence J. *The Complete Films of Ingrid Bergman.* New York: Carol Communications, 1989. 0-8065-0972-4, 241p. Quirk gives an overview of Bergman's career and then discusses all of her films, including their plots and critical reviews.

Taylor, John Russell. *Ingrid Bergman.* New York: St. Martin's, 1983. 0-312-41796-9, 127p. Taylor thinks that Bergman did not have to choose to be either a great star or a mother because she could be both. In this adulatory biography with photographs, Taylor includes chapters on Bergman's life in Sweden, the United States, and Italy.

BERNADETTE (1844–1879)

Religious   France

Bernadette helped establish Lourdes as a pilgrim shrine and nursed soldiers during the Franco-Prussian War, endeavors that gained her sainthood. Born

Bernadette Soubirous in Lourdes on January 7, 1844, to a poor miller with eight other children, she began to have asthma attacks at six. When she was eleven, a cholera epidemic struck the area, but she recovered. She had her first catechism class on January 21, 1858, and her first apparition several days later on February 11. By April 7, she had had seventeen visions of the Virgin Mary and received knowledge that the Virgin had imparted miraculous powers of healing to the waters of the River Gave near a grotto in Lourdes. On June 3, she took her first Holy Communion, and, while tending her sheep on July 16, 1862, she had her eighteenth vision. The Virgin requested that a chapel be built in the area and told Bernadette how to find a spring that had been forgotten. After seven cures occurred at the spring, the Roman Catholic church declared Bernadette's visions as authentic. The Lourdes grotto became a shrine for pilgrims when people were healed there in 1858, and thousands witnessed Bernadette's transfigurations. In 1866, Bernadette joined the Sisters of Charity at Nevers and continued religious and charitable work. Before she died in 1879, she had been near enough death to receive extreme unction four times. She was beatified in 1925 and canonized in 1933, with her feast day occurring on April 16.

BIBLIOGRAPHY

Laurentin, Rene. *Bernadette of Lourdes: A Life Based on Authenticated Documents*. Trans. John Drury. Minneapolis: Winston, 1979. 0-030-51156-9, 243p. Laurentin relates names, events, and documented conversations that place Bernadette at Lourdes from 1844 to 1866 and at Nevers from 1866 to 1879. When word of her apparitions spread, she had to have protection from the public. The second part of the biography covers her religious life and the various difficulties during her time with the Sisters of Charity.

Lynch, John W. *Bernadette—The Only Witness*. Boston: St. Paul Editions, 1981. 0-8198-1104-1, 184p. This readable biography, based on the research of L'abbé René Laurentin and Reverend André Ravier, tells about Bernadette's life and her family background as well as the activities that led to her canonization.

Ravier, André. *Bernadette*. Trans. Barbara Wall. Photos. Helmuth Nils Loose. Cleveland, OH: Collins, 1979. 0-529-05672-0, 63p. In this biography of Bernadette, Ravier documents her life of poverty and illiteracy before she began to receive visions of the Virgin Mary. He continues with her experiences in the convent and the attitudes of her superiors and inquisitors. He also inserts a calendar of the Virgin's appearances in 1858.

BERNHARDT, SARAH (1844-1923)

Actor   France

Rosine Bernhard, known by her stage name of Sarah Bernhardt, was the best-known stage figure of her time. Born in Paris on October 22 or 23, 1844, Bernhardt was the daughter of a courtesan. She was educated in a convent and at the Paris Conservatoire before making her unnoticed debut at the Comédie Française in 1862. She gained recognition in 1869 at the Théâtre de l'Odéon playing in *Le Passant*, a comedy by François Coppée. Recalled to the Comédie Française in 1872, Bernhardt played the leading role in *Phèdre* (1874), followed by the queen in *Ruy Blas* (1872) and Doña Sol in *Hernani* (1877), to great acclaim. She began to travel with her own company in 1879 and left the Comédie the next year. She appeared regularly in London and New York City and toured internationally. In Paris, she managed or owned various theaters, including the Théâtre des Nations, since renamed the Théâtre Sarah Bernhardt, in which she often appeared. Among her most successful performances were those in *La Dame aux Camelias, Adrienne Lecouvreur, Fedora, Theodora, La Tosca,* and *Cleopatre*. She played the title role in a French version of Shakespeare's *Hamlet* (1899) and *L'Aiglon* (1901), a play about Napoleon. Famous for her slim beauty and bell-like voice, people called her the "divine Sarah." Bernhardt had a leg amputated when seventy, but she refused to abandon the stage, playing for troops in World War I and acting until her death. She wrote two plays, a work on acting, and her memoirs as well as exhibited her sculpture and painting. Bernhardt was made a member of the Legion of Honor in 1914.

BIBLIOGRAPHY

Aston, Elaine. *Sarah Bernhardt: A French Actress on the English Stage*. New York: Berg, St. Martin's, 1989. 0-85496-019-8, 173p. Since the French condemned Bernhardt for her independence and determination, Aston looks at the English reaction to her as an actress by relying on newspaper reviews for production dates and critical responses to Bernhardt's acting. In this standard biography, Aston decides that people loved her because she brought pleasure to them and helped them.

Brandon, Ruth. *Being Divine: A Biography of Sarah Bernhardt*. London: Mandarin, 1992. 0-7493-1233-5, 466p. Since Bernhardt was an extraordinarily famous person, Brandon looks for a symbolic significance or secret to her particular magic. She examines Bernhardt as a phenomenon of her time and place and identifies Bernhardt as the first popular culture goddess to use the media.

Emboden, William A. *Sarah Bernhardt*. New York: Macmillan, 1975. No ISBN, 176p. The photographs accompanying Emboden's text confirm Bernhardt's ability to create mood through her impersonations. Emboden uses the photographs as a method of trying to understand Bernhardt and her diversified interests.

Gold, Arthur, and Robert Fizdale. *The Divine Sarah: A Life of Sarah Bernhardt*. New York: Knopf, 1991. 0-394-52879-4, 351p. Gold and Fizdale use Bernhardt's letters and writings; press reports; diaries; memoirs; and letters from critics, lovers, admirers, fellow actors, friends, and enemies, most of them unpublished, to evoke a sense of her and the social and theatrical times of Paris at the end of the nineteenth century. The collection of approximately one hundred family photographs and publicity shots exposes an intelligent woman who wanted control over all aspects of her life.

Skinner, Cornelia Otis. *Madame Sarah*. 1966. New York: Paragon House, 1988. Paper, 1-55778-107-9, 356p. Skinner examines Bernhardt to see whether she can understand why admirers called Bernhardt the "eighth wonder of the world," "incandescent light," and "idol." Skinner's biography, which reads like a novel, also tries to find a truth in the contradictions and rumors about Bernhardt's behavior to see whether she really was the greatest French personality since **Joan of Arc**.

BESANT, ANNIE (1847–1933)

Activist   England

Annie Besant was a pioneer in the struggle for birth control and women's rights and head of the theosophist movement. She was born on October 1, 1847, and when her father died, Besant was five. When she was eight, Ellen Marryat educated Besant at her Devon home; Besant became intensely religious, longing to be a Christian martyr while practicing extreme behaviors of fasting and self-flagellation. At twenty, she married a clergyman but hated the subjugation of marriage, losing her faith when her two children became ill. She left her husband in 1873 and began her activism. She wrote about atheism, women's rights, Irish home rule and land-tenure reform, the evils of British imperialism, and birth control; these writings cost her custody of her daughter. She then joined the Fabian Society, the Marxist Social Democratic Federation, and finally Madame **Helena Blavatsky's** Theosophical Society after reading *The Secret Doctrine* (1888). At Blavatsky's death, Besant became leader and went to India. She adopted Indian clothes, always wearing a white sari; learned Sanskrit; and translated the *Bhagavad-Gita*. She wanted to help the Indians whom the British had oppressed, and she battled child marriage, seclusion of women, and the caste system, while establishing several schools. She then began to fight for home rule but disagreed with Gandhi's civil disobedience.

BIBLIOGRAPHY

Dinnage, Rosemary. *Annie Besant.* New York: Penguin, 1986. Paper, 0-14-008663-3, 127p. Dinnage sees Besant as a pioneer who, at the same time, remained a product of the Victorian age. Although always committed to social betterment, her religiousness restrained her, even in India. Dinnage thinks that Besant was always searching for spiritual fulfillment.

Muthanna, I. M. *Mother Besant and Mahatma Gandhi.* Tamil Nadu, India: Thenpulam, 1986. No ISBN, 460p. In this comparative study of Mother Besant and Gandhiji (Mahatma Gandhi), Muthanna tries to show the unique role that Mother Besant had in the regeneration of India and its struggle for freedom from British rule.

Raj Kumar. *Annie Besant's Rise to Power in Indian Politics, 1914–1917.* New Delhi, India: Concept, 1981. No ISBN, 182p. Raj looks at Besant's role in the politics of India during the First World War by examining her style and her method of organization when she became the president of the Indian National Congress, the height of Indian politics at the time.

Taylor, Anne. *Annie Besant: A Biography.* New York: Oxford University Press, 1992. 0-19-211796-3, 383p. Taylor covers Besant's life chronologically, paying careful attention to detail, in this recommended biography. She shows how Besant used her political perceptions, superb oratory skills, and religious mysticism to entice the Hindus. She indicates that Besant's pursuit of justice and willingness to defy any authority standing in its way are what meshed the political and spiritual strands of her life and led her to Theosophy.

BESSMERTNOVA, NATALIA (1941–)

Ballerina   Russia

Natalia Bessmertnova is an acclaimed ballerina. Born July 19, 1941, in Moscow, she has been compared to five others who have been able to express in their dance the ideas and sentiments of their society, including **Anna Pavlova,** Olga Spesivtseva, Marinia Semenova, **Galina Ulanova,** and **Maya Plisetskaya.** Bessmertnova has used all of their abilities—romanticism, musical expressiveness, broad dancing, and lyricism. Her slim body, thin arms, and long hands, as well as her ability to interpret Giselle, gained her entry to the Bolshoi Ballet at twenty. As a product of the Moscow School of Dance, she gained recognition in 1963 dancing leading roles of Shirin in *Legend of Love*, Odette-Odile in *Swan Lake*, Phrygia in *Spartacus*, Aurora in *The Sleeping Beauty*, Kitri in *Don Quixote,* and Masha in *The Nutcracker.* When she married Yuri Grigorovich, her choreographer, he led her away from the classic roles into new and modern ballets, devising Anasthasia in *Ivan the Terrible* especially for her. Among her prizes, Bessmertnova won the prestigious State Prize of the United Soviet Socialist Republics, the gold medal at the Varna Ballet Contest, and the Anna Pavlova Prize from the Paris Academy of Dance.

BIBLIOGRAPHY

Atlas, Helen V. *Natalia Bessmertnova.* Photography Mira. Brooklyn, NY: Dance Horizons, 1975. 0-87127-067-6, 23p. This pictorial rendition of Bessmertnova's roles contains only five pages of text.

Demidov, A. *A Bolshoi Ballerina, Natalia Bessmertnova.* Trans. Yuri S. Shirokov. London: Macdonald, 1986. 0-356-12367-7, 64p. The photographs complement the text to illustrate Bessmertnova's artistic career. Demidov discusses the various roles that she has danced and how she has interpreted these roles with her various partners.

BHUTTO, BENAZIR (1953–)

Politician   Pakistan

Benazir Bhutto has served twice as the prime minister of Pakistan. As the daughter of the former president of Pakistan, born on July 21, 1953, she attended Oxford University in England and was president of the Oxford Union while an undergraduate. She returned to Pakistan in 1977 and began a diplomatic career. In 1979, General Zia ul Haq led a military coup and overthrew her father and executed him. She became active in opposing the military dictatorship of General Zia, and he kept her under house arrest until 1984. She went into exile in 1985 but returned the following year to lead the Pakistan People's Party. She was arrested and imprisoned, but she continued campaigning after her release. She married a wealthy man, Asif Zardari, in 1987. The next year, her political party won a large number of seats, and she became the first woman prime minister of Pakistan. She was removed from office, but corruption charges against her were dismissed in August 1990. After a period of political turmoil, both she and her party returned to power in October 1993. She was again removed under charges of corruption in 1996.

BIBLIOGRAPHY

Bhutto, Benazir. *Daughter of Destiny: An Autobiography.* New York: Simon and Schuster, 1989. 0-671-66983-4, 411p. Bhutto wrote her autobiography when a friend remarked that what is not recorded is not known. Since Bhutto had experienced the martial law in Pakistan and been imprisoned, she could tell about the transformation of her society into a democracy from a dictatorship, starting with the assassination of her father and ending in 1988 before her election. An epilogue discusses General Zia's death in an airplane crash, and an editor's note tells of the results of the ensuing elections when Bhutto was elected.

Bokhari, Sajjad. *Mohtarma Benazir Bhutto, the Leader of Today.* Lahore, India: Fiction House, 1993. No ISBN, 229p. In a laudatory look at Benazir Bhutto, Bokhari thinks that Bhutto has done a wonderful job of taking over her father's work, although evil forces have tried to defeat her. Bokhari notes that Bhutto's concerns for autonomy, a self-reliant economy, and Pakistanhood have always come first. The text includes some of Bhutto's speeches and photographs.

Hughes, Libby. *From Prison to Prime Minister: A Biography of Benazir Bhutto.* New York: Dillon, 1990. 0-87518-438-3, 128p. Hughes uses sources from interviews and periodicals to re-create Bhutto's life while a happy child, pursuing undergraduate work at Radcliffe, continuing graduate studies at Oxford, and dealing courageously with the power struggle of her family against General Zia. This biography for young adults also presents differences, such as Bhutto's arranged marriage, between Pakistan and Western countries.

BINGEN, HILDEGARD of. *See* HILDEGARD of BINGEN.

BIRGITTA (1303?–1373)
Religious   Sweden

Birgitta renounced her secular life, became a charity worker, and started the Order of the Most Holy Savior, which, after her death, earned her sainthood. Birgitta's father was a judge and landowner in the province of Uppland when she was born. Her mother died when Birgitta was twelve, and a maternal aunt educated her. During this time, she told her friends about religious visions of Christ crucified she had had at seven and ten. In 1316, her father married her to Ulf, who was five years older, but supposedly the marriage was not consummated, at her request, until later. She raised eight children and, as the lady of Ulvåsa, became known for her charity. She established a special building for the poor and sick and nursed them herself. When her children helped her in the hospital, her neighbors expressed concern about the germs to which they were exposed. In 1341, she and her husband went on a pilgrimage to Santiago de Copostela in Spain. When Ulf became ill at Arras on their way back in early 1342, Birgitta prayed to France's St. Denis, and Ulf recovered. He died the next year in Sweden, however, and Birgitta renounced the world as her extraordinary visions became more frequent. In one of her visions, she claimed that Christ commanded her to found a strict new religious order that would help reform monastic life. For this purpose, she visited Jerusalem and moved to Rome, remaining there for the rest of her life, urging ecclesiastical reform (especially the return to Rome of the Avignon popes), establishing a house of hospitality for pilgrims from the north, and counseling the rich and poor. She received papal confirmation of her order in 1370 and started the Order of the Most Holy Savior. She was canonized in 1391, with her feast day occurring on July 23.

BIBLIOGRAPHY
Andersson, Aron. *St. Bridget [Birgitta] of Sweden.* London: Catholic Truth Society, 1980. Paper, 0-8518-3296-2, 141p. Andersson introduces Birgitta in his recommended biography, using her own words in a florilegium. He discusses her life and the development of her order, emphasizing the monastic and contemplative life along with its tradition of hospitality and charity.

Bridget [Birgitta]. *Life and Selected Revelations.* Trans. Albert Ryle Kezel. New York: Paulist Press, 1990. 0-8091-0434-2, 350p. The edited text presents Birgitta's life and her revelations, which earned her position as one of the most important women of the later Middle Ages. Her revelations were the basis on which she lived her life and made decisions concerning her religious order.

Butkovich, Anthony. *Revelations; Saint Birgitta of Sweden.* Los Angeles: Ecumenical Foundation of America, 1972. No ISBN, 110p. Butkovich thinks that Birgitta tried to preserve and reform the church through her works as the Hundred Years' War was beginning between England and France, the papacy had moved from Rome to Avignon, the Turks were invading the Byzantine Empire, and the "black death" threatened. He reviews her most important revelations, prophecies, and devotions.

BISHOP, ISABELLA LUCY (1832–1904)
Traveler and Writer   England

Isabella Bird Bishop became a world traveler and wrote extensively about her journeys. Born on October 15, 1832, she had delicate health, suffering from a spinal illness. She learned to ride and swim in an attempt to combat her weaknesses during her family's moves to various locations where her clergyman father found work. In 1854, after an operation, she spent several months in America, about which she wrote in *An Englishwoman in America* (1856). In 1857, she returned to America and studied the religious revival, an interest fueled by her family's evangelical leanings. Her travels, a way for her to supposedly rest from her poor health, took her to Australia, New Zealand, and the Pacific. In 1879, she traveled to America's Rocky Mountains and became friends with "Rocky Mountain Jim," who proposed marriage. She followed this journey with a trip to Japan. After her sister Henrietta died in 1881, she married Dr. John Bishop. He died in 1886, and his influence led her to study medicine in London before going to the Indian cities of Punjab and Kashmir, where she founded two medical hospitals. Famous from writing about her experiences, she returned to London and became the first woman fellow of the Royal Geographical Society (1892). A final journey took her eight thousand miles across Canada, Japan, and Korea to China on the Tibetan border. She established three hospitals on her way and published *The Yangtse Valley and Beyond* (1899) as well as a book of photographs (1900) about this trip. She was packed for another journey when she died.

BIBLIOGRAPHY
Barr, Pat. A *Curious Life for a Lady; the Story of Isabella Bird, a Remarkable Victorian Traveller.* Garden City, NY: Doubleday, 1970. No ISBN, 347p. Isabella Bird (Bishop), a woman of four feet, eleven inches, began traveling when she was forty to help her poor health. In an intriguing biography, Barr tells of Bird's journeys climbing Mauna Loa, following cattle through the Rockies, traversing a pass on the border of Tibet in a snowstorm, facing a Chinese mob, and establishing hospitals as charitable work. She relates that Bird wanted to avoid the empire and never visited or wrote about India.

Bird, Isabella L. *Unbeaten Tracks in Japan.* 1880. Boston: Beacon, 1987. Paperback, 0-8070-7015-7, 332p. Bird catalogs the months she spent in Japan in 1878 as a single woman in her mid-forties. She describes her adventures and her interpreter, a young man with the lowly interests of teahouse girls and sweetmeats. The book is a series of forty-four "letters" to her sister

Henrietta, which were edited and published, each one a description of an adventure.

Bird, Isabella L. *A Lady's Life in the Rocky Mountains.* 1879. London: Virago, 1991. 0-86068-267-6, 4296p. In these seventeen letters to her sister Henrietta, Bird describes her experiences in the Rocky Mountains which she visited in 1873. The collected letters were published as one volume.

BLACKWELL, ELIZABETH (1821–1910)
Physician   England

Elizabeth Blackwell, the first woman doctor, spent her life helping poor women and children who needed medical care. Born in Bristol on February 3, 1821, she came with her family, practicing Dissenters, to the United States in 1832. When her father died in debt, she and her sister, raised to think they were equal to males, opened a girls' school in Cincinnati to help support the family. When a friend was dying from cancer, she told Blackwell that she might not have suffered so much if she had had a female doctor. Blackwell applied to twenty-eight medical schools, and the Geneva Medical School of Geneva College (now Hobart and William Smith Colleges) accepted her, almost as a joke, but in 1849, she received her doctor of medicine degree in front of twenty thousand people. She returned to England as the first woman doctor and continued her studies there and in Paris. In Paris, she contracted purulent ophthalmia from a baby, which caused her to lose an eye and ended her chance to become a surgeon. She returned to America the next year and began a dispensary in New York tenement houses that eventually became the New York Infirmary for Indigent Women and Children. In 1858, she went back to England to lecture and stayed to help the women who wanted to attend medical school, finally settling there in 1869. She aided in founding the National Health Society in 1871 and became the chair of gynecology at the new London School of Medicine for Women in 1874. She fought against legal control of prostitution, vaccination, and animal experimentation and helped women gain opportunities to become physicians.

BIBLIOGRAPHY

Blackwell, Elizabeth. *Pioneer Work in Opening the Medical Profession to Women; Autobiographical Sketches.* 1895. New York: Source Book, 1970. 0-876810-80-6, 264p. Blackwell says that she wrote her autobiography because her adopted daughter Kitty requested it. She dedicated it to Kitty and included comments, letters, and diary extracts as part of her memories.

Brown, Jordan. *Elizabeth Blackwell.* New York: Chelsea House, 1989. 1-55546-642-7, 111p. This documented biography, appropriate for young adults, gives a thorough picture of Blackwell's life, showing her personality and determination.

Kline, Nancy. *Elizabeth Blackwell: A Doctor's Triumph.* Berkeley, CA: Conari, 1997. 1-57324-057-5, 190p. This biography for young adults covers Blackwell's life, showing both her frustrations and her achievements as the first female doctor. Kline emphasizes Blackwell's social pioneer work in establishing health care centers for women and children both in New York and in London.

Schleichert, Elizabeth. *The Life of Elizabeth Blackwell.* Illus. Antonio Castro. Frederick, MD: Twenty-First Century, 1992. 0-941477-66-5, 80p. Schlei-

chert's authentic biography for young adults covers Blackwell's life with a good overview of her achievements but without dwelling on the hardships.
Wilson, Dorothy Clarke. *Lone Woman; the Story of Elizabeth Blackwell, the First Woman Doctor*. Boston: Little, Brown, 1970. No ISBN, 469p. This biography begins on October 20, 1847, at a meeting created by Wilson that might have occurred when the men at Geneva decided to admit Blackwell. Although a fictional biography, it has a bibliography.

BLANCHE of CASTILE (1188–1252)
Queen of France   Spain

Blanche of Castile became the queen of France at the death of her husband, Louis VIII, and expanded territory controlled by the country. The daughter of Alonso VIII of Castile and the granddaughter of Henry II of England, Blanche was betrothed at eleven to the future Louis VIII to cement a treaty between France and England. In 1216, Blanche claimed the English throne as she supported Louis' attempt to invade. At his death, Blanche became regent and guardian of their children. She and her son, Louis IX, ruled France from 1226 to 1234, during which she quelled forceful barons by wearing white while riding a white horse in 1226 to lead her troops, defeated Henry III's attacks in 1230, and expanded territory including Blois, Chartres, Sancerre, Toulouse, and Provence through agreements and marriage treaties. Student uprisings in 1229, lasting for four years, were more difficult to overcome, and the university relocated outside Paris during those years. She retained her influence over Louis IX after he ascended the throne in 1236 and began her second regency in 1248 when he left on a crusade. She then had to negotiate for his release after the battle of El Mansurah. Her daughter, Isabel of France, was a humanist scholar who established the Abbey of Longchamps and chose the convent over marriage. Another daughter, Marguerite, founded many hospitals and schools.
BIBLIOGRAPHY
Pernoud, Regine. *Blanche of Castile*. Trans. Henry Noel. New York: Coward, McCann and Geoghegan, 1975. 0-698-10595-8, 319p. Pernoud's researched biography gives background information about the life of Blanche, who at the age of twelve was already married to Louis and preparing to be queen.

BLAVATSKY, HELENA (1831–1891)
Writer and Philosopher   Russia

Madame Blavatsky, an intelligent woman with diverse interests, led the Theosophical Society. Helena Hahn was born on August 12, 1831, to German parents in Yekaterinoslav (now Dnepropetrovsk, Ukraine). She married a much older man when she was sixteen but left him after a few months. For the next twenty years, she traveled in Europe, Asia, and the United States and later claimed to have studied for seven years under Hindu masters in the East. After nearly drowning at sea, she turned to spiritualism and claimed to possess psychic powers. In 1873, Madame Blavatsky, as she was always known, went to New York City. Within two years, she became one of the founders, and eventually the central figure, of the Theosophical Society, a small, international group of occultists who believed that reincarnation was the only way for a human to become purified. Although she became an American citizen, she established a new headquarters in India in 1878. There, she faced dissension, charges of plagiarism and fraud, and notoriety but always maintained that the masters had passed on to her their own uncommonly developed spiritual state. She refused to accept money, lived simply, and died without property. During her life, she asserted many scientific theories about which people laughed but that have become more probable as scientists extend their knowledge of the universe.

BIBLIOGRAPHY

Cranston, S. L. *HPB: The Extraordinary Life and Influence of Helena Blavatsky, Founder of the Modern Theosophical Movement.* New York: Putnam, 1993. 0-87477-688-0; paper, 0-87477-769-0, 648p. This exhaustive examination of Blavatsky focuses on her teachings, her life, and the ten thousand previously untranslated pages of articles, letters, and recent materials published in Russian. Cranston discusses Blavatsky's abilities as a scientist, poet, pianist, painter, philosopher writer, educator, and tireless warrior for truth.

Johnson, K. Paul. *The Masters Revealed: Madam Blavatsky and the Myth of the Great White Lodge.* Albany: State University of New York Press, 1994. 0-7914-2063-9; paper, 0-7914-2064-7, 288p. Johnson gives a balanced view of Blavatsky in revealing that she spoke Russian, Georgian, French, English, Arabic, Italian, and Sanskrit; was a complex, overweight woman with physical illnesses; had a fearsome temper and a psychic gift; and assumed multiple personalities. He shows respect for her work and sees her socially idealistic and fiercely political life as a search for spiritual truth.

Leonard, Maurice. *Madame Blavatsky: Medium, Mystic and Magician.* New York: Regency, 1977. No ISBN, 115p. This account compliments Madame Blavatsky's originality of thought which she revealed in *Isis Unveiled* and *The Secret Doctrine.* Leonard thinks that Blavatsky's refusal to obey Victorian sexual codes is what caused people to react to her negatively. He believes that if she was a fraud, she was a good one, and if she was genuine, her message was significant.

Meade, Marion. *Madame Blavatsky, the Woman Behind the Myth.* New York: Putnam, 1980. 0-399-12376-8, 528 p. Meade traces Blavatsky's life from her Russian childhood through her early travels in Egypt and Western Europe to her emergence as a public figure with the founding of the Theosophical Society in New York. She sees Blavatsky as a former Russian aristocrat who survived by using her wit, charm, courage, and occasional deceit. Meade concludes in this objective and recommended biography that Blavatsky might have been her own most willing victim.

Wachtmeister, Constance. *Reminiscences of H. P. Blavatsky and the Secret Doctrine.* Wheaton, IL: Theosophical Publishing House, 1976. Paper, 0-8356-0488-8, 141p. Various people who knew Blavatsky while she was in Europe compiling *The Secret Doctrine* give their impressions of her in this biography. They and the press sometimes acknowledged her courage in presenting thoughts and theories at variance with the materialistic science of the day, and most marvel at her energy during bad health as she sacrificed to write the book.

BLIXEN, KAREN. *See* **DINESEN, ISAK.**

BODICHON, BARBARA LEIGH (1827–1891)
Activist and Educator   England

Barbara Bodichon campaigned for equality at home and simultaneously pursued her watercolor painting. Born Barbara Smith on April 18, 1827, her father, a member of Parliament, gave his sons and daughters an equal education. He provided his daughters with an income to make them independent. For Bodichon, he financed and deeded the Westminster School for Infants, and she then established the Portman Hall School, nondenominational and coeducational. She also became an accomplished watercolorist, having studied with Jean-Baptiste Camille Corot. She believed that women should have equality in both the home and the state and wrote and petitioned for the Married Women's Property Acts so that married women could have control over their own money. In *Women and Work* (1857), she argued that women should be paid because work gave them independence and dignity and often kept them healthy. She married Dr. Eugène Bodichon and began spending part of each year with him in Algeria. She helped launch *The Englishwoman's Journal*, a magazine to which she contributed articles with more effective content than style. In 1866, she helped found the Woman Suffrage Committee because she thought that women should be allowed to vote and to pursue a higher education. As a member of the Society of Female Artists, she exhibited her landscapes of the countryside and Algeria around London, and some still hang in Girton College, the Cambridge college for women that Bodichon helped found. Her poor health stopped her public campaigning, but she continued to paint and exhibit. She left the money inherited from her father to her heirs and bequeathed to Girton College the money she earned from selling over two hundred of her paintings.

BIBLIOGRAPHY

Bodichon, Barbara Leigh Smith. *An American Diary, 1857–8*. Ed. Joseph W. Reed, Jr. London: Routledge and K. Paul, 1972. 0-7100-7330-5, 198p. For specialized readers, the text includes Bodichon's diary for the year 1857–1858 when she was on a visit to the United States. Bodichon wanted to see specific things such as a school for the "coloured," and her responses to it and to other places give a view of the United States to a foreigner in the mid-nineteenth century. The editor has added a brief biography of her and an essay on the English visitors who came to the United States during the twenty years prior to the Civil War.

Herstein, Sheila R. *A Mid-Victorian Feminist, Barbara Leigh Smith Bodichon*. New Haven, CT: Yale University Press, 1985. 0-300-03317-6, 205p. Herstein explores the political, social, and religious environment in which Bodichon lived and the radical Unitarian circle of her childhood in this scholarly biography. She traces Bodichon's activism and her strong ability to organize as she continued her family's tradition of removing inequities from English law. Her *Laws Concerning Women* gave impetus to the fight for women's rights in England.

BOLEYN, ANNE (1507–1536)
Queen   England

After Anne Boleyn became the wife of Henry VIII, she was crowned queen. The daughter of Sir Thomas Boleyn (later, the earl of Wiltshire and Ormonde),

she spent two years at the French court from 1519 to 1521. When she returned to England, several men began pursuing her, including the heir to the earldom of Northumberland and Henry VIII. After a six-year courtship, Henry married Anne secretly in January 1533, before Thomas Cranmer, archbishop of Canterbury, pronounced Henry's divorce from his first wife, Catherine of Aragon. In June, Anne was crowned queen, and in September, she gave birth to the future queen **Elizabeth I.** Anne's strength of will, her intellect, and her subtle ways matched or bettered Henry who was vain, indecisive, and superficial. Early in 1536, however, Anne had a miscarriage, and four months later, Henry wanted to remarry. On May 2, Anne was imprisoned in the Tower of London on charges of adultery with her own brother, three gentlemen of the privy chamber, and a musician of the court. Other accusations against her included mocking the king, laughing at him, making fun of his ballads, and saying that he was impotent. Proof of his impotence would make Elizabeth illegitimate and the child Anne miscarried the son of someone else. Additionally, Anne was charged with conspiring against the king's life and of trying to kill Henry's daughter and illegitimate son. No record of the evidence or of the defense, if any, remains. Henry and Jane Seymour were betrothed the day after Anne's beheading, on May 20.

BIBLIOGRAPHY

Erickson, Carolly. *Mistress Anne.* New York: Summit Books, 1984. 0-671-41747-9, 288p.   In this good introduction to Anne, Erickson thinks the choice of Anne for Henry's second wife seems unusual because Anne had the disfigurements of a mole on her neck and a sixth finger on one hand, markings ominously symbolic to the society in which she lived. With no royal blood and neither the political nor the monetary advantage of Henry's first wife, **Katherine** [*sic*] **of Aragon,** Anne caused the rift between Henry and the pope.

Friedmann, Paul. *Anne Boleyn: A Chapter of English History, 1527–1536.* 1884. New York, AMS, 1973. 2 vols. 0-404-09050-8. Friedmann's biography, with marginal notes, was definitive until the 1960s, when additional information appeared giving a new view of Anne Boleyn. Friedmann's sources are the English correspondence of Henry, his ministers, and subordinate agents; the correspondence of Charles V (Catherine of Aragon's brother), Charles' aunt, sister, brother, and ministers as it relates to England; and the French correspondence. Other sources are diaries, chronicles, memoirs of contemporaries, accounts compiled by seemingly trustworthy sources, and miscellaneous documents.

Ives, Eric W. *Anne Boleyn.* New York: Blackwell, 1986. 0-631-160655, 451p. Ives explores Anne Boleyn's European education, her upbringing, the secret of her power and success, and her love for Henry VIII. He sees her marriage and its destruction from a different view by suggesting that Anne, presiding over the English court, was more the mistress of her destiny than others have considered.

Lofts, Norah. *Anne Boleyn.* New York: Coward, McCann and Geoghegan, 1979. 0-698-11005-6, 192p. Lofts comments that when Anne Boleyn was born, no one bothered to record the date or the place of birth, but when she died, all knew every detail. Lofts uses diaries, letters, and accounts of the period to capture this willful and ambitious woman who loved jokes and masquerades and who, for a few years, dominated an equally willful king, changing English history.

Warnicke, Retha M. *The Rise and Fall of Anne Boleyn: Family Politics at the Court of Henry VIII.* Cambridge: Cambridge University Press, 1989. 0-521-37000-0, 326p. In her well-researched and scholarly biography, Warnicke looks at the family politics in Henry VIII's court and believes that Anne's miscarriage of a deformed child in January 1536 branded her as a witch, causing Henry to have her executed four months later. Warnicke thinks Anne possibly risked herself to marry Henry to raise the Boleyn family's status.

BONAPARTE, JOSEPHINE (1763–1814)
Empress   Martinique

Josephine Bonaparte became the empress of France as the wife of Napoleon. Marie Josèphe Rose Tascher de la Pagerie, born in Martinique on June 23, 1763, to a sugar plantation owner where the slaves called her Yeyette (a corruption of Rosette), went to Paris at fifteen to live with her aunt who had arranged a marriage for her with Alexandre de Beauharnais, a family friend. By 1785, she demanded a separation because of his indifference to her, and she went back to Martinique. In 1789, she returned to Paris where her salon became a meeting place for the Deputies of the Assembly, which included her former husband. He was imprisoned and guillotined while Josephine was imprisoned in the Carmes. In 1795, she was liberated, and in 1796, married Napoleon in a civil ceremony. He changed her name to Josephine, based on her middle name of "Josèphe." She went with Napoleon to Italy but remained in Paris while he fought in Egypt, collecting a fortune from military suppliers with her various dealings. She also created a court attractive to foreign ambassadors, artists, and writers. In 1804, she and Napoleon remarried with full religious ritual on the eve of their joint coronation as emperor and empress. In 1809, however, they divorced against her will so that he could marry Mary Louise, the Austrian archduchess, in hope of her bearing an heir. Josephine retired to Malmaison, retaining the titles of duchess of Navarre and empress. At her death, twenty thousand people filed by her coffin, and eyewitnesses reported that Napoleon mourned her privately, since his legal wife still lived, by visiting her grave before his exile.

BIBLIOGRAPHY

Aronson, Theo. *Napoleon and Josephine: A Love Story.* New York: St. Martin's, 1990. 0-312-05135-2, 317p. Aronson used contemporary sources that he trusted and letters as the documentation for his domestic history of a marriage. He exhibits political events only when they directly affected Napoleon and Josephine's relationship and established that they were happiest together when they stayed at Malmaison.

Bruce, Evangeline. *Napoleon and Josephine: The Improbable Marriage.* New York: Scribner's, 1995. 0-02-517810-5, 555p. Bruce views the changes of Napoleon and Josephine's marriage as symbolic of their times. She thinks that Napoleon always loved Josephine and would have stayed with her if she could have had a child. The epilogue discusses the fate of other Bonapartes after Napoleon's fortunes changed.

Cartland, Barbara. *Josephine, Empress of France.* London: Arrow, 1973. 0-099-08100-8, 191p. In this recommended biography, Cartland examines Josephine's behavior as woman and mother rather than as empress. She thinks that history has misrepresented Josephine but that Josephine was partially to blame because of her erratic behavior of changing political loyalties when she thought necessary.

Epton, Nora. *Josephine: The Empress and Her Children*. New York: Norton, 1976. 0-393-07500-1, 230p. Epton looks at Josephine as mother to her two children, Eugène and Hortense, but the title misleads because the book discusses Josephine's personality and sense of responsibility.

Redoute, Pierre-Joseph *Roses for an Empress*. Trans. Anna Bennett. London: Sidgwick and Jackson, 1983. 0-283-98983-1, 117p. Redoute's story of Josephine's life is based on letters and reports from people who knew her. He illustrated it with pictures of places where she lived and of flowers that she loved.

BONHEUR, ROSA (1822–1899)
Artist   France

Rosa Bonheur's idea that nature is always true and beautiful and her knowledge of animal anatomy and ability to portray special characteristics of a breed in her paintings were unsurpassed in the nineteenth century. Born on March 16, 1822, she later trained under her father, painter Raymond Bonheur, because women could not attend art schools where nude models worked. Her mother died when Bonheur was very young, and Bonheur plagued her father to let her study art. At the Louvre, she copied old masters and found that she preferred landscapes with animals. The French government acquired her first major painting, *Ploughing in Nivernais* (1848), for the Louvre. Her father believed in the equality of women, and she wore men's clothes, first to enter slaughterhouses and study animal anatomy, but then as a norm after the French police approved her request to do so in 1852. She broke from academic rules with her individuality, but wealthy factory owners and merchants bought her pictures because they could understand them. Queen **Victoria** requested a private viewing of *The Horse Fair* (1853–5), now at the Metropolitan Museum of Art in New York along with *Weaning the Calves* (1887). When Buffalo Bill Cody's show stayed outside Paris for seven months in 1889, she painted his animals. In 1894, she became the first woman to receive the Grand Cross of the French Legion of Honor. She refused to marry and lived nearly forty years on her estate near Fontainebleau with her friend Nathalie Micas. Throughout her life, she was an eccentric maverick whose ambition led her to declare that she married art, a demanding spouse.

BIBLIOGRAPHY

Ashton, Dore, and Denise Browne Hare. *Rosa Bonheur: A Life and a Legend*. New York: Viking, 1981. 0-670-60813-0, 206p. The authors place Bonheur in her times and look at how they affected her development as an artist whose adulation and public interest seem out of proportion with her talent. They see her as an original individual whose life and work coincided with a need in others, both in her time and the present, in their recommended and accessible biography.

Shriver, Rosalia. *Rosa Bonheur*. Philadelphia: Art Alliance, 1982. 0-87982-037-3, 111p. Shriver looks at the success of Bonheur in a man's world with the nobility of Europe admiring her. Although self-educated, Bonheur became one of the foremost animal painters of the nineteenth century.

Stanton, Theodore, ed. *Reminiscences of Rosa Bonheur*. 1910. New York: Hacker Art Books, 1976. 0-87817-09-6, 413p. Bonheur tells of such things as her early life, family, confidante, travels, the war of 1870, and love of animals, and the text also includes comments about her by people who knew her. Among the topics Stanton discloses are Bonheur's masculine attire, love of tobacco, musical tastes, favorite authors, artistic tendencies, dislike of journalists, her sickness, and her death.

BOOTH, CATHERINE (1829–1890)
Evangelist   England

Catherine Booth helped to establish the Salvation Army and gained a reputation as a superb preacher who spoke for the poor and needy. Born in Ashbourne, Derbyshire, on January 17, 1829, to John Mumford, a coach builder and a Wesleyan lay preacher, Catherine grew up in a strict, religious home, and her ill health kept her from attending school. In 1844, Catherine associated with the Wesleyan Church, assured of "eternal salvation," but four years later, she joined the "reform movement" and was excommunicated, not believing the Sacraments necessary for salvation. She met William Booth at the reformers' chapel where he had recently become pastor and married him in 1855. The two led revivals throughout England before settling in London in 1865 and developing the People's Mission, where they preached to all classes of society. Since Catherine was acceptable to the wealthy economic class as well as the poor, the Booths collected money for the family and for the poor of London's East End. By 1877, the mission had become the Salvation Army, with its ranks open to women preachers and some of its work directed toward helping prostitutes. Although in continuing ill health, Booth wrote for the army's *War Cry*, lobbied for female suffrage, and spoke against the social purity agitation. She gave her final public address in 1888, and over thirty-six thousand people supposedly attended her funeral.

BIBLIOGRAPHY
Barnes, Cyril J. *Words of Catherine Booth*. London: Salvationist, 1981. Paper, 0-8541-2379-2, 85p. Barnes places Catherine Booth's statements in their geographical and historical settings, giving insight about the bases of her comments. The thirty-three different situations recreate her life and her power as a woman preacher with the "courage of ten men."
Bramwell-Booth, Catherine. *Catherine Booth: The Story of Her Loves*. London: Hodder and Stoughton, 1970. 0-340-1060-8, 477p. The granddaughter of Catherine Booth wants Booth's story to be a challenge to people to have the kind of zeal that Booth had when she founded the Salvation Army. Bramwell's information in this recommended biography comes from William Stead, a man independent of Salvation Army loyalties who recorded his impressions of Booth. Booth's loves were William Booth, souls, the Salvation Army, children, mankind, and God.
Green, Roger J. *Catherine Booth: A Biography of the Cofounder of the Salvation Army*. Grand Rapids, MI: Baker, 1996. Green's balanced biography, with documentation, attempts to re-create Booth's ability to persuade people through facts rather than empty rhetoric.

BORGIA, LUCREZIA (1480–1519)
Patron   Italy

Lucrezia Borgia gained a reputation as a terrible woman, but she was a patron of the arts who advanced the cultural life of her time. She was born in Rome on April 18, 1480, daughter of Rodrigo Borgia, a Spanish cardinal who later became Pope Alexander VI. Her father arranged three marriages for her for political reasons. When her first marriage at thirteen to Giovanni Sforza of Pesaro was no longer useful, her father, having become pope, annulled it in 1497. He then married her to Alfonso of Aragon, a nephew of the king of Naples. When the pope needed another alliance, her husband had to flee, but Cesare, Lucrezia's brother, commanded Alfonso's bodyguard to kill him in 1500. She went to the family estates, and when she reappeared with a child, she became the subject of scandals most likely perpetrated when her first husband said that the child resulted from her incestuous liaison with Cesare. The following year, Lucrezia married Alfonso I, duke of Este, who in 1505 inherited the duchy of Ferrara. When her father died in 1503, Borgia was able to escape the political intrigues of her family, and she established a court at Ferrara where the foremost artists, writers, including Aristo, and scholars of the time gathered. As a patron of the arts, she gained many friends, but after 1510, she became more interested in religion. Because of her unscrupulous relatives, her reputation suffered, but historians agree that charges of crime and vice against her have no historical proof.

BIBLIOGRAPHY
Erlanger, Rachel. *Lucrezia Borgia: A Biography*. New York: Hawthorn Books, 1978. 0-8015-4725-3, 372p. Erlanger wonders how people who knew Borgia in Ferrara could praise her virtue and her goodness, including her third husband, who married her unwillingly but mourned her death, if she were the evil person reported to have used poison to destroy her enemies. Erlanger's conclusion in this accessible biography is that a poet angry at the murder of Borgia's second husband may have perpetrated the story by comparing her to Thaïs in her epitaph.

Gregorovius, Ferdinand Adolf. *Lucrezia Borgia according to Original Documents and Correspondence of Her Day*. Trans. Constance MacNab. 1903. London: New English Library, 1969. 0-450-00300-0, 189p. The text uses mementos and documents of Borgia's day from the Este family archives in Rome, Ferrara, and Modena and from the Gonzaga family in Manua to expose her life in Rome and in Ferrara. Gregorovius notes that the use of the Christian church for advancement contrasts with conduct expected in the church and makes the Borgias appear especially fiendish.

BOUDICCA (d. c. 60–62)
Queen   Britain

Boudicca, formerly called "Boadicea," became queen of the Iceni, a tribe inhabiting the territory of the present-day counties of Norfolk and Suffolk, at the death of her husband, King Prasutagus (d. c. 47–60). After Prasutagus died, the Romans seized the Iceni territory, tortured and beat Boudicca, raped her daughters, and enslaved the noblest Iceni. Boudicca gathered a large army, destroyed the Roman colony of Camulodunum (now Colchester), marched on Londinium and Veralamium (now London and Saint Albans), and sacked them.

According to the Roman historian Tacitus, her troops killed some seventy thousand Romans. Suetonius, Roman governor of Britain, had been fighting the Druids in Anglesey, but he rushed back to advance against her and destroy her force. In despair, Boudicca killed herself by taking poison on the battlefield.

BIBLIOGRAPHY

Fraser, Antonia. *The Warrior Queens: The Legends and the Lives of the Women Who Have Led Their Nations in War.* New York: Knopf, 1989. 0-394-54939-2, 383p. In this collective biography, Fraser examines the situations that have placed women in roles throughout history where they have had to defend their people. She recounts Boudicca's foiled attempt to rescue the Iceni and other tribes from British rule and the bravery she exhibited while facing the Roman troops.

Somerset Fry, Plantagenet. *Boudicca.* London: W. H. Allen, 1978. 0-491-02074-0, 118p. With six chapters giving background on the Celts in Europe and Britain as well as Boudicca, Somerset Fry says that he can only surmise about Boudicca's life. One can know nothing for certain about her except that she led the revolt against the Romans, almost winning, and that she killed herself with poison.

Webster, Graham. *Boudica, the British Revolt against Rome A.D. 60.* Totowa, NJ: Rowman and Littlefield, 1978. 0-8476-6043-5, 152p. The history of Boudica [*sic*] remained unknown until Boccaccio discovered the manuscripts of Tacitus at Monte Cassino and published them in Italy in 1534. Webster clarifies that Boudica means "Victoria" and has been misspelled as Boadicea through the years. Tacitus's father-in-law, Agricola, went to England in A.D. 78 and told him about this woman. Webster's other major sources are archaeological digs and aerial reconnaissance. Both Somerset and Webster have written enlightening biographies.

BOULANGER, LILI (1893–1918)

Composer   France

Boulanger studied composition at the Paris Conservatoire and was the first woman to win the Grand Prix de Rome for her cantata, *Faust et Hélène*, in 1913, when she was only nineteen. She was born in Paris on August 21, 1893, to a composer and his wife, a much younger former voice student. Débussy and the impressionists influenced Boulanger, but her growth did not stop with her prize. She continued to develop her personal style, especially in the use of sacred texts and the symbolist poets. Among the places that she lived and worked in France were Paris, Gargenville, Compiègne, Bayonne, Arcachon, Biarritz, St. Raphaël, Nice, and Mézy. She also lived in both Florence and Rome, Italy; Bad Kreuznach and Frankfurt in Germany; and Scheveningen, Wittebroecke, and The Hague in the Netherlands. Her music was a symbol of French art and spirit during and after World War I and also symbolic of women's artistic liberation. Although she was ill for much of her life, she continued to work, slowing only to help families of musicians during the war years. During the last two years of her life, she wrote vocal music and sacred compositions. Among her other works are *Pour les Funérals d'un Soldat* and *Vieille Prière Bouddhique*.

BIBLIOGRAPHY

Rosenstiel, Leonie. *The Life and Works of Lili Boulanger.* Rutherford, NJ: Fairleigh Dickinson University Press, 1978. 0-8386-1796-4, 315p. Rosenstiel discovered as a Juilliard violin student that no full-length work about Boulanger existed. She used primary sources previously unavailable in library, archival, and field research as well as personal interviews and correspondence with Boulanger's friends and family. Rosenstiel's research helps her relate why Boulanger might have composed a particular type of work at a particular time in her life. Additional information from family photographs, records, documents, and personal reminiscences makes the biography a fine scholarly study of Boulanger's life as well as her extant compositions.

BOULANGER, NADIA (1887–1979)
Musician and Educator   **France**

Nadia Boulanger may have been the most influential music teacher in the twentieth century, but as a young child, she hated music. On 16 September, 1887, she was born in Paris as the daughter of a composer and his voice student, forty-three years younger, who had followed him from Russia. When Boulanger was three, she heard a fire siren outside, went inside and re-created the sound on the piano; she kept playing. By thirteen, she was performing on the organ and the piano, and at seventeen, she started teaching and supervising her sister **Lili Boulanger**'s education. Boulanger competed for the Prix de Rome which her sister won but placed only second, so she stopped composing and began teaching full-time in order to support herself and her mother. She said that she based her whole teaching career on understanding others rather than having them understand her. Her nickname "Tender Tyrant" showed that she was demanding, and she very seldom complimented students. She taught constantly, eating during and napping between lessons so that she could earn as much as the men who had to work only half as hard to earn the same. She taught Dinu Lipatti, Yehudi Menuhin, Leonard Bernstein, Joe Raposi, Aaron Copland, Philip Glass, Lennox Berkeley, Thea Musgrave, Quincy Jones, and Virgil Thompson. She was the first woman to conduct a symphony orchestra in London (1937), to conduct subscription concerts with the Boston Symphony Orchestra (1938) and the New York Philharmonic (1939), and to conduct the Hallé Orchestra (1963). She premiered Stravinsky's concerto for wind instruments, *Dumbarton Oaks*, in Washington, D.C. (1938). She performed and recorded baroque and Renaissance music, which helped revive their popularity. She felt that music was moral and that music students had to be passionate about what they did. Among her many awards were honorary doctorates from Oxford and Harvard and a commandership of the Légion d'Honneur.

BIBLIOGRAPHY
Campbell, Don. *Master Teacher: Nadia Boulanger*. Laurel, MD: Pastoral, 1984. 0-912405-03-1, 151p. Campbell's work is not a biography but a collection of impressions, reflections, and photographs that serve as a tribute to Boulanger. Campbell met her when he was thirteen and never forgot the experience. Throughout her life, Boulanger did not want to give her inner views or her personal history, but, toward the end of her life, she began to define herself in a few areas. Campbell thinks that no pure definition of her exists but that no other woman in history parallels her influence.

Kendall, Alan. *The Tender Tyrant, Nadia Boulanger: A Life Devoted to Music: A Biography*. Wilton, CT: Lyceum Books, 1977. Paper, 0-915336-18-9, 144p. Kendall presents a portrait of Boulanger and her world rather than a full biography. Since Boulanger's work is her life, Kendall sees no way to separate the two. He instead looks at her significance as a composer, pianist, conductor, critic, and, mainly, teacher in a readable and well-researched work.

Monsaingeon, Bruno. *Mademoiselle, Conversations with Nadia Boulanger.* Manchester, England: Carcanet, 1985. 0-85635-603-4, 141p. Monsaingeon creates a series of questions that he asks Boulanger and then uses interview transcripts, excerpts from her writings, and real conversations in answering them. He succeeds in creating the voice of a teacher who helped musicians find the music inside them in this readable and recommended view of Boulanger. Boulanger wanted students to create as they were capable, and she steadily urged them onward.

Rosenstiel, Leonie. *Nadia Boulanger: A Life in Music.* New York: Norton, 1982. 0-393-01495-9, 427p. In a popular biography, Rosenstiel shows how Boulanger might have gained the accolade of having helped American music gain worldwide recognition by examining her roles as organist, conductor, sometime composer, and one of the greatest teachers in the twentieth century. Boulanger gave Rosenstiel access to previously unavailable personal papers and records. Additionally, Rosenstiel interviewed persons from different facets of Boulanger's life.

Spycket, Jérome. *Nadia Boulanger.* Trans. M. M. Shriver. Pendragon, NY: Pendragon, 1992. 0-945193-38-6, 176p. Spycket uses primary sources of photographs, quotations, and facsimiles of letters in an outline of Boulanger's life which he says is not a biography. He shows her, however, as a musician, teacher, and friend through the photographs, the comments of her students and peers, and her own insights.

BOURGEOIS, LOUISE (1911–)
Sculptor
France

Louise Bourgeois became one of the twentieth-century's major sculptors. Born on December 25, 1911 into a family of tapestry weavers in France, Bourgeois learned to draw the outlines for repairs to the tapestries and how to do the repairs. At the Sorbonne, she started to major in mathematics, but she switched to art. She married in 1938 and moved with her husband to the United States. At her first one-woman exhibit in New York in 1949, critics identified her as a major sculptor. She uses wood, wax, marble, metal, or latex to create an organic quality in her sculptures. Many of her works display confined, helpless, or frustrated but universal women. She also depicts family units or people who have a common goal. The trepidation, guilt, and pain in her work are also the world of her daily life. She received some of her inspiration for her sculptures when she flew over the Sahara Desert and observed the clusters of huts, isolated from the rest of the world. Her use of the "found" object and her surrealistic approach require tenacity, and her constant scrutiny of a thing shows that she is a compulsive recorder of emotional, visual, and personal historical data.

BIBLIOGRAPHY
Bernadac, Marie-Laure. *Louise Bourgeois.* New York: Flammarion, Abbeville, 1996. 2-08013-600-3, 192p. Bernadac chronologically overviews Bourgeois' career with 150 illustrations of her work and accompanying interpretation. Bernadac sees Bourgeois, neglected for many years, as original and sensual. She investigates Bourgeois' symbolic works as well as her most re-

cent "cells," in which she demonstrates that her art, a magical act, is emotional and erotic.

Bourgeois, Louise, and Lawrence Rinder. *Louise Bourgeois: Drawings and Observations.* Boston: Bulfinch Press, 1995. 0-8212-2299-6, 192p. In a series of interviews with Bourgeois, Rinder realized that Bourgeois's drawings represent her emotions and, therefore, are an autonomous and discrete body of work independent from her sculpture. Bourgeois often writes notes and comments on her drawings, which act as a monologue with self. Rinder explores how her drawings are woven into her personal history, and he includes photographs of Bourgeois' drawings with explanations of their relevance to her life.

Gardner, Paul. *Louise Bourgeois.* New York: Universe, 1993. 0-87663-639-3, 112p. This readable biography of Bourgeois is brief but thorough, with a careful look at her thoughts and how they translate into her work. Photographs of her sculptures illustrate the text.

Kotik, Charlotta, Terrie Sultan, and Christian Leigh. *Louise Bourgeois: The Locus of Memory, Works 1982–1993.* New York: Harry N. Abrams, 1994. 0-8109-3127-3, 144p. Three essays by different writers present views of Bourgeois' work. One gives an overview of her life and its influences, one discusses her art, and the third presents her rise in the art world after people began to realize her value. Photographs from each period help to emphasize her achievement.

Kuspit, Donald B. *Bourgeois.* New York: Vintage, 1988. 0-394-74792-5, 109p. In this interview with Bourgeois about her art, she speaks about the forces of her parents' relationship and her childhood. The framework of feminism helped her to understand the autobiographical statements of her work in the "new subjectivism" of the 1980s and the acknowledgment that the finding and restoring techniques learned in her youth are part of her artistic method.

BOWEN, ELIZABETH (1899–1973)

Writer   Ireland

Elizabeth Bowen was a fiction writer, critic, and biographer who won prizes for her work. Born in County Cork on June 7, 1899, the daughter of a wealthy barrister and landowner, Elizabeth Cole moved at seven to England with her mother. After education at Harpenden Hall, Hertfordshire, and Downe House School in Kent, she worked in a Dublin hospital treating shell-shocked cases during World War I. She moved to London and married Alan Cameron in 1923, the same year she published her first collection of short stories, *Encounters.* Her first novel, *The Hotel* (1927), was the first of a string of stories where she examined the illusions of youth and the subsequent betrayals of adulthood. She wrote constantly as she tried to show the abyss between public beliefs and private intuitions. Her themes appear in *The Death of the Heart* (1938) and *The Heat of the Day* (1949), a war story. She was also a perceptive literary critic and biographer, publishing *English Novelists* and *Collected Impressions* (1950) in these fields. In 1969, her novel *Eva Trout* won the James Tait Black Memorial Prize. Trinity College, Dublin, and Oxford gave her honorary doctorates, and she received a Commendation of the British Empire in 1948.

BIBLIOGRAPHY
Glendinning, Victoria. *Elizabeth Bowen*. New York: Knopf, 1978. 0-394-40533-1, 331p. Glendinning sees Bowen as the link between Virginia Woolf and Iris Murdoch or Muriel Spark. The readable text looks at her life and explores her vital, indefatigable, sociable, independent, hardworking, brave, kindhearted, and perceptive personality. Glendinning uses neither psychological interpretations of her actions nor critical interpretations of her work. The book includes many anecdotes and ignites an interest in Bowen, her unusual life, and her work.

Halperin, John. *Eminent Georgians: The Lives of King George V, Elizabeth Bowen, St. John Philby, and Nancy Astor*. New York: St. Martin's, 1995. 0-312-12661-1, 242p. In this collective biography of people who lived during the Edwardian 1930s and 1940s, Halperin creates a brief but interesting and conversational life of Bowen. He shows how she and the others represented Victorian tradition and its conflicts with evolving modernism.

Hoogland, Renee C. *Elizabeth Bowen: A Reputation in Writing*. New York: New York University Press, 1994. 0-8147-3501-0; paper, 0-8147-3511-8, 369p. In an analytically dense biography, Hoogland examines Bowen's life through the lens of lesbian studies since Bowen was a married woman who had several lesbian affairs.

Jordan, Heather Bryant. *How Will the Heart Endure: Elizabeth Bowen and the Landscape of War*. Ann Arbor: University of Michigan Press, 1992. 0-472-10218-4, 253p. Careful research shows that Bowen was a writer who had to face her dual allegiances to England and to Ireland as well as to identify the problems of her generation, so often at war. Jordan adds to Glendinning's biography by interpreting the social contexts of Bowen's major novels.

BRAUN, LILY (1865–1916)

Scholar and Activist   Germany

As an unorthodox Marxist, Lily von Kretschman Braun campaigned against patriarchy and capitalism. She was born in Halberstadt on July 2, 1865, into the upper class, whose restrictions she came to hate. By the time she reached her twenties, she had become attracted to radical political movements. She chose socialism and feminism as her major causes. Her first husband died, and she then married socialist writer and politician Heinrich Stammte. Braun taught and wrote literary criticism, publishing *Aus Goethes Freundeskreisen* (1892). While involved with the socialists, she expressed her strong feminist views in *Die Frauenfrage* (1901) by asserting that the political economy rested on female labor, and Social Democratic Party leaders expelled her. They thought that women's issues were secondary to those of working-class members in general. Her best-known book is *Im Schatten der Titanen* (1908), with her militant and radical views expressed in another book, *Memoiren einer Sozialistin* (1909–11). She was a political organizer as well as writer, housewife, and mother but collapsed and died at a relatively young age.

BIBLIOGRAPHY
Meyer, Alfred G. *The Feminism and Socialism of Lily Braun*. Bloomington: Indiana University Press, 1985. 0-253-32169-7, 235p. In studying Braun's life, Meyer thinks that she was committed to class warfare but that she

wanted a war of decency rather than death. He shows that she hated exploitation of any kind and never relinquished her beliefs.

BREMER, FREDRIKA (1801–1865)
Writer Sweden

As a feminist who believed that women should have rights, Fredrika Bremer expressed her views in her novels. She was born near Åbo, Finland, on August 17, 1801, moving with her family to a country estate near Stockholm, Sweden, when she was three. During her youth, her mother forbade Bremer's talking to visitors or servants, sheltering her from the world's evils. Bremer toured Europe in 1820–21, and when she returned home, she became involved in charity work. She anonymously published *Sketches of Everyday Life* (1828) to raise funds. It attracted little notice, but her *The H. Family* (1829), a novel of domestic life and manners, was an immediate success. Her father died in 1830, and she began traveling widely and publishing other works, gaining popularity abroad. *The House* won her a gold medal from the Swedish Academy in 1844. Her visits to Europe, Palestine, and the United States furnished material for the three volumes of her *Homes of the New World* (1853–54). Her later novels covered education and emancipation of women. She was a member of reform movements and women's charity organizations advocating women's rights to dispose of their own property. She helped nurse during the cholera epidemic of 1853, founded an orphanage, and started a school to train female teachers. In 1854, during the Crimean War, she called for an international peace movement, and her novel *Hertha* (1856) caused an uproar with its feminist theme. In 1885, twenty years after her death, the first Swedish women's association was named for her.

BIBLIOGRAPHY
Bremer, Fredrika. *Life, Letters, and Posthumous Works of Fredrika Bremer.* Trans. Fredrerick Milow. 1868. New York: AMS, 1976. 0-404-56708-8, 439p. The text includes a biographical overview, Bremer's brief autobiography, and letters that she wrote to friends and family members.

Elert, Claes-Christian, and Gunnar Eriksson. *Suppression, Struggle, and Success: Studies on Three Representatives of Cultural Life in Sweden: Fredrika Bremer, Andreas Kempe, and Linnaeus.* Stockholm: Almqvist and Wiksell, 1982. 91-7174-099-6, 105p. The authors give an overview of Bremer's life and accomplishments and attempt to discover how Bremer could write so well after being so sheltered.

Stendahl, Brita K. *The Education of a Self-Made Woman: Fredrika Bremer, 1801–1865.* Lewiston, ME: Edwin Mellen, 1994. 0-7734-9098-1, 206p. In this analytical biography, Stendahl investigates Bremer's life to find out where she got her strength after growing up with so much disappointment and depression. She sees Bremer as the instigator of Sweden's women's movement by erasing barriers from around her own life. Stendahl shows that Bremer, although she did not devise specific programs, envisioned a more compassionate future.

BRITTAIN, VERA (1896?–1970)
Writer and Activist   England

Vera Brittain was both a nonfiction writer and a lecturer who advocated pacifism, women's rights, and internationalism. After a December 29, 1896?, birthdate and growing up in Staffordshire, with her education at St. Monica's,
Kingswood, Brittain attended Somerville College, Oxford. During World War
I, she served as a Voluntary Aid Detachment nurse, while both her brother and
her fiancé died. She wrote about this pain in *Testament of Youth* (1933) and
gained worldwide fame. In 1925, she married a political philosopher at McGill
University in Canada, and they had two children. One of her books, *Testament
of Friendship* (1940), told about her friend the novelist Winifred Holtby, whom
Brittain met while she attended Oxford and with whom Brittain lived both before and during her marriage. The pacifism of Brittain's pamphlet *Seed of
Chaos* (1944) shocked American readers. *Testament of Experience* (1957) gives
a historical record of her life and the times from 1925 to 1950. She made seven
international lecture tours about nuclear disarmament, pacifism, and, as a dedicated member of the Anglican Church, reconciliation. She always combined
personal narrative with historical and political analysis in her twenty books
and thousands of journalistic pieces.

BIBLIOGRAPHY

Berry, Paul, and Mark Bostridge. *Vera Brittain: A Life.* London: Chatto and
    Windus, 1995. 0-7011-2679-5, 581p. Berry knew Brittain personally and
    was her literary executor. He and Bostridge, with unused manuscript mate-
    rial and other careful research, tell a balanced story of Brittain's life, her
    unusual arrangement with her husband and her friend Winifred Holtby,
    and her struggle to become a successful writer.

Brittain, Vera. *Testament of Friendship: The Story of Winifred Holtby.* New
    York: Seaview, 1981. 0-87223-679-X, 442p. Brittain wrote this biography
    of Holtby fifteen years after Holtby died of Bright's disease at thirty-seven.
    In telling of their sixteen-year friendship, Brittain reveals a great deal about
    herself.

Brittain, Vera. *Testament of Youth.* 1933. New York: Viking, 1989. Paper, 0-
    14-012251-6, 672p. Brittain remembers what she saw as a volunteer nurse
    and the losses that she had during World War I with the death of her
    brother and her fiancé. What she experienced separated her from any secu-
    rity of childhood and shaped her into a strong pacifist committed to social
    justice.

Gorham, Deborah. *Vera Brittain: A Feminist Life.* Cambridge, MA: Blackwell,
    1996. 0-631-14715-2, 330p. Gorham thinks Brittain made an important
    and original contribution by integrating imaginative and political writing to
    reconcile the ideals of creativity and historical truth. Gorham uses unpub-
    lished documentation that Brittain left about her life to show her strengths
    and weaknesses in this analytical and accessible biography focusing on Brit-
    tain's feminist attitudes.

Kennard, Jean E. *Vera Brittain and Winifred Holtby: A Working Partnership.*
    Hanover, NH: University Press of New England, 1989. 0-87451-474-6; pa-
    per, 0-87451-482-7, 224p. Kennard's biography shows Brittain and her
    friend Winifred Holtby spending much of their time speaking for those
    who could not voice their problems. It also examines Brittain's strong fe-
    male friendship as a means of self-definition and as an intellectual influ-
    ence. This readable biography imparts important information about their

understanding of each other and asserts that the two were not lesbians. University of New Hampshire Book Prize.

BRONTË, ANNE (1820–1849)
Writer   England

Although **Charlotte Brontë** seems to have perpetrated the idea that Anne Brontë was a lesser writer because Charlotte disapproved of the content of *Tenant of Wildfell Hall,* many critics think that Anne was a major writer and must be judged on her own merit. The youngest of the Brontë sisters, born on January 17, 1820, Anne seems to have been determined to become independent and successful outside her home. She had a very brief formal education and worked as a governess for several families when she was nineteen. Since she was quite shy, however, she stayed at her father's parsonage for the rest of her life. She wrote and published *Agnes Grey* (1847) and *Tenant of Wildfell Hall* (1848) using the pseudonym "Acton Bell." The later work caused such a scandal that a second edition had to be published within a month. Anne portrayed vice truthfully and claimed equal legal rights for women, while her view of religious dogma shocked Victorian society. Her novels give a realistic picture of country life for the middle class in early nineteenth-century England. Her earliest poems date from when she was sixteen, and she wrote fifty-nine in total. Always sickly, she developed tuberculosis and collapsed on a trip to Scarborough with **Charlotte** after **Emily** died.

BIBLIOGRAPHY
Chitham, Edward. *A Life of Anne Brontë.* Cambridge, MA: Blackwell, 1991. 0-631-16616-5, 216p. Since Chitham thinks that using Anne's semiautobiographical *Agnes Grey* to understand her life is somewhat circular and that the two published diary papers cannot be trusted because of publisher carelessness, he has used the only extant original papers. He also used weather records to surmise what Anne was experiencing when writing a dated poem as well as topography records of the places where she lived as the bases for his recommended biography.

Frawley, Maria H. *Anne Brontë.* New York: Twayne, 1996. 0-8057-7060-7, 171p. In this scholarly analysis, Frawley thinks that Brontë's work deals not only with autobiographical subjects of her daily life but also with the broader aspects of self-understanding, self-representation, and dilemmas of identity. Frawley uses previously unknown primary sources, including Brontë's Bible, her diary papers, and her music manuscript books, in interpreting the social and psychological dimensions of identity in her work.

Gerin, Winifred. *Anne Brontë.* Lanham, MD: Rowman and Littlefield, 1975. 0-8747-1797-3, 372p. Gerin based this biography, the first about Anne, on autobiographical elements in *Agnes Grey.* She also used texts of letters or editions of poems and novels from the whole family that may not have had textual authenticity. She thinks that writing poetry helped Anne escape her solitude.

Harrison, Ada M., and Derek Stanford. *Anne Brontë, Her Life and Work.* 1959. Hamden, CT: Archon, 1970. 0-208-00987-6, 252p. In two parts, one on Anne's life and the other on her novels and poems, the authors try to present Anne through her own merits rather than through Charlotte's eyes. Charlotte destroyed many of Anne's papers after her death so that Charlotte's view about Anne has been the one prevailing longest.

Langland, Elizabeth. *Anne Brontë: The Other One.* Totowa, NJ: Barnes and Noble, 1989. 0-389-20865-5, 172p. Langland shows that Anne was an important force in the novel's development toward realism, in the theory of the novel, and in feminist criticism. She looks at Anne's life by focusing on the tensions and divergences among the sisters, the influences on Anne, her two major works, and critical commentary.

BRONTË, CHARLOTTE (1816–1855)
Writer   England

Contemporary comments about Charlotte Brontë's major work, *Jane Eyre,* included that it was "a wicked book" and that the author was someone "to keep one's daughters away from." Born on April 21, 1816, to an eccentric father who did not particularly like children, Charlotte's mother died when Charlotte was five, and she became, in essence, the family's mother. Her feeling that she was ugly caused her to turn around when talking to people so they would not have to look at her. At nineteen, she went to work as a teacher and governess, the only jobs open to women, so that she could earn money to send her brother Branwell to school. She hated the work but made herself do it. When Charlotte found a book of poems that her sisters Emily and Anne were secretly writing, she suggested that they publish them under the names Currer, Ellis, and Acton Bell—male names that would protect them from their brother and father as well as critics prejudiced against women writers. Although the book sold only two copies, she continued to write. She began her book *Jane Eyre* after nursing her father through an eye operation and while suffering an intense toothache. When asked how she could write about something that she had not experienced, she said that she thought about a subject or situation many nights before falling asleep so that eventually she felt as if she had. She eventually married a man who pursued her so persistently that she pitied him, but his disapproval of women writers caused her to stop writing. She died nine months later, most likely of complications from pregnancy.

BIBLIOGRAPHY

Goldring, Maude. *Charlotte Brontë, the Woman: A Study.* Norwood, PA: Norwood Editions, 1977. 0-8482-0960-6, 95p. Charlotte Brontë, to Goldring, was a woman who suffered and was despondent as she "waited" for whatever was to come in her life; however, Brontë was always able to grapple with her moods and talk herself back into moderation. Goldring thinks that Brontë shows her emotion only in her novels, not in her letters or her life.

Gordon, Lyndall. *Charlotte Brontë: A Passionate Life.* New York: Norton, 1995. 0-393-03722-3, 416p. According to Gordon, Charlotte Brontë, author of *Jane Eyre* and *Villette,* was a very resourceful woman, impatient, sarcastic and strong, and committed to her writing. He shows in this balanced biography, which should be the first choice for any reader, how she survived during a time inhospitable to women and how she incorporated autobiographical elements into her novels along with the concept of the "shadow." Cheltenham Prize.

Moglen, Helene. *Charlotte Brontë: The Self Conceived.* New York: Norton, 1976. 0-393-07505-2, 256p. Moglen tries to show the two dimensions of Brontë in the life she lived and the life she wrote about in her books. This interpretation is a psychosexual and social interpretation under a feminist light that interprets Brontë through characters in her novels. Moglen thinks that Brontë's pregnancy probably killed her since she did not particularly like children, and pregnancy would most likely have horrified her.

Peters, Margot. *Unquiet Soul: A Biography of Charlotte Brontë*. Garden City, NY: Doubleday, 1975. 0-385-06622-8, 460p. Peters thinks that the tension in living both dutifully and unconventionally made Brontë's novels good. Brontë knew that life could be nothing other than a battle between conformity and rebellion, and, although she knew the conventional notions of womanhood, she did not agree with them.

Winnifrith, Tom. *A New Life of Charlotte Brontë*. New York: St. Martin's, 1988. 0-312-01578-X, 136p. Winnifrith titles his chapters with Brontë's roles as pupil, writer, teacher, author, and wife; her travel to Belgium; and her books *Jane Eyre*, *Shirley*, and *Villette*. He examines her as a "whole" person rather than as part of a particular school of criticism and finds her rather unpleasant but admirable.

BRONTË, EMILY (1818–1848)
Writer   England

Emily Brontë became famous for her extraordinary novel, *Wuthering Heights*, which critics called "demonic," "sickening," and "shocking." The middle daughter, born on July 30, 1818, she rarely talked, running in and out of rooms to retrieve books without speaking to anyone who happened to be there. Her nickname became the "Major" because she dominated the older Charlotte. She seemed to like animals better than humans, but she was sometimes unreasonable to her animals as well. One time she beat her dog for sleeping on her clean, white bedspread. After she wrote *Wuthering Heights*, Charlotte said that the chapters she had read kept her awake at night. Emily's brother Branwell died of alcohol poisoning and tuberculosis after *Wuthering Heights* was published, and at his funeral, Emily caught a cold and never completely recovered. She continued to do her chores and refused treatment until two hours before she died. Her coffin measured only sixteen inches across.

BIBLIOGRAPHY

Chitham, Edward. *A Life of Emily Brontë*. New York: Blackwell, 1987. 0-631-14751-9, 284p. Chitham's "investigative biography" looks at the facts known, some information that seems to be factual from which conclusions can be drawn, and some theory including places, objects, and people that Brontë must have seen but for which no record exists.

Davies, Stevie. *Emily Brontë, the Artist as a Free Woman*. Manchester, England: Carcanet, 1983. 0-85365-489-7, 170p. The biography discusses Brontë's life, her poetry, and her novel. Davies interprets Brontë's life in terms of her poetry and of her one novel, *Wuthering Heights*, and offers a viable introduction to her.

Frank, Katherine. *A Chainless Soul: A Life of Emily Brontë*. Boston: Houghton Mifflin, 1990. 0-395-42508-5, 302p. Frank uses recent scholarship about social and literary history of the nineteenth century as a way to understand Emily Brontë better. She shows her as troubled, austere, and solitary, but not passive. She thinks that Brontë suffered from anorexia nervosa and, using this condition as a basis, speculates what hunger did to shape her life and her writing as well as her body.

Gerin, Winifred. *Emily Brontë: A Biography*. 1971. New York: Oxford University Press, 1990. Paper, 0-19-281251-3, 290p. Emily Brontë had the reputation of having sprung full-grown when she published her one novel, as

Athena did from the head of Zeus. After living in the Brontë town of Haworth for ten years, Gerin tries to find the reasons for the major changes in the last few years of Brontë's life through the meager bits of documented fact.

Moore, Virginia. *The Life and Eager Death of Emily Brontë, a Biography*. 1936. New York: Haskell House, 1971. 0-8383-1345-0, 383p. After reading Charlotte's many letters, Anne's two letters, and Emily's three letters as well as all the poetry and prose, Moore tries to interpret Emily Brontë's life. She thinks that Heathcliff and the iron man of the poems are psychological interpretations of Brontë's life and that even the setting of Haworth, with its mountain-steep main street, influenced Brontë's strong emotion in her writing.

BROWNING, ELIZABETH BARRETT (1806–1861)
Poet   England

Elizabeth Barrett Browning gained lasting renown with her collection of love poems, *Sonnets from the Portuguese*. Born on March 6, 1806, at Coxhoe near Durham, she moved to a country house with her family near the Malvern hills, which she grew to love. Her father was proud of her talent, and when she was eleven or twelve, he arranged for fifty copies of her epic *The Battle of Marathon* to be published. She studied both Latin and Greek and translated works as well. At fifteen, she became ill, probably with a spinal injury. She continued publishing her poems as an invalid and was well known to other authors of the time, including Wordsworth, who asked twice to visit her. After her second volume of poems was published in 1844 to critical claim both in England and in the United States, Robert Browning wrote her a letter in which he stated "I do, as I say, love these books [her poetry] with all my heart—and I love you too." They met six months later, and although Browning was six years younger, he never doubted that he would marry her, invalid or not. His own mother was happily older than his father, but Barrett's had not been. Her father demanded that his twelve children not marry. But Elizabeth Barrett defied him by running away to Italy with Robert Browning after a twenty-month courtship by letter. They settled permanently in Florence where a child was born two years later. Barrett Browning published *Aurora Leigh* in 1856 to public acclaim and critical concern as a barely disguised story of her life in which she pondered some of the major social ills of her day, including poverty, unemployment, prostitution, and unsavory living conditions. Her poetry was effusive, and *Sonnets from the Portuguese* remained her best work since the sonnet form controlled her enthusiasm.

BIBLIOGRAPHY

Forster, Margaret. *Elizabeth Barrett Browning: A Biography*. New York: Doubleday, 1989. 0-385-24959-4, 400p. Forster's recommended, introductory biography relies on new material available on Barrett Browning's life that Philip Kelley has uncovered since 1959 and the new feminism that has caused a revived interest in her poetry. Forster used hundreds of letters covering Barrett Browning's childhood, adolescence, and adult life before she married as well as many after she married to show that Browning has become one of the literary "grandmothers." Royal Society of Literature Award.

Grylls, R. Glynn. *Mrs. Browning: The Story of Elizabeth Barrett*. London: Weidenfeld and Nicolson, 1980. 0-297-77802-1, 162p. Grylls covers Barrett

Browning's life, mainly after her marriage, with excerpts from poems and letters interspersed through the text.

Markus, Julia. *Dared and Done: The Marriage of Elizabeth Barrett and Robert Browning.* New York: Knopf, 1995. 0-679-41602-1, 382p. Using Barrett Browning's unpublished correspondence and many other documents, Markus relates the story of the Brownings' courtship by letter, their marriage, and their life in Italy. She also investigates their backgrounds, including Browning's Creole heritage, and how they affected their work.

Mermin, Dorothy. *Elizabeth Barrett Browning: The Origins of a New Poetry.* Chicago: University of Chicago Press, 1989. 0-226-52038-2, 310p. In this scholarly biography, Mermin posits that Barrett Browning was the first Victorian poet and the first major woman poet in England. Mermin also emphasizes that Barrett Browning is an originator of a new poetry and that she developed strategies to escape gender traps, such as learning Greek and fantasizing about wearing men's clothing. Mermin thinks the key to Barrett Browning's work is her search to find a woman's place in a man's world of poetry.

Stone, Marjorie. *Elizabeth Barrett Browning.* New York: St. Martin's, 1995. 0-312-12210-1, 254p. For this scholarly biography, Stone uses neglected manuscripts as a basis for comparing Browning to her contemporary female writers such as Gaskell and to discuss her innovative poetic development. Stone thinks that Browning's refusal to create self-sacrificing heroines was her way of rejecting dominant males and concludes that males have unfairly relegated Browning to minor literary status.

BURDETT-COUTTS, ANGELA (1814–1906)

Philanthropist   England

Angela Burdett-Coutts showed Victorian women that philanthropy could be a woman's profession. Born into a wealthy family on April 21, 1814, Burdett-Coutts had the privilege of travel and private tutors, and her governess became a trusted friend who influenced her fervor for the Evangelical Church. At twenty-three in 1837, Burdett-Coutts became famous because her stepgrandmother left her an entire fortune, making her England's wealthiest woman. Her friends were politicians, such as Peel, Disraeli, and Gladstone, and writers, including Charles Dickens. Dickens helped her organize her contributions to the Ragged School Union and to Urania Cottage in Shepherd's Bush, a place for prostitutes to find respite. She supported churches in London and endowed bishops in South Africa and Australia. She tried to keep food prices down in poor areas of London and established a middle-class housing development in Highgate. In 1871, she became the first woman to rise to the peerage in her own right, and in 1872, she was the first woman presented with freedom of the City of London. She gave more money for African exploration and provided nurses for the Zulu War. She founded an establishment in Australia to aid the borigines and began a relief fund for refugees of the 1877 Russo-Turkish War. When she was sixty-seven, she married a twenty-seven-year-old man, although she had refused many proposals after she became wealthy and even made one to a family friend forty-five years older, who politely declined. She is buried in Westminster Abbey.

BIBLIOGRAPHY

Healey, Edna. *Lady Unknown: The Life of Angela Burdett-Coutts.* New York: Coward, McCann, and Geoghegan, 1978. 0-698-10939-2, 253p. Papers previously unavailable help Healey give the first thorough picture of Burdett-Coutts. Although a popular biography, it is well researched and entertaining, but it offers little insight on Burdett-Coutts as a philanthropist in the Victorian age.

BURNETT, FRANCES HODGSON (1849–1924)

Writer   England

Ironically, Frances Hodgson Burnett's two most famous books obscured her reputation as a serious novelist of realism. Burnett, born on November 24, 1849, was one of the five children under the age of eight whom her mother had to support when Burnett's father died. The family left Manchester, England, to live with her mother's brother in rural Tennessee when Burnett was fifteen. Since Burnett felt responsible for supporting the family when a teenager, she picked wild grapes to earn money for the postage to mail her first stories to publishers. Although almost everyone admired her writing and acclaimed her critically, many thought her conceited. Her nickname was "Fluffy," and she wore lacy chiffon dresses and cloaks lined with ermine and satin over her plump body, along with her black velvet hats. She married and divorced twice because marriage interfered with her work, but she adored her two sons. Burnett's idea for *The Secret Garden* came from the rose garden at her English house, planted with three hundred French rose bushes. She was "ahead of her time," because she was probably the first woman to be seen smoking in public and let her books be made into movies. When she brought a lawsuit against someone who dramatized *Little Lord Fauntleroy* without her permission in 1888, she began the fight leading to the British Copyright Act, passed in 1911.

BIBLIOGRAPHY

Burnett, Frances Hodgson. *The One I Knew the Best of All.* Illus. Reginald B. Birch. 1893. New York: Arno, 1980. 0-405-12828-2, 325p. Burnett calls herself the Small Person, the only child that she really knew well. Among the anecdotes is a recounting of the acceptance of Small Person's first two stories. The editor was not sure Burnett had written the first one and asked for a second one to verify. Then he bought both of them.

Carpenter, Angelica Shirley, and Jean Shirley. *Frances Hodgson Burnett: Beyond the Secret Garden.* Minneapolis: Lerner, 1990. 0-8225-4905-0, 128p. This biography uses as a main source *The Romantick Lady,* in which Burnett's son Vivian wrote frankly about her. The text covers her early years in Manchester, her life in Tennessee until 1868, her days in Paris, and her return to the United States.

Thwaite, Ann. *Waiting for the Party: The Life of Frances Hodgson Burnett.* 1974. Lincoln, MA: David R. Godine, 1991. Paper, 0-87923-790-2, 288p. In chapters divided according to the periods in Burnett's life, Thwaite thinks that Burnett wrote stories that she would have liked to have happen in real life but that her own life was often unhappy and frustrating. She sees Burnett as always waiting for the "party" rather than actually attending it.

BURNEY, FANNY (1752–1840)

Writer   England

Fanny Burney wrote novels, and her journals of life in the early nineteenth century give a clear picture of contemporary people, customs, and court life. She was born in King's Lynn on June 13, 1752, the daughter of the musical historian Charles Burney. Illiterate until she was eight, she began reading her father's books, including sermons, histories, and conduct books. She kept a diary in which she recorded conversation, delineated character, and described events. Her stepmother suggested that she might be writing something for which she could be condemned, but when Burney let her read it, she saw that it was not what one usually read in a private diary. Burney acknowledged herself as author of her first novel, *Evelina*, published anonymously in 1778, when her father praised it. She then became friends with such writers as Samuel Johnson, Edmund Burke, and members of the famous Literary Club. In 1793, while anti-French sentiment pervaded London, she bravely married a French Royalist refugee, General Alexandre d'Arblay. Burney's (Madame d'Arblay) fame rests principally on her diary, which she began on May 30, 1768, and kept for seventeen years. Burney's nickname "Fanny" may have caused critics to patronize her, and some said that her writing became stodgy when she started writing under her married name of Madame d'Arblay. Her other novels, *Cecilia* (1782), *Camilla* (1796), and *The Wanderer* (1814), are sentimental but entertaining descriptions of innocent young women entering society.

BIBLIOGRAPHY

Burney, Fanny. *The Early Journals and Letters of Fanny Burney*. Vols. 1 and 2, *1768–1773 and 1774–1777*. Ed. Lars E. Troide. Toronto: McGill-Queen's University Press, 1988 and 1990. Vol. 1, 0-7735-0539-3, 311p. Vol. 2, 0-7735-0538-5, 353p. Burney's journals and letters show her close observation of those around her, including the monotonous Thomas Barlow, who tried to get her to marry him in 1775, and Dr. Johnson, who was somewhat clumsy and awkward. She also reveals her own susceptibility to illness and shows that she had an understanding of the society in which she lived and was able to communicate the habits and the dialogue of the people around her.

Devlin, D. D. *The Novels and Journals of Fanny Burney*. New York: St. Martin's, 1987. 0-312-00034-0, 118p. In a brief look at Burney's novels, Devlin indicates that she was aware of what was going on around her, even though she did not dwell on the French Revolution or other events of her time. Her reactions were neither simple nor predictable, and therefore, they defy labeling.

Doody, Margaret Anne. *Frances Burney: The Life in the Works*. New Brunswick, NJ: Rutgers University Press, 1988. Paper, 0-8135-1355-3, 441p. Doody shows Burney as examining her society's structure, functions, and beliefs and revealing its perverseness through her characters. In this balanced view of Burney, Doody says that, even though violence was part of Burney's writing, with suicide one of the major motives, Burney espoused integrity, independence, and generosity.

Epstein, Julia. *The Iron Pen: Frances Burney and the Politics of Women's Writing*. Madison: University of Wisconsin Press, 1989. 0-299-11940-8; paper, 0-299-11944-0, 276p. Epstein sees Burney as a conflicted but self-conscious social reformer who wrote about aggressive violence with novels tied to the social institutions of class, family, marriage, lineage, and inheritance in this scholarly biography. Epstein thinks that **Jane Austen**, the **Brontës**, or **George Eliot** might not have been able to write as they did without Burney's heroines breaking the rules before them.

Kilpatrick, Sarah. *Fanny Burney.* New York: Stein and Day, 1981. 0-8128-2761-9, 232p. To show Burney's self-sufficiency from the time she was fifteen, Kilpatrick has written a popular and easily accessible biography in which she tells of Burney's burning her early writing. The biography discusses the two men influential in her early life, her father and family friend Samuel Crisp, against whom she measured all other men; her court appointment; and her love-match husband, General D'Arblay, married at forty for twenty years.

BUTLER, JOSEPHINE (1828–1906)
Activist   England

Josephine Butler championed a variety of causes during her life, including an international movement against prostitution and the "white-slave" trade. The youngest and favorite of her father, a chief Whig agent in Northumbria, Josephine Elizabeth Grey heard much political controversy from his friends while growing up and straightforward Christian convictions from her mother. She married George Butler, a teacher later to become the canon of Winchester, in 1852, who calmed her and helped her plan her activism. Butler supported higher education for women and campaigned for repeal of the Contagious Diseases Act from 1869, after she published *Women's Work and Women's Culture*, to 1886. She saw that any working-class woman even suspected of being a prostitute lost her reputation when the "morals" police approached her about compulsory registration, licensing, and medical examination. Butler succeeded in this campaign because she had learned lobbying from her father, and she used the contacts that she had made while growing up. She later visited the Continent to organize an international movement against prostitution and "white-slave" trade. One of her last concerns was to fight child prostitution. She also wrote *Personal Reminiscences of a Great Crusade* (1896) and *Life of St. Catherine of Siena* (1898).

BIBLIOGRAPHY
Boyd, Nancy. *Three Victorian Women Who Changed Their World: Josephine Butler, Octavia Hill, Florence Nightingale.* New York: Oxford University Press, 1982. 0-19-520271-6, 276p. Boyd surveys Josephine Butler's life and accomplishments against the historical background of her times to show the magnitude of her achievements and her legacy. Although the style is rather plodding, the text is informative and laudatory.

Butler, Josephine Elizabeth Grey. *Personal Reminiscences of a Great Crusade.* 1911. Westport, CT: Hyperion, 1976. 0-88355-257-4, 245p. Butler discusses the various causes with which she was involved and the persons with whom she corresponded, such as Victor Hugo in France and Guiseppe Mazzini in Italy, during her lifetime. Her zeal emerges through her anecdotes.

Petrie, Glen. *A Singular Iniquity; the Campaigns of Josephine Butler.* New York: Viking, 1971. 0-670-64711-X, 317p. Petrie bases this biography on letters, journals, and unpublished manuscripts that detail the conditions that Butler found in England and the Continent during her fierce battles for equality of the sexes. Protected by her social rank, she overcame her personal reticence and the public's scorn because of her religious beliefs to show how licensed prostitution could be detrimental to the women. At the end of her life, she had begun trying to help Russian Jews.

Williamson, Joseph. *Josephine Butler, the Forgotten Saint.* Leighton Buzzard, England: Faith, 1977. 0-71640-485-0, 122p. Williamson was a member of a lower economic class who witnessed the work that Butler did for prostitutes in East London. He wanted to laud her willingness to work with people in a different class from her own. He quotes Butler extensively, tells of her talents as an accomplished musician and artist, and generally approves of everything about her.

BUTT, CLARA (1872–1936)
Opera Singer   **England**

A conductor supposedly asked the musicians to play more loudly when Clara Butt was singing because they could not be heard over her large contralto voice which became famous in opera and concert halls. She was born on February 1, 1872, in London where she studied at the Royal College of Music. She made her debut at the Royal Albert Hall as Ursula in Sullivan's *Golden Legend* in 1892, and three days later she sang in Gluck's *Orfeo* at the Lyceum Theater. She based her success on ballads and oratorios, however, rather than opera. Her voice was famous for its beauty and its strength, qualities complemented by heavy orchestration in the cycle *Sea Pictures* (1899), which Sir Edward Elgar composed especially for her. She toured the United States first in 1899 and again in 1913. She married in 1900, and she and her baritone husband, R. Kennerley Rumford, entertained audiences with their English ballads. During World War I, she donated the proceeds from one of her tours to pay for musicians to give concerts around England, the profits going to the Red Cross. She also performed in these concerts herself, one in Westminster Abbey where a fly flew into her mouth while she was singing; she had to swallow it in order to continue. In 1920, she received the Dame of the British Empire for her services during the war. Other activities included recording on the gramophone, becoming involved in anticommunist activities, and traveling to India in 1927, where she visited Annie Besant.

BIBLIOGRAPHY
Ponder, Winifred. *Clara Butt, Her Life-Story.* 1928. New York: Da Capo, 1978. 0-306-77529-8, 261p. Ponder lauds Butt's career and charitable contributions in her biography. Butt kept neither diary nor letters, and Ponder had to gather information from family and friends. Ponder makes disconcerting shifts between present and past tense which are stylistically weak but understandable since her book was published while Butt still lived.

$$\mathfrak{C}$$

CABALLÉ, MONTSERRAT (1933–)
Opera Singer   **Spain**

Montserrat Caballé is one of the twentieth century's major international operatic sopranos. She has lived in Barcelona since her April 12, 1933, birth. She enjoys enormous acclaim for her concert repertoire and stage roles from Rossini to Puccini, in contemporary opera, in Zarzuela, and in the German tradition of Wagner and Strauss. She has sung at Covent Garden, Glyndebourne, the Metropolitan Opera, La Scala, Mexico City, and other main houses and has made many recordings during her forty-year career. Her consummate singing voice, her accomplished theatrical interpretations, and her support of younger singers such as José Carreas make her an important operatic legacy.

BIBLIOGRAPHY
Pullen, Robert, and Stephen Taylor. *Montserrat Caballé: Casta Diva.* Boston: Northeastern University Press, 1995. 1-55553-228-4, 464p. Pullen and Taylor's biography of Caballé admires her accomplishments and includes lengthy descriptions of her performances. They present Caballé as an intelligent, loving, and humorous woman.

CABRINI, FRANCESCA XAVIER (1850–1917)
Religious   **Italy**

"Mother Cabrini" founded sixty-seven houses of the Missionary Sisters of the Sacred Heart in major international cities to lodge over five thousand children and nurse over one hundred thousand. Cabrini was born in Sant 'Angelo, Lodigliano (Lombardy) on July 15, 1850, the youngest of thirteen children. She had already decided by her first communion at the age of seven that she would become a missionary. Her delicate health first kept her out of the convent, so she began supervising and reforming an orphanage in 1874. In 1880, she founded the Missionary Sisters of the Sacred Heart, using a former Franciscan convent as her headquarters. Pope Leo XIII urged her to go to the United States, instead of China, and work among the Italian immigrants. In New York after 1889, she established schools and organized visits to prisons. She had never traveled until she was thirty-seven, when she first crossed the ocean, but she made thirty-six additional trips. In 1946, the church canonized her, and she became the first American saint.

BIBLIOGRAPHY

Daughters of St. Paul. *Mother Cabrini.* Boston: St. Paul Editions, 1977. No ISBN, 168p. The Daughters of St. Paul published this adulatory biography based on data obtained from books, pamphlets, magazines, and newspaper articles furnished by the Missionary Sisters of the Sacred Heart, Mother Cabrini's order.

Lorit, Sergio C. *Frances Cabrini: A Saint for America.* Trans. Jerry Hearne. New York: New City, 1988. 0-911782-63-X, 141p. Lorit traces Mother Cabrini's life in Italy and her concern for those in need, including impoverished Italian immigrants and children orphaned by industrial accidents in the United States. Lorit lauds Cabrini's achievements without documentation.

Saverio de Maria, Madre. *Mother Frances Xavier Cabrini.* Trans. Rose Basile Green. Chicago: Missionary Sisters of the Sacred Heart of Jesus, 1984. 0-8453-4764-0, 371p. Saverio tries to reveal Mother Cabrini's inner life in a reasonably authentic biography by using her comments and those of others who knew her that articulate her attitudes, perceptions, meditations, decisions, and pursuits as a spiritual pioneer of social justice.

CALCUTTA, TERESA of. *See* TERESA of CALCUTTA.

CAMBRIDGE, ADA (1844–1926)
Writer   England

Ada Cambridge's writing raised questions about the status and roles of women, society's treatment of the aged, and the nature and existence of God. She was born in Norfolk as the second of ten children on November 21, 1844. Her father was a gentleman farmer, and she was educated privately. By the time she met and married George Cross at twenty-six, she had published short stories, poems, and a book of hymns. They left almost immediately for Australia, where her husband was to be a missionary priest, and eventually settled in Melbourne. In her eighteen novels, she encouraged women to think for themselves and find the inner freedom to make choices but knew that the relationship between men and women was the most central issue of life. She attracted a wide English readership but was modest about her success, regarding herself fortunate to be described as the foremost female novelist and compared to William Thackeray, **George Eliot,** and **Charlotte Brontë.** Her best works were *A Marked Man, The Three Miss Kings, Not All in Vain, Fidelis,* and *Materfamilias.* After her death, she became a victim of conservatism in Australian literature, a movement that replaced her reputation with the myth of the frail clergyman's wife writing romantic fiction of dubious value.

BIBLIOGRAPHY

Beilby, Raymond, and Cecil Hadgraft. *Ada Cambridge, Tasma, and Rosa Praed.* New York: Oxford University Press, 1979. 0-19-550509-3, 48p. In a collective biography, Beilby and Hadgraft examine Cambridge's life and work and find her to be one of Australia's most important female writers.

Bradstock, Margaret, and Louise Wakeling. *Rattling the Orthodoxies: A Life of Ada Cambridge.* New York: Penguin, 1991. 0-14-012998-7, 269p. The authors disclose parallels between Cambridge's life and fiction and think that her reputation suffered after the 1900s when male critics considered colonial women writers as class-bound, Anglophile, and interested only in feminine concerns. Cambridge's "alternate truths," however, challenged her male contemporaries.

Cambridge, Ada. *Thirty Years in Australia.* Kensington, New South Wales, Austria: New South Wales University Press, 1989. 0-86840-020-3, 251p. Cambridge presents daily life in Australia as well as her social and political views over a period of thirty years. The text includes unpublished works, correspondence, personal papers, early newspapers, and microfilms of publishers' archives.

Tate, Audrey Patricia. *Ada Cambridge: Her Life and Work, 1844–1926.* Portland, OR: International Specialized Book Services, 1991. 0-522-84410-3, 319p. Tate wants to retain an authentic picture of Cambridge, so she deliberately uses Cambridge's own words as much as possible to show a young girl of mid-Victorian England who came to view herself as an Australian woman.

CAMERON, JULIA MARGARET (1815–1879)

Photographer   **India**

Julia Margaret Cameron's portraits reveal a perception of the subjects unlike other Victorian photography. Her father was a Scotsman in the Bengal Civil Service, and she was born in Calcutta on June 11, 1850. Her parents died when she was young, and she returned to Europe, attending schools in England and France. Back in India, she met and married Charles Cameron, a reformer of the Indian legal system. She used her energy to raise money for Irish famine victims in 1846 and her several children. When the children left home, she became depressed, and her daughter gave her an old wooden camera. Without previous knowledge of photography, she worked for a year to learn the fundamental skills. From 1864, everything in her life became subject to her photography. She preferred pictures of faces only because people's clothing exposed their social class. Among the people she captured were Alfred Lord Tennyson, Anthony Trollope, Robert Browning, Thomas Carlyle, and Charles Darwin. Contemporaries criticized her lack of professional training, but her husband's encouragement and her own faith in her ability kept her working.

BIBLIOGRAPHY

Gernsheim, Helmut. *Julia Margaret Cameron: Her Life and Photographic Work.* London: Gordon Fraser, 1975. 0-900406-61-5, 200p. The first half of Gernsheim's text is a biography of Cameron, with the second half a reproduction of her photographs.

Hill, Brian. *Julia Margaret Cameron: A Victorian Family Portrait.* London: Owen, 1973. 0-7206-0472-9, 203p. Hill discusses Cameron and her six siblings, the Pattle sisters. Although he includes much about her sisters, his emphasis remains on Cameron, known for her eccentricity and eclectic friendships.

Lutkish, Joanne. *Cameron, Her Work and Career.* Rochester, NY: International Museum of Photography, 1986. Paper, 0-935398-13-9, 103p. Lutkish examines Cameron's life and work for an exhibition at the George Eastman House in 1986. It incorporates reproductions of her photographs.

Ovenden, Graham, ed. *A Victorian Album: Julia Margaret Cameron and Her Circle*. London: Secker and Warburg, 1975. 0-436-35416-0, 252p. This work is a brief biography, with the main section featuring Cameron's pictures to clarify her view of photography.

CARPENTER, MARY (1807–1877)
Educator   England

Mary Carpenter first advocated higher education for women and later promoted female involvement in public life as well. Born on April 3, 1807, to a famous Unitarian minister and teacher, she later attended his school. After working as a governess for two years, she and her mother opened a girls' school in Bristol. In 1835, she founded the Working and Visiting Society as a basis for working with neglected children, and in 1846, she founded a "ragged" school in the Bristol slums. An essay she wrote influenced discussion about reformatory schools, but since she disagreed with the punitive atmosphere in existing schools, she established her own reformatory for boys at Kingswood in 1852. After the Youthful Offenders Act of 1854 recognized her schools, she opened several reformatories for girls. She then established industrial schools. She visited India on four occasions and spoke on such topics as women's education and the penal system. About her visits she wrote *Our Convicts, The Last Days of Rammohun Roy,* and *Six Months in India.* She founded the National India Association in 1870, and, after researching American, Canadian, and European reform systems, she lectured about them.

BIBLIOGRAPHY
Carpenter, J. Estlin. *The Life and Work of Mary Carpenter.* 1881. Montclair, NJ: Patterson Smith, 1974. 0-87585-145-2, 404p. The author chronicles the events in Carpenter's life through letters, books, papers, and the institutions to which she belonged and those that she established. The author thinks Carpenter's interests were singular and without much variety. Many complete letters appear in the text.

Manton, Jo. *Mary Carpenter and the Children of the Streets.* London: Heinemann, 1976. 0-435-32569-8, 268p. In this authentic biography, Manton shows that Carpenter sacrificed her intellectual interests, but enjoyed minor pleasures in life, painting, and helping needy children.

CARR, EMILY (1871–1945)
Artist   Canada

Emily Carr, an important female Canadian painter, was beloved for her paintings of Indian villages, totem poles, and the forests of the West Coast and was an award-winning writer. After her birth on December 12, 1871, Carr grew up in Victoria, British Columbia, before studying in San Francisco and in London. In 1902, she became ill and returned to Canada, but seven years later, she decided to study in Paris at the Académie Colarossi. While in Paris, she broke with earlier Victorian concepts, and her invigorated brush strokes revealed her as a forerunner of abstract expressionism. When she returned to Canada, no one acknowledged her work, and she briefly stopped painting. Trips she made to the forests in British Columbia and her interest in Native American culture influenced her resumed work, and she began to create totems and trees that re-sembled living beings. Critics responded positively, and in 1933, she joined the Canadian Group of Painters. In 1940, her lack of energy and poor health led her to writing. She published tales about Canadian life, *Klee Wyck* (1941), *The Book of Small* (1942), and *The House of All Sorts* (1944). *Klee Wyck* won the Governor General's Award for nonfiction. Three other books, one her autobiography, appeared after her death, in 1953.

BIBLIOGRAPHY

Blanchard, Paula. *The Life of Emily Carr*. Seattle: University of Washington Press, 1987. 0-295-96546-0, 331p. This readable biography gives insight into the complexities of Carr's life by looking at its recurring themes, inner conflicts, and illnesses of her middle years. Blanchard speculates about her life from a feminist view and wonders what in her life led her to succeed. Sources include the published autobiographies, unpublished stories, letters, and journals.

Gowers, Ruth. *Emily Carr*. New York: Berg, St. Martin's, 1987. 0-907582-95-8, 126p. Gowers was Carr's friend, and she presents Carr's career from a personal perspective. She says that some saw Carr as a cranky oddball, and others as a lonely, misunderstood genius, but always honest.

Tippett, Maria. *Emily Carr, a Biography*. New York: Oxford University Press, 1979. 0-19-540314-2, 314p. In this fully researched and balanced biography, Tippett employs quotes from diary notes, letters, and sketches to present the personal, artistic, literary, and religious aspects of Carr's life. Tippett concludes that Carr was aggressive and demanding when she wanted or deserved something not yet received.

Shadbolt, Doris. *Emily Carr*. Seattle: University of Washington Press, 1990. 0-295-97003-0, 240p. Shadbolt, an art historian, clearly describes Carr's life and analyzes her work. She connects each of Carr's works to where Carr lived and with whom she was friends during that period of her life. Shadbolt thinks that Carr was successful in her goal of expressing Canada in her art.

Walker, Stephanie Kirkwood. *This Woman in Particular: Contexts for the Biographical Image of Emily Carr*. Waterloo, Ontario, Canada: Wilfrid Laurier University, 1996. 0-88920-263-X, 212p. Walker looks at each of Carr's biographies to see how the biographer created Carr's story. This academic examination is an assessment of biography as a genre, making no attempt to add new information about Carr's life.

CARREÑO, TERESA (1853–1917)

Instrumentalist, Composer, and Conductor   Venezuela

Teresa Carreño played and composed piano pieces and conducted orchestras. Expected to lead the life of a South American lady, after her December 22, 1853, birth, she revealed musical talent, and piano lessons from her father and from Gottschalk, a famous teacher, prepared her to play a New York concert at the age of eight and for President Lincoln in the White House at ten. After study in Paris with Georges Mathias and Anton Rubinstein, she premiered MacDowell's *D Minor Piano Concerto* in 1888. In 1893, she made her debut in Berlin and became renowned throughout Europe. Her immense power allowed her to play pieces such as Beethoven's *Emperor*, Liszt's *Concerto in E flat*, and Tchaikovsky's *Piano Concerto*, along with Grieg's *Piano Concerto*. In 1907, she toured Australia. She spoke five languages, and, in addition to her piano performances, she sang and conducted. She married four times, changing her career with each husband. She performed with one husband, a violinist; formed and managed an opera company with another husband, a baritone; changed her piano style with a third husband, a pianist; and finally settled with her second husband's brother.

BIBLIOGRAPHY

Milinowski, Marta. *Teresa Carreño: "By the Grace of God."* 1940. New York: Da Capo, 1977. 0-306-70870-1, 410p. Although Milinowski wrote and published the first edition of this balanced popular biography before 1970, it is the only work available in English about Carreño.

CARTLAND, BARBARA (1902–)
Writer   England

Barbara Cartland has had her novels translated into almost every language. Born in Edgbaston, Birmingham on 9 July, 1902, Mary Barbara Hamilton published her first novel, *Jigsaw*, in 1923, and has since produced well over four hundred best-selling books—biography, food, health and beauty, autobiography, and novels of chaste romantic love designed for women readers. During World War II, she served in the Auxiliary Territorial Services and was the lady welfare officer and librarian in Bedfordshire. An ardent advocate of health foods and fitness for the elderly, she has championed causes like the St. John's Ambulance Brigade and various nursing organizations. She founded campsites for Romanies (Gypsies), which they called "Barbaraville." She became the president of the National Association of Health in 1966. She earned a place in the *Guinness Book of World Records* in 1983 for writing twenty-six books during that year. She is also a Dame of Grace of St. John of Jerusalem.

BIBLIOGRAPHY

Cartland, Barbara. *I Seek the Miraculous*. New York: Dutton, 1978. 0-525-13081-0, 248p. In one-page chapters, Cartland recounts incidences and inspirations at home or from places where she has traveled with her second husband.

Robyns, Gwen. *Barbara Cartland*. New York: Doubleday, 1985. 0-385-19818-3, 435p. Robyns quotes Cartland as saying that she wrote every day because she thought her romantic novels could help people. Robyns quotes readers who say that Cartland changed their lives. Supposedly a definitive biography, Robyns had the approval and help of the family for her research and produced a readable, popular biography with photographs.

CASTILE, BLANCHE of. *See* BLANCHE of CASTILE.

CASTILE, ISABELLA of. *See* ISABELLA of SPAIN.

CASTELLANOS, ROSARIO (1925–1974)
Writer   Mexico

Rosario Castellanos wrote award-winning fiction about exile and taught her views at colleges abroad before beginning to serve her country as a diplomat. Castellanos' parents wanted a son when she was born on May 25, 1925. When their son died while Castellanos was still a child, she experienced their feelings of disappointment as they lamented that the boy had died instead of the girl. Her father's library augmented her education, but its loneliness added to her feeling like an outsider in her own family. Other people's rejections also concerned her, and she worked with, and wrote about, Mexico's ignored native Indians. She refused to accept class discrimination, traditions, and prejudices in the closed social structure of Comitán in southern Chiapas where she lived. She also wrote about women and their societal roles. In 1957, her first published book won two prestigious awards. She taught at the University of Mexico and at several colleges in the United States before being appointed Mexican ambassador to Israel in 1971, where she did her best writing before her accidental death. Mexico gave her a state funeral and buried her in the Tomb of National Heroes.

BIBLIOGRAPHY
Bonifaz Caballero, Oscar. *Remembering Rosario: A Personal Glimpse into the Life and Works of Rosario Castellanos.* Trans. Myralyn F. Allgood. Potomac, MD: Scripta Humanistica, 1990. 0-916379-72-8, 68p. The biography looks at Castellanos from her childhood to maturity. It examines the wit and irony in both her poetry and her life.

O'Connell, Joanna. *Prospero's Daughter: The Prose of Rosario Castellanos.* Austin: University of Texas Press, 1995. 0-292-76041-8, 263p. This scholarly, well-documented overview of Castellanos's life and her work includes thorough interpretations of her writing.

CASTLE, BARBARA (1911–)
Politician   **England**

Barbara Castle has been an important force in British politics, serving at the local and national levels during her career. After her birth on October 6, 1911, in Chesterfield, Derbyshire, as the youngest of a tax inspector's three children, and education at Bradford Girls' Grammar School and St. Hugh's College, Oxford, where she had a scholarship, Barbara Betts worked in local government before World War II. Her father had exposed her to socialism with his concern for the miners in their area of England and the refugees from the Spanish civil war. She became one of the youngest members elected to the St. Pancras Borough Council and was also a member of the Metropolitan Water Board. She entered Parliament in 1945 as a member of Labour for Blackburn. During the 1950s, she was a "Bevanite," outspoken in her defense of radical causes. She attained cabinet rank as minister of overseas development. As a controversial minister of transport, she introduced a seventy-miles-per-hour speed limit and a "breathalyzer" test for drunken drivers. In the newly created post of secretary of state for employment and productivity, she dealt with the government's difficult prices and incomes policy, taking the Equal Pay Act through Parliament in 1970. In 1974, she became minister of health and social security, then vice-chairman of the Socialist Group in the European Parliament, where she led the British Labour Group from 1979 to 1985 and was vice president of the Socialist Group. Her diaries, published in 1980 and 1984, raised much controversy.

BIBLIOGRAPHY

Castle, Barbara. *The Castle Diaries, 1964–70.* London: Weidenfeld and Nicolson, 1984. 0-297-78374-2, 858p. This volume of Castle's diaries, covering the years 1964 to 1970, contains information about her political life. Although loosely written, it shows the extra effort that a woman in public office must make when she has a family at home.

Castle, Barbara. *The Castle Diaries, 1974–76.* London: Weidenfeld and Nicolson, 1980. 0-297-77420-4, 788p. This account covers Castle's two years as secretary of state for social services in Harold Wilson's government from 1974 to 1976. Cabinet discussions, internal Labour Party politics, development of social welfare policies, the European Economic Community referendum, relations between ministers and civil servants reveal British politics.

Castle, Barbara. *Fighting All the Way.* Philadelphia: Trans-Atlantic, 1993. 0-333-59031-7, 626p. Castle relates the story of a twentieth-century politician and the battles during her career. She begins with her childhood, continues to her tenure at Oxford, and then covers her life on the fringes of London journalism. She concludes with discussions of political life in this readable autobiography.

De'ath, Wilfred. *Barbara Castle: A Portrait from Life.* Brighton, England: Clifton, 1970. 0-901255-15-7, 126p. The text includes the results of interviews with people who knew Barbara Castle during different times of her life. Their impressions are conversational, easy to read, and revealing of Castle's personality and demeanor in a variety of situations.

CASTRO, ROSALÍA de (1837–1885)

Poet   Spain

Rosalía de Castro used the folklore from her Galician heritage in her writing and universalized human experience. Born illegitimate on February 24, 1837, her mother traveled in secrecy for her birth and then gave her to her father's sisters, although de Castro did not know that their brother, a priest, was her father until she was seven. After she married, she had seven children but continued her writing, in which she pursued the themes of pain and sorrow of poverty contrasted with the joy of life. She also explored the condition of woman as a person and as an artist. People in Galicia think of her as their tribal singer because she captured the Galician belief in the unseen but known and rescued the culture from oblivion. Critics regard her as one of the major nineteenth-century Spanish poets, marking the beginning of the modern period in Spanish literature. She wrote her last and best work, *The Sar*, in the Castilian dialect.

BIBLIOGRAPHY

Kulp-Hill, Kathleen. *Rosalia de Castro.* Boston: Twayne, 1977. 0-8057-6282-5, 147p. In a critical analysis, Kulp-Hill examines de Castro's life and works in terms of her Galician culture, showing how she became a symbol of its land and heritage. Kulp-Hill sees de Castro's poetry as containing inexhaustible depths of beauty and meaning.

CATHERINE of ARAGON (1485–1536)
Queen   Spain and England

Catherine of Aragon married Henry VIII of England, but her inability to produce a male heir caused him to divorce her and separate from the Catholic Church. The youngest daughter of Ferdinand V and **Isabella I**, king and queen of Aragon and Castile, she was born on December 16, 1485. In 1501, she married the fifteen-year-old Prince Arthur, Prince of Wales, son and heir of Henry VII; he died six months later. A papal dispensation enabled Henry to marry the widow of his brother in 1503, but because of other complications, they were not married until 1509, seven weeks after Henry's accession to the throne. Between 1510 and 1514, Catherine bore four children, all of whom died in infancy. In 1516, Princess Mary, later, Queen **Mary I**, was born. In the following years, Henry's infidelities and his anxiety for a son soured the marriage so that he asked for an annulment. The pope opposed, but Henry secretly married **Anne Boleyn**, and Archbishop Thomas Cranmer gave the annulment a few months later. Catherine, passively resistant throughout, went into retirement. In 1534, the pope pronounced her marriage valid, provoking Henry's final break with Rome and the onset of the Reformation in England. Catherine refused to accept either the title of "princess dowager" or the Act of Succession (1534), which declared Princess Mary illegitimate.

BIBLIOGRAPHY

Du Boys, Albert. *Catharine of Aragon and the Sources of the English Reformation.* 1881. New York: B. Franklin, 1968. 2 vols. No ISBN. Du Boys follows Catharine's [sic] life from her first marriage to Frederick, Prince of Wales, through the divorce proceedings with Henry VIII. Catharine's only ally was her brother Charles I of Spain.

Luke, Mary M. *Catherine the Queen.* New York: Coward-McCann, 1967. No ISBN, 510p. Luke uses letters, quotations, and conversations from authenticated sources to show that Henry was faithful to Catherine for almost a quarter century, but she did not have a son who survived. Luke shows Catherine as loving, with her supporters calling her "queen" of the "earthly queens."

Mattingly, Garrett. *Catherine of Aragon.* New York: Vintage, 1960. No ISBN, 343p. Mattingly confirms Catherine as a strong influence, with the Spanish Embassy capitulating to her personality and her decisions. After Henry remarried, Catherine hoped that Mary could restore the Catholic religion from her throne, but Catherine could not foresee that Henry's third wife would have a son who lived long enough for the Reformation to change world history.

Weir, Alison. *The Six Wives of Henry VIII.* New York: Grove, 1992. 0-8021-1497-0, 643p. The text looks at Henry VIII's six wives from the perspective of the Tudor times, using private papers, letters, diaries, and diplomatic sources. It shows the political machinations behind Henry's decision to divorce Catherine and the ways that his administrators achieved Henry's goal.

CATHERINE II of RUSSIA (1729–1796)

Empress   Germany and Russia

Catherine II earned the title "the Great" for her foreign policy by adding more land to Russia than Peter. Born on May 2, 1729, Catherine began her rise when Empress **Elizabeth of Russia** invited her, a German princess, Sophia Auguste Friedrike, to come to Moscow to visit her court. Seemingly intelligent and submissive, Elizabeth married Sophia to the grand duke Peter, her son and tsar-to-be. The French-speaking Sophia began to study Russian and the Russian Orthodox faith. After converting, she changed her name to Catherine. Catherine's son Paul was not the child of her disinterested husband, Peter, but of a court nobleman. Catherine began a series of affairs, one with Gregory Orlov, who with his brothers deposed Peter and killed him after Catherine was on the throne. After her lavish coronation, she started corresponding with some of the greatest thinkers of the day, including Diderot, Mazzini, and Voltaire. She tried to give serfs freedom but defeated them in an ensuing uprising by calling her troops from Turkey to fight at home. Catherine realized the dangers of liberty and equality, so instead of asking the masters to be easier on the serfs, she passed a law in 1785 allowing them to treat the serfs in any way necessary. While monarch, she claimed parts of Poland and Turkey with its warm-water port on the Black Sea, began the first Russian school with math and science as well as the arts for females, and beautified St. Petersburg.

BIBLIOGRAPHY

Alexander, John. *Catherine the Great*. New York: Oxford University Press, 1989. 0-19-505236-6, 418p. Scholarly study and popular gossip account for balance in this biography, which emphasizes Catherine's personality, actions, policies, and the events that people remember. Alexander looks at her mental and physical health and analytically examines her sexuality based on documentation from letters, court ceremonial journals, manuscript sources, and unpublished dissertations in a biography appropriate for academics.

De Madariaga, Isabel. *Catherine the Great: A Short History*. New Haven, CT: Yale University Press, 1990. 0-300-04845-9, 240p. De Madariaga notes that Catherine was a ruler of her times, admired by some and suspected by others who saw the discrepancies between what she proclaimed as her objectives and her actual achievements.

Erickson, Carolly. *Great Catherine*. New York: Crown, 1994. 0-517-59091-3, 392p. Erickson looks at Catherine's memoirs, which stop before she became empress, and writings, letters, dispatches of visiting ambassadors, memoirs of contemporaries in Russia and Europe, contemporary descriptions of Russian society and the court by visitors, and political and administrative documents to see what Catherine achieved during her reign in a sympathetic and balanced account that reads like a good novel.

Nikolaev, Vsevolod, and Albert Parry. *The Loves of Catherine the Great*. New York: Coward, McCann, and Geoghegan, 1982. 0-698-11201-6, 287p. Authenticated eighteenth-century Russian, French, and German memoirs, correspondence, diplomatic reports, and other historical documents tell about Catherine, the builder and absolute ruler of a domain of thirty-six million people from Central Europe across Asia.

Troyat, Henry. *Catherine the Great.* Trans. Joan Pinkham. New York: Meridian, 1994. 0-452-01120-5, 377p. Troyat uses memoirs, personal letters, diplomatic dispatches, and public documents in his thorough presentation of Catherine.

CATHERINE of SIENA (1347–1380)
Religious   **Italy**

Catherine of Siena devoted her life to helping the poor and promoting peace. Originally named Caterine Benincasa, she was born in Siena on March 25, 1347, as the twenty-third child of a dyer. She probably learned to read at an early age but could not write until she was an adult. As a child, she claimed to have visions, and at sixteen, she joined the Third Order of Saint Dominic in Siena, where she became noted for her gift of contemplation and her devotion to the poor. She soon began to dictate letters about spiritual matters that won her even more admiration, and her enthusiasm converted many sinners. In 1374 Raymond of Capua, future master general of the Dominican order, became her spiritual director and was from then on closely associated with all her activities. Christ's stigmata were supposedly imprinted on her body in 1375. In 1376 Catherine journeyed to Avignon to plead with Pope Gregory XI on behalf of Florence, tried to promote peace in Italy, and encouraged a crusade to recover the Holy Land. Deeply distressed by the Great Schism in 1378, she went to Rome to support Pope Urban VI and work for unity. She wrote devotional pieces, letters, and poems; her *Dialogue,* a work on mysticism, was translated in 1896. She died in Rome, and Pope Pius II canonized her in 1461. She became a doctor of the church in 1970, with her feast day April 29.

BIBLIOGRAPHY
Baldwin, Anne B. *Catherine of Siena: A Biography.* Huntington, IN: Our Sunday Visitor Publications Division, 1987. Paper, 0-87973-510-4, 192p. The text looks at Catherine's life, her decisions, and her legacy.
Giordani, Igino. *Saint Catherine of Siena, Doctor of the Church.* Trans. Thomas J. Tobin. Boston: St. Paul Editions, 1975. No ISBN, 258p. The text gives an undocumented accounting of Catherine's life.
Meade, Catherine M. *My Nature Is Fire: Saint Catherine of Siena.* New York: Alba House, 1991. 0-8189-0615-4, 192p. To Meade, Catherine was a woman whose human struggle to become like her creator helped her to change her society. Meade introduces Catherine's deep, interior prayer life as a constant effort for spiritual satisfaction.
Noffke, Suzanne. *Catherine of Siena: Vision through a Distant Eye.* Collegeville, MN: Liturgical Press, 1996. 0-8146-5311-1, 267p. Noffke's documented biography notes that Catherine had uncompromising drive and determination even as a young child. Meditation was one of her gifts, and she worked to improve her world through helping the church.

CAVELL, EDITH (1865–1915)
Nurse   **England**

As a nurse Edith Cavell went to Brussels and helped soldiers escape through the underground of her hospital during World War I. Born on December 4, 1865, to a clergyman, Edith Louisa worked first as a governess and then studied at London Hospital. She helped during the typhoid epidemic, and in 1907, she became the matron at Birkendael Medical Institute, a large training center for nurses in Brussels. After the Germans invaded in World War I, the center became a Red Cross hospital. She treated the wounded regardless of their home country. On August 5, 1915, the Germans arrested her for harboring two hundred French, British, and Belgian soldiers and having helped them escape from Belgium. The escaping soldiers became drunk in town and told people about their situation. American and Spanish ministers to Germany requested a stay of execution, but the Germans ignored them. After her court-martial, the Germans shot her on October 12. Many thousands attended her memorial service at Westminster Abbey, and a commemorative statue was erected in Saint Martin's Place, Trafalgar Square, London.

BIBLIOGRAPHY

De Leeuw, Adele. *Edith Cavell; Nurse, Spy, Heroine*. Illus. Charles Brey. New York: Putnam, 1968. No ISBN, 95p. This fictional biography without documentation includes one chapter about Cavell's early life, with the remainder focused on her experiences as a nurse in London and in Brussels before the Germans accused her of, and executed her for, spying.

Ryder, Rowland. *Edith Cavell*. New York: Stein and Day, 1975. 0-8128-1868-7, 278p. Ryder's carefully documented book on Cavell notes that she would have lived a life of relative obscurity if she had not faced German military inefficiency in August 1914.

CENTLIVRE, SUSANNA (1667?–1723)

Playwright and Actor   **England**

Susanna Centlivre was one of the leading comic dramatists of the eighteenth century and England's most prolific playwright from 1700 to 1722. She was born in either Ireland or England on November 20, 1667?, but when she was fifteen, she ran away from her Irish home to Liverpool. After two husbands died in duels, she began writing her own plays and acting in them around the provinces. *The Perjured Husband* (1700) was her first play, and *The Gamester* (1705) was her first popular success. Her plays had strong characters and entertaining dialogue, which allowed many actors to gain acclaim while keeping them in performance throughout the seventeenth and eighteenth centuries. *A Busy Body* and *The Wonder! A Woman Keeps a Secret* lasted into the nineteenth century. In 1706, she married Joseph Centlivre, the chief cook for Queen **Anne of England**. In 1712, they moved to London, where she kept a salon attracting well-known literary figures. In total, Centlivre wrote nineteen plays, numerous poems, and witty love letters.

BIBLIOGRAPHY

Bowyer, John Wilson. *The Celebrated Mrs. Centlivre*. 1952. Westport, CT: Greenwood, 1968. No ISBN, 267p. Bowyer's carefully documented and accessible, scholarly study presents Centlivre's life, her writing, the history of the stage at her time, and her friends in the literary community. Bowyer suggests that Centlivre's decision to marry while writing made the profession acceptable for women.

Lock, F. P. *Susanna Centlivre*. Boston: Twayne, 1979. 0-8057-6744-4, 155p. This critical look at Centlivre's life and work exposes Centlivre as an opportunist but simultaneously original and authentic. Although well documented, the biography is ponderous reading.

CERRITO, FANNY (1817–1909)
Ballerina and Choreographer Italy

Fanny Cerrito made her ballet debut in Naples when she was fifteen. She was born on May 11, 1817, to a second lieutenant of the Fantriola Regiment and his wife. After she started performing, critics recognized her talent, and she began touring in Italy and Austria with an engagement at La Scala for 1838 and at Her Majesty's Theatre in London for 1840. She danced in *Lac des Fées, Alma, La Vivandière,* and *Ondine.* Queen **Victoria** requested a Royal Command Performance of the *pas de deux* from *Ondine* in 1843. Two years later, she married her regular partner, Saint-Léon, and he created a ballet for her, *La Fille de Marbre,* which she danced at her Paris Opéra debut in 1847. She left him in 1851 while continuing to dance at the Opéra, performing in other ballets as well as her own, *Gemma,* in 1854. She danced in Russia for Alexander II for two of her last three seasons. She retired in 1857 and continued to live in Paris until her death.

BIBLIOGRAPHY
Guest, Ivor. *Fanny Cerrito.* 1956. London: Dance Books, 1974. 0-903102-08-0, 176p. Guest's carefully researched, scholarly biography of Cerrito's life includes illustrations. He includes information about her performances and the state of ballet during her lifetime.

CHAMINADE, CÉCILE (1857–1944)
Instrumentalist and Composer France

Cécile Chaminade wrote over two hundred piano pieces and was also a popular pianist. The third of their six children, she was born on August 8, 1857, to a violinist father and a mother who was both a pianist and singer. Her wealthy family lived in Paris and traveled in Europe. She first composed church music when she was eight, and she saw her first opera in 1868, *Les Hugenots.* At eighteen, she made her musical debut, soon after playing for Liszt, who compared her style to Chopin's. After Bizet's disastrous première of *Carmen* in 1875, which she attended, she had great sympathy for musicians' suffering from critics' responses and was careful about her own performing decisions. Her most popular performances were those of her own work as she toured widely, especially in England after 1892. She also made recordings of her own compositions of *Callirhoö, Les Amazones,* and *Consertstück.*

BIBLIOGRAPHY
Citron, Marcia J. *Cecile Chaminade: A Bio-Bibliography.* Westport, CT: Greenwood, 1988. 0-313-25319-6, 243p. Citron's biobibliography is the first scholarly book on Chaminade, with the brief biography portion based on the primary sources owned by Chaminade's heirs. It also contains criticisms written about the performances of all her works. The text, thoroughly documented, is appropriate for the academic reader.

CHAMORRO, VIOLETA (1929–)
Politician Nicaragua

Violeta Barrios de Chamorro became the president of Nicaragua in hopes of its becoming a democratic republic. She was born in Rivas; her father was a rancher who traveled among his properties. Educated at Colegio Francés, a boarding school in Granada, she thought music would be her profession because she loved to play the piano. For college, she attended Blackstone in Virginia, but her father died when she was eighteen, and she had to return home to assume her mother's domestic duties while her mother retreated into her room. Chamorro married her brother's friend, and his life in politics exiled her to Costa Rica during Somoza's government and took her back to the country before he was assassinated. With her children and grandchildren supporting her, she ran for the presidency of Nicaragua, defeating Daniel Ortega, after serving a year in the Sandinista junta.

BIBLIOGRAPHY

Chamorro, Violeta, Guido Fernandez, and Sonia Cruz de Baltodano. *Dreams of the Heart: The Autobiography of President Violeta Barrios de Chamorro of Nicaragua.* New York: Simon and Schuster, 1996. 0-684-81055-7, 352p. Chamorro says that she entered politics in Nicaragua with a desire for knowledge and wisdom and to achieve things for the greater good of her country. Her autobiography gives background about the Somoza and Sandinista governments, cultural expectations, and her life.

CHANEL, COCO (1883–1971)

Couturier   France

Coco Chanel founded a couture house in Paris in which she designed and sold her well-designed clothes, graceful jewelry, and elegant perfumes. Born into a poor family in Saumur, Maine-et-Loire on August 19, 1883, Gabrielle Bonheur Chanel's mother died when she was young, and her father disappeared after placing her and her sister in an orphan's home. She watched her Aunt Julia decorate hats before going to Deauville to work for a milliner and, in 1914, opened her own millinery shop in Paris. In World War I, she worked as a nurse, but after the war, she founded a couture house on the rue Cambon while living at the Ritz Hotel on the same street. Her casual clothes of the 1920s discarded the inner corset and created the classic Chanel look, consisting of casual but extremely well cut wool jersey suits with straight, collarless cardigan jackets and short, full-cut skirts, worn with art deco costume jewelry and a sailor hat over short hair. She also created several perfumes, including Chanel No. 5. By the 1930s, she owned four businesses and factories making perfumes, jewelry, and textiles. She closed her house in 1939 and designed nothing during World War II but revived it in 1954. Americans began buying her clothes and helped her understated Chanel look regain its appeal.

BIBLIOGRAPHY

Charles-Roux, Edmonde. *Chanel: Her Life, Her World, and the Woman behind the Legend She Herself Created.* Trans. Nancy Amphoux. New York: Knopf, 1975. 0-394-47613-1, 380p. This thorough biography reveals a woman who wanted nothing frivolous but broke rules in business as necessary and thought that being copied well was good for her business. She wanted to be known as a craftsman.

De La Haye, Amy, and Shelley Tobin. *Chanel, the Couturiere at Work.* Woodstock, NY: Overlook, 1994. 0-87951-570-8, 136p. The authors document Chanel's success as hard work and a willingness to exploit every person she knew and every situation in which she found herself. The straightforward and interesting text traces Chanel's life and her couture house through Karl Lagerfeld into the 1990s.

Kennett, Frances. *Coco: The Life and Loves of Gabrielle Chanel*. Illus. Natacha Ledwidge. London: V. Gollancz, 1989. 0-575-04595-7, 160p. Kennett posits that Chanel's early life as Gabriel, which she wanted to hide, gave her discipline, personal austerity, and respect for homemaking, all qualities important to her work.

Mackrell, Alice. *Coco Chanel*. New York: Holmes and Meier, 1992. 0-8419-1301-3, 95p. In a brief look at Chanel's life and achievements through the designs of her clothes, jewelry, and perfume, Mackrell shows that Chanel's designs were especially appropriate for twentieth-century women.

Madsen, Axel. *Chanel: A Woman of Her Own*. New York: H. Holt, 1990. 0-8050-0961-2, 388 p. Madsen recalls legends that Chanel created to hide her bastard beginning and life in a poorhouse as a young girl. In this popular biography, Madsen includes anecdotes about all aspects of Chanel's life, especially her love of wealth and fame and distrust of solitude.

CHANTAL, JEANNE-FRANÇOISE de (1572–1641)
Religious   **France**

Baroness Jeanne-Françoise de Chantal founded the Visitation Order and treated victims of the plague during 1628. She was born January 28, 1572, in Dijon. After four children, her husband died in a hunting accident. Three years later, she heard St. Francis de Sales preach at Lent, and she placed herself under his spiritual direction. She arranged her eldest daughter's marriage, provided for her adolescent son, and took her other two daughters with her to Annecy, where she founded her order with Francis. By the time she died en route to Paris on a visit to see Queen **Anne of Austria**, the Visitation Order had eighty-six houses.

BIBLIOGRAPHY
Francis, de Sales, Saint. *Francis de Sales, Jane de Chantal: Letters of Spiritual Direction*. Trans. Peronne Marie Thibert. New York: Paulist Press, 1988. Paper, 0-8091-2990-6, 296p. The letters of de Chantal begin with the outburst "Live Jesus" and reveal a woman who saw Jesus as the center of her life. The editors also include a helpful overview of the times.

Ravier, Andre. *Saint Jeanne de Chantal: Noble Lady, Holy Woman*. Trans. Mary Emily Hamilton. San Francisco: Ignatius Press, 1989. 0-89870-267-4, 231p. Ravier uses the memoirs of de Chantal's intelligent and charming grandniece by marriage and private secretary for her last nine years, Mother de Chaugy, as a basis for his information.

Wright, Wendy M. *Bond of Perfection: Jeanne de Chantal and Francois de Sales*. New York: Paulist Press, 1985. Paper, 0-8091-2727-X, 254p. Using original manuscripts, Wright discusses the life of Jeanne de Chantal, with major emphasis on her friendship with Francis de Sales.

CHARRIERE, ISABELLE de (1740–1805)
Writer   **The Netherlands**

Isabelle de Charriere was a novelist who wrote in both German and French during the age of revolution and Romanticism and criticized aristocratic privilege, moral conventions, religious orthodoxy, and poverty. Isabelle Agnes Elizabeth was born in the Netherlands on October 20, 1740, and moved to Switzerland. She rejected several admirers, including the biographer James

Boswell, before she married her brother's Swiss tutor, St. Hyacinthe de Charriere, in 1766. Among her novels were *Lettres Neuchateloises* (1784), *Caliste, Ou Lettres Écrites de Lausanne* (1785–88), and *Trois Femmes* (1797). Her novels revealed philosophical reflection and psychological insight but lacked plot coherence.

BIBLIOGRAPHY

Allison, Jenene J. *Revealing Difference: The Fiction of Isabelle de Charriere.* Newark: University of Delaware Press, 1995. 0-87413-566-4, 171p. This feminist treatment of de Charriere's works references her life as necessary to elucidate the text and to show her view of eighteenth century women.

Jaeger, Kathleen M. *Male and Female Roles in the Eighteenth Century: The Challenge to Replacement and Displacement in the Novels of Isabelle de Charriere.* New York: Peter Lang, 1994. 0-8204-2179-0, 241p. This scholarly biography, suitable for academics, is a discussion of de Charriere's novels, following a brief introduction to her life.

West, Anthony. *Mortal Wounds.* New York: McGraw-Hill, 1973. 0-07-069475-3, 371p. West features three female authors, **Madame de Staël**, de Charriere, and **George Sand**, with the longest segment covering Madame de Staël. He asserts that de Charriere was a much superior talent to Madame de Staël in his brief section introducing her. Although opinionated, West's assessment is an accessible introduction to de Charriere.

CHIANG CH'ING (1910–1991)
Revolutionary   China

Chiang Ch'ing (Jiang Qing) gained fame as the wife of Mao, China's communist leader. To escape her unsatisfactory life with her violent father and domestic servant mother, Chiang Ch'ing created a fantasy world that included a series of lovers. She went to Shanghai and became involved in the theater before going to the war front and meeting Mao. As the new arrival, she attracted Mao, a man needing feminine attention although married twice and twenty years older. She married him and supported his policies, and after his death, she expected to become the empress. Instead, a tribunal convicted her of helping Mao and perpetrating crimes during the Cultural Revolution. In her defense, she retorted that she was Mao's dog who did what he told her to do. She had strong willpower and refused to let anyone take away her spirit; she was always battling.

BIBLIOGRAPHY

Singko, Ly. *The Fall of Madam Mao.* New York: Vantage, 1979. 0-533-03678-X, 136p. Singko focuses on 1976, when Madam [*sic*] Mao grabbed power with three others after Mao's death, and they were suddenly arrested and kept from leading the country. Singko bases most of his information on his own experiences as a participant in the revolutionary struggle, himself knowing three of those arrested, including "Madam Mao."

Tai, Dwan L. *Chiang Ch'ing: The Emergence of a Revolutionary Political Leader.* Hicksville, NY: Exposition, 1974. 0-682-48060-6, 222p. Tai tells Qing's story using the unofficial voices of China; eyewitnesses' oral accounts; the testimony of those Chinese now outside China who knew, hated, or loved her; and documents from the Peking elite. The text posits that even with her complex qualities, Qing probably went to trial for Mao's crimes rather than merely her own.

Terrill, Ross. *Madame Mao: The White-Boned Demon*. New York: Simon and Schuster, 1992. 0-671-74484-4, 448p. Terrill calls Madame Mao "Jiang Qing." He tells her life as she evolved from actor to top political leader as the wife of Mao. He asserts that her petulance and courage might have instigated some of the most brutal acts of the Cultural Revolution. Based on previously unavailable documents and recollections from the family, Terrill has written an interesting, popular biography that looks at the personal side of Chinese politics.

Witke, Roxane. *Comrade Chiang Ch'ing*. Boston: Little, Brown, 1977. 0-316-94900-0, 549p. Witke says that her biography is authorized because Ching asked that it be published; Ching, however, did not read the text for final approval. The result is a thorough, well-documented, and balanced biography based on all the resources that Witke could find about Chiang Ch'ing.

CHISHOLM, CAROLINE (1808–1877)
Philanthropist   England

Caroline Chisholm worked to improve conditions for women in England and India and especially immigrant women and their families in Australia. Born May 30, 1808, as the youngest of four children of a prosperous Northampton farmer, Caroline Jones had an evangelical upbringing. The condition of her marriage to Archibald Chisholm in 1830 was that she wanted to continue the charity work which she had already started. In India, she founded the Female School of Industry for the Daughters of European Soldiers in Madras. In Australia, she took many of the destitute, single, immigrant women into her own home while pressuring the governor to provide her a building to open a Female Immigrants' Home. She opened the first free labor registry, extending service to all the unemployed, surveyed employment opportunities, and arranged for immigrants to work in the region. By 1845, she campaigned in London for families to join the immigrants and eventually achieved her goals when the Family Colonization Loan Society was established in 1849, a vehicle through which immigrants could obtain loans for passage, to be repaid when they settled. A principal guarantor was **Angela Burdett-Coutts**. The discovery of gold in Australia, however, ensured the project's success. When the Chisholms returned to Australia in 1854, they had no money, but public and private funds helped them go into business while she continued to work for land reform, helping girls gain education, and suffrage.

BIBLIOGRAPHY
Bogle, Joanna. *Caroline Chisholm: The Emigrant's Friend*. Ridgefield, CT: Morehouse, 1994. 0-85244-205-X, 157p. This accessible and well-researched biography shows Chisholm as she championed independent emigrant families.

Hoban, Mary. *Fifty-One Pieces of Wedding Cake: A Biography of Caroline Chisholm*. Kilmore, Victoria, Australia: Lowden, 1973. 0-9097-0627-1, 436p. Hoban documents this biography from Chisholm's writing and from immigrants whom she helped. She sees Chisholm as an Australian national treasure and thinks that she should be recognized and remembered as such.

Kiddle, Margaret. *Caroline Chisholm*. 1969. Portland, OR: International Specialized Book Services, 1990. 0-5228-4428-6, 208p. Kiddle describes Chisholm's energy, human sympathy, administrative ability, personal charm and dignity, and undying faith in her cause in this biography. Kiddle thinks that Chisholm was the greatest woman pioneer in Australia's history, looking for neither material reward nor public position.

CHRISTIE, AGATHA (1890–1976)
Writer   England

Agatha Christie began writing in 1920 with her famous detective, Hercule Poirot, appearing in her first book, *Mysterious Affair at Styles*, and in later detective novels, she introduced a female detective, Jane Marple. Born Agatha Miller in Torquay on September 15, 1890, she was educated privately before she went to Paris to study singing and piano. She married Archibald Christie in 1914, and she worked as a volunteer nurse at a Red Cross hospital during World War I in Torquay. She divorced her alcoholic husband, and in 1930, she married Max Mallowan, an archaeologist whom she accompanied on excavations each year to such places as Syria and Iraq. When World War II began, she worked in the dispensary of University College Hospital. Throughout, she continued to write, publishing over seventy books, short stories, and plays such as *The Mousetrap* (1952) and *Witness for the Prosecution* (1953). Her novels, with their surprising plot twists, have sold over 100 million copies and have been translated into over one hundred languages. She received numerous awards including the New York Drama Critics' Circle Award and, in 1971, Dame Commander of the Order of the British Empire.

BIBLIOGRAPHY
Christie, Agatha. *An Autobiography*. 1977. New York: Berkley, 1991. Paper, 0-425-12739-7, 542p. Christie says she began writing her autobiography when she was sixty in Nimrud, Iraq, and finished it fifteen years later. She discusses her childhood, marriages, motherhood, divorce, and success as an author, wanting to remember the happier parts of life.

Morgan, Janet P. *Agatha Christie: A Biography*. New York: Knopf, 1985. 0-394-52554-X, 393p. Morgan bases her authorized and accessible biography on letters Christie wrote and received, manuscripts and plotting books, photograph albums and scrapbooks, diaries and address books, and receipts and accounts saved from before Christie's grandparents' day.

Osborne, Charles. *The Life and Crimes of Agatha Christie*. Chicago: Contemporary Books, 1990. 0-8092-4107-2, 357p. Osborne examines all of Christie's writing, including nonfiction, stories for children, poetry, plays, and films, as well as six novels under the pseudonym of Mary Westmacott. Osborne began reading Christie in high school Latin class and confides that he thinks she is a very good writer.

Robyns, Gwen. *The Mystery of Agatha Christie*. Garden City, NY: Doubleday, 1978. 0-385-12623-9, 247p. Since Christie, a private person, would not talk to Robyns, Robyns spoke to over a hundred people to re-create Christie's story. Robyns' recommended biography describes Christie as complex, with a personal life of passion, anger, and anguish but a steady character of tenacity, insight, sensitivity, professionalism, and a fanatical craving for personal privacy.

CHRISTINA (1626–1689)
Queen   Sweden

Queen Christina of Sweden was a patron of the arts and of learning. She was born on December 8, 1626, and her father, Gustav II Adolphus, died before she came of age. She ruled under the regency of five crown officers until old enough to be crowned in 1644. The final years of the Thirty Years' War, dissension in the Swedish Diet, and attempted revolts disturbed her reign. Before she abdicated in 1654, she proclaimed her cousin Charles X Gustav as her successor. She then embraced Roman Catholicism and unsuccessfully attempted to take the thrones of Naples in 1656 and Poland in 1667. Among the artists she supported as patroness were Scarlatti, Bernini, and Corelli.

BIBLIOGRAPHY
Akerman, Susanna. *Queen Christina of Sweden and Her Circle: The Transformation of a Seventeenth-Century Philosophical Libertine.* Kinderhook, NY: E. J. Brill, 1991. 90-04-09310-9, 339p. In this biography, Akerman identifies Queen Christina as a "philosophical libertine." Her interpretation takes into account seventeenth-century thinkers and possible reasons for Queen Christina's abdication and conversion to Catholicism. The complex text is appropriate only for serious scholars.

Cartland, Barbara. *The Outrageous Queen: A Biography of Christina of Sweden.* London: Corgi, 1974. 0-552-09534-6, 221p. Cartland bases dialogue in this biography of Christina on actual, documented statements. The researched biography reads like a novel but is undocumented. Cartland examines Christina's life and her times to understand her actions and the bases for her often unexpected decisions.

Masson, Georgina. *Queen Christina.* London: Heron, 1970. No ISBN, 419p. Queen Christina's character and her hopes are clear in this scholarly biography, in which Masson uses her autobiography, letters, and maxims as a basis for the study. Masson incorporates Christina's delight in pageantry and her ability to function in international intrigues.

CIBBER, SUSANNAH 1714–1766
Opera Singer and Actor   England

Susannah Cibber was a leading lady of tragedy at Drury Lane and Handel's chosen singer for his compositions. Born Susannah Arne, she was the daughter of a Covent Garden upholsterer and sister to a composer. At eighteen, she made her singing debut at the Haymarket Theatre, and at twenty, she married Drury Lane's manager, Theophilus Cibber, who coached her to her first major success in Voltaire's *Zaïre* (1736). Theophilus, a rogue, spent his wife's money and betrayed her so that he could sue her in court for adultery. Although his award was paltry, she had to leave the stage for several years. When she returned, she became Garrick's most famous partner. Throughout, she continued to sing in concerts and opera, and Handel wrote his contralto roles in both *Acis and Galatea* and *Messiah* for her. At her death, the theater world mourned and visited her grave in Westminster Abbey.

BIBLIOGRAPHY
Nash, Mary. *The Provoked Wife: The Life and Times of Susannah Cibber.* Boston: Little, Brown, 1977. 0-316-59831-3, 369p. Cibber's last performance was in *The Provoked Wife* with Garrick. This well-researched biography,

which reads like a novel, is a history of the London stage for thirty years, a look at music during the time of Handel, and a revelation of Cibber's response to her husband's provocations and to the people she knew.

CIXOUS, HÉLÈNE (1937–)
Scholar and Intellectual   Algeria

Hélène Cixous is an influential contemporary intellectual in France. Born in Oran on June 5, 1937, Hélène and her Jewish family remained in Algeria after her physician father died when she was eleven. She graduated from the Lycée Bugeaud there in 1954 and then went to France. She married, began teaching, and continued her studies for two further degrees in English during the next three years. She and her husband separated in 1964, and she began lecturing at the Sorbonne. In May 1968, she became involved in the student uprisings in Nanterre, where she had moved. When her doctorate with a dissertation on James Joyce was approved, she became a professor at Vincennes. Her work explores the relationship between psychoanalysis and language, the involvement of the reader and the writer within the literary text. Her work on submerged memories, *Dedans*, won the Prix Médicis in 1969. Other plays, prefaces, and essays have followed.

BIBLIOGRAPHY
Conley, Verena Andermatt. *Hélène Cixous: Writing the Feminine*. Lincoln: University of Nebraska Press, 1984. 0-8032-1424-3, 181p. Conley explores Cixous's belief that to write is to live and concludes that her life and writing are inextricably woven together. This erudite look at Cixous's writing references her personal life when appropriate. Although difficult because of its abstraction, it is one of the few books about Cixous.

Sellers, Susan. *Helene Cixous: Authorship, Autobiography, and Love*. Cambridge, MA: Blackwell, 1996. 0-7456-1254-7, 191p. This work of criticism contains limited biographical background on Cixous as it explores the development of her thirty-six works of fiction and drama and examines her theory of *écriture féminine*. Sellers sees a relationship between Cixous's own losses when a child and her writing.

CLARE of ASSISI (1194–1253)
Religious   Italy

After she refused two offers of marriage, Clare, under the influence of Francis of Assisi, decided to follow a religious vocation and started the "Poor Clares." She was born on July 16, 1194, as Clare di Favarone of the Offreduccio family. At eighteen, she left the closed social system of her home by departing via the house's door of the dead. She entered a Benedictine house but found that some of the other women also wanted to live like the Franciscans. Francis helped her to set up a separate community in Assisi, and Clare became the abbess. She had to persuade Innocent III and then Gregory IX that the Poor Clares should be granted the "Privilege of Poverty" and live entirely from the donations made to them rather than to accept a regular income. The order was much more austere than any previous women's order, with the prayer life of the group especially important which Clare saw as a force vital for the church and society in general. She was canonized in 1255.

BIBLIOGRAPHY

Bargellini, Piero. *The Little Flowers of Saint Clare*. Trans. Edmund O'Gorman. Ann Arbor, MI: Servant, 1993. 0-89283-823-X, 174p. Bargellini, in his biography suitable for young adults, has accumulated a series of undocumented incidents through which he describes Clare's life, beginning with her Palm Sunday decision to leave her family to follow the spiritual model of Francis of Assisi.

Bodo, Murray. *Clare: A Light in the Garden*. Rev. ed. Cincinnati, OH: St. Anthony Messenger, 1992. 0-86716-122-1, 126p. In this revised biography, Bodo uses an informal style to discuss the friendship between Clare and Francis of Assisi.

Karper, Karen. *Clare: Her Light and Her Song*. Chicago: Franciscan Herald, 1990. 0-8199-0870-3, 401p. Karper's accessible, documented, and researched biography places Clare within her times to show how monumental her achievements were.

Peterson, Ingrid J. *Clare of Assisi: A Biographical Study*. Quincy, IL: Franciscan Press, 1993. 0-685-70885-3, 436p. Peterson uses Clare's few letters and a testament as well as contemporary medieval scholarship and contends that Clare was already leading a religious life before Francis of Assisi converted. She sees Clare as representative of women in her century who made the choice of entering a traditional cloister rather than an arranged marriage.

CLAUDEL, CAMILLE (1864–1943)
Sculptor   France

Camille Claudel was a sculptor influenced by the work and life of Auguste Rodin. Claudel was born on December 8, 1864, as the daughter of a wealthy government worker who, with her brother Paul (a poet and diplomat), encouraged her to study art. When the family moved to Paris in 1881, she met Rodin and became his model and lover for over fifteen years, angering her family and Rodin's former lover during the process. Her work exhibits an expressiveness and emotion similar to Rodin's. Her pieces include *Buste de Jeune Fille* (1887), a portrait of Rodin (1892), and *Le Jeune Romain* (1885). She also worked on larger groups of mythological figures. After her relationship with Rodin ended, she had a mental collapse, and her parents admitted her to an asylum in 1913, where she stayed for the remainder of her life.

BIBLIOGRAPHY

Paris, Reine-Marie. *Camille: The Life of Camille Claudel, Rodin's Muse and Mistress*. Trans. Liliane Emery Tuck. New York: Arcade, 1988. Paper, 1-55970-025-4, 258p. Paris concludes that, although Claudel lived until 1943, she was mentally dead in 1910. In this interesting look at Claudel, Paris asserts that her brother's name as a poet and playwright has overshadowed hers but that she had an originality in her humanist sculptures that should receive recognition.

Delbee, Anne. *Camille Claudel: Une Femme*. Trans. Carol Cosman. San Francisco: Mercury House, 1992. 1-56279-026-9, 373p. Delbee did not know about Claudel until she read something written by Paul Claudel, her brother. Delbee's research revealed a woman who deserves more critical acclaim than the pity that her unfortunate circumstances have attracted and about whom Delbee wanted to write. Her biography is readable and revealing.

CLEOPATRA (69–30 B.C.)

Queen   Egypt

Almost all information available about Cleopatra, the woman descended from the Macedonian Greek royal line of Alexander the Great and who became the last ruler of that line and queen of Egypt at age eighteen in 51 B.C., comes from her enemies or from Plutarch, who lived one hundred years later. She reigned jointly with her brother Ptolemy XIII, ten, who was also nominally her husband until her brother's advisers drove her out of Egypt by the time she was twenty. In Syria, she raised an army, but Julius Caesar arrived to capture Alexandria for the Romans, and she had herself rolled inside a rug and carried into the guarded palace to meet him and join forces. They defeated Ptolemy XIII, and Cleopatra again ruled, this time with her even younger brother, Ptolemy XIV. Caesar stayed in Egypt, and they had a son, Ptolemy Caesar. When Caesar returned to Rome, Cleopatra and her child followed him but went back to Egypt after his assassination. She then captivated Mark Antony with her wealth and beauty, and he offered her the protection that she needed. Supposedly, she experimented with poisons in order to kill herself as painlessly as possible instead of being taken prisoner, and she probably decided on the bite of an asp. During her twenty-one-year rule, when women had no power, she fought for control in the ways that she knew. Of all the Ptolemies, she is the only one who spoke Egyptian; the others spoke only their native Greek. If she had succeeded with her plans, she and her descendants would have ruled the Western world instead of Rome.

BIBLIOGRAPHY

Bradford, Ernle Dusgate Selby. *Cleopatra.* San Diego: Harcourt Brace Jovanovich, 1972. 0-15-118140-3, 279p.   Bradford defends Cleopatra in this readable biography about her attempts to run her country and keep her throne. It emphasizes the corruption of the Hellenistic Greeks, but the illustrations augment the information.

Brooks, Polly Schoyer. *Cleopatra: Goddess of Egypt, Enemy of Rome.* New York: HarperCollins, 1995. 0-06-023607-8, 151p.   Starting with the words of Plutarch that Cleopatra's "actual beauty was not itself remarkable . . . but the contact of her presence . . . was irresistible," Brooks gives a readable, well-researched portrait of a woman warrior, educated and intelligent, who knew how to minimize the odds against her and refused to allow any human or any empire to rule her.

Grant, Michael. *Cleopatra.* New York: Simon and Schuster, 1973. 0-671-21521-3, 301p.   This scholarly biography of Cleopatra is readable and filled with information about the times in which she lived, using all of the resources available about her. An intriguing source is the revealing faces on ancient coins.

Lindsay, Jack. *Cleopatra.* New York: Coward, McCann, and Geoghegan, 1971. No ISBN, 560p.   Lindsay presents a scholarly view of the Egyptian court system, the dynastic rivalries, and the role of prevailing religious thought in analyzing Cleopatra's decisions while queen.

Nardo, Don. *The Importance of Cleopatra.* San Diego: Lucent, 1994. 1-56006-023-9, 112p.   Nardo believes that the racism and sexism of Cleopatra's contemporaries induced them to spread falsehoods about Cleopatra as a manipulator who planned her seductions of Julius Caesar and Mark Anthony. In this well-documented biography, Nardo attempts to show her as a beloved ruler whose subjects supported her.

COLET, LOUISE (1810–1876)
Writer and Poet   **France**

Louise Revoil Colet was a novelist, poet, journalist, and dramatist also noted for her friendships with many writers. She was born August 15, 1810, to an Aix-en-Provence businessman and, when twenty-four, married an impoverished musician for an escape to Paris and a writing career. Two years later, she published her first poetry, *Fleurs du Midi*. Her Paris salon attracted literary figures, including Victor Hugo, Baudelaire, Alexandre Dumas, **George Sand**, Alfred de Musset, and Alfred de Vigny. Gustave Flaubert also attended and was not as well known as Colet during their one-year affair and seven-year friendship, after which she supposedly became the model for Madame Bovary. Colet supported the Italian Risorgimento in 1861 and the Paris Commune of 1871 but fiercely criticized the Catholic Church. Later, she denounced the Second Empire's immorality and materialism. The philosopher Victor Cousin helped her to gain prizes and a pension for her writing.

BIBLIOGRAPHY
du Plessix Gray, Francine. *Rage and Fire: A Life of Louise Colet*. New York: Simon and Schuster, 1994. 0-671-74238-8, 416p. In this biography, du Plessix Gray uses letters to recount Colet's sexual liaisons and her self-promotion. Colet had to support herself and her family with her writing but refused to compromise her independence by remarrying. She, however, had no illusions about sexual relationships as a mode of survival, although Flaubert almost relegated her to literary obscurity.

COLETTE (1873–1954)
Writer   **France**

Colette was a writer who won critical acclaim for her work of over fifty novels. Born Sidonie-Gabrielle in Saint-Sauveur-en-Puisaye on January 28, 1873, she was the daughter of a tax collector and was educated in her village and at her home under her mother's influence. Her family moved to town when she was seventeen, and she met "Monsieur Willy," the music critic and novelist Henri Gauthier-Villars, whom she married. They moved to Paris, and, when he discovered her literary ability, he forced her to write her first novels, publishing them under his name after adding several racy passages. In 1904, she left him and began to write animal stories, fictionalized reminiscences, and idylls of rural life with strong characters like her mother. She then became a music hall and mime artist before marrying and having a child. She nursed the wounded during World War I at her St. Mâlo estate and received the Chevalier of the Légion d'Honneur in 1920. After a second divorce, she became a newspaper fiction editor, columnist, and critic and led an unconventional life for her times since it and her work symbolized both female loneliness and sexuality. Because of her several marriages, she was not allowed to be buried in a Catholic cemetery, but thousands attended her state funeral. Among her many honors were election to the Académie Royale de Belge in 1935, the only woman in the Académie Goncourt in 1945, and Grand Officer of the Légion d'Honneur in 1953. One of her novels was *Gigi* (1944).

BIBLIOGRAPHY

Crosland, Margaret. *Colette—the Difficulty of Loving: A Biography*. Indianapolis: Bobbs-Merrill, 1974. 0-672-51760-4, 284p. Crosland's readable biography covers Colette's early years at Saint-Sauveur with her mother, where she learned to love trees, flowers, and animals; her unfortunate marriage to Willy; her love for her second husband; and her time with her third spouse.

Lottman, Herbert R. *Colette: A Life*. Boston: Little, Brown, 1991. 0-316-53361-0, 344p. Lottman's biography, using unpublished information, shows the evolution of Colette's artistic creations and their relationship to her life as they began to change her readers' perceptions of the way men and women related to each other.

Mitchell, Yvonne. *Colette: A Taste for Life*. New York: Harcourt Brace Jovanovich, 1977. 0-15-618550-4, 240p. This popular biography with illustrations presents the works of Colette with understanding and love. It describes an exciting and dynamic woman who wrote well about love and nature from her childhood through her adult life.

Richardson, Joanna. *Colette*. New York: Franklin Watts, 1984. 0-531-09824-9, 276 p. Using new sources, including testimony from Colette's two stepsons, Richardson shows Colette's two faces in a thorough, well-documented biography.

Sarde, Michel. *Colette: A Biography*. 1980. New York: William Morrow, 1989. Paper, 0-688-00390-7, 479p. Sarde includes unpublished manuscripts, letters, and newly discovered documents as well as personal interviews with Colette in an intriguing and recommended story of Colette and her work, written from a feminist viewpoint.

COLONNA, VITTORIA (1490–1549)

Poet   Italy

Vittoria Colonna was a poet known for her sonnets and her friends. Born into an aristocratic family of Naples, with her father the constable to Ferdinand II, Vittoria Colonna was betrothed as a child to the marquis of Ferrara and married to him at nineteen. In 1511, he fought in northern Italy and died nine years later from wounds received. After his death, Colonna wrote over one hundred poems showing her grief as it progressed toward religious contemplation. Known for her kindness, gentleness, and charity, Colonna had many friends, including intellectuals of her time such as Castiglione and Tasso. In 1538, she moved to Rome, where she began a platonic friendship with Michelangelo in which they exchanged letters and sonnets. In 1540, she entered a convent and stayed cloistered for the last years of her life. Michelangelo was with her when she died.

BIBLIOGRAPHY

Jerrold, Maud. *Vittoria Colonna, with Some Account of Her Friends and Her Times*. 1906. Freeport, NY: Books for Libraries, 1969. 0-8369-5153-0, 336p. Jerrold's biography of Colonna includes information about her contemporaries, such as **Gaspara Stampa**, since not much documentation about Colonna's life remains. Pedantic and stylistically dated, it is the only biographical work available to apprise contemporary readers of Colonna's existence.

COMNENA, ANNA (1083–1148?)
Scholar   Byzantium

Anna Comnena continued her husband's work after his death by writing the *Alexiad*, a history in fifteen books, which she completed in 1148. Born on December 1, 1083, as the daughter of the emperor Alexius I Comnenus, Comnena had a strong education in which she studied literature, philosophy, history, and geography. She also knew much about medicine and nursing. She and her mother, the empress Irene, tried to get her father to change his succession to her husband, the Byzantine soldier and historian Nicephorus Bryennius, instead of his son and Comnena's brother, Emperor John II Comnenus. Her father refused, so she conspired to depose her brother. After the plot failed, she retired to a convent and worked on *The Alexiad*, the only work which Anna wrote that reveals anything about her life. Thaunus mentioned it first in 1223 in his history, which was not published until 1618. A dissertation published in Thuringia during 1766 mentioned it the second time. Although the work excessively glorifies her father and his family, it is a valuable historical resource for the period during which the first crusade took place.

BIBLIOGRAPHY
Buckler, Georgina Grenfell. *Anna Comnena: A Study*. London: Oxford University Press, 1968. No ISBN, 558p. Buckler examines Anna Comnena's personality, character, education, and her value as a historian and writer. The text gives insights into Comnena's life and uses references from *The Alexiad* to show how she related to the history of her times.
Dalven, Rae. *Anna Comnena*. New York: Twayne, 1972. No ISBN, 186p. After giving the historical background of the state of Byzantium from 1025 to 1081, the text examines Anna's life as a Byzantine princess and educated historian as well as the contemporary situation in Byzantium while she lived.

COMPTON-BURNETT, IVY (1884–1969)
Writer   England

Ivy Compton-Burnett analyzed the family life of upper-class Edwardian England in a series of sophisticated, ironic novels in which vice goes unpunished, and virtue goes unrewarded. Born on June 5, 1884, as the eldest of seven children of her father's second wife in a Middlesex family that already had five children from his first marriage, Compton-Burnett became the governess for the younger children after she finished her classical education at Royal Holloway College in London. Her tyrannical reputation caused discord, and during the next twelve years, a favorite brother died, and two younger sisters committed a joint suicide. In 1919, she moved into a flat with Margaret Jourdain and resumed her writing. Her novels, written in terse dialogue and relying on melodramatic devices, include *A God and His Gifts* (1963) and *The Last and the First* (1971). In 1967, she became a Dame of the British Empire.

BIBLIOGRAPHY
Sprigge, Elizabeth. *The Life of Ivy Compton-Burnett*. New York: G. Braziller, 1973. 0-8076-0685-5, 191p. Sprigge was a personal friend of Compton-Burnett, and her biography gives a friend's view without documentation or research. It is a chatty approach to the life of a private figure, but it offers

information about Compton-Burnett's childhood that was not previously available.

Spurling, Hilary. *Ivy, the Life of I. Compton-Burnett*. New York: Knopf, 1984. 0-394-47029-X, 621p. Spurling's insightful and definitive biography recaptures Compton-Burnett's happy childhood, along with the tragic losses of her later life. Duff Cooper Memorial Prize and Royal Society of Literature Award.

CORRIGAN, MAIREAD (1944–)
Activist   Ireland

Mairead Corrigan was awarded the Nobel Peace Prize along with **Betty Williams** for trying to bring peace to Northern Ireland. As the second child of five girls and two boys, born in Belfast on January 27, 1944, Corrigan attended St. Vincent's School but left at fourteen to work in a textile factory and then as a secretary at the Guinness brewery. She volunteered with the Legion of Mary, a Catholic club to help handicapped children. Although she first sympathized with Republicans, she became outraged by the British army and its activities in Belfast after a gunman's getaway car killed her sister's three children. She, Betty Williams, and Ciaran McKeaun founded the Northern Irish Peace Movement in 1976. Corrigan and Betty Williams traveled abroad to campaign for help, including Russia and Thailand. Corrigan was distressed about the low impact of the movement on Northern Irish affairs, and she became chair of the peace movement again in 1980. After her sister committed suicide in the same year, Corrigan married her brother-in-law.

BIBLIOGRAPHY
Deutsch, Richard. *Mairead Corrigan, Betty Williams*. Trans. Jack Bernard. Woodbury, NY: Barron's, 1977. 0-8120-5268-4, 204p. Interviews with Corrigan and Williams show the frustration they felt and why they worked for the peace movement. The balanced and readable biography gives a fair evaluation of the Irish situation.

O'Donnell, Dalry. *The Peace People of Northern Ireland*. Camberwell, Victoria, Australia: Widescope, 1977. 0869320157, 122p. This conversational biography of two women, Mairead Corrigan and Betty Williams, describes why and how they initiated the peace movement in Northern Ireland. Background on the Irish problems in Ulster puts their contribution in a quasi-religious context.

CRAIK, DINAH (1826–1887)
Writer   England

Dinah Mulock Craik was a well-known and competent writer, often measured against **George Eliot**. After her birth on April 20, 1826, as the daughter of a Nonconformist clergyman in Stoke-on-Trent, Staffordshire, she was educated at Brampton House Academy in Newcastle under Lyme. By thirteen, she had a job teaching Latin at the small school where her mother taught. A series of family tragedies left her and one remaining brother on her mother's small estate. She began writing and sold the copyrights for her first three books but grew into an independent and self-supporting woman before she married at forty George Lilli Craik, a partner and editor in the Macmillan publishing house. She had managed the proceeds from her book sales wisely and helped struggling authors. She wrote about single and working women whose emotional needs were unfulfilled and those with social and legal problems. When male critics identified her as a women's novelist, they paid less attention to her books. She wrote twenty novels, twelve children's books, and more than 150 short stories and essays, which appeared in periodicals during the forty-one years that she worked. *John Halifax, Gentleman*, a popular rags-to-riches story that now seems Victorian, has been continuously in print since its publication in 1856. Her most popular mid-Victorian work of advice and counsel was called *A Woman's Thoughts about Women*.

BIBLIOGRAPHY

Mitchell, Sally. *Dinah Mulock Craik*. Boston: Twayne, 1983. 0-8057-6850-5, 146p. Since Craik disliked literary biography, she has not been the subject of a biography or critical study. She was reticent to discuss her own circumstances, and she systematically destroyed letters, while forbidding her friends to produce memoirs. Mitchell discusses the phenomenon of popularity and the relationship between Craik and her public in this scholarly study.

CRAWFORD, ISABELLA (1850–1887)
Poet   Ireland

Isabella Crawford was Canada's first important female poet. She was supposedly born December 25, 1850, although contradictory information exists, as the sixth child of her father, in Dublin, Ireland. As the only surviving daughter, Crawford moved to Canada with her family when she was eight. She was educated at home and never left for more than a month. Although very few verifiable facts are available about her life, her only published book of poetry, *Old Spookses' Pass, Malcolm's Katie, and Other Poems* (1884), shows her deep love of the Canadian landscape and the influence of Canadian culture.

BIBLIOGRAPHY

Galvin, Elizabeth. *Isabella Valancy Crawford: We Scarcely Knew Her*. Toronto: Natural Heritage, Natural History, 1994. 0-9204748-0, 135p. Galvin wants to present what she knows about Crawford without a critical analysis of her work or comparing her to others. The well-documented and researched text is clear and accessible.

Farmiloe, Dorothy Alicia. *Isabella Valancy Crawford: The Life and the Legends*. Ottawa, Canada: Tecumseh, 1983. 0-91966-265-X, 90p. Farmiloe's biography uses published material, unpublished manuscripts, and the Crawford family history in a carefully documented biography. It presents a brief picture of Crawford, whom Farmiloe compares to Emily Dickinson in her decision to stay close to home rather than travel widely.

CRUZ, JUANA INÉS de la (1651?–1695)
Scholar and Poet   Mexico

Juana Inés de la Cruz was a scholar and writer recognized as one of the most significant intellectuals of her time. Born near the volcano Popocatatépetl on November 12, 1651?, as the illegitimate child of a *hidalgo* father and a Mexican mother, she lived with her grandparents. With an extraordinary interest in learning, Inés de la Cruz was probably the greatest poet born in Mexico. She taught herself by studying wherever she could find books, but she could not marry as she had no dowry. By the age of fourteen, she had established her reputation, and she was invited to court as a lady-in-waiting to the viceroy's wife, Marquesa de Mancera. Someone paid for her to enter the Order of St. Jerome, and she went there with her books, saying she had no interest in marriage and wanted only a place for quiet study. Between 1669 and 1690, she collected the largest library in South America and entertained the greatest thinkers and scientists of the times. Throughout her life she wrote poetry in various languages, but the bishop of Puebla hated women, especially intelligent ones, and he finally found a way to stop her writing when she defended a woman's right to learn and attacked the oppression of the Inquisition. She sold her library of four thousand books and collection of musical and scientific instruments and quietly gave the money to the poor of Mexico City. When the plague broke out in Mexico City in 1695, she stayed to nurse the nuns who had fallen ill and others in the city before dying herself.

BIBLIOGRAPHY

Flynn, Gerard C. *Sor Juana Inés de la Cruz*. New York: Twayne, 1971. No ISBN, 123p. Flynn covers the life of Sor (sister) Juana in one chapter and makes critical commentary on her poetry and theater in the rest by incorporating her philosophy with what people have said about her.

Juana Inés de la Cruz. *A Woman of Genius: The Intellectual Autobiography of Sor Juana Inés de la Cruz*. Trans. and Intro. Margaret Sayers Peden. Photographs Gabriel North Seymour. Salisbury, CT: Lime Rock, 1982. 0-915998-15-7, 181p. Juana's *La Respuesta* is one of the few sources of biographical information available about her. This edition integrates photographs of religious subjects with Juana's own description of her life and thought.

Paz, Octavio. *Sor Juana: Or, the Traps of Faith*. Trans. Margaret Sayers Peden. Cambridge, MA: Belknap Press, 1988. 0-674-82105-X, 547p. This scholarly and comprehensive biography re-creates the era in which Sor Juana lived, with Paz seeing her as an important voice in literature, the last poet of Spain's golden age.

Warnke, Frank J. *Three Women Poets: Renaissance and Baroque: Louise Labé, Gaspara Stampa, and Sor Juana Inés de la Cruz*. Trans. Frank J. Warnke. Lewisburg, PA: Bucknell University Press, 1987. 0-8387-5089-3, 135p. Warnke wants to make these three poets accessible to modern readers. He tells of Juana's life and identifies her as a baroque poet because her work is intellectual, witty, and full of paradox and contradiction.

CUNARD, NANCY (1896–1965)

Activist and Businesswoman   **England**

Nancy Cunard devoted herself to social and political causes, especially racial equality in the United States and the Spanish civil war. As the only child of wealthy parents, Cunard married an Australian Guards officer but kept her intellectual interests hidden with a mask of social engagements. She divorced, and in 1928, she founded the Hours Press with a printing press purchased from an American newspaperman and used it to support writers such as Robert Graves, Ezra Pound, Samuel Beckett, and George Moore. She shocked everyone when she began living with an African-American jazz pianist, Henry Crowder, in London. After they left for Austria, she wrote a scathing piece called *Black Man and White Ladyship, an Anniversary*, in which she condemned the attitudes of British society, including her mother. With Crowder, she collected an anthology on black art, which was published in 1934. When the Spanish civil war began in 1937, she joined the International Brigade and went to Spain, where she reported for the *Manchester Guardian* and the *Associated Negro Press*. Afterward, she helped Spanish war refugees, Franco's prisoners, and Venice's gondoliers.

BIBLIOGRAPHY

Chisholm, Anne. *Nancy Cunard: A Biography*. New York: Knopf, 1979. 0-394-49200-5, 366p. Chisholm bases her biography of Cunard on personal interviews and unpublished letters and diaries. It is a carefully researched look at an heiress who refused to sit around and count her money.

Ford, Hugh D. *Nancy Cunard: Brave Poet, Indomitable Rebel, 1896–1965*. Philadelphia: Chilton, 1968. No ISBN, 383p. Rather than an extensive biography, this work contains contributions from over fifty friends and admirers as well as selections from Cunard's own writing. Her personality and beliefs become clear in this collection as each person captures some aspect of her life and relates it lovingly.

CURIE, MARIE (1867–1934)

Scientist   **Poland**

Marie Curie made major discoveries in both chemistry and physics that won Nobel Prizes. Born on November 11, 1867, Marya Sklodwska had a father who taught high school physics, but law prevented her from studying past secondary school. At twenty-three, Marya arrived in Paris, changed her name to Marie, learned French and physics simultaneously, and graduated first in her class. She met the Sorbonne's chief of labs, Pierre Curie, with whom she began to work, and they married. Madame Curie decided to use Henri Becquerel's work on X-rays as a basis for her doctor of science research (she was the first female doctor of science in Europe), and in it, she identified two new elements, polonium and radium. The Curies also discovered "induced radioactivity"—anything near radium became radioactive. She won two Nobel Prizes, one for physics on fundamental research in radioactivity (1903) and one for chemistry (1912) after discovering radium and polonium. She became the first woman professor at the Sorbonne, and then during World War I, she created a portable X-ray machine to take to the front so that doctors could more quickly locate shrapnel in soldiers' bodies. She died from radiation sickness.

BIBLIOGRAPHY

Birch, Beverly. *Marie Curie's Search for Radium*. Hauppauge, NY: Barron's, 1996. 0-8120-6621-9, 68p. Birch reports a balanced story of Marie Curie and her work in a readable biography for young adults illustrated with appropriate photographs.

Grady, Sean M. *Marie Curie*. San Diego: Lucent, 1992. 1-56006-033-6, 111p. Grady's well-documented and carefully researched biography of Marie Curie addresses her accomplishments and is suitable for young adults.

Pflaum, Rosalynd. *Grand Obsession: Madame Curie and Her World*. New York: Doubleday, 1989. 0-385-26135-7, 496p. The text gives a balanced account of the lives of Madame Curie, her husband, and their daughter and son-in-law. It includes much scientific information, clearly explained, and the French disdain for them as outsiders, although they made some of science's most important contributions.

Quinn, Susan. *Marie Curie: A Life.* New York: Simon and Schuster, 1995. 0-671-67542-7, 496p. The journal that Marie Curie wrote after her husband, Pierre's, sudden death and letters later to Paul Langevin, the married man with whom she had an affair, became available for researchers in 1990. Quinn uses these sources in her well-researched and recommended biography to relate that Curie neglected her two daughters in her despair and that her affair almost cost the revocation of her Nobel Prize, but World War I took the attention of the French public from her indiscretion.

Reid, Robert William. *Marie Curie.* New York: Saturday Review, 1974. 0-84150-317-6, 349p. Marie Curie's life becomes accessible to all readers in Reid's biography. Using private papers in French and English and the newspapers of the day, Reid shows her and her relationship to the other scientific minds of her day, such as Lord Kelvin, Joliot, Bohr, Becquerel, and Einstein, so that the work is also a scientific history of the time.

𝔇

DABROWSKA, MARIA (1889–1965)
Writer   **Poland**

Maria Dabrowska (also Dombrowska) was an acclaimed novelist and journalist. Born on October 6, 1889, as Marja Szumska near Kalisz, she attended private boarding school in Warsaw before going to school in Belgium and enrolling at the University of Lausanne in Switzerland. She also lived in France before World War II. Her four-volume epic narrative, *Noce I Dnie* (Nights and Days), deemed one of the best works in Polish, is a saga in which she follows a family through several generations. She also wrote articles for Polish newspapers on political and economic reform as well as the cooperative movement, subjects of concern throughout her life. Although she expressed her opinions, sometimes opposite those of government, in her writing, she received a state funeral at her death.

BIBLIOGRAPHY
Folejewski, Zbigniew. *Maria Dabrowska*. New York, Twayne, 1970. 0-8057-2260-2, 123p. Folejewski examines Dabrowska's intellectual background and literary heritage, with an analysis of her work and concern about the lack of English translation.

DANILOVA, ALEXANDRA (1904–1997)
Ballerina   **Russia**

Alexandra Danilova devoted her life to ballet and earned awards for stunning performances. "Choura" was born in Peterhof on January 20, 1904, and trained in St. Petersburg in the Russian tradition. She joined the Mariinsky, now Kirov, Theatre and became a soloist there in 1922. She became a ballerina with Diaghilev's Ballets Russes in 1927, where she created new roles for Balanchin. Critics compared her facial features to a Botticelli painting, and she said that in Russia she was known for her "cameo" face. She also danced with the Monte Carlo Opéra Ballet and the Ballets Russes de Monte Carlo. In the

1950s, she visited London with her own company and staged ballets at the Metropolitan Opera, the New York City Ballet, and La Scala in Milan. Afterward, she taught and staged productions at the New York School of Ballet and, in 1977, gave a performance of an aging ballerina in the film *The Turning Point*. In 1985, she received the Capezio Dance Award.

BIBLIOGRAPHY

Danilova, Alexandra. *Choura: The Memoirs of Alexandra Danilova*. New York: Knopf, 1986. 0-394-50539-5, 213p. Although Danilova never achieved the status of **Anna Pavlova** or **Margot Fonteyn**, she devoted her life to dance. In her memoirs, she discusses her relationships, including anecdotes about people such as Stravinsky and **Coco Chanel**, and shares her teaching methods from the School of American Ballet.

Twysden, A. E. *Alexandra Danilova*. New York: Kamin Dance, 1947. No ISBN, 175p. Twysden became Danilova's official biographer and, in a positive view, reports what Danilova and her friends told her.

DARK, ELEANOR (1901–1985)

Writer   Australia

Eleanor Dark was an important Australian novelist whose birth date was August 26, 1901. Her mother died when she was thirteen, and her father remarried. She wanted justice for women and a strong family system, and she used these themes in her work. Among her novels are *Slow Dawning* (1932), *Sun across the Sky* (1937), *The Little Company* (1945), *Storm of Time* (1948), *No Barrier* (1953), and *Lantana Lane* (1959). *The Timeless Land* (1941) is a trilogy that covers the years 1788–1814 in New South Wales. Two of her works, *Prelude to Christopher* (1934) and *Return to Coolami* (1936), won the Australian Literature Society gold medal.

BIBLIOGRAPHY

Day, A. Grove. *Eleanor Dark*. Boston: Twayne, 1976. 0-8057-6224-8, 168p. This biocritical volume discusses Dark's life, her major works, and her important historical novels set in Australia.

DAVID-NEEL, ALEXANDRA (1868–1969)

Traveler and Writer   France

Alexandra David-Neel made extraordinary journeys to Central Asia and the mountains of Tibet where no other Western woman traveler had been, after teaching herself to speak Tibetan and being fascinated with Buddhism. She was born October 24, 1868, in Paris and became interested in Central Asia as a child. She first toured the Far and Middle East and North Africa as an opera singer and returned there when her estranged husband financed many of her travels. Among other accomplishments, she got herself ordained as a Tibetan lama and disguised herself as a Tibetan beggar woman to became the first European woman to enter the city of Lhasa. Among the people she met on her travels were Prince Sidkeong of Sikkim and the Dalai Lama. She wrote many books about her travels and about her belief in Buddhism.

BIBLIOGRAPHY

David-Neel, Alexandra. *My Journey to Lhasa*. 1927. Boston: Beacon, 1993. 0-8070-5903-X, 310p. David-Neel learned Sanskrit and Buddhist philosophy and learned to speak Tibetan so that she could communicate when she reached Lhasa. She recounts her experiences along with the loneliness, nostalgia, and depression that interfered with her objectivity.

Foster, Barbara M., and Michael Foster. *Forbidden Journey: The Life of Alexandra David-Neel*. San Francisco: Harper and Row, 1987. 0-06-250345-6, 363p. This well-documented and balanced scholarly biography reads like a novel, and its subject, David-Neel, had experiences that are often found only in fiction.

Middleton, Ruth. *Alexandra David-Neel: Portrait of an Adventurer*. Boston: Shambhala, 1989. 0-87773-413-5, 206p. Middleton begins her biography with David-Neel as a little girl facing a gendarme and refusing to give her name. When asked where she had been, she replied, "I have been in the woods, searching for my own tree." Middleton uses metaphor for David-Neel's life, travels, and studies.

DAVIES, EMILY (1830–1921)
Educator and Activist   England

Emily Davies believed that women should have equal education and suffrage rights. Daughter of a Southampton clergyman and schoolteacher on April 22, 1830, Davies received her education at a day school and at home before moving with her family to Durham in 1840. After noting the restrictions attached to achievements by **Elizabeth Garrett Anderson** and **Dorothea Beale**, Davies used more subtle approaches to getting what she wanted for women by starting a branch of the Society for Promoting the Employment of Women. After her father's death in 1861, she moved to London and became the editor of the *English Woman's Journal*. Davies lobbied for women to take the Local Cambridge Examination on an experimental basis. In 1865, Cambridge opened the exam to women. In 1867, Davies opened her own college for women at Benslow House, Hitchin, Hertfordshire, with five students. These students took the Cambridge examinations privately, and in 1873, the college moved to Cambridge and became Girton College for Women in 1874, later a Cambridge University school. She also authored two books on women's education, including *Thoughts on Some Questions Relating to Women 1860–1908* and served on several education boards. She was a suffragette and helped to organize the first suffrage petition, which John Stuart Mill presented in 1866.

BIBLIOGRAPHY
Bennett, Daphne. *Emily Davies and the Liberation of Women: 1830–1921*. New York: Trafalgar Square, 1991. 0-233-98494-1, 279p. In this biography, Bennett uses personal correspondence and papers to show Emily Davies' hard fight for a women's college at Cambridge, her female friendships, and her reliance on her friend Henry Tomkinson.

Stephen, Barbara Nightingale. *Emily Davies and Girton College*. Westport, CT: Hyperion, 1976. 0-8835-5282-5, 387p. Stephen uses Davies' papers to create a well-documented and scholarly account of Davies, Madame Bodichon, and other founders of Girton. She notes the revolutionary work that they accomplished and the history of the early years of the college.

DE CASTRO, ROSALÍA *See* CASTRO, ROSALÍA de.

DE CHANTAL, JEANNE-FRANÇOISE. *See* CHANTAL, JEANNE-FRANÇOISE de.

DE CHARRIERE, ISABELLE. *See* CHARRIERE, ISABELLE de.

DEFFAND, MARIE du (1697–1780)
Intellectual   France

Marie du Deffand ran a salon in Paris that attracted many intellectuals. She was born on September 25, 1697, as the third of four children of the Vichy-Chamrond family, which was respectable but no longer wealthy. She received her education in a Paris convent, married a relation in 1718 but separated four years later, and became the leader of a decadent group in the court of her lover, the regent Philippe II, duc d'Orléans. Her salon prospered from 1753 until her death, although she condescended to attending *Encyclopédistes*. She lived with the politician Jean-François Henault until his death. Various intrigues and her worsening eyesight changed the clientele of her salon, but she disclosed her intelligence, independence, wit, and culture in her letters to friends such as Voltaire and Walpole.

BIBLIOGRAPHY
Craveri, Benedetta. *Madame du Deffand and Her World.* Trans. Teresa Waugh. London: P. Halban, 1994. 1-870015-51-7, 481p. This biography reads like a novel as it carefully and thoroughly documents Du Deffand's life and world.

DE LA FAYETTE, MADAME. *See* LA FAYETTE, MADAME de.

DE LA PARRA, TERESA. *See* PARRA, TERESA de la.

DELAUNAY, SONIA (1885–1979)
Artist   Ukraine

Sonia Delaunay became one of the innovators of modern art in her use of strong colors and shapes for unusual subjects. Born on November 14, 1885, as the daughter of a Jewish factory owner, Sophia Terk lived in St. Petersburg with an uncle. She wanted to be a mathematician, but, after studying with a draftsman, she went to Paris and became an artist. Van Gogh, Gauguin, and the Fauves influenced her with their bold colors and forms. Her marriage of convenience lasted only one year before she married Robert Delaunay, with whom she developed the concepts of Orphism and Simultanism. She painted unusual subjects and "designed" poetry. After the family fortune disappeared in the Russian Revolution of 1917, she started designing textiles and other soft materials and painted murals with Robert for the Paris Exposition of 1937. After Robert's death in 1941 and during the Nazi occupation of France, she moved to Grasse and then to Toulouse. In 1953, she mounted her first solo exhibition since 1916 and exhibited at the Louvre in 1964, the only living woman to exhibit there.

BIBLIOGRAPHY
Baron, Stanley, and Jacques Damase. *Sonia Delaunay: The Life of an Artist.* New York: Harry N. Abrams, 1995. 0-8109-3222-9, 208p. Baron's full ac-

cess to Delaunay's journals and personal records and Damase's knowledge of her work after writing the first monograph on Delaunay gave them the basis to write her full biography, with accompanying photographs.

Damase, Jacques. *Sonia Delaunay: Fashion and Fabrics.* Trans. Shaun Whiteside. New York: Harry N. Abrams, 1991. 0-8109-3204-0, 176p. Damase shows Delaunay's experiments with color and form in this visual record of her career. He traces the progress of her designs from sketches to completed garments in their original fabrics but does not examine the artistic value of her career.

Madsen, Axel. *Sonia Delaunay: Artist of the Lost Generation.* New York: McGraw-Hill, 1989. 0-07-039457-1, 357p. In the first full biography of Sonia Delaunay, Madsen uses her diaries and journals as a basis for presenting her as the modern artist who changed fashion and graphic design in the 1920s and after. Black-and-white illustrations augment the text.

DELEDDA, GRAZIA (1871–1936)
Writer   Italy

Grazia Deledda wrote about Sardinia in her work, and her last novel was possibly the one most responsible for her 1926 award of the Nobel Prize in literature. Deledda's father was mayor in the town of Nuovo, Sardinia, where she was born on September 27, 1871. She finished her formal education at fourth grade level, continued reading nineteenth-century fiction, and published her first story at fifteen and her first novel at seventeen. Then she became a regular contributor to magazines. In 1899, she married Palmiro Modesani and moved to Rome. She began writing novels at the rate of almost one a year, using a direct style to show dilemmas, including "religiosity" of ordinary Sardinian people. Her study of Sardinian folklore and the man-earth mythical cycle helped her to express ancient Bronze Age Sardinia. Some of the best known of her thirty-three novels are *Tesore* (1897), *Il vecchio della montagna* (1900), *Elias Portolu* (1903), *Conere* (1908), *L'incendio dell'oliveto* (1920), and *La madre* (1920).

BIBLIOGRAPHY

Aste, Mario. *Grazia Deledda: Ethnic Novelist.* Potomac, MD: Scripta Humanistica, 1990. 0-916379-72-8, 102p. Aste thinks that Deledda has been neglected during the twentieth century because her readers must understand the life, culture, and letters of Sardinia to appreciate the depth of her work.

Merry, Bruce. *Women in Modern Italian Literature: Four Studies Based on the Work of Grazia Deledda, Alba De Cespedes, Natalia Ginzburg, and Dacia Maraini.* Townsville, Australia: James Cook University of North Queensland, 1990. 0-86443-318-2, 229p. Merry discusses the integration of Deledda's work with her life, noting that her women characters have a longer memory, better skill at dissimulation, and better strategies for coping with adversity than their brothers, husbands, and fathers.

Balducci, Carolyn. *A Self-Made Woman: Biography of Nobel-Prize-Winner Grazia Deledda.* Boston: Houghton Mifflin, 1975. 0-395-21914-0, 200p. Balducci's researched but undocumented biography is the first one of Deledda in English. Balducci investigates the times and how Deledda contributed to changes in Italian laws for women.

DE LOS ÁNGELES, VICTORIA. *See* ÁNGELES, VICTORIA de los.

DE MAINTENON, FRANÇOISE. *See* MAINTENON, FRANÇOISE de.

DE MEDICI, CATHERINE. *See* MEDICI, CATHERINE de.

DE PISAN, CHRISTINE (1364–c.1430)
Scholar and Poet   Italy

Christine De Pisan wrote history, philosophy, and poetry as well as biography. She was born in Venice, Italy, the daughter of a scholar who became Charles V of France's court astrologer and physician. Her childhood was spent at the French court from 1369, and Charles V's library became her university. She later wrote Charles V's biography. She became a widow at the age of twenty-five, when her husband died of the plague. Thereafter, she worked to support her family of three children by writing for several nobles. Her first poems, ballades of lost love, were immediately popular and made her France's first woman of letters. To counter courtly love attitudes, she wrote prose works defending women and an account of their heroic deeds. She wrote an autobiography, *La vision de Christine* (Christine's Vision, 1405), in reply to her detractors. She believed in woman's rights and attacked men who belittled them, such as Ovid. She thought women should be educated, and her views often became supporting arguments in debate. She left a detailed record of her inner life for posterity.

BIBLIOGRAPHY
Willard, Charity Cannon. *Christine De Pisan: Her Life and Works.* New York: Persea, 1984. 0-89255-084-8, 266p. Willard's distinctive literary biography of De Pisan incorporates life in early fifteenth-century France. It offers close readings of De Pisan's diverse work, which people read for over one hundred years after her death.

DE POMPADOUR, MADAME. *See* POMPADOUR, MADAME de.

DE SCUDÉRY, MADELEINE. *See* SCUDÉRY, MADELEINE de.

DE SÉVIGNÉ, MARIE. *See* SÉVIGNÉ, MARIE de.

DESPARD, CHARLOTTE (1844–1939)
Activist   Scotland

Charlotte Despard was an activist who fought for suffrage, the rights of the poor, and Irish freedom. Born in Edinburgh on June 15, 1844, Charlotte French was daughter to a naval commander who died when she was nine. Her mother eventually entered an asylum, and the siblings went to live with relatives. During that time, French visited a York rope factory and realized that other, less fortunate young people her age worked in squalid conditions. After marrying an Irish merchant and traveling with him for twenty years, she moved into London slums and devoted herself to the poor by opening a child welfare center and founding a workingmen's club. Disagreeing with the **Pankhursts**, she started the Women's Freedom League in 1907. Then she campaigned against taxation without representation and toured the country advocating suffrage. Her brother John French became the lord lieutenant of Ireland from 1918 to 1921. She worked with the Sinn Fein as a Republican speaker and founder of the Irish Workers' College in Dublin. She spoke against General Franco during the Spanish civil war, and, when she was ninety-one, she spoke at an anti-Nazi demonstration in Hyde Park.

BIBLIOGRAPHY

Linklater, Andro. *An Unhusbanded Life: Charlotte Despard: Suffragette, Socialist, and Sinn Feiner*. London: Hutchinson, 1980. 0-09-140040-6, 270p. Linklater bases this biography on the personal reminiscences of Despard's relatives, her ward, her friends and neighbors in Northern Ireland, and archives in various museums. This documented biography relates anecdotes of Despard's long life and how she championed her many causes.

Mulvihill, Margaret. *Charlotte Despard: A Biography*. London: Pandora, 1989. 0-86358-213-3, 211p. Using Despard's diaries for the years 1913 to 1926, an autobiographical fragment, novels, letters, and family papers, Mulvihill has written a readable biography that probes all aspects of Despard's life. She scrutinizes Despard in light of her times and her causes, including vegetarianism, passivism, socialism, and feminism.

DE STAËL, MADAME. *See* STAËL, ANNE LOUISE de.

DEUTSCH, HELENE (1884–1982)

Psychoanalyst   Poland

Helene Deutsch explored the emotional life of women in her seminal *The Psychology of Women*. As the youngest child in a Galician family of a lawyer born on October 9, 1884, Deutsch studied secretly and won admission to law school. In 1907, she entered the medical school of Vienna University. During her last year there in 1912, she married a doctor, Felix Deutsch. As a physician she began seven years of neurological and psychiatric training. While men fought in World War I, she directed the civilian women's section of the psychiatric department. She met Sigmund Freud in 1916, was one of the first four women he analyzed, and became the second woman admitted to the Vienna Psychoanalytical Society. From 1925 to 1933, she was the director of the Vienna Psychoanalytic Institute, but, as a Jew, she had to leave. People in the United States knew her as a subtle woman who treated them with Old World courtesy.

BIBLIOGRAPHY

Deutsch, Helene. *Confrontations with Myself: An Epilogue*. New York: Norton, 1973. 0-393-07472-2, 217p. In these memoirs, Deutsch, as an eighty-nine-year-old woman, reflects honestly on her past, including her youth in Poland and her recollection of Freud and his circle. She acknowledges some of her mistakes and wonders about other decisions.

Roazen, Paul. *Helene Deutsch: A Psychoanalyst's Life*. New Brunswick, NJ: Transaction, 1992. 1-56000-552-1 371p. Roazen knew Deutsch, and his work is her authorized and recommended biography. He tries to present a balanced picture so that the negative as well as positive aspects of her work will be apparent.

Sayers, Janet. *Mothers of Psychoanalysis: Helene Deutsch, Karen Horney, Anna Freud, Melanie Klein*. New York: Norton, 1991. 0-393-03041-5, 319p.

Sayers looks at each one of these psychoanalysts in terms of their roles as mothers or their femaleness, in Freudian terms. A short overview of Helene Deutsch's life and her contribution to psychoanalysis is a good introduction.

DE VALOIS, NINETTE (1898–)
Ballerina and Choreographer   **Ireland**

Dame Ninette de Valois finally realized her goal for a British National Ballet in 1956. Born in County Wicklow, Eire, on June 6, 1898, Edris Stannus attended theater school in London and performed with a touring children's theater before she became the principal dancer with the British National Opera in 1918. In 1922, she danced with Massin and Lydia Lopokova before becoming a soloist with Diaghilev's Ballets Russes in 1923. Three years later, she opened the Academy of Choreographic Art in London, and **Lilian Baylis** allowed her to stage dances for Old Vic performances. Among the theaters where she served as choreographic director were the Old Vic, the Festival Theatre in Cambridge, and the Abbey Theatre in Dublin. De Valois's experience with the ballet, plays, opera, music hall, revue, musical comedy, and pantomime prepared her to help Lilian Baylis form the Vic-Wells Ballet (later the Sadler's Wells Theatre Ballet). In 1947, she founded the National School of Ballet in Turkey and advised ballets in Canada and Iran. In 1947, she became a Dame Commander of the British Empire and in 1957, a Dame of the British Empire. In 1974, she was the first female recipient of the Erasmus Prize Foundation Award.

BIBLIOGRAPHY
Walker, Kathrine Sorley. *Ninette De Valois: Idealist Without Illusions.* London: H. Hamilton, 1987. 0-241-12386-0, 373p. In addition to her historical overview of twentieth-century dance, Walker shows that de Valois's many experiences prepared her to contribute her talents in unique ways to the ballet world.

DEVLIN, BERNADETTE (1947–)
Politician   **Ireland**

Bernadette Devlin McAliskey is an Irish politician. She was born on April 23, 1947; her father was a road sweeper's son, and her mother raised Devlin and her poor Catholic family of five brothers and sisters in Dungannon, County Tyrone. After Devlin started attending Queen's University in Belfast as a scholarship student, she joined protest movements. In 1969, the Independent Party for Mid-Ulster elected her a member of Parliament. As the youngest member of the House, at twenty-one, since William Pitt, she attacked British policy and lead Catholic rioters in the Battle of Bogside, for which she served four months in prison. When she had a child out of wedlock in 1971, she lost Catholic support, and, although she married Michael McAliskey in 1973, she did not stand in the General Election. In 1979, she lost in a bid to win a seat in the European Parliament, and, after a quiet period, she supported the Irish Republican Army (IRA) hunger strikers in 1980, established the Independent Socialist Part of Ireland in 1975, and became involved in movements in other countries, including Spain.

BIBLIOGRAPHY
Devlin, Bernadette. *The Price of My Soul.* New York: Knopf, 1969. No ISBN, 224p. Devlin's anecdotes relate her beliefs, personality, and sacrifices along with the economic, social, and political situation of Northern Ireland.
Target, G. W. *Bernadette: The Story of Bernadette Devlin.* London: Hodder and Stoughton, 1975. 0-340-16543-X, 384p. Using newspaper articles and interviews with people who knew Devlin, and Devlin herself, Target presents Devlin and a clear picture of Northern Ireland during recent times.

DÍAZ, NIDIA (1952–)

Revolutionary   El Salvador

Nidia Díaz, María Marta Valladares, has been a revolutionary fighting for Salvadorian freedom from military rule and an activist for woman's rights. She was born on November 11, 1952, in San Salvador as the third of four children. She began to fight for social jusitce at thirteen, when she participated in pastoral and literacy campaigns sponsored by social and Christian organizations. She later became part of the Salvadoran revolutionary movement leadership, and during the same period, she completed four years of psychology study. In 1985, when she was seriously wounded in combat, Americans working for Oliver North captured her, questioned her for sixteen days, and held her in solitary confinement for six months before releasing her on October 24, 1985, with other political prisoners in exchange for the daughter of President Duarte. She was named president of the "Mélida Anaya Montes" Salvadoran Union for Women's Liberation. Appointed to the Political-Diplomatic Commission of the Frente Farabundo Martí de Liberación Nacional (FMLN) in 1987, she was named director of the FMLN's Commission for the Protection and Promotion for Human Rights. She went to Geneva as a delegate in 1990.

BIBLIOGRAPHY
Diaz, Nidia. *I Was Never Alone: A Prison Diary from El Salvador.* New York: Ocean, Talman, 1992. 1-875284-13-3, 210p. Diaz wrote while in prison and says that the book reflects her revolutionary ideology rather than personal emotions because she wanted to reveal no feelings to her captors. But she relates, with immediacy, the struggles of Salvadorans as well as her own for political, economic, and social freedom.

DIETRICH, MARLENE (1901–1992)

Actor   Germany

Marlene Dietrich began making silent movies in the 1920s and became a film star. Born in Berlin on December 27, 1901, Maria Magdalene was the daughter of a Royal Prussian Police officer who died when she was very young. She wanted to become a concert violinist and studied at the Hochschüle fur Musik in Berlin, but a wrist injury thwarted her plans. She turned to the stage and Max Reinhardt's Deutsche Theaterschüle and began her film career in 1923. She and her Czech husband, Rudolf Sieber, moved to the United States, and she became an international star in *The Blue Angel* (1930). Among her movies of that era were *Morocco, Dishonored, Shanghai Express,* and *Blonde Empress.* She refused to work in Germany before World War II, and her movies were subsequently banned there. During World War II, she spent time entertaining the troops, and both the American and French governments decorated her. She continued to make films but had more success as a cabaret star.

BIBLIOGRAPHY

Bach, Steven. *Marlene Dietrich: Life and Legend.* New York: William Morrow, 1992. 0-688-07119-8, 626p. Bach uses reviews of Dietrich's films, plays, songs, and nearly one hundred accompanying photographs to find an intelligent woman and artist who survived the Hollywood star system, two world wars, performances in Europe on a grueling schedule, and a series of lovers.

Dietrich, Marlene. *Marlene.* New York: Grove, 1989. 0-8021-1117-3, 273p. Dietrich enjoys pointing to mistakes made about her life in other biographies, but she refuses to tell the truth in her own memoirs, contradicting herself within the text.

Riva, Maria. *Marlene Dietrich.* New York: Knopf, 1993. 0-394-58692-1, 789p. Riva, her mother's companion and confidant, portrays Dietrich in this popular biography as devoted to "romance" rather than to sex.

Spoto, Donald. *Blue Angel: The Life of Marlene Dietrich.* New York: Doubleday, 1992. 0-385-42553-8, 335p. Spoto's earlier photo-essay is the basis for this full biography of Dietrich. He has added extensive research and insightful interpretations of her film work and demonstrates how she learned to "market" herself.

Walker, Alexander. *Dietrich.* New York: Harper and Row, 1984. 0-06-015319-9, 207p. Walker thinks that Dietrich played on the heroic qualities of militarism and romanticized war to develop her persona. With excellent illustrations, the book presents a survey of Dietrich's films rather than a full biography.

DINESEN, ISAK (1885–1962)

Writer   Denmark

Isak Dinesen (Karen Blixen's pseudonym) became famous for her description of her experience in Africa managing a coffee plantation. She was born on April 17, 1885, in Copenhagen, where she first studied. Thinking that she would be an artist, Blixen went to Paris and Rome before marrying her cousin, Baron Bror Blixen-Finecke, in 1914, and moving with him to Kenya. They divorced seven years later, but she continued to administer the plantation. She had to leave in 1931, when her finances failed, but she had begun writing during Kenya's rainy seasons and publishing stories under the name "Osceola." She decided to become a professional after returning to her family in Denmark, and her first English publication was *Seven Gothic Tales* (1934). She became ill and during that time wrote her famous memoirs, *Out of Africa* (1937), in which she discussed her syphilis, contracted from her husband, and an affair she had after their separation. During the Nazi occupation of Denmark, she published, under the name "Pierre Andrezel," a melodrama allegorically depicting the unscrupulous oppression. Among her other works are *Winters' Tales* and *Enraged.*

BIBLIOGRAPHY

Dinesen, Isak. *Out of Africa.* New York: Modern Library, 1992. 0-679-60021-3, 399p. Dinesen remembers her experiences in Kenya managing a coffee farm. The book relates the events beginning with her arrival, her husband's departure in 1921 after giving her syphilis, her affair with a man who later died in a 1929 plane crash, and her forced departure in 1931 as a result of financial difficulties.

Henriksen, Aage. *Isak Dinesen/Karen Blixen: The Work and the Life.* Trans. William Mischler. New York: St. Martin's, 1988. 0-312-01777-4, 197p. Six separate segments cover different aspects of Blixen in this readable biography. Henriksen knew Blixen well, and he uses an informal tone in his insights about how her work reflects her life and personality.

Migel, Parmenia. *Tania: A Biography and Memoir of Isak Dinesen.* 1967. New York: McGraw-Hill, 1987. Paper, 0-07-041909-4, 325p. In 1950, Dinesen asked Migel to write her biography. Migel pictures Dinesen as a writer whose magical personality and work belong in the Romantic period rather than the twentieth century. Four parts cover the places she lived and visited and contemplate the legend Dinesen created about herself.

Pelensky, Olga Anastasia. *Isak Dinesen: The Life and Imagination of a Seducer.* Athens: Ohio University Press, 1991. 0-8214-0968-9, 218p. Pelensky concludes from her research that the military shaped Dinesen's life because of a psychic split between Dinesen men and Westenholz women, with her soldier father as the single biggest force on her imagination. This psychological, scholarly biography also asserts that the influence of the Danish feudal society, nihilism, and Dinesen's desire to create herself as an aesthetic object were undercurrents in her life as aristocrat, adventurer, and author.

Thurman, Judith. *Isak Dinesen: The Life of a Storyteller.* 1982. New York: Picador, 1995. 0-312-13525-4, 495p. Thurman bases her biography on Dinesen's letters, diaries, first drafts, and personal papers. She scrutinizes Blixen's personas from her childhood in Denmark to her return and writing success after living in Kenya. Thurman correlates the events in Dinesen's life with episodes from her writing in a commendable, well-written, and thorough biography. National Book Award.

Westenholz, Anders. *The Power of Aries: Myth and Reality in Karen Blixen's Life.* Trans. Lise Kure-Jensen. Baton Rouge: Louisiana State University Press, 1987. 0-8071-1261-5, 127p. In this analytical biography, Westenholz thinks that Blixen created her own reality in her first major work, *Seven Gothic Tales*, and spent her life trying to avoid being consumed, like the character Pellegrina in her later work. However, Blixen would not reveal herself to others, and Westenholz tries to find the answer to her personality in her work and in her life.

DING LING (1904?–1986)
Writer   China

Ding Ling was an activist and writer who won Soviet awards for her work as well as condemnation and prison. Her family from the Hunan province was gentry, and her mother educated Jiang Bingzhi (Ding Ling is her pseudonym) until she went to study in Taoynan at seventeen. She became concerned about the equality of women, and in 1919, after the May 4 Movement, she went to Changsa to attend a coeducational school. In 1925, she began publishing her short stories with romantic heroines critical of the old ways as they struggle for independence and fulfillment. She became active in a group of left-wing writers, and after her husband's, Hu's, execution in 1931, she became more committed to the Left and wrote socialist-realist fiction like *Shuii* (Flood, 1931). After she joined the Communist Party, Kuomintang agents imprisoned her in

1933 for three years. She escaped in the disguise of a Manchurian soldier to join Mao Zedong (Tse-Tung) and his forces in the Yenan province. Her novel about these experiences, *Sang-Kan-ho-Shang* (The Sun Shines over the Sangkan River), won the 1957 Stalin Prize. The party then condemned her as a reactionary in 1957, told her not to write, and expelled her to northeast China, where she worked as a peasant farmer for twelve years. In 1966, the Cultural Revolution publicly humiliated her, and in 1970, leaders imprisoned her in Beijing for five years of solitary confinement. Three years of exile in a mountain village of Shanxi province followed until 1979, when the Communist Party reinstated her and cleared her name.

BIBLIOGRAPHY

Chang, Jun-mei. *Ting Ling, Her Life and Her Work*. Taipei, China: Institute of International Relations, 1978. No ISBN, 170p. This biography relates Ting Ling's [*sic*] case to its historical context and reviews her life and work as a product of her time. Chang thinks that she is not a major literary figure but that she represents what women have endured.

Feuerwerker, Yi-tsi M. *Ding Ling's Fiction: Ideology and Narrative in Modern Chinese Literatures*. Cambridge, MA: Harvard University Press, 1982. 0-674-20765-3, 216p. Feuerwerker did not know whether Ding Ling was living while she worked on this book, but when the Communist Party rehabilitated Ding Ling in 1979, Feuerwerker went to China and interviewed her and those who had known her while she was exiled to the Great Northern Wilderness state farms. Feuerwerker focuses on Ding Ling's narrative writings and their ability to show a response to, and a resistance of, political pressure.

DRABBLE, MARGARET (1939–)
Writer   England

Margaret Drabble has had a major influence on British fiction through her portrayal of the concerns inherent in middle-class women. After her birth in Sheffield, Yorkshire, on June 5, 1939, Drabble was educated at the Mount School, York, and Newnham College, Cambridge, where she took a double first in English. She married Clive Swift in 1960, had three children, divorced in 1975, and married Michael Holroyd in 1982. *The Millstone*, her third novel, won the Llewellyn Rhys Memorial Prize in 1966. She has written other novels, including *The Middle Ground* (1980) and *The Radiant Way* (1987), as well as a biography of Arnold Bennett (1974) and *A Writer's Britain* (1979). She served as editor of the most recent *Oxford Companion to British Literature*. The American Academy of Arts and Letters gave her the E. M. Forster Award in 1973, and she has chaired the National Book League since 1980.

BIBLIOGRAPHY

Creighton, Joanne V. *Margaret Drabble*. New York: Methuen, 1985. Paper, 0-416-38390-4, 127p. Creighton looks at Drabble's life and her work and tries to show how they mesh. She includes Drabble's comments on marriage, motherhood, and various other topics and critiques Drabble's work.

Sadler, Lynn Veach. *Margaret Drabble*. Boston: Twayne, 1986. 0-8057-6907-2, 152p. Sadler sees that Drabble, while remaining true to herself, remains true to the human spirit and condition. This biography shows her as a storyteller of manners and character in contemporary Britain.

DROSTE-HÜLSHOFF, ANNETTE von (1797–1848)
Poet   Germany

Contemporaries considered Annette von Droste-Hülshoff Germany's greatest female poet in her time. After her birth in Westphalia on January 10, 1797, von Droste-Hülshoff's mother discouraged her education, but she began writing poetry at seven. As an adult, she wrote an epic, *Das Hospiz am Grossen Sant Bernard* (1928), and began traveling and meeting famous people, including the Grimm brothers. In the 1830s, she expanded to ballads, lyrics, and prose, in an attempt to amuse her own class. Her best poetry appeared after she became devoted to her protégé, Levin Schücking, seventeen years younger. She published a novella, *Die Judenbuche*, as well. When Schücking rejected her in 1843 to marry another, she quit writing. In her works, she used natural realism and demonstrated a preoccupation with the supernatural and evil. In her early poetry, not published until after her death, she expressed strong religious doubts. Her lack of formal education probably allowed her to have independence of choice in subject and genre.

BIBLIOGRAPHY
Guthrie, John. *Annette von Droste-Hülshoff: A German Poet between Romanticism and Realism.* Herndon, VA: Berg, 1989. 0-85496-174-7, 128p. Guthrie confirms that von Droste-Hülshoff deserves the reputation that she had during her lifetime. He emphasizes her individuality but, at the same time, he recognizes her conservatism and dislike of change.

DU DEFFAND, MARIE. *See* DEFFAND, MARIE du.

DU MAURIER, DAPHNE (1907–1989)
Writer   England

Daphne du Maurier became famous for her novel *Rebecca*, set in Cornwall, where she lived most of her life. Born on May 13, 1907, she was the second daughter of a renowned actor and theater manager who had created the role of "Bulldog Drummond." Her mother was also an actor, and her grandfather an author. Du Maurier was educated at home with her sisters and then in Paris. She published her first novel, *The Loving Spirit*, when she was twenty-four. She continued to write after marrying in 1932 and published *Rebecca* in 1938. She wrote romantic, Gothic, and historical fiction, including *Frenchman's Creek* (1942), *The King's General* (1946), and *My Cousin Rachel* (1952). She also wrote short stories and biography.

BIBLIOGRAPHY
Du Maurier, Daphne. *Myself When Young: The Shaping of a Writer.* Boston: Hall, 1978. 0-8161-6611-0, 329p. Du Maurier recalls her youth by referring to the diaries that she kept and using the language in which she wrote them to tell about her early days in Cornwall. She reveals few innermost thoughts but establishes Cornwall's influence on her plots and characters.

Forster, Margaret. *Daphne du Maurier: The Secret Life of the Renowned Storyteller.* New York: Doubleday, 1993. 0-385-42068-4, 457p. Forster uses du Maurier's correspondence to link du Maurier's books to her mental state while writing each. Forster emphasizes, with details about her bisexual attractions and longtime infatuation with **Gertrude Lawrence**, that du Maurier insisted that writing was her life. She died when she stopped writing.

Shallcross, Martyn. *The Private World of Daphne du Maurier*. New York: St. Martin's, 1992. 0-312-07072-1, 192p. Shallcross met du Maurier when he was only four. He renewed his acquaintance over the years and, in this straightforward biography, tries to show her childhood and solitary adult life. He also discusses the various film versions of her novels as well as her relationships with their producers.

DU PRÉ, JACQUELINE (1945–1987)
Instrumentalist   England

Jacqueline du Pré made her reputation as a cellist performing throughout the world. Born on January 26, 1945, she studied at the London Violoncello School before attending the Guildhall School of Music, where renowned cellists such as Rostropovich instructed her. She made her professional debut at the Wigmore Hall in London during 1961 and began a career that soon won international acclaim. She married pianist Daniel Barenboim in 1967, and they gave many recitals and made many recordings together. Her technique and style were especially appropriate for concertos by Haydn, Schumann, Elgar, Boccherini, Dvořák, and Delius. In 1968, she debuted *Romanze*, which Alexander Goehr wrote for her. In the early 1970s, the onset of multiple sclerosis stopped her performances, but she continued to teach master classes. In 1976, she was created an Officer of the British Empire.

BIBLIOGRAPHY
Easton, Carol. *Jacqueline du Pré: A Life*. New York: Summit, 1989. 0671695916, 224p. Easton met du Pré after multiple sclerosis had stopped du Pré from performing and offered to read to her. During their friendship, du Pré suggested that Easton write the biography. Easton bases her story on anecdotes of at least one hundred friends, musicians, and teachers outside the family, showing du Pré as brave but distressed with her sudden shift from concert cellist to invalid.

DURAS, MARGUERITE (1914–1996)
Writer and Filmmaker   Indochina (Vietnam)

Margaret Duras has won awards for her fiction and her films. After her April 4, 1914, birth and childhood in Indochina, Duras saw the effects of political events on humans. At seventeen, she left Saigon for Paris and worked briefly before beginning to write. Her personal knowledge of Indochina's woes formed her pacifist political viewpoint. In 1950, her book, *Un barrage contre le Pacifique* (A Sea of Troubles), established her reputation and disapproval of colonialism. Many of her protagonists are women living on the fringes of society, and they or other characters numb their difficulties with alcohol. She won the Prix Goncourt in 1984 for *L'Amante Anglaise*, a semiautobiographical novel. She wrote screenplays, such as her adaption of *Hiroshima Mon Amour* (1959). In 1966, she began directing films and established her ability to show tension between images and sound track in experimental, low-budget films. She prefers not to be called a feminist writer, but she illustrates her political views through her female protagonists.

BIBLIOGRAPHY
Duras, Marguerite, and Xaviere Gauthier. *Woman to Woman*. Trans. Katharine A. Jensen. Lincoln: University of Nebraska Press, 1987. 0-8032-1672-6,

200p. This series of interviews with Duras remains unedited because Gauthier did not want to lose the sense of the discussion, words, or silences. She and Duras discuss Duras's life, her approach to writing, and the writing itself in an enlightening exchange.

Glassman, Deborah. *Marguerite Duras: Fascinating Vision and Narrative Cure.* Cranberry, NJ: Fairleigh Dickinson University Press, 1991. 0-8386-3337-4, 152p. In this accessible study of Duras and how she imposes order through her narratives, Glassman examines an early novel, *Moderato Cantabile*, and the related film, *Hiroshima Mon Amour*, the "India cycle," and Duras's autobiographical phase in *L'Amant*.

Harvey, Robert, and Hélène Volat. *Marguerite Duras: A Bio-Bibliography.* Westport, CT: Greenwood Press, 1997. 0-313-28898-4, 273p. This scholarly text contains a brief biography of Duras with her comments about life and the place of history followed by a chronology of dates important to her. The other sections of the book include a bibliography of primary sources as well as separate secondary source bibliographies on Duras' writing and her films.

Vircondelet, Alain. *Duras: A Biography.* Normal, IL: Dalkey Archive, 1994. 1-56478-065-1, 378p. Vircondelet studies the films, screenplays, and novels of Duras in this literary biography and discovers a subversive and defiant woman, unwilling to be tamed either in her life or in her work.

DUSE, ELEANORA (1858–1924)
Actor   Italy

Eleanora Duse achieved international fame as an actress. She was born on October 3, 1858, to a father more interested in painting than acting and a mother of farming stock who began acting out of necessity after her marriage. Duse, on stage at four, was a seasoned trouper at seven. As a teen, when her mother was ill, Duse played her roles. Her mother's early death grieved Duse, but she recovered for her first major success in 1878 with *Les Fourchambaults*. She toured as a leading lady the next year with Erneste Rossi and won acclaim. In 1881, she visited Russia and, four years later, Latin America. She and Rossi founded a successful company rivaling **Sarah Bernhardt**'s. Some of her best roles were Ibsen's *Hedda Gabler, The Doll's House, Rosmersholm*, and *Lady from the Sea*. Shaw admired her, and Chekhov supposedly used her as a model for *The Seagull*. Although she retired in 1914, she returned to the stage in 1921 and toured the United States in 1923.

BIBLIOGRAPHY
De Bonis, Sofia. *Eleonora Duse: The Story of Her Life.* 1924. New York: B. Blom, 1971. No ISBN, 308p. In this adulatory and effusive, undocumented biography, De Bonis, who knew Duse, attempts to tell the "simple, true story" of Duse from birth to death. The text includes photographs.

Noccioli, Guido. *Duse on Tour: Guido Noccioli's Diaries, 1906–1907.* Trans. Giovanni Pontiero. Amherst: University of Massachusetts Press, 1982. 0-87023-369-6, 178p. Noccioli kept a diary of the year, 1906–07, when he went with Duse on her second tour of South America. He provides a daily account of Duse in rehearsal and performance at the peak of her career. This readable account reveals what being on tour in the early twentieth century with a famous actress was like.

Pontiero, Giovanni. *Eleonora Duse, in Life and Art*. New York: P. Lang, 1986. 3-8204-8974-6, 462p. This thoroughly researched, documented, and balanced biography is most likely the definitive work on Duse's life. Pontiero concentrated on Duse's vast correspondence, revealing her inner tensions and oscillating moods, precarious health, financial worries, bad emotional attachments, and conflicting responsibilities of motherhood.

Stokes, John, Michael R. Booth, and Susan Bassnett. *Bernhardt, Terry, Duse: The Actress in Her Time*. New York: Cambridge University Press, 1988. 0-521-25615-1, 192p. In this biography of three women working in the same profession at the same time in history, the authors have used letters, reviews, promptbooks, photographs, recordings, and eyewitness accounts to analyze the women's work and their lives.

Weaver, William. *Duse, a Biography*. San Diego, CA: Harcourt Brace Jovanovich, 1984. 0-15-126690-5, 383p. Letters, newspaper reviews, and memoirs from Duse's contemporaries aided Weaver in the creation of his biography. He shows her as prima donna, patriot, and friend, with illustrations of her major roles.

𝔈

EARDLEY, JOAN (1921–1963)
Artist   Scotland

Joan Eardley became a painter with a speciality of simple subjects such as harbor scenes and workers. She was born May 18, 1921, the daughter of an English army officer in the First World War who never recovered from gassing in the trenches. She lived near Horsham in Sussex, and, after her father's suicide when she was seven, she and her mother and sister went to live in London. She received her first encouragement in art from a teacher at St. Helens and later trained at the Glasgow School of Art. After World War II, she went to Italy but returned to Glasgow and taught evening classes, devoting her days to painting the Glasgow tenements where she lived. She also painted at Catterline, a fishing village south of Aberdeen. The social themes in her work, revealed with dark colors, are women and children of the slums, interior scenes of fishing cottages, and ports. In 1963, she became a Royal Scottish Academician, and her paintings appear in major British galleries.

BIBLIOGRAPHY
Buchanan, William. *Joan Eardley*. Edinburgh, Scotland: Edinburgh University Press, 1976. 0-85224-301-4, 91p. Buchanan gives a brief overview of, and introduction to, Eardley's life and work, with plates of her pictures.

Oliver, Cordelia. *Joan Eardley, RSA*. Photos Audrey Walker and Oscar Marzaroli. Edinburgh, Scotland: Mainstream, 1989. 1-85158-166-9, 120p. Oliver's biography examines Eardley's life and uses accompanying black-and-white and color reproductions of her work to illustrate various influences, including van Gogh. Oliver suggests that Eardley died before receiving the international recognition that she deserved.

EBERHARDT, ISABELLE (1877–1904)
Traveler and Writer   Switzerland

Isabelle Eberhardt became a writer after converting to Islam and settling in Morocco. She was born on February 17, 1877, as the illegitimate child of a tutor, Alexander Trophimowsky, and her mother who had left her Russian husband. Trophimowsky raised her as a boy, educating her so that, at sixteen, she spoke six languages, including Arabic. Suicidal as a teenager and often ill, she developed a dependence on drugs and alcohol. In 1897, she and her mother went to West Africa, and her mother died there after they had converted to Islam. Under a pseudonym, Eberhardt wrote articles for Paris journals about Islamic Africa and visited the Algerian Sahara dressed as a male Arab student gathering stories about drug use and sex orgies. Because of her notoriety, someone tried to assassinate her, and a famous trial afterward caused her expulsion from Algeria. She then married a young Arab army officer and returned. On a trip to Morocco, she became ill, and the day after she left the hospital of her own accord, she drowned in a flash flood. Her writings appeared in five books published after her death.

BIBLIOGRAPHY
Eberhardt, Isabelle. *The Passionate Nomad: The Diary of Isabelle Eberhardt.* Ed. Rana Kabbani. New York: Beacon, 1988. Paper, 0-8070-7103-X, 116p. Kabbani, Eberhardt's editor, suggests that Eberhardt was not the romantic that she seemed but a rebel. Eberhardt describes her feelings of exile from 1900 to 1903 but omits details of her life in a country few Europeans had seen.

Hart, Ursula Kingsmill. *Two Ladies of Colonial Algeria: The Lives and Times of Aurelie Picard and Isabelle Eberhardt.* Athens: Ohio University Center for International Studies, 1987. 0-89680-143-8, 140p. Hart gives a brief overview of Eberhardt's life, and, since Eberhardt married an Algerian Muslim who had French citizenship, Hart tries to make a case that Eberhardt was both a mystic and a forerunner of the Algerian nationalist movement.

Kobak, Annette. *Isabelle: The Life of Isabelle Eberhardt.* New York: Knopf, 1989. 0-394-57691-8, 258p. Carefully researched and detailed, Kobak's intriguing biography of the unorthodox Isabelle Eberhardt scrutinizes a woman about whom police and army intelligence reported various scandals. Some believe that the French caused Eberhardt's troubles, including trying to assassinate her.

Mackworth, Cecily. *The Destiny of Isabelle Eberhardt.* New York: Ecco, 1975. 0-912946-22-9, 228p. Mackworth tells Eberhardt's story based on her diaries, letters, and short stories. This undocumented biography seems and reads like a novel.

EBNER-ESCHENBACH, MARIE (1830–1916)
Writer   Austria

Marie Ebner-Eschenbach wrote novellas about the differences in social and economic classes, earning the status of the foremost woman writer in the German realist period. She was born in Moravia at Adislawitz Castle on September 13, 1830, and lived there and in Vienna before marrying her cousin in 1848. She had tried writing poetry as a girl, but after she and her husband moved to Vienna in 1863, her writing experiments led her to the novella. She wrote stories about class life, showing concern for the poor from a conservative viewpoint. Her best story was probably *Das Gemeindekind* (1887), in which a murderer's son tries to find a place for himself in society. She wanted more justice for the world, and she fought for it with rationality and love being the two principal forces of both her personality and her fiction. She reveals her own life in her fiction and uses her own name or a variation of it for many of her protagonists. The University of Vienna awarded her a doctorate in 1900, the first woman to receive the honor from that institution.

BIBLIOGRAPHY

Klostermaier, Doris M. *Marie von Ebner-Eschenbach: The Victory of a Tenacious Will.* Riverside, CA: Ariadne, 1997. 1-57241-038-8, 348p. Klostermaier uses Ebner-Eschenbach's unpublished correspondences, notebook entries, and reviews, as well as published monographs and essays, to verify that Ebner-Eschenbach deserved her reputation as Austria's most prominent nineteenth-century woman writer. Since she wanted to be understood through her work, she destroyed many papers, and Klostermaier has also examined Ebner-Eschenbach's works carefully to see how she revealed herself in her fiction. This biography is well researched and accessible.

Steiner, Carl. *Of Reason and Love: The Life and Works of Marie von Ebner-Eschenbach.* Riverside, CA: Ariadne, 1994. 0-929497-77-5, 233p. In this straightforward biography, Steiner gives a comprehensive picture of von Ebner-Eschenbach's life and a critical analysis of her work. Steiner sees her as a major figure in Austrian and German literature regardless of gender.

EDGEWORTH, MARIA (1767–1849)

Writer   England

Maria Edgeworth defended a woman's right to write and gave advice about educating the young. Born on January 1, 1767, in Blackbourton, Oxfordshire, she was educated in Derby and in London. Her mother died when she was only six. The family settled on their Irish estate in 1782, where her father, an agricultural reformer, began increasing the productivity of the estate and improving the lives of his farmers. Edgeworth and her father were very close, although in his remarriage, her fathered nineteen more children. Maria began teaching them, helping on the family estate, and started writing with her first book, *Letters for Literary Ladies*, appearing in 1795. In it, she defended her right to translate. She then wrote children's stories and a textbook with her father about teaching children, called *Practical Education* (1798), which critics liked. It made the family famous. In 1800, she published an adult novel, *Castle Rackrent*. She went to France in 1802 and romanced a Swedish officer but supposedly refused to marry him because of her family duties. She continued to earn much money from writing, and, during the Irish famine of 1846, she organized relief measures for the community around her estate.

BIBLIOGRAPHY

Butler, Marilyn. *Maria Edgeworth: A Literary Biography.* Oxford, England: Clarendon, 1972. No ISBN, 531p. Butler's definitive biography indicates that Edgeworth wrote her own novels, with her father editing them. Butler thinks that Edgeworth presented social and economic circumstances in her writing that introduced the mid-Victorian novel.

Clarke, Isabel Constance. *Maria Edgeworth, Her Family and Friends.* 1949. Philadelphia: R. West, 1976. 0-8492-0418-6, 208p. Clarke tries to reconstruct Edgeworth's story from all available sources and focuses first on a picture of Edgeworth. In a researched but casual biography, Clarke sees Edgeworth as an amiable personality and basically agreeable.

Inglis-Jones, Elisabeth. *The Great Maria: Portrait of Maria Edgeworth.* 1959. Westport, CT: Greenwood Press, 1978. 0-313-20428-4, 265p. In a relatively balanced and reasonable introduction to Edgeworth, Inglis-Jones uses letters that Edgeworth wrote her family, unpublished papers, and a privately printed *Memoir of Maria Edgeworth* from 1863 as her main sources.

Kowaleski-Wallace, Elizabeth. *Their Fathers' Daughters: Hannah More, Maria Edgeworth, and Patriarchal Complicity.* New York: Oxford University Press, 1991. 0-19-506853-X, 256p. This carefully documented and scholarly analysis looks at selected aspects of the biographical, autobiographical, and fictional work of More and Edgeworth to investigate a motivation for their attraction to patriarchy.

Newcomer, James. *Maria Edgeworth.* Lewisburg, PA: Bucknell University Press, 1973. 0-8387-7761-9, 94p. Newcomer gives a brief overview of Edgeworth's life and work that is merely an introduction.

ELEANOR of AQUITAINE (1122–1202)
Queen   France

Called "Grandmother of Europe" for the alliances she made for her daughters, Eleanor was also mother and wife of kings. Born in 1122, Eleanor inherited the duchy of Aquitaine and Poitiers in 1137 and married Louis, who became the king of France as Louis VII. She dedicated the abbey church of St. Denis, the first Gothic building, in 1144, and the next year, she had her first of ten children. In 1147, she joined Louis on the Second Crusade, taking a large company of women. Four years later she met Duke Henry of Normandy, and the next year she divorced Louis and married him. In 1153, she bore the first of Henry's five sons, William. In 1154, Henry and Eleanor became king and queen of England, stretching from Scotland's borders to those of Spain. In 1166, as a result of Henry's affair with Rosamond, Eleanor returned to France and established the court of love in Poitiers, a place for poets, musicians, scholars, and intellectuals to meet and socialize. She also supported education and religious institutions from this position. When Eleanor backed her sons' rebellion against Henry in 1173, Henry imprisoned her. In 1189, Henry died, and Richard, the new king, freed her. In 1194, after Germans captured Richard, Eleanor traveled across the Alps to ransom him. John became king at Richard's death in 1199, and Eleanor died in 1204, eleven years before the English made John sign the Magna Carta.

BIBLIOGRAPHY

Meade, Marion. *Eleanor of Aquitaine: A Biography.* New York: Hawthorn Books, 1977. 0-8015-2231-5, 389p. In this popular biography of Eleanor, Meade places her as the key political figure of the twelfth century.

Owen, D. D. R. *Eleanor of Aquitaine: Queen and Legend.* Cambridge, MA: Blackwell, 1993. 0-631-17072-3, 256p. Owen attempts to separate the human Eleanor from the stories and legends that have surrounded her and concludes that Eleanor was a model for Guinevere, the protagonist of Arthurian romances.

Pernoud, Regine. *Eleanor of Aquitaine*. Trans. Peter Wiles. New York: Coward-McCann, 1968. No ISBN, 286p. Eleanor appears here as sympathetic wife, lover, and mother in this readable, popular biography. Although based on fact, Pernoud interprets as necessary to understand Eleanor. Prix Historia.

Seward, Desmond. *Eleanor of Aquitaine*. New York: Times, 1979. 0-8129-0749-3, 264p. This biography is well written but without supportive evidence for some of its suppositions. It offers nothing new about Eleanor but shows the power that she held over her children, especially Richard I.

ELEANOR of CASTILE (1246–1290)
Queen of England   Spain

Eleanor of Castile became the queen of England when she married Edward I of England. She was the daughter of Ferdinand III of Castile and Joan of Ponthieu. When she married Edward, her half brother Alfonso X of Castile gave Edward his claim to Gascony. When Henry III's opponents seized power in England in 1264, Eleanor was able to escape safely to this French claim. Later, she went with Edward on a crusade from 1270 to 1273 and supposedly saved his life in Acre. When he ascended the throne, Eleanor was accused of mistreating their tenants although most likely her enemies spread the story. Her devotion to Edward helped bring out his better qualities, and, when she died, Edward erected Eleanor Crosses (several still remain) at each place her coffin stopped on its way to London.

BIBLIOGRAPHY
Parsons, John Carmi. *Eleanor of Castile: Queen and Society in Thirteenth-Century England*. New York: St. Martin's, 1995. 0-312-08649-0, 364p. Parsons examines Eleanor's role in thirteenth-century society and culture in his definitive biography. He finds her, a loyal wife, to have understood the intellectual advantage of networking as a way to gather wealth, property, and power. He also investigates the myth of "good Queen Eleanor."

ELIOT, GEORGE (1819–1880)
Writer   England

George Eliot won critical renown as a novelist with her first novel, *Adam Bede* (1859), and has kept it since. Born Mary Anne Evans in Warwickshire on November 22, 1819, where her father was a landowner's agent, she attended local boarding schools. As a religious and intelligent young girl, she was also a talented musician. After her mother's death, she looked after the household and began to help charities in the community. When she moved to Coventry with her father in 1841, she met the freethinker Charles Bray, his wife, and his sister-in-law. Her ensuing religious doubts fueled by these friendships caused her to break with her father. Simultaneously, she was translating Strauss's *Life of Jesus* and Spinoza's *Tractatus theologio-politicus*. She spent time in Geneva before moving to London and becoming an assistant editor of the *Westminster Review*. She and George Henry Lewes started living together in 1854, but Lewes' wife would not divorce him. Evans started writing fiction in 1856, with Lewes' encouragement, especially since they needed money to support his family as well. The critical success and the popular audience she won with her first novel continued with *Mill on the Floss* (1860), *Silas Marner* (1861), and *Ro-*

mola (1862), supposedly based on the personality of **Barbara Bodichon**. Her second period of writing produced the novels *Felix Holt* (1866), *Middlemarch* (1871), and *Daniel Deronda* (1876). She also wrote poetry and satire.

BIBLIOGRAPHY

Bodenheimer, Rosemarie. *The Real Life of Mary Ann Evans: George Eliot, Her Letters and Fiction.* Ithaca, NY: Cornell University Press, 1994. 0-8014-2988-9, 295p. Bodenheimer posits that Evans' letters juxtaposed to Eliot's fiction give insight into the woman and the writer. She examines the "fiction" in fact or letters and the "fact" in fiction.

David, Deirdre. *Intellectual Women and Victorian Patriarchy: Harriet Martineau, Elizabeth Barrett Browning, George Eliot.* Ithaca, NY: Cornell University Press, 1987. 0-8014-1965-4, 273p. Although Eliot was not an exile from Victorian culture and society, she defied the patriarchal injunctions against female authorship. David explores writing as the business of her life, her celebrity, her intellect, and her control of the language.

Karl, Frederick Robert. *George Eliot: Voice of a Century: A Biography.* New York: Norton, 1995. 0-393-03785-1, 708p. Karl's discovery of an exchange of letters between Eliot and Herbert Spencer is the basis of his book on Eliot. The rather laborious text includes much research, but it sheds little new light on Eliot the woman.

McSweeney, Kerry. *George Eliot (Mary Ann Evans): A Literary Life.* New York: St. Martin's, 1991. 0-312-06574-4, 156p. McSweeney looks at Eliot's development as a novelist by examining her work and noting the biographical events, intellectual ideas, and social context in which Eliot wrote, along with commentary from contemporary critics.

Taylor, Ina. *A Woman of Contradictions: The Life of George Eliot.* New York: William Morrow, 1990. 0-688-09405-8, 255p. Taylor suggests in a carefully researched and recommended biography that the Cross (1968) and Haight (1969) biographies of Eliot were hagiography rather than careful looks at Eliot's life and work. She sees Eliot as the antithesis of the Victorian female with her assertiveness, her sensuality, and her materialistic interests.

ELIZABETH I of ENGLAND (1533–1603)

Queen   England

Elizabeth I ruled over the flowering of the English Renaissance. Daughter of Henry VIII and **Anne Boleyn**, Elizabeth was born on September 7, 1533, but was declared illegitimate in 1536, when her mother was executed. She was well educated and raised as a Protestant, and in 1549, she rejected the advances of Thomas Seymour, lord high admiral of England, who was subsequently executed for treason. Jane Seymour's son became Edward VI at Henry's death, and Mary ascended at Edward's death. **Mary I of England** suspected Elizabeth's Protestant affiliations and imprisoned her in the Tower. At Mary's death, the public preferred Elizabeth's Protestant connections and religious tolerance. She repealed Mary's Catholic legislation and established the Church of England. When the Spanish invaded in 1588, Elizabeth's navy defeated Philip II's armada. Although she allowed marriage negotiations to continue throughout her reign with foreign suitors, she never married because she knew that her successor, James VI of Scotland, was Protestant. She had court favorites such as Robert Dudley, earl of Leicester, and Robert Devereaux, earl of Essex (until his rebelliousness led to her executing him in 1601). Exploration flourished under her rule with Sir Francis Drake and Sir Walter Raleigh, but at home, a famine caused unrest. Her rule over Ireland allowed the British to enrich themselves at the expense of the natives, and a rebellion in 1597 under Hugh O'Neill, the earl of Tyrone, occurred. She continually perpetuated the concept of the "Virgin Queen."

BIBLIOGRAPHY

Erickson, Carolly. *The First Elizabeth.* New York: Summit, 1983. 0-671-41746-0, 446p. Erickson shows Elizabeth as manipulator, diplomat, and flirt in this entertaining and accessible biography. Her precarious childhood, in which a healthy child at seven months old was considered marriageable, prepared her to be a politician who withstood pressures to marry during her forty years as England's monarch.

Hackett, Helen. *Virgin Mother, Maiden Queen: Elizabeth I and the Cult of the Virgin Mary.* New York: St. Martin's, 1995. 0-312-12481-3, 303p. Elizabeth called herself "virgin mother, maiden queen." Hackett's critical and academic biography of Elizabeth examines the mythical aspects of her reign that either she or others perpetrated, including that she represented the Virgin Mary in a Protestant England.

Hibbert, Christopher. *The Virgin Queen: Elizabeth I, Genius of the Golden Age.* Reading, MA: Addison-Wesley, 1991. 0-201-15626-1, 287p. Hibbert's biography is a readable account of Elizabeth I's personal life with anecdotes, gossip, and illustrations.

Plowden, Alison. *Marriage with My Kingdom: The Courtships of Elizabeth I.* New York: Stein and Day, 1977. 0-8128-2338-9, 216p. Plowden's well-researched biography, using contemporary sources of the times, suggests that Elizabeth's possible liaisons in marriage were tools to overcome the Spanish, French, Austrian, and lesser Scandinavian kingdoms and that she never seriously considered marriage.

Somerset, Anne. *Elizabeth I.* New York: Knopf, 1991. 0-394-54435-8, 636p. Somerset's carefully researched and thoroughly documented look at Elizabeth I exposes motivations and backgrounds of the people over whom Elizabeth I had to keep control and explores Elizabeth's complexities and inconsistencies.

ELIZABETH II of ENGLAND (1926–)

Queen   England

Elizabeth II ascended the throne of England in 1953. Christened Elizabeth Alexandra Mary, the first child of Prince Albert, duke of York, and Elizabeth, born on April 21, 1926, never expected to be queen. She was educated privately by governesses and at a small school near Windsor Castle. Although she had to restrict her activities when her father unexpectedly became King George VI, she trained as a driver in the Auxiliary Territorial Service in 1944 during World War II. In 1947, she and Lieutenant Philip Mountbatten were engaged and then married at Westminster Abbey. In 1951, she had to start representing her father, who was ill, at state occasions abroad. In 1952, while she was in Kenya, she heard that he had died and that she was queen. She has toured the world for the Commonwealth, and as queen, is head of the Anglican Church and of the British Commonwealth.

BIBLIOGRAPHY

Bradford, Sarah. *Elizabeth: A Biography.* New York: Farrar, Straus, and Giroux, 1996. 0-374-14749-3, 564p. Bradford's biography of Elizabeth gives a careful and balanced account of her life, including public appearances and private agonies such as Prince Philip's indiscretions.

Davies, Nicholas. *Queen Elizabeth II: A Woman Who Is Not Amused.* Secaucus, NJ: Birch Lane, Carol, 1994. 1-55972-217-7, 640p. Davies thinks that Britain's monarchy is living its last days, and he explores the life of its monarch, Elizabeth II, in this popular biography. He fills her story with sensation, infidelity, and poor parenting decisions, although sometimes his documentation does not support his statements.

Flamini, Roland. *Sovereign: Elizabeth II and the Windsor Dynasty.* New York: Delacorte, 1991. 0-385-29917-6, 440p. Flamini's biography was published to coincide with Queen Elizabeth's sixty-fifth birthday, but it adds little since the years of 1983, giving only a little more political background than other biographies.

Harris, Kenneth. *The Queen.* New York: St. Martin's, 1995. 0-312-11878-3, 368p. Harris's biography of Elizabeth II gives a balanced, chronological overview of her life, emphasizing her conscientiousness.

Higham, Charles, and Roy Moseley. *Elizabeth and Philip: The Untold Story of the Queen of England and Her Prince.* New York: Doubleday, 1991. 0-385-26321-X, 516p. This biography, seemingly based on rumor, adds nothing new about the royal family or Queen Elizabeth.

ELIZABETH of HUNGARY (1207–1231)

Religious   **Hungary**

Elizabeth served people in need until her health failed when she was only twenty-four. When she was only fourteen, the daughter of King Andrew II of Hungary married Ludwig IV of Thuringia. Even though the marriage was arranged, the two loved each other, but Ludwig died while on a crusade. His brother drove Elizabeth out of the court by saying that her charitable endeavors were bankrupting the monarchy. After she provided for her three children, she joined an order of St. Francis and spent the rest of her life caring for the poor and the sick. Her confessor, Conrad of Marburg, was harsh and insensitive although intelligent, but he could not break her spirit. She was canonized in 1235.

BIBLIOGRAPHY

Uminski, Sigmund H. *The Royal Beggar: The Story of Saint Elizabeth of Hungary.* New York: Polish Publication Society, 1971. No ISBN, 71p. In this documented hagiography of Elizabeth, Uminski says that Conrad of Marburg, her inquisitor, eventually killed her with his intense questioning.

ELIZABETH of RUSSIA (1709–1762)

Empress   **Russia**

Elizabeth ruled Russia for twenty years, making her court competitive with the great capitals of Europe. As the daughter of Peter I, Elizabeth was intelligent and charming. She deposed the infant Ivan IV and his regent, Empress Anna, in 1741 after which she abolished the cabinet system of government but left business of the reign to her advisers. She founded the University of Moscow and the Academy of Arts in St. Petersburg. She helped the economy grow by establishing banks and developing eastern Russia. Her foreign policy saw success in the war against Sweden in 1741–1743 and in the alliances with France and Austria against Prussia in the Seven Years' War from 1756 to 1763.

BIBLIOGRAPHY

Anisimov, Evgeny V. *Empress Elizabeth: Her Reign and Her Russia, 1741–1761*. Trans. John T. Alexander. 1986. Gulf Breeze, FL: Academic International, 1995. 0-87569-140-4, 277p. In this well-documented and readable biography, Anisimov re-creates the times in which Empress Elizabeth lived and discusses the atmosphere that made her accession to the Russian throne possible.

Longworth, Philip. *The Three Empresses: Catherine I, Anne and Elizabeth of Russia*. London: Constable, 1972. 0-09-458040-5, 242p. Longworth compares the three empresses, Catherine I, Anne, and Elizabeth, because he sees them as succeeding in a man's world, although they were unprepared. Using diaries, memoirs, letters, and dispatches of the time, Longworth notes that Elizabeth helped corrupt her society while simultaneously pioneering Western fashions, sponsoring opera and theater, and supporting the Russian ballet.

ELIZABETH, QUEEN MOTHER (1900–)

Queen   England

Elizabeth became queen when her husband, George VI, had to become king at the abdication of his brother. Elizabeth Angela Marguerite Bowes-Lyon was the ninth of ten children, born at St. Paul's Waldenbury, Hitchin, Hertfordshire, on August 4, 1900. Her family descended from Robert the Bruce and owned a castle at Glamis, Scotland, where she spent her childhood and received her education. During World War I, she and her family cared for soldiers. In 1920, she met Prince Albert, "Bertie," but would not marry him until 1924. Two daughters, **Elizabeth II** and Margaret, were born in 1926 and 1928, respectively. The family enjoyed traveling and living quietly until Edward VIII abdicated in 1938. Elizabeth refused to leave London during the blitz, visiting areas of the city that the Germans had bombed. When her husband died, and her daughter became queen, she took the title "Queen Mother." In 1979, she became the 160th Warden of the Cinque Ports, the first woman in this position for nine hundred years.

BIBLIOGRAPHY

Donaldson, Frances Lonsdale. *King George VI and Queen Elizabeth*. Philadelphia: Lippincott, 1977. 0-397-01229-2, 127p. In this biography, Donaldson uses personal letters, diaries, recollections of friends, and photographs to show the warmth and courage in the leadership of George VI and Queen Elizabeth during one of the most difficult English reigns after the abdication and during World War II.

Morrow, Ann. *The Queen Mother*. Briarcliff Manor, NY: Stein and Day, 1985. 0-8128-3012-1, 241p. Morrow, a journalist, portrays the Elizabeth at home and in public in this biography. She includes many anecdotes and photographs in her colorful and entertaining account.

Mortimer, Penelope. *Queen Mother: An Alternative Portrait of Her Life and Times*. North Pomfret, VT: Trafalgar Square, 1996. 0-233-98972-2, 320p. Mortimer reveals the Queen Mother as the most endearing member of the royal family because of the stability and honor she has emitted. This popular biography is gossipy, well written, and enjoyable.

ELSSLER, FANNY (1810–1884)
Ballerina   Austria

Fanny Elssler was an engaging ballerina who delighted audiences in Europe and the United States. Franjziske Elssler, born June 23, 1810, was a member of a large and poor family; her father was copyist and valet to Haydn. She began dancing as a child with her sister and left Austria when fourteen to dance in Italy. At sixteen, the prince of Salerno pressured her into a liaison, but in Vienna the elderly intellectual Baron Von Gentz protected her. She had two children but refused to marry because she did not want to jeopardize her independence. She and her sister danced in London and Berlin before she made her debut in *La Tempête* at the Paris Opéra. Veron, her manager, encouraged professional competition between Elssler's dramatic, passionate style and **Marie Taglioni's** spiritual portrayals. Queen **Victoria** requested a royal command performance of Elssler and **Fanny Cerrito** dancing a *pas de deux*. In 1840, Elssler toured the United States, the first ballerina to do so, and, when she returned to Europe later than expected, the Paris Opéra sued her for breach of contract. She performed instead in London, La Scala in Milan, St. Petersburg, and Moscow.

BIBLIOGRAPHY
Guest, Ivor Forbes. *Fanny Elssler.* Middletown, CT: Wesleyan University Press, 1970. 0-8195-402-2, 284p. This well-researched but boring biography balances the private life of Elssler with her public life and contains reproductions of paintings, prints, and miniatures of Elssler.

EMECHETA, BUCHI (1944–)
Writer   Nigeria

Buchi Emecheta is one of Africa's most acclaimed contemporary women writers. The daughter of Jeremy and Alice Emecheta, born on July 21, 1944, she decided as a young girl that she would attend Western schools like her brother rather than become a second-class citizen. Her father died when she was nine, and her mother was "inherited" by her dead husband's brother. Emecheta went to live with her mother's cousin in Lagos and "borrowed" money for a scholarship application that won her four years at the prestigious Methodist Girls' High School. Instead of attending university as she wanted, she married and followed her husband to London, but when he burned the manuscript of her first book because he thought it would shame his family, she took her five children and left. She raised her children, and by the time she had obtained bachelor's and master's degrees from London University, she had written three novels. She has published thirteen novels, three autobiographical works, four children's books, and a collection of photographs, with translations into fourteen different languages. She received an honorary doctor of literature from Fairleigh Dickinson University.

BIBLIOGRAPHY
Emecheta, Buchi. *Head Above Water.* London: Heinemann, 1994. 0-435-90993-2, 229p. The autobiography spans Emecheta's life from Nigeria to England while writing as a single mother. She reveals her life and the pro-

cess of becoming an internationally acclaimed author writing in her fourth language.

Umeh, Marie, ed. *Emerging Perspectives on Buchi Emecheta.* Trenton, NJ: Africa World, 1995. 0-86543-454-9, 490p. This collection of essays about Emecheta's life and work also contains an interview with her. This book is essential for any reader wanting to know what Emecheta thinks important and reasons for her choice of subjects and themes for her fiction.

EVANS, EDITH (1888–1976)

Actor   England

Dame Edith Evans was a professional actress with flawless technique who always acted kindly and correctly whether onstage or offstage. Born in the Pimlico section of London on February 8, 1888, as daughter of a civil servant who disliked reading and a mother who read voraciously, Evans left school at fourteen to become apprenticed to a milliner and began acting as an amateur. In 1912, she appeared in Cambridge, and William Poel liked her work. He took her to London, where she starred in *Troilus and Cressida* under his direction. In 1924, she showed her comedy skill in Congreve's *The Way of the World.* For the next twenty years, she played Shakespearean roles at the Old Vic, Restoration comedy, Shaw, Chekhov, and the definitive Lady Bracknell in Wilde's *The Importance of Being Earnest.* She also played in movies, among them *Look Back in Anger* and *Tom Jones.* She received the Dame of the British Empire in 1946 for her service to the theater and London, Oxford, and Cambridge awarded her honorary degrees.

BIBLIOGRAPHY

Batters, Jean. *Edith Evans: A Personal Memoir.* London: Hart-Davis MacGibbon, 1977. 0-246-10994-7, 159p. Batters, Evans' secretary for twenty-five years, recalls Dame Edith as wonderful or maddening, a woman without natural beauty who could transform herself into a charmer.

Forbes, Bryan. *Dame Edith Evans, Ned's Girl.* Boston: Little, Brown, 1977. 0-316-28875-6, 297p. Evans wanted no authorized biography, but Forbes, her executor, wanted to write about her. After Forbes drafted interviews, Evans read the passages and refused to let Forbes omit any unfavorable but true information. The balanced biography covers her life.

$\mathfrak{F}$

FAITHFULL, EMILY (1835–1895)
Businesswoman   **England**

Emily Faithfull started a printing business, for which she hired only women, in 1857. As the youngest daughter to a clergyman, born on May 27, 1835, Faithfull's education taught her that women had limited choices in careers. After reading about the women who had helped with the new printing industry in the fifteenth century, she became the secretary of the first Society for Promoting Employment of Women in 1859, and the next year, she founded the Victoria Press in London. When she encouraged women to sit on stools while working when men who were doing the heavy lifting in the same shop could see them, people called her immoral. Her work showed excellence, however, and in 1862, she became the Printer and Publisher in Ordinary to the Queen. In addition to managing her firm, she lectured in London and in the United States, gave dramatic readings, wrote poetry and prose, helped with the *English Woman's Journal* and *Victoria Magazine,* and founded an International Musical, Dramatic and Literary Society. Her printing business continued after her death.

BIBLIOGRAPHY
Ratcliffe, Eric. *The Caxton of Her Age: The Career and Family Background of Emily Faithfull (1835–95).* Upton-upon-Severn, Worcestershire, England: Images, 1993. 1-897817-24-X, 96p. Ratcliffe highlights the actions and dedication of Faithfull to her chosen field. His biography, with references, is an accessible although loosely written overview of her life and work.
Stone, James S. *Emily Faithfull, Victorian Champion of Women's Rights.* Toronto: P. D. Meany, 1994. 0-88835-040-6, 336p. Stone exhibits much support for Faithfull's significance in the women's movement during the 1860s. He details her work for women's higher education, job training, equitable property rights, and suffrage in a text that catalogs many facts about her life.

FALLACI, ORIANA (1930–)
Writer   Italy

Oriana Fallaci has won awards for her investigative journalism. She was born in Florence on June 29, 1930, oldest daughter to an antifascist cabinetmaker. She attended the Liceo Galileo Galilei and says that she was a child of the Resistance during World War II, fighting under the name "Emilia." She began her journalism career while still a teenager as a special correspondent for an Italian newspaper. After a brief stint in medical school, she worked as a war correspondent in Vietnam, the Middle East, and South America. In Italy, she has won the St. Vincent Prize for Journalism twice, based on her interviews with supposedly inaccessible people such as the Ayatollah Khomeini. She has also written novels and nonfiction.

BIBLIOGRAPHY
Arico, Santo L. *Oriana Fallaci: The Woman and the Myth*. Carbondale: Southern Illinois University Press, 1997. 0-8093-2153-X. Arico examines Fallaci's life and career in a carefully researched and entertaining biography.

Fallaci, Oriana. *Interview with History*. New York: Liveright, 1976. 0-87140-590-3, 376p. Although a series of interviews with political leaders of the 1960s, Fallaci reveals much about her own opinions and attitudes in her reporting.

Gatt-Rutter, John. *Oriana Fallaci: The Rhetoric of Freedom*. Washington, DC: Berg, 1996. 1-85973-074-4, 212p. Although primarily a study of Fallaci's works, Gatt-Rutter acknowledges that Fallaci's life is inextricabily infused in her choice of subject and how she presented it.

FARJEON, ELEANOR (1881–1965)
Writer   England

Eleanor Farjeon wrote fantasies and children's stories, gaining a huge following of readers and winning awards. She was born on February 13, 1881, to a Jewish father who was always writing, so Farjeon thought she should write and began at age five. "Nellie" received her education at home, reading in her father's library of nine thousand books. For her children's books, she was the first recipient of the international Hans Christian Andersen Award and of the Regina Medal of the Catholic Library Association. She also received the Carnegie Medal in 1956 and was nominated in 1959 for Dame of the British Empire. Late in her life, she became a Catholic. Outstanding work in children's books today can earn a Farjeon Award.

BIBLIOGRAPHY
Farjeon, Annabel. *Morning Has Broken: A Biography of Eleanor Farjeon*. London: J. MacRae, 1986. 0-86203-225-3, 315p. Farjeon uses both published and unpublished memoirs and writing as bases for this carefully documented and balanced biography. It includes many details of Farjeon's life and relationships, since almost everyone she met and liked became one of her friends.

FARRENC, JEANNE-LOUISE (1804–1875)

Composer and Instrumentalist   France

Louise Farrenc was an accomplished pianist, composer of distinction, and editor of early keyboard music. Born on May 31, 1804, into an artistic family, she began piano and theory at six and by fifteen began studying composition and orchestration. She became the only woman in the nineteenth century to be a professor of piano at the Paris Conservatoire, but she functioned outside the cultural mainstream of midcentury Paris, preferring to follow her own interests. She worked on the little-known late sonatas of Beethoven, favoring abstract forms of the sonata and the symphony. In 1861, she won the first Académie des Beaux Arts Prix Chartier and won it again in 1869. She quietly pursued her career as a teacher, composer mainly of chamber music, and forerunner of the musical renaissance of the 1870s.

BIBLIOGRAPHY

Friedland, Bea. *Louise Farrenc, 1804-1875: Composer, Performer, Scholar.* Ann Arbor, MI: UMI Research, 1980. 0-8357-1111-0, 269p. Friedland traces the course of Farrenc's musical career and surveys the opinion of her contemporaries, finding her a rare musical personality in this scholarly, documented, and technical biography with musical references.

FAWCETT, MILLICENT (1847–1929)

Activist   England

Millicent Garrett Fawcett campaigned for woman's rights and suffrage. She was born on June 11, 1847, in Aldeburgh, Suffolk, the daughter of a merchant. After attending formal school as a teenager, she, her sister Elizabeth Garrett Anderson, and Emily Davies became concerned about women's inequality. She served on the first suffrage committee in 1867 and worked for the married Woman's Property Act. After her husband died in 1884, she led a separate society for woman's rights, but in 1897, united with the National Union of Women Suffrage Societies and became president. Her trips to Ireland, stand against home rule, and inquiries into South African Boer War concentration camps made her famous. Fawcett spoke throughout England and lobbied Parliament members for suffrage and other rights, stopping only during World War I. She also wrote nonfiction, including *Life of Queen Victoria* (1895), *Women's Suffrage* (1912), and *Women's Victory and After* (1918). In 1925, she received the honor of Dame of the British Empire.

BIBLIOGRAPHY

Fawcett, Millicent. *What I Remember.* New York: Hyperion, 0-88355-261-2, 271p. In Fawcett's family, the oldest child had died soon after birth, so Fawcett was never sure whether she had the good fortune of being the seventh, or merely eighth, child. Her recollections also cover her activities as a champion of woman's rights and suffrage.

Rubinstein, David. *A Different World for Women: The Life of Millicent Garrett Fawcett.* Columbus: Ohio State University Press, 1991. 0-8142-0564-X, 320p. In this balanced and thoroughly documented biography, Rubinstein shows Fawcett as a woman of exceptional talent and achievement who became a principal although controversial leader of the suffragist movement.

FERRIER, SUSAN (1782–1854)
Writer   Scotland

Susan Ferrier wrote the first Scottish novels of manners containing complex, contradictory characters. Born on September 7, 1782, as the tenth child of a clerk in Edinburgh, she became a housekeeper for her father when she was fifteen. She seemed ordinary to persons outside her circle, but to those she knew, she revealed a sharp wit and a strong sense of the ridiculous. Friends of her father's who visited the house included Sir Walter Scott. Ferrier wrote her book *Marriage* in 1810 but did not publish it until 1818. After that, Scott encouraged and supported her writing with its reputation for representing her society so well from a woman's point of view. She wrote *The Inheritance* (1824) and *Destiny* (1831) before becoming an Evangelical. When she joined the Free Church, she ceased to write and devoted her life to charity and campaigns against drink and slavery.

BIBLIOGRAPHY
Cullinan, Mary. *Susan Ferrier*. Boston: Twayne, 1984. 0-8057-6878-5, 135p.
  Cullinan discusses Ferrier's life and her work as a conservative social satirist who made her place in Scottish fiction with only three novels, all competent observations of her society.

FIELDS, GRACIE (1898–1979)
Entertainer   England

Gracie Fields' comic songs and sentimental ballads and especially her films delighted English audiences. Born on January 9, 1898, in Rochdale, Lancashire, as May Stansfield to a cargo boat engineer and a mother determined for her to succeed, she began performing as a child and became a professional at the age of twelve. For ten years, beginning in 1915, she toured the country in Archie Pitt's revues, marrying him in 1923. Five years later, she made the first of nine Royal Command Performances. During the depression, she kept her performances happy, and by 1938, she was supposedly the highest-paid performer in the world. In 1940, after divorcing Pitt, she married an Italian. Since he was unwelcome in England during the war, she went to Hollywood, made films, and entertained British troops on the front. Although she spent nearly forty years abroad, her British audiences continued calling her "Our Gracie." In 1979, she became a Dame of the British Empire.

BIBLIOGRAPHY
Burgess, Muriel, with Tommy Keen. *Gracie Fields*. London: W. H. Allen, 1980. 0-491-02623-4, 125p. In this well-documented biography of Fields, Burgess gives an overview of Fields' life. Burgess also traces the ebb and flow of popular opinion when people, without all the facts, called Fields a traitor in 1940 but welcomed her home when she performed for troops during World War II.
Moules, Joan. *Our Gracie: The Life of Dame Gracie Fields*. London: R. Hale, 1983. 0-7090-1010-9, 247p. Moules thinks that Fields was the greatest female artist ever to perform in Britain. In this biased but enjoyable biography, Moules looks at Fields as comedienne, singer of serious and comic songs, and actress.

FIRST, RUTH (1925–1982)
Writer and Revolutionary   South Africa

Ruth First worked for, and wrote about, changing South Africa's political balance so that all races would have freedom. As the daughter of middle-class Jewish socialist parents who had immigrated to South Africa from the Baltics, First joined the Communist Party while a university student. She campaigned first for black mine workers and then black farmworkers. In Johannesburg, she edited journals, which the government soon banned and for which they tried her and her husband at the Treason Trial. They were acquitted, but in 1963, after publication of *South West Africa*, she was arrested and in solitary confinement for six months (retold in the film *A World Apart*). She left South Africa for England and taught at Manchester and the University of Durham. In 1979, she went to Mozambique to teach, and there a letter bomb killed her. Throughout her life, she published books about her experiences and her concerns.

BIBLIOGRAPHY

First, Ruth. *117 days*. New York: Monthly Review Press, 1989. 0-85345-790-5, 170p. First recounts questions that authorities asked her during her solitary confinement and embellishes her answers with anecdotes about people she had known throughout her life.

Pinnock, Don. *Ruth First*. Cape Town, South Africa: Maskew Miller Longman, 1995. 68p. The text covers First and her political concerns as a South African communist activist.

FLAGSTAD, KIRSTEN (1895–1962)
Opera Singer   Norway

Kirsten Flagstad memorized the part of Elsa in Wagner's *Lohengrin* when she was only ten but made her professional debut in d'Albert's *Tiefland*. Born on July 12, 1895, she remained in Scandinavia until she went to Bayreuth, Germany, in 1933 to sing small roles. In 1935, she sang the Wagner roles of Sieglinde, Isolde, and Brünhilde in New York. The next year, she debuted at Covent Garden, singing roles of Isolde, Senta, Brünhilde, and Kundry. When her second husband joined the Nazi Party of Norway (Quisling), the United States began to suspect her loyalty, although she accepted invitations to sing only in neutral countries. People picketed her performances in the United States until 1952. After her retirement, she helped the new Norwegian State Opera.

BIBLIOGRAPHY

Vogt, Howard. *Flagstad: Singer of the Century*. New York: Secker and Warburg, 1987. 0-436-55800-9, 300p. Vogt's biography, using Rein's authorized biography, includes long passages about Flagstad's devotion to music but not much about her return to Nazi-occupied Norway or her hostility toward her daughter and the tenor Lauritz Melchior.

FONTEYN, MARGOT (1919–1991)
Ballerina   England

Margot Fonteyn became a ballerina of international renown. Born on May 18, 1919, Peggy Hookham lived in China, the United States, and Southeast Asia as a child, but was the first international ballerina to have the majority of her training in England. When fifteen, she joined the Vic-Wells Ballet School, with her first performance being a snowflake in *Casse Noisette*. The next year, she became a soloist with her first starring role as Young Tregennis in de Valois' *Haunted Ballroom*, and the same year, she danced Odette. She studied in Paris with Olgo Preobrajenska and Mathilde Kschessingskaya before appearing throughout the world in a variety of classic roles and new ballets created by choreographers such as Frederick Ashton. In 1954, she became president of the Royal Academy of Dancing; the next year, she married Dr. Roberto Arias, a politician from Panama, moved to his home, and experienced a different world of diplomacy and politics. The same year, she became a Dame of the British Empire. In 1959, she became Guest Artist to the Royal Ballet. She began her partnership with Rudolf Nureyev in 1962, which helped to popularize ballet.

BIBLIOGRAPHY

Bland, Alexander. *Fonteyn and Nureyev: The Story of a Partnership*. New York: Times, 1979. 0-8129-0860-0, 207p. The text discusses the professional and personal relationship between Fonteyn and Nureyev during the ten years they danced together, with accompanying photographs.

Crickmay, Anthony, and Mary Clarke. *Margot Fonteyn*. Brooklyn, NY: Dance Horizons, 1976. 0-87127-086-2, 20p. Crickmay and Clarke discuss Fonteyn's hard work and discipline, allowing her to become a great ballerina. This brief overview of her life, undocumented, includes photographs of her practicing or in performance.

Fonteyn, Margot, Dame. *Margot Fonteyn: Autobiography*. New York: Knopf, 1976. 0-394-48570-X, 266p. Fonteyn presents an account of her life and career by recalling some of the great moments of the Royal Ballet and the different excitement in her marriage to a politician whom a would-be assassin crippled. She emphasizes her life outside ballet.

Money, Keith. *Fonteyn and Nureyev: The Great Years*. New York: Harvill, HarperCollins, 1994. 0-00-271375-6, 256p. Money's biography for dance aficionados includes many previously unpublished photographs of Fonteyn and Nureyev. They show the artists informally and also their emotional power and style in performance that won them box office sellouts. Money's commentary discusses situations in which he took the photographs. He says that the young Nureyev renewed the aging Fonteyn's career, but they complemented each other admirably.

Money, Keith. *Fonteyn: The Making of a Legend*. New York: Reynal, 1974. 0-688-61163-X, 318p. Over eight hundred photographs of Fonteyn in almost all of her roles reveal her talent. The brief text contains review excerpts so that Fonteyn's life emerges visually.

FRAME, JANET (1924–)

Writer   New Zealand

Janet Frame found an international audience for her writing before New Zealanders recognized her worth. A native of Oamaru, near Dunedin, born on July 28, 1924, and daughter of an impoverished railway engineer, Frame attended Otago University and became a teacher before shifting to nurse-companion. She suffered mental problems and spent many years intermittently in hospitals, where she read the classics and began to write. She moved to London in 1956, and wrote about her hospital experience in *Faces in the Water* (1961). Her writing has universalized the experience of being a New Zealander and has explored the difficulties of communication and establishing a personal view. She won the Commonwealth Prize for Literature, the New Zealand Scholarship in Letters, and the Turnovsky Prize. She has been both a Robert Burns and a Sargeson fellow as well as an Additional Member of the Order of New Zealand and an honorary foreign member of the American Academy of Arts and Letters. She was awarded the Dame Commander of the British Empire and honorary doctorates from the University of Otago and the University of Waikato along, with the Massey University Medal.

BIBLIOGRAPHY
Alley, Elizabeth, ed. *The Inward Sun: Celebrating the Life and Work of Janet Frame.* Wellington, New Zealand: Daphne Brasell Associates, 1994. 0-908896-39-5, 214p. This collection of diverse, personal essays in honor of Janet Frame shows how others reacted to her writing and how it influenced their lives.

Evans, Patrick. *Janet Frame.* Boston: Twayne, 1977. 0-8057-6254-X, 228p. Evans examines Frame's life and the universality of her writing, which contains a mythic importance beyond her local New Zealand upbringing.

Frame, Janet. *To the Is-land: An Autobiography.* New York: G. Braziller, 1982. 0-8076-1042-9, 253p. In this autobiography, Frame recalls tales of childhood and adolescence, interspersing them with her own experiences so that she gains more depth than most in describing the activities of a child.

FRANCO, VERONICA (1546–1591)
Poet   Italy

Veronica Franco wrote poetry and thought that she had the right to choose the men whom she loved. A native and citizen of Venice, Franco's family was neither rich nor powerful, and her mother became a courtesan. Franco married a doctor but left him for a series of love affairs, including liaisons with two poets and King Henri III of France. Although women could not participate in Venice's intellectual society, publishing houses printed their opinions. Franco's poetry and letters, written mainly between 1570 and 1580, and her independence disturbed the authorities. In 1580, the Inquisition charged her with witchcraft or the power to make men fall in love with her. She won her trial using a language of self-defense in which she countered that men maltreated women. As a Venetian courtesan, however, she was expected to provide cultivated company and good conversation. Her poetry was energetic and sexually explicit for her times, but she recognized that women whom men had abandoned needed help. The same year as her trial, she announced that women of the streets needed a home, and the year she died, a home for them was opened, with two of her wills leaving them money. Critics neglected her work after her death, but in the twentieth century, volumes of her poems and letters have been reissued.

BIBLIOGRAPHY
Rosenthal, Margaret F. *The Honest Courtesan: Veronica Franco, Citizen and Writer in Sixteenth-Century Venice.* Chicago: University of Chicago Press, 1992. 0-226-72811-0, 391p. This first major study of Franco is a scholarly, well-documented accounting of her life, her times, and her work.

FRANK, ANNE (1929–1945)
Writer   The Netherlands

After Anne Frank's Jewish family moved into the back second-story rooms of a warehouse and office facing an Amsterdam canal during the German Occupation of Holland in World War II, she kept a diary of their days inside. Born on June 12, 1929, into a comfortable, Jewish middle-class family, she attended school in Amsterdam before the war. In the cramped living space with six other people who had to keep quiet during the day and invisible from the windows at all times, she expressed her feelings about this situation and her hopes for escape and returning to a normal life. After three years, someone told the Germans of their location, and they were transported. She died of typhus in Bergen-Belsen, and only her father survived. A friend gave him Anne's diary and her other writings which had been left in their hiding place, and he published the diary in 1947 as *Het Achterhuis* (The Diary of a Young Girl). It has been translated into thirty languages, while the house where she hid is now open to the public with an extensive display of memorabilia about Anne and her family and Jews in Amsterdam during the war.

BIBLIOGRAPHY

Frank, Anne. *The Diary of a Young Girl: The Definitive Edition.* Ed. Otto H. Frank and Mirjam Pressler. Trans. Susan Massotty. New York: Doubleday, 1995. 0-385-47378-8, 352p. This edition of Anne Frank's diary, including previously unpublished photographs, contains over 30 percent more material than the original edition published in 1947.

Gies, Miep. *Anne Frank Remembered: The Story of the Woman Who Helped to Hide the Frank Family.* New York: Simon and Schuster, 1988. Paper, 0-671-66234-1, 256p. Gies aided the Frank family when they needed a place to hide in Amsterdam. She discusses the drama of this situation and her interaction with Frank.

Lindwer, Willy. *The Last Seven Months of Anne Frank.* Trans. Alison Marsschaert. New York: Anchor, 1992. Paper, 0-385-42360-8, 204p. Each of the six Dutch Holocaust survivors whom Lindwer interviewed and filmed knew Anne Frank. They tell about her final days as well as their own backgrounds, their Nazi capture, their experiences in the camps, and what happened to them when they were liberated.

Van Der Rol, Ruud, and Rian Verhoeven. *Anne Frank: Beyond the Diary: A Photographic Remembrance.* Trans. Tony Langham and Plym Peters. New York: Puffin, 1995. Paper, 0-14-036926-0, 128p. This look at Anne Frank explores the meanings behind her diary and how they reveal universal needs and longings of young females. It includes diary excerpts and photographs from her childhood. *Christopher Award, American Library Association Notable Book, A Publishers' Weekly Nonfiction Book of the Year, Booklist Editor's Choice, Mildred L. Batchelder Honor, and Bulletin Blue Ribbon.*

FRANKLIN, MILES (1879–1954)
Writer   Australia

Miles Franklin wrote about Australia in her novels. Born into a pioneer family trying to farm in Talbingo, New South Wales, on October 14, 1879, Stella Marian Sarah was educated at home and at a local school. She worked as a governess from 1897, giving her money to the family. She began her first novel at eighteen and finished it six months later. In it she put her feelings of oddness, plainness, of being unloved, her passions, and her ambition. She sent it to Henry Lawson, and he helped her publish it in England in 1901 as *My Brilliant Career.* It brought her great fame, to which she had difficulty adjusting. In 1902, she became affiliated with feminist groups, and then she became more interested in Christian Science. In 1906, after refusing a proposal of marriage, she went to the United States where she met Jane Addams and helped the Women's Trade Union League. She went to Macedonia with a Scottish women's hospital unit in the second half of World War I. In World War II, she refused to support the nationalist view. She won a prize for her book *All That Swagger* (1936), receiving congratulations from friends around the globe. The Miles Franklin Award is the annual literary prize in Australia.

BIBLIOGRAPHY

Coleman, Verna. *Miles Franklin in America: Her Unknown (Brilliant) Career.* London: Angus and Robertson, 1981. 0-207-14536-9, 219p. Coleman used Franklin's pocket diaries from 1909 to 1916, manuscripts, and pictures to trace Franklin's personas in America as Stella Franklin, in London as Brent of Bin Bin, and in Australia as Miles Franklin.

Franklin, Miles. *Childhood at Brindabella: My First Ten Years.* Sydney: Angus and Robertson, 1974. 0-207-13150-3, 162p. Franklin wrote this autobiography in 1952–1953 about her first ten years, recalling herself wearing a red nightdress at ten months. She wanted to show a happy childhood to contrast with many memoirs detailing unhappy ones.

Franklin, Miles. *My Congenials: Miles Franklin and Friends in Letters.* Ed. Jill Roe. Pymble, New South Wales, Australia: Angus and Robertson, 1993. Vol. 1, 0-207-16925-X, 351p. Franklin was a prolific letter writer because friends or congenials could ease life's difficulties. Only eight letters survive from the 1880s, but these letters cover 1879–1938.

Franklin, Miles. *My Congenials: Miles Franklin and Friends in Letters.* Ed. Jill Roe. Pymble, New South Wales, Australia: Angus and Robertson, 1993. Vol. 2, 0-207-17860-7, 356p. Roe has arranged Franklin's letters chronologically and added commentary as necessary. In 1952, Franklin received 438 letters.

Roderick, Colin Arthur. *Miles Franklin: Her Brilliant Career.* New York: Rigby, 1982. 0-7270-1696-2, 199p. Roderick's thoroughly researched biography of Franklin and her family includes labeled photographs with an annotated chronology following the main text.

FRANKLIN, ROSALIND (1920–1958)

Scientist   England

Rosalind (Elsie) Franklin was one of the persons who discovered and explained the double-helical structure of the DNA molecule. She was born on July 25, 1920, into a family of Orthodox Jews who were activists. Her father pursued a variety of commitments, including voluntary work at the Working Men's College. He was a vice principal who had been unable to attend either Oxford or Cambridge because of his military service and his early marriage. Franklin's mother's family had given her an intellectual background. Franklin studied at St. Paul's Girls' School and then went to Cambridge University and became a researcher in physical chemistry and molecular biology. She worked with a variety of associations doing research that involved the physical structure of coals and carbons and the structure of DNA and viruses. She died at thirty-seven and did not receive the credit granted to the other two persons working on DNA, James Watson and Frederick Crick, with the 1962 Nobel Prize. However, the discovery would not have occurred as soon or perhaps at all without her contribution.

BIBLIOGRAPHY

Sayre, Anne. *Rosalind Franklin and DNA.* New York: Norton, 1975. 0-393-07493-5, 221p. Sayre begins her story of Franklin by noting that in *The Double Helix,* James Watson referred to a "Rosy." None of Rosalind Franklin's friends had ever called her "Rosy," so Sayre sees Watson's casual attitude as a way of dismissing Franklin's contributions to the discovery of DNA. Sayre relates Franklin's singular desire to be a scientist, attitudes toward women in science, and the misstatements that Watson made in his book.

FREUD, ANNA (1895–1982)

Psychoanalyst   Austria

Anna Freud followed her father into psychoanalysis, excelled in the study of child psychology, and developed important theories. Born on December 3, 1895, as the youngest child of Sigmund Freud, Anna Freud left school to teach and then became her father's secretary and pupil. She became an active member of the International Psychoanalytical Association in 1922, and in 1925, she became secretary of the Vienna Training Institute, directed by **Helene Deutsch.** During the next two years, she started observing children and gave a series of lectures about their behavior. She followed the "Continental" school and wrote *The Ego and the Mechanisms of Defence* (1937). When the Nazis threatened Austrian Jews, Freud moved to England with her father in 1938. After his death, she continued her work and in 1952, became the director of the Hampstead Child Therapy Clinic. She returned to Vienna in 1971, and received an honorary doctorate from Vienna University the next year. She also received honors from other universities for her work on child psychology.

BIBLIOGRAPHY

Coles, Robert. *Anna Freud: The Dream of Psychoanalysis.* Boston: Addison-Wesley, 1992. 0-201-57707-0, 220p. While using some of Freud's unpublished letters and his personal interviews with her, Coles makes this readable biography an important resource. Coles traces her stages of teacher, theorist, healer, leader, idealist, and writer and places her within the historical and physical setting in which they occurred.

Freud, Anna. *Anna Freud's Letters to Eva Rosenfeld.* Ed. Peter Heller. Trans. Mary Weigand. Madison, CT: International Universities, 1992. 0-8236-0152-8, 210p. These letters, written between 1920 and 1932, give a perspective of friendship and life prior to World War II. During this time, Freud was caring for her ailing father and building her own professional identity and career.

Peters, Uwe Henrik. *Anna Freud: A Life Dedicated to Children.* New York: Schocken, 1985. 0-8052-3910-3, 281p. Peters uses a combination of brief vignettes to show Freud's devotion to her father, her personal strength, and her humility.

Sayers, Janet. *Mothers of Psychoanalysis: Helene Deutsch, Karen Horney, Anna Freud, Melanie Klein.* New York: Norton, 1991. 0-393-03041-5, 319p. Sayers looks at each one of these psychoanalysts in terms of their roles as mothers, in Freudian terms. Each identified the importance of the mother in her work. A short overview of Anna Freud's life and her contribution to psychoanalysis is a good introduction.

Young-Bruehl, Elisabeth. *Anna Freud: A Biography.* New York: Summit, 1988. 0-671-61696-X, 527p. The first authorized biography after Freud's death, Young-Bruehl probes psychoanalysis as well as Freud. Based on correspondence, manuscripts, poetry, dream interpretations, and interviews with Freud's friends, colleagues, and analysands, Young-Bruehl presents a sympathetic and thorough life.

FRY, ELIZABETH (1780–1845)
Activist
England

As a member of a famous Quaker family from Norfolk, Elizabeth Gurney exposed the pitiable state of women in prison, lunatics, and the poor. She was born on May 21, 1780, to a wool stapling and spinning factory owner who had been barred from attending university and holding civil office because he was a Friend. Fry's mother died when Fry was twelve, and at eighteen, Fry became an Anglican. When she married Joseph Fry, she returned to the Friends. She became concerned about conditions at Newgate Prison in London, and in 1817, she established a prisoners' aid society to help the women and children. She campaigned for improvements in the conditions for prisoners being transported to Australia, and during the 1820s, she toured prisons throughout the country and demanded reform. She also identified the need for employment and adequate housing for the poor in London. Her husband's bankruptcy in 1828 stopped many of her public activities, but she continued visiting those in need. Her achievement was extraordinary because, even while raising ten children, she made males listen to the needs of the poor.

BIBLIOGRAPHY
Rose, June. *Elizabeth Fry.* New York: St. Martin's, 1981. 0-312-24248-4, 218p. Rose studied the 561,000 words of Fry's journals to write the book, and her well-documented biography of Fry is readable and recommended.

Whitney, Janet. *Elizabeth Fry, Quaker Heroine.* 1937. New York: B. Blom, 1972. No ISBN, 327p. Whitney has researched Fry's life, and this fictional biography with created dialogue reads like a novel. Although suitable for young adult readers, Rose's authentic biography is preferable.

G

GALLI-CURCI, AMELITA (1889–1963)
Opera Singer   **Italy**

Amelita Galli-Curci's commercial recordings after her rise to renown as an opera star rivaled those of the Italian tenor Enrico Caruso in popularity. Born in Milan on November 18, 1889, into a family with musical interests, she began studying piano at five and saw her first opera, *Les Hugenots*, at seven. She attended the German International Institute and the Liceo Alessandro Manzoni, where she learned languages. She taught herself how to sing and used cylinder recordings of her voice to check her progress. She made her debut in 1909 in Rome and sang with the Chicago Opera Association from 1916 to 1925 and in New York from 1920 to 1930 as one of the most renowned coloraturas of all time, portraying roles in operas such as Delibes' *Lakme* and Donizetti's *Lucia di Lammermoor*. A thyroid condition forced her to retire in 1930.

BIBLIOGRAPHY
Le Massena, C. E. *Galli-Curci's Life of Song.* Beverly Hills, CA: Monitor, 1978. 0-91773-40-0, 280p. Le Massena thinks that Galli-Curci had the advantages of talent, environment, and aesthetic development in her family and Italian culture, and she supports it with examples in a popular biography that appends an interview in which Galli-Curci emphasizes the importance of simplicity. Photographs highlight the text.

GANDHI, INDIRA (1917–1984)
Politician   **India**

Indira Gandhi became the first female leader of a country with the second largest population in the world of 500 million. Indira Nehru was born on November 19, 1917, to Jawaharlal Nehru, a man who opposed the British rule of India, and she watched him go back and forth to prison for speaking against the British government. As a teenager, she, too, became active in politics and the movement for independence, spending most of 1942 in jail. The same year, she married Feroze Gandhi (no relation to Mohandas Gandhi). When India won independence in 1947, Indira Gandhi's father became the prime minister, and, when accompanying her father on his travels, Gandhi pursued her own political career. In 1959, as chairperson of the ruling Congress Party, she tried to get women and young people concerned about social issues, and in 1964, after her father's death, she was elected to the Indian Parliament, where she became minister of information and broadcasting. Her father's successor died in 1966, and people picked her to become the prime minister of the Indian democracy. She instituted programs to fight hunger, created "fair price" shops to stabilize the price of rice, combated the severe poverty, and worked to stop ethnic problems. Economic conditions worsened, however, and in 1975, she declared a state of emergency and changed the rule from a democracy to her personal control. In 1977, she lost reelection, but in 1980, she returned to office. In 1984, a Sikh on her security force assassinated her.

BIBLIOGRAPHY
Carras, Mary C. *Indira Gandhi: In the Crucible of Leadership: A Political Biography*. Boston: Beacon, 1979. 0-8070-0242-9, 289p. In her balanced biography, Carras is sympathetic to Gandhi after interviewing her, although she thinks that Gandhi might have lost her power because of her indecision and her lack of a clear strategy.

Jayakar, Pupul. *Indira Gandhi: An Intimate Biography*. New York: Pantheon, 1993. 0-679-42479-2, 448p. Jayakar, one of Gandhi's intimate friends for over thirty years, presents a balanced and recommended look at her public and private lives based on her memories, taped interviews, contemporary diaries, and correspondence. Jayakar's young Gandhi, lonely but ambitious and idealistic, sacrificed her marriage and her relationship to her sons.

Malhotra, Inder. *Indira Gandhi: A Personal and Political Biography*. Boston: Northeastern University Press, 1991. 1-55553-095-8, 363p. Malhotra's biography of Gandhi is well written and balanced. He incorporates contemporary history into his portrait of Gandhi both in and out of office after interviewing Gandhi many times while a journalist, which allows him material not available elsewhere.

Masani, Zareer. *Indira Gandhi: A Biography*. New York: T. Y. Crowell, 1976. 0-690-00169-X, 341p. With the cooperation of Gandhi and access to her correspondence, Masani creates a background of Indian history in which he assesses her performance as prime minister.

Moraes, Dom F. *Indira Gandhi*. Boston: Little, Brown, 1980. 0-316-58191-7, 336p. Moraes knew Gandhi well and interviewed her many times. He gives a reasonably balanced view of her and her government in a well-written and accessible biography by noting her tendency to care about people but also to be able to rapidly discard them.

GARBO, GRETA (1905–1990)
Actor   Sweden

Greta Garbo became a familiar face in Hollywood as a silent film star. Greta Lovisa Gustafsson was born into a poor Stockholm family on September 18, 1905, in a four-room cold-water walk-up with her father poor or out of work throughout her childhood. Her father died, and at fourteen she worked in a barbershop. When she changed jobs to salesgirl, her short role in a publicity film led to her eventual enrollment in the Royal Dramatic Theatre School.

Mauritz Stiller chose her to play in *The Story of Gösta Berling* in 1924, became her manager, and took her with him to Hollywood. She became a silent film star in *The Torrent* (1926). Stiller left, but Garbo stayed and made ten silent films before *Anna Christie* in 1930. Films included *Mata Hari, The Grand Hotel, Queen Christina,* and *Anna Karenina.* Her last film, during World War II, was a failure. She quit films but received a special Academy Award in 1954 for her work.

BIBLIOGRAPHY

Paris, Barry. *Garbo: A Biography.* New York: Knopf, 1995. 0-394-58020-6, 654p. This biography of Garbo, based on fifty years of correspondence with screenwriter Salka Viertel and one hundred hours of taped telephone conversations with confidant and New York art dealer Sam Green, is the definitive biography now available about Garbo's life.

Payne, Robert. *The Great Garbo.* New York: Praeger, 1976. 0-275-34000-7, 297p. In this short, undocumented biography, Payne recounts the unimportant movies that propelled Garbo to fame, emphasizing the misconceptions about her in Hollywood and examining the "face" and "presence" she became for the movie industry.

Vickers, Hugo. *Loving Garbo: The Story of Greta Garbo, Cecil Beaton, and Mercedes de Acosta.* New York: Random House, 1994. 0-679-41301-4, 333p. Vickers has used previously unpublished entries from Beaton's diaries and letters from Beaton to Garbo as well as interviews and other sources to tell about these relationships and café society in the 1930s to 1950s.

Walker, Alexander. *Garbo: A Portrait.* New York: Macmillan, 1980. 0-02-622950-1, 191p. In this valuable portrait of Garbo, Walker has used the Metro-Goldwyn-Mayer files of studio memos, contracts, telegrams, and letters of the 1920s through the 1940s.

GARDEN, MARY (1874–1967)

Opera Singer   Scotland

Mary Garden became known for her performance of the operatic role in Debussy's *Mélisande,* and she recorded many of Debussy's songs with him. She was born in Scotland on February 20, 1874, and came to the United States as a child, where she studied singing in Chicago. Scheduled to open as Micaela in *Carmen* in Paris in 1900, she debuted earlier in Charpentier's *Louise* when the star collapsed. Massenet asked her to debut his *Chérubin* in 1905 and his *Thaïs* at the Manhattan Opera House in 1907. Garden's characterization through gesture, vocal inflection, and controversial costume made her more famous than her singing. From 1910 to 1930, she starred at the Chicago Opera and served as its director for the 1921–1922 season. Her last operatic performance was in 1934 at the Opéra Comique.

BIBLIOGRAPHY

Garden, Mary, and Louis Biancolli. *Mary Garden's Story.* 1951. New York: Arno, 1980. 0-405-12840-1, 302p. Garden remembers first singing at five and enjoying the experience of entertaining. In this memoir with accompanying photographs, she describes the places where she sang and the people whom she met.

Turnbull, Michael. *Mary Garden.* Portland, OR: Timber, 1997. 1-57467-017-4, 250p. In this biography, Turnbull captures the substance of the private Garden and shows how she learned to promote herself. It includes notes from a master class about her approach and interpretation of various roles.

GASKELL, ELIZABETH (1810–1865)
Writer   **England**

Mrs. Gaskell gained fame with realistic novels full of careful details. One year after Elizabeth Stevenson was born on September 29, 1810, in London to a Unitarian minister and his wife, her mother died. Her aunt in Cheshire raised her, and when fifteen, she attended Avonbank School, Stratford, for two years. After her father and brother died, she stayed with a variety of relatives before marrying William Gaskell, a Unitarian minster and college English teacher, in 1832. When her baby son William died of scarlet fever in 1845, she published her first novel, *Mary Barton,* in which she chastised contemporary employment conditions. It was a success, and she began contributing to magazines, including Dickens' *Household Words.* In *Ruth* and *North and South,* she discussed subjects such as a girl who has been unwillingly seduced and impregnated. After meeting **Charlotte Brontë** and visiting her at Haworth in 1853, she wrote Brontë's biography.

BIBLIOGRAPHY
Bonaparte, Felicia. *The Gypsy-Bachelor of Manchester: The Life of Mrs. Gaskell's Demon.* Charlottesville: University Press of Virginia, 1992. 0-8139-1390-X, 310p. An examination of Gaskell's work by theme, image, diction, characters, and plot leads Bonaparte to assert that Gaskell had an antithetical self opposing the feminine angel, an inner demon or "gypsy-bachelor."

Flint, Kate. *Elizabeth Gaskell.* Plymouth, England: Northcote House, 1995. 0-7463-0718-7, 74p. A brief biography precedes an analysis of how Gaskell's major fiction reflected her own thoughts and life, emphasizing the theme of conflicting senses of identity.

Gerin, Winifred. *Elizabeth Gaskell: A Biography.* 1980. New York: Oxford University Press, 1990. 0-19-281296-3, 318p. Gerin's well-researched and documented biography of Gaskell is recommended for her writing and for her revelations about Gaskell. Whitbread Award.

Spencer, Jane. *Elizabeth Gaskell.* New York: St. Martin's, 1993. 0-312-06058-0, 156p. In her introductory biography, Spencer uses Gaskell's letters and some of the recent feminist criticisms of her work to show her conflicts as a woman artist in the Victorian period and a Unitarian woman on the fringes of society lacking self-confidence.

Uglow, Jennifer S. *Elizabeth Gaskell: A Habit of Stories.* New York: Farrar, Straus, and Giroux, 1993. 0-374-14751-5, 690p. Uglow's excellent biography reveals a highly accomplished novelist who represented the most positive values of Victorianism. As well as being a good wife and mother, Gaskell was radically against social injustice.

GENTILESCHI, ARTEMISIA (1590–c. 1642)
Artist   Italy

Artemisia Gentileschi was an artist who knew Michelangelo. Born on July 8, 1590, as the eldest child and only daughter of a painter who trained her and boasted of her achievements, Gentileschi's mother died when she was twelve. In 1612, her father brought a rape case against Agostino Tassi after Tassi had promised to marry Gentileschi and then delayed unreasonably. The resulting publicity gave her independence, and she moved to Florence two years later. In two more years, when she was only twenty-three, she became a member of the Florentine Accademia del Disegno. She was the only known female follower of Caravaggio, but she used his realism differently from his male followers. Michelangelo commissioned her work for the ceiling of Casa Buonarroti while she was working on her *Judith and Holofernes* and *Judith and Her Maidservant*. She worked in Rome before moving to Naples, remaining there except for a visit to England with her father in 1639 at Charles I's request. She had many other commissions but seems to have died in poverty.

BIBLIOGRAPHY
Garrard, Mary D. *Artemisia Gentileschi: The Image of the Female Hero in Italian Baroque Art.* Princeton, NJ: Princeton University Press, 1989. 0-691-04050-8, 607p. Garrard explores the scholarly premise that women's art is inescapably, if unconsciously, different from men's because the sexes are socialized to different experiences. She sees Gentileschi's art as radically different in expression and in interpretation of traditional themes from that of men contemporary to her.

GERTRUDE of HELFTA (1256–c. 1302)
Mystic   Germany

Gertrude von Helfta, called Gertrude the Great, went to live with nuns at Helfta, a Cistercian abbey in Saxony, when she was only five. Other than the information that she was a choir-nun, indicating her noble birth, nothing is known about her early life. When she was twenty-five, a vision of Christ called her to devote her life to sacred writings instead of the secular. She became an influential mystic who described her visions in *Exercitia spiritualia septem* and *Legatio divinae pietatis*. She and another nun began the cult of the adoration of the Sacred Heart.

BIBLIOGRAPHY
Finnegan, Mary Jeremy. *The Women of Helfta: Scholars and Mystics.* 1962. Athens: University of Georgia Press, 1991. 0-8203-1291-6, 171p. In this scholarly text, Finnegan tells the story of Gertrude the Great, looks at the influences on her life, and analyzes her writings for their literary and devotional content.
Gertrude. *The Herald of Divine Love.* Trans. Margaret Winkworth. New York: Paulist Press, 1993. 0-8091-0458-X, 259p. Winkworth's introduction to Gertrude and translation of her work include an analysis of her literary style and as much about the times in which she lived as necessary to clarify her background.
Gertrude. *The Herald of God's Loving Kindness.* Trans. Alexandra Barratt. Kalamazoo, MI: Cistercian, 1991. 0-87907-055-2, 186p. Barratt includes a

biographical and historical introduction based on knowledge about Gertrude in this translation of her religious writings.

GILMORE, MARY JANE (1865–1962)

Poet   Australia

Dame Mary Jane Gilmore was called "crusader and poet," "our great national poet," and "Australia's best-loved writer" for her nine major books of verse and three of prose. Born August 16, 1865, in New South Wales, she was the first child of Donald Cameron of Scotland, a mailman turned carpenter, and May Ann Beattie from Ulster. Gilmore moved with her family to Wagga Wagga at one and stayed there to teach in the area schools. In 1896, she left to join William Lane's utopian "New Australia" settlement in Paraguay, South America. There she met and married a shearer, William Gilmore, and they returned to Australia in 1902. Her socialist sympathies led her to campaign for the betterment of the sick and the helpless through her newspaper column in the Sydney *Worker* for over twenty years, along with her poetry and prose. In 1937, she became Dame of the British Empire. She was given a full ceremonial funeral in 1962, the first in Australia since the death of Henry Lawson in 1922.

BIBLIOGRAPHY

Gilmore, Mary Cameron. *More Recollections*. Sydney: Angus and Robertson, 1935. No ISBN, 268p. In this memoir, Gilmore compares wild horses in South America and Australia and discusses mirage and soak, flint-lock and rifle, grist, dogs, axes, china silk, swan-hopping, aboriginal antiquities, snakes and medicine, persecution, and black surgery, along with other superstitions and rumors.

Gilmore, Mary Cameron, Dame. *Old Days, Old Ways: A Book of Recollections.* Illus. Robert Avitabile. 1962. North Ryde, New South Wales, Australia: Angus and Robertson, 1986. 0-207-15016-8, 248p. Gilmore writes about the aborigines and their traditions in this memoir. Among the topics are hunting regulations to preserve the natural food supply and the similarity between their way of counting and that of the Guaranis of Paraguay in South America.

Lawson, Sylvia. *Mary Gilmore*. New York: Oxford University Press, 1967. No ISBN, 30p. Lawson's brief introduction to Gilmore scans her life, her writing, and her commitment to her beliefs.

Wilde, W. H. *Courage and Grace: A Biography of Dame Mary Gilmore.* Portland, OR: International Specialized Book Services, 1988. 0-522-84368-9, 490p. Wilde's carefully researched and thoroughly documented, definitive biography of Gilmore starts with a description of the crowds of people and the innumerable baskets of flowers at Gilmore's state funeral.

GINZBURG, NATALIA (1916–1991)

Writer   Italy

Natalia Ginzburg became an award-winning writer in Italy for her fiction. Born as Natalia Levi on July 14, 1916, into an intellectual Jewish family in Palermo, she grew up in Turin, where her father was a professor. Antifascist groups met at their home before she married Leone Ginzburg in 1938, who was imprisoned for underground activities in 1940 and who died four years later. She began writing under the pseudonym Alessandra Tornimparte and published *La*

Strada Che Va in Città in 1942. Other novels covered a variety of topics, including politics, the Italian Resistance, and life during the war. She won the Strega Prize for *Lessico famigliare*, an autobiographical novel about her family, in 1964. Her seemingly simple style presents bitter heroines who face their loneliness with humor. She often uses the omniscient narrator, but she manipulates the process so that the reader can still identify directly with her protagonists and their problems of communicating with others.

BIBLIOGRAPHY

Bullock, Alan. *Natalia Ginzburg: Human Relationships in a Changing World.* New York: Berg, 1991. 0-85496-178-X, 261p. In this biography, Bullock uses interviews, prefaces, journal pieces, theater reviews, and essays in his introduction to Ginzburg, along with a critical analysis of her style and subject matter.

Ginzburg, Natalia. *Family Sayings.* Trans. D. M. Low. 1967. New York: Seaver, Henry Holt, 1986. 0-8050-0152-2, 181p. Ginzburg prefaces this record of her family by saying that although it is factual, she wants readers to treat it like a novel. Her recollections of childhood and adolescence incorporate what Italy was like during her time.

GLANVILLE-HICKS, PEGGY (1912–1990)

Composer   Australia

Peggy Glanville-Hicks was an accomplished composer and music critic who supported the work of other musicians. Born December 29, 1912, she stayed in Australia to study at the Melbourne Conservatorium before going to London's Royal College of Music under Vaughan Williams and to Paris with Nadia Boulanger. Her *Choral Suite*, which debuted in London in 1938, was the first Australian work performed at a festival for the International Society for Contemporary Music. After she married Stanley Bate, an English composer, they founded Les Trois Arts in 1940, a ballet company based in London. Two years later, she moved to New York and became an American citizen in 1948. She helped to reestablish European artists after World War II by founding the International Music Fund with Carleton Sprague Smith. Among her positions and achievements were the director of the New York Composer's Forum, commissions for operas, and a ballet, *The Masque of the Wild Man*, performed at the first Spoleto Festival in 1958. She founded the Artists' Company to promote American opera and served as *New York Herald Tribune* music critic. She moved to Athens, Greece, in 1959 and became interested in the demotic music of the Aegean before returning to Australia in 1976.

BIBLIOGRAPHY

Hayes, Deborah. *Peggy Glanville-Hicks: A Bio-Bibliography.* Westport, CT: Greenwood Press, 1990. 0-313-26422-8, 274p. Hayes divides the text into two major sections, one on Glanville-Hicks' biography and the other on her works and performances including records, writings by her, and writings about her. Although only an overview, it is the only introduction to Glanville-Hicks' life.

GOEPPERT-MAYER, MARIA (1906–1972)

Scientist   Poland

Maria Goeppert-Mayer's model of nuclear structure won her the shared Nobel Prize in physics in 1963 as the first woman since Marie Curie to win the prize. Born in Kattowitz on June 28, 1906, Goeppert-Mayer's upper-middle-class father was a professor of medicine, and before marriage, her mother had been a French and piano teacher. Her father awakened her curiosity in the world around her, and she received her doctorate from Göttingen in 1930 before marrying Joseph Mayer in the same year. In 1931, they moved to the United States, where she worked at Johns Hopkins and at Columbia to separate uranium isotopes. In 1945, she went to the Institute of Nuclear Studies at the University of Chicago where Enrico Fermi interested her in nuclear physics. In 1956, she was elected to the National Academy of Sciences, and in 1960, she took a professorship at the University of California.

BIBLIOGRAPHY

Dash, Joan. *A Life of One's Own; Three Gifted Women and the Men They Married.* New York: Harper and Row, 1973. 0-06-010949-1, 388p. This long biographical sketch tells of the influences of Goeppert-Mayer's childhood that helped her in her adult life. Dash's thesis is that Goeppert-Mayer was successful because her husband supported her career.

GOLDMAN, EMMA (1869–1940)

Revolutionary   Lithuania

Emma Goldman devoted her life to her political goals, trying to achieve them in any way possible. She was born on June 27, 1896, and grew up in Kovno before her family moved to St. Petersburg in 1881. In 1886, she and her half sister emigrated to the United States and lived in Rochester, New York, where she worked in a glove factory. She married and divorced soon after, as her interest in socialism was rising during the Haymarket anarchist trial of 1886. In 1889, she moved to New York City and met Alexander Berkman, with whom she tried to assassinate Henry Frick during the Pittsburgh steel strike in 1892. Out of jail after a year, Goldman went to Austria, where anarchists taught her to organize and speak against injustice. Then she attempted to assassinate President McKinley and was arrested; edited the anarchist monthly *Mother Earth,* advocating woman's rights in marriage, child rearing, sex, and birth control; and opposed conscription in World War I. After she and Berkman were deported to Russia in 1921, they realized that the Bolsheviks had failed. Goldman wanted to return to America but was allowed only to visit briefly in 1934.

BIBLIOGRAPHY

Chalberg, John. *Emma Goldman: American Individualist.* New York: Harper-Collins, 1991. 0-673-52102-8, 196p. Chalberg shows Goldman as a restless person, moving from one place to another and from one lover to another without finding fulfillment.

Falk, Candace. *Love, Anarchy, and Emma Goldman.* Rev. ed. New Brunswick, NJ: Rutgers University Press, 1990. 0-8135-1512-2, 388p. Falk begins Goldman's story in midlife, when Goldman was struggling to write her autobiography. Falk has selected letters and developed themes raising questions about Goldman's ideology and personal life.

Gay, Kathlyn, and Martin Gay. *Emma Goldman*. San Diego: Lucent, 1997. 1-56006-024-7, 128p. The Gays' researched and documented biography, appropriate for young adults, gives an overview of Goldman's life and her advocacy for individual rights against government oppression, with accompanying photographs.

Wexler, Alice. *Emma Goldman in Exile: From the Russian Revolution to the Spanish Civil War*. Boston: Beacon, 1989. 0-8070-7004-1, 301p. By looking at Goldman's last twenty years. Wexler posits that Goldman was not the individual she wanted to be but was a mythmaker who tried to control people to keep them from thinking of her as an outsider.

GOLDSTEIN, VIDA (1869–1949)
Activist   Australia

Vida Goldstein was the first woman nominated for the Australian Parliament and worked for suffrage and improved social conditions. Born in Portland, Victoria, on April 13, 1869, she received her education in social work and politics at Melbourne Presbyterian College. After graduation, she began campaigning against the poverty inherent in slums and labor conditions in sweatshops. She and her sister opened a school, but, as she studied more sociology and economics, she left the school to spend her time on the women's movement. She wanted women to have property rights in marriage and rights in divorce and wanted to improve working conditions for the shop assistants. She represented Australia and New Zealand at the Women's Suffrage Conference in Washington, D.C., during 1902, and in 1903, she founded the Women's Federal Political Association. When women were allowed to vote in 1908, she began a new paper called *The Woman Voter*. As she aged, she became more conservative but went to Europe to speak and work for peace.

BIBLIOGRAPHY
Bomford, Janette M. *That Dangerous and Persuasive Woman: Vida Goldstein*. Portland, OR: International Specialized Book Services, 1993. 0-522-84542-8, 264p. Bomford's biography, the only one full-length, is well documented and thorough, showing Goldstein's consistency of belief and practice in demanding rights decades before people were ready to concede they were appropriate. Bomford uses events and facts for evidence because few of Goldstein's personal records remain.

GÓMEZ de AVELLANEDA, GERTRUDIS (1814–1873)
Playwright and Poet   Cuba

Gertrudis Gómez de Avellaneda, called "la Avellandeda," was one of the Romantic period's foremost playwrights and poets. She was born on March 23, 1814, in Puerto Príncipe as the daughter of a Spanish naval officer. When she was twenty-two, she went to Spain, where she lived, except for four years beginning in 1859, when she returned to Cuba and greatly influenced its literature. Her poetry reveals personal suffering with slight pessimism and ranks with the most poignant lyrics in the Spanish language. She based her plays on historical figures. She published her first poems anonymously but then took credit and gained fame for her work. Throughout her life, she struggled for woman's rights and for justice, with interest in a wide range of social problems.

BIBLIOGRAPHY
Gómez de Avellaneda y Arteaga, Gertrudis. *Sab, and Autobiography*. Trans.
    Nina M. Scott. Austin: University of Texas Press, 1993. 0-292-77655-1,
    157p. Scott translates Gomez de Avellaneda y Arteaga's novel *Sab* and in-
    cludes a translation of her autobiography written at twenty-five.
Harter, Hugh A. *Gertrudis Gómez de Avellaneda*. Boston: Twayne, 1981. 0-
    8057-6441-0, 182p. In his critical analysis of Gómez de Avellaneda's
    work, which he compares in popularity to that of George Sand, Harter
    notes that her legacy has been victim to a political debate as to whether she
    was loyal to Cuba or to Spain.

GONNE, MAUD (1866–1953)

Revolutionary   England

Maud Gonne MacBride was an Irish actor and revolutionary for the Irish cause
who became famous because she refused to marry William Butler Yeats, and he
wrote about her in his poetry. She was born December 21, 1866, in Surrey before her father was transferred to the Curragh, England's largest military base
in Ireland. Gonne's mother died when Gonne was five, and she went to France
for her education and returned to Dublin with her father when she was sixteen.
Back in France, convalescing from tuberculosis, she fell in love with a journalist and had two children with him but left after ten years to support the Irish
cause. In 1900, she founded the Inghinidhe Na Eireann (Daughters of Ireland),
a women's group. Yeats met her in 1889, proposed in 1899, and never recovered from her refusal. She played Cathleen in his drama *Cathleen Ni Houlihan*
in 1902. She became Catholic and married John MacBride, another revolutionary, but they soon separated. He was executed after the Easter Rising of 1916.
In 1917, she returned from Paris to participate in the Republican movement,
was arrested, and spent six months in Holloway Prison. She founded soup
kitchens, schools, and hospitals during the Troubles, always demanding total
Irish independence. At six-feet tall, she filled a room with her presence, and
some saw her as an Irish Joan of Arc, while others used the term "Maudgon-
ning" in reference to the actions of a reckless, flamboyant agitator.

BIBLIOGRAPHY
Cardozo, Nancy. *Maud Gonne*. 1978. New York: New Amsterdam, 1990. 0-
    941533-95-6, 468p. This biography, readable and thoroughly researched,
    with photographs, shows that Gonne was not the idol that Yeats created.
Gonne, Maud. *The Autobiography of Maud Gonne: A Servant of the Queen*.
    Eds. A. Norman Jeffares and Anna MacBride White. Chicago: University of
    Chicago Press, 1995. 0-226-30251-2, 378p. Maud Gonne wrote her auto-
    biography because she needed money. Her son wanted to hide family un-
    pleasantries and she wanted to avoid lawsuits, so Gonne is less than truthful
    about many circumstances such as her divorce, her illegitimate daughter,
    and her affair with Millevoye.
Levenson, Samuel. *Maud Gonne*. New York: Reader's Digest, 1976. 0-88349-
    089-7, 436p. This biography shows an understanding of the historical and
    literary importance of Maude Gonne by re-creating Ireland at the turn of
    the century, picturing her as a selfless Irish patriot best remembered for her
    relationship with Yeats.
MacBride, Maud Gonne, and W. B. Yeats. *The Gonne-Yeats Letters
    1893–1938*. Eds. Anna MacBride White and A. Norman Jeffares. New

York: Norton, 1993. 0-393-03445-3, 544p. Although "Willie and Maud" both believed in Ireland, the occult, and drama as the way that Ireland's genius would reveal itself, they disagreed on their personal values. Yeats was basically a pragmatist; Gonne was an idealist. In 372 letters from Gonne and 28 from Yeats, they describe their projects.

Ward, Margaret. *Maud Gonne: A Life*. San Francisco: HarperCollins, 1993. 0-04-440889-7, 320p. Ward has carefully researched Maud Gonne Mac-Bride's background to write a balanced biography about her complex life supporting Irish freedom and woman's rights through picketing, lobbying, raising funds, and founding a female nationalist group.

GONZÁLES, LUISA (1904–)
Writer and Activist   Costa Rica

Luisa Gonzáles is a celebrated writer and speaker championing the rights of women and children. Born on April 25, 1904, in a poverty-stricken barrio of San José, she became the first in her family to obtain the Costa Rican equivalent of a high school education. She taught school for fourteen years to help the poor but realized that education alone could not change their lives. She knew that they would have to alter their social situation. She joined the Communist Party, which she thought would help. She was fired because of her political activism, and she and her husband, a university professor, established a free school for workers, offering classes in Costa Rican history. She then founded the Costa Rica Women's Alliance, advocating the rights of working women, including the peasants, and supported the Sandinistas in Nicaragua. She has published on a wide range of topics and received the Costa Rican Aquileo J. Echeverría award for outstanding achievement in literature in 1970 and in 1974.

BIBLIOGRAPHY
Gonzáles, Luisa. *At the Bottom: A Woman's Life in Central America*. Berkeley, CA: New Earth, 1994. 0-915117-12-6, 121p. Gonzáles recalls her life up to 1932, when she was in her late twenties. She gives a view of everyday events in the early part of the century although much of the life she describes remains the same.

GOODALL, JANE (1934–)
Scientist   England

Jane Goodall is one of the most respected scientists studying animals in the field. Born on April 3, 1934, Goodall received a stuffed animal chimpanzee when she was eighteen months old. After reading *Tarzan* and *The Jungle Book*, she decided that she would study animals in Africa when she grew up. She did and took her stuffed chimpanzee with her. When she got to Africa, Louis Leakey arranged for her to study chimpanzees at the Gombe Stream Research on Lake Tanganyika in Tanzania. As she observed them more closely than any other human, she discovered that they were not violent; they greeted each other with kisses and helped each other to groom. She saw that they hunted, ate meat, and used tools, so she named them based on their distinguishing characteristics. In 1961, she presented her findings, but men were critical of her research methods. However, Cambridge University accepted her, and she received a doctorate in ethology. She and her Dutch husband had a son in

1967, and she raised him using chimpanzee child-rearing techniques of breast-feeding, cradling, and keeping him nearby constantly. When she started lecturing that women needed to stay with their children more, she angered feminists. In 1991, she received the Edinburgh Medal honoring scientists who have made a contribution to the understanding and well-being of humanity and in 1995, the Hubbard Medal, honoring distinction, exploration, discovery, and research from the National Geographic Society.

BIBLIOGRAPHY

Goodall, Jane. *My Life with the Chimpanzees*. New York: Pocket, 1988. Paper, 0-671-66095-0, 123p. In this autobiography for young adults, Goodall tells how she planned to go to Africa, met Leakey, went into the field, and learned to record long sessions of observation.

Goodall, Jane. *Through a Window: My Thirty Years with the Chimpanzees of Gombe*. Boston: Houghton Mifflin, 1990. 0-395-50081-8, 268p. Goodall tells about the generations of chimpanzees that she and her Tasmanian workers have studied and about their own lives in this profession. The chimpanzee personalities make this book seem more like a novel than an autobiographical approach to a scientific study.

Montgomery, Sy. *Walking with the Great Apes: Jane Goodall, Dian Fossey, Birute Galdikas*. Boston: Houghton Mifflin, 1991. 0-395-51597-1, 280p. By comparing the three approaches of these women to the primates, the reader sees very different temperaments and emotional bonds leading to similar results. Jane Goodall has been cautious and diplomatic but effective in her careful recording of each action and response.

Pratt, Paula Bryant. *Jane Goodall*. San Diego: Lucent, 1997. 1-56006-082-4, 112p. Pratt's researched and documented biography is appropriate for young adults. She gives an overview of Goodall's life and work with accompanying photographs.

GORDIMER, NADINE (1923–)

Writer   South Africa

Nadine Gordimer's novels probe the English in South Africa, the Afrikaans-speaking whites, and the horrible life of the blacks. Born on November 20, 1923, she lived in Springs, Transvaal, as a child, and attended a convent school. She started writing at nine, with her first fiction published at thirteen. She later attended the University of Wiwatersrand, Johannesburg. She married her first husband in 1949 and published short stories the same year. In 1953, she published her first novel, *The Lying Days*, in which the protagonist strives to separate herself from the prejudices of her childhood. In 1954, Gordimer remarried, and her second husband was a Jewish refugee from the Nazis. The South African government banned many of her books, but she has been a visiting lecturer in the United States since 1961. She won the Booker McConnell Prize for *The Conservationist* in 1974 and the Nobel Prize in literature in 1991.

BIBLIOGRAPHY

Gordimer, Nadine. *Conversations with Nadine Gordimer*. Eds. Nancy Topping Bazin and Marilyn Dallman Seymour. Jackson: University Press of Mississippi, 1990. 0-87805-444-8, 321p. This series of interviews covering Gordimer's life from 1959 to 1986 discusses her childhood, upbringing, life in South Africa, and her work.

Gordimer, Nadine. *The Essential Gesture: Writing, Politics and Places.* Ed. Stephen Clingman. New York: Penguin, 1989. 0-14-012212-5, 356p. Gordimer talks about her life as a white living in South Africa and the alienation, first, of being a minority of race and, secondly, of being a minority within her own community by opposing apartheid.

GRAY, EILEEN (1878–1976)
Architect and Designer   Ireland

Eileen Gray created a career for herself designing furniture and houses with a variety of materials including lacquer, plastics, steel, and glass. She was born on August 9, 1878, at Brownwood, Enniscorthy, County Wexford, and studied painting at the Slade School in London. In Paris during 1907, she became an apprentice to Sugawara, a Japanese lacquerist. When World War I began, she left art to drive an ambulance. After the war, she and Sugawara started studios in London and in Paris, where she became famous for her handmade furniture. She also designed houses that prefigured modernism with their use of space. In World War II, the Germans interned her as an enemy, and, although she lived in France afterward, she refused to socialize. Gray continued to design, and in the 1970s, she became a Royal Designer for Industry. She was inducted into the Royal Society of Arts in 1972 and the next year became a fellow of the Royal Institute of Irish Architects.

BIBLIOGRAPHY
Adam, Peter. *Eileen Gray: Architect/Designer.* New York: Harry N. Abrams, 1987. 0-8109-0996-0, 400p. Adam's biography of Eileen Gray is a straightforward look at her career from her lacquer screens through her houses filled with her own designs. Photographs and drawings illustrate the text.

Garner, Philippe. *Eileen Gray: Design and Architecture, 1878–1976.* Cologne, Germany: Benedikt Taschen Verlag, 1993. 3-82289-356-0, 160p. The text, in German, English, and French, gives a biographical sketch of Gray with color photographs showing her style and development.

Johnson, J. Stewart. *Eileen Gray, Designer.* London: Debrett's Peerage for Museum of Modern Art, 1979. 0-87070-307-2, 67p. Johnson bases his life of Gray on papers and chronologies surveyed after her death including a daybook and list of customers, a notebook with instructions for preparing lacquer, correspondence with a craftsman named Inagaki, bills, letters, and photographs.

GREENAWAY, KATHERINE (1846–1901)
Artist   England

Kate Greenaway became an important illustrator using children and idyllic country scenes as subjects in England in the late nineteenth century. She was born on March 17, 1846, into a modest family that she was able to support through the fame and wealth gained while in her thirties. As they moved into larger homes, she was able to have gardens like the ones depicted in so many of her drawings. She had personal disappointments including a failed relationship with the Victorian critic John Ruskin that did not materialize as she wished.

BIBLIOGRAPHY

Engen, Rodney. *Kate Greenaway: A Biography*. New York: Schocken, 1981. 0-8052-3775-5, 240p. Based on correspondence and interviews with Greenaway's descendants, Engen's scholarly biography, with Greenaway's illustrations, shows that Greenaway was somewhat insecure and needed to keep making money for her family. He also suggests that Ruskin was not cruel in their relationship but mentally unstable.

Holme, Bryan. *The Kate Greenaway Book*. New York: Viking, 1976. 0-670-41183-3, 141p. Holme presents nearly two hundred of Kate Greenaway's illustrations, giving an insight into the meticulousness and whimsicality of her work, with a brief biographical commentary.

Taylor, Ina. *The Art of Kate Greenaway: A Nostalgic Portrait of Childhood*. Gretna, LA: Pelican, 1991. 0-88289-867-1, 128p. Taylor examines Greenaway's life and some of her triumphs and disappointments while additionally presenting a view of life in Victorian England for an unmarried woman capable of supporting herself.

GREGORY, AUGUSTA (1852–1932)

Writer   Ireland

Lady Augusta Gregory wanted to restore Irish culture and independence, and her plays and activities in Dublin with the Abbey Theatre helped her work toward these ideals. Born on March 15, 1852, as her father's twelfth of sixteen children by two wives, Isabella Augusta Persse was educated privately at Roxborough, County Galway. At twenty-eight, she met Sir William Gregory, sixty-three, who lived close by her family at Coole Park and married him in 1881. After his death eleven years later, she met William Butler Yeats and joined him in advocating a national folklore. She began supporting the Irish Literary Theatre in 1899 and became a codirector of the Abbey Theatre in 1904 and manager in 1909. Her ability to administer and to raise money kept the theater in business. Her home, Coole Park, was the center for Irish Renaissance writers such as Yeats, William Synge, Bernard Shaw, and others who met for discussion. She learned Gaelic and translated some of the old sagas, including *Guchulain of Muirthemne* and *Gods and Fighting Men*. Then she began writing plays, publishing over forty before her death.

BIBLIOGRAPHY

Mikhail, E. H. *Lady Gregory: Interviews and Recollections*. London: Macmillan, 1977. 0-333-22327-6, 113p. This biographical collection of anecdotal essays written by people who knew and liked Lady Gregory tells about her after her marriage and includes a description of the peaceful life at Coole Park and Gregory's commitment to Irish literature and drama while directing the Abbey Theatre.

Stevenson, Mary Lou Kohfeldt. *Lady Gregory: The Woman behind the Irish Renaissance*. New York: Atheneum, 1985. 0-689-11486-9, 366p. This carefully documented and readable biography reveals Lady Gregory's background and work and contains information about Irish history and politics.

GUYON, JEANNE MARIE (1648–1717)
Writer   France

Jeanne Guyon developed the concept of quietism, which taught indifference to everything, even salvation. Born on April 13, 1648, she spent most of her childhood in various convents because her father was too old and her mother disinterested in raising her. Jeanne Marie de Bouvier De La Mothe married, when she was sixteen, Jacques Guyon, an invalid in his thirties. After his death twelve years later, she did as she had always wanted: devote herself to prayer and travel through Europe explaining her doctrine. In Paris, her seeming immorality led to her arrest, but **Madame de Maintenon** helped free her. Guyon became influential in the court, and the future archbishop of Cambrais, Abbé François Fénelon, began to support her. She wanted a trial in 1695 to clear her name, but the Commission of Issy condemned her instead, and she was again arrested. Released in 1702, she spent the rest of her life in Blois. Whether she was saint or sinner remains unclear, but she had good intentions.

BIBLIOGRAPHY
Guyon, Madame. *Sweet Smelling Myrrh: The Autobiography of Madame Guyon.* Ed. Abbie C. Morrow. Trans. Warner Hutchinson. 1980. Salem, OH: Schmul, 1996. 0-88019-348-4, 192p. Guyon wrote her autobiography during her first imprisonment in 1688, but she added to it and revised it in 1709. It reveals perceptions of Louis XIV's French hierarchy.

Coslet, Dorothy. *Madame Jeanne Guyon: Child of Another World.* Fort Washington, PA: Christian Literature Crusade, 1992. 0-87508-144-4, 219p. Coslet's fictional biography retells Guyon's life beginning with her escape to Switzerland from family members who questioned her religious views. Coslet describes the various trials, real and psychological, that Guyon had to endure in order to stay true to her own beliefs.

Thompson, Phyllis. *Madame Guyon, Martyr of the Holy Spirit.* London: Hodder and Stoughton, 1986. 0-340-40175-3, 191p. Thompson based her biography on Guyon's autobiography and created a readable but biased story of a woman whose spiritual life she appreciated.

GWYN, ELEANOR (c. 1650–1687)
Actor   England

Eleanor Gwyn was a well-known actor in London during the seventeenth century. Other than her birth date of February 2, 1650, not much is known about her early life. Records show that Gwyn played several comedy parts after the London plague of 1665, performed at the Theatre Royal until 1671, and played other theaters before returning to Drury Lane in the 1680s. She was illiterate, but her comic ability made her an effective and entertaining heroine. Charles II became interested in Gwyn and replaced his mistress, the duchess of Portsmouth, with her. Her wit, unpretentiousness, and lack of greed made her one of the best loved and most respected women in British history. Although her family members had committed a variety of socially unacceptable crimes, she did not abandon them when she became famous. One of her sons by the king became the duke of St. Albans, and her influence helped found London's Chelsea Hospital.

BIBLIOGRAPHY
Bax, Clifford. *Pretty Witty Nell: An Account of Nell Gwyn and Her Environment.* 1932. North Stratford, NH: Ayer, 1972. 0-405-08243-6, 261p. Bax documents Gwyn's life but uses a condescending tone throughout as he places her within the times in which she lived.
Bevan, Bryan. *Nell Gwyn, Vivacious Mistress of Charles II.* New York: Roy, 1970. No ISBN, 190p. Bevan carefully documents this well-written and recommended look at Nell Gwyn.
MacGregor-Hastie, Roy. *Nell Gwyn.* London: Hale, 1987. 0-7090-3099-1, 205p. In this readable biography with an emphasis on historical aspects, MacGregor-Hastie posits that Nell Gwyn's life reveals both the good and bad attitudes of Restoration England.

GWYNNE-VAUGHN, HELEN (1879–1967)

Scientist   England

Helen Gwynne-Vaughn became head and, later, professor of botany at Birkbeck College, London, where she was an authority on fungi, and helped to organize women during World War I. Helen Charlotte Isabella was born January 21, 1879, in Westminster. Her father died of typhoid on a vacation with her mother when Gwynne-Vaughn was only five. Educated at Cheltenham Ladies' College and King's College, London, Gwynne-Vaughn majored in botany. In World War I, she organized and later was controller of the Women's Army Auxiliary Air Force in France in 1917, becoming the commandant in 1918. Between wars, she was married only four years before her husband died of consumption, but she continued her teaching. In World War II, she again served the Women's Auxiliary Territorial Service as chief controller. In 1944, she retired from Birkbeck. She received a Dame of the British Empire in 1919 and a Dame Grand Cross of the Order of the British Empire in 1929 for her public and scientific services.

BIBLIOGRAPHY
Izzard, Molly. *A Heroine in Her Time: A Life of Dame Helen Gwynne-Vaughan, 1879–1967.* New York: St. Martin's, 1969. 0-333-06977-3, 368p. Izzard used a manuscript that Dame Helen wrote in 1950 about her life, and in a balanced biography, Izzard sees how women's ideas about themselves have changed.

$\mathfrak{H}$

HALL, RADCLYFFE (1883–1943)
Writer   England

Radclyffe Hall was a prizewinning writer. Marguerite Hall, born but unwanted
in Bournemouth on August 12, 1883, later attended King's College, London,
and a German university. After becoming financially independent at twenty-
one, she started writing poetry. She published her first volume in 1906 and followed it with three more volumes, eight novels, and then short stories. Her
novel *Adam's Breed* (1926) won the Prix Femina Vie Heureuse and the James
Tait Black Memorial Prize. Her most notorious novel was *The Well of Loneliness* (1928), which was banned because of its lesbian content and the thin disguise of her homosexuality. She thought sexual inversion was a trick of nature
that deserved sympathy. She met Lady Troubridge, her lifelong lover and companion, and called herself "John" while living with Troubridge in London, Sussex, and Paris. In 1930, she received the Gold Medal of the Eichelbergher
Humane Award.

BIBLIOGRAPHY
Baker, Michael. *Our Three Selves: The Life of Radclyffe Hall.* New York: Wil-
    liam Morrow, 1985. 0-688-04385-2, 386p. Baker says that Hall never kept
    a diary or wrote many letters until she became famous so he quotes from
    her prose and poetry to show her prevailing concerns and preoccupations
    in this thorough and balanced biography with photographs.
Castle, Terry. *Noel Coward and Radclyffe Hall: Kindred Spirits.* New York:
    Columbia University Press, 1996. 0-231-10596-7, 149p. When examining
    the friendship between Radclyffe Hall and Noel Coward, Castle also looks
    at male and female homosexual friendships through the years.
Dickson, Lovat. *Radclyffe Hall at the Well of Loneliness: A Sapphic Chronicle.*
    New York: Scribner's, 1975. 0-684-14530-8, 236p. This well-documented
    biography discusses Hall's life and relationship with Una Troubridge.

Troubridge, Una Vincenzo. *The Life of Radclyffe Hall*. 1961. New York: Arno, 1975. 0-405-07355-0, 189p. Troubridge writes about her life with John (Hall) as a series of letters, a personal and accessible but biased view.

HANOVER, SOPHIA of. *See* SOPHIA of HANOVER.

HANSON-DYER, LOUISE (1884–1962)

Businesswoman   **Australia and France**

Louise Hanson-Dyer established Éditions du Oiseau-Lyre, a music publishing business that helped to revive early music. Born in Melbourne on July 19, 1884, Louise Berta Mosson later studied piano in Edinburgh and at the Royal College of Music in London. After marrying James Dyer, she helped establish the British Music Society in Melbourne. They moved to London in 1927 and then to Paris, where she first purchased the copyright to Couperin's works, and to those of Purcell and Blow, for publication through her press. When her husband died, she remarried and called herself Hanson-Dyer. In the 1950s, her publishing house issued long-playing records of eighteenth-century music, and she continued to publish Australians like **Peggy Glanville-Hicks** and Margaret Sutherland. She was the first Australian woman to be cited in the *Harvard Dictionary of Music*.

BIBLIOGRAPHY
Davidson, Jim. *Lyrebird Rising: Louise Hanson–Dyer of Oiseau-Lyre, 1884-1962*. Portland, OR: Amadeus, 1994. 0-931340-72-1, 578p. Davidson used the Oiseau-Lyre archives in Paris and Monaco, books from Hanson-Dyer's own library, and private papers, periodicals, secondary sources, and interviews to re-create the triad of Australia, Britain, and France in Hanson-Dyer's life in this readable but scholarly biography.

HATSHEPSUT (1503–1482 B.C.)

Queen   **Egypt**

Hatshepsut was the first woman pharaoh and ruler of Egypt in two thousand years. The daughter of Thutmose I, she married her half-brother, Thutmose II. When he died, Hatshepsut became regent to his young heir, Thutmose III. Two years later, she appropriated the title of pharaoh. She fought in Nubia and other places, but her reign was generally peaceful, prosperous, and productive. She had a mortuary temple constructed at Deir el-Bahri in Thebes showing scenes of her birth and her achievements, such as bringing the obelisks to the temple at Karnak and retrieving cargoes from the expedition to Punt on the Red Sea. After her murder, Thutmose removed her followers from their exalted positions and continued to rule. By the time he died, he had tarnished her reputation and smashed her statues.

BIBLIOGRAPHY
Hatchett, John F. *Hatshepsut, a Beautiful African Queen of the Nile*. Rev. ed. Hampton, VA: United Brothers and United Sisters Communications, 1991. No ISBN, 48p. This unorthodox and brief attempt at a biography is a biased and weak view of Hatshepsut with the single aim of showing that she was African.

Hussein, Amr. *Hatshepsut*. Trans. Samia M. Shereef. Cairo, Egypt: A. Hussein,
    1989. No ISBN, 112p. This brief, disjointed overview of Hatshepsut's ac-
    complishments during her reign includes photographs and diagrams of tem-
    ples connected to her name. A travel guide might be more appropriate.

HAYWOOD, ELIZA (1693?–1756)
Playwright   England

Eliza Haywood first wrote plays and novels to earn money for her family, but
she became the most popular and prolific woman writer of her age. The daughter of a London tradesman, she married Valentine Haywood in 1717. Four
years later, he left her with two small children, and she began writing for
money. She had been acting since childhood in Dublin and London, so she began writing plays. Her first play, *A Wife to Be Left*, debuted at Drury Lane in
1723. She found, however, that her fiction was better. She wrote forty romantic novels between 1719 and 1730, demonstrating that she was both an arbiter
of passion and a strong moralizer. With Daniel Defoe, she collaborated on a series of pamphlets before changing her focus in the 1750s to domestic realism.
She also contributed to *The Tea Table* and *The Female Spectator*.

BIBLIOGRAPHY
Schofield, Mary Anne. *Eliza Haywood*. Boston: Twayne, 1985. 0-8057-6913-
    7, 139p. Since Haywood left neither facts nor fiction about her life,
    Schofield looked in her books to find clues to her life and work. Schofield
    emphasizes Haywood's use of a double writing technique to show women
    as exploited and enslaved.

HEAD, BESSIE (1937–1986)
Writer   South Africa

Bessie Head, a novelist and short story writer, believed that literature should
both entertain and teach. Born on July 6, 1937, in Pietermaritzburg, the
daughter of a white mother and a black father who worked in the family stable,
Head was raised in a foster home as "colored" after her mother was committed
to an asylum and committed suicide when Head was one. Head became a
teacher before leaving her husband when she was in her early twenties and going to Botswana. She became a citizen, and her novels, set in Botswana, include
When Rain Clouds Gather (1969), *Maru* (1971), and *A Question of Power*
(1973). She survived sexism, racism, and apartheid as well as abuses as an orphan, woman, and outsider. Yet in her work, she always emphasized hope for a
better world, basing themes on her experiences. She additionally wrote short
stories and a history of the life of the community in which she lived before she
died of hepatitis.

BIBLIOGRAPHY
Abrahams, Cecil. *The Tragic Life: Bessie Head and Literature in Southern Af-
    rica*. Trenton, NJ: Africa World, 1990. 0-86543-176-0, 131p. This work is
    not a traditional biography, but the scholarly essays about Head's life and
    work establish her life as an inextricable part of her work.
Head, Bessie. *A Woman Alone: Autobiographical Writings*. Ed. Craig MacKen-
    zie. Portsmouth, NH: Heinemann, 1990. 0-435-90578-3, 107p. MacKen-
    zie has arranged the autobiographical pieces chronologically according to

when Head wrote them to show her early life in South Africa, exile in Botswana, and then Botswanan citizenship.

Ola, Virginia Uzoma. *The Life and Works of Bessie Head.* Lewiston, ME: Edwin Mellen, 1994. 0-7734-9018-3, 91p. This brief, scholarly overview of Bessie Head's life illustrates how Head's beliefs controlled her work.

HELFTA, GERTRUDE of. *See* GERTRUDE of HELFTA.

HÉLOÏSE (1101–1163)
Intellectual and Abbess   **France**

Héloïse, an intellectual, spent most of her life in a religious order. Orphaned at an early age, she went to live in Paris with her uncle, the cleric and canon Fulbert. She was fluent in Latin and might also have known Hebrew and Greek, which was highly unusual for a female. When she was sixteen, Abelard, twenty years older, began instructing her for free. Abelard moved into Fulbert's house and paid rent. But after Héloïse and Abelard had an affair, she went to Brittany, Abelard's home, to have their son, first refusing to marry him and ruin his academic future. Fulbert promised not to tell of their marriage, but he did, and even worse, had unsavory men castrate Abelard. Both Abelard and Héloïse joined religious orders, but Héloïse never thought of herself as serving God because God had not aided her. Abelard gave her land, which he called the Paraclete, meaning "intercessor" or "comforter," for her convent. Héloïse's letters to Abelard through the years show that she always loved him, and when he died, she had his body moved to the Paraclete, where she served as abbess, and requested to be buried next to him. Later their bodies were moved to Père Lachaise cemetery in Paris.

BIBLIOGRAPHY
Ericson, Donald E. *Abelard and Héloïse: The Most Celebrated Lovers of the Middle Ages, Their Lives, Their Love, Their Letters.* New York: Bennett-Edwards, 1990. 0-9617271-1-X, 166p. Ericson speculates in his account of Héloïse's relationship with Abelard that Fulbert might have been her father. Clerics were forbidden to marry, and some had children out of wedlock whom they helped raise as their "nieces" and "nephews."

McLeod, Enid. *Héloïse: A Biography.* 1938. London: Chatto and Windus, 1971. No ISBN, 318p. McLeod gives a full study of Héloïse's life, using newly translated letters, to show the main events and the fine balance between her mind, character, and heart. McLeod thinks she was the most distinguished woman, at least of her century, if not of all time.

Pernoud, Régine. *Héloïse and Abelard.* Trans. Peter Wiles. New York: Stein and Day, 1973. 0-8128-1558-0, 256p. Pernoud posits that all Paris knew about Héloïse's intelligence and that Abelard would have heard about, or seen, her before they officially met. Although a scholarly account, the text reads like a novel.

Robertson, D. W., Jr. *Abelard and Héloïse.* Ed. Norman F. Cantor. New York: Dial, 1972. 0-02-4343-6, 238p. Over half of the text focuses on Abelard's life and his writings, but Robertson comments that, without Héloïse, Abelard might not have written at all.

HENIE, SONIA (1912–1969)
Ice-Skater and Actor   Norway

Sonia Henie was an Olympic ice-skating champion, professional skater, and actor. Born on April 8, 1912, she went ice-skating with her brother as a two-year-old and began working toward becoming the Norwegian ice-skating champion. In 1923, she won, and in 1927, she became the World Champion, winning the competition nine more times. She won Olympic Gold Medals in 1928, 1932, and 1936 before going to Hollywood, starring in eleven films, and becoming an American citizen. During her third marriage to Norwegian shipowner Niels Onstad, she built a large collection of Impressionist and Postimpressionist art, which they donated to Oslo in 1968 before she died of leukemia.

BIBLIOGRAPHY
Axe, John. *Collectible Sonja Henie*. Riverdale, MD: Hobby House, 1979. Paper, 0-87588-146-7, 48p. A brief biographical profile of Henie precedes revealing photographs of the collectible items resulting from her career, including posters, magazine covers, and dolls, with descriptions of their significance.

Strait, Raymond, and Leif Henie. *Queen of Ice, Queen of Shadows: The Unsuspected Life of Sonja Henie*. 1985. Chelsea, MI: Scarborough House, 1990. Paper, 0-8128-8518-X, 339p. The authors, one of whom is Henie's brother, focus on Henie as calculating and immoral in a biased biography.

HENSEL, FANNY MENDELSSOHN (1805–1847)
Instrumentalist and Composer   Germany

Fanny Mendelssohn was a talented pianist and composer. She was born on November 14, 1805, and received her initial training from her mother. She then studied in Berlin with Ludwig Berger for piano and Carl Zelter for composition. In 1816, at eleven, she went to Paris, and by thirteen, she could play Bach's forty-eight preludes and fugues from memory. Since her father saw her only as a future housewife and did not want her to compete with her brother, Felix, he discouraged her continuance of music study and composition, so in 1829, she married the painter Wilhelm Hensel. They traveled to Italy, and when they returned to Berlin, she organized concerts on Sunday afternoons in their apartment. She continued to compose, setting music to some of her husband's poems. In 1845, she began publishing her music, issuing twelve collections before her death. Her music, similar to her brother's, included piano pieces, a piano trio, and songs. Felix took credit for at least two of her songs.

BIBLIOGRAPHY
Tillard, Françoise. *Fanny Mendelssohn*. Trans. Camille Naish. Portland, OR: Amadeus, 1996. 0-931340-96-9, 400p. Tillard's readable biography, using letters and documents, is the first to be published on Mendelssohn. Although Tillard may be biased toward Fanny at the expense of Felix, Tillard shows how nineteenth-century attitudes thwarted Mendelssohn's career, even though she might have been the more talented sibling.

HEPWORTH, BARBARA (1903–1975)
Sculptor   England

Dame Barbara Hepworth was a sculptor whose abstract pieces are displayed around the world. Born on January 10, 1903, the daughter of a Yorkshire county surveyor, Hepworth attended the Leeds College of Art and the Royal Academy of Art in London and won a scholarship to Italy. She was a member of a radical artists' group, the Seven and Five Society, and when she married her second husband, painter Ben Nicholson, she worked with the abstract groups Unit One and Abstraction-Creation. Her first work was stylized, and as she matured, it turned to abstract form. They moved to St. Ives, Cornwall, in 1939, and Hepworth developed her style, which resembles the work of her friend Henry Moore. She became a Dame Commander of the British Empire in 1958, and seven years later, a Dame of the British Empire. She later created the Dag Hammerskjöld Memorial at the United Nations building in New York.

BIBLIOGRAPHY

Curtis, Penelope, and Alan G. Wilkinson. *Barbara Hepworth: A Retrospective.* Seattle: University of Washington Press, 1995. 1-85437-141-X, 168p. Curtis and Wilkinson give a chronological account of Hepworth and her stylistic development as her interest in non-Western art and a truth-to-materials attitude matured from abstraction to multipart structures. They include an extensive biography and a list of Hepworth's public commissions, along with photographs.

Festing, Sally. *Barbara Hepworth: A Life of Forms.* New York: Viking, 1995. 0-670-84303-2, 343p. This balanced, well-documented, and readable biography with photographs helps to show that Hepworth was gifted but that her last works were mixed in quality.

Gardiner, Margaret. *Barbara Hepworth: A Memoir.* 1982. Edinburgh, Scotland: Salamander, 1994. Paper, 0-85331-674-0, 63p. Gardiner, a dear friend, reveals Hepworth's vibrance and her willingness to help whenever someone needed it.

Hepworth, Barbara. *A Pictorial Autobiography.* New York: Praeger, 1970. No ISBN, 127p. Barbara Hepworth tells her life story from her Yorkshire childhood and student days at the Royal College to her studio in St. Ives. The autobiography includes 344 shots of cats, catalog covers, certificates of honors received, and her works.

HERSCHEL, CAROLINE (1750–1848)
Astronomer   Germany

Caroline Lucretia Herschel executed many of the calculations for her brother's astronomical conclusions while discovering fourteen nebulae and eight comets between 1786 and 1797 on her own. After her birth on March 16, 1750, she learned little more than how to play the violin and helped her mother manage the household while growing up until she went to Bath, England, with her brother Sir William. She trained there as a singer while her brother taught music until their last performance in 1782. She kept house for Sir William and helped him with his astronomical research for George III, including grinding and polishing mirrors and mathematical calculations. In 1798, she submitted original work to the Royal Astronomical Society, and thirty years later, the society awarded her its gold medal and elected her to honorary membership. She also received medals from the kings of Denmark and Prussia.

BIBLIOGRAPHY

Ashton, Helen, and Katharine Davies. *I Had a Sister: A Study of Mary Lamb, Dorothy Wordsworth, Caroline Herschel, Cassandra Austen.* 1937. Philadelphia: R. West, 1977. 0-849-20105-5, 286p. The authors examine the lives of four women, including Herschel, who, working in their brothers' shadows, made stunning astronomical discoveries.

Robinson, Ella May. *Stars in Her Heart.* Washington, DC: Review and Herald, 1971. No ISBN, 127p. Robinson bases fictional biography dialogue on Herschel's own letters, journals, and daybook as well as those of others, along with recorded incidents or well-known facts.

Stott, Carole. *Into the Unknown.* New York: Hampstead, 1989. 0-531-19513-9, 45p. This brief collective biography, appropriate for young adults, contains an explanation of Caroline Herschel's achievement in a formerly masculine profession.

HESS, MYRA (1890–1966)

Instrumentalist   England

Myra Hess was a pianist of international renown. Born on February 25, 1890, into a London family of Jewish ancestry that made uniforms, she began to take piano when she was only five. At the age of twelve, she won a scholarship to the Royal Academy of Music in London. At seventeen, she made her debut performing Beethoven's Fourth Piano Concerto, conducted by Sir Thomas Beecham. That work plus her transcription of Bach's Cantata No. 147, "Jesu, Joy of Man's Desiring," were signature works. She played Schumann and Mozart as well and performed with her cousin in duets in tours of Europe and the United States. While in London during World War II, she organized luncheon concerts at the National Gallery, since all the halls were closed, engaged various performers, and played herself. She became a Dame of the British Empire in 1941 as recognition of her services to the public. Cambridge, London, and other universities awarded her honorary doctorates.

BIBLIOGRAPHY

McKenna, Marian C. *Myra Hess: A Portrait.* London: Hamilton, 1976. 0-241-89522-7, 319p. McKenna has written a documented and balanced, scholarly biography based on letters, speeches, books, interviews, newspapers, National Gallery records, unpublished materials, and information from Hess's secretary.

HILDEGARD of BINGEN (1098–1179)

Mystic   Germany

Hildegard was a musician, artist, healer, dramatist, and writer who described her visions. As the last of ten children whose mother was Mechtild, Hildegard entered a Benedictine convent at the age of seven and took vows at fourteen. Her visions began then, and when she was thirty-two in 1136, she became abbess at Diessem. After her community began to grow, she moved it to Bingen, where she wrote *Scivias* in which she described her visions as well as hymns, poetry, and a morality play. She was an accomplished artist and musician, and musicologists think that her hymns may be the earliest extant mass music compose by a female. Since her learning also extended to science and medicine, she was known as the "Sibyl of the Rhine." She wrote on natural history about subjects such as minerals, animals, elements, plants, circulation of the blood, and mental instability. She freely offered advice to Henry III, Frederick Barbarossa, and Pope Eugenius III and helped to mobilize support for the Second Crusade.

BIBLIOGRAPHY

Flanagan, Sabina. *Hildegard of Bingen, 1098–1179: A Visionary Life.* New York: Routledge, 1989. 0-415-01340-2, 230p. This reflective biography sets the story of Hildegard in her own age and shows her as a woman of vision and power whose visions might have been migraines. The text includes a summary of Hildegard's writings on religion, theology, medicine, and music in chronological order, and it places them in their cultural milieu.

Godefridus. *The Life of the Holy Hildegard.* Trans. James McGrath. 1980. Collegeville, MN: Liturgical Press, 1995. Paper, 0-8146-2244-5, 134p. This short and accessible overview of Hildegard's life describes the variety of her writings in subjects including theology, philosophy, anthropology and cosmology, music, natural science, and medicine.

Hildegard of Bingen. *Creation and Christ: The Wisdom of Hildegard of Bingen.* Trans. Edmund Colledge and James Walsh. Mahwah, NJ: Paulist Press, 1996. 0-8091-3674-0, 96p. After an introduction to Hildegard of Bingen's life and work, Walsh and Colledge's translation shows that her visions helped her understand the power of beauty within creation and to want an order in which to try to transform other souls.

Hildegard, Saint. *The Letters of Hildegard of Bingen.* Trans. Joseph L. Baird and Radd K. Ehrman. New York: Oxford University Press, 1994. 0-19-508937-5. 227p. The introduction to Saint Hildegard's letters discusses the genre of medieval letters so that their particular form becomes more understandable. The correspondence translated here discloses her early visions, her responses to situations in the convent, and the final conflict in her life when the clergy of Mainz placed her and her nuns under interdict for burying an excommunicated man.

Ulrich, Ingeborg. *Hildegard of Bingen: Mystic, Healer, Companion of Angels.* Trans. Linda M. Maloney. Collegeville, MN: Liturgical Press, 1993. 0-8146-2132-5, 256p. This biography is a series of disjointed "diary" entries from Hildegard's writings. Ulrich has collected and organized them so that they reveal the thoughts of Hildegard throughout her daily life.

HODGKINS, FRANCES (1869–1947)
Artist   New Zealand

Contemporary critics see Frances Hodgkins as one of the most innovative artists of her day at the forefront of British modernism. She was born in Dunedin on April 28, 1869, and her father, a lawyer, taught her to paint with watercolors before she attended art school. She then taught piano to earn money for a trip to Europe, and from 1901 to 1904, she saw Italy, France, Morocco, and the Netherlands. Although she returned to New Zealand and Wellington, she received no recognition, and she went back to Paris in 1907. She taught and then opened her own watercolor school, mainly for women. She exhibited in New Zealand and Australia before settling in St. Ives, Cornwall, at the outbreak of World War I. In Cornwall, she began painting in oils, and after the war, she moved to various places in England, where she taught sketching classes. She never had a permanent home and moved whereever she could make sales, find models and studio space, and work outside without street urchins interfering. Finally, in 1928, she won critical acclaim from her exhibit at Claridges Gallery in London, and the Seven and Five Society, a group of progressive painters, asked her to join. Her later work contrasts with her early Postimpressionist style through its stylization. Critics now see her work as innovative.

BIBLIOGRAPHY

Buchanan, Iain, Michael Dunn, and Elizabeth Eastmond. *Frances Hodgkins: Paintings and Drawings.* Auckland, New Zealand: Auckland University Press, 1994. 1-86940-105-0, 185p. This critical biography looks at different periods of Hodgkins' art life and analyzes her works.

Hodgkins, Frances. *Letters of Frances Hodgkins.* Ed. Linda Gill. New York: Oxford University Press, 1993. 1-86940-081-X, 584p. Of 992 of Hodgkins' surviving letters, 616 appear here. Gill has inserted biographical information and a friend's comment that Hodgkins wrote as she painted, "with brilliant patches of colour and . . . snap and go."

McCormick, E. H. *Portrait of Frances Hodgkins.* Oxford, England: Oxford University Press, 1981. 0-19-547991-6, 159p. This well-written and documented biography with illustrations is a good introduction to Hodgkins and her painting.

HOODLESS, ADELAIDE (1857–1910)
Activist   Canada

Perhaps the best-known Canadian internationally, Adelaide Hoodless campaigned for giving mothers health education that would help them improve conditions in their homes. Born on February 27, 1857, she grew up as the youngest of twelve children on a Brantford, Ontario, farm, before marrying John Hoodless, a wealthy businessman. Their fourth son died from contaminated milk, and Hoodless began her crusade. She formed the first Women's Institute for farm women in 1897. Government officials thought that scientific training and nutrition were too expensive to offer to citizens so she taught the courses herself at the Hamilton Young Women's Christian Association (YWCA) in 1889. She offered a household science class the next year and became president of the YWCA in 1892, after which she opened a school of domestic science with funds solicited from a tobacco magnate. Some saw her as a candidate for sainthood who worked to improve family life in Canada; others such as academics and critics saw her as a barrier to the feminist cause, an ultraconservative whose desire to maintain middle-class standards was a detriment to the women's movement.

BIBLIOGRAPHY

MacDonald, Cheryl Emily. *Adelaide Hoodless, Domestic Crusader.* Toronto: Dundurn, 1986. 1-55002-018-8, 183p. This first full-length biography of Hoodless, documented and well written, presents a balanced view of a Victorian woman who had energy and ambition to work for what she thought was important.

HORNEY, KAREN (1885–1952)
Psychoanalyst   Germany

Karen Horney was a psychoanalyst, teacher, writer, and researcher who developed a theory of female psychology. Born in Hamburg on September 15, 1885, the daughter of a Norwegian sea captain who did not approve of education for females, Karen Danielson decided when she was twelve that she wanted to study medicine. She attended medical school at the University of Freiburg and at Göttingen. Over the next six years, she studied in Berlin, attained her degree with a thesis on traumatic psychoses, married, and had three daughters. During World War I, she worked in the Berlin Sanitorium and military neuropsychiatric hospital, but after the war, she started work at the Berlin Psychoanalytic Institute, where she challenged Freud's view of human nature by saying that women envied male power, not their penises. She separated from her husband and began the second phase of her career in the United States, where she developed her theory of personality. She suggested that children clinging to their parents were not oedipal but abnormal. When her ideas distressed the New York Psychoanalytic Society, she resigned in 1941 and founded the Association for the Advancement of Psychoanalysis and the American Institute of Psychoanalysis. The Karen Horney Clinic in New York is named for her.

BIBLIOGRAPHY

Jones, Constance. *Karen Horney*. New York: Chelsea House, 1989. 1-55546-659-1, 111p. This balanced biography for young adults focuses on fighting within the psychoanalytic community, introducing Freudian theory and explaining Horney's rebellion against it.

Paris, Bernard J. *Karen Horney: A Psychoanalyst's Search for Self-Understanding*. New Haven, CT: Yale University Press, 1994. 0-300-05956-6, 270p. In this academic biography, Paris examines various stages of Horney's thought to show how her experiences influenced her ideas. He uses new sources, including Horney's letters to her daughters.

Quinn, Susan. *A Mind of Her Own: The Life of Karen Horney*. Reading, MA: Addison-Wesley, 1988. 0-201-15573-7, 479p. Quinn uses many anecdotes in this detailed and authoritative biography based on diaries, letters, and interviews to reveal Horney as a shrewd and self-centered woman whose revisions to Freud's concepts evolved from her clinical experiences with women. The text is sympathetic, with clear explanations of Horney's theories and their development.

Rubins, Jack L. *Karen Horney: Gentle Rebel of Psychoanalysis*. New York: Dial, 1978. 0-8037-4425-0, 362p. Rubins relates Horney's theories to her life to show that her views have been incorporated into orthodox psychoanalysis. He includes recollections of her colleagues, friends, students, and her three daughters in this "popular" but pedantic biography.

HUNGARY, ELIZABETH of. *See* ELIZABETH of HUNGARY.

𝔍

ICHIYO, HIGUCHI (1872–1896)
Writer and Poet   **Japan**

Higuchi Ichiyo was the first writer of consequence in the Meiji period of 1868–1912 and the first woman writer of stature in modern Japan. She was born in Toyko on May 2, 1872, and after her father died when she was fifteen, she had to live with her mother in a poor area of town where they ran a paper shop. She educated herself and spent what little time she had after work, when she felt well enough, to write. In her few productive years she wrote some of the most important work of her time, in four thousand classical poems, discursive essays, twenty-one short stories, and a multivolume diary. As a Japanese fiction writer, Higuchi is best known for settings in and around Tokyo's pleasure district including *Oetsugomori* (1894) and *Takekurabe* (1895). She also had the ability to re-create the emotions of women and children. She died of tuberculosis when only twenty-four. Her diary was published as *Wakabakage*, an autobiographical novel, in the year she died.

BIBLIOGRAPHY

Danly, Robert Lyons. *In the Shade of Spring Leaves: The Life and Writings of Higuchi Ichiyo, a Woman of Letters in Meiji Japan.* New Haven, CT: Yale University Press, 1981. 0-300-02614-5, 355p. This literary biography with critical digression concentrates on Ichiyo's short stories and the diary because Danly and other critics think that the poetry is below first-rate. It is a readable but scholarly biography. National Book Award.

INCHBALD, ELIZABETH (1753–1821)
Actor and Playwright   **England**

Elizabeth Inchbald was England's principal dramatist during the eighteenth century as well as novelist, actor, and literary critic. Born Elizabeth Simpson on October 15, 1753 as the eighth of nine children in a Roman Catholic family, her father was a farmer in Bury St. Edmunds who died when she was eight. She never attended school because she had a pronounced stammer, but she read a lot. She ran away from home to join her brother George onstage before marrying Joseph Inchbald, a painter and actor, in 1772. She and Joseph played together in the provinces and in London, even with her speech defect. Joseph died seven years later, and, although beautiful and the recipient of several proposals, she never remarried. Ten years later, she retired from acting and began writing. She produced successful comedies based on French and German models, contributed to *Edinburgh Review*, and was a novelist. From 1806 to 1809, she served as the editor of *The British Theater*, a twenty-five–volume collection of British plays. Elizabeth Inchbald's adaptation of Kotzebue's play *Lovers' Vows* appears in Austen's *Mansfield Park*, causing disarray in the household. Her friends thought of Inchbald as a witty and loving liberal with integrity.

BIBLIOGRAPHY

Littlewood, Samuel Robinson. *Elizabeth Inchbald and Her Circle; the Life Story of a Charming Woman (1753–1821).* Folcroft, PA: Folcroft Library Editions, 1973. 0-8414-2285-5, 135p. Littlewood consulted Inchbald's diaries and letters and James Boaden's *Memoirs* freely in this thorough and accessible biography of Inchbald's life, work, and interaction with her friends.

Manvell, Roger. *Elizabeth Inchbald: England's Principal Woman Dramatist and Independent Woman of Letters in 18th Century London: A Biographical Study.* Lanham, MD: University Press of America, 1987. 0-8191-6633-2, 221p. Manvell looks at the life and work of Inchbald, using letters, the memoirs of James Boaden, comments from her contemporaries, and drama critics of the late eighteenth century.

INGLIS, ELSIE MAUD (1864–1917)

Physician   India

Elsie Inglis had two passions—surgery and suffrage—and in her memory are the Elsie Inglis Unit of the Scottish Women's Hospitals, a children's home in Serbia, and a wing of the Royal Infirmary of Edinburgh. Inglis's Scottish father served in the Indian civil service, and she was born on a Himalayan hill station. She went to England for her schooling and eventually attended the Edinburgh School of Medicine, which Sophia Jex-Blake founded and ran. Disenchanted, she went to Glasgow and founded a rival Medical College for Women with her father's support, where she won the right to study surgery with men. She passed the Scottish Triple Qualification in 1892, and seven years later, she became a physician. She founded a maternity center that became the Elsie Inglis Hospital, lectured in favor of suffrage, and raised money to send female workers to the World War I front in Serbia and France.

BIBLIOGRAPHY

Leneman, Leah. *In the Service of Life: The Story of Elsie Inglis and the Scottish Women's Hospitals.* Edinburgh, Scotland: Mercat, 1994. 1-873644-26-4, 274p. Using personal letters and diaries as a basis, Leneman recounts Inglis's work during World War I to organize a women's-only medical unit of doctors, nurses, orderlies, and ambulance drivers. Although scorned, the unit succeeded in every way.

ISABELLA of SPAIN (1451–1504)
Queen   Spain

Isabella became the queen of Spain by becoming her brother's heir and uniting Castile with Aragón when she married Ferdinand. Born the daughter of the king and queen of Castile on April 22, 1451, near Ávila in Spain, Isabella was not in the line of succession to the throne, but her brother Henry was not a good king. The powerful Castilian nobles urged her to take the throne. To keep Castile out of war, she agreed to be Henry's heir if he could be king while he lived. As an intelligent female and an expert horsewoman, she was prepared to rule. In 1469, she chose to marry Ferdinand, crown prince of Aragón, because she wanted Spain united under the Catholic religion. When she wanted changes, Ferdinand would lead campaigns, and she would visit nobles on horseback to extract money. The two set up a national police force, improved the roads, and controlled moneymaking in their attempts to make Spain strong again. All of her decisions focused on creating a Catholic Spain, including giving Columbus the money to take Catholicism to India by going west. The year Columbus left, Isabella expelled the Moors from Granada and the Jews from the country. The Inquisition occurred under her reign, but some speculate that she was unaware of its horrors.

BIBLIOGRAPHY

Carroll, Warren Hasty. *Isabel of Spain: The Catholic Queen.* Front Royal, VA: Christendom, 1991. Paper, 0-931888-42-5, 385p. Carroll's thoroughly documented and researched biography of Isabel is accessible, although scholarly. He covers Isabel's times and life in a well-written account.

Fraser, Antonia. *The Warrior Queens: The Legends and the Lives of the Women Who Have Led Their Nations in War.* New York: Knopf, 1989. 0-394-54939-2, 383p. Fraser examines Isabella of Castile, a queen in her own right, as she asserted herself to unite her and her husband's territories under the same Catholic rule.

Liss, Peggy K. *Isabel the Queen: Life and Times.* New York: Oxford University Press, 1992. 0-19-507356-8, 416p. Using many primary sources, Liss has carefully researched this academic biography of Isabel and chronologically arranged a political and social history that attempts to explain her life within the religious and social contexts of her time.

Rubin, Nancy. *Isabella of Castile: The First Renaissance Queen.* New York: St. Martin's, 1991. 0-312-05878-0, 468p. Rubin begins her carefully researched and documented biography with Isabella's first appearance as recognized queen in 1474, after Enrique had declared her to succeed him in 1469.

J

JACKSON, GLENDA (1936–)
Actor   **England**

Glenda Jackson is an award-winning actor in film and onstage. Born on May 9, 1936, as the eldest of four girls to a bricklayer father and a mother who worked for people in their homes in Birkenhead, Jackson moved at three with the family to Hoylake, Cheshire, where she received her education at West Kirby Grammar School for Girls. When she was fifteen, she saw *The Merchant of Venice* at Stratford, which inspired her to consider acting while working at a chemist's. She took elocution and dance lessons and joined an amateur theater group. Her efforts led to a scholarship to the Royal Academy of Dramatic Arts in 1954. She had a variety of parts in repertory and appeared in the film *This Sporting Life* in 1963 before joining the Royal Shakespeare Company the next year. She played in London and on Broadway before moving into films, where she won two Academy Awards, one for *Women in Love* and the other for *A Touch of Class*. In 1978, she became a Dame Commander of the British Empire. Five years later, she began to produce plays for the new United British Artists and helped to form a Women's Playhouse Trust. A socialist and member of the Labour Party all of her life, she won a seat in the House of Commons in 1992.

BIBLIOGRAPHY
Woodward, Ian. *Glenda Jackson: A Study in Fire and Ice*. New York: St. Martin's, 1985. 0-312-32914-8, 225p. Woodward sees Jackson as a woman of contradictions in this balanced, popular biography that discusses her and her work. One colleague said she was dour, but people in her town all went to the theater on the days Jackson's films played.

JADWIGA of POLAND (1371–1399)
Queen   Poland

Jadwiga became the queen of Poland and established diplomatic relations with other countries as necessary to begin the greatest two hundred years of Polish history. The daughter of Louis d'Anjou, the king of Hungary and Poland, Jadwiga was betrothed at the age of four to Duke William of Habsburg. When her father died in 1384, she succeeded to the Polish crown, with her sister Maria becoming the queen of Hungary. Her early betrothal was broken, and after a treaty promising the union of Poland and Lithuania, the conversion of Lithuania to Christianity, and the payment of substantial damages to the rejected Austrian duke, she sacrificed her real love to marry the grand prince of Lithuania, Jogaila (Polish for Jagiello or the Christian Wladyslaw II), in 1386 to start the Jagiellian dynasty. He was twenty years older, but together they ruled for nineteen years. For the first five years, she was supposedly the tool of her advisers, but during the next four years, she began negotiations with her Luxembourg brother-in-law so that in 1392, she could establish a compromise between her husband and his cousin Witold. The last part of her reign was diplomatic, and she postponed an unavoidable war. She died in 1399 in childbirth, and her husband followed her advice to marry a granddaughter of Casimir the Great as a way to consolidate his position in Poland. She was also an influential patron of learning and the arts, especially of church music, and she reestablished the University of Kraków. The pope beatified her on his visit to Poland in 1979.

BIBLIOGRAPHY
Halecki, Oskar. *Jadwiga of Anjou and the Rise of East Central Europe.* New York: Columbia University Press, 1991. 0-88033-206-9, 400p. This scholarly but readable biography includes much history to show how important the liaisons that Jadwiga created were for the future of Poland.

JAMES, PHYLISS DOROTHY (1920–)
Writer   England

P. D. James is an award-winning novelist who creates a sense of place with credible characters who show what can happen when people reach a breaking point. She was born in Oxford on August 3, 1920 as the eldest child of an Inland Revenue official. She attended the Cambridge Girls' High School and worked in the theater before World War II. During the war, she became a Red Cross nurse and worked in the Ministry of Food. After her husband, a physician, came home from World War II and suffered schizophrenia, she began working in hospital administration. She then joined the home office, first in the police department, where she became involved with the forensic science service, and then in the criminal law department, where she specialized in juvenile delinquency. She started writing at forty-two, publishing her first novel in 1962. She has introduced Commander Adam Dalgleish, a detective and minor poet, and Cordelia Gray as the protagonists. She won an Edgar for *Daughters*, a Silver Dagger for *Shroud of the Nightingale* and *The Black Tower*, and a Crime Writers Association Diamond Dagger for *A Taste for Death*. Three of her books were chosen as Book-of-the-Month-Club selections. She began to write full-time in 1979 as a serious novelist in a popular genre and was made an Officer of the Order of the British Empire in 1984.

BIBLIOGRAPHY

Gidez, Richard B. *P. D. James*. Boston: Twayne, 1986. 0-8057-6924-2, 153p. Gidez gives a biographical sketch of James along with a descriptive and critical analysis of James' work as a traditional novelist writing crime fiction.

Siebenheller, Norma. *P. D. James*. New York: Ungar, 1981. 0-8044-2817-4, 154p. Siebenheller looks at James in the middle of her career and shows how James' husband's war injury and her own work experiences have contributed to the content of her carefully crafted novels focusing on crime plot or detective.

JAMESON, ANNA (1794–1860)

Writer   Ireland

Anna Jameson wrote literary criticism and travel biographies. Born in Dublin, Anna Brownell Murphy was the oldest daughter of a miniaturist. Four years later, the family moved to Cumberland and then to London. She received a poor education but became a governess to the marquis of Wincester when she was only sixteen. Her first engagement to Robert Jameson broke off, but after she went to Italy as a governess, she returned and married him in 1825. The marriage was unhappy, and she fictionalized it in *The Diary of an Ennuyée*. The book was a major success, and with her career started, she added other works, essays on women in Shakespearean plays, and four volumes titled *Sacred and Legendary Art*. She eventually began to sell her work, separated from her husband in 1836, and supported her mother, sisters, and niece with her writing. Among her friends were **Fanny Kemble, Elizabeth Barrett Browning,** Jane Welse Carlyle, **Barbara Bodichon,** and Lady Noel Byron. She was widely read in England and America for her literary and art criticism and for her travel biographies. In the last few years of her life, she started to lecture about the Sisters of Charity and to discuss the important role of women as reformers and educators.

BIBLIOGRAPHY

Johnston, Judith. *Anna Jameson: Victorian, Feminist, Woman of Letters*. Brookfield, VT: Ashgate, 1997. 1-85928-379-9, 272p. In a well-researched biography, Johnston presents Jameson as an accomplished writer who worked to change conceptions of women.

Thomas, Clara. *Love and Work Enough: The Life of Anna Jameson*. 1967. Ann Arbor, MI: Books on Demand. 0-8357-4150-8, 272p. Thomas uses out-of-print sources, printed references, manuscript letters, the Lovelace-Byron papers, and two hundred letters between Lady Byron and Anna Jameson for this well-documented and scholarly biography. She considers what influenced Jameson to write a particular piece, the public for which it was designed, and its reception by the nineteenth-century literary world as demonstrated through contemporary reviews.

JANSSON, TOVE (1914–)

Writer   Finland

Tove Jansson has written and illustrated books for adults and children that have won many prizes. She was born August 9, 1914, as the daughter of a sculptor and a designer. She had no formal training but read a lot while studying book design and painting. Her Moomintroll books, set in a fantastic world, feature the Moomins, who offer the security of family life. Among the prizes she has won are the Tolland Prize from the Swedish Literature Society in Finland, the Swedish Academy Prize, the Topelius Prize, and the coveted Hans Christian Andersen Medal. Her books have been translated into at least twenty-five languages.

BIBLIOGRAPHY

Jansson, Tove. *Sculptor's Daughter*. London: Ernest Benn, 1969. 0-510-04411-5, 175p. In this autobiography, Jansson recalls scenes from her childhood and writes vignettes focusing on nineteen separate incidences.

Jones, W. Glyn. *Tove Jansson*. Boston: Twayne, 1984. 0-8057-6563-8, 177p. Jones presents a critical study of some of Jansson's work with a brief biography of her life up until 1966.

JEKYLL, GERTRUDE (1843–1932)

Horticulturalist   **England**

Gertrude Jekyll designed gardens, creating atmosphere with native plants. Born into a wealthy family on November 29, 1843, as the second daughter and fourth surviving child, Jekyll had little formal education but showed her artistic talent by wanting to study painting and work with silver, woodcarving, and embroidery. She traveled widely, socialized with other upper-class members, and suggested decorating ideas for her friends, including the duke of Westminster. When her eyesight began to fail as she reached her late thirties, she began gardening. After she met Edward Lutyens in 1889, a young architect, she began to design gardens for many of his houses based on the colors of the French impressionist painters. Together they designed over three hundred gardens. English cottage gardens also inspired her, and she used many scented but less flamboyant flowers such as honeysuckle, pinks, and mignonette. New trends that she supported and about which she wrote were "wild" gardens, trailing climbers, silver and white borders, herb gardens, and "bedding out" of formal Victorian gardens.

BIBLIOGRAPHY

Brown, Jane. *Gardens of a Golden Afternoon: The Story of a Partnership, Edwin Lutyens and Gertrude Jekyll*. New York: Penguin, 1994. 0-14-017563-6, 208p. This overview of Jekyll's life contains especially intriguing photographs of drawings and gardens that Jekyll created with Sir Edward Lutyens. The biography is well documented and readable.

Massingham, Betty. *Miss Jekyll: Portrait of a Great Gardener*. 1973. North Pomfret, VT: David and Charles, 1982. 0-7153-5757-3, 195p. Massingham's biography is a description of the life and times of Jekyll based on her writings and philosophy "to live by faith." She emphasizes Jekyll's training as an artist and the way she dealt with her myopia.

Tankard, Judith B., and Michael R. Van Valkenburgh. *Gertrude Jekyll: A Vision of Garden and Wood*. New York: Harry N. Abrams, 1989. 0-8109-1158-2, 148p. Tankard and Van Valkenburgh used the information about Jekyll's garden plans and photographs discovered at the University of California at Berkeley for a well-researched text, including photographs of Jekyll's own garden.

JEX-BLAKE, SOPHIA (1840–1912)
Physician   England

Sophia Louisa Jex-Blake was the first female doctor in Scotland, and she opened a medical school for women in Edinburgh before men's schools would admit them. Jex-Blake was born January 21, 1840, into a privileged family. She had a private education that allowed her to progress to a tutorship in mathematics at Queen's College in London and in Germany. At twenty-five, she sailed to Boston to study teaching in the United States but volunteered at the New England Hospital for Women and Children and found medicine to be a more worthy cause. After rejection by the Harvard Medical School for being female, she registered at the Women's Medical College of New York Infirmary, but her father's death compelled her return to England. She and four other women then gained acceptance to the Edinburgh Medical School in 1869, although hostility kept them from graduating. In 1874, she founded the London School of Medicine for Women before graduating from the University of Bern in 1877 with her thesis on puerperal fever. Her views clashed with those of **Elizabeth Garrett Anderson**, so in 1878, she left London for Edinburgh, where she opened a dispensary. Eight years later it became the Edinburgh Hospital for Women and Children. In 1894, women were admitted into the Edinburgh Medical School, allowing her to close her school because it was no longer needed.

BIBLIOGRAPHY
Roberts, Shirley. *Sophia Jex-Blake: A Woman Pioneer in Nineteenth Century Medical Reform.* New York: Routledge, 1993. 0-415-08753-8, 207p. This well-documented biography gives a straightforward and chronological account of Jex-Blake's life.

JHABVALA, RUTH PRAWLER (1927–)
Writer   Germany and India

Ruth Prawler Jhabvala is a critically acclaimed novelist who writes about the English experience in India. Born on May 7, 1927, in Cologne, Germany, to Polish parents who emigrated to England in 1939 to flee Nazi Germany, Ruth Prawler attended Chiswick High School and Queen Mary College, University of London, attaining a master's degree in English literature. In 1951, she met and married an Indian architect and went to India with him. She published her first novel about her adopted country in 1955 and followed it with others. She began a film collaboration as a screen writer with the producer Ismail Ivory and the director James Merchant in 1963 that continued through many successful movies and television plays, such as *The Europeans* (1979), *Quartet* (1981), *Heat and Dust* (1982), *The Bostonians* (1984), and *A Room with a View* (1986). She shows the misunderstandings between classes and cultures with a careful subtlety and has received a variety of awards, including the Booker Prize and the MacArthur.

BIBLIOGRAPHY
Bailur, Jayanti. *Ruth Prawer Jhabvala: Fiction and Film.* New Delhi, India: Arnold, 1992. No ISBN, 132p. Bailur thinks that Jhabvala's fiction is based on her life. The text is mainly interpretation and criticism, but it presents Jhabvala's personal views on a variety of topics.

Crane, Ralph J. *Ruth Prawler Jhabvala*. New York: Scribner's, 1992. 0-8057-7030-5, 110p. Crane introduces Jhabvala's fiction in this critical assessment and includes a biographical overview.

JOAN of ARC (1412?–1431)
Martyr   France

With little formal education, Joan of Arc helped the French overcome the English occupation. She was born on January 6, 1412?, in Domrémy, where, at twelve, she heard someone speaking to her. She heard the voice on other occasions and said that it was the Archangel Michael, the defender of France, who was asking her to be a good girl so that God would help her and France. Joan believed that Michael had sent her three directives: go to Orléans to lift the siege, have the king crowned, and drive the English from France. The archangel promised Joan that the commander of a nearby castle would help her. When she met with Charles, he asked her why he should believe her, and she told him something in private that left him visibly affected. She and her troops floated down the Loire River to Orléans, where she demanded that the British surrender. They laughed, and the French won their first battle. On the next day, May 5, 1429, they won a second battle, and finally a third battle, which saved Orléans. The Burgundian troops captured her outside Compiègne in 1430, tried her, and convicted her of immodesty and blasphemy. In 1431, she was burned on the scaffold in Rouen. In 1455, her family requested a new trial, and the verdict was reversed. In 1920, the Roman Catholic Church canonized her as a saint.

BIBLIOGRAPHY
Banfield, Susan. *Joan of Arc*. New York: Chelsea House, 1985. 0-87754-556-1, 112p. This biography for young adults covers Joan of Arc's life and is well documented, with photographs and reproductions illustrating the text.
Brooks, Polly Schoyer. *Beyond the Myth: The Story of Joan of Arc*. New York: Lippincott, 1990. 0-397-32422-7, 176p. Brooks demonstrates how people could believe in Joan by giving extensive background and being careful to differentiate among fact, speculation and legend. Chicago Bulletin Blue Ribbon.
Gies, Frances. *Joan of Arc: The Legend and the Reality*. New York: Harper and Row, 1981. 0-690-01942-4, 306p. This carefully documented, scholarly biography of Joan includes her legacy, what others have said about her since her death.
Smith, John Holland. *Joan of Arc*. New York: Scribner's, 1973. 0-684-13515-9, 232p. Smith explores Joan's life through the responses that she made to the interrogators at her trial and draws several conclusions in his well-researched but pedantic biography.
Warner, Marina. *Joan of Arc: The Image of Female Heroism*. New York: Knopf, 1981. 0-394-41145-5, 349p. Warner covers Joan of Arc's life, death, and legacy. Warner tries to restore Joan to her own context by re-creating the religious beliefs and political struggles that made her activities acceptable and intelligible.

JOHN, GWEN (1876–1939)
Artist   Wales

Gwen John was a prizewinning artist who viewed her subject matter with si-
multaneous detachment and intense personal involvement. Although born in
Haverfordwest, Pembrokeshire, on June 22, 1876, as the second of four children, John and her family moved after her mother's death seven years later to
Tenby in order to escape the nonpermissive attitudes of their aunts. She attended the Slade Art School with her brother, studied figure drawing, and won
the Nettleship Prize. In Paris during 1898, she studied at Whistler's Académie
Carmen, and in 1900, began exhibiting in London at the English Art Club. In
1903, however, she returned to Paris to live and became a model for, and then
a lover of, Auguste Rodin, as well as a friend of Rainer Maria Rilke. She hated
publicity and reluctantly exhibited her work, probably only because she needed
the money. Her main goal was to paint and draw as well as she could. Her
other concerns were people and her cats. In 1910, John Quinn from New York,
a lawyer, saw her work and wanted to buy all of it, but she would not sell everything. She eventually met Quinn in 1921, and after his death in 1924, his
family continued to purchase whatever she would sell. She was interested in
mysticism and became a Catholic, spending time with the Dominican Sisters
who lived in Meudon. As she retreated from society, her colors became more
muted and her figures more elongated.

BIBLIOGRAPHY
Chitty, Susan, Lady. *Gwen John*. New York: Franklin Watts, 1987. 0-531-
    15035-6, 223p. Chitty notes in a balanced and accessible, scholarly biogra-
    phy that John did not sign her paintings, and they can be dated only by the
    color of the cats in them. She painted women, children, cats, the backs of
    people in church, and landscapes outside the window and inside her room.
Taubman, Mary. *Gwen John: The Artist and Her Work*. Ithaca, NY: Cornell
    University Press, 1986. 0-8014-1894-1, 136p. Taubman looks at John's
    life and reproductions of her work, seeing the self as subject as the unifying
    theme running through all of her work.
Thomas, Alison. *Portraits of Women: Gwen John and Her Forgotten Contempo-
    raries*. Cambridge, MA: Polity, 1994. 0-7456-0661-X, 259p. Thomas's em-
    phasis in this collective, carefully researched biography is Gwen John, an
    artist who realized that she could not create if burdened with a family.

JORDAN, DOROTHY (1761–1816)
Actor   Ireland

Dorothy Jordan became the most famous comic actor of her time, rivaled only
by **Sarah Siddons,** and kept performing for over thirty years. Bland, born near
Waterford and baptized on November 22, 1761, was the daughter of Captain
Bland, a wealthy man stationed in Wales, and Grace Philipps, the actor daughter of a clergyman. She debuted in Dublin eight years before opening at Drury
Lane in *The Country Girl* on October l, 1785. Her singing voice and her legs,
displayed in her most popular roles when she impersonated a man, charmed
her audiences. In 1790, she began a liaison with the duke of Clarence, later
William IV. It lasted until 1811, when his family determined that he needed legitimate heirs and a wife who had not been illegitimate herself, but she bore
him ten children and made him a loving companion. She also paid many of his

debts since she continued to work and shrewdly dealt with Richard Brinsley
Sheridan, the Drury Theater's playwright and manager. After the separation
from William IV, she had to leave her home and her children, but she kept performing in London and the provinces. A son-in-law, however, needed funds,
which she supplied, but to escape debtor's prison, she had to go to Paris where
she died alone.

BIBLIOGRAPHY
Jerrold, Clare Armstrong. *The Story of Dorothy Jordan.* New York: B. Blom,
      1969. No ISBN, 429p. This well-researched but biased biography about
      Bland suggests that prior biographers mistreated her because they sup-
      ported royalty and the decision of William IV's family rather than Bland.
Tomalin, Claire. *Mrs. Jordan's Profession: The Actress and the Prince.* New
      York: Knopf, 1995. 0-679-41071-6, 414p. Tomalin's well-researched and
      well-written biography based on Jordan's many letters includes vivid scenes
      from the theater and from Jordan's life to show the social and political
      structure of her times as well as the sexual atmosphere where a lower-class
      woman had to accept the advances of nobility but was often carelessly dis-
      carded when necessary.

JUANA INÉS de la CRUZ. *See* CRUZ, JUANA INÉS de la.

JULIAN of NORWICH (1343–1416?)
Mystic   England

Little is known about Julian of Norwich's life except that she probably lived
outside the walls of St. Julian's Church in Norwich, where she may have served
as an anchoress. She may have attended a school that a community of Benedictine nuns ran near her home at Carrow. Although she probably did not read
Latin, she was well read. In 1373, she suffered a serious illness that a series of
sixteen revelations ended. She received these in a state of ecstasy, and they
lasted five hours. One other vision followed the next day. The visions concerned the Passion, the Holy Trinity, and the Virgin Mother. As she thought
about them twenty years later, she wrote or dictated *XVI Revelations of ivine
Love.* Her account is interwoven with reflections on the mysteries of faith,
prayer, and the divine love of God. The revelations are considered to be one of
the most remarkable documents of the medieval period because Julian of Norwich was the first female writer in English.

BIBLIOGRAPHY
Baker, Denise B. *Julian of Norwich's Showings: From Vision to Book.* Prince-
      ton, NJ: Princeton University Press, 1994. 0-691-03631-4, 244p. Baker's
      scholarly look at Julian of Norwich's showings, both the short and long
      form, reveals a Christian mystic and original theologian who was the first
      woman to write in English.
Jantzen, Grace. *Julian of Norwich: Mystic and Theologian.* New York: Paulist
      Press, 1988. 0-8091-2992-2, 230p. Jantzen's scholarly biography of Julian
      of Norwich, researched and documented, looks at her as mystic and theolo-
      gian. She examines Julian's writings and her religious experiences in their
      fourteenth-century context as well as in their appropriateness for the twen-
      tieth.
Julian of Norwich. *The Life and the Soul: The Wisdom of Julian of Norwich.*
      Trans. Edmund Colledge and James Walsh. Mahwah, NJ: Paulist Press,

1996. 0-8091-3673-2, 96p. An extensive introduction to Julian of Norwich's life prefaces her writings, in which she shows that she received revelations from a God who is nurturing, compassionate, and merciful to those who seek.

Nuth, Joan. *Wisdom's Daughter: The Theology of Julian of Norwich.* New York: Crossroad, 1991. 0-8245-1132-8, 260p. Nuth reveals Julian of Norwich as a visionary and spiritual writer in this scholarly biography. She analyzes Julian in relation to medieval history and theology and shows Julian's approach to the maternal love of God as mother through a layer of thoughtful feminist theological theory.

Pelphrey, Brant. *Christ Our Mother: Julian of Norwich.* Wilmington, DE: M. Glazier, 1989. 0-89453-623-0, 271p. This well-documented, readable biography examines Julian, her visions, and her writings. Pelphrey's clarity makes this biography a good introduction to Julian of Norwich.

JULIANA of THE NETHERLANDS (1909–)
Queen   The Netherlands

Juliana became first the princess regent and then the queen of the Netherlands when her mother, Wilhelmina, abdicated in 1948. Born on April 30, 1909, to Wilhelmina and Prince Henry, Juliana studied at home before entering the University of Leyden. She received an honorary degree, which she said she did not earn. Juliana married Prince Bernhard in 1937 and escaped to Canada during the German Occupation, returning to the Netherlands via England in 1944. She had four daughters, the second of whom lost almost all her sight when two. Juliana sought help, and when a faith healer said that praying would heal the child, Juliana pursued this course; it failed and was one of many disagreements with her husband. When her daughters married, neither she nor her Dutch subjects quite approved of their choices. Although her marriage and her personal life remained stressful, her subjects loved and supported her. She abdicated in 1980 in favor of her daughter Beatrix.

BIBLIOGRAPHY
Hoffman, William. *Queen Juliana: The Story of the Richest Woman in the World.* New York: Harcourt Brace Jovanovich, 1979. 0-15-146531-2, 250p. This readable and entertaining popular biography presents a balanced view of Juliana and the problems in her marriage and with her children. Hoffman shows that the rich may have money, but they cannot buy such things as sight for a daughter.

𝕶

KAHLO, FRIDA (1907–1954)

Artist   Mexico

Frida Kahlo's reputation for her art with its personal statements has increased since her death. Born in Coyoicoán, Mexico City, on July 6, 1907, as one of the five children of a Mexican woman and a German-Jewish immigrant photographer, Kahlo contracted polio and had to spend a year in bed. She had a shrunken leg, but she refused to let it interfere with her life. In 1925, she had a freak accident when an electric trolley plowed into a bus on which she was riding and impaled her on a steel handrail, injuring her spine, ribs, pelvis, collarbone, and foot. While recovering at home, she painted her first self-portrait. She painted many more and gave them to her friends to express her friendship. After their second meeting, she and Diego Rivera began courting and married one year later. Kahlo soon became interested in traditional Mexican *exvoto* paintings, works giving thanks to a saint, the Madonna, or Christ for a blessing performed in the artist's behalf. They often showed a healed limb or a person recovered from an illness. After her husband gave her a long, ruffled dress from Tehuantepec, she began wearing such dresses because they hid her leg and politically supported the women of Tehuantepec who had run their society. Her husband arranged the first public exhibit of her works in 1953, but she had to attend on a stretcher because she was ill.

BIBLIOGRAPHY

Drucker, Malka. *Frida Kahlo: Torment and Triumph in Her Life and Art*. New York: Bantam, 1991. 0-553-07165-3, 160p. Drucker's readable biography, carefully researched, discusses Kahlo's life with emphasis on her nationalism and political activism.

Herrera, Hayden. *Frida, a Biography of Frida Kahlo*. New York: Harper and Row, 1983. 0-06-011843-1, 507p. Herrera gives both a narrative of Kahlo's life and a critical assessment of her work in this carefully documented and recommended biography, using quotes from Kahlo's letters and diaries and interviews with collectors, confidantes, and other artists.

Kahlo, Frida. *The Diary of Frida Kahlo: An Intimate Self-Portrait*. New York: Harry N. Abrams, 1995. 0-8109-3221-0, 295p. This translation of Kahlo's diary includes drawings and watercolors, with the text disclosing her verbal puns and strong emotions.

Kahlo, Frida. *The Letters of Frida Kahlo: Cartas Apasionadas*. Ed. Martha Zamora. San Francisco, CA: Chronicle, 1995. 0-8118-1124-7, 102p. Zamora has collected eighty letters from Kahlo's correspondence, ranging from love letters to her first boyfriend to business letters to her doctors, which reveal her humor and intelligence.

Zamora, Martha, and Marilyn S. Smith. *Frida Kahlo: The Brush of Anguish*. San Francisco: Chronicle, 1990. 0-8770-1746-8, 143p. Zamora and Smith add little new information on Kahlo but create a balanced account, noting her disability but not feeling sorry for her.

KAIN, KAREN (1951–)
Ballerina   **Canada**

Karen Kain is Canada's most popular ballerina. Born in Hamilton, Ontario, on March 28, 1951, Kain was one of four children. Her mother took Kain to see Celia Franca dance *Giselle* when she was nine, and Kain declared that she would be a ballerina. She trained with the Canadian Ballet School and joined the company in 1969, becoming its principal dancer in 1970, dancing the major classical leads as well as interpreting roles by contemporary choreographers. In 1973, she and her partner Frank Augustyn won the Moscow International Ballet Competition. She was a partner of Rudolf Nureyev and a guest artist at the Ballet de Marseille, where she created a leading role in Roland Petit's *Les Intermittences du Coeur* (1974).

BIBLIOGRAPHY
Darling, Christopher, and John Fraser. *Kain and Augustyn: A Photographic Study*. London: Studio Vista, 1978. 0-289-70837-0, 160p. This "biography" is a series of photographs of Kain and her partner Augustyn in performance. Although not thorough, the photographs reveal expressions and poses showing her serious approach to her profession.

Street, David, and David Mason. *Karen Kain: Lady of Dance*. New York: McGraw-Hill Ryerson, 1978. 0-07-082705-2, 127p. The illustrations, including pictures that Kain drew and labeled as a child, are as important as the text in this view of Karen Kain and her grueling schedule of a ballerina with long hours of training and lessons.

KARINSKA, BARBARA (1886–1983)
Costume Designer   **Ukraine**

Barbara Karinska was a major costume designer for film, theater, and ballet. Born on October 3, 1886, in Kharkov as the eldest of a respected Ukrainian textile merchant's ten children, Karinska first designed costumes for her wealthy family's performances, using embroidery. As a young girl, she had governesses, and she decided to study law in Moscow. There she met her husband, and they emigrated to Paris, where Karinska began embroidering Liberty scarves and making costumes for the Comédie Française. After she met George Balanchin in 1932, she began designing costumes for the Monte Carlo Ballet and the Ballets Russes, using designs of Chagall, Dali, and Matisse as inspiration. In 1938, she went to Hollywood and designed for films such as *Kismet* and *Gaslight*. Two years later, she opened a business in New York, and after her authentic costumes for *Joan of Arc* won her an academy award in 1948, she designed for plays and opera. The work she did in her collaboration with George Balanchin and the New York City Ballet from 1949 to 1977 showed her striking style and bold color as well as her careful attention to detail. A "Karinska" label in a waistband, since tutus have no collars, assured the very best. In 1961, she was the only designer to ever win the Capezio Dance Award.

BIBLIOGRAPHY
Bentley, Toni. *Costumes by Karinska*. New York: Harry N. Abrams, 1995. 0-8109-3516-3, 192p. The interesting anecdotes about Karinska's life, which was so closely integrated with her work, make this biography especially enjoyable. Photographs exhibit her elegant costumes.

KARSAVINA, TAMARA (1885–1978)

Ballerina   **Russia**

Tamara Karsavina danced in Russia and Europe before settling in England and mentoring young dancers. Born in St. Petersburg on March 9, 1885, in a family where her father and grandfather had been actors, Tamara Platonovna studied at the Imperial Ballet School after her mother decided she would become a dancer. She joined the Marinsky as a soloist in 1902 but challenged the management before leaving to dance with Diaghilev in Paris during 1909 and 1910 and in Monte Carlo for the 1911 season. Among her special performances were Fokin's choreography of *Les Sylphides* (1908), *The Firebird* (1910), *Carnaval* (1911), *Petrushka* (1911), and *Le Spectre de la Rose* (1911). Karsavina returned to St. Petersburg in 1915 for the birth of her child and to dance with the Marinsky company again. In 1919, she rejoined Diaghilev, although she lived in London where she became vice president of the Royal Academy of Dancing and appeared as a guest artist for the Ballet Rambert's first season in 1930. She taught young dancers, such as **Margot Fonteyn,** who later used her techniques as soloists.

BIBLIOGRAPHY
Karsavina, Tamara. *Theatre Street: The Reminiscences of Tamara Karsavina*. London: Dance Books, 1981. 0-903102-47-1, 362p. Karsavina surveys her life from childhood through the Russian Revolution and years after, focusing on her schooling, dancing at the Maryinsky Theater, her tours to Europe, the war, and Diaghilev's influence. Photographs accompany the text.
Lifar, Serge. *The Three Graces: Anna Pavlova, Tamara Karsavina, Olga Spessivtzeva; the Legends and the Truth*. Trans. Gerard Hopkins. London: Cassell, 1959. No ISBN, 255p. In an undocumented, collective biography, Lifar covers the early careers and greatness of Pavlova, Karsavina, and Olga Spessivtzeva after introducing some of the best dancers of prior centuries including **Taglioni, Elssler,** and Grisi.

KAUFFMANN, ANGELICA (1741–1807)

Artist   **Switzerland**

Angelica Kauffmann became an artist with a reputation for fine portraits and paintings with historical and allegorical subjects. She was born on October 30,

1741, to a portrait and religious painter who recognized her artistic talent when she was very young. Her first commission came when she was only eleven. She refused to limit her subjects to those typically "feminine," working also on historical pictures and classical subjects. In 1762 and after, she traveled with her father to Florence, Rome, and Naples. She was elected to the Accademia di San Luca, and in Venice, the wife of the British ambassador, Lady Wentworth, coerced her into coming to England. In London, her flirtatiousness gained her a reputation along with her paintings. She exhibited with the Royal Academy as a founder member and, after secretly marrying in 1767, discovered that her husband was a bigamist. After he died in 1781, she married another painter, and they moved to Rome, where she established a studio. She was one of most successful women artists in England until the end of the nineteenth century, with European royalty and nobility as her patrons.

BIBLIOGRAPHY

Mayer, Dorothy Moulton, Lady. *Angelica Kauffmann, R. A., 1741–1807.* Gerrards Cross, England: Smythe, 1972. 0-900675-68-3, 192p. Mayer's researched, readable, and accessible biography of Kauffmann reads like fiction as it looks at her life and includes reproductions of her work.

Roworth, Wendy Wassyng, ed. *Angelica Kauffmann: A Continental Artist in Georgian England.* London: Reaktion, 1992. 0-948462-41-8,216p. Roworth places Kauffmann in her times, examines how she could have been a woman and successful at such a time in history, and gives reasons for the phenomenon with documentation and reproductions.

KELLY, PETRA (1947–1992)

Politician   Germany

Petra Kelly became involved with the European government and helped to form the Green Party in Germany. Born in Gunzburg, Bavaria, on November 29, 1947, Kelly received her education in Germany before moving to Columbus, Georgia, with her stepfather, an officer in the American army hospital service. She then studied in Washington, D.C., at the American University, where she volunteered on the presidential campaigns of Hubert Humphrey and Robert Kennedy while demonstrating against the Vietnam War and American nuclear defense policy. When her ten-year-old sister died of cancer, she founded a group to further research on the disease in children. She returned to Europe in 1970 and began working with the European Economic Community in Brussels on environmental issues. In 1972, she joined both the West German Association of Environmental Protection Action Groups and the German Social Democratic Party. She left the party in 1979 because of its stands on nuclear defense, health, and women. She and several friends then founded the Green Party. Its success with her as the national candidate in European elections gave her international coverage and won her the Alternative Nobel Prize in 1982 and the American Peace Woman of the Year Award in 1983. In the same year, she became one of seventeen Green Party members in the West German Parliament. She wrote several books, including *Fighting for Hope* (1984) and *Hiroshima* (1985).

BIBLIOGRAPHY

Parkin, Sara. *The Life and Death of Petra Kelly.* San Francisco: Pandora, 1995. 0-04-440896-X, 230p. Parkin was Kelly's friend and fellow politician, and after Kelly's lover shot Kelly in the head and then killed himself, Parkin wrote this balanced biography.

KEMBLE, FANNY (1809–1893)

Actor   England

Fanny Kemble was an actor and writer. Born on November 27, 1809, as the daughter of an actor/manager and the niece of Sarah Siddons, Frances Anne began acting early, appearing as Juliet to her father's Mercutio at Covent Garden when she was only twenty. Her successful performance revived her father's company, with her roles including Lady Macbeth, Constance, Mariana, Beatrice, Portia, and Queen Katherine. In 1833, she visited the United States and became an intense abolitionist. The next year she married a Georgia planter, Pierce Butler, without knowing that he owned slaves. She left him in 1845 and returned to acting, giving a series of Shakespearean readings in England before returning to the United States to live. She published several pieces of writing, but her autobiography is best remembered because of her honesty. She offended people with her candid comments, but she was very intelligent, with a good sense of humor that they admired.

BIBLIOGRAPHY

Furnas, J. C. *Fanny Kemble: Leading Lady of the Nineteenth Century Stage.* New York: Dial, 1982. 0-312-28162-5, 494p. In a carefully crafted biography, Furnas balances the story of Fanny with a view of nineteenth-century American life.

Marshall, Dorothy. *Fanny Kemble.* London: Weidenfeld and Nicolson, 1977. 0-297-77282-1, 280p. Marshall examines Kemble's life, and with details unavailable in other biographies, reveals the social and political background in which Kemble lived.

Rushmore, Robert. *Fanny Kemble.* New York: Crowell-Collier, 1970. No ISBN, 213p. Rushmore uses excerpts from Kemble's journals and letters to disclose her life as an actress and wife with background about the social history of the times.

Wright, Constance. *Fanny Kemble and the Lovely Land.* New York: Dodd, Mead, 1972. 0-396-06645-3, 242p. Wright's readable biography, based on Kemble's papers and journal, focuses not on Kemble's stage career but on her relationship with her husband, her growing disgust at his ownership of slaves, and her friendships with New England freethinkers and the slaves working for her husband.

KEMPE, MARGERY (1364–c. 1440)

Mystic   England

Margery Kempe was a mystic who wrote about her experiences. The father of Margery Brunham was mayor in their town of Lynn, Norfolk, and after she married John Kempe, a burgess, she had fourteen children. She tried to run businesses such as a brewery and a horsemill but was unsuccessful. After her first child, she had an attack of madness, which ended when she had a vision of Christ. She and her husband were so grateful for the end of her condition that they made a pilgrimage to Canterbury to offer thanks at the cathedral. She began to condemn all pleasure, and in 1413, she and her husband took a vow of chastity. She spent time visiting shrines and people connected with the church around England, and then she went to the Holy Land and returned via Italy. She wrote about her travels, her mystical experiences, and her concerns for those who have sinned between 1431 and 1438 in the oldest extant autobiography in English.

BIBLIOGRAPHY

Atkinson, Clarissa W. *Mystic and Pilgrim: The "Book" and the World of Margery Kempe*. Ithaca, NY: Cornell University Press, 1983. Paper, 0-8014-9895-3, 242p. Kempe's autobiography, rediscovered in 1934, is the basis for Atkinson's biography. She examines Kempe in light of sociological and religious contexts of the fifteenth century.

Neuburger, Verena E. *Margery Kempe: A Study in Early English Feminism*. New York: P. Lang, 1994. 3-906752-65-8, 219p. Neuburger scrutinizes Margery Kempe and contrasts her work with Julian of Norwich's. Neuburger's conclusion indicates that Kempe was the first feminist.

Staley, Lynn. *Margery Kempe's Dissenting Fictions*. University Park: Pennsylvania State University Press, 1994. 0-271-01030-4, 224p. Staley looks at *The Book of Margery Kempe* in relation to the social and religious aspects of fifteenth-century English culture, finding that it offers an understanding of sacred biography and of Kempe's English national identity.

KENNEDY, MARGARET (1896–1967)

Writer   **England**

Margaret Kennedy was novelist, playwright, and journalist. She was born in London on April 23 (Shakespeare's supposed birthday), 1896, as the eldest of four children; her father was a barrister. She studied history at Cheltenham College and Somerville College, Oxford. Her first book was nonfiction, but she preferred novels and wrote sixteen of them. Her most critically acclaimed were *The Constant Nymph* (1924) and its sequel, *The Fool of the Family* (1930). Among her plays was *Escape Me Never* (1933). She also wrote two critical works and short stories. Her themes break from convention in their pursuit of personal fulfillment. She received awards such as the James Tait Black Memorial Prize and Literary Guild and Book Society Choices. In 1939, Bell's palsy curtailed her activity.

BIBLIOGRAPHY

Powell, Violet Georgiana. *The Constant Novelist: A Study of Margaret Kennedy, 1896-1967*. London: Heinemann, 1983. 0-434-59951-4, 219p. Powell uses Kennedy's journal, a chronicle of the years before the war, and other sources in this well-researched, readable biography discussing Kennedy's life and the times.

KENNY, ELIZABETH (1880–1952)

Nurse   **Australia**

Elizabeth Kenny used her nursing skills to find a way to rehabilitate poliomyelitis victims. Born on September 20, 1880, she grew up in New South Wales, and one day, she broke her wrist. When the doctor explained how bones weld to muscles, she decided to help her frail brother. She succeeded in building his muscles and decided to help others as well, refusing marriage to a man who disapproved of her choice. She worked in the back country, treating infantile paralysis with heat and moisture followed by exercise. Her patients recovered, while those treated with casts on their limbs did not. She joined the Australian army nursing corps in World War I, earning the military rank of "Sister" (first lieutenant). She continued rehabilitating victims of paralytic diseases by stimulation and reeducation of the muscles, establishing a clinic in Townsville in 1933, and in England in 1937. She demonstrated her methods, which were successful when those of trained doctors were not, at the Mayo Clinic in Minneapolis during 1940 and in other countries.

BIBLIOGRAPHY

Cohn, Victor. *Sister Kenny: The Woman Who Challenged the Doctors.* Minneapolis: University of Minnesota Press, 1975. 0-8166-0755-9, 302p. This balanced biography of Kenny presents her as frail, brave, selfless, idealistic, and tireless but also vain, flamboyant, domineering, and intolerant.

Crofford, Emily. *Healing Warrior: A Story about Sister Elizabeth Kenny.* Illus. Steve Michaels. Minneapolis: Carolrhoda, 1989. ISBN 0-87614-382-6, 64p. This biography for young adult readers gives an overview of the importance of Sister Kenny's life and work, which earned her the title of mother of "modern physical rehabilitation."

KERR, DEBORAH (1921–)

Actor   Scotland

Deborah Jane Kerr-Trimmer became a stage and screen actress using the professional name of Deborah Kerr. After her birth in Helensburgh on September 30, 1921, as the daughter of a civil engineer from Glasgow, she had the influence of two dominating grandmothers. She trained as a dancer and joined the *corps-de-ballet* of a Sadler's Wells production of *Prometheus* (1938) but decided that she would act instead. She appeared in repertory in Oxford before making her film début in *Contraband* (1940). After success in Britain, she went to Hollywood and eventually played in *From Here to Eternity* (1953). She received six Academy Award nominations before retiring from the screen in 1969. Other awards include the New York Film Critics' Best Performance; the *Photoplay* Gold Medal Best Actress; Variety Club Best Film Actress; *Prix Fermina* Universal Cinema, Belgium, Best Actress; Sorrento Film Festival Best English Actress; and the Los Angeles Drama Critics' Circle Award. She has continued to work in the theater.

BIBLIOGRAPHY

Braun, Eric. *Deborah Kerr.* New York: St. Martin's, 1978. 0-312-18895-1, 264p. In this popular biography, Braun discusses Kerr's life and admires her work by quoting critics who wrote about her stage and film performances. He includes photographs.

KING, JESSIE (1875–1949)

Artist   Scotland

Jessie Marion King, the most important Scottish illustrator of the twentieth century, became an internationally known designer and illustrator. Born in New Kilpatrick (now Bearsden) on March 20, 1875, she was the daughter of a minister. After studying at the Glasgow School of Art from 1895 to 1899, she won a scholarship traveling to Germany and Italy. She became a book illustrator, often sought after, and a designer of jewelry, wallpaper, batik, and pottery. She helped Mackintosh decorate its Scottish Pavilion at the Exposizione Nazionale in Turin, and she won a gold medal for her design of a book cover. She also designed fabrics and silver for Liberty's of London. She moved to Paris with her husband but returned to Scotland at the outbreak of World War I. In her studio, she used old chamber pots to keep her colors and exhibited her work throughout her life.

BIBLIOGRAPHY

White, Colin. *The Enchanted World of Jessie M. King.* Edinburgh, Scotland: Canongate, 1989. 0-86241-235-8, 164p. In a well-written and researched biography of King's life with illustration reproductions, White used family papers and old photographs to show King as an illustrator of dreams, combining the Celtic past by blending reality and fantasy.

KINGSLEY, MARY (1862–1900)

Anthropologist   **England**

Mary Henrietta Kingsley was an explorer who traveled throughout Africa collecting a variety of living animal and other species that she brought back to England. She was born on October 13, 1862, as the daughter of doctor and an innkeeper's daughter. With little formal education and an ability to act practically, she left home as soon as her father died. She went to the Canary Islands and then to West Africa, where she stayed for two years, trading with bush Africans and paying for food and shelter with tobacco, fishhooks, matches, and rubber. She wore a heavy black skirt, a high-necked blouse, a hat, and carried an umbrella on her journeys, unafraid to mix with various tribes and to learn their languages. She saw herself as equal to those she met and knew that eating with possible enemies was better than fighting with them. She studied seamanship; paddled a canoe through mangrove swamps; met species such as gorillas, crocodiles, and hippopotami; and climbed to the top of Cameroon Mountain, the highest point in West Africa. The British Museum named for her three of the insects, reptiles, and fish that she had collected. She wrote about her two trips, disapproving of missionary meddling and supporting African political causes against the British. She died in South Africa of enteric fever and was buried at sea.

BIBLIOGRAPHY

Blunt, Alison. *Travel, Gender, and Imperialism: Mary Kingsley and West Africa.* New York: Guilford, 1994. 0-89862-347-2, 190p. This well-documented, scholarly work on the travels and travel writing of Kingsley uses Kingsley's work and letters as a primary source to study the social, ideological, and logistical significance of women traveling alone during Kingsley's time.

Frank, Katherine. *A Voyager Out: The Life of Mary Kingsley.* Boston: Houghton Mifflin, 1986. 0-317-53370-3, 333p. In her definitive study of Kingsley, Frank employs previously unpublished sources, along with printed information, to reveal Kingsley's experience as she traveled in Africa after staying at home with her family until she was thirty.

Myer, Valerie Grosvenor. *A Victorian Lady in Africa: The Story of Mary Kingsley.* Southampton, England: Ashford, 1989. 1-85253-099-5, 221p. Myer's readable and entertaining biography without documentation probes Kingsley's unusual life.

Pearce, R. D. *Mary Kingsley: Light at the Heart of Darkness.* Oxford: Kensal, 1990. 0-946041-61-X, 174p. Pearce's scholarly and feminist biography, thoroughly documented and based on new information about Kingsley's life, shows a complex woman who understood her times and lived in them while simultaneously rebelling.

KLEIN, MELANIE (1882–1960)

Psychoanalyst   Austria

Melanie Reizes Klein, an Austrian psychoanalyst, studied problems of character and personality and applied the results in her treatment of children. Klein was born in Vienna on March 30, 1882, and watched her own mother interact with her children before training in Budapest and Berlin with two Freudians, Ferenczi and Karl Abraham. In 1926, Ernest Jones, Freud's biographer, invited her and her three children to London. Klein analyzed a child under three, and her techniques using play are now prevalent in children's clinics. She created her theory from her mother's behavior and Freud's ideas, believing that the struggle occurring between a child's life instinct and envy of the mother in the first four months of life formed human nature. She wanted to integrate the various parts of a child's personality by making the child's unconscious conscious. Her most important work was identifying the range of patients who could be psychoanalyzed by looking at the origins of psychosis, paranoid-schizoid illness, and depression. She also researched the psychological aspects of ethics, thinking, aesthetics, and groups.

BIBLIOGRAPHY
Segal, Julia. *Melanie Klein.* Thousand Oaks, CA: Sage, 1992. Paper, 0-8039-8476-6, 160p. Segal examines Klein's life, her major theoretical and practical contributions, criticisms of her work, and her influence, using Klein's letters and her unpublished autobiography in an accessible biography.

KNIGHT, LAURA (1877–1970)

Artist   England

Dame Laura Knight became a painter who specialized first in portraits and then landscapes and ballet studies. Laura Johnson was born on August 4, 1887, as the third in a family of girls, her father having left home before her birth and dying not long after. She attended Long Eaton Derbyshire and then the Nottingham School of Art. She very early formed her socialist views, and when she moved to Cornwall with her husband in 1903, their friends included Bernard Shaw, **Anna Pavlova**, T. E. Lawrence, and Augustus John, brother of Gwyn. Knight's first acclaimed painting was *Daughters of the Sun* in 1910. After World War I, Gypsy bands and the circus intrigued her, and she followed them for years, painting scenes of the performers. She became an associate of the Royal Academy of Art in 1927 and was made a Dame of the British Empire in 1929. She became a full member of the Royal Academy in 1936, but women could not attend the annual members' banquet until 1967.

BIBLIOGRAPHY
Bolling, G. Fredric, and Valerie A. Withington. *The Graphic Work of Laura Knight: Including a Catalogue Raisonne of Her Prints.* Brookfield, VT: Ashgate, 1993. 0-85967-939-X, 154p. The text, using Knight's words about a particular scene or the nature of a drawing, examines Knight's drawing and published prints with full-page illustrations grouped according to theme and subject.

Dunbar, Janet. *Laura Knight*. London: Collins, 1975. 0-00-211489-5, 237p. Dunbar's researched and readable biography of Knight's life contains several photographs of her family but none of her art as Dunbar searches for the reason Knight has been almost forgotten since her death.

Fox, Caroline. *Dame Laura Knight*. Oxford: Phaidon, 1988. 0-7148-2447-X, 128p. This researched and readable biography, based on Knight's autobiographies, contains photographs of Knight's work, including her sketches from the Nuremberg war trials.

KNIPPER-CHEHKOVA, OLGA (1868–1959)

Actor   Russia

Olga Knipper-Chehkova became a Russian actor known for her poetical interpretations of Chehkov's plays. Born Olga Leonardovna in Glazov on September 9, 1868, her father an engineer, she studied drama at the Moscow Philharmonic Society and made her debut at the Moscow Art Theatre. She married Chehkov in 1901, and after his death three years later, she continued to play lead roles at the Moscow Art Theatre. She began to play comic parts after the revolution and played in films. She spent three years touring in Russia, Europe, and the United States and survived Stalin's years to experience Khrushchev's revival of Western relations. She played Arkadina in *The Seagull*, Helena Andreyevna in *Uncle Vanya,* and Anna Petrovna in *Ivanov*, but is best remembered as Masha in *Three Sisters*. She was eighty when she last appeared in *The Cherry Orchard*. She died as a People's Artist of the Soviet Union.

BIBLIOGRAPHY
Pitcher, Harvey J. *Chekhov's Leading Lady: A Portrait of the Actress Olga Knipper*. New York: Franklin Watts, 1980. 0-531-09918-0, 288p. Pitcher presents a balanced portrait of both Chekhov and Knipper in a well-documented and accessible biography based on letters and photographs.

KOLLONTAI, ALEXANDRA (1872–1952)

Revolutionary   Russia

Alexandra Mikhaylovna Kollontai was a Russian revolutionary, feminist, and politician. Born in St. Petersburg on March 31, 1872, her aristocrat father was a general in the Imperial Army, and her mother was daughter of a Finnish wood merchant. Servants raised her in both St. Petersburg and Finland, and she read to educate herself. She refused to become a debutante, wanting to study abroad, but her father allowed her to travel only in Europe. After her marriage and the birth of her son, she began writing short stories rebelling against domesticity. She saw a textile factory in 1896 and, appalled by the conditions, began her advocacy of the working class. Already a student of Marx and Engels, she began to study economics and become interested in other socialists such as **Rosa Luxemburg**. She was exiled for the two books she wrote expressing her views, but she toured Europe and the United States to support pacifism and oppose conscription. She returned to Russia in 1917 after the revolution and met Lenin who appointed her commissar for public welfare (the only woman in the first Bolshevik government). She tried to get reforms for women such as free love, easier divorce, and collective child care. She disliked the slow change and campaigned for her causes, but Stalin effectively exiled her as minister to

Norway, then Mexico, and finally Sweden. She continued to record her beliefs about children and the place of women while she was stationed abroad.

BIBLIOGRAPHY

Clements, Barbara Evans. *Bolshevik Feminist: The Life of Aleksandra Kollontai.* Bloomington: Indiana University Press, 1979. 0-253-31209-4, 352p. Clemments' recommended biography reveals style, research, and knowledge in its telling of Kollontai, a woman who chose to endure the loneliness of independence.

Farnsworth, Beatrice. *Aleksandra Kollontai: Socialism, Feminism, and the Bolshevik Revolution.* Stanford, CA: Stanford University Press, 1980. 0-8047-1073-2, 432p. Farnsworth emphasizes the conflict that Kollontai had with the Communist Party over the "woman question," and she evaluates Kollontai's life carefully, contributing information about early Bolshevism and relationships among members, the difficulty of recruiting women into the party, and the disagreement among Russian women about the "woman question," based on Kollontai's own writing, the memoirs of Stalin's wife, Krupskaya, and earlier Soviet women's magazines.

Porter, Cathy. *Alexandra Kollontai: The Lonely Struggle of the Woman Who Defied Lenin.* New York: Dial, 1980. 0-8037-0129-2, 553p. Porter makes unsubstantiated generalizations, leaning toward feminism and Bolshevism in this biography of Kollontai.

KOLLWITZ, KÄTHE (1867–1945)

Artist and Sculptor   Germany

Käthe Kollwitz, an artist and sculptor, became known for her powerful pieces speaking against hunger, alcoholism, abortion, and most of all, war. Käthe Schmidt was born on July 8, 1867, in East Prussia, where her father was a Free Congregation preacher. She studied in art schools in Königsberg, Berlin, and Munich before marrying Karl Kollwitz, a medical student and moving to Berlin. There, her pictures about an industrial revolt in Silesia in the 1840s earned her a gold medal nomination, but the kaiser vetoed her award. After teaching and traveling abroad, she produced two other cycles, *The Peasants' War* and *Images of Wretchedness.* During World War I, her son Peter died, and her following work reflected her anguish over war, poverty, and death. She created the poster *Bread!,* which functioned as a vehicle for strikers in Berlin during 1920, and *Vienna Is Dying! Save Its Children!* in the same year. In 1928, she became professor of graphics at the Prussian Academy, but the Nazis made her resign in 1933, and she finished a tribute to her son, *Father and Mother,* the same year. Her last print cycle was *Death,* completed in 1935. Her grandson died on the Russian front in 1942.

BIBLIOGRAPHY

Kearns, Martha. *Käthe Kollwitz: Woman and Artist.* Old Westbury, NY: Feminist Press, 1976. 0-912670-15-0, 237p. The text leans toward politicizing Kollwitz's feminism and is not as well researched as it could be, although it includes an annotated bibliography of Kollwitz's life and works.

Klein, Mina C., and H. Arthur Klein. *Käthe Kollwitz: Life in Art.* New York: Holt, Rinehart, and Winston, 1972. 0-03-086362-7, 183p. Klein identifies her recommended introduction as both an "art book" and a biography because she has focused primarily on Kollwitz's art, but she thinks nonspecialists should know how Kollwitz's achievements are inextricably related to her personal life.

Kollwitz, Käthe. *Käthe Kollwitz: Artist of the People*. London: South Bank Centre, 1995. 1-85332-135-4, 47p. The text includes a brief chronology of Kollwitz's life, followed by labeled photographs of her work demonstrating the emotions that she projected through her art.

Kollwitz, Käthe. *The Diary and Letters of Käthe Kollwitz*. Trans. Richard Winston and Clara Winston. Evanston, IL: Northwestern University Press, 1988. 0-8101-0760-0, 200p. These diary entries reveal the struggles of Kollwitz as both master and servant to her art. They show her as mother and wife with lighthearted and happy memories as well as despairing ones.

Nagel, Otto. *Käthe Kollwitz*. Trans. Stella Humphries. Greenwich, CT: New York Graphic Society, 1971. 0-8212-0401-7, 261p. In a recommended biography, Nagel, a fellow artist and friend, surveys Kollwitz's life in childhood, as a physician's wife in Berlin, suffering through the Nazis, and her death. Accompanying productions of prints, drawings, and the cycles show the scope and character of her art.

KOVALEVSKAYA, SOFYA (1850–1891)

Mathematician   Russia

A radical nihilist thinker, Sofya Vasilyevna Kovalevskaya was the most notable female mathematician of the nineteenth century. Born January 15, 1850, to a well-educated and multilingual colonel of the artillery, Vasily Vasilievich Krukovskoi, and a society mother who had little influence on her early life, Kovalevskaya constantly gazed at the lithographed notes of a calculus course on the wallpaper of one of the rooms of their estate. She read a lot, and when she interpreted the symbols in a trigonometry book unknown to her tutor, a family friend encouraged her father to let her pursue mathematics. By seventeen, she had begun studying differential and integral calculus. She could study further only abroad, so she arranged a marriage of convenience to obtain a passport and left for Heidelberg. She eventually joined Karl Weierstrass at the University of Berlin and became the first woman in modern times to receive a doctorate in mathematics, the first to hold a chair in the subject outside Renaissance Italy (at Stockholm University), and the first on the board of a scientific journal (*Acta Mathematica*). In 1888, she won the Prix Bordin of the French Academy of Sciences, for which the prize money was increased to indicate the importance of her work. The next year, she received a similar prize from the Swedish Academy of Sciences, and the Imperial Academy of Sciences in Russia grudgingly elected her a member.

BIBLIOGRAPHY

Cooke, Roger. *The Mathematics of Sofya Kovalevskaya*. New York: Springer-Verlag, 1984. 0-387-96030-9, 234p. Cooke sets the theoretical background for Kovalevskaya's mathematics in this scholarly examination of her work and includes her relationships to many of the mathematicians of her day.

Kennedy, Don H. *Little Sparrow: A Portrait of Sophia Kovalevsky*. Athens: Ohio University Press, 1982. 0-8214-0703-1, 341p. Kennedy uses published memoirs and correspondence as well as Kovalevsky family memories to relate her drive toward achievement and overcoming her feelings of inadequacy.

Koblitz, Ann Hibner. *A Convergence of Lives: Sofia Kovalevskaia, Scientist, Writer, Revolutionary*. 1983. New Brunswick, NJ: Rutgers University Press, 1993. 0-8135-1962-4, 305p. Koblitz bases her particularly accessible biography on Swedish and Russian archival material and photographs, without dwelling on the technicalities of Kovalevskaia's mathematics, to place Kovalevskaia in the social and political contexts of her times.

Kovalevskaia, S. V. *A Russian Childhood*. Trans. and ed. Beatrice Stillman. New York: Springer-Verlag, 1978. 0-387-9034-8, 250p. Kovalevskaia recreates the social history of a wealthy landowning gentry family during a time shaped by the emancipation of the serfs, the rebellion of children against their fathers, and the rise of radical political groups thinking that science could bring a just social order.

KULISCIOFF, ANNA (1857–1925)
Activist   Russia

Anna Kuliscioff was an active socialist and feminist in Italy. She was born at Simferopol in the Crimea on January 9, 1857, and later studied at the Zürich Polytechnic, where she met Russians who also believed Bakunin's ideas. When the Russian government disapproved of her political activities, she went into exile in 1877. In Florence, she was arrested for activism in Italian politics, but she helped her friend Andrew Coska found a socialist party. In 1884, her interest in Marxism led her to move to Milan with Filippo Turati. There she qualified in medicine and began to minister to the working classes. She simultaneously became concerned about women's lower social and economic status. Her desire for a law to protect women and children at work caused a split within the socialist organization, and in 1901, she opposed Turati and the majority of the party by demanding that the Party support woman's rights. She helped to create the *Unione Femminile Nazionale Socialista* while editing a newspaper for working-class women and continued her activism until her death.

BIBLIOGRAPHY
LaVigna, Claire. *Anna Kuliscioff: From Russian Populism to Italian Socialism*. New York: Garland, 1991. 0-8240-2542-3, 245p. This scholarly biography of Kuliscioff covers her life until 1913 and includes her Italian years, her relationship with Coska, the Union, the formation of the Italian Socialist Party, Marxism, her crusade for women and children, and her disagreement with party members over her goals.

𝕷

LABÉ, LOUISE (c. 1520–1566)
Poet   **France**

Louise Charlieu Labé was a poet who believed that women were the intellectual equals of men. As the daughter of a Lyons rope maker in a Renaissance
center encouraging education for women of the nobility, she could speak Italian and Latin as a young girl. She also learned horsemanship and the use of
arms. Her marriage to Ennemond Perrin, thirty years older, was one of convenience, and she continued liaisons with other men, including contemporary intellectuals and writers. She wrote mainly about physical desire in her poetry,
with her intense tone compensating for the narrow subject matter. In her poetry, nothing outside her passion and her beloved existed. In 1555, her *Oeuvres*
was published, and her sonnets show Petrarch's influence, although they do not
treat love in the same way.

BIBLIOGRAPHY

Baker, Deborah Lesko. *The Subject of Desire: Petrarchan Poetics and the Female Voice in Louise Labé*. Purdue, IN: Purdue University Press, 1996. 1-
55753-088-2, 249p. Baker discusses Labé not in a biography but in a critical analysis of her work in which she sees Labé express erotic desire within
and against Renaissance literary authority and tradition.

Cameron, Keith. *Louise Labé: Renaissance Poet and Feminist*. New York:
Berg, St. Martin's, 1990. 0-85496-618-8, 100p. Cameron places Labé in
her times with a brief historical account of Lyons in this carefully documented, scholarly account of Labé and her work, including translations.

Warnke, Frank J. *Three Women Poets: Renaissance and Baroque: Louise Labé,
Gaspara Stampa, and Sor Juana Ines De La Cruz*. Trans. Frank J. Warnke.
Lewisburg, PA: Bucknell University Press, 1987. 0-8387-5089-3, 135p.
Warnke gives a short introduction to Labé's life and translations of some of
her poems in this academic, collective biography.

LA FAYETTE, MADAME de (1634–1693)
Writer   France

Madame de La Fayette was a novelist whose works have become classics in French literature. Marie-Madeleine Pioche de La Vergne was baptized on March 18, 1634. Her family was not in the highest noblity, but her tutor educated her well, teaching her to love literature. She married above her station to the comte de La Fayette in 1655, a widower eighteen years older. After two sons, she returned to Paris, and he remained in Auvergne on his estates. She published her first novel, *Princesse de Montpensier*, anonymously in 1662, and, after publishing *La Princesse de Clèves* in 1678, she immediately became successful. She counted among her friends the poet Ségrais, Henrietta Anne of England, **Madame de Sévigné**, and de La Rochefoucauld. Although Madame de La Fayette suffered from ill health most of her life, she wrote three more works, which were published posthumously.

BIBLIOGRAPHY
Haig, Stirling. *Madame de La Fayette*. New York: Twayne, 1970. No ISBN, 164p. In a scholarly, somewhat pedantic, critical biography on Madame de La Fayette, Haig thinks that she was probably not the creator of the first psychological novel in France but was the first to use psychology in her characters. He sees her as the end of a literary tradition rather than the beginning of one.

LAFORET, CARMEN (1921–)
Writer   Spain

Carmen Laforet, an award-winning novelist, discusses the importance of religion on women's lives and the effect of the Spanish civil war on families of survivors, using the paradigm of family to reflect society at large. She was born in Barcelona on September 6, 1921, and, after a childhood in Las Palmas on the Canary Islands, she returned to the mainland at eighteen to study humanities and law. After moving to Madrid and marrying a journalist, she published her first novel in 1944, a semiautobiographical work titled *Nada*. It won the Premio Nadal, bringing her immediate international fame with its translation into many languages. Her work explores the conflicts between dreams and aspirations, recalling the themes in *Don Quixote*. She converted to Roman Catholicism in 1952, and this influenced her subject matter through her last published work in 1963.

BIBLIOGRAPHY
Johnson, Roberta. *Carmen Laforet*. Boston: Twayne, 1981. 0-8057-6443-7, 153p. Johnson, in her introduction to Laforet's life and works, observes that Laforet's Premio Nadal award helped other women write about important subjects within their own lives, such as sibling relationships, marriage, motherhood, spinsterhood, the church, confinement, and discrimination.

LAGERLÖF, SELMA (1858–1949)
Writer   Sweden

Selma Lagerlöf was a novelist who won the Nobel Prize in literature in 1909. Three years after her birth on November 20, 1858, on her family's estate of Mårbacka in Värmland, Sweden, the daughter of a lieutenant, a lameness struck her from which she never completely recovered. During her youth, she heard the folktales of her people and adapted them in her writing, which she began while she was teaching in a girls' junior high school after she had studied at a teachers' college for gifted women in Stockholm. She published her first novel in 1891, *Gosta Berlings Saga*. Her second novel, *Antikrists Mirakler* (The Miracles of the Anti-Christ), concerned modern society in Italy. During the literary renaissance of the 1890s, she was Sweden's most important novelist. In 1901 and 1902, when she published a two-volume work titled *Jerusalem*, she cemented her reputation. She used money from the Nobel Prize to repurchase the family estate, which had been sold during the family's economic distress after her father's death.

BIBLIOGRAPHY

Berendsohn, Walter Arthur. *Selma Lagerlöf: Her Life and Work*. Trans. George F. Timpson. Port Washington, NY: Kennikat, 1968. No ISBN, 136p. Berendsohn recounts Lagerlöf's life, examines her works, and assesses her art and message in a somewhat dated biography. For a source other than Lagerlöf's own writing, Berendsohn is more accessible than Edstrom's scholarly analysis.

Edstrom, Vivi Blom. *Selma Lagerlöf*. Trans. Barbara Lide. Boston: Twayne, 1984. 0-8057-6587-5, 151p. Edstrom's critical analysis of Lagerlöf's work contains a brief overview of her life and examines the theme of confrontation between the masculine and the feminine, with the ability of women to influence men morally through goodness and love.

Lagerlöf, Selma. *Memories of Mårbacka*. Notes Greta Anderson. Iowa City, IA: Penfield, 1996. 1-57216-048-9, 198p. Anderson has organized a series of short, family, ancestral tales that give insight into Lagerlöf's family and the relationship of its members, especially her admiration for her father, even though his business sense caused the family to lose its home after his death.

Lagerlöf, Selma. *Memories of My Childhood: Further Years at Mårbacka*. Trans. Velma Swanston Howard. 1934. Millwood, NY: Kraus Reprint, 1975. 0-527-54010-2, 290p. Lagerlöf gives a child's view of situations in the anecdotes she recalls about hearing adult stories but not understanding until she was older what they meant. The text becomes more stylistically complex as Lagerlöf matures.

LASKER-SCHÜLER, ELSE (1869–1945)

Poet   Germany

Else Lasker-Schüler was an important German lyric poet. She was born on February 11, 1869, in Elberfeld of Jewish parentage. She married and settled in Berlin, where she frequented avant-garde literary circles and began publishing her poetry during the formation of the expressionist movement. After a divorce and remarriage, she published more poetry, along with short stories, novels, and plays. In 1932, she won the German Kleist Prize for her body of work. The next year, when the Nazis came to power in Germany, she had to flee to Switzerland. She often gave money to people in need, leaving herself in poverty, and she spent her last years that way, dying in Jerusalem. Her poetry employs fantasy, symbolism, and personal evocations of her own childhood along with themes of romantic passion, religion, and art.

BIBLIOGRAPHY

Heizer, Donna K. *Jewish-German Identity in the Orientalist Literature of Else Lasker-Schüler, Friedrich Wolf, and Franz Werfel.* Columbia, SC: Camden House, 1996. 1-57113-025-X, 116p. With a thesis that Germans considered Jews to be Orientals, Heizer examines the lives of three German writers, including Lasker-Schüler, to see how they handled the situation between 1900 and 1933. In a well-researched and documented text, Heizer analyzes the constructed cultural identity in Lasker-Schüler's work.

Schwertfeger, Ruth. *Else Lasker-Schüler: Inside This Deathly Solitude.* New York: Berg, St. Martin's, 1991. 0-85496-177-1, 116p. Schwertfeger looks at the eccentricities of Lasker-Schüler's life and work in her accessible biography.

Cohn, Hans W. *Else Lasker-Schüler, the Broken World.* London: Cambridge University Press, 1974. 0-521-20292-2, 162p. Cohn analyzes Lasker-Schüler's poetry, with no English translations, in terms of her psyche after he presents an outline of her life in an informal, somewhat inappropriate tone.

LAURENCE, MARGARET (1926–1987)

Writer   Canada

Margaret Laurence was a novelist who won awards for her stories set in Canada. Originally Jean Margaret Wemyss, born on July 18, 1926, she lived in Neepawa, Manitoba, where her stepmother raised her after her parents died when she was young. She decided to become a writer, and after attending United College in Winnipeg, she worked as a reporter for the *Winnipeg Citizen*, a newspaper supporting trade unions. After her marriage in 1947, she lived in various places around the globe, including Somalia and Ghana. She returned to Canada for five years but left for England, where she wrote her books about her hometown of Neepawa, called the "Manawaka" novels. Her novels *A Jest of God* (1966) and *The Diviners* (1974) (banned in Canadian schools because of its overt sexuality) both won the Governor General's Award. After she returned to Canada, she was the writer-in-residence at Toronto University. Other works were children's books, short stories, and a study of African literature.

BIBLIOGRAPHY

Bailey, Don. *Memories of Margaret: My Friendship with Margaret Laurence.* Scarborough, Ontario, Canada: Prentice-Hall, 1989. 0-13-574393-1, 237p. Bailey, a minister, credits Laurence with saving his life and, in his balanced memoir, shows her willing to find the humor beneath despair.

Laurence, Margaret. *Dance on the Earth: A Memoir.* Toronto: McClelland and Stewart, 1989. 0-7710-4746-0, 298p. Laurence's daughter finished her mother's autobiography, gone through two drafts before Laurence died.

Laurence, Margaret. *A Very Large Soul: Selected Letters from Margaret Laurence to Canadian Writers.* Ed. J. A. Wainwright. Dunvegan, Ontario, Canada: Cormorant, 1995. 0-920953-87-5, 264p. The letters here were addressed to Canadian writers who responded to questions about their first encounter with Laurence. They describe their actual meetings, letters, works of hers they read, their relationship, and what she said to them or to other writers to influence them.

Morley, Patricia A. *Margaret Laurence.* Boston: Twayne, 1981. 0-8057-6433-X, 171p. This critical analysis of Laurence's life and writings divides her writing into two periods—her writing with Canada as a setting and her work resulting from Africa.

Sparrow, Fiona. *Into Africa with Margaret Laurence*. Toronto: ECW, 1992. 1-55011-169-8, 251p. In this well-documented, scholarly biography, Sparrow discusses the influence of Africa on Laurence's work.

LAWRENCE, GERTRUDE (1901–1952)

Actor   **England**

Gertrude Lawrence won awards for her acting in light comedy. She was born on July 4, 1901, in London as Gertrud Alexandra Dagma Lawrence Klasen to a Danish father and an Irish mother. Her father was an interlocutor in the theater, and her mother played small parts. Lawrence first appeared onstage at two and danced in a London pantomime when she was nine. She studied dancing, elocution, and acting at the Italia Conti Dancing Academy and at the Convent of Sacré Coeur in Streatham. She played in the provinces for seven years before understudying **Beatrice Lillie**, who broke her leg by falling off a horse. Lawrence then traveled to New York with Lillie and *Charlot's Revues*. When she returned to London, Noel Coward wrote *Private Lives* for her. She subsequently appeared in such plays as *Skylark, Tonight at 8:30, Lady in the Dark, Pygmalion, The King and I*, and *The Glass Menagerie*. During World War II, she performed for both British and American troops in both Europe and the Pacific and became a staff assistant in the American Red Cross and a colonel in the United States Auxiliary Ambulance Corps. After the war, she helped direct the School of Dramatic Arts at Columbia University. Among her awards were the New York Academy gold medal for best performance, the Comedia Matinee Club's most outstanding theatrical performance, and an honorary degree from Ithaca College.

BIBLIOGRAPHY

Morley, Sheridan. *Gertrude Lawrence, a Biography*. New York: McGraw-Hill, 1981. 0-07-043149-3, 228p. Well researched and well written, Morley's biography of Gertrude Lawrence, best known to American audiences as Anna in *The King and I*, shows her career, presents her rather egotistical personality, and discusses her relationships with her friends, including Noel Coward.

Aldrich, Richard Stoddard. *Gertrude Lawrence as Mrs. A; an Intimate Biography of the Great Star*. 1954. Westport, CT: Greenwood Press, 1969. 0-8371-2469-7, 414p. Aldrich, Lawrence's husband, wrote this popular, biased biography, with photographs.

LAWSON, LOUISA (1848–1902)

Writer and Activist   **Australia**

Louisa Lawson was a social reformer, writer, and founder of Australia's first women's magazine. She was born in Guntawang, New South Wales, on February 17, 1848. At eighteen, she married a gold digger and former sailor and gave birth to a son in a tent near a gold mine. Nine years later, she wanted a local school and started campaigning for it, but she was not allowed to attend the town meeting discussions because she was female. She left her husband in 1883, took her children to Sydney, and supported them with her sewing. After demanding that only women be hired to help her on *The Dawn* in 1888, she had to fight the printing unions. She worked on *The Dawn* for seventeen years and during the same time founded a place for working girls to live called Darlinghurst Hostel. The lack of progress in woman's rights frustrated her, but women gained the right to vote just before her death.

BIBLIOGRAPHY

Ollif, Lorna. *Louisa Lawson: Henry Lawson's Crusading Mother.* Adelaide, Australia: Rigby, 1978. 0-7270-0587-1, 148p. Ollif's accessible biography of Lawson is well researched. Ollif suggests that Lawson was the first literary genius of Australia, a better writer than her renowned son Henry.

LEAKEY, MARY NICOL (1913–1996)

Archaeologist   England

Mary Leakey found fossil evidence of a hominid in Olduvai Gorge that was the world's earliest human, a Zinjanthropus, 1.75 million years old. Born on February 6, 1913, to parents enormously interested in Egyptology, Mary Nicol went to France with them as a young girl and became interested in archaeology and cave art. On her first dig, she began to think like an archaeologist, wondering about sorting into age and type. Leakey hated school and never enrolled in college, but she began attending lectures on geology and archaeology. Finally, Dorothy Liddell accepted her as a part of a dig at an important Stone Age site at Hembury, and in 1930, Leakey created drawings of the Stone Age tools. Another archaeologist asked her to do the drawings of Egyptian stone tools for her book, and Louis Leakey requested her services for his study, *Adam's Ancestors.* She also married him, moved to Kenya, and began working on important excavations such as Hyrax Hill, where she found a Neolithic settlement of stone-walled houses and a cemetery with nineteen burial mounds. She made a number of additional important finds, including Iron Age tools, a Stone Age settlement at Olorgesailie, the oldest bones in Africa, and hominid footprints made 3.6 million years. When she finally attended Oxford, she went to collect an honorary degree.

BIBLIOGRAPHY

Lambert, Lisa A. *The Leakeys.* Vero Beach, FL: Rourke, 1993. 0-86625-492-7, 111p. In this biography for young adults, Lambert discloses sacrifices and successes in the Leakey family's life.

Leakey, Mary D. *Disclosing the Past.* Garden City, NY: Doubleday, 1984. 0-385-18961-3, 224p. Leakey traces her childhood, early interest in art and archaeology, years working with her husband, and those following his death, when she continued her fieldwork at Olduvai and Laetoli.

Leakey, Mary D. *Olduvai Gorge: My Search for Early Man.* London: Collins, 1979. 0-00-211613-8, 187p. Leakey describes her life on Olduvai Plain from when she first arrived through her experiences with the digs, the camp, aspects of dating and digging, the beds, tools, fossil fauna, and the effects of this environment and research on her life.

Morell, Virginia. *Ancestral Passions: The Leakey Family and the Quest for Humankind's Beginnings.* New York: Simon and Schuster, 1995. 0-684-80192-2, 639p. Letters, journals, interviews, and articles provide a thorough basis of research to aid Morell's story of the Leakey family's searches along the Olduvai and the ensuing personal conflicts.

LECOUVREUR, ADRIENNE (1692–1730)

Actor   France

Adrienne Lecouvreur, an actor with the Comédie-Française, played important roles in the productions of such playwrights as La Motte, Crébillon, and Voltaire. She was born on April 5, 1692, the daughter of a hatmaker in Damery, and moved to Paris when she was ten. She began acting when she was fourteen, and she stayed with the Comédie-Française for thirteen years. Her anti-academic approach to acting and concern that costumes reflect the historical period of the play helped establish her reputation. She had several affairs, and Scribe wrote a play about her, *Adrienne Lecouvreur*. When she died suddenly, with Voltaire at her side, the church would not allow her burial, so her friends interred her at night.

BIBLIOGRAPHY

Richtman, Jack. *Adrienne Lecouvreur: The Actress and the Age; a Biography*. Englewood Cliffs, NJ: Prentice-Hall, 1971. 0-13-008698-3, 240p. In this well-documented and readable biography, Richtman tries to separate the truth from the legend about Lecouver. What he finds is that the truth is more interesting.

LE GALLIENNE, EVA (1899–1991)

Actor and Theater Manager   England

Eva Le Gallienne won awards for her attempts to establish a national theater. She was born January 11, 1899, to a well-known writer and a Danish mother who was a Danish newspaper correspondent working in London. After her parents' marriage failed, Le Gallienne and her mother moved to Paris, and she studied at the College Sévigné, a school preparing girls for the Sorbonne. In 1926, Le Gallienne founded the Civic Repertory Theater of New York, the first nonprofit American theater. She tried unsuccessfully to found a national noncommercial theater of quality that would be accessible to everyone. Throughout her life, she refused to sacrifice her art for popular success, starring in such plays as *Hedda Gabler, Liliom, The Cherry Orchard, Peter Pan, Camille, Mary Stuart, The Royal Family*, and *The Dream Watcher*. Her translations of Ibsen made his work available for the English-speaking stage. In 1977, the American National Theatre and Academy gave her the National Artist Award. In 1986, President Reagan presented her with the National Medal of the Arts, the highest award for an artist in the United States.

BIBLIOGRAPHY

Schanke, Robert A. *Eva Le Gallienne: A Bio-Bibliography*. New York: Greenwood Press, 1989. 0-313-26096-6, 208p. Shanke has divided this scholarly look at Le Gallienne into a biography of her life and career, a chronology focusing on the highlights of her career, a list of productions, an annotated bibliography of her writings, and one of writings about her.

Schanke, Robert A. *Shattered Applause: The Lives of Eva Le Gallienne*. Carbondale: Southern Illinois University Press, 1992. 0-8093-1820-2, 319p. Schanke's biography covers Le Gallienne's life and posits the unprovable thesis that her overt lesbianism affected her ability to love others.

Sheehy, Helen. *Eva Le Gallienne: A Biography*. New York: Knopf, 1996. 0-679-41117-8, 544p. Using Le Gallienne's diaries and correspondence, Sheehy discusses many of the details of Le Gallienne's life, which will interest her fans and theater students, demonstrating Le Gallienne's importance to twentieth-century theater.

LEHMANN, LOTTE (1888–1976)

Opera Singer   Germany

Lotte Lehmann was not only an internationally acclaimed soprano but also a writer and gifted painter. Born on February 27, 1888, in Perleberg, her father was a junior official in a national benevolent society. When the family moved to Berlin, Lehmann was fourteen. She auditioned at a music school, and when the head of the school said that she would be able to sing professionally, her family helped her find money for the first term. She made her debut at the Hamburg Opera in 1908, in London in 1914, and in Vienna in 1916. In the years after, Strauss chose her for the premieres of his operas *Die Frau ohne Schatten* (1919) and *Intermezzo* (1924). She also sang Strauss's *Ariadne auf Naxos* and *Arabella*. Other composers whom she performed during this period included Massenet, Tchaikovsky, and Puccini. She made her American debut as Sieglinde in *Die Walküre* in 1930. Toscanini called her "the greatest artist in the world," and Puccini preferred her Suor Angelica to all other singers. When Hitler infiltrated Austria, Lehmann left for the United States. In addition to her singing, she wrote poetry, a novel, and music criticism. She also offered master classes after her retirement and continued to pursue her painting.

BIBLIOGRAPHY

Glass, Beaumont. *Lotte Lehmann, a Life in Opera and Song.* Santa Barbara, CA: Capra, 1988. 0-88496-277-6, 330p. Glass uses available documents and letters for his popular, balanced biography, incorporating, where possible, the words of Lehmann herself and those who saw her perform.

Jefferson, Alan. *Lotte Lehmann, 1888–1976.* London: J. MacRae, 1988. 0-8620-3311-X, 333p. Jefferson could not obtain Lehmann's private papers, but he used sources from around the world and from her friends in his well-documented, scholarly biography.

Lehmann, Lotte. *My Many Lives.* Trans. Frances Holden. 1948. Westport, CT: Greenwood Press, 1974. 0-8371-7361-2, 262p. Lehmann's account will especially interest aspiring opera singers when she explains the acting in, and singing of, the roles Elsa, Elisabeth, Eva, Sieglinde, Lenore, Manon Lescaut, Marguerite, and Tatjana.

LEHMANN, ROSAMOND (1901–1990)

Writer   England

Rosamond Lehmann, a critically acclaimed novelist, remained active in the literary world throughout her life. She was one of four children, born on February 3, 1901, in the family of a Liberal member of Parliament who was once a noted athlete and scholar. After her private education, she received a scholarship to Girton College, Cambridge. Her first novel, *Dusty Answer*, published in 1927, was a success that caused controversy because it revealed the passions of a young girl in society. She remarried and then published a novel dealing with homosexuality. Subsequent novels discussed unhappy marriage, adultery, and abortion. She stopped writing after World War II until she wrote *A Sea-Grape Tree*, published in 1970. Her daughter died in 1958, making her seek solace with people who claimed to communicate with the dead; she became president of the College of Psychic Studies. She also served as the international vice president of PEN and as a member of the Council of the Society of Authors. In 1982, she was awarded the Dame Commander of the British Empire.

BIBLIOGRAPHY

Lestourgeon, Diana E. *Rosamond Lehmann*. Boston: Irvington, 1965. 0-8290-1723-2, 157p. Lestourgeon sketches the background of this autobiographical writer because she sees Lehmann's life as the way to understand both the merits and limitations in her work. Lestourgeon discusses each novel in chronological order to show the development of Lehmann's talent.

Siegel, Ruth. *Rosamond Lehmann: A Thirties Writer*. New York: Peter Lang, 1989. 0-8204-1046-2, 194p. Siegel posits that Lehmann shows the feminine experience of causality, betrayal, and the failed search for identity in this carefully documented, critical biography with extensive references to, and interpretations of, Lehmann's work.

Simons, Judy. *Rosamond Lehmann*. New York: St. Martin's, 1992. 0-312-07208-2, 160p. In this scholarly analysis of Lehmann and her works, Simons focuses on her seven novels by looking at the political aspects of romance and how changes in sexual passion reflected evolving moral codes.

Tindall, Gillian. *Rosamond Lehmann, an Appreciation*. London: Chatto and Windus, Hogarth, 1985. 0-7011-2706-6, 201p. Tindall sees Lehmann's own life as surfacing within her work without disguise, and she analyzes Lehmann's works and the aspects of her life revealed within them.

LEIGH, VIVIEN (1913–1967)

Actor **England**

Vivien Leigh was a renowned actor who won awards for her stage and screen portrayals. Born Vivian Hartley in Darjeeling, India, on November 5, 1913, where her father was a businessman, she returned to England when she was seven and received her education at the Convent of the Sacred Heart in Roehampton. At thirteen, she attended various schools in France, Italy, and Bavaria. At eighteen, she entered the Royal Academy of Dramatic Art. Three years later, she married a barrister, and after two years at home, she returned to the stage. Her success led to a role with Laurence Olivier in *Fire over England* in 1935 and as Ophelia in Olivier's production of *Hamlet*. In 1939, she played in *Gone with the Wind* and divorced her husband. The next year, she married Olivier. During World War II, she continued playing onstage and touring for the armed forces. In 1951, after playing Blanche in the stage version of *A Streetcar Named Desire*, she re-created the role on film, winning her second Oscar. She continued to play at Stratford-upon-Avon in the 1950s, but she stopped acting when she began having problems with nervousness.

BIBLIOGRAPHY

Edwards, Anne. *Vivien Leigh: A Biography*. New York: Simon and Schuster, 1977. 0-671-22496-4, 319p. In this popular, well-researched, accessible, and recommended biography, Edwards discusses Leigh's career and her life.

Molt, Cynthia M. *Vivien Leigh: A Bio-Bibliography*. Westport, CT: Greenwood Press, 1992. 0-313-27578-5, 303p. This analytical text includes a straightforward biography of Vivient Leigh as well as a listing of her stage, television, and radio appearances; a discography; a chronology; and a filmography.

Taylor, John Russell. *Vivien Leigh*. London: Elm Tree Books, 1984. 0-241-11333-4, 128p. Taylor met Leigh once for an interview and notes that the encounter was short and cold but that Leigh was an actor whom no one has replaced since her death. He continues with a balanced overview of her life and career with photographs.

Vickers, Hugo. *Vivien Leigh*. Boston: Little, Brown, 1989. 0-316-90245-4, 411p. In this thoroughly researched biography, Vickers reveals original materials about Leigh's parents, uses the papers of Leigh's surviving daughter, and includes anecdotes about Leigh's private life.

Walker, Alexander. *Vivien: The Life of Vivien Leigh*. New York: Weidenfeld and Nicolson, 1987. 1-55584-080-9, 342p. After meeting Leigh once, Walker tries to give a balanced picture of her in his readable, well-researched, and documented biography.

LENYA, LOTTE (1898–1981)
Entertainer   Austria

Lotte Lenya's original musical style established her reputation in Berlin during the 1920s and 1930s. Karoline Wilhelmine Blamauer was born on January 18, 1898, and during World War I, she studied drama and ballet in Zurich. In 1920, she went to Berlin where she became more interested in acting. She worked with the playwright George Kaiser, who introduced her to Kurt Weill, the man she married in 1926. Their collaborations led to her participation in his musical *Mahagonny* (1927), with their big success in 1928 of *Die Dreigroschenoper*. In 1933, they left for the United States and settled in New York. The two continued to work together, with Lenya's musical abilities guiding *The Eternal Road* (1937) and *The Firebrand of Florence* (1945).

BIBLIOGRAPHY
Spoto, Donald. *Lenya: A Life*. Boston: Little, Brown, 1989. 0-316-80725-7, 416p. This well-written, carefully documented, popular biography presents Lenya starting with her excellent reviews for work in *Cabaret* on Broadway and in Boston.

Weill, Kurt, and Lotte Lenya. *Speak Low (When You Speak Love): The Letters of Kurt Weill and Lotte Lenya*. Ed. and trans. Lys Symonette and Kim H. Kowalke. Berkeley: University of California Press, 1996. 0-520-07853-5, 554p. The editors include Lenya's brief autobiography about her early years and then proceed chronologically through 410 extant letters between Weill and Lenya from 1924 to 1948.

LESSING, DORIS (1919–)
Writer   Rhodesia (Zimbabwe)

Doris Lessing, a novelist and short story writer, looks at women's difficulties with independence. She was born as Doris Taylor on October 22, 1919, in Kermanshah, Iran, where her father served in the British army and her mother was a nurse. She then moved with her family to Rhodesia (Zimbabwe) when she was five and lived there for twenty-five years before going to England. While living in Rhodesia, she became a member of the Communist Party. She described her arrival in England in her book *In Pursuit of the English*. Concerned with the racial situation in Rhodesia, she discussed it in her first novel, *The Grass Is Singing* (1951). Her earlier novels expressed the conflicts inherent between intellectual pursuit and political activism. Much of her later work is set in southern Africa. Her *Children of Violence*, the first volume of which was published in 1952 and the last in 1969, explored her disappointment in communism. In her work of the 1970s, she became more spiritual in her approach. In recent books, she has moved away from mysticism.

BIBLIOGRAPHY

Fishburn, Katherine. *Doris Lessing: Life, Work, and Criticism*. Fredricton, New Brunswick, Canada: York, 1987. 0-919966-60-8, 33p. This brief biography introduces Lessing, lists her works, and imparts some of the critical responses to it.

Ingersoll, Earl G., ed. *Doris Lessing: Conversations*. Princeton, NJ: Ontario Review, 1994. 0-86538-080-5, 248p. Ingersoll has collated twenty-four conversations from the 1960s to 1993 to show Lessing's articulate and often controversial views on marriage and the family, politics, and mysticism.

Lessing, Doris. *African Laughter: Four Visits to Zimbabwe*. New York: HarperCollins, 1992. 0-06-016854-4, 416p. Lessing grew up in Southern Rhodesia, left for twenty-five years because she opposed the white minority government, returned in 1982 to write about the new government, again six years later, and then two more times in the 1990s. In this autobiographical memoir, Lessing reflects on coming home, memory, and place in incidents and anecdotes about the remote countryside and the conflicted city streets.

Lessing, Doris. *Going Home*. New York: HarperCollins, 1996. Paper, 0-06-097630-6, 320p. Lessing tells of her first journey back to Africa and Southern Rhodesia in 1956, where she grew up. Her love of Africa remained, while her hatred of "white supremacy" and other distasteful practices continued.

Lessing, Doris. *Under My Skin: Volume One of My Autobiography, to 1949*. New York: HarperCollins, 1994. 0-06-017150-2, 419p. Lessing recounts her youth in Southern Rhodesia (now Zimbabwe), her young married life in Salisbury, and her communist years during World World II, showing an ability to comment about her youth in such a way that it becomes universal.

LEVI-MONTALCINI, RITA (1909–)

Physician   Italy

Rita Levi-Montalcini won a shared Nobel Prize in physiology in 1986 for her discovery of a bodily substance that stimulates and influences the growth of nerve cells. She was born on April 22, 1909, of Jewish parentage. She later studied medicine at the University of Turin, where she researched the effects that peripheral tissues have on nerve cell growth. She hid in Florence during the German occupation of Italy (1943–1945) but resumed research at Turin after the war. In 1947 she accepted a post at Washington University, St. Louis, Missouri, with the zoologist Viktor Hamburger. They traced the nerve-growth factor in a mouse tumor transplanted into a chick embryo and called it NGF. She discovered that the NGF helped nerve-tissue culture grow and, with her co-winner for the Nobel, isolated the nerve-growth factor. She continued to work in the field and moved to Rome for further research.

BIBLIOGRAPHY

Dash, Joan. *A Life of One's Own; Three Gifted Women and the Men They Married*. New York: Harper and Row, 1973. 0-06-010949-1, 388p. This long biographical sketch tells of the influences of Levi-Montalcini's childhood that helped her in her adult life. Dash's thesis is that Levi-Montalcini was successful because her husband supported her career.

Levi-Montalcini, Rita. *In Praise of Imperfection: My Life and Work.* Trans. Luigi Attardi. New York: Basic Books, 1988. 0-465-03217-6, 220p. Levi-Montalcini recounts her life beginning with her childhood in Turin and through being a medical student and her decision to move to the United States.

LEWALD, FANNY (1811–1889)
Writer   Germany

Fanny Lewald, one of the most important German woman writers of the nineteenth century, won fame for her novels about problems in marriage and the injustice of the social system. Although born into a Königsberg Jewish family on March 24, 1811, Lewald converted to the Lutheran Church so that she could marry a theologian, but he died before they could marry. Her first novels, *Clementine* (1842), *Jenny* (1843), and *Eine Lebensfrage* (1945), gained her fame. They dealt with controversy such as forced marriage, the German-Jewish princess, the emancipation of Jews in Germany, and the dissolution of a failed marriage by divorce. In 1845, she met the novelist and schoolmaster Adolf Stahr, with whom she lived before marrying him after his divorce nine years later. She traveled widely and published about her experiences in the British Isles and Italy. Lewald's later books were multivolume family sagas creating realistic portraits. Critics saw her work as ranking with that of **George Eliot** and **George Sand,** but she fell out of favor, possibly because, in addition to being female, she was Jewish.

BIBLIOGRAPHY
Lewald, Fanny. *The Education of Fanny Lewald: An Autobiography.* Trans. Hanna Ballin Lewis. Albany: State University of New York Press, 1992. 0-7914-1147-8, 341p. Lewis has included less than 50 percent of the original three volumes of Lewald's autobiography, published in 1871. She retains the separate chapters but paraphrases what she has omitted to show Lewald's advanced ideas about emancipating women and the struggle to be self-supporting.

LEYSTER, JUDITH (1609–1660)
Artist   The Netherlands

Judith Leyster became a genre painter with the support of her family and the instruction of Frans Hals. He greatly influenced her work, but she developed her own style and became known for the vitality and happiness apparent in her paintings. Born in Haarlem on July 28, 1609, to a smallware weaver who became a brewer, she was the eighth of nine children. She spent time in Utrecht but returned to Haarlem from 1628 until 1637. She used bold, detailed strokes to convey positive moods of everyday life and family scenes of women and children in such works as *The Gay Cavaliers, The Flute Player,* and *The Proposition.* She pictured these ordinary life experiences and temptations on her canvases to show what she considered to be moral. In 1633, she became a member of the painters' guild of St. Luke and opened her own student studio, which gave her financial success. She married in 1636, and she and her husband moved to Amsterdam the following year, where, as a mother, she produced fewer works.

BIBLIOGRAPHY

Leyster, Judith, James A. Welu, and P. Biesboer. *Judith Leyster: A Dutch Master and Her World.* New Haven, CT: Yale University Press, 1993. 0-300-05564-1, 391p. This biographical catalog on Leyster and analysis of her work includes eight essays and discussions of sixteen of her works, giving insight about her economic environment, her marriage, her position in society as the one female member of the artists' guild, and her paintings.

LILLIE, BEATRICE (1898–1989)
Entertainer   Canada

Beatrice Lillie gained fame as a revue artist who created characters with her songs, some of them written specifically for her. She was born May 29, 1898, to immigrant parents from England and Northern Ireland. After growing up in Canada and studying at St. Agnes College in Belleville, Ontario, she went with her mother and sister to England. When André Charlot saw her perform, he hired her for *Not Likely!* in 1914. She continued to work for him throughout World War I, often appearing in top hat and tails. Some called her the female "Charlie Chaplin," based on her interpretations of her music. She married Robert Peel; in 1920, he became Sir Robert and she became Lady Peel. Since they needed money to keep the family's land, she returned to the stage after the birth of a son. Her husband died in 1934, and she continued to perform in New York, Chicago, Los Angeles, and London. In World War II, she entertained the troops and mourned her son, killed in action. Among her stage shows were *An Evening with Beatrice Lillie* and *Auntie Mame.* She also appeared in films, two of her most famous being *Around the World in Eighty Days* (1956) and *Thoroughly Modern Millie* (1967).

BIBLIOGRAPHY

Laffey, Bruce. *Beatrice Lillie: The Funniest Woman in the World.* New York: Wynwood, 1989. 0-922066-22-1, 296p. Laffey, in his readable, popular biography, indicates that he adored Lillie's never-ending optimism and vitality, even when she had intense unhappiness in her life.

Lillie, Beatrice, John Philip, and James Brough. *Every Other Inch a Lady.* Garden City, NY: Doubleday, 1972. No ISBN, 360p. Lillie fills this entertaining, enjoyable autobiography with anecdotes. Among them is her comment that her mother used to say that her family and Bernard Shaw were "distantly related, though she never mentioned the mileage." Lillie says that her philosophy of life is a preference to always look for the best and not brood on the bad.

LIND, JENNY (1820–1887)
Opera Singer   Sweden

Jenny Lind, called the "Swedish Nightingale," received international acclaim. Born on October 6, 1820, she grew up in Stockholm and studied at the Royal Opera School after making her first stage appearance in vaudeville at ten. She made her opera debut when she was eighteen as Agathe in Weber's *Der Freischütz.* Her voice was already strained three years later, and she had to rest it. Critics applauded her rejuvenated voice after her performances in 1842, as Bellini's *Norma* and in 1834 at the Berlin Opera. Her final operatic appearance was in 1849 in London. Among the roles she sang were Marie in Donizetti's *The Daughters of the Regiment* and Amalia in Verdi's *I Masnadieri*. She began touring the United States in 1850, performing in recitals. After her retirement from the stage, she sang for charities and became a professor of singing at the Royal College of Music in London. At her death, she was the first woman to be buried in Westminster Abbey's Poets' Corner.

BIBLIOGRAPHY

Kyle, Elisabeth. *The Swedish Nightingale: Jenny Lind*. New York: Holt, Rinehart, and Winston, 1966. Nc ISBN, 223p. This fictional biography about Lind, suitable for young adults, is undocumented but contains a bibliography.

Maude, Jenny Maria Catherine Goldschmidt. *The Life of Jenny Lind*. 1926. New York: Arno, 1977. 0-405-09694-1, 222p. Maude's biography of Lind, her mother, is researched but uncritical and stylistically dated.

Wagenknecht, Edward. *Jenny Lind*. 1959. New York: Da Capo, 1980. 0-306-76045-2, 230p. Wagenknecht calls his biography of Lind a portrait or "psychograph." He includes new material in this carefully documented, researched, and recommended study of her art life and her personal life.

Ware, W. Porter, and Thaddeus C. Lockard, Jr. *P. T. Barnum Presents Jenny Lind: The American Tour of the Swedish Nightingale*. Baton Rouge: Louisiana State University Press, 1980. 0-8071-0687-9, 204p. Ware and Lockard recount Jenny Lind's twenty-two months on tour with the impresario P. T. Barnum, which made them both rich and relieved Lind from operatic performances during the period.

LINDGREN, ASTRID (1907–)

Writer   Sweden

Astrid Lindgren's works for children have earned her awards, prizes, honorary degrees, and her name on at least thirty-four schools in Germany alone. Born on November 14, 1907, in Vimmerby, she gained fame in 1945 with the first of three books featuring Pippi Longstocking, a girl strong beyond measure with no parental control. Lindgren followed her with characters such as Ronia the Robber's Daughter and Emil. Her stories merge the ephemeral with the archetypal, the local with the universal. She has also written literary fairy tales. An advocate of world peace and animal rights, she has spoken publicly on these issues.

BIBLIOGRAPHY

Metcalf, Eva-Maria. *Astrid Lindgren*. New York: Twayne, 1995. 0-8057-4525-4, 157p. This critical biography shows Lindgren as one of the twentieth century's great storytellers. It discusses her life and major themes as well as the sociohistorical context of her work in a straightforward, academic style.

LISIEUX, THÉRÈSE of. *See* THÉRÈSE of LISIEUX.

LISPECTOR, CLARICE (1925–1977)

Writer   Ukraine

Clarice Lispector has written novels showing her control of language and structure that have made her one of Brazil's and South America's most popular writers. After her birth in the Ukraine on December 10, 1925, she and her family emigrated to Brazil, living in Recife and Rio de Janeiro. She wrote her first novel at nineteen. After studying law, she married a diplomat and lived abroad, including eight years in the United States. She divorced in 1959 and returned to Brazil, where she continued her writing, bringing her total work to nine novels, six collections of stories, four children's books, translations, interviews, and nonfiction pieces. She showed a constant concern over the way "things" in the physical world cause often wholly unexpected responses in a person's consciousness. She was less interested in events themselves than how they affected people's minds. Very little happens in her stories, with plots being nonexistent and narratives blurring between poetry and prose. Her novel *Um sopro de vida* (A Breath of Life) is often compared to the work of **Virginia Woolf**, Hermann Hesse, and Andre Gide. As the first generation of Brazil's modernist movement, she created a new kind of prose fiction, a "new narrative" for Latin America, focusing on the mythopoeic, philosophical, and linguistic aspects of being and human consciousness, through language resembling that of James Joyce. Much of her work, exploring human alienation and frustration, has been translated into other languages.

BIBLIOGRAPHY

Fitz, Earl E. *Clarice Lispector*. Boston: Twayne, 1985. 0-8057-6605-7, 160p. This critical biography discusses the internal aspects of Lispector's work while talking about the external factors that have affected her career.

Marting, Diane E. *Clarice Lispector: A Bio-Bibliography*. Westport, CT: Greenwood Press, 1993. 0-313-27803-2, 368p.   This scholarly text has biographical information as it relates to Lispector's writing. It discusses her major works in detail, devoting individual chapters to each one.

LLOYD, MARIE (1870–1922)

Entertainer   England

Marie Lloyd became one of the most famous and most accomplished twentieth-century music hall performers. She was born Matilda Alice Victoria Wood on February 12, 1870, in Hoxton to a waiter and flower maker as the eldest of his eleven children. At fifteen, she appeared at the Royal Eagle Music Hall as Bella Delmere but changed her name soon after to Marie Lloyd. She became the principal girl in the Drury Lane pantomime in 1891, and through the next years, performed at all of England's leading music halls. She followed these triumphs with tours of the United States, South Africa, and Australia. She married three times, had a difficult life, and was considered scandalous during her day when arrested in New York and interned on Ellis Island as undesirable. She had poor teeth and drank, but she made people happy with her performances in music halls.

BIBLIOGRAPHY

Baker, Richard Anthony. *Marie Lloyd: Queen of the Music-Halls*. London: R. Hale, 1990. 0-7090-4135-7, 192p. This balanced and entertaining but undocumented biography of Lloyd discusses the background of the music hall and its importance for the East End of London in its craving for entertainment.

Farson, Daniel. *Marie Lloyd and Music Halls*. London: Tom Stacey, 1972. 0-8546-8082-9, 176p. Farson examines the history of music halls and and how they made Lloyd's success possible as well as how her unique presence continued their popularity.

Jacob, Naomi Ellington. *"Our Marie," Marie Lloyd: A Biography*. Bath, England: Cedric Chivers, 1972. 0-85594-721-7, 287p. Jacob disapproved of Farson's writing about Lloyd because she thought that she, as Lloyd's friend, would be the only one who knew Lloyd well enough to tell Lloyd's "tragedy." In this fictional biography, Jacob imparts her biased view of Lloyd and her career, their own relationship, and Lloyd's other friends, omitting unpleasant information.

LONG, MARGUERITE (1874–1966)
Instrumentalist   **France**

Marguerite Long gained a reputation for her insightful piano interpretations of twentieth-century music. Born on November 13, 1874, she later studed in Nîmes and Paris and taught at the Paris Conservatoire from 1906 to 1940, and became one of the first women appointed to professor there in 1920 and the first woman to teach a classe superieure at the Conservatoire. She was never well known outside France, but she worked with the composers Débussy, Ravel, and Fauré as interpreter and the authoritative performer of their piano music. She gave the premieres of Ravel's *Tombeau de Couperin* and his *Piano Concerto in G*, with him conducting. She published scholarly books on Debussy (1960) and Fauré (1963), with her book on Ravel appearing after her death, in 1971. She promoted twentieth-century French music and served as a mentor to generations of French pianists. In 1943, she and Jacques Thibaud started an international piano and violin competition under their own names.

BIBLIOGRAPHY
Dunoyer, Cecilia. *Marguerite Long: A Life in French Music, 1874-1966*. Bloomington: Indiana University Press, 1993. 0-253-31839-4, 256p. Dunoyer's thorough and well-written biography, the first on Long, uses previously unpublished archival documents, letters, and interviews to show Long and the music scene in Paris and to establish Long's role as an artist and pedagogue.

LONSDALE, KATHLEEN (1903–1971)
Scientist   **Ireland**

Kathleen Lonsdale received many honors for her work as a crystallographer, physicist, and chemist. Born January 28, 1903, the youngest of a postmaster's ten children, Kathleen Yardley lived in Newbridge, Ireland, where she attended Downshall Elementary School before she and her family moved to England. At sixteen, for the highest marks on an exam in geography and physical geography from the Royal Geographical Society, she won a scholarship to attend Bedford College, London, and study mathematics. The next year, she won a scholarship to university and changed her specialty to physics. As head of her class, she was invited to join a team of scientists to do radiographic studies of crystal structures in organic compounds at University College, London, and the Royal Institution. Other aspects of her scientific work included theory of space groups, divergent beam X-ray photography of crystals, and diffuse X-ray single crystal reflection. She married in 1927, had three children, and traveled widely as a member of the Society of Friends. In 1945, she became the first woman fellow of the Royal Society. In 1956, she became Dame Commander of the British Empire, and the next year she received the Royal Society's Davy Medal. She held positions such as a chair in chemistry, vice president of the Royal Society, president of the British Association, and president of the International Union of Crystallography.

BIBLIOGRAPHY

Hodgkin, Dorothy Crowfoot. *Kathleen Lonsdale: A Biographical Memoir.* London: Royal Society, 1976. 0-85403-078-6, 47p. Hodgkin's brief account comes from Lonsdale's notes about her life and work in her Personal Record for the Royal Society, from published and unpublished biographical notes, and from conversations with Lonsdale's husband, her three children, and other members of her family.

LOPOKOVA, LYDIA (1892–1981)

Ballerina   Russia

After becoming a ballerina in Russia, Lydia Lopokova danced in Europe, and with her husband, she founded the Arts Theatre in Cambridge, England. Lopokova was born in St. Petersburg on October 21, 1892, and made her first appearance onstage at nine. She graduated at seventeen from the Imperial Ballet School and became a member of the Marinsky corps de ballet. In 1910, she joined Diaghilev's Ballets Russes, creating the role of Columbine in *Carnaval* and replacing **Tamara Karsavina** in *The Firebird* during the following year. She went to the United States to dance, and when she returned to London, she rejoined Diaghilev for *Les femmes de Bonne Humeur, La Boutique Fantasque,* and *The Sleeping Princess.* She married Maynard Keynes in 1921 and became a supporter of the British ballet. She danced for the Camargo Society, theVic-Wells Ballet, and the Old Vic. She also had several stage roles, such as Olivia in *Twelfth Night,* Nora in *A Doll's House,* Hilda in *Master Builder,* and Celimène in *Le Misanthrope.* Although she withdrew somewhat from the ballet after her husband's death, she served as a member of the Arts Council of Great Britain.

BIBLIOGRAPHY

Keynes, Milo, ed. *Lydia Lopokova.* New York: St. Martin's, 1983. 0-312-50039-4, 238p. The variety of responses from contributors shows different aspects of Lopokova's life and makes an interesting collection, gathered by her nephew.

Lopokova, Lydia, and John Maynard Keynes. *Lydia and Maynard: The letters of Lydia Lopokova and John Maynard Keynes.* Eds. Polly Hill and Richard Keynes. New York: Scribner's, 1989. 0-684-19202-0, 367p. The daily letters of the first three years of a fifteen-year correspondence give a view of Lopokova's response to someone she loves, although they add little insight about her private thoughts.

LOREN, SOPHIA (1934–)

Actor   Italy

Sophia Loren, an international actor, has won awards for her work. Originally Sofia Scicolone, she was born illegitimate in Rome on September 20, 1934, and raised in Naples. After leaving normal school, Loren won a beauty contest at fourteen, and she and her mother went to Rome to work as extras on the movie *Quo Vadis*. She won more contests and began modeling for magazines before she met Carlo Ponti at fifteen. He gave her a contract and made her an Italian movie star over the next ten years. She then went to Hollywood, where she had roles in movies as the stereotypical sex goddess. She returned to Italy and won the Cannes Film Festival Award and the American Academy Award for her role in *Two Women* (1960). She married Ponti in Italy, but Italy would not recognize his earlier divorce, so to avoid charges of bigamy, they moved to France and became French citizens so that they could legally marry.

BIBLIOGRAPHY

Hotchner, A. E. *Sophia, Living and Loving: Her Own Story*. New York: William Morrow, 1979. 0-688-03428-4, 256p. This autobiography of Loren is a first-person memoir in which Hotchner quotes friends and relatives to support Loren's comments.

Levy, Alan. *Forever, Sophia: An Intimate Portrait*. New York: St. Martin's, 1986. 0-312-29883-8, 264p. After Levy visited with Loren many times, he wrote this book as an honest and affectionate look at her life, even though it is not an authorized biography.

Shaw, Sam. *Sophia Loren in the Camera Eye*. New York: Hamlyn, 1980. 0-600-34155-0, 160p. Shaw's photographs and recollections are a homage to Loren, and he tries to show the happy moments in her life. The photographs display her in a variety of roles from small parts to leads.

Zec, Donald. *Sophia*. New York: McKay, 1975. 0-679-50547-4, 263p. This popular biography is readable with undocumented dialogue, photographs, and a bibliography.

LOVELACE, AUGUSTA ADA (1815–1852)

Mathematician   England

Augusta Lovelace was a mathematician whose understanding of symbolic logic was honored with the naming of a universal computer language called ADA. Although she was the legitimate daughter of Lord Byron, born December 10, 1815, her autocratic mother never allowed her to meet her father. She was mechanically inclined, liked geography, designed model ships, and taught herself geometry from a book before William Frend instructed her in astronomy and mathematics. She met Charles Babbage, the inventor of the calculating machine, in 1833, and began to correspond with him. She translated an Italian paper on the "different engine," and her translation became three times longer than the original paper and contained radical ideas far beyond those in Babbage's design, thereby displaying her understanding of this programmed computer's principles. After she married Lord William King in 1835 and had three children, her mother continued to supervise her. She used her mathematical skills in a secret gambling system, but she lost much money and died from uterine cancer, still in debt. Not until her papers surfaced in 1954 did anyone know of her true mathematical genius.

BIBLIOGRAPHY

Moore, Doris Langley-Levy. *Ada, Countess of Lovelace: Byron's Legitimate Daughter*. London: J. Murray, 1977. 0-7195-3384-8, 397p. Based on previously unpublished family papers and including many details, the text examines Lovelace's life in an aristocratic but emotionally starved family.

Stein, Dorothy. *Ada: A Life and Legacy*. Cambridge, MA: MIT Press, 1985. 0-262-19242-X, 368p. Stein approaches Lovelace's life from the mathematical, scientific, and medical aspects. The resulting biography is a well-written and thoroughly researched work.

Wade, Mary Dodson. *Ada Byron Lovelace: The Lady and the Computer*. New York: Dillon, Macmillan, 1994. 0-87518-598-3, 128p. This biography, suitable for young adults, tells Lovelace's story, the times in which she lived, her problems with gambling, and the affair that she tried to keep from her husband.

LUTYENS, ELIZABETH (1906–1983)
Composer   England

Agnes Elizabeth Lutyens was a prolific composer of orchestral, instrumental, and chamber pieces. Born on July 9, 1906, she was the daughter of an architect and studied in Paris at the École Normale before she returned to London and the Royal College of Music. She became involved in supporting the work of other composers, such as Britten and Rawsthorne, around 1933 with the founding of the Macnaghten-Lemare concerts. Although composing at this time, she withdrew all of her music, including that performed in her 1932 debut. She was interested in radical techniques that critics condemned until the 1960s. She composed over 140 works, each looking at the medium with which she was working in a different way. She also wrote stage works and used her own librettos. Some of these were *Infidelio* (1954), *Time Off!—Not a Ghost of a Chance!* (1968), *Isis and Osiris* (1970), and *The Goldfish Bowl* (1975). Her most important orchestra pieces include *Concertante* (1950) and *Music for Orchestra* (1955, 1962, and 1963). Much of her work has been completed on commission, and she has used vocal texts from sources such as Rimbaud, Wittgenstein, Joseph Conrad, James Joyce, African verse, Chaucer, and Japanese poetry. She became a Dame Commander of the British Empire in 1969.

BIBLIOGRAPHY

Harries, Meirion, and Susie Harries. *A Pilgrim Soul: The Life and Work of Elisabeth Lutyens*. Boston: Faber and Faber, 1989. 0-571-1612-1, 324p. For a popular but technical biography, the Harries used Lutyens' papers, letters, manuscripts, notebooks, diaries, programs, and press cuttings in their biography of "Twelve-tone Lizzie," a bohemian, aristocratic woman working in a man's world who never thought that she had received ample recognition.

Lutyens, Elisabeth. *A Goldfish Bowl*. London: Cassell, 1972. 0-304-93663-4, 330p. In this readable and well-written memoir, Lutyens chronicles her life and the difficulties of motherhood balanced with creation. Lutyens's version of herself took shape in letters she wrote to her mother when she was between the ages of ten and forty.

LUXEMBURG, ROSA (1871–1919)
Revolutionary   Poland and Russia

Rosa Luxemburg, a socialist, feminist, and pacifist, founded the German Communist Party. Her Jewish family lived in Zamosc, Russian Poland, but moved to Warsaw when she was three, where her father moved in intellectual circles. As the youngest of five children, born on March 5, 1871, Luxemburg was lame and tiny but never shy. At seventeen, she joined a Polish socialist organization, but her illegal activities were discovered, and her friends had to help her cross the border to Zurich to escape prosecution. While studying philosophy, economics, and law, she met Leo Jogiches, with whom she founded the Social Democratic Party of Poland in 1893. She traveled around Europe for several years, generally avoiding arrest until 1907, when she became an instructor of economics for party officials. In 1914, her most famous work, *The Accumulation of Capital*, appeared, in which she opposed nationalism because she thought it destroyed international worker solidarity. German socialists supporting World War I disturbed her, and she spent most of the war in prison organizing the Spartacus League with **Clara Zetkin**. This radical group became the German Communist Party and opposed the moderate socialist government. She supported the Spartacus uprising in 1919, but when the police found and arrested the rebels, they grabbed, beat, and then shot them. After her murderers threw her body into Berlin's Landwehr Canal, they were acquitted.

BIBLIOGRAPHY

Abraham, Richard. *Rosa Luxemburg: A Life for the International*. New York: Berg, 1989. 0-85496-182-8, 178p. Abraham gives a picture of the public life of Rosa Luxemburg by including what other people have said about her, but his approach provides only a brief introduction to her and some of her beliefs.

Ettinger, Elzbieta. *Rosa Luxemburg: A Life*. Boston: Beacon, 1986. 0-8070-7007-6, 286p. Ettinger's well-written biography of Luxemburg, based on material newly available from Poland, is more personal than Abraham's since she discusses in detail Luxemburg's relationship with Leo Jogiches, her longtime lover and then good friend.

Luxemburg, Rosa. *Comrade and Lover: Rosa Luxemburg's Letters to Leo Jogiches*. Trans. Elzbieta Ettinger. Cambridge, MA: MIT Press, 1979. 0-262-05021-8, 206p. In these letters written to Leo Jogiches between 1893 and 1914, Luxemburg reveals her thoughts and the tenets of German social democracy before World War I.

Luxemburg, Rosa. *The Letters of Rosa Luxemburg*. Ed. Stephen Eric Bronner. 1978. Atlantic Highlands, NJ: Humanities Press, 1993. 0-391-03789-7, 307p. These letters cover twenty-five years of correspondence to a variety of people, disclosing personal aspects of Luxemburg's life.

Shepardson, Donald E. *Rosa Luxemburg and the Noble Dream*. New York: Peter Lang, 1996. 0-8204-2739-X, 171p. This readable, well-documented look at Luxemburg's life and her beliefs concludes that she would have been happy with the mass revolution that downed a communism gone awry because she espoused the noble dream of democratic socialism.

$\mathfrak{M}$

MACARTHUR, ELIZABETH (1766–1850)
Businesswoman   **England and Australia**

Elizabeth Macarthur, a pioneer in Australia, made New South Wales an important world wool market. Elizabeth Veale was born on August 14, 1766, into a wealthy farming family and received her education in Devon. After she married John Macarthur in 1788, they went to New South Wales via convict ship for his military service. In transit, she gave birth to a daughter, who died before they reached Australia. As the first free woman in the colonies, she had culture and influenced military and administrative matters. Her husband, working as paymaster, inspector of public works, and businessman, acquired a fortune as well as land grants with which he built Elizabeth Farm, the first Australian estate with formal gardens and a huge home for their nine children. He rebelled against Governor Bligh in 1809, however, and had to leave the country. Elizabeth ran their business, increasing their merino flocks, establishing New South Wales as an area in which to produce wool, and expanding sales into the English market. She continued to help after his return, and at his death, she and her sons increased both their business and their wealth.

BIBLIOGRAPHY

Bickel, Lennard. *Australia's First Lady: The Story of Elizabeth Macarthur.* North Sydney, New South Wales, Australia: Allen and Unwin, 1991. 0-04-442231-8, 219p. Bickel's biography is well documented, with many anecdotes about Macarthur's experiences.

King, Hazel. *Elizabeth Macarthur and Her World.* Forest Grove, OR: International Scholarly Book Services, 1980. 0-424-00080-6, 227p. This well-documented, accessible, scholarly biography, using documents and letters in the collection of Macarthur Papers in the Mitchell Library of Sydney, presents Macarthur's life.

MACAULAY, CATHERINE (1731–1791)
Scholar   England

Catherine Macaulay became interested in Greek and Roman history and adapted her interests to write an eight-volume history of England. She was born on April 2, 1731, at Olantigh in Wye, Kent, to a wealthy landowner and his second wife, who died in childbirth when Catherine was two. Her father secluded himself, and Catherine educated herself privately by reading from his library. When she was in her twenties, she began her work, publishing the first volume of *History of England* in 1763. Her husband died in 1766, and she continued her work after his death, moving to Bath in 1774 and visiting Paris twice within the next three years. She was well respected for her history and for her political pamphlets, and members of society sought her but gossiped at her marriage to a man of twenty-one when she was forty-seven. After she completed her history of England in 1783, she and her husband visited the American colonies, with which she had great sympathy, and they became good friends with George Washington.

BIBLIOGRAPHY
Hill, Bridget. *The Republican Virago: The Life and Times of Catharine Macaulay, Historian*. New York: Oxford University Press, 1992. 0-19-812978-5, 263p. With no extant family papers and only fragmentary and anecdotal material available, Hill, in a thoroughly researched and documented biography, confirms Macaulay as an important historical figure who influenced English radicalism and American and French revolutionary ideas.

MACAULAY, ROSE (1881–1958)
Writer   England

Rose Macaulay was an award-winning novelist who was also a poet, journalist, historian, anthologist, broadcaster, and letterwriter. She was born in Rugby, Warwickshire, on August 1, 1881, where her father was assistant master at Rugby school, the second daughter instead of the son that her mother wanted. She went to Genoa, Italy, to live before returning to England and Oxford High School. She followed it with Sommerville College, where she studied history. In London after Oxford, she socialized with other writers and published her first novel, *Abbots Verney*, in 1906. After World War I, she received the Prix Femina Vie Heureuse for *Dangerous Ages* (1921). Throughout her career, she wrote journal and newspaper pieces on a variety of subjects. During World War II, she served as a voluntary ambulance driver, but after the war, she wrote several travel books and won the James Tait Black Memorial Prize for her novel *The Towers of Trebizond* (1956). In 1958, she was honored as Dame of the British Empire.

BIBLIOGRAPHY
Babington Smith, Constance. *Rose Macaulay*. London: Collins, 1972. 0-002-11720-7, 254p. This tactful biography shows the parallels between Macaulay's life and her writing, with excerpts from her work. Babington Smith sees as a central focus of Macaulay's life her love for a married man who died in 1942 and whose widow Macaulay did not want to embarrass.

Bensen, Alice Rhodus. *Rose Macaulay*. New York: Twayne, 1969. No ISBN, 184p. Bensen's biography shows that Macaulay's writing was closely associated with her life, so it includes critical analyses of her works.

Crawford, Alice. *Paradise Pursued: The Novels of Rose Macaulay*. Cranbury, NJ: Fairleigh Dickinson University Press, 1995. 0-8386-3573-3, 213p. Crawford uses Macaulay's papers from Trinity College, Cambridge, including juvenilia; letters from the Bodleian in Oxford; and her BBC broadcasts in her carefully documented, scholarly, and critical assessment. She sees Macaulay's novels as united in a lengthy process toward the pursuit of paradise as Macaulay asked questions about how one should live one's life and what basic goodness one should desire.

Emery, Jane. *Rose Macaulay: A Writer's Life*. London: J. Murray, 1991. 0-7195-4768-7, 381p. Emery's thoroughly researched, balanced, and recommended biography contemplates whether Macaulay's conversational skills were more valuable than her writing.

MACBRIDE, MAUD GONNE. *See* GONNE, MAUD.

MacDONALD, FLORA (1722–1790)
Revolutionary   Scotland

Flora MacDonald, a Scottish Jacobite, aided Prince Charles Edward in his escape after the Battle of Culloden Moor in 1746. Born in South Uist in the Hebrides Islands, she was the third child of a gentleman farmer who died when she was two. Her mother had three small children and two farms twenty miles apart to oversee. MacDonald was educated at home with Gaelic as her first language, and, when she was thirteen, Lady Clanranald, wife of the chief of her clan, adopted her. She could play the spinet, sing, and dance and had social graces, but she could also milk a cow, make butter and cheese, and walk or ride forty miles a day. After the Battle of Culloden, she disguised herself as a maid to take the prince from Benbecula to Portree. She married Allan MacDonald in an arranged marriage and went to North Carolina with him, where, in the American colonies, he became a brigadier general. When he was taken prisoner in 1779, MacDonald returned to Scotland. He was freed two years later, and they settled in Kingsburgh, Scotland. Few contemporary descriptions of her exist because she kept no journal, but history records her as unassuming, self-confident, gentle yet resolute, devoted to her family yet extraordinary because she captured Scotland's imagination. In the last year of her life, she dictated *Memorial* in honor of Sir John MacPherson.

BIBLIOGRAPHY
MacLeod, Ruairidh H. *Flora MacDonald: The Jacobite Heroine in Scotland and North America*. London: Shepheard-Walwyn, 1995. 0-85683-147-6, 255p. MacLeod says that the only source for much of MacDonald's life in America is her *Memorial*. However, since 1938, new material about the 1745 uprising has become available, and it, along with North Carolina records, includes original material about Flora and her husband. MacLeod has written a balanced, well-documented, and readable, scholarly biography of MacDonald's life.

MACPHAIL, AGNES (1890–1954)
Politician   Canada

Agnes Macphail was Canada's first woman member of Parliament (MP). She was born Agnes Campbell in Grey County, Ontario, on March 24, 1890. After her education at Stratford Normal School, she became a schoolteacher and became involved with the woman suffrage movement. In 1921, she was elected as an MP for the United Farmers of Ontario, the first woman to enter the House of Commons. She served as the sole woman for seventeen of her nineteen years. When first elected, she voted with the Progressive Party, but she joined the "Ginger Group" in 1924 and became a leader of the Co-operative Commonwealth Federation of Canada. In 1925, she changed the spelling of her name to "Macphail" from "MacPhail." She served in the Ontario legislature from 1943 until 1951 and represented Canada in the Assembly of the League of Nations. She was an outspoken feminist committed to equality and human rights, first as a radical and then as a social democrat.

BIBLIOGRAPHY

Crowley, Terence Allan. *Agnes Macphail and the Politics of Equality*. Toronto: J. Lorimer, 1990. 1-55028-328-6, 240p. Crowley's balanced and well-documented biography is a recommended account of Macphail, a woman committed to populist politics who concealed her private life.

Pennington, Doris. *Agnes Macphail, Reformer: Canada's First Female M.P.* Toronto: Simon and Pierre, 1989. 0-88924-212-7, 261p. This is a well-researched, scholarly approach to Macphail's life with special emphasis on her political career.

MAHLER, ALMA (1879–1964)
Instrumentalist   **Austria**

Alma Mahler was a gifted pianist who helped her husband and others by critiquing their music. Born on August 31, 1879, in Vienna to the artist and dreamer, Emil Schindler, Mahler met intellectuals and artists in Vienna throughout her life. When she met Gustav Mahler, the most powerful man in the music world, in 1901, he was twenty years older, but she married him. As a composition pupil, she understood Mahler's music, gave him advice, and devoted much of her time to copying his scores. After he died, she married Walter Gropius and stayed with him through the Bauhaus success. At fifty, she married Franz Werfel. She was a fascist and an anti-Semite but married two Jews. She knew Hans Pfitzner, Alexander von Zemlinsky, Arnold Schoenberg, Thomas Mann, and Oskar Kokoschka and was the center of her Viennese culture between the two world wars.

BIBLIOGRAPHY

Giroud, Francoise. *Alma Mahler, Or, the Art of Being Loved*. New York: Oxford University Press, 1992. 0-19-816156-5, 162p. Not as flattering as other biographies, Giroud uses diaries, letters, and secondary sources to depict Mahler as a woman seeking dominance over the men in her life, including her three husbands.

Keegan, Susanne. *The Bride of the Wind: The Life and Times of Alma Mahler-Werfel*. New York: Viking, 1992. 0-670-80513-0, 346p. Keegan's balanced biography of Mahler is both sympathetic with her situation and critical of her morals. It shows Mahler in the midst of Viennese social life and seriously examines her compositions.

Monson, Karen. *Alma Mahler, Muse to Genius: From Fin-de-siecle Vienna to Hollywood's Heyday*. Boston: Houghton Mifflin, 1983. 0-395-32213-8, 348p. Monson's biography is a well-documented resource about a complex woman who knew how to make men think that they were unique.

Sorell, Walter. *Three Women: Lives of Sex and Genius*. Indianapolis: Bobbs-Merrill, 1975. 0-672-51750-7, 234p. The women whom Sorell discusses in interesting but short biographies—Alma Mahler-Werfel, Gertrude Stein, and Andreas-Salomé—inspired some of the greatest artists of the century. He thinks that Mahler-Werfel was passive with her artistic powers but also less fulfilled and ambivalent because she wanted to possess men but not be possessed.

MAINTENON, FRANÇOISE de (1635–1719)

Consort   France

Madame de Maintenon became influential in her lover Louis XIV's court by reducing the corruption and incompetence. Françoise d'Aubigné was born in the Niort, Poitou, prison, on November 27, 1635, into a Huguenot family. Her Calvinist aunt educated her until she was seven, and when she was ten, after her father was released from prison, the family went to Martinique. Her mother died when she was eighteen, and her aunt sent her to live with a disabled poet, Paul Scarron, twenty-five years older, whom she married. When he died in 1660, she went to live in a convent. Her friend Marie de Montespan became the king's mistress and employed Scarron as governess for their children. With the king's payments, Scarron bought the Château de Maintenon in 1674, and the king made her a marquise in 1675. Louis XIV hired her as lady-in-waiting to the dauphine in 1679, and the next year, she became Louis's mistress. After Queen Marie Thérèse died in 1683, the king married her. Their relationship lasted thirty-two years. She founded Saint-Cyr, the Maison Royale de Saint Louis for impoverished, aristocratic girls, and retired there when the king died.

BIBLIOGRAPHY
Barnard, Howard Clive. *Madame de Maintenon and Saint-Cyr*. 1932. Menston, Yorkshire, England: Scholar, 1971. 0-85409-702-3, 240p. Barnard thinks that Madame de Maintenon's main contribution was to education. In this carefully documented biography, Barnard discusses Saint-Cyr, which Madame de Maintenon founded based on educational practices for males.
De Polnay, Peter. *Madame de Maintenon*. London: Heron Books, 1969. No ISBN, 339p. De Polnay suggests that Madame de Maintenon gave the second half of Louis XIV's reign a dignity that he could not have achieved without her. Although entertaining, this biography is undocumented.
Haldane, Charlotte. *Madame de Maintenon: Uncrowned Queen of France*. Indianapolis: Bobbs-Merrill, 1970. No ISBN, 310p. Haldane notes that Madame de Maintenon's thousands of letters reveal her personality but that she burned almost her entire correspondence with Louis XIV, so that no direct evidence of their relationship either before or after their marriage exists. Haldane uses other documents as well to re-create this readable biography of a woman whom original biographers maligned unjustly.

MAKAROVA, NATALIA (1940–)

Ballerina   Russia

Natalia Makarova is a classical ballerina who has performed throughout the world. She was born in St. Petersburg on November 21, 1940, where she attended the Vaganova School and joined the Kirov ballet. She appeared as

Giselle at Covent Garden in London and toured the United States in 1961. She appeared as Odette-Odile and as Aurora in critically acclaimed performances in the Soviet Union before defecting to the West after a European tour in 1970. She joined the American Ballet Theatre in New York and has made guest appearances in the United States and Great Britain, where she has played both classical and modern ballet roles.

BIBLIOGRAPHY

Austin, Richard. *Natalia Makarova: Ballerina.* Brooklyn, NY: Dance Horizons, 1978. 0-87127-103-6, 139p. Austin uses photographs and Makarova's own words from discussions with her to present her artistic career rather than her private life, but he admits being unable to solve the mystery of her genius.

Makarova, Natalia. *A Dance Autobiography.* Ed. Gennady Smakov. Photos Dina Makarova and others. New York: Knopf, 1979. 0-394-50141-1, 366p. In this autobiography with photographs, Makarova spends more time discussing the technical aspects of preparing for specific roles than she does in revealing herself.

MALIBRAN, MARIA (1808–1836)

Opera Singer   Spain

Maria Felicita Malibran was a mezzo-soprano who won critical acclaim throughout the world. She was born on March 24, 1808, to tenor Manuel Garcia, and he was her first teacher. Malibran made her formal debut at the King's Theatre in London as Rosina in Rossini's *The Barber of Seville* in 1825. Her father then took her and the rest of his opera company to New York for the first season of Italian opera in the United States. On this tour, she married Eugène Malibran, probably to escape her father, and soon left him. After two years, she returned to Europe and made her Paris debut in 1828 in Rossini's *Semiramide.* The next four years she commuted between London and Paris and appeared in all of Italy's major opera houses. Composers who wanted her to sing their music included Chopin, Liszt, and Mendelssohn. Her marriage to Malibran was annulled, and she had a son with Charles de Bériot before marrying him in 1836. She died a few months later in a riding accident.

BIBLIOGRAPHY

Bushnell, Howard. *Maria Malibran: A Biography of the Singer.* University Park: Pennsylvania State University Press, 1979. 0-271-00222-0, 264p. Using unpublished sources and letters in this well-documented biography of Malibran, Bushnell also reveals the nineteenth-century world of opera.

Fitzlyon, April. *Maria Malibran: Diva of the Romantic Age.* Chicago: Souvenir Press, 1987. 0-285-65030-0, 330p. Fitzlyon shows that Malibran's contemporary public treated her, an opera diva, like a cult figure. She influenced novels, artists, and poets of her time.

MANDELA, WINNIE (1934–)

Activist   South Africa

Winnie Mandela is a political activist whose work in South Africa helped to stop the policy of apartheid. Born in Pondoland, part of Transkei, on September 26, 1934, she was a member of the Tembu royal house. Because of inheritance laws, her mother had wanted a boy. In Johannesburg, Mandela obtained a social science diploma and became a hospital social worker before marrying Nelson Mandela, a lawyer and member of the African National Congress (ANC), in 1958. She became active in the Women's League of the ANC, which was declared illegal in 1961, the same year the government captured and sentenced her husband to life imprisonment. It banned and restricted her. During his absence, Mandela became the spokesperson for the ANC and was imprisoned in 1966 for almost a year. In 1976 after the Soweto uprising, the government banished her to the outskirts of the Orange Free State Town of Brandforth and primitive conditions. She broke the ban in 1978 and received a suspended sentence. She again broke the ban in 1985 and won the Third World Prize before returning to Soweto to live. After being convicted of a nonpolitical crime in the 1990s, she regained confidence and was reelected to the presidency of the Women's League. She has continued to stand for justice in South Africa.

BIBLIOGRAPHY

Gilbey, Emma. *The Lady: The Life and Times of Winnie Mandela.* London: Vintage, 1994. 0-09-938801-4, 328p. Gilbey's biography of Mandela is a carefully researched, well-written, and balanced attempt to understand how Mandela could, in recent years, become an apologist for some of the worst excesses of black South Africa's armed struggle.

MANSFIELD, KATHERINE (1888–1923)
Writer   New Zealand

Katherine Mansfield has long been considered one of the twentieth century's best short story writers. She was born in Wellington, New Zealand, on October 14, 1888, as one of a successful businessman's six children. She published a short story in a high school paper when she was nine and at fifteen went to London to attend Queen's College. She remained in Europe for the rest of her life except for the years 1906–1908, when she studied music in New Zealand. In 1909, she received her first pay for a story. She also married that same year but left her husband the next day. Her first volume of short stories, *In a German Pension*, dealt with her experience in Germany while pregnant (not with her husband's child) before she miscarried. Among the writers with whom she socialized in London were **Virginia Woolf**, D. H. Lawrence, and John Middleton Murry, the man with whom she began to live in 1912 and whom she married in 1918. She and Murry founded a magazine in 1916, but her health soon began to deteriorate, and she went to the south of France to recuperate. Her most famous work, *Prelude*, describes her childhood in New Zealand. Murry edited and published her letters and journals after her death from tuberculosis.

BIBLIOGRAPHY

Alpers, Antony. *The Life of Katherine Mansfield.* New York: Viking, 1980. 0-670-42805-1, 466p. Alpers uses newly opened manuscript collections, private papers, and personal contacts to present Mansfield the writer and the woman. New Zealand Literary Fund of Queen Elizabeth II Arts Council.

Boddy, Gillian. *Katherine Mansfield: The Woman and the Writer.* New York: Penguin, 1988. 0-14-008632-3, 325p. In Mansfield's collection of papers, letters, and notebooks, Boddy found an enigmatic woman who was rebel, dreamer, musician, and mimic and describes her in a well-researched and readable introduction.

Meyers, Jeffrey. *Katherine Mansfield: A Biography*. New York: New Directions, 1980. 0-8112-075-1, 306p. Like Alpers, Meyers has carefully researched his subject and given a balanced view of Mansfield's life.

Moore, James. *Gurdjieff and Mansfield*. Boston: Routledge and Kegan Paul, 1980. 0-7100-0488-5, 261p. This biography covers the last years of Mansfield's life after she moved to Fontainebleau and glosses over facts to make the questionable point that Gurdjieff, a friend, was more important to Mansfield than Murry.

MARGARET of SCOTLAND (1046?–1093)

Queen of Scotland   Hungary

As the queen of Malcolm III of Scotland, Margaret persuaded him to initiate a series of ecclesiastical reforms that transformed the religious and cultural life of Scotland. She was the oldest of three children of the Anglo-Saxon prince Edward Atheling and his Hungarian wife, Agatha. Margaret grew up in the court of Hungary, and when the politics became unfavorable, went with her family to Scotland. In 1070, she married Malcolm. She founded the Holy Trinity Abbey at Dunfermline, restored many churches, and devoted herself to the care of the sick and the poor. Canonized in 1249, she is considered the patroness of Scotland.

BIBLIOGRAPHY
Nagy, Kazmer. *St. Margaret of Scotland and Hungary*. Glasgow: John S. Burns, 1973. No ISBN, 63p. Nagy relies on Anglo-Saxon sources and Hungarian historiography to trace the lineage of Margaret through her mother, although most sources on her are exclusively in England.

MARGARET of VALOIS (1553–1615)

Consort   France

Marguerite of Valois is the first woman known in history to have written her autobiography. She was a royal daughter to **Catherine de Medici** born on May 14, 1553, but she never became the queen of France. She was intelligent, with great presence of mind and an exceptional education. She was lonely, and for political reasons, she often was imprisoned in her room. She might have been a political victim of the attempt to unite the Protestants and Catholics in France since the Night of St. Bartholomew disturbed her wedding ceremonies to Henri de Navarre. Her happiest years with her husband were when they lived away from the French court in Gascogne for several years where inhabitants of Flanders adored her. When her husband became king, he also became Catholic, but he had already decided to divorce her. In 1576, she began attending lectures and, during her enforced solitude, began to study. After her long sojourn in Auvergne, she abandoned politics for literature and engendered an academy of some importance for the history of literary ideas. She is not to be confused with Marguerite d'Angoulême, also known as **Marguerite of Navarre**.

BIBLIOGRAPHY
Haldane, Charlotte. *Queen of Hearts: Marguerite of Valois ("La Reine Margot")*. London: Constable, 1968. 0-486-11894-0, 307p. Haldane uses Marguerite's memoirs and her correspondence, especially during the years of negotiation for her divorce, as well as prior biographers in this readable bi-

ography with a balanced view of Marguerite and the attitudes toward her during and after her lifetime.

Marguerite, Queen. *Memoirs of Marguerite de Valois*. Trans. Liselotte Dieckmann. 1628. Seattle: Papers on French Seventeenth Century Literature, 1987. No ISBN, 160p. Marguerite's memoirs show France during the Counter-Reformation in a way no history of the period can match. They are a valuable contribution, although she merely reports rather than reflects about clothes, followers, court intrigues, and extravagant parties.

Sealy, Robert J. *The Myth of the Reine Margot: Toward the Elimination of a Legend*. New York: P. Lang, 1994. 0-8204-2480-3, 226p. Sealy believes that historical figures take on the aspects of the fictions that writers may perpetrate, and Sealy thinks that *Le Divorce Satyrique*, which portrayed Marguerite solely as a woman who loved pleasure, misrepresented her. His purpose is to show how fiction has distorted the historical image of Margot (Marguerite).

Strage, Mark. *Women of Power: The Life and Times of Catherine de Medici*. New York: Harcourt Brace Jovanovich, 1976. 0-15-198370-4, 368p. Strage believes that Catherine de' Medici was the most important woman in Europe while she lived and that she, Diane de Poitier (Catherine's husband's mistress), and Marguerite de Valois (Catherine's daughter) had no rights but still managed to dominate their times.

MARGARET of YORK (1446–1503)

Activist and Politician   England

Margaret of York, duchess of Burgundy, was an influence on the northern provinces, especially Belgium, during the lifetime of her husband, Charles the Bold of Burgundy. She was born May 3, 1446, daughter of Richard, duke of York, and Cecily Neville, with her brothers slated to become Edward IV and Richard III, kings of England. In 1468, she married Charles as his third wife and became a useful political adviser and negotiator for him. She has received more attention in Belgium than in England because in English history she has appeared as a pawn in Edward IV's foreign policy and a thorn to Henry VII. She aggravated the Tudor paranoia against the house of York, which led to her family's destruction. In Europe, after Charles died in 1477, she helped arrange the Habsburg marriage of her stepdaughter, Marie of Burgundy, to Maximilian of Austria, a critically important move. She helped Maximilian to establish the Habsburg presence in the Low Countries and was a guide and mentor to the young Philip. Her determination kept the duchy of Burgundy from succumbing to the Valois dukes, and she remained an implacable enemy of Louis XI of France. Because of her control, France was unable to annex the Low Countries until the eighteenth century. The modern kingdom of Belgium owes much of its preservation from French influence to her. She was also interested in religious matters. Her love of fine books led her to become a patroness of the printer William Caxton, which kept her at the forefront of educated lay opinion and printing technology.

BIBLIOGRAPHY

Weightman, Christine B. *Margaret of York, Duchess of Burgundy, 1446–1503*. New York: St. Martin's, 1989. 0-312-03104-1, 244p. This well documented, scholarly biography attempts to provide a whole picture of Margaret by examining her political activity and its motivation along with her lifestyle. Weightman investigates how a woman at the end of the fifteenth century could ensure her own personal survival and prosperity in the face of a series of disasters that led to her representing a failed alliance and removed her most powerful relations in both England and Burgundy. Margaret, however, used her talents for the advancement of others as well as for her own benefit.

MARGUERITE of NAVARRE (1492–1549)
Writer and Intellectual   **France**

Marguerite of Navarre (also known as de Valois or d'Angoulême) was an intellectual. Born on May 14, 1492, the daughter of Charles d'Orléans, count of Angoulême, and Louise of Savoy, she learned Hebrew, Latin, Italian, German, and Spanish from her mother and philosophy, history, and theology from tutors. In 1508, she appeared at the court of Louis XII, but she married the duke of Alençon in 1509 and disappeared until her brother Francis I ascended the throne. She became his hostess, and in 1517, he gave her the duchy of Berry which contained the University of Bourges. In this position, she attracted the leading scholars to the university and initiated new disciplines. When Spain imprisoned Francis in 1525, she negotiated his release and the Treaty of Cambrai. The same year, her husband died, and two years later, she married Henri D'Albret, king of Navarre. She became isolated from Francis's court again, but she helped her husband with political reforms and established a court at Nérac, which became a haven for intellectuals and religious reformers persecuted by the Catholic church. She wrote religious verse, of which the church also disapproved, and published it in *Le Miroir de l'Âme Pécheresse* (1531). Her best-known work was *Heptameron*, short stories that resembled those by Boccaccio in his *Decameron,* published after her death.

BIBLIOGRAPHY
Chamberlin, E. R. *Marguerite of Navarre.* New York, Dial, 1974. 0-8037-5207-5, 296p. This well-researched, well-written, and balanced biography gives an overview of Marguerite of Navarre's life and her accomplishments.

MARIA THERESA (1717–1780)
Empress   **Austria**

Maria Theresa became the empress of Austria, archduchess of Austria, and queen of Bohemia and led her country in 1740 after the death of her father. She was born in Vienna on May 13, 1717, as the eldest of three daughters to the Holy Roman Emperor Charles VI and his wife, Elizabeth. He passed an act that allowed the female line to succeed him. In 1736, he married Theresa to Francis Stephen, who became the duke of Tuscany. They had sixteen children, ten of whom survived to adulthood, including Marie Antoinette. When Maria Theresa was only twenty-three, her father died, and she changed from a frivolous twenty-three-year-old to an autocratic ruler. She had her husband crowned emperor in 1745 and created new taxes to pay for an army, which defended her right to the throne when Frederick the Great of Prussia challenged her in the War of the Austrian Succession. She limited the power of the nobles, changed civil service, and placed the church under state control. Although she ceded Silesia to Russia so that the war could end in 1748, she determined to regain her lands, and in 1756, after she had cut her ties with England, she made treaties with France and Russia that began the Seven Years' War. Francis died in 1765, and she began new reforms of centralization along with the architectural, social, and cultural development of Vienna.

BIBLIOGRAPHY

Bright, James Franck. *Maria Theresa.* 1897. Freeport, NY: Books for Libraries, 1971. 0-8369-5761-X, 224p. This undocumented biography suggests that Maria Theresa's problems evolved from her ministers because they would never have listened to a younger woman.

Crankshaw, Edward. *Maria Theresa.* 1969. Philadelphia: Trans-Atlantic, 1996. 0-09-465030-6, 384p. Crankshaw's readable, researched, and recommended, popular biography examines Maria Theresa's accession to the throne, the life in the Vienna court, the influence of government policy, and her services as Queen Mother.

Fraser, Antonia. *The Warrior Queens: The Legends and the Lives of the Women Who Have Led Their Nations in War.* New York: Knopf, 1989. 0-394-54939-2, 383p. Fraser examines the situations that have placed women in roles where they have had to defend their people. Fraser briefly describes Maria Theresa's attributes as an eighteenth-century ruler.

McGill, William J., Jr. *Maria Theresa.* New York: Twayne, 1972. No ISBN, 169p. McGill's balanced biography posits that Maria Theresa was the most important ruler in Habsburg history, royal yet devoted, pragmatic yet pursuing reform.

MARIE ANTOINETTE (1755–1793)

Queen   France

Marie Antoinette became wife of the French dauphin Louis when she was fifteen, with their marriage forming an alliance between Austria and France. Born on November 2, 1755, as the eleventh daughter of the Holy Roman Emperor Francis I and **Maria Theresa**, the French continued to distrust Austria and Marie after she arrived to marry the dauphin. By the time Louis became king in 1774, Marie had her own group of friends and was a notorious spendthrift. Rumors paired her with a number of liaisons, some false and some probably factual. After she had a son, she spent less money but did not seem to understand economics. As her political power became stronger, she influenced Louis to keep feudalism without restricting royal prerogative as the National Guard had demanded. In 1789, when she and the king were brought to Paris, she was particularly unpopular. In 1791, the government seized her from Varennes, where the royal family was attempting to escape. She tried to negotiate and continued to ask for Austrian aid. In 1792, during the final invasion of the Tuilleries, the people captured her and Louis. After accusing them of treason, they executed Louis and imprisoned Marie in the Conciergerie. They tried her on October 14, 1793, before the Revolutionary Tribunal and guillotined her two days later. Her surviving son, Louis XVII, died two years later while still in prison.

BIBLIOGRAPHY

Cronin, Vincent. *Louis and Antoinette.* London: Collins, 1974. 0-002-11494-1, 455p. Using new sources, Cronin presents Marie Antoinette and her husband in this balanced, readable biography as good, industrious, kind, thrifty, and happily married.

Erickson, Carolly. *To the Scaffold: The Life of Marie Antoinette.* New York: William Morrow, 1991. 0-688-07301-8, 384p. This carefully researched and recommended popular biography reveals a Marie Antoinette who is rather likable, although uninterested in the skills that would have made her a competent queen.

Farr, Evelyn. *Marie Antoinette and Count Axel Fersen: The Untold Love Story.* Chester Springs, PA: Peter Owen, Dufour, 1996. 0-7206-0960-7, 256p. This accessible and balanced biography reveals that Marie Antoinette was mismatched to the French heir and that her affair with Count Fersen was a lasting love. Farr uses recently available correspondence and documents to reconstruct Marie Antoinette's relationship and Fersen's attempts to save Antoinette from the guillotine before his own death as a victim of court conspiracy.

Loomis, Stanley. *The Fatal Friendship: Marie Antoinette, Count Fersen and the Flight to Varennes.* London: Davis-Poynter, 1972. 0-7067-0047-3, 341p. Loomis tells the story of Marie Antoinette and her supposed lover Count Fersen's escape to Varennes in a researched biography that reads like a novel.

Seward, Desmond. *Marie Antoinette.* New York: St. Martin's, 1981. 0-312-51467-0, 297p. Seward suggests that Marie Antoinette was guillotined not for her participation in the revolution but for her aloofness and Austrian heritage.

MARKHAM, BERYL (1902–1986)

Aviator   England

Beryl Markham was the first woman aviator to fly solo across the Atlantic. She was born on October 26, 1902, in Leicestershire and went with her father to his farm in Kenya when she was four, leaving her mother and brother in England. There she learned to speak Swahili, Nandi, and Masai and learned about racehorse training and breeding. When a financial crisis ruined the farm, her father left her with one horse and went to Peru. At eighteen, she became the first woman in Africa to receive a trainer's license, and the next year, her horse won the prestigious Kenya St. Leger race. As a beautiful woman, she had many admirers, and she married several of them. She first married a rugby player. Then she married Mansfield Markham and had a child. During their marriage, the duke of Gloucester became infatuated with her, and Markham's husband sued and won. They remained married, although separated, until 1942. Markham learned to fly in the 1920s and by 1931 had become a pilot taking mail and passengers throughout East Africa. In 1936, she flew across the Atlantic from east to west. After she crash-landed in Nova Scotia, New York welcomed her with a ticker-tape parade. She went to California, divorced, and married Raoul Schumacher, who helped her write about her bush-flying and Africa in *West with the Night.* They divorced after five years, and she returned to Africa to train winning racehorses in Kenya, Rhodesia, and South Africa.

BIBLIOGRAPHY

Gourley, Catherine. *Beryl Markham: Never Turn Back.* Berkeley, CA: Conari, 1997. 1-57324-073-7, 150p. In this biography for young adults, Gourley posits that Markham's childhood experiences of being abandoned by her mother and taken to Kenya by her father formed her into a risk-taker and a free spirit. Markham defied the stereotypical female roles considered appropriate for her times to become an aviatrix, writer, adventurer, and horse trainer.

Lovell, Mary S. *Straight on till Morning: The Biography of Beryl Markham.* New York: St. Martin's, 1987. 0-312-01096-6, 408p. Lovell's straightforward biography of Markham includes gossip and revelations about people whom Markham knew as it presents a woman so unusual that, although researched, its content reads like fiction.

Markham, Beryl. *West with the Night.* 1942. New York: Farrar, Straus, and Giroux, 1982. 0-86547-118-5, 320p. Markham describes her love of Africa and its lessons on life in this memoir, emphasizing the beauty of the jungles and deserts below and the skies above as she flew her airplane into its vastness.

Trzebinski, Errol. *The Lives of Beryl Markham: Out of Africa's Hidden Free Spirit and Denys Finch Hatton's Last Great Love.* New York: Norton, 1993. 0-393-03556-5, 396p. In this well-researched biography, Trzebinski reveals Markham's remarkable love life, including background about the man she stalked (the lover of **Isak Dinesen**) and won before he died in a plane crash as well as her affairs with the Prince of Wales and his brother.

MARKIEWICZ, CONSTANCE (1868–1927)
Politician											England and Ireland

Constance Markiewicz was an Irish nationalist politician. She was born in London on February 4, 1868, but received her education from governesses on the family estate in Lissadell, County Sligo, Ireland. She studied art first at the Slade School in London and then in Paris. There she met Count Casimir Markiewicz, a Polish painter, and married him. They lived in Paris and the Ukraine before returning to Dublin in 1903, where Markiewicz became involved with Ireland's revival, joining the Gaelic League, the Abbey Theatre, and **Maud Gonne**'s Daughters of Ireland. Markiewicz helped found the United Arts Club in 1907 and the youth movement of Na Fianna in 1909. People called her "Madame" and the "Red Countess" as she became an active participant in the Dublin strike of 1913 and the Easter Rising in 1916, leading a group of soldiers before being captured and condemned to death. Her sentence changed to life imprisonment, she left prison in 1917 during the amnesty and was elected as a member of Parliament (MP) for Dublin. Although the first female MP in the British Isles, she refused to go to Westminster in protest against the government. Dublin South elected her to Parliament in 1923, but she kept going to prison and staged a hunger strike in protest of Irish laws. In 1926, she joined the Fianna Fail party and the next year was reelected to Parliament.

BIBLIOGRAPHY

Norman, Diana. *Terrible Beauty: A Life of Constance Markievicz, 1868–1927.* London: Hodder and Stoughton, 1987. 0-340-39525-7, 320p. In this thorough and well-documented, scholarly biography of Markievicz, Norman includes early twentieth-century Irish history. Norman posits that people remember Markievicz for killing a policeman because men try to denigrate women until the woman disappears from history, regardless of what they have done to make society a better institution.

O'Faolain, Sean. *Constance Markievicz.* London: Cresset, 1987. 0-09-17289-5, 220p. This is a popular biography, but O'Faolain makes assertions about Markievicz that he cannot prove. His casual commentary destroys any validity the work might have for a scholar interested in Markievicz or in a balanced picture of the times.

Van Voris, Jacqueline. *Constance de Markievicz.* Long Island, NY: Feminist Press, 1972. 0-912670-04-5, 143p. This brief introduction to Markievicz's life is readable but undocumented.

MARKOVA, ALICIA (1910–)
Ballerina   England

Alicia Markova was a ballerina who danced throughout Europe and the United States during her career. Born Lillian Alicia Marks in London, daughter of a Jewish engineer and an Irishwoman from Cork, she made her first professional appearance when she was only ten. At thirteen, after training, she appeared with the Legal Ballet Group, and Diaghilev hired her the following year. At sixteen, she danced the title role in Balanchin's *Le Rossignol.* After 1929, she danced with Blum at Drury Lane in London and then at the Metropolitan Opera House in New York. In the mid-1930s, she was the first *prima ballerina* of the Vic-Wells Ballet. She also performed with the Rambert Ballet Club founded by **Marie Rambert.** From 1935 to 1938, she took her own corps, the Markova-Dolin Ballet, into the provinces, and during World War II, she danced with the American Ballet Theater in New York. She cofounded the London Festival Ballet in 1950 and became the vice president of the Royal Academy of Dancing in 1958. In 1963, the year she retired, she received the Dame of the British Empire and became the director of the New York Metropolitan Opera Ballet, a post she kept until 1969 to become a professor of ballet at the University of Cincinnati Conservatory of Music. She gave master classes in London and Paris, appeared on television, and served as president of the London Festival Ballet in 1986.

BIBLIOGRAPHY
Markova, Alicia. *Markova Remembers.* Boston: Little, Brown, 1986. 0-316-54625-9, 192p. Makarova shares memories and photographs from her childhood, remembering her meeting with Pavlova after a performance when she told her to always take good care of her teeth and to have a cologne rub after dancing.

MARTINEAU, HARRIET (1802–1876)
Writer and Intellectual   England

Harriet Martineau was a novelist, political economist, and children's writer. She was born in Norwich on June 12, 1802, to a Huguenot textile manufacturer. She received an education equal to her brother's, but as a child, she was nervous and had the onset of deafness. In 1826, her father went bankrupt and then died, followed soon by her brother and fiancé. She decided to become independent, and by 1831, she had won prizes for her essays published in the *Unitarian Journal.* Because of her education, she was able to write and publish a twenty-five–volume series, *Illustrations of Political Economy,* in 1834. Based on the ideas of Mill, James, and Ricardo, it was so successful that cabinet ministers invited her to address Parliament. She followed with other multivolume books. In 1837, she visited America and wrote *Society in America.* Her first novel, *Deerbook,* appeared in 1839. An illness forced her to stay at home, and she began writing children's stories. Hypnotic treatment seemed to cure her illness, and she became interested in mesmerism. During the next few years, she moved and traveled before writing for the *London Daily News* in the 1950s on subjects such as agricultural economics, her opposition to licensed prostitution, her support for the Married Women's Property Bill, and her concern about poor women's working conditions. When doctors told her that she was incurably ill in 1854, she wrote her *Autobiography*, published posthumously.

BIBLIOGRAPHY

David, Deirdre. *Intellectual Women and Victorian Patriarchy: Harriet Martineau, Elizabeth Barrett Browning, George Eliot*. Ithaca, NY: Cornell University Press, 1987. 0-8014-1965-4, 273p. David's scholarly study shows three women, including Martineau, who did not become exiles from Victorian culture and society when they defied the patriarchal injunctions against female authorship. Martineau made writing the business of her life, gained celebrity, used her intellect, and showed her control of the language as a strong, ambitious writer.

Hoecker-Drysdale, Susan. *Harriet Martineau, First Woman Sociologist*. New York: Berg, St. Martin's, 1992. 0-85496-645-5, 190p. This intellectual biography shows Martineau as a significant figure in British social science and nineteenth-century sociological thought.

Martineau, Harriet. *Harriet Martineau's Autobiography*. Ed. Gaby Weiner. London: Virago, 1983. Vol. 1, paper, 0-86068-425-3. Vol. 2, paper, 0-86068-430-X. This readable portrayal of Martineau's life is a stylistically dated but good introduction, although biased, since Martineau said her duty was to write her autobiography.

Martineau, Harriet. *Harriet Martineau's Letters to Fanny Wedgwood*. Ed. Elisabeth Sanders Arbuckle. Stanford, CA: Stanford University Press, 1983. 0-8047-1146-1, 329p. Martineau's letters reveal her views about literary and scientific leaders, including Dickens, Darwin, and Carlyle, as well as the political issues of her time, gossip, and candid opinion.

Pichanick, Valerie Kossew. *Harriet Martineau, the Woman and Her Work, 1802–76*. Ann Arbor, MI: University of Michigan Press, 1980. 0-472-10002-4, 301p. Pichanick's thoroughly researched and documented scholarly biography of Martineau profiles a woman who lived in an age of transition and recognized it.

MARY, QUEEN to GEORGE V (1867–1953)

Queen Consort   England

Victoria Mary Augusta Louise Olga Pauline Claudine Agnes of Teck, the queen consort of George V and mother of both Edward VIII and George VI, won international acclaim for her charity and hospital work during World War I. She was born on May 26, 1867, daughter of Princess Mary Adelaide, cousin of Queen **Victoria** and the German nobleman Francis Alexander, duke of Teck, in Kensington Palace, London. As a young girl, she lived in Florence and attained culture. In 1893 she married George, then duke of York, and in 1911 was crowned with him in Westminster Abbey. She developed the concept of the "Working Queen," who, although conservative and frugal, believed in progress. She coped with the abdication of her son Edward VIII, although she disapproved of his decision and the reason behind it. After George V's death, she, as dowager queen, was not expected to remarry. She had interest in the main religious and political movements of her day and knew women who were

working for reform. Her efforts to improve life for the British people made her
a popular figure.

BIBLIOGRAPHY

Bloom, Ursula. *The Great Queen Consort*. London: Hale, 1976. 0-7091-5659-
6, 168p. From a first-person point of view, Bloom tells the story of Mary
of Teck. The book, undocumented and unindexed, is a laudatory, popular
biography that interprets the word "great" from the title to mean "best."

Edwards, Anne. *Matriarch: Queen Mary and the House of Windsor*. New York:
William Morrow, 1984. 0-688-03511-6, 527p. Edwards has written a definitive biography of Queen Mary, carefully documented. It reads like a
novel and should be selected as the source of choice about Mary as a queen
and as a Queen Mother.

Jackman, S. W. *The People's Princess: A Portrait of H.R.H. Princess Mary,
Duchess of Teck*. Berkshire, England: Kensal, 1984. 0-946041-19-9, 213p.
This loosely written biography of Mary is easily readable and includes spe-
cifics about her royal connections.

Wakeford, Geoffrey. *Three Consort Queens: Adelaide, Alexandra and Mary*.
London: Hale, 1971. 0-7091-2017-6, 207p. This chatty look at three consort queens describes their personalities and their contributions to the British monarchy. A popular, collective biography, it is readable and
entertaining.

Warwick, Christopher, ed. *Queen Mary's Photograph Albums*. London: Sidgwick and Jackson, 1989. 0-283-99853-9, 152p. Warwick has selected photographs from the ten thousand that Mary collected in thirty-three albums
and labeled with her own hand. This biographical sketch, complemented by
the revealing photographs, presents different "facts" rather than attempting
to be definitive.

MARY, QUEEN of SCOTS (1542–1587)

Queen   Scotland

Mary was the queen of Scotland, ascending to the throne when she was only
six days old. Born on December 7, 1542, she was the only child of James V of
Scotland and the French Mary of Guise. Her mother betrothed her to the
French dauphin (later, Francis II) and sent Mary to France when she was five to
be educated at the court of Henri II and **Catherine de Medici**. Mary learned
Latin, Italian, Spanish, and some Greek and spoke French as her first language.
When she married Francis, they had a treaty that stated that a male heir would
unite the two thrones. But the year after Francis became king, he died, and
Mary returned to Scotland in 1561. Mary's Catholic supporters challenged the
succession of **Elizabeth I** of England, but instead she married Henry Stewart,
Earl of Darnley, who murdered her secretary, Rizzio, before her eyes. When
their son was born, Mary became involved with James Hepburn, the earl of
Bothwell. Darnley was murdered in January 1565, and people suspected Bothwell but could not prove his guilt. In March, Bothwell abducted Mary, divorced his wife, and married Mary. The Scots rebelled, exiled Bothwell to
prison, and banished Mary to Lochleven Castle before putting James, her illegitimate brother, on the throne. She fled to England after her supporters lost
an uprising where Elizabeth feared Mary's rivalry and kept her in captivity for
nineteen years, refusing to execute her, until Babington's plot was revealed.
Elizabeth signed papers, and Mary was executed at the age of forty-four.

BIBLIOGRAPHY

Cowan, Ian Borthwick. *The Enigma of Mary Stuart.* London: Gollancz, 1971. 0-575-00674-9, 222p.   Cowan relies on prior biographies and histories containing opinions of Mary. In examining the arguments both for and against her, he says the evidence has changed little, but interpretations of it have. He thinks that her marriage to Darnley in 1565 began the controversies.

Fraser, Antonia. *Mary, Queen of Scots.* 1969. New York: Greenwich House, 1983. 0-517-41424-4, 613p. This biography, for the mature young adult and general reader, shows sound scholarship and tells a good story about this queen. The text includes over one hundred photographs. James Tait Black Memorial Prize.

Hamilton and Brandon, Angus Alan Douglas-Hamilton, Duke of. *Maria R: Mary Queen of Scots, the Crucial Years.* Edinburgh: Mainstream, 1991. 1-85158-363-7, 312p.   Hamilton concentrates on the year Mary married Darnley, 1565, and the year of her son's coronation, 1567, and sees them as the pivotal years of her problems. Beautiful illustrations, a history of the times, and insight about some of the minor characters in Mary's life fill the text.

Stepanek, Sally. *Mary, Queen of Scots.* New York: Chelsea House, 1987. 0-87754-540-5, 112p.   Stepanek begins this biography for young adults wondering whether Mary Stuart was a martyr for her faith and country or responsible for murder, adultery, and deceit. The only extant remains of her life are colorful tapestries or melancholy letters and poems. Mary's passions ruled her kingdom, especially in the battle between Catholics and Protestants.

Wormald, Jenny. *Mary Queen of Scots: A Study in Failure.* London: G. Philip, 1988. 0-540-01131-2, 206p. Wormald finds that Mary had little wit and no judgment. Rather than "mad or bad," Wormald finds her to be "just very sad" in this readable and carefully researched biography.

MARY I of ENGLAND (1516–1558)

Queen   England

Known as "Bloody Mary," Mary Tudor became the queen of England after the death of her half brother Edward. She was the daughter of Henry VIII and **Catherine of Aragon**, born at Greenwich Palace on February 18, 1516. Linacre, Vives, and her mother gave her an excellent education, but she was always to be a victim of politics, used for any advantage of her father's kingdom. Henry arranged marriage with Charles V, the Holy Roman Emperor, but that failed, and she became the Princess of Wales in 1525. In 1527, Henry began divorce proceedings against Catherine, and Mary's loyalty to her mother separated them, causing Henry to declare her illegitimate in 1536. She had to act as lady-in-waiting to the baby **Elizabeth I.** Charles V suggested that Mary accept the illegitimacy stigma and renounce the church so that she could gain succession rights, but Mary continued to celebrate the Latin mass. When Edward VI died in 1553, and Lady Jane Grey's supporters seized the throne, Mary had to flee. She finally returned and ascended to the throne when she was thirty-seven, the first woman to rule alone in England, but two decisions destroyed her. She decided to marry Philip of Spain, eleven years younger, and to restore the church and the pope. To do so, she had to burn at least three hundred people for heresy and so earned the name "Bloody Mary." When Parliament would not let Philip become king, he returned to Spain, and England found itself in the war between France and Spain, during which Mary lost Calais. She had a series of false pregnancies and was quite lonely before her death at forty-two.

BIBLIOGRAPHY

Erickson, Carolly. *Bloody Mary: The Life of Mary Tudor*. New York: William Morrow, 1993. 0-688-11641-8, 533p. Erickson sees Mary as a survivor who outlasted illness, her mother's martyrdom, and her father's torments. It is a carefully researched, thoroughly documented, and accessible biography of Mary Tudor's life.

Loades, David. *Mary Tudor: A Life*. Cambridge, MA: Blackwell, 1989. 0-631-15453-1, 352p. One of the best biographies of Mary in both a wide range of scholarship and argument, Loades shows Mary as an industrious but ineffective ruler who died just as some of her policies were coming to fruition. Using many recently discovered sources contemporary to Mary's times, Loades shows her as a gentle and pious woman who supported policies that gained her infamy instead of admiration.

Waldman, Milton. *The Lady Mary: A Biography of Mary Tudor, 1516–1558*. London: Collins, 1972. 0-002-11486-0, 224p. Waldman spends more time discussing the times than Mary Tudor, but in his balanced discussion of her life and legacy, he emphasizes her childhood and the years between the 1530s and 1540s that affected her reign.

Weir, Alison. *The Children of Henry VIII*. New York: Ballantine, 1996. 0-345-39118-7, 400p. Weir's entertaining and balanced biography of Henry VIII's children makes many strange, modern-day families seem normal. Mary's Catholicism cut short her reign.

MARY II of ENGLAND (1662–1694)

Queen   England

Mary II married the Dutch Protestant William of Orange in an arranged marriage, and when she and William came to England from Holland to help with the deposition of her father James II, Mary became the queen of England. Born April 30, 1662, to James II and his converted Catholic wife, Mary was educated as a Protestant with her sister **Anne**. When she returned to England with William for the "Glorious Revolution," she announced that William would be crowned with her as a joint sovereign. William was displeased but had no choice. When William fought in campaigns on the Continent and in Ireland, Mary ably led the country, but when he returned, she withdrew from public scrutiny. She was intelligent and interested in science, theology, and geography, but she seemed discontent from her childlessness and her husband's unfaithfulness. Her subjects loved her blameless and selfless devotion to them. She died from smallpox.

BIBLIOGRAPHY

Hamilton, Elizabeth, Lady. *William's Mary: A Biography of Mary II*. New York: Taplinger, 1972. 0-8008-824-8, 369p. Using the diaries of Pepys and Evelyn, Hamilton presents Mary II in a scholarly biography, well written and balanced in its presentation of both Mary and the times in which she lived.

Miller, John. *The Life and Times of William and Mary*. London: Weidenfeld and Nicolson, 1974. 0-297-76760-7, 224p. Miller's biography, suitable for young adults, is researched and accessible, with illustrations and reproductions.

Zee, Henri A. van der, and Barbara van der Zee. *William and Mary*. New York: Knopf, 1973. 0-394-48092-9, 526p. This popular biography of Mary and William is well written and well documented.

MATUTE, ANA MARIA (1926–)
Writer   **Spain**

Ana Maria Matute is a novelist, short story writer, and creator of children's fiction who has won many literary prizes. She was born in Barcelona and suffered ill health as a child before enduring an unhappy experience at college. The civil war began when she was ten, and it is an important theme in her work. During her time in Spain under Franco, response to her politically volatile work was quiet. In 1958, her novel *Los hijos muertos* (The Dead Children) was published and won an award. Since she empathized with the poor rather than the party in power, critics were cautious in their acclaim. She published a trilogy in the 1960s, *Los mercaderes* (The Merchants), which tells about a young girl and her psychological problems from the beginning of the civil war to her present time.

BIBLIOGRAPHY
Diaz, Janet Winecoff. *Ana Maria Matute*. New York: Twayne, 1971. No ISBN, 165p. Diaz says that her intent in this critical biography is to present Matute's life and works. She sees Matute's experiences from her early years—exposure to the Castilian countryside, peasants, and the emotional impact of the civil war—as frequent and obsessive themes in her writing.
Jones, Margaret E. W. *The Literary World of Ana Maria Matute*. Lexington: University Press of Kentucky, 1970. 0-8131-1228-1, 143p. Jones' brief biography of Matute precedes a critical examination of her writing for autobiographical elements that might explain what she means.

MCALISKEY, BERNADETTE. *See* DEVLIN, BERNADETTE.

McAULEY, CATHERINE (1778–1841)
Religious   **Ireland**

Catherine McAuley founded Our Blessed Lady of Mercy in Dublin in 1827, which four years later became the order of the Sisters of Mercy. She was born September 29, 1778, to a man engaged in a variety of trades and a mother who had no interest in either religion or the poor. After her father's death, her mother squandered the family money. When she died in 1798, McAuley went to live with a couple who adopted her after her selfless nursing of the woman and the family. The man made her heir to his sizable estate. She took the money back to Dublin, and instead of joining society, she worked with the poor of the city, becoming superior of the Sisters of Mercy, the order that she founded in 1831.

BIBLIOGRAPHY
Breault, William. *The Lady from Dublin*. Boston: Quinlan, 1986. 0-9333411-6-4, 127p. Breault has illustrated his introduction to McAuley with pen-and-ink drawings.

Bolster, M. Angela. *Catherine McAuley in Her Own Words*. Dublin: Dublin Diocesan Office for Causes, 1978. No ISBN, 100p. Bolster divides her undocumented biography of McAuley, based on McAuley's writings and archives available at Drumconda, into segments referring to McAuley's life as heiress, foundress, legislator, ambassador, and witness.

Regan, M. Joanna, and Isabelle Keiss. *Tender Courage: A Reflection on the Life and Spirit of Catherine McAuley, First Sister of Mercy*. Chicago: Franciscan Herald, 1988. 0-8199-0197-3, 158p. This readable and laudatory biography of McAuley, based on sparse memoirs of companions, the oral tradition of her sayings, notebooks containing novice responses to her, and her letters, reveals her life.

Sullivan, Mary C. *Catherine McAuley and the Tradition of Mercy*. Notre Dame, IN: University of Notre Dame Press, 1995. 0-268-00811-6, 420p. Sullivan's well-documented, scholarly biography contains manuscripts by and about McAuley with commentaries on their significance for revealing her thought and activity.

McMILLAN, MARGARET (1860–1931)
Writer   England

Dame Margaret McMillan was a British journalist, lecturer, and propagandist for education. She was born into a Scottish family in New York on July 19, 1860, but her father died in 1865, and her family returned to Inverness, where they attended school. McMillan prepared to be a governess by studying music in Frankfurt and languages in Switzerland before going to London. In London, she became an active member of socialist groups and of the suffrage movement. In 1893, she went north to Bradford and became one of the first members of the new Independent Labour Party. The next year, she was elected to the Bradford School Board, and five years later, she instituted government medical inspections of schools. Attacking the causes and consequences of poverty, McMillan was a pivotal figure in early childhood education as the first to champion the benefits of nursery school. She joined her sister Rachel in London in 1902 where they lobbied for school health care. They opened a children's clinic in Bow and in Deptford in 1910 where children could get dental, ear, and eye care, with the government paying. The two sisters set up camps for children and established an infants' school in 1913, which was completed in 1917 and named after Rachel. McMillan's colleagues admired her, and she had an effect on educational practice worldwide. She became a Dame Commander of the British Empire in 1917 and a Companion of Honour in 1930.

BIBLIOGRAPHY
Bradburn, Elizabeth. *Margaret McMillan: Portrait of a Pioneer*. New York: Routledge, 1989. 0-415-01254-6, 267p. Bradburn's well-researched and readable biography includes information from McMillan's earlier biographers and McMillan's own words, where possible, to emphasize her passion for educational improvement.

Steedman, Carolyn. *Childhood, Culture, and Class in Britain: Margaret McMillan, 1860–1931*. Trenton, NJ: Rutgers University Press, 1990. 0-8135-1539-4, 343p. In a scholarly account of the cultural history of the times during which Margaret McMillan lived and a biography of her life, Steedman gives an informed and detailed discussion of McMillan's achievements.

MECHTILD of MAGDEBURG (1210–1297)
Mystic   Germany

Mechtild of Magdeburg was a mystic who lived a life of prayer and austerity and wrote about it. She had noble parents from Saxony and experienced her first mystical encounter when only twelve. She wanted to live only for God, so she became a Beguine at Magdeburg in 1230, living under Dominican rules. She reported incredible experiences while criticizing the clergy that led them to force her departure. The Cistercian convent at Helfta took her in 1270, although she was sick and nearly blind. Christ supposedly said to her that she would see his divinity flowing into all people who lived without cunning, and her writings (in Low German rather than Latin) were collected under a title reflecting this assertion, *Das fliessende Licht des Gottheit* (The Flowing Light of the Godhead). Her lifelong friend, the Dominican Heinrich of Halle, collected and preserved her writing. She influenced German medieval mysticism and may be the Matelda to whom Dante refers in the *Purgatorio* in Cantos 27 through 33.

BIBLIOGRAPHY
Beer, Frances. *Women and Mystical Experience in the Middle Ages*. Rochester, NY: Boydell, 1992. 0-85115-302-X, 174p. Among the topics that Beer scrutinizes in the lives and times of **Hildegard of Bingen**, Mechthild of Magdeburg, and **Julian of Norwich** are their views of empowerment, physical body, creation, independence, and attitudes toward other women.

Finnegan, Mary Jeremy. *The Women of Helfta: Scholars and Mystics*. 1962. Athens: University of Georgia Press, 1991. 0-8203-1291-6, 171p. The women of Helfta were thirteenth-century nuns, Gertrude the Great, Mechtild of Hackeborn, and Mechtild of Magdeburg, who lived in a Cistercian convent in Saxony. Each wrote, was a mystic, and directed souls. Mechtild of Magdeburg's writings reflect both a lay and monastic view because of her acquaintance with the courtly love tradition. Finnegan examines the influences on her life and her writings.

Mechthild of Magdeburg. *Flowing Light of the Divinity*. Trans. Christiane Mesch Galvani. New York: Garland, 1991. 0-8240-7737-7, 280p. The translator suggests that to move linearly through Mechthild's work will keep a reader from understanding it because women writers do not follow the sense of closure that male writers may have. Mechthild's book details her visions.

MEDICI, CATHERINE de (1519–1589)
Queen   Italy

Catherine de Medici became queen of France when Henri II, her husband, became king and was the mother of the last three Valois kings. She was born in Florence on April 13, 1519, the daughter of Lorenzo de Medici, duke of Urbino, and granddaughter of Lorenzo the Magnificent. Her parents died before she was a month old from consumption and puerpal fever, and Cardinal Giulo de Medici took her to Rome as her guardian. In 1533, at fourteen, she married Henri, duke of Orléans, the future Henri II of France, second son of Francis I. She became queen on her husband's accession in 1547 but was constantly humiliated by Henry's mistress, Diane of Poitiers, who ruled him completely. After Henri died in 1559, she acted as queen regent during the brief reign of her eldest son, Francis II, the first husband of **Mary, Queen of Scots**. She was also queen regent during the minority of her second son, Charles IX, who succeeded to the throne in 1560 and whom she dominated throughout his reign. In the same year, she arranged for her daughter, Elizabeth of Valois (1545–68), to become the third wife of the powerful Roman Catholic king of Spain, Philip II. In the religious wars of 1562–1569, she first supported the Protestants and then the Guises, which has traditionally implicated her in the St. Bartholomew's Day Massacre of 1572. The same year, Catherine married her daughter, **Margaret of Valois**, to the Protestant king Henry of Navarre, who later became Henry IV, king of France. Her third son, Henri of Anjou, having been elected king of Poland in 1573, succeeded to the French throne in 1574 as Henri III; but her political influence waned throughout his troubled reign. Catherine was also a patron of the arts—building a new wing of the Louvre Museum, constructing the Tuilleries gardens, and erecting the chateau of Monceau. Her personal library contained numerous rare manuscripts.

BIBLIOGRAPHY

Heritier, Jean. *Catherine de Medici*. Trans. Charlotte Haldane. New York: St. Martin's, 1963. No ISBN, 480p. Heritier recounts Catherine's political methods and shows that they were reasonable for those who were ruling in Machiavelli's Italy and in her France in this accessible biography.

Mahoney, Irene. *Madame Catherine*. New York: Coward, McCann, and Geoghegan, 1975. 0-698-10617-2, 381p. Letters, diaries, memoirs, and ambassador and secret agent reports, along with gossip document this biography of the Sinister Queen, called by her enemies an atheist, murderer, employer of magicians, sorcerer, defier of the pope, and seller-out to Italy. Mahoney sees in her a cultivated Florentine, faithful wife, and persistent negotiator but does not think that she actually found the "real" Catherine.

Ross Williamson, Hugh. *Catherine de' Medici*. New York: Viking, 1973. 0-670-20696-2, 288p. Ross emphasizes a Catherine who tried to conciliate the Catholics and the Huguenots rather than the one associated with the St. Bartholomew's Day Massacre. The work, an eminently readable but undocumented biography, seems biased toward Catherine and Catholicism.

Sichel, Edith Helen. *Catherine De' Medici and the French Reformation*. London: Dawson, 1969. 0-7129-0417-4, 329p. Sichel thinks that Catherine had a rudderless mind and was enigmatic and abnormal. She examines her life in terms of the times and those who knew her but thinks that the Reformation failed in France because of Catherine's strong control.

Sichel, Edith Helen. *The Later Years of Catherine De' Medici*. London: Dawson, 1969. 0-7129-039-4, 446p. To understand why Catherine gave the command that caused the tragedy on the Eve of St. Bartholomew, Sichel examines her within the times of her later years, when religion was used for power and to cover many ills.

MEIR, GOLDA (1898–1978)

Politician   Russia and Israel

Golda Meir sacrificed her personal life for her dream of a free, independent Jewish nation. Born Goldie Mabovitz in Kiev, Russia (Ukraine), on May 3, 1898, she and her nontraditional family (her parents married without the help of the traditional matchmaker) escaped from Russia in 1906. She spent her later childhood in a Milwaukee ghetto, where her sister Shana, nine years older, taught her to read and write. Meir ran away from an arranged marriage to Denver, where she attended Shana's Zionist meeting. She returned to Milwaukee to finish high school, teaching English at night to immigrants. She began speaking at Zionism rallies, inspiring listeners in English, Yiddish, and Russian. At nineteen in 1918, she attended the Jewish Congress in Philadelphia, married Morris Myerson, and went to Palestine to live on a kibbutz. She loved Palestine and changed her name to "Golda" in honor of the new phase of her life. She raised two children there but spent most of her time working toward a free Israel, eventually sacrificing her family. She was a delegate to the World Zionist Conference and a member of the Jewish Agency for Palestine, led the fighting in Jerusalem against the Arabs after Israel's partitioning, and was the only female among the twenty-four signers of the Israeli Declaration of Independence. Her governmental positions included first ambassador to the Soviet Union, minister of labor and social insurance, Israeli delegate to the United Nations, and Israel's fourth premier.

BIBLIOGRAPHY

Mann, Peggy. *Golda; the Life of Israel's Prime Minister*. New York: Coward, McCann, and Geoghegan, 1971. No ISBN, 287p. This biography of Golda Meir presents her life in a balanced text with specific information about the age-old Arab-Israeli conflict and the creation of the state of Israel.

Martin, Ralph G. *Golda Meir: The Romantic Years*. New York: Scribner's, 1988. 0-684-19017-6, 422p. Martin traces Meir's life through 1948 and shows her political successes and her personal failures in an undocumented biography.

Meir, Golda. *My Life*. New York: Putnam, 1975. 0-399-11669-9, 480p. As Meir recounts her life from her early days in Russia to her immigration to Palestine in the 1920s, she describes the conflicts of being a politician, wife, and mother.

Morris, Terry. *Shalom Golda*. New York: Hawthorn, 1971. No ISBN, 208p. Morris effectively portrays Meir's positive attributes and deals straightforwardly with her status as a woman.

MEITNER, LISE (1878–1968)
Mathematician and Scientist   Austria

Lise Meitner was a mathematician and physicist whose experiments led to an understanding of nuclear fission. She was born into a large Viennese Jewish family on November 7, 1878, but raised as a Protestant. She received a general education, but her interest in physics led to a doctorate from the University of Vienna in 1906. Interested in radioactivity, she went to Berlin to study with Planck in 1907. Since no women were allowed in the laboratory, she had difficulty doing her experimentation, but she and Otto Hahn refitted a carpenter's shop for radiation measurement. In 1912, Meitner joined the Kaiser-Wilhelm Institut für Chimie. During World War I, while serving as both a nurse and a radiographer, she continued to measure substances for radioactivity, and near the end of the war, she and Hahn discovered the element protactinium. She became head of the Physics Department at the Kaiser-Wilhelm Institut and, in 1926, professor of physics at the University of Berlin, working with gamma and beta rays. To escape Nazi Germany in 1938, she went to the Netherlands. An invitation to work at the Nobel Institute in Stockholm allowed her to publish her paper describing nuclear fission. Although a coworker later received the Nobel Prize for the discovery, she did not. She was a visiting professor in the United States, and afterward the Swedish Atomic Energy Commission gave her a laboratory. When she retired in 1960, she moved to Cambridge, England. In 1966, she was the first woman to receive the Fermi Award from the Atomic Energy Commission, but she refused to work with scientists trying to build a nuclear fission bomb.

BIBLIOGRAPHY

Sime, Ruth Lewin. *Lise Meitner: A Life in Physics.* Berkeley: University of California Press, 1996. 0-520-08906-5, 526p. In this biography, suitable for young adults, Sime uses correspondence between Meitner and her colleague Otto Hahn to show that Meitner actually explained what happened when neurons fired at uranium and thus was the real discoverer of nuclear fission. From other careful research, Sime reveals a human integrity in Meitner's personality that balanced her analytical and scientific mind.

MELBA, NELLIE (1861–1931)
Opera Singer   Australia

Nellie Melba was an Australian soprano who sang in opera houses around the world and for whom *Pêche Melba* and melba toast were named. She was born Nellie Mitchell on May 19, 1861, in Melbourne as the third child of Scottish parents who both loved music. She studied piano and organ as a young girl, but when she sang at a school concert at six, the audience wanted to hear an encore. In 1887, she made her debut as Gilda in Verdi's *Rigoletto* at the Brussels opera house. The next year, she played Lucia in Donizetti's *Lucia di Lammermoor* at Covent Garden and sang there regularly for the next twenty-five years. Massenet nicknamed her "Madame Stradivarius" for the quality of her voice. She also sang in Paris, at the La Scala in Milan, and at the Metropolitan in New York. She toured the United States in 1897 and 1898. During return trips to Australia, she organized three of the opera seasons. After funding Red Cross work during World War I, she became Dame of the British Empire in 1918. She made over 150 recordings reflecting her ability to manipulate demanding coloratura roles. She was one of the few singers at Covent Garden who could choose who would sing performances with her.

BIBLIOGRAPHY

Casey, Maie, Lady. *Melba Re-Visited.* Melbourne, Australia: M. Casey, 1975. 0-959748-61-X, 30p. Casey first saw Melba perform when Casey was nine years old. Her short and biased rendering remembers Nellie with fondness.

Hetherington, John Aikman. *Nellie Melba: A Biography.* 1968. Concord, MA: Paul, 1996. Paper, 0-522-84697-1, 312p. This popular biography, carefully researched, reads like a novel. Hetherington has presented a balanced view of Melba and included photographs.

Melba, Nellie. *Melodies and Memories.* Intro. John Cargher. 1971. Melbourne, Australia: Nelson, 1980. 0-170-05668-6, 253p. Cargher notes that all written about Melba is probably true. She was a famous singer and prima donna who was not always a nice person, but in her times, opera singers were still the mistresses of nobles, rich patrons, or impresarios.

Murphy, Agnes G. *Melba: A Biography.* 1909. New York: Da Capo, 1977. 0-306-77428-3, 348p. This popular biography recounts the positive aspects of Melba's career.

Radic, Therese. *Melba, the Voice of Australia.* Saint Louis, MO: MMB Music,

1986. 0-918812-45-3, 214p. In her balanced and recommended biography, Radic notes that Melba was called vexatious daughter, runaway wife, bad mother, loose woman, divorcée, mistress of the pretender to the French throne, fat soprano, vain, vulgar, imperious and a snob, lover of second-class music, and foul-mouth. But in reality, she was a self-made woman whose miraculous voice helped her amass a fortune and win international acclaim.

MENCHÚ, RIGOBERTA (1959–)
Activist   Guatemala

Rigoberta Menchú won the Nobel Peace Prize in 1992 for her efforts to save the peasants in her country. Menchú, a Maya-Quiché Indian, was born in Chimel, a hamlet near San Miguel de Upsantán, capital of El Quiché in Guatemala. She began picking coffee beans on a Guatemalan plantation when she was only eight, never having the opportunity to attend school, and saw two brothers and a friend die from the pesticides that had been sprayed on coffee and cotton fields. In discussions after Catholic prayer services, Menchú, twelve, began to see injustice and poor living conditions as things possible to change. Employees in the city treated her terribly, and in the late 1970s, wealthy landowners, with government support, began to take farmland from her village. Farmers began to resist with the Comite Unidad Campesino, (Committee for Campesino Unity). Her father was severely beaten, and while he was recovering, she took over his crusade and began to speak for the people, because she had learned to read and write while in the convents. By twenty, Menchú had seen her entire family die. She saw her beaten brother doused with gasoline and burned in the street. In 1980, her father and others occupied the Spanish Embassy, and the government burned it with them inside. Then her mother was captured, raped, beaten, and left to die. Menchú escaped to Mexico in 1981 and wrote a book about her experiences. As a founding member of the Unified Representation of the Guatemala Opposition (RUOG), a group of exiled Guatemalan leaders who worked to publicize the cause of peasants in the world community, she tried to return to Guatemala in 1988 but was arrested. She was allowed to return to exile, but after she won the Nobel Prize in 1992, she was able to come back to Guatemala under protection of international representatives.

BIBLIOGRAPHY

Brill, Marlene Targ. *Journey for Peace: The Story of Rigoberta Menchú*. New York: Lodestar, 1996. 0-525-67524-8, 48p. This biography of Menchú is appropriate for the youngest adults. Using information found in Menchú's autobiography, United Nations publications, and interviews with people participating in the international peace movement, Brill explains the horrors that Menchú observed as a young girl and that she has tried to change.

Lazo, Caroline. *Rigoberta Menchú*. New York: Dillon, 1994. 0-87518-619-X, 64p. Rigoberta Menchú realized the power of the spoken word as a young girl of Mayan ancestry in Guatemala during the 1970s. She saw that the Indian dialects allowed the people to talk without the Spanish-speaking minority of wealthy landowners and military leaders understanding them, but they needed Spanish to protest, and she taught herself in order to begin securing human rights.

Menchú, Rigoberta. *I, Rigoberta Menchú: An Indian Woman in Guatemala*. Ed. Elisabeth Burgos-Debray. Trans. Ann Wright. London: Verso, 1984. 0-

86091-083-0, 251p. Menchú describes the reality of life in the Guatemalan peasant system and of migrant workers on the coffee planations with insights about Mayan social systems. It includes an excellent explanation of the Central American political and social scene.

MENDILOW, MYRIAM (1909–1989)
Activist   Israel

Myriam Mendilow's tireless efforts provided the elderly of Jerusalem with a place to meet others. Born into the Salz family in Safed, Palestine, high in the hills, she was early influenced by her mother's desire to know about the world and to read books of which her father did not approve. Her mother sent her to school when public school for girls was unknown, and Mendilow was academically prepared to follow her sister abroad to study in Paris after World War I in 1924. She returned to teach in Aleppo and in 1930 went to Jerusalem to teach. After World War II, the family moved to England, but they returned to Jerusalem. For the first time, Mendilow saw the lonely, poor, and old immigrants who had left their countries and had no family. She had a party for them but realized they needed more. She raised money for permanent clubs and found that the elderly could make crafts to sell as well. She established Lifeline, a group of workshops for different crafts, and was investigating the elderly's medical deficiencies at her death. At her death, the Jerusalem newspaper called Myriam Mendilow the "mother of Jerusalem."

BIBLIOGRAPHY
Cytron, Barry, and Phyllis Cytron. *Myriam Mendilow: Mother of Jerusalem.* Minneapolis: Lerner, 1994. 0-8225-4919-0, 128p. Suitable for young adults, this accessible biography of Mendilow shows how her work paralleled the growth and change of Palestine into Jerusalem and the change of some orthodox Jews to understanding the needs of others outside their families.

MERCOURI, MELINA (1925–1994)
Actor and Politician   Greece

Melina Mercouri won international fame as an actor before she became the minister of culture for Greece's first socialist government. She was born on October 18, 1925, into a prominent Athenian family interested in politics. After she graduated from the Drama School of the National Theatre of Greece, she starred at twenty in Eugene O'Neill's *Mourning Becomes Electra*. She followed it with a variety of roles, including the film *Never on Sunday*, for which she won international recognition. After a Greek military coup in 1967, she opposed the junta throughout Europe and the United States and lost her citizenship. At its defeat in 1974, she returned to Greece and supported Papandreou's government. She became a deputy from Piraeus and, as minister of culture, increased arts funding and tried to retrieve the Elgin Marbles from England.

BIBLIOGRAPHY
Mecouri, Melina. *I Was Born Greek.* 1971. Garden City, NY: Doubleday, 1971. No ISBN, 253p. Mecouri says that she is neither modest nor reserved, and she writes about her life and those that she knows as well as her love of Greece.

MICHEL, LOUISE (1830–1905)
Revolutionary   France

Louise Michel was a socialist and a revolutionary. She was born on May 9, 1830, as the illegitimate daughter of a landowner and a Vroncourt servant near Domrémy. Her grandfather educated her broadly, and after his death, her father returned to the estate. His wife wanted Michel to leave, and she went to school at Chaumont, where she prepared to teach. After criticizing the Second Empire in 1852, she lost her first teaching job. Four years later, she went to Paris, took courses in physics and chemistry, taught, joined secret Republican clubs, and published several novels with social protest themes. In the Franco-Prussian War, she supported the Committee of Vigilance in the eighteenth arrondissement, and, with her lover, became even more radical as one of the last defenders in Montmartre cemetery in May 1871. Imprisoned in Versailles, she was sentenced to life imprisonment in New Caledonia, and her lover was executed. While Michel remained in prison for ten years, she studied botany, taught, and wrote poetry. When the amnesty of 1881 freed her, she returned to Paris and participated in the same political activities. She was imprisoned several times, but after the death of her mother in 1885, she became depressed. When she was freed from prison in 1889, she led strikes but fled to London before the government could certify her as insane and confine her for life. One anarchist who visited her in London was **Emma Goldman**. In 1895, Michel returned to Paris and continued her activism until her death.

BIBLIOGRAPHY
Michel, Louise. *The Memoirs of Louise Michel, the Red Virgin.* Ed. and trans. Bullitt Lowry and Elizabeth Ellington Gunter. Birmingham: University of Alabama Press, 1981. 0-8173-0062-7, 220p. Michel's anarchism was emotional, not theoretical, since she was ill read in contemporary and historical revolutionary writing. The translators have reorganized her memoirs so that they give an orderly view of her life through 1886.

Thomas, Edith. *Louise Michel.* Trans. Penelope Williams. Montreal: Black Rose, 1980. 0-919619-08-2, 443p. Thomas suggests that Michel wrote too much about herself, but she uses Michel's writings in this researched, documented, and recommended biography to understand her better and to look for the real person behind the public speeches and the battles.

MISTINGUETT (1874–1956)
Entertainer   France

Mistinguett was one of the most original performers of comedy in Paris. Jeanne-Marie Bourgeois was born in Enghien on April 5, 1874, into a large family. She began her career when sixteen at the Casino de Paris with the name "Mistinguett." Twenty years later, she was still popular at the Moulin-Rouge and the Folies Bergère, where she performed with Maurice Chevalier. She insured her legs for 1 million francs and wore flamboyant hats and costumes onstage. People loved her comedy, with her best performance probably coming in *Sans-Gêne* in 1921. She retired in 1951 and wrote her reminiscences. Her song "My Man" was popularized by Fanny Brice in the Broadway play, *Funny Girl*.

BIBLIOGRAPHY
Bret, David. *The Mistinguett Legend.* New York: St. Martin's, 1991. 0-312-05471-8, 262p. This popular biography talks not only about Mistinguett,

the performer, but also about music hall life in France during the first half of the twentieth century. Bret exposes Mistinguett's many lovers and the accusations of bad temper but notes that she wanted her performances to be perfect and had to keep others at a distance when necessary.

MISTRAL, GABRIELA (1889–1957)
Poet   Chile

Gabriela Mistral was a Nobel Prize–winning poet who became a symbol of the national aspirations of her country. A green-eyed, dark-skinned mixture (*una mestiza de vasca*) of Indian and Basque origin, born on April 7, 1889, Lucila Godoy y Alcayága was sometimes blamed unjustly for the circumstances of her birth, such as being accused in school of stealing books. After teaching for a while, she met a young man who shared her love of poetry. Three years later, the police contacted her to say that he had committed suicide with one of her postcards in his pocket. She wrote "The Sonnets of Death" for him but kept the poems five years before entering them in a contest under the assumed name "Gabriela Mistral." "Gabriela" stood for "angel who bears good news," and "Mistral" for the north wind blowing into southern France. After winning the contest, she attended in disguise and heard someone else read her poetry. The name Gabriela Mistral was famous in Chile from that day in 1914. When Chile's officials saw the high regard of other Spanish-speaking nations toward her, they named her consul and allowed her to go anywhere she chose and paid her expenses. She lived in the United States (where her first poetry was published), France, Portugal, and Spain. In her writing, she pleaded for better treatment of women, children, the poor, mestizos, and Indians and donated the profits from one of her books to orphans of the Spanish civil war. At the end of World War II, her slightly deformed nephew had an unhappy love affair, took poison, and died. The Nobel Prize in literature could not console her grief for this second suicide in her life, and by the time she died in 1957, she had grieved herself to ninety pounds.

BIBLIOGRAPHY

Castleman, William J. *Beauty and the Mission of the Teacher: The Life of Gabriela Mistral of Chile, Teacher, Poetess, Friend of the Helpless, Nobel Laureate.* Smithtown, NY: Exposition, 1982. 0-682-49853-X, 116p. This thoroughly accessible life of Mistral, recommended for young adults, is divided into short sections examining her family, her life, and her work.

Gazarian-Gautier, Marie-Lise. *Gabriela Mistral, the Teacher from the Valley of Elqui.* Chicago: Franciscan Herald, 1975. 0-81990-544-5, 168p. Gazarian-Gautier's carefully documented and thorough biography, based on interviews with Mistral and other information as well as her works, shows Mistral as a "Christian" writer with concern for the poor and oppressed.

Horan, Elizabeth. *Gabriela Mistral: An Artist and Her People.* Washington, DC: Organization of American States, 1994. 0-8270-3277-3, 216p. This scholarly biography of Mistral places her in the context of Chilean women and society. Horan looks at her life and her works from a feminist aspect, along with Chile's battles over women working outside the home, getting an education, and being exposed to secularism.

Posner, Geraldine. *Mistral, Neruda, Huidobro, Three Figures in Chilean Literature.* Washington, DC: Embassy of Chile, 1979. No ISBN, 30p. Posner's brief introduction of Mistral's life quotes her and her mother.

MITCHISON, NAOMI (1897–1996)
Writer   England

Dame Naomi Mitchison was a novelist who excelled in historical fiction. Born November 1, 1897, Naomi Mary Margaret Haldane, daughter of a scientist, grew up in Oxford and attended the Dragon School before becoming a "home student" at the college that would become St. Anne's. During World War I, she worked as a volunteer nurse before marrying G. R. Mitchison, a lawyer and, later, Labour member of Parliament. She published her first novel, *The Conquered*, in 1923 and followed it with over seventy books. She was the first woman writer in the English-speaking world to revise mythology and history from a woman's point of view (before 1931) and to present androgynies and sexual alternatives to conventional dualism and heterosexuality. In 1935, she identified contradictions in the upper-middle-class alliance of communism, socialism, and feminism. Her over one thousand publications include autobiography, travel, history, poetry, and children's books (including one on her role as a great grandmother). After she and her husband moved to Argyll in 1937, she became an influential writer in the Scottish Renaissance, blending Celtic mythology and socialist politics. She served in various political capacities, such as the Argyll County Council, the Highland Panel, and the Highlands and Islands Advisory Council. She traveled all over the world, became an honorary member of an African tribe, and received many awards, including honorary degrees from the University of Stirling, the University of Strathclyde, and St. Anne's College in Oxford. The queen gave her the Order of the British Empire.

BIBLIOGRAPHY
Benton, Jill Kathryn. *Naomi Mitchison: A Century of Experiment in Life and Letters*. Boston: Pandora, 1990. 0-04-440460-3, 192p.   Benton used Mitchison's private papers and published work in a well-documented biography of Mitchison and thinks that Mitchison's life shows what women of the twentieth century have faced.

Mitchison, Naomi. *All Change Here: Girlhood and Marriage*. London: Bodley Head, 1975. 0-370-10485-4, 158p. Mitchison says that recalling her adolescence was difficult. She discovered, as she wrote, that she was tracing her development as a writer from 1910 until 1917.

Mitchison, Naomi. *Among You Taking Notes: The Wartime Diary of Naomi Mitchison, 1939–1945*. London: V. Gollancz, 1985. 0-575-03561-7, 352p. Mitchison took part in the social research organization Mass-Observation, which wanted to create a science of humans. She edited and published this wartime diary forty years after she wrote it.

Mitchison, Naomi. *Mucking Around: Five Continents over Fifty Years*. London: V. Gollancz, 1981. 0-575-02945-5, 147p. Mitchison uses her diaries to remind herself of life in England between the wars from 1920 to 1940 and muses why one should have to endure two wars in one lifetime.

Mitchison, Naomi. *Small Talk: Memories of an Edwardian Childhood*. London: Bodley Head, 1973. 0-370-10490-0, 132p. Mitchison uses her diaries to reconstruct her early life, with a view of a middle-class family in Oxford, where her father was a fellow at New College.

MNOUCHKINE, ARIANNE (1938–)
Director   France

Ariane Mnouchkine is a leading theater director in Europe. Her father was a French film producer, and Mnouchkine became involved in drama at Oxford University. When she returned to Paris in 1961, she founded a student theater group and directed a film called *Ghenghis Khan* inside Roman ruins. In 1964, she founded Théâtre du Soleil, an alternative theater with forty student actors. Then she studied at Jacques Lecoq's mime school and taught her troupe what she learned. In 1968, the group started looking at other theatrical traditions and added commedia dell'arte, Chinese, and Greek aspects to their work. Their success in Milan led the French government to provide an old warehouse as a permanent home. Among the later productions have been *L'Âge d'Or* (1975), *Molière* (1978), *Mephisto* (1979), and Cixous' play *L'Indiade*. Mnouchkine continues to direct her company.

BIBLIOGRAPHY
Kiernander, Adrian. *Ariane Mnouchkine and the Théâtre du Soleil*. New York: Cambridge University Press, 1993. 0-521-36139-7, 172p. In this first full-length study of Mnouchkine and her work, Kiernander relates an insider's view, since she worked with the Théâtre du Soleil in 1985. She focuses on the company and its structure, Mnouchkine's working methods and modes of operation, and Mnouchkine's achievements.

MODERSOHN-BECKER, PAULA (1876–1907)
Artist   Germany

Paula Modersohn-Becker was one of the twentieth century's major painters. Born in Dresden on February 8, 1876, she stayed there until twelve, when her family moved to Bremen. Four years later, she went to London to attend St. John's Wood School of Art and followed it with art studies in Berlin. After critics disapproved of her first exhibition in 1899, she left for Paris and spent time at the Académie Colarossi and the École des Beaux Arts. In 1901, she returned to Germany to marry Otto Modersohn. She liked the symbolists, especially van Gogh and Gauguin, and her portraits of country women such as *Old Peasant Woman* (1904) show their influence. Cézanne inspired her last works, and her paintings were both realistic and symbolic. In her rather short career, Modersohn-Becker painted over four hundred pictures and developed a style from naturalism to flattened and monumental forms showing that she was more independent than the German expressionists with whom she is often identified. Although her paintings were considered crass and inappropriate while she lived, she has gained recognition as an important figure painter in this century.

BIBLIOGRAPHY
Modersohn-Becker, Paula. *The Letters and Journals of Paula Modersohn-Becker*. Trans. Alessandra Comini. Metuchen, NJ: Scarecrow, 1980. 0-8108-1344-0, 344p. Letters and journals arranged chronologically reveal that Modersohn-Becker's subjects came from real-life sources. She also shows the conflict between what society expected of her as a married woman and what she craved for herself as an artist.
Perry, Gillian. *Paula Modersohn-Becker, Her Life and Work*. London: Women's, 1979. 0-7043-282-6, 149p. Perry uses letters and diaries to

document this biography of Modersohn-Becker. Instead of focusing on her husband and friends, Perry analyzes the artist's subjects, which included women, peasants, and self-portraits.

MODJESKA, HELENA (1844–1909)
Actor   Poland

Helena Modjeska was an actor recognized as one of the finest tragedians of the nineteenth century. She was born on October 12, 1844, as one of a Cracow teacher's ten children. She ran away from home at sixteen to form a theatrical company with her husband, Gustave Zimajer. She joined a Warsaw company in 1868, playing in *Adrienne Lecouvreur*. For the next few years, she played Shakespearean, Greek, and modern roles in the Polish theater before she and her second husband, an aristocrat, emigrated to the United States. When they could not survive on a ranch, she returned to the stage, learning English so that she could debut in San Francisco using the native language. She toured Poland and the United States before she went to London and performed until 1900. Among her best roles were Ophelia and Lady Macbeth. She retired from the stage in 1903 with a farewell performance at the Metropolitan Opera House in New York.

BIBLIOGRAPHY
Altemus, Jameson Torr. *Helena Modjeska*. 1883. New York: B. Blom, 1971. No ISBN, 217p. Altemus presents an undocumented overview of Modjeska's life written while she was alive.

Coleman, Marion. *Fair Rosalind: The American Career of Helena Modjeska*. Cheshire, CT: Cherry Hill, 1969. 0-910366-29-9, 1019p. This thorough, documented, and readable, definitive biography of Modjeska focuses on her American career, although it also covers her life in Europe. Coleman anguishes that Modjeska has been forgotten as one of the major Shakespearean actors in late nineteenth-century America.

Madame Modjeska, Countess Bozenta: Polish-American Actress and American Poets. Buffalo, NY: State University of New York at Buffalo Council on International Studies and Programs, 1993. 0-924197-14-5, 124p. This atypical biography is a collection of poems and a play using Modjeska's life as a basis. It is obviously a loving portrait that reveals some of her character traits.

Modjeska, Helena O. *Memories and Impressions: An Autobiography*. 1910. Temecula, CA: Reprint Services, 1991. 0-7812-8286-1, 571p. Modjeska gives an overview of her life and times from 1848 onward in this autobiography. Descriptions of her travels, performances, and experiences in the United States and Poland provide a readable account from both a historical and a personal perspective.

MONTESSORI, MARIA (1870–1952)
Physician   Italy

Maria Montessori's ideas are the basis of today's preschool and day-care programs, but her philosophy influences all areas of education. She was born on August 31, 1870, in Chiaravalle to an old-fashioned, conservative gentleman father and a well-educated, patriotic mother. They moved to Rome when Maria was five. When she was seven, Italy established a new public school system that required both boys and girls to have an education. She disliked the system because it encouraged everyone to think alike. Rebelling against the idea that women must be either homemakers or teachers, she became the first woman in Italy to earn a medical degree. Afterward, she established a school in Rome for mentally retarded children. By using educational materials that she developed, she was able to teach the children enough to pass the state exams for their primary education certificate, the average level of schooling for most Italians at that time. In 1907, she opened Casa dei Bambini (Children's House) in San Lorenzo, a poor section of Rome where children who stayed home while their parents worked would have somewhere to go. Her first sixty students ranged in ages from two and one-half to seven and were allowed to use any of the available resources at learning stations established around the room. Each activity focused on an educational purpose while training the senses. The students learned mathematics, language, science, geography, and practical skills like cleaning, preparing food, and dressing. She expected them to learn self-confidence and self-discipline. Educators heard about her schools and came from all over the world to observe. In 1915, the first Montessori nursery school opened in the United States, but the method was not widely used until the 1950s.

BIBLIOGRAPHY

Kramer, Rita. *Maria Montessori: A Biography*. New York: Putnam, 1976. 0-399-11304-5, 410p. Montessori's son and daughter-in-law shared documents and memories with Kramer so she could identify, in a documented and researched popular biography, the intellectual influences on Montessori's thought and the role of her personality in her work.

Packard, Rosa Covington. *The Hidden Hinge*. Greenwich, CT: Fides, 1972. 0-8190-0074-4, 229p. Packard discusses Montessori's life and her discoveries, how adults can prepare to work with children, and what children, according to Montessori, need before they reach the age of four.

Pollard, Michael. *Marie Montessori*. Milwaukee: Gareth Stevens, 1990. 0-8368-0217-9, 68p. This text for young adults carefully describes the educational activities that Montessori researched and identified to help children learn.

Shephard, Marie Tennent. *Maria Montessori: Teacher of Teachers*. Minneapolis: Lerner, 1996. 0-8225-4952-2, 128p. This biography for young adults discusses Montessori's life as a young girl attending a boys' school and surviving the stigmas to become the first Italian female physician.

Standing, E. M. *Maria Montessori: Her Life and Work*. 1957. New York: Dutton, 1989. 0-452-25624-0, 382p. Standing has written a readable, documented, popular biography that explores Montessori's life and accomplishments as important contributions to the well-being and education of children.

MONTGOMERY, LUCY MAUD (1874–1942)
Writer   Canada

Lucy Montgomery was a novelist whose stories about Anne of Green Gables won her lasting fame. She was born on November 30, 1874, in Clifton on Prince Edward Island to a father who frequently traveled and a mother who died before Montgomery was two. After the age of seven, Montgomery lived with her intolerant grandparents and began making journal entries when she was nine, preparing herself to be a writer in a place where women did not aspire to such professions, and published first at sixteen. After studying at Prince of Wales College in Charlottetown and Dalhousie College, Halifax, Nova Scotia, she qualified to teach school. She returned to Cavendish to care for her grandmother for thirteen years and squandered her sleep so that she could write. Her first book was *Anne of Green Gables* (1908), and it was a major success. She wrote several sequels, with *Rilla of Ingleside* (1921) describing in detail the impact of World War I on the island community. In 1911, she married the Reverend Ewan MacDonald and moved to his home in Leaskdale, Ontario. Her work is sometimes satirical, but she captures the mysteries and terrors of childhood in her stories.

BIBLIOGRAPHY

Andronik, Catherine M. *Kindred Spirit: A Biography of L. M. Montgomery, Creator of Anne of Green Gables*. New York: Atheneum, 1993. 0-689-31671-2, 160p. Andronik's balanced biography, based on Montgomery's journals, reveals Montgomery's life with her grandparents and a marriage that disappointed her. Andronik documents the places, incidents, and people from Montgomery's life that she used in her Anne of Green Gables books.

Bruce, Harry. *Maud: The Life of L. M. Montgomery*. New York: Bantam, 1992. 0-553-08770-3, 176p. In this well-written biography, suitable for young adults, Bruce uses Montgomery's journals as a resource, focusing on Montgomery's perseverance up to the age of thirty-six, when she married.

Gillen, Mollie. *Lucy Maud Montgomery*. Don Mills, Ontario, Canada: Fitzhenry and Whiteside, 1978. 0-88902-244-5, 62p. This is a brief, researched introduction to Montgomery's life, with photographs. Gillen's biography gives a quick overview of Montgomery's life and work.

Rubio, Mary, and Elizabeth Waterston, eds. *The Selected Journals of L. M. Montgomery*. New York: Oxford University Press, 1993. Vol. 1, 0-19-540503-X, 424p. Vol. 2, 0-19-540586-2, 464p. Vol. 3, 0-19-540936-1, 443p. Rubio and Waterston have edited Montgomery's journals, which she kept "locked up." Volume 1 covers her childhood until 1911; volume 2 stretches across World War I; and volume 3 covers from 1921 to 1929. In this intriguing primary source, Montgomery reveals her private thoughts and concerns.

Rubio, Mary, and Elizabeth Waterston. *Writing a Life: L. M. Montgomery*. East Haven, CT: InBook, 1995. 1-55022-220-1, 133p. Three tensions straining Montgomery were her role as a woman expected to marry and raise children, writing for a lucrative popular market, and the scorn of academic critics for the appeal of her books. Rubio and Waterston see Montgomery as subversive by using secret messages of rebellion and resistance against authority in her sunny stories in a readable and well-researched analysis.

MOODIE, SUSANNAH (1803–1885)

Writer   England

Susannah Moodie wrote about her pioneer experiences in Canada. Born in Bungay, Suffolk, as Susannah Strickland, on December 6, 1803, she and her sister began to write to support the family after her father's death in 1818. They published in ladies' journals, including Strickland's collection of country life stories, *La Belle Assemblée*. In 1831, she moved to London, where she met and married John Moodie. They worked together in the Anti-Slavery Society while she published abolitionist tracts. They emigrated to Canada in 1832 and settled first on a farm before they moved into the backwoods to clear their own land. John Moodie helped quell the 1837 rebellion and was appointed sheriff. From 1840 to 1844, Susannah Moodie wrote sketches of pioneer life for the *Literary Garland.* These vignettes later appeared in a collection titled *Roughing It in the Bush; or, Forest Life in Canada* (1852) and *Life in the Clearings* (1853). She wrote fiction and helped her husband edit the high-quality *Victoria Magazine* for working people.

BIBLIOGRAPHY

Moodie, Susanna. *Roughing It in the Bush; or, Forest Life in Canada.* Intro. Margaret Atwood. 1852. Boston: Beacon, 1987. Paper, 0-8070-7023-8, 518p. Moodie's firsthand account describes her family of English emigrants and its attempt to establish a homestead in upper Canada in the early part of the nineteenth century. Moodie presents both the physical and spiritual experience of the effort while including anecdotes about situations and people whom she met.

Moodie, Susanna. *Letters of Love and Duty: The Correspondence of Susanna and John Moodie.* Ed. Carl Ballstadt, Elizabeth Hopkins, and Michael Peterman. Toronto: University of Toronto Press, 1993. 0-8020-5708-X, 360p. The editors use newly found letters that describe John and Susanna Moodie's relationship and join the letters with pertinent biographical information, giving a view of the Moodies' lives in the Canadian bush.

Moodie, Susanna. *Life in the Clearings: To Which Is Added this Author's Introduction to Mark Hurdlestone.* Ed. Robert L. McDougall. 1853. Toronto: Macmillan, 1976. 0-7705-1409-X, 298p. Moodie recounts her youth in England, where she was a woman of refinement with a taste for things literary. When she came to Canada, she decided to write so that people like her would not make the mistake of thinking that another country would be civilized like England.

Shields, Carol. *Susanna Moodie: Voice and Vision.* Ottawa, Canada: Borealis, 1977. 0-919594-46-8, 81p. Shields says that Moodie was not a particularly good writer because she wrote for pay. Shields thinks that Moodie was a pioneer who happened to write, in this critical but balanced look that also examines the themes apparent in her writing, such as the complexity and variability of human personality, the opposition and interaction of male and female roles, and the debate about the nature of society.

MORE, HANNAH (1745–1833)
Writer   England

Hannah More was a poet, playwright, and tract writer. She was a schoolteacher's fourth of five daughters born in Fishponds, Bristol, on February 2, 1745. At her sisters' school, she was first a pupil and then a teacher. She was engaged to a Mr. Turner for six years, but he paid her two hundred pounds a year instead of marrying. She took the money to London and wrote tragedies with one of her friends, the actor Garrick, in which she revealed social and cultural expectations of the time. Her subject matter became more serious in *Sacred Dramas* (1782), poems, and an essay, *Estimate of the Religion of the Fashionable World* (1790). Finally, she wrote moral tracts for the poor such as *Village Politics by Will Chip* (1793) and *Cheap Repository Tracts,* beginning in 1795.

Afterward, she and a sister started a school in the mining district of Mendips, Somerset, because she wanted to improve the standards of women's education.

BIBLIOGRAPHY

Demers, Patricia. *The World of Hannah More*. Lexington: University Press of Kentucky, 1996. 0-8131-1978-2, 208p. This documented, literary biography anchors More's life in her work by examining the entire span of her career. Demers says that More passionately believed that education was an antidote to both the "immorality of the upper ranks and the feckless improvidence of the lower orders."

Ford, Charles Howard. *Hannah More: A Critical Biography*. New York: P. Lang, 1996. 0-8204-2798-5, 309p. Ford examines in a critical\ biography how More overcame the hazards of being a woman in a man's world and sees her as a reformer rather than a reactionary. His study deciphers her coded and ambiguous passages on feminine place and education to expose an angry woman hiding behind a proper lady and her works.

Kowaleski-Wallace, Elizabeth. *Their Fathers' Daughters: Hannah More, Maria Edgeworth, and Patriarchal Complicity*. New York: Oxford University Press, 1991. 0-19-506853-X, 256p. This carefully documented and scholarly analysis looks at selected aspects of the biographical, autobiographical, and fictional work of More to investigate a motivation for her attraction to patriarchy.

MOREAU, JEANNE (1928–)

Actor   France

Jeanne Moreau is both an actor known for her portrayals of independent women and a film director. She was born in Paris on January 23, 1928, to parents who wanted a boy. Her mother was an English Tiller Girl (dancer), and her father a French restaurant owner. Moreau studied at the Paris Conservatory of Dramatic Art and began performing with the Comédie Française when she was twenty. She later worked with the Théâtre National Populaire. In the 1950s she started acting in films, and her collaboration with Louis Malle established her reputation. In the next few years, she worked with Roger Vadim, Peter Brook, Antonioni, Truffaut, and Demy. In each of these performances, whether in English or French, she played an independent or isolated woman. By 1965, she had become France's biggest box office draw. She has continued to star in films, and in the 1970s, she directed several. Her major awards include Best Actress at Cannes, French Film Actress of the Year, Melbourne Festival, Karlovy-Vary Festival, Best Foreign Actress for the British Film Academy, Prix de L'ACIC, Prix de l'Académie Charles Cros, Prix Brigadier, Prix de la Critique, Officer of the French National Order of Merit, Légion d'Honneur, Officer of the National Order, and the Leon d'Or at the Venice Film Festival for her entire career.

BIBLIOGRAPHY

Gray, Marianne. *La Moreau: A Biography of Jeanne Moreau*. New York: Donald I. Fine, 1996. 1-55611-487-7, 250p. Gray's popular biography, for which she used interviews, films, and business discussions with Moreau, reads like a novel as it recounts Moreau's life.

MORGAN, SYDNEY (1783–1859)
Writer   Ireland

Lady Sydney Morgan wrote lively novels, verse, and travel books. Sydney
Owenson was born on December 25, 1783, in Dublin as the daughter of a theatrical manager. She attended Madame Terson's Academy in Clontarf and Mrs.
Anderson's "finishing school" on Earl Street. Her mother died when she was
thirteen, and the family had financial difficulties. She helped support her family by working as a governess and as an author of sentimental poems and novels. She married a surgeon in 1812, Thomas Charles Morgan, and he was later
knighted. In 1837, she received a government pension.

BIBLIOGRAPHY
Campbell, Mary. *Lady Morgan: The Life and Times of Sydney Owenson.* New
    York: Pandora, 1988. 0-86358-115-3, 250p. Campbell presents Lady Mor-
    gan as a writer whose personal life was as important as her professional life
    as a writer. She uses anecdotes from Morgan's memoirs and other sources
    as documentation along with historical aspects of the times in which Mor-
    gan lived.
Morgan, (Sydney). *Lady Morgan's Memoirs: Autobiography, Diaries, and Corre-
    spondence.* 1862. New York: AMS Press, 1975. 2 vols. 0-404-56793-2.
    Morgan's memoirs give an overview of her rather vain personality and the
    dramatic imagination that controlled her life.
Newcomer, James. *Lady Morgan the Novelist.* Lewisburg, PA: Bucknell Univer-
    sity Press, 1990. 0-8387-5177-6, 98p. Newcomer attempts to reaffirm
    Lady Morgan's considerable achievement rather than to rehabilitate her
    reputation. By analyzing the novels and one drama in his documented biog-
    raphy, he focuses on the woman and her writing, seeing her as both realistic
    and idealistic in trying to do good for Ireland and to promote freedom for
    all.
Stevenson, Lionel. *The Wild Irish Girl: The Life of Sydney Owenson, Lady Mor-
    gan (1776–1859).* 1936. New York: Russell and Russell, 1969. No ISBN,
    330p. In his readable, well-documented, and researched biography, Steven-
    son thinks that Morgan was the first successful woman author to rise to so-
    cial, intellectual, and financial prestige from her businesslike exploitation
    of her literary talent.

MORISOT, BERTHE (1841–1895)
Artist   France

Berthe Morisot was a painter both influenced by, and influential on, the work
of the impressionists. Born Berthe Marie Pauline in Bourges on January 14,
1841, her mother encouraged her to take drawing lessons when she was young,
and she studied under Guichard in 1858 and Corot after 1861. In the Salons of
1864-1874, she exhibited her landscapes and her portraits. Manet suggested
that she use more outline in her work, and she encouraged him to use lighter
colors. In 1874, she married Manet's brother, and she disregarded Manet's advice by exhibiting her work in the impressionist exhibition of that year. She
had difficulty reconciling her roles as woman, mother, and artist, as she revealed in her letters to her sister Emma, who gave up painting when she married in 1869. Morisot showed her works in Paris, London, Brussels, and Boston
and gave an exhibition of her works in 1892.

BIBLIOGRAPHY

Adler, Kathleen, and Tamar Garb. *Berthe Morisot*. Ithaca, NY: Cornell University Press, 1987. 0-8014-2038-5, 128p. Adler and Garb focus on five issues relevant to Morisot in reconstructing what being a woman artist in nineteenth-century France would have been like, the status of women in Morisot's social class, how she reconciled her private and public lives, her education and background, her contacts with other artists, and her relationships with the impressionists.

Edelstein, T. J., ed. *Perspectives on Morisot*. New York: Hudson Hills, 1990. 1-55595-049-3, 120p. This examination of Morisot's life and work includes seven essays by female art historians which conclude that she was not as strong a feminist as once thought because her mother goaded her into an art career. Then when the Salon jury rejected her paintings, she unwillingly broke with the accepted art styles of the time.

Higonnet, Anne. *Berthe Morisot*. New York: HarperCollins, 1990. 0-06-016232-5, 240p. Higonnet suggests, after consulting previously unpublished journals and letters, that Morisot portrayed a "feminine visual culture" while pursuing an "unfeminine" career and that she succeeded without too much personal sacrifice.

Higonnet, Anne. *Berthe Morisot's Images of Women*. Boston: Harvard University Press, 1992. 0-674-06798-3, 311p. In this look at Morisot, Higonnet examines her in terms of her times and as a woman artist. She looks at Morisot's subjects of family females and examines how her work shows middle-class femininity.

MURDOCH, IRIS (1919–)
Writer   England

Dame Iris Murdoch is a novelist and philosopher. She was born in Dublin on July 15, 1919, and although she received her education in London at the Froebel Educational Institute and Badminton School before attending Somerville College at Oxford, she considers herself thoroughly Irish. She became interested in stories through *Kim* and *Treasure Island* and Carroll's "Alice books." Her first love was shot as a spy in occupied Bulgaria during World War II. She then worked with the United Nations Relief and Rehabilitation Administration in London before going to Belgium and Austria to work in displaced persons' camps. After the war, she studied philosophy at Newnham College, Cambridge, and became a tutor in philosophy at St. Anne's College, Oxford, in 1948. After her first publication in philosophy, *Sartre, Romantic Rationalist* (1953), she began to write novels. The first ones were somewhat Gothic, but others often dealt with commitment and loyalty in a world that seems irrational. After she married a scholar and critic in 1958, she continued to write philosophy as well as drama and has won several awards and prizes, including the Booker Prize for *The Sea, the Sea* in 1978. Her play *Art and Eros* appeared at the National Theater in 1980.

BIBLIOGRAPHY

Baldanza, Frank. *Iris Murdoch*. New York: Twayne, 1974. 0-8057-1410-3, 187p. This academic, critical biography mainly looks at Murdoch's work. Difficult to read, it is for a scholarly audience.

Spear, Hilda D. *Iris Murdoch*. New York: St. Martin's, 1995. 0-312-12596-8, 139p. In her recommended biography, Spear suggests events in Murdoch's early life that might have influenced particular plotlines, but Murdoch's refusal to write her autobiography or autobiographical novels makes some of these assertions mere speculations.

MURPHY, EMILY (1868–1933)
Magistrate   Canada

Emily Murphy was a lawyer and writer who supported feminist ideals. She was born Emily Gowan Ferguson on March 14, 1868, in one of the leading families in Cooksville, Ontario, her father a landowner and businessman, and received her education from Bishop Strachan School in Toronto. She married a rector and traveling missionary in 1887, and after the birth of two daughters, they moved to Swan River, Manitoba, and then to Edmonton, Alberta. Murphy denounced alcohol and rural poverty while supporting suffrage and woman's rights in divorce and sexual assault. She suggested a Women's Court, which was established in 1916, and as its head, she became the first female magistrate in the British Empire. When the defense lawyer she faced as a magistrate claimed that Murphy was "not even a person" under British law because a British act passed in 1876 said that women were subject to legal penalties but had no legal rights or privileges, she countered, and the Supreme Court of Alberta upheld her position. After a debate about a woman's running for the Senate, in 1929, women were finally considered "persons" and thereby eligible to run for the Senate's seats. In 1931, Murphy resigned as magistrate but continued to supervise Alberta's prisons and asylums. She kept a diary from which she took anecdotes to include in her novels.

BIBLIOGRAPHY
James, Donna. *Emily Murphy*. Don Mills, Ontario, Canada: Fitzhenry and Whiteside, 1977. 0-88902-234-8, 63p. This straightforward and brief biography covers Murphy's life and career.

Mander, Christine. *Emily Murphy, Rebel: First Female Magistrate in the British Empire*. Toronto: Simon and Pierre, 1985. 0-88924-173-2, 150p. Mander uses references from Murphy's writings to support Murphy's advocacy for action and common sense in her thorough biography.

MYRDAL, ALVA (1902–1986)
Diplomat   Sweden

Alva Myrdal devoted most of her life trying to solve the problem of nuclear armaments piling up throughout the world. Born January 31, 1902, the daughter of a farmer, she grew up in Uppsala, Sweden. She left school at fifteen because her family did not expect females to advance. But she took a job doing people's taxes and saved money to further her education. The University of Stockholm admitted her, even though she had no secondary education, with the stipulation that she keep up with the college work. After graduating in 1922, she married Gunnar Myrdal, a man who, like her, believed that life could be better. In 1949, she became the head of the United Nations' Department of Social Welfare, where she worked with problems of women, children, education, and housing. Then in Europe, at the United Nations Educational, Scientific, and Cultural Organization (UNESCO), she helped Europe's universities revive after World War II. In 1955, she became the Swedish ambassador to India, Burma (now Myanmar), and Ceylon (now Sri Lanka). She began learning about nuclear weapons as the Cold War spread, and as an elected member of the Swe-den Senate of the *Riksdag* in 1961, she began to stress the role of disarmament. Although a pacifist, she had supported Finland's effort to repeal the Soviet in-vasion, and she supported the Allies fighting against Hitler. In 1964, she began to study the problems of apartheid in South Africa, and in 1966, she joined sev-enteen other nations at the disarmament meeting in Geneva. But in 1965, she founded the Stockholm International Peace Research Institute. For her work, she first received the Albert Einstein Peace Prize and then, in 1982, the Nobel Peace Prize for continuing to clamor against aggression and terrorism, "the conscience of the disarmament movement."

BIBLIOGRAPHY

Bok, Sissela. *Alva Myrdal: A Daughter's Memoir.* Reading, MA: Addison-Wesley, 1991. 0-201-57086-6, 375p. In this biography of her mother, Bok has studied articles, diary excerpts, letters, and notes written in the margins of Myrdal's texts. Instead of a definitive biography, Bok tells Myrdal's life as she both witnessed and heard about it.

N

NAIDU, SAROJINI (1879–1949)
Poet and Activist   India

Sarojini Naidu was a feminist, politician, and poet who wrote Indo-Anglian poetry. Born on February 13, 1879, in Hyderabad, a city of Hindu-Muslim culture, into a Brahmin family, Sarojini Chattopadhyay passed the exam to enter
the University of Madras when she was twelve. At sixteen she went to study at
King's College, London, and then Girton College, Cambridge. She met members of the Rhymer's Club, and Edmund Gosse advised her to write about the
occupations, faiths, festivals, legends, myths, and rituals of India. She married
Dr. G. R. Naidu, against her family's wishes because he was not Brahmin, and
worked with him on organizing flood relief in Hyderabad, for which she won
the Kaiser-I-Hind gold medal in 1908. She began to publish her poetry during
this period, and her collections, using Indian themes and scenes, were *The Bird
of Time* (1912), *The Golden Threshold* (1916), and *The Broken Wing* (1917).
She met Gandhi in 1914 and Nehru in 1916, encounters that began her political career. Later, she went to the United States and Canada as Gandhi's emis-
sary and traveled with him to London. She became president of the Indian
National Congress at the Kanpur session in 1925, and in 1932, she went to jail
for participating in the civil disobedience movement. She always tried to promote peace and culture between the Hindus and the Muslims as well as the Indians and the British.

BIBLIOGRAPHY
Dwivedi, A. N. *Sarojini Naidu and Her Poetry*. Allhabad, India: Kitab Mahal,
    1981. No ISBN, 164p. This critical-analytical appraisal of Naidu and her
    poetry is a balance between biography and criticism.
Khan, Izzat Yar. *Sarojini Naidu, the Poet*. New Delhi, India: S. Chand, 1983.
    No ISBN, 276p. Khan suggests in this adequate study of Naidu that her re-
    fusal to belong to a literary movement or to participate in the modernist's
    search for new forms and new language kept her readers' respect.

Mishra, L. N. *The Poetry of Sarojini Naidu*. Delhi, India: B. R., 1995. 81-7018-833-4, 149p. In Mishra's discussions of Naidu's poetry, she includes a biography in which she explores the influences in Naidu's life that led her to writing poems.

Prasad, Deobrata. *Sarojini Naidu and Her Art of Poetry*. Delhi, India: Capital Publishing House, 1988. 81-85157-27-8, 216p. Prasad, a poet, looks at Naidu in a carefully researched biography and discusses her poetry's imagery, symbolism, style, and mysticism.

Sharma, K. K. *Perspectives on Sarojini Naidu*. Ghaziabad, India: Vimal Prakashan, 1989. No ISBN, 224p. Sharma lauds Naidu's poetry and says that, although her output was small, she was one of the foremost Indian English writers.

NAVARRE, MARGUERITE of. *See* MARGUERITE of NAVARRE.

NEFERTITI (c. 1300 B.C.)

Queen   Egypt

Nefertiti became the queen of Egypt as the wife of Akhenaton. The daughter of Queen Tiy and Amenhotep III, she promoted and then rejected her husband's new religion, which worshiped the sun god Aten as the main Egyptian deity. She raised her half brother Tutankhamen and educated him and, after Amenhotep III died, arranged Tutankhamen's marriage and had him crowned at Karnak, ensuring continuation of her power. He then reinstated the old religion. She has been known only to scholars since the nineteenth century, and information about her comes almost wholly from sites, monuments, inscriptions, and artifacts.

BIBLIOGRAPHY

Samson, Julia. *Nefertiti and Cleopatra: Queen-Monarchs of Ancient Egypt*. London: Rubicon, 1985. Paper, 0-948695-00-5, 149p. Samson bases her biography of Nefertiti on Sir William Petrie's finds from Amarna and Luxor beginning in 1891. She examines Nefertiti's corule with her husband, her sun worship, her home, and her legacy, with highlighting illustrations.

Vandenberg, Philipp. *Nefertiti: An Archaeological Biography*. Trans. Ruth Hein. Philadelphia: Lippincott, 1978. 0-397-01256-X, 161p. In this intriguing biography of Nefertiti, Vandenberg uses archaeological data as a basis for Nefertiti's life.

NIGHTINGALE, FLORENCE (1820–1910)

Nurse   England

Florence Nightingale developed the philosophical base of modern Western secular nursing. She was born May 15, 1820, in Florence, Italy, as the second daughter in a wealthy family. Her parents and tutors gave her a private education in the classical mode, with emphasis on languages, literature, philosophy, history, and mathematics. At seventeen, she thought that God had called her into service, but her parents would not allow her to follow her "calling" and become a nurse. She became a health field administrator, first as the superintendent of the London Institution for the Care of Sick Gentlewomen in Distressed Circumstances. In 1854, she took thirty-eight nurses to the Crimea, and as their superintendent for a few months, lowered the death rate among wounded soldiers from 42 percent to 2.2 percent. She reformed the English Army Medical School, established military statistics, initiated formalized nursing education at St. Thomas' Hospital, London, and reformed hygienic standards in India. She wrote over twelve thousand letters, monographs, and books, and Queen Victoria appointed her as the first woman Order of Merit award.

BIBLIOGRAPHY

Boyd, Nancy. *Three Victorian Women Who Changed Their World: Josephine Butler, Octavia Hill, Florence Nightingale.* New York: Oxford University Press, 1982. 0-19-520271-6, 276p. Boyd gives an overview of the life and accomplishments of Florence Nightingale after an introduction giving the historical background in which Nightingale lived to show the magnitude of her accomplishments and her legacy.

Huxley, Elspeth Joscelin Grant. *Florence Nightingale.* London: Weidenfeld and Nicolson, 1975. 0-296-76771-2, 254p. Huxley's biography of Nightingale presents an enlightening picture of a woman who defied her family's wishes in her refusal to marry, her decision to help the sick and wounded, and her willingness to involve herself with the military.

Selanders, Louise C. *Florence Nightingale: An Environmental Adaptation.* Thousand Oaks, CA: Sage, 1993. 0-8039-4859-X, 38p. Selanders discusses Nightingale's life and times, her nursing theory, and a comparison of her nursing theory with the American Nurses' Association's contemporary standards and concludes that her theory serves as a brilliant model for current practice.

Shor, Donnali. *Florence Nightingale.* Illus. Gianni Renna. Englewood Cliffs, NJ: Silver Burdett, 1990. 0-382-09978-8, 104p. For young adults, Shor's authentic biography overviews Nightingale's life, including her call to nursing, her service in the Crimean, and her legacy to the Red Cross.

Smith, F. B. *Florence Nightingale: Reputation and Power.* New York: St. Martin's, 1982. 0-312-29649-5, 216p. Using the Nightingale Papers and manuscripts prepared by Nightingale's friends, Smith tries to understand Nightingale's power and her reputation rather than cover her life. In his recommended biography, Nightingale could be ruthless or a liar whenever necessary to further her interests.

NIJINSKA, BRONISLAVA (1891–1972)

Choreographer   Russia

Bronislava Nijinska was a choreographer who created works for dancers around the world. She was the third child of professional dancers in Minsk, born on January 8, 1891, only one hour after her parents finished performing in Glinka's opera *A Life of the Tsar.* She studied at the Imperial Theatrical School in St. Petersburg and at the Maryinsky. She graduated in 1908 and became a soloist with the Maryinsky company before dancing with Diaghilev in Paris in 1909. She remained in Russia during World War I, starting her own school in Kiev. In 1921, she returned to Diaghilev and became his principal choreographer, creating eight ballets for him beginning in 1923. Her innovative work in Paris in the 1920s and 1930s reflected the modern aesthetic that was emerging at the time. She mounted ballets at the Colón Theatre in Buenos Aires, the Opéra Russe in Paris, and then her own company. After 1938, she worked mainly in the United States, establishing a school in California. She choreographed over seventy ballets in addition to dance sequences for numerous films, operas, and other stage productions.

BIBLIOGRAPHY

Baer, Nancy Van Norman. *Bronislava Nijinska: A Dancer's Legacy*. San Francisco: Fine Arts Museums of San Francisco, 1986. 0-88401-048-1, 103p. Baer's appreciative and straightforward overview of Nijinska's life and work with photographs shows her method of choreographic notation and the designs that transferred her ideas into reality.

Nijinska, Bronislava. *Bronislava Nijinska—Early Memoirs*. Trans. Irina Nijinska and Jean Rawlinson. Intro. Anna Kisselgoff. Durham, NC: Duke University Press, 1992. 0-8223-1295-6, 546p. Nijinska's memoirs document her growth as an artist, her work with her brother, ballet in prerevolutionary Russia, and life in Russia at the turn of the century.

NIN, ANAÏS (1903–1977)

Writer   **France**

Anaïs Nin's work, showing influences of the surrealists and psychoanalysis, is a series of diaries in which she explores her life. She was born on February 21, 1903, in Neuilly, the daughter of a Spanish concert pianist and composer. Her parents divorced while she was young, and she moved first to Cuba, and then, when she was eleven, to New York City with her mother. The same year, Nin began to write her diaries and decided to leave the public schools and read books from the public library for her education. In the early 1930s, she returned to France and began her literary career with a book on D. H. Lawrence. Its appeal to Henry Miller, the American author, led to their affair and lifelong friendship. At the beginning of World War II, she came back to New York and began to publish her five-volume *roman fleuve* (continuous novel) through her own press, Gemor. Although many admired her work, not until she published the first volume of her diaries in 1966 did she gain critical acclaim. Before and after she died, fourteen volumes or versions of her diary were published, including *Henry and June: From the Unexpurgated Diary*; *Incest: From the Unexpurgated Diary*; and *Fire: From the Unexpurgated Diary*. Critics mention her unique expression of individuality and her insights based on her psychoanalysis with Otto Rank.

BIBLIOGRAPHY

Bair, Deirdre. *Anaïs Nin: A Biography*. New York: Putnam, 1995. 0-399-13988-5, 654p. Bair thinks that Nin was a major "minor" writer whose work tried to "make it new" with its sex, examination of self, and psychoanalytic basis. In a carefully researched and documented, definitive biography, Bair uses either written or spoken testimony from persons who knew Nin, whether Nin mentioned them in her diaries or not, and over 250,000 unedited pages of the diaries and correspondence.

DuBow, Wendy M., ed. *Conversations with Anaïs Nin*. Jackson: University Press of Mississippi, 1994. 0-87805-719-6, 254p. DuBow edits twenty-four interviews with Nin, with eight new ones, which occurred between 1965 and 1976. Nin discusses her work, her attitude toward the women's movement, and her own philosophy but stays inside her personally constructed persona, refusing to mention her husbands.

Fitch, Noel Riley. *The Erotic Life of Anaïs Nin.* Boston: Little, Brown, 1993. 0-316-28428-9, 528p.   Basing the rest of Nin's life on her father's seduction of her as a child and later the incestous relationship she had with him as a method of gaining control, Fitch examines Nin's other liaisons with a variety of men and her bigamous life, married to one man in New York and another in California. Unpublished materials and interviews helped Fitch reach her conclusions that Nin's diaries fictionalized her life.

Franklin, Benjamin V., ed. *Recollections of Anaïs Nin.* Athens: University of Ohio Press, 1996. 0-8214-1164-0, 173p.   Franklin, fascinated by Nin's work, met her several times and decided to create an honest and accurate picture of her through the eyes of people who knew her. Their cogent remarks reveal an enigmatic woman who wanted her work to appear on college syllabi but did not want to be criticized in any form.

Snyder, Robert. *Anaïs Nin Observed: From a Film Portrait of a Woman as Artist.* Chicago: Swallow, 1976. 0-8040-0708-X, 115p.   Snyder's work, based on his motion picture *Anaïs Nin Observed,* is a collection of photographs with text describing their significance to the events in her life.

NOETHER, EMMY (1882–1935)
Mathematician   Germany

Emmy Noether was a mathematician. Born in Erlangen on March 23, 1882, as the first child of a Jewish professor of mathematics at the university, she and her brother shared their father's interests. A family friend, Paul Gordon, tutored her during her relatively normal childhood and then directed her doctoral thesis. David Hilbert persuaded Noether to come to Göttingen to continue her research on the mathematical formulation of the theory of relativity and the axiomatic method of mathematics. As a woman, she could not be formally appointed, but she gave lectures announced under Hilbert's name. After World War I, she received a low salary for her lectures, but when she published a paper on differential operators, scholars recognized her abilities in modern abstract algebra. Among her achievements were abstract axiomatic algebra, the ascending chain condition, the unified theory of noncommutative algebras and their representations, and the proof that every simple algebra over an algebraic number field is cyclic. When the Nazis came in 1933, she lost her appointment, but Bryn Mawr College in the United States hired her. She was the only woman included in the "Men of Modern Mathematics" display at the 1964 World's Fair.

BIBLIOGRAPHY
Brewer, James W., and Martha K. Smith. *Emmy Noether: A Tribute to Her Life and Work.* New York: Marcel Dekker, 1981. 0-8247-1550-0, 180p.   In this carefully documented and thoroughly researched biography, the authors mix biographical information with Noether's mathematical achievements, which will especially interest mathematicians and science historians.

Dick, Auguste. *Emmy Noether, 1882–1935.* Trans. H. I. Blocher. Boston: Birkhauser, 1981. 3-764-33019-8, 193p.   Dick's straightforward, well-written, and well-researched biography presents Noether's life and the theoretical bases of her accomplishments.

NORTON, CAROLINE (1808–1877)
Writer   England

Caroline Norton believed that married women should have rights. She was born Caroline Elizabeth Sarah Sheridan on March 22, 1808, one of a civil servant's seven children. An aunt raised her, and after her father died when she was nine, she went to school in Surrey. At nineteen, she married the barrister George Norton, a member of Parliament. Their financial difficulties influenced her to publish her verse in *The Sorrows of Rosalie* (1829). Two years later, she began to edit a court magazine, *La Belle Assemblée*, and then *English Annual*. Her husband brought suit against Lord Melbourne in 1836 for alienating her affection, but she had no representative at the trial because, as a woman, she lacked legal status. When the suit failed, she battled to keep her three sons, and her pamphlet *A Plain Letter* influenced the passage of the 1839 Infant Custody Bill. Although her children were returned to her, the youngest died soon after in 1842. After 1845, she lived alone and wrote, but Norton sued her for his legal debt so that he could take her money from copyright interests. She subsequently wrote in favor of the Divorce Bill and the first Married Women's Property Bill in *English Laws for Women in the Nineteenth Century and a Letter to the Queen*. After her husband died in 1875, she remarried but died a few months later.

BIBLIOGRAPHY
Norton, Caroline Sheridan. *The Letters of Caroline Norton to Lord Melbourne.* Ed. James O. Hoge and Clarke Olney. Columbus: Ohio State University Press, 1974. 0-8142-0208-X, 182p. The text presents the letters that Caroline Norton wrote between 1831 and 1848 to Lord Melbourne, during which time her husband filed suit against them. Although her letters show gaiety and flirtation, they indicate that she still had affection for her husband.

Chedzoy, Alan. *A Scandalous Woman: The Story of Caroline Norton.* London: Allison and Busby, 1992. 0-85031-838-6, 312p. This well-documented biography of Caroline Norton reads like fiction as Chedzoy creates Norton's situation when her husband accused her of having an affair with Lord Melbourne.

NORWICH, JULIAN of. *See* JULIAN of NORWICH.

NUR JAHAN (d. 1645)
Empress   India

Nur Jahan was a Moghul Indian empress. Born in a caravan traveling from Tehran to India to parents of noble lineage who had fled misfortune in Persia, she was the daughter of the Persian official of the Moghuls, Mihr-ur-Nisa. After her husband's death, she became Emperor Jahangir's stepmother's lady-in-waiting. The emperor fell in love with her and married her when she was forty. As his favorite wife, he gave her relatives high positions in the court. Her brother became the chief minister, and her niece Mumtaz (buried in the Taj Mahal) married the heir to the throne. Nur Jahan, devoted to her husband, helped him to moderate his drinking and opium smoking, but he gave her complete authority, which she held for sixteen years. She issued decrees in the empire and became the only woman ruler of India to issue coins in her name. She increased the splendor of the court with spectacles, polo games, tiger hunting, and art collections. She disrupted political stability by changing allegiances based on her family's alliances. Civil war erupted between 1623 and 1626, but when she won and tried to punish the opposition, another rebellion defeated her. Her opponent seized full power at her husband's death and retired her to private life in Lahore with a generous pension.

BIBLIOGRAPHY

Anand, Sugam. *History of Begum Nurjahan*. New Delhi, India: Radha, 1992. 81-85484-39-2, 187p. Anand's balanced and thoroughly documented, scholarly biography describes Nurjahan [sic] and evaluates her support for women establishing their own identities and leading self-reliant lives while she ruled.

Findly, Ellison B. *Nur Jahan, Empress of Mughal India*. New York: Oxford University Press, 1993. 0-19-507488-2, 424p. This thoroughly documented biography examines Nur Jahan's reputation, based on the only source available, her emperor husband's memoirs about himself, and tries to assess her contribution to India.

Pant, Chandra. *Nur Jahan and Her Family*. Allahabad, India: Dandewal, 1978. No ISBN, 109p. This well-documented but poorly proofread academic biography illustrates that Nur Jahan is one of the most enigmatic women in history. Pant posits that her family members were qualified for their positions in government.

NZINGA (1582?–1663)

Queen   Angola

Mbande Nzinga kept political stability in Angola as its queen. Her brother, the king of Ndongo, sent her to negotiate with the Portuguese in 1622, and she persuaded them to recognize Angola's independence after receiving Christian baptism and the name Dona Ana de Souza. When her brother died in 1624, she became queen of Ndongo from 1624 to 1626 and of Matamba from 1630 to 1663 while leading the nation's struggle against the Portuguese domination. Although Portuguese drove her east and tried to take her off the throne, she organized an army, conquered and ruled Matamba, developed alliances, and controlled slave routes for the next thirty years. She allied with the Dutch in the 1640s, the war with the Portuguese did not end until 1654. She stayed on the throne until her death.

BIBLIOGRAPHY

Glasgow, Roy Arthur. *Nzinga: Warrior Queen/King*. Boone, NC: Parkway, 1994. 0-963575-23-6. Glasgow discusses the achievements of Nzinga while keeping the Portuguese from taking control of her country.

Sweetman, David. *Queen Nzinga; the Woman Who Saved Her People*. London: Longman, 1971. 0-582-64529-8, 40p. In a series for young adults, this brief, fictional biography attributes undocumented emotions to Nzinga as it describes her achievements.

OCAMPO, VICTORIA (1891–1978)
Writer   **Argentina**

Victoria Ocampo was a writer and literary editor who exposed Latin America to authors from around the world through her publishing. Born in a wealthy family as the oldest of six children, Ocampo learned to speak several languages fluently. She entered an arranged marriage but soon left her husband to live alone and establish a Buenos Aires literary salon. She introduced many international writers to South America, including Rabindranath Tagore and **Virginia Woolf**. She wanted South America to extend its literary pursuits, and her journal *Sur* influenced many of the continent's writers. She advocated woman's rights but opposed **Eva Perón**. She never wanted to write like the classic writers of world renown; she wanted to write only as a unique woman.

BIBLIOGRAPHY
Dyson, Ketaki Kushari. *In Your Blossoming Flower-Garden: Rabindranath Tagore and Victoria Ocampo.* New Delhi, India: Sahitya Akademi, 1988. No ISBN, 477p. Dyson examines Ocampo's correspondence with Tagore, who was twenty-nine years older, to show how she became his exotic muse after they met in Argentina during 1924.

Meyer, Doris. *Victoria Ocampo: Against the Wind and the Tide.* Austin: University of Texas Press, 1989. Paper, 0-292-78710-3, 348p. In a carefully documented and scholarly biography, Meyer gives a balanced view of the life of Ocampo as she faced social standards that she refused to accept and determined what she wanted to write.

OLIPHANT, MARGARET (1828–1897)
Writer   **Scotland**

Margaret Oliphant was an accomplished novelist whose work supported her family during Victorian literature's golden age. Born on April 4, 1828, in Wallyford, Midlothian, as the daughter of a customs official, Oliphant had a close relationship with her mother, who encouraged her writing. Oliphant wrote her first novel when seventeen and wrote three more before she married her cousin, Francis Oliphant, in 1852. He died, leaving her with two children and pregnant with a third, but she prized her name of Oliphant Wilson Oliphant and continued to use it. She wrote constantly to support her family, and her production included ninety-eight novels, fifty or more short stories, twenty-five works of nonfiction, and over four hundred articles, mainly for *Blackwood's Magazine*. Her children all died before she did, and her autobiographies reveal the pain of losing them. Some of her most popular works described religious life in an English country town.

BIBLIOGRAPHY

Jay, Elisabeth. *Mrs Oliphant, "A Fiction to Herself": A Literary Life*. New York: Oxford University Press, 1995. 0-19-812875-4, 355p. Jay examines Oliphant's life as a professional writer who was both creator and creation of the social world in which she lived in this thoroughly documented and recommended biography.

Oliphant, Mrs. *The Autobiography of Mrs. Oliphant*. Ed. Mrs. Harry Coghill. Chicago: University of Chicago Press, 1988. 0-226-62651-2, 161p. In this view of her life and her society, Oliphant relates her exclusion from the domestic and professional advantages afforded male writers.

Williams, Merryn. *Margaret Oliphant: A Critical Biography*. New York: St. Martin's, 1986. 0-312-51447-6, 217p. Williams' biography of Oliphant includes lengthy plot summaries of her work in an attempt to show the family, social, and economic forces shaping her life as well as the issues of a woman writing in Victorian times.

OTTESEN-JENSEN, ELISE (1886–1973)

Activist   Sweden

Elise Ottesen-Jensen worked to find creative ways of presenting sex education. She was born on January 2, 1886, to a clergyman in Høyland, and after attending school locally and in Bergen, Norway, she was attracted to medicine, but the family could not support her interest. Instead, she began studying with a practicing dentist so that she could become licensed after three years. An explosion in the lab, however, severed her thumbs and little finger and altered her life. While she was attending Kristiania Commerical College, her younger, unmarried sister became pregnant, and her father sent the sister to Denmark to have the child so that the family would not be stigmatized. Furious at her father's callous behavior, Ottesen-Jensen began campaigning for creative ways of providing sex education. In 1945, she initiated the International Planned Parenthood Federation and advocated family planning.

BIBLIOGRAPHY

Linder, Doris H. *Crusader for Sex Education: Elise Ottensen-Jensen [sic] (1886–1973) in Scandinavia and on the International Scene*. Lanham, MD: University Press of America, 1996. 0-7618-0333-5, 319p. Linder uses uses Ottesen-Jensen's papers and letters to write a straightforward, well-researched, and accessible biography.

PAN CH'AO (45?–115?)
Writer and Scholar   **China**

Pan Ch'ao served as Ts 'ao Ta-ku or historian in the court of the eastern Han emperor Ho. Her scholar father and cultured mother trained her, along with her brothers, who also were recognized scholars. She married, but her husband died young and left her a widow. In 101, she successfully petitioned the emperor for the return of her brother, a Chinese general. Pan Ch'ao occupied the post of historian of the court in fact but not in title, since she was female; however, she was the first, if not only, woman to attain such a distinction. In her position, she also served as lady-in-waiting and instructress to the young empress and her other ladies-in-waiting. Pan Ch'ao finished the *Han Shu, or History of the Former Han Dynasty*, started by her father and brother. She also wrote a treatise on education, *Lessons for Women*, in 106, a work on feminine morality that is most likely the earliest extant document about women's education. Other surviving works are four narrative poems and two memorials to the throne. Dates are unimportant in Chinese culture, so neither her birth nor death date is certain.

BIBLIOGRAPHY

Swann, Nancy Lee. *Pan Ch'ao: Foremost Woman Scholar of China.* New York: Russell and Russell, 1968. No ISBN, 179p. To translate Pan Ch'ao's work, Swann had to know the history, philosophy, and ancient usages of the language. She covers the age in which Pan Ch'ao lived, her family, her life, her literary output, and her life as a Chinese woman. Swann sees Pan Ch'ao as a moralist and examines her philosophy of life along with the qualities of her literary style.

PANKHURST, CHRISTABEL (1880–1958)
Activist and Lawyer   England

Christabel Pankhurst was a writer, lawyer, and advocate for suffrage. Born on September 22, 1880, she was educated at home, at Manchester High School, and in Switzerland. While she studied law at Victoria University, Manchester, she joined the North of England Society for Women's Suffrage and the Manchester Trade Union Council. She and her sister **Sylvia** formed a women's branch of the Independent Labour Party in 1903. After her arrest in a protest during a Liberal meeting at the Free Trade Hall in Manchester, the *Daily Mail* coined the term "suffragette." In 1904, Lincoln's Inn refused to accept her into the bar because she was a woman, but in 1905, she won a prize for international law, and the following year, she won another prize for her legal career. In 1912, the government threatened her with conspiracy, and she fled to Paris. When she returned to London, she voiced her concern about sexual and political repression and wrote articles on venereal disease and prostitution. In later life, she became interested in the Second Advent religious movement, about which she spoke and wrote, and in 1940, settled in California.

BIBLIOGRAPHY
Castle, Barbara. *Sylvia and Christabel Pankhurst*. New York: Viking Penguin, 1987. 0-14-008761-3, 158p. This documented, readable biography contains photographs of the Pankhursts and their campaigns.

Mitchell, David J. *Queen Christabel: A Biography of Christabel Pankhurst*. London: Macdonald and Jane's, 1977. 0-354-04152-5, 397p. In his carefully documented and readable biography, Mitchell believes that Pankhurst's imprisonment for asking the Liberal Party about votes for women made suffrage an important issue.

Noble, Iris. *Emmeline and Her Daughters: The Pankhurst Suffragettes*. Folkestone, England: Bailey and Swinfen, 1974. 0-561-00222-3, 191p. Noble's fictionalized biography for young adults describes the lives of the Pankhursts and their stand for suffrage.

PANKHURST, EMMELINE (1857–1928)
Activist   England

Often referred to as "Mrs. Pankhurst," Emmeline Pankhurst led the militant Women's Social and Political Union before World War I. Born on July 14, 1857, the eldest of ten children, Emmeline Goulden attended boarding schools in Manchester and Paris before marrying Richard Pankhurst in 1879. In Manchester, she worked on the Suffrage Committee and the Married Women's Property Committee, with her lawyer husband drafting the bill. After 1884, they joined the Fabian Society and then the Independent Labour Party. Her husband was too politically radical for the London bar so she managed a shop to support the family until his death. With her daughter **Christabel**, she formed the Women's Social and Political Union in 1903, which became militant in 1905 after Christabel was arrested. In London, with her daughter **Sylvia**, she organized and led marches, inspiring crowds with her superb oratory. In the years before World War I, she was arrested thirteen times and went on a hunger strike. During World War I, she recruited, and after the war, she adopted four orphans. Just before she died, women won the right to vote.

BIBLIOGRAPHY

Noble, Iris. *Emmeline and Her Daughters: The Pankhurst Suffragettes*. Folkestone, England: Bailey and Swinfen, 1974. 0-561-00222-3, 191p. Noble's fictionalized biography for young adults describes the lives of the Pankhursts and their stand for suffrage.

Pankhurst, Emmeline. *My Own Story*. Westport, CT: Greenwood Press, 1985. 0-313-24926-1, 364p. Pankhurst's autobiography is her view of women's vigilance to get the vote during the early twentieth century in England.

PANKHURST, SYLVIA (1882–1960)

Activist   England

Sylvia Pankhurst was an artist who turned to activism. She was born in May 5, 1882, in Manchester, the second of five children. Her father died when she was fifteen and left her committed to his socialist ideals. She attended the Municipal School of Art, winning prizes and a scholarship to study in Venice and later in London at the Royal Academy. Along with her mother and sister, she helped to found the Women's Social and Political Union. She used her talent to create banners, murals, and posters and also painted studies of women at work. She was arrested thirteen times, and during a hunger strike, someone forced her to eat. She broke with her mother at the beginning of World War I because she was violently opposed to the war. During the war, she founded a pacifist socialist journal, *Worker's Dreadnought*; started a **Montessori** school; managed clinics and restaurants; and published antiwar propaganda for which she was fined. In 1920, she stowed away on a Soviet ship and met Lenin. She was a member of the British Communist Party but refused to relinquish publication of her journal and was expelled. In 1928, she would not name her child's father because of the attitudes toward unwed mothers, and in the 1930s, she wrote a history of the suffragette movement and a biography of her mother and began to protest against Italian fascism. She then moved to Ethiopia and edited *Ethiopian News* for twenty years.

BIBLIOGRAPHY

Castle, Barbara. *Sylvia and Christabel Pankhurst*. New York: Viking Penguin, 1987. 0-14-008761-3, 158p. This documented and readable biography contains photographs of the Pankhursts and suffragette activities.

Noble, Iris. *Emmeline and Her Daughters: The Pankhurst Suffragettes*. Folkestone, England: Bailey and Swinfen, 1974. 0-561-00222-3, 191p. Noble's fictionalized biography for young adults describes the lives of the Pankhursts and their stand for suffrage.

Pankhurst, Richard, and Ian Bullock, eds. *Sylvia Pankhurst: From Artist to Anti-fascist*. New York: St. Martin's, 1992. 0-312-06840-9, 210p. Written by Pankhurst's son, the biography mainly connects Pankhurst to her art which critics think was much less successful than her writing.

Romero, Patricia W. *E. Sylvia Pankhurst: Portrait of a Radical*. New Haven, CT: Yale University Press, 1987. 0-300-03691-4, 334p. Romero, in a well-researched and readable life of Pankhurst, discusses a complex woman who focused on the fringes of the Pan-Africanist, monarchist, antifascist, communist, socialist, and feminist groups.

Taylor, Rosemary. *In Letters of Gold: The Story of Sylvia Pankhurst and the East London Federation of the Suffragettes in Bow.* London: Stepney, 1993. Paper, 0-950-52418-2, 46p. This brief biography introduces Pankhurst to young adults and includes photographs and illustrations of activities associated with her causes.

PARDO BAZÁN, EMILIA (1851–1921)
Writer   **Spain**

Condesa de Emilia Pardo Bazán, an ardent feminist, championed naturalism in her writing. Born in La Coruña on September 16, 1851, she married an older man at sixteen and moved to Madrid. Her early works reflected her interest in philosophy, with her first novels and a series of essays asserting that French naturalism should be introduced in Spanish realistic fiction, a stance which distressed the Spanish intelligensia. In 1890, she shifted her interest from realism to Christian idealism, reflected in her last two novels. In addition to writing plays, short stories, and literary criticism, she ran a literary salon in Madrid. She advised about public education and became the first woman professor of Romance literature at Madrid in 1916.

BIBLIOGRAPHY
Gonzalez-Arias, Francisca. *Portrait of a Woman as Artist: Emilia Pardo Bazán and the Modern Novel in France and Spain.* New York: Garland, 1992. 0-8240-0687-9, 230p. Gonzalez-Arias follows Pardo Bazán's intellectual development and the evolution of her art by analyzing four of her novels in a well-documented, scholarly text with quotes in Spanish.

Hemingway, Maurice. *Emilia Pardo Bazan: The Making of a Novelist.* New York: Cambridge University Press, 1983. 0-521-24466-8, 190p. Hemingway's exposition on Pardo Bazán is a scholarly, critical work with limited biographical information on Spain's greatest woman novelist.

Pattison, Walter Thomas. *Emilia Pardo Bazán.* New York: Twayne, 1971. 0-8057-2120-7, 134p. To Pattison, Pardo Bazán is an important writer, and in his look at her life and major work, he emphasizes her strong personality and beliefs.

PARRA, TERESA de la (1895–1936)
Writer   **Venezuela**

Anna Teresa Sanojo de la Parra became a novelist who wrote about women and their inner lives. Born in Paris on October 5, 1895, and educated there, she returned to Caracas when she was a young woman. She began to write ficitionalized autobiography from the point of view of an eighteen-year-old aristocratic girl who has lived in Paris and has difficulty adjusting to conventional Venezuelan society. Strong women in the family influenced her, but she was more interested in enjoying life than performing its duties. The books, which gained immediate attention, were *Diario de una señorita que se fastidia* (1922) and *Ifigenía* (1924). In her later works, she remembered her childhood, such as *Memorías de mama Blanca* (1929). She never married, although many men pursued her, and returned to Europe in her later years, seeking a cure for tuberculosis.

BIBLIOGRAPHY
Lemaitre, Louis Antoine. *Between Flight and Longing: The Journey of Teresa de la Parra*. New York: Vantage, 1986. 0-533-06649-2, 229p. Lemaitre views Parra's life as one of imagination, myth, and lived experience transmuted into art in this well-written biography.

PATERSON, EMMA (1848–1886)

Activist   England

Emma Paterson was a trade unionist. Born Emma Anne Smith in London on April 5, 1848, her father, a headmaster, encouraged her education. After his death, she worked as the assistant secretary at the Working Men's Club and Institute Union where she met her husband. On their visit to the United States, Paterson found models for women's industrial organizations, which she wrote about in April 1874. She wanted a general union of women workers in England, and three months later, she founded the Women's Provident and Protective League. She organized women by trades, starting with bookbinding (which she knew best), then dressmaking, millinery, and upholstery. The next year, she became the first woman to attend the Trade Union Congress in Glasgow; she wanted women factory inspectors, but she opposed legislation to protect women because she thought that it might hurt instead of help. For the rest of her life, she worked for reform, including learning the printing trade and founding the Women's Printing Society.

BIBLIOGRAPHY
Goldman, Harold. *Emma Paterson: She Led Women into a Man's World*. Woodstock, NY: Beekman, 1973. 0-8464-0372-2, 127p. Goldman notes that Paterson is considered the "real pioneer of modern women's trade unions" as the first identifiable woman from a working-class background to try to solve the problems of women at work without sacrificing their individuality.

PATTI, ADELINA (1843–1919)

Opera Singer   Spain

Adelina Patti was an internationally recognized soprano famous for her comedy opera roles. She was born in Madrid on February 19, 1843. Her father, a tenor, prepared her to sing in New York at seven, and she made her operatic debut there at sixteen singing Donizetti's Lucia. She debuted as Amina in Bellini's *La Sonnambula* in London, Paris, and Vienna during the next two years. She then sang in London for twenty-five seasons in over thirty different roles, with Rossini's *The Barber of Seville* as one of her best. Her voice, an unusually high, rich, ringing soprano, earned her the name "Queen of Song" and made her wealthy. She gave her last performance in France in 1897 and her last one in the United States in 1903. In retirement she lived in Craig-y-nos Castle near Swansea and in 1898 became a naturalized British citizen. She continued to sing in charity concerts until her death.

BIBLIOGRAPHY
Cone, John Frederick. *Adelina Patti: Queen of Hearts*. Portland, OR: Amadeus, 1993. 0-931340-60-8, 400p. Cone follows Patti's career, her husbands, friends, triumphs, and rivalries with other singers by using quotes from critics and composers, including Verdi when her *La Traviata* delighted him,

and photographs, against a backdrop of nineteenth-century opera business and performance expectations. This recommended biography reads like a novel.

Klein, Hermann. *The Reign of Patti.* 1920. New York: Arno, 1977. 0-405-09686-0, 470p. Klein covers Patti's whole career of over fifty-six years from the time she made her debut as a child prodigy in New York in 1850 at age seven, in a balanced and readable but stylistically dated biography.

Lauw, Louisa. *Fourteen Years with Adelina Patti: Reminiscences of Louisa Lauw.* Trans. Jeremiah Loder. Intro. James Camner. Milan, Italy: La Scala Autographs, 1977. No ISBN, 68p. As Patti's friend and traveling companion from 1863 to 1877, during which Patti had her London, Paris, and Vienna debuts, Lauw discloses her travels and times with the diva.

PAVLOVA, ANNA (1881–1931)
Ballerina   **Russia**

Pavlova was a ballet dancer who introduced the beauty of ballet to the world by leaving Russia to dance for anyone who would come to her performances, from the peasant to the potentate. Born daughter of a laundress on January 31, 1881, Anna Pavlova lived with her mother, who, although poor, took her to a ballet in St. Petersburg when she was eight. Pavlova knew that she must dance, not in the chorus, but alone like the Italian ballerina **Maria Taglioni**. Not able to enter the Imperial Ballet School in St. Petersburg until she was ten, she quickly learned, although teachers discouraged her attempt at acrobatic techniques because of her frailness. Throughout her life, Pavlova wanted to dance for everyone, not just the wealthy who could afford the front row seats. She traveled extensively, supporting the orchestra and dancers of her company with performances in Europe, England, and the United States. For the second half of her life, she also taught abroad and made her dancing, even when ill, a gift of beauty for others. One night when she could not go onstage, her friends, including Sol Hurok and Sergei Diaghilev, knew that her illness was serious, and she soon died from lung disease.

BIBLIOGRAPHY
Fonteyn, Margot. *Pavlova: Portrait of a Dancer.* New York: Viking, 1984. 0-670-54394-2, 159p. Fonteyn's commentary about Pavlova complements press materials and photographs so that she shows objective enthusiasm for her subject.

Kerensky, Oleg. *Anna Pavlova.* New York: Dutton, 1973. 0-525-17658-6, 160p. In trying to build a picture of Pavlova as an artist and a woman, Kerensky uses the firsthand impressions of choreographers, films, company members, and photographs covering her life.

Lazzarini, John, and Roberta Lazzarini. *Pavlova: Repertoire of a Legend.* New York: Schirmer, 1980. 0-02-871970-0, 224p. This biography took years of research and travel for the Lazzarinis to find their material, and they have collected photographs from ninety of Pavlova's roles to give a dance history of her career.

Levine, Ellen. *Anna Pavlova: Genius of the Dance.* New York: Scholastic, 1995. 0-590-44304-6, 132p. Levine's young adult biography presents Pavlova's life along with discussions of choreography, technique, and style in several of her ballets and the revolutionary times in which she lived.

Money, Keith. *Anna Pavlova, Her Life and Art.* New York: Knopf, 1982. 0-394-42786-6, 425p. This well-written book contains unpublished photographs and information recently translated from the Russian about Pavlova.

PECHEY-PHIPSON, EDITH (1845–1908)
Physician   England

Edith Pechey-Phipson was one of the first female physicians in England. She was born October 7, 1845, as the daughter of a Baptist minister who had attended Edinburgh University and a scholar mother. Pechey became a teacher, but medical school attracted her when she was twenty-four, and she decided to study with **Sophia Jex-Blake.** After becoming an assistant in a Liverpool maternity hospital, she applied to qualify for the license of midwifery in Edinburgh. Since no legal grounds for denying women a right to take the test existed, examiners decided to resign rather than certify a woman. She passed her medical examinations in Berne and became a physician in 1877. Soon she established a successful practice in Leeds and became a lecturer on hygiene at the London School of Medicine for Women. Although nominated for dean of the school, she accepted a position in Bombay, India, as the head of Cama Hospital for women and children. There she married a merchant and later became the first woman to hold a position on the Senate of the University of India. In 1906, she and her husband returned to England permanently.

BIBLIOGRAPHY
Lutzker, Edythe. *Edith Pechey-Phipson, M.D.: The Story of England's Foremost Pioneering Woman Doctor.* New York: Exposition, 1973. 0-682-47597-1, 259p. Lutzker bases her balanced biography of Pechey-Phipson on letters, available archival papers, valuable photographs, and information from the places where Pechy-Phipson worked that Lutzker visited.

PEETERS, CLARA (1594?–1657?)
Artist   Belgium

Clara Peeters was a still-life painter. She grew up in Antwerp and painted some of the earliest still-lifes known in the Netherlands before she was twenty. Her subjects were often food and tableware, and she liked to show light reflected in the goblets or from jewelry. Her latest extant work was dated 1657, although the only certain fact about her life is that she married Henrik Joossen in 1639.

Decoteau, Pamela Hibbs. *Clara Peeters: 1594–ca. 1640: And the Development of Still-life Painting in Northern Europe.* Lingen: Luca Verlag, 1992. 3-923641-38-9, 199p. This oversize biography designates Peeters as one of the originators of still-life paintings in the Netherlands. Because nothing is known about her life, this collection analyzes her thirty-one works and suggests what people, times, and places might have influenced them.

PERÓN, EVA (1919–1952)
Politician   Argentina

Perón is both revered and reviled in Argentina today as the wife of, and ruler with, Juan Perón. María Eva Duarte, born May 7, 1919, was a daughter in the "second family" of her father, but he died when she was seven, leaving the family in poverty. She left home at fifteen to go to Buenos Aires, where she told her friends "I will be somebody." She got a job in a soap opera, and three years later, she had her own show. When she was twenty-five, she met Juan Perón, a forty-eight-year-old widower who, like her, was born into poverty but had limitless ambition. After her campaign to free Perón from political imprisonment and their dual campaign for his presidency, she began changing the balance of wealth in Argentina. She established the Eva Perón Foundation and dispensed money to whomever and whenever she wanted. In 1947, Argentinean women gained the right to vote, largely from her efforts. She campaigned for women to receive equal pay in the workplace and to be paid for work they did at home. On the other hand, the Peróns did not appreciate disagreement and imprisoned or exiled opponents. Perón had laws changed so that he could succeed himself as president, but soon after, Eva went into the hospital with cancer and died after the election. Millions came to Buenos Aires for her funeral.

BIBLIOGRAPHY

Barnes, John. *Evita, First Lady: A Biography of Eva Perón*. New York: Grove, 1978. Paper, 0-8021-3479-3, 195p. With a chronological, objective account, Barnes' balanced biography demonstrates that Evita was an important populist politician.

Fraser, Nicholas. *Eva Perón*. New York: Norton, 1985. 0-393-30238-5, 144p. Well researched and carefully documented, Fraser's biography of Perón is generally balanced and objective in its coverage of her achievements for urban workers and the poor and her handling of organized labor and lower-income groups to further her own political objectives.

Perón, Eva. *Evita: Eva Duarte Perón Tells Her Own Story*. 1953. New York: Two Continents, 1978. 0-906071-07-0, 235p. Perón dedicates her autobiography to her husband, who helped her, a "sparrow," to fly like a "condor." In it she discusses her early life and her poverty, her rejection as an actor, and how Perón helped Argentina's disadvantaged.

Sava, George. *Mourning Becomes Argentina*. Bognor Regis, England: New Horizon, 1978. 0-86116-119-X, 208p. Sava, a physician, met Perón several times, and in a chatty but recommended biography based on the memoirs she gave him, concludes that the rich hated her for giving their money to the poor but that the poor adored her.

Taylor, J. M. *Eva Perón: The Myths of a Woman*. Chicago: University of Chicago Press, 1981. Paper, 0-226-79144-0, 196p. Taylor exposes myths surrounding Perón as lady of hope, menace, revolutionary, feminist, or mystical metaphysical leader and suggests that each myth evolved from what a group looking at Perón wanted from her.

PIAF, EDITH (1915–1963)
Entertainer   France

Edith Piaf became known for her songs with their undercurrents of sadness and nostalgia. Edith Giovanna Gassion was born in Paris on December 19, 1915, daughter of an acrobat and a café singer. Her father named her Edith for **Edith Cavell**, the British nurse whom the Germans had executed the previous day. Her mother abandoned her at birth, and her grandmother raised her. When she was a child, meningitis blinded her for four years, and her father encouraged her to sing. After attending the École Primaire Bernay, she started singing in the streets at fifteen. She graduated to cabaret, and became known as Piaf, from the Parisian slang for "sparrow." After her radio debut in 1936, she appeared in plays and films during and after World War II. In 1947 she toured Europe and the United States. Despite her phenomenal success, her life was marred by unhappiness and illness. Among her best-remembered songs are "La vie en rose," which she wrote for herself, and "Non, je ne regrette rien." Forty thousand people mourned at her funeral, and Soviets observed a two-minute silence in her memory.

BIBLIOGRAPHY

Berteaut, Simone. *Piaf; a Biography*. New York: Harper and Row, 1972. 0-06-010313-2, 488p. In a biography that reads like a novel, Berteaut, Piaf's half sister, tells Piaf's story from her birth on the sidewalks of Paris, through her early youth living in a brothel, to her many adult triumphs and trials.

Bret, David. *The Piaf Legend*. New York: Parkwest, Robson, 1989. 0-86051-627-X, 188p. In his popular, well-documented biography of Piaf, Bret tries to identify the quality that attracted so many people to her.

Lange, Monique. *Piaf*. Trans. Richard S. Woodward. New York: Seaver, 1981. 0-394-51806-3, 256p. Lange uses photographs, unpublished documents, letters, and personal interviews to show a Piaf who was sometimes cruel, sometimes generous, dramatic or funny, and amazingly famous.

Piaf, Edith. *My Life*. Trans. Margaret Crosland. Chester Springs, PA: Dufour Editions, 1990. 0-7206-0797-3, 144p. Piaf dictated an autobiography before she died, telling about her rise from poverty, her philosophy, her religious beliefs, and her generosity as well as the scandals following her forays into drugs, alcohol, and sex.

PISAN, CHRISTINE DE. *See* DE PISAN, CHRISTINE.

PLISETSKAYA, MAYA (1925–)

Ballerina   **Russia**

Maya Plisetskaya represented the ideal of the Russian ballerina for her dancing at the Bolshoi Ballet. Born in a Moscow dancing family on November 20, 1925, she trained at the Bolshoi Theatre Ballet School, becoming first a soloist and then principal dancer after 1943. She had a dazzling, fast technique that allowed her to shine in roles such as Odile/Odette in *Swan Lake*. With charisma both on- and offstage, she was allowed to travel when most Soviet artists had to stay in the Soviet Union. Her awards include First Prize Budapest International Competition and People's Artist of the United Socialist Soviet Republics in 1959, People's Artist of Russian States Federation of the Soviet Republic in 1951, Anna Pavlova Prize in 1962, Lenin Prize in 1964, and Hero of Socialist Labor in 1985.

BIBLIOGRAPHY

Voznesensky, Andrei. *Maya Plisetskaya*. Trans. Kathleen Cook. Moscow: Progress, 1976. No ISBN, 152p. Readable text accompanies photographs of Plisetskaya showing her extraordinary facial expressions in performance. Voznesensky thinks that she revived Taglioni's Romanticism in her dancing.

POMPADOUR, MADAME de (1721–1764)

Intellectual   France

Madame de Pompadour, the mistress of Louis XV, influenced many of the political and architectural decisions of her time. Jeanne-Antoinette Poisson, born December 29, 1721, was the daughter of a financial speculator who fled the country under scandal when she was four. From her mother and sister, she received a thorough cultural and intellectual education. She married Charles-Guilllaume, Le Normant d'Étoiles, and after legally separating from him, she began her relationship with Louis XV and became the marquise. She lived at Versailles and was friendly with everyone, including Queen Marie, an excessively religious woman. De Pompadour established her friendship with Louis so that after he no longer saw her exclusively, she still influenced his appointments. With her brother, the marquis de Merigny, she initiated the building of the École Militaire, Place de la Concorde, the Petit Trianon, and the Château de Bellevue, and her love of decorative crafts lent support to the new porcelain factory at Sèvres. Voltaire was one of her friends, as well as the authors of the *Encyclopédie*.

Mitford, Nancy. *Madame de Pompadour.* 1968. New York: Dutton, 1984. Paper, 0-525-48146-X, 304p. Mitford speaks kindly of Madame de Pompadour in this biography, describing her rise to power and her ability to collect art objects. The text includes many illustrations of portraits, paintings, and artifacts in Madame de Pompadour's collection reflecting her taste.

POPOVA, LIUBOV (1889–1924)

Artist   Russia

Liubov Popova became a leading member of the suprematist group and then forged her art in the glory of the Communist Party. Born in Moscow as Liubov Eding on April 24, 1889, into the family of a businessman and philanthropist, she studied there before visiting Italy and France, where cubism influenced her. After returning to Russia in 1913, she exhibited with the futurists in St. Petersburg and Moscow. During the revolution, she designed posters, and in 1918, she met Tatlin, the founder of Soviet constructivism, who encouraged her to exhibit her work in the Moscow Constructivist show of 1921. She taught at the Vkhutemas Art Training School, at Gvitma, and at Proleckult, where she worked on street decorations and designs for populist theater. In the year before her death, she designed textiles for the First State Textile Print Factory, Moscow, where she was given a memorial exhibition in 1924. Her work was especially important for its exploration of abstract color values.

BIBLIOGRAPHY

Sarab'ianov, Dmitrii Vladimirovich, and Natalia Adaskina. *Popova.* New York: Harry N. Abrams, 1990. 0-8109-3701-8, 396p. The authors discuss Popova's artistic development from 1912 to 1924 and her attempt to attach politics to modern art with both color and black-and-white illustrations of her work and the twenty-one texts that she wrote.

Dabrowski, Magdalena. *Liubov Popova.* New York: Harry N. Abrams, 1991. 0-8109-6090-7, 135p. Dabrowski furnishes the main essay in this catalog of Popova's New York exhibit in 1991, with other essays discussing her working methods and materials. Plates illustrate the text.

POTTER, BEATRIX (1866–1943)
Artist   England

Beatrix Potter became known as a writer and illustrator of books for children after publication of such works as *The Tale of Peter Rabbit* (1900). Born in London on July 6, 1866, as the daughter of a wealthy lawyer, Helen Beatrix received her education from various governesses and drew pictures on holidays in Scotland and the Lake District. When she was twenty-seven, she created a series of illustrated letters to amuse a sick child. She privately published *The Tale of Peter Rabbit* in 1900 and *The Tailor of Gloucester* two years later. Frederick Warne republished them along with twenty-two other books over the next thirty years. Potter lived with her parents until she was thirty-nine. She became engaged to Warne's son against her parents' wishes, but, when he died a few months later, she left home anyway, moving to Sawrey in the Lake District. At forty-seven, she married William Heelis, against her parents' wishes. In her last thirty years, she stopped writing to become a successful hill-farmer.

BIBLIOGRAPHY
Grinstein, Alexander. *The Remarkable Beatrix Potter*. Madison, CT: International Universities, 1995. 0-8236-5789-2, 328p. After a brief background on Potter and a presentation of her journal dating from 1881 to 1897, Grinstein applies psychoanalytic theory to thirty of her stories, chronologically according to the date she wrote them, to see what they reveal about her life.

Lane, Margaret. *The Tale of Beatrix Potter; A Biography*. New York: Frederick Warne, 1985. 0-7232-3266-0, 174p. Using passages from her earlier book about Potter and Potter's journal, letters, and illustrations, Lane observes Potter's character and balances her parents' Victorian mores, her independence as a country woman and sheep farmer, and the relationship between her works and their purpose as children's entertainment.

Taylor, Judy. *Beatrix Potter: Artist, Storyteller, and Countrywoman*. 1986. New York: Penguin, 1997. Paper, 0-7232-4175-9, 224p. Taylor consulted over eight hundred of Potter's letters and papers and places Potter's life in historical perspective to show a lonely and sensitive Potter but always energetic and courageous before she became an astute businesswoman when married as Mrs. Heelis.

Taylor, Judy, ed. *Beatrix Potter's Letters*. New York: Viking, Penguin, 1990. 0-7232-3437-X, 478p. Along with unpublished sketches, photographic reproductions of Potter's illustrated letters, and color plates, Taylor has included over four hundred of Potter's letters to permit Potter to tell in her own words about the social needs of her times, including discussions of weather, finances, and farming.

Taylor, Judy, ed. *"So I Shall Tell You a Story . . .": Encounters with Beatrix Potter*. New York: Viking, Frederick Warne, 1993. 0-7232-4025-6, 224p. This collection contains essays written by people who have either met Potter or loved her stories. At least one of the interpretive essays uses a Freudian analysis, and Taylor has included some of Potter's illustrations.

PRESTON, MARGARET ROSE (1875–1963)
Artist   Australia

Influenced by aboriginal painting, Margaret Rose Preston painted still-lifes of Australian flowers as the foremost Australian female painter between the wars. She was born in Port Adelaide, South Australia, on April 29, 1875, to a Scottish marine engineer and a Quaker mother, who called her Rose. When she went to Sydney, she attended the Girls' School, but she left two years later to study art in Melbourne at the National Gallery School. In 1904, she went to Munich to attend the Government Art School for Women and traveled widely in Europe before returning to Australia in 1919. Later travels in the South Pacific Islands, Southeast Asia, China, Africa, and India also influenced her still-lifes, wood and linocut engravings, and graphics.

BIBLIOGRAPHY

Butel, Elizabeth. *Margaret Preston: The Art of Constant Rearrangement.* New York: Viking, 1986. 0-670-81131-9, 100p. Butel says that Preston demanded recognition for a truly indigenous Australian national art and thought it should be the study of aboriginal art. Financially independent, she used it as her own subject matter.

North, Ian, Humphrey McQueen, and Isobel Seivl, eds. *The Art of Margaret Preston.* Adelaide, Australia: Art Gallery Board of South Australia, 1980. 0-7243-5564-2, 87p. This catalog includes a brief autobiography of Preston; reproductions of her works from her color paintings, geometric modern phase, and aboriginal period; and explanatory notes.

PRICHARD, KATHARINE (1883–1969)
Writer   Fiji

Katharine Susannah Prichard was an award-winning writer. She was born in Levuka, Fiji, on December 4, 1883, the day that a hurricane struck the island, where her father was the editor of the *Fiji Times.* She studied in Melbourne and worked as a journalist there before traveling to London in 1908. After four years back in Australia, she again went to London and published her first novel, *The Pioneers* (1915), which won the colonial section of a publisher's competition. In 1916, she returned to Australia, and over the next fifty years, produced twelve novels, many poems, plays, and short stories, and an autobiography. In 1920, she became a founding member of the Australian Communist Party. Her later work reflects her socialist beliefs, especially the Australian goldfields trilogy: *The Roaring Nineties* (1946), *Golden Miles* (1948), and *Winged Seeds* (1950). Her son wrote a play about her life called *Wild Weeds and Wind Flowers* (1975).

BIBLIOGRAPHY

Beasley, Jack. *A Gallop of Fire: Katharine Susannah Prichard: On Guard for Humanity: A Study of Creative Personality.* Earlwood, Australia: Wedgetail, 1993. 0-958913-83-8, 187p. Beasley's documented biography and scholarly study looks at Prichard in terms of her writing, her life, and Australia's history but without benefit of Prichard's private papers, because she burned all of them.

Drake-Brockman, Henrietta. *Katharine Susannah Prichard.* New York: Oxford University Press, 1967. No ISBN, 56p. Drake-Brockman's well-researched but brief overview of Prichard's life and career includes short analyses of her writings to show how events in her life influenced her subject matter and her choices.

Throssell, Ric. *Wild Weeds and Windflowers*. North Ryde, New South Wales, Australia: Angus and Robertson, 1990. 0-207-13241-0, 273p. What Throssell re-creates about his mother through documentation with letters and other pertinent papers are the facets of her life, including war, depression, revolution, and the militant political movements in Australia about which she cared so much.

PYM, BARBARA (1913–1980)
Writer   England

Barbara Pym is now recognized as the leading post–World War II British novelist. Born in Oswestry, Shropshire, on June 2, 1913, she studied English language and literature at Huyton College, near Liverpool, and St. Hilda's College, Oxford. She then taught English in Poland but returned before the outbreak of World War II. She worked as a postal censor in Bristol at the beginning of the war and then in the Women's Royal Naval Service, which took her to Naples in 1943. In 1946, she began working at the International African Institute in London, where she remained. In the 1950s she published her first novel, written just after she finished college, and a series of satirical novels on English middle-class society and parish life. From 1961 to 1977 her supposedly anachronistic subject matter caused publishers to reject her novels, but in 1977, critics in *The Times Literary Supplement* noted that she was an underrated writer. When she published *Quartet in Autumn* (1977), her reputation returned. She wrote from a woman's point of view, revealing life for a woman with a subtle, ironic truth, aware that women, rather than the men they knew, must validate their lives. In 1979, the year after her first novels appeared in the United States, she became a fellow of the Royal Society of Literature.

BIBLIOGRAPHY
Allen, Orphia J. *Barbara Pym: Writing a Life*. Lanham, MD: Scarecrow, 1994. 0-8108-2875-8, 262p. Allen includes biographical information, interpretations of Pym's novels, a summary of critical issues in her work, and a bibliography in her academic but readable analysis.

Holt, Hazel. *A Lot to Ask: A Life of Barbara Pym*. New York: Dutton, 1991. 0-525-24937-0, 308p. Using Pym's letters and diaries and her own knowledge of the International African Institute in London, where Pym worked, Holt's biography of Pym compares to a Pym novel as it places Pym in her time and shows her relationship to her work.

Nardin, Jane. *Barbara Pym*. Boston: Twayne, 1985. 0-8057-6897-1, 154p. This critical biography examines Pym's life with emphasis on the themes and techniques in her work that make it unique.

Pym, Barbara. *A Very Private Eye: An Autobiography in Diaries and Letters*. Ed. Hazel Holt and Hilary Pym. New York: Dutton, 1984. 0-525-24234-1, 358p. This collection from diary and notebook entries as well as letters chronicles two periods in her life, 1932 to 1946, when she was at Oxford, and 1963 to 1980, the time during which she could not get her works published. Readers of her work will want to see this autobiography, and others may find a way to her work through this introduction.

Wyatt-Brown, Anne M. *Barbara Pym: A Critical Biography*. St. Louis: University of Missouri Press, 1992. 0-8262-0820-7, 232p. Wyatt-Brown tries to show in her accessible biography and psychological study, based on Pym's unpublished manuscripts, literary notebooks, and discarded fragments of information, how Pym's art allowed her to triumph over social constraints, both those imposed upon her and those she unwittingly brought upon herself.

$\mathfrak{R}$

RACHEL (1820?–1858)
Actor   Switzerland

Élisa Félix, known as Rachel, was an actor. Born on February 28, 1820?, in Mumpf as the daughter of Jewish peddlers, she sang on the streets of France for money, first in Lyons and then in Paris. She studied at Saint-Aulaire's drama school and at the Conservatoire d'Art Dramatique until her father made her work. An influential critic, impressed with her performance in *La Vendéenne*, helped her get a position with the Comédie-Française, where she eventually played all of the female roles in the dramas of Corneille and Racine and was successful in Legouve's *Adrienne Lecouvreur*. During her tours in Europe, the United States, and Russia, her passionate stage presence earned her the reputation as the best actor of the time.

BIBLIOGRAPHY
Gribble, Francis Henry. *Rachel, Her Stage Life and Her Real Life*. 1911. New York: Ayer, 1972. 0-405-08582-6, 275p. Gribble uses previously unpublished documents and other French biographies as resources in a stylistically dated biography to describe Rachel's international acclaim.

RADCLIFFE, ANN (1764–1823)
Writer   England

Ann Radcliffe was a novelist best known for her work *The Mysteries of Udolpho* (1794). Born Ann Ward in London on July 9, 1764, she received a "female" education of music lessons, drawing, and writing, in Bath before marrying William Radcliffe in 1787. To amuse herself, she began writing Gothic novels. She set seven of her books, after the first two, in the Pyrenees or the Alps. Each one has romantic heroes, practical heroines, and supernatural elements. During her career, she had a high reputation, but she stopped writing and retired to her estates in 1797. She influenced Byron, Shelley, and others, who imitated her "gothick romances."

BIBLIOGRAPHY

Miles, Robert. *Ann Radcliffe: The Great Enchantress*. New York: St. Martin's, 1995. 0-7190-3828-6, 201p. In this carefully documented, critical biography, Miles views Radcliffe in the context of her social origins, the "middling" classes, and examines her texts to find aesthetic depth, development in "intentional" ways, and discussions of dysfunctional nuclear families with fathers and daughters clashing.

Rogers, Deborah D. *Ann Radcliffe: A Bio-Bibliography*. Westport, CT: Greenwood Press, 1996. 0-313-28379-6, 232p. Rogers uses new material from an extant Radcliffe manuscript in this scholarly biography on her and adds an annotated bibliography of works by and about Radcliffe in several languages.

Rogers, Deborah D., ed. *The Critical Response to Ann Radcliffe*. Westport, CT: Greenwood Press, 1993. 0-313-28031-2, 320p. Rogers has collected ninety-three documents on Radcliffe, including contemporary reviews, letters, diary entries, and the most important critical assessments of her work.

RAMBERT, MARIE (1888–1982)
Choreographer   Poland and England

Marie Rambert became a ballet dancer, teacher, and choreographer. Born on February 20, 1888, into an intellectual family, Cyvia Rambam's father was a bookseller. In 1905, he sent her to Paris to study medicine and escape the revolutionary fervor in Warsaw. Instead, she began dancing after seeing **Anna Pavlova** and Isadora Duncan. She gave private performances before attending the Dalcroze Summer School in Geneva. Then she went to the Academy of Eurhythmics in Dresden and started teaching. After helping Nijinsky with choreography for *Sacre du printemps*, she went to South America with Diaghilev's Ballets Russes in 1913. She arrived in London in 1917, became a British citizen the next year, and married Ashley Dukes, a playwright. By 1920, she had established a dance school, which evolved into a dance company presenting classical and new ballets while promoting collaboration between painters, musicians, and choreographers. In 1935, it became the Ballet Rambert. The company's work and its tours through Europe, the Middle and Far East, Europe, and Scandinavia merited her the Légion d'Honneur in 1957. She remained closely associated with Ballet Rambert through its change to a modern dance company in the 1960s. A strong supporter of young British choreographers, dancers, and designers, she was created a dame in 1962. In 1972, she became vice president of the Royal Academy of Dancing.

BIBLIOGRAPHY

Clarke, Mary. *Dancers of Mercury; the Story of Ballet Rambert*. London: A. and C. Black, 1962. No ISBN, 240p. Clarke's biography of Rambert discusses her creation of the Ballet Rambert while recounting a history of ballet in the early part of the twentieth century.

Rambert, Marie. *Quicksilver: The Autobiography of Marie Rambert*. New York: St. Martin's, 1972. 0-333-08942-1, 231p. This entertaining memoir of "Quicksilver," the little girl who could not stay still, gives not only Rambert's life but also the story of her theater, first named "Ballet Club," then "Mercury," and finally "Ballet Rambert" at its New York producer's request.

RAND, AYN (1905–1982)

Writer   Russia

In her work, Ayn Rand espouses "objectivism," the philosophy that defends individualism and egoism and refutes the concept of a collective mind. Allisa Rosenbaum was born to a Jewish family in St. Petersburg, Russia, on February 2, 1905. She taught herself to read and write before elementary school age, and by the time she was nine, she had decided to be a writer. After Lenin and Trotsky overthrew the government, her father lost everything. Rand hated the Bolshevik policies and decided she would prove them wrong by writing about people "as they could be, not as they are." Although she was always in favor of intellectual equality, she never concerned herself with what she considered "women's" issues. She graduated from the University of Leningrad in 1924 at nineteen with a degree in history and left for New York, knowing no English. She renamed herself "Ayn" for a version of "Allisa" and "Rand" because it was the name on her typewriter. She married Frank O'Connor in 1929, and, although she had married only for a visa to stay in the United States, she remained married for fifty years. She later had a thirteen-year liaison with a man twenty-five years younger when she was in her fifties. Her writings include *The Fountainhead* (1943) and *Atlas Shrugged* (1957). Persons in a Library of Congress survey said that she was second only to the Bible in influencing their lives.

BIBLIOGRAPHY

Baker, James T. *Ayn Rand.* New York: Scribner's, 1987. 0-8057-7497-1, 184p. Baker gives an overview of Rand's life, work, themes, and theory of "objectivism" in a scholarly, well-written biography.

Branden, Barbara. *The Passion of Ayn Rand—A Biography.* New York: Doubleday, 1986. 0-385-24388-X, 464p. Barbara Branden's popular and balanced biography recalls her nineteen-year friendship with Rand. She mentions Rand's eyes, which, in their intensity, rarely reflected inward.

Branden, Nathaniel. *Judgement Day—My Years with Ayn Rand.* Boston: Houghton Mifflin, 1989. 0-395-46107-3, 436p. Nathaniel Branden's chatty, subjective biography of Rand tells too much about Branden himself, because he and Rand had an affair.

Rand, Ayn. *Letters of Ayn Rand.* Ed. Leondard Peikoff. New York: Dutton, 1995. 0-525-93946-6, 720p. These letters from 1926 to 1982 to a variety of people reveal Rand's ambition as well as her advice to aspiring writers as she continued to believe that altruism and self-sacrifice were unworthy in face of voluntary cooperation and conscious choice.

Sciabarra, Chris Matthew. *Ayn Rand: The Russian Rad.* University Park: Pennsylvania State University Press, 1995. 0-271-01440-7, 472p. Sciabarra returns to Rand's Russian roots and argues in this critical biography that she may have rejected Russian religion and Marxism but that she understood and kept the belief that mind and matter are singular so that thought and action or reason and feeling work together.

RANKIN, ANNABELLE (1908–1986)

Politician   Australia

Dame Annabelle Rankin was a politician who became the first Australian woman of ministerial rank and first female head of a diplomatic mission. She was born on July 28, 1908, in Brisbane, Queensland, Australia, the daughter of a colonel, and was educated in Toowomba, Queensland. She began her public career during World War II as assistant commissioner of the Young Men's Christian Association, where she looked after the welfare work of the women's services. After the war in 1946, she created the Junior Red Cross in Queensland and was elected to the Senate as the first Queensland woman to enter federal politics. She served on a number of committees, and twenty years later, she became a member of Parliament, where she was minister of housing and high commissioner to New Zealand. She was created a dame in 1957.

BIBLIOGRAPHY

Browne, Waveney. *A Woman of Distinction: The Honourable Dame Annabelle Rankin D.B.E.* Ascot, Queensland, Australia: Boolarong, 1981. 0-908175-21-3, 136p. Browne used quotes from letters and other sources for this informal biography, disregarding strict chronological sequence to record Rankin's charming, gracious, kind, and unpretentious service to her community.

RATHBONE, ELEANOR (1872–1946)
Politician   England

Eleanor Rathbone, a member of Parliament, was an active suffragist, the originator of the Family Allowance Plan, and an advocate for increased governmental responsibility for the rights of women throughout the empire in India, Africa, and the Middle East. Born on May 12, 1872, in Liverpool as the eighth of ten children in a merchant family with a Quaker background, she lived in both Liverpool and London, where her father was a Liberal member of Parliament. She studied classics at Somerville College, Oxford. When she returned to Liverpool, she began working with the Women's Industrial Council and the Central Relief Society and was the leading speaker for the local Women's Suffrage Society. She understood the problems of poverty and the injustices for women in this stratum of society, although she herself was economically secure. She became a member of Parliament at the first election in which all women could vote in Britain. She supported an improved franchise for Indian women and the enactment of a Family Allowance Plan. Before World War II, she visited India, Palestine, Yugoslavia, Rumania, and Czechoslovakia. She then became a strong supporter of Zionism, working with displaced persons and Jewish refugees in Europe. She received honorary degrees from Liverpool University in 1931 and Oxford in 1938.

BIBLIOGRAPHY

Stobaugh, Beverly Parker. *Women and Parliament, 1918–1970.* Hicksville, NY: Exposition, 1978. 0-682-49056-3, 152p. Stobaugh studies the women who came to Parliament in this collective biography and includes an overview of Eleanor Rathbone, who served from 1929 to 1946.

Alberti, Johanna. *Eleanor Rathbone.* Thousand Oaks, CA: Sage, 1996. 0-8039-8875-3, 200p. Alberti's straightforward biography is scholarly but uninspired; however, it is the most recent and most thoroughly documented presentation, showing Rathbone's belief that Britain had a moral responsibility to help individuals and countries threatened by Fascism or other movements.

RATUSHINSKAYA, IRINA (1954–)
Poet   **Russia**

Irina Ratushinskaya is a poet whose work is often compared to that of Boris Pasternak. She was born in Odessa on March 4, 1954, into a Polish family, but her parents wanted her to be accepted as Russian so they refused to let her learn Polish. When she was fourteen, she began to write poetry. After the University of Odessa, where she studied physics and mathematics, she was a lecturer at the Odessa Pedagogical Institute but lost her job when she refused to serve on a committee choosing Jewish students by quota. She married in 1979 physicist and human rights activist Igor Gerashzenko, but authorities refused to let them emigrate, arresting them when they demonstrated for Andrei Sikharov. For her activities and her poetry, authorities convicted her of anti-Soviet agitation, sentencing her to seven years of hard labor and five years of internal exile. She lived for four years, 138 days in freezing cells. During imprisonment, she wrote 150 poems on bars of soap with burned match sticks and memorized them before washing them away. Because groups in the West campaigned for her, she and her husband received a three-month release to go to the United Kingdom for her glaucoma treatment. When she remained, Soviets stripped her citizenship. She has lived in the United States, mainly in Chicago, where she has been the poet-in-residence at Northwestern University.

BIBLIOGRAPHY
Ratushinskaya, Irina. *In the Beginning*. New York: Knopf, 1991. 0-394-57141-X, 317p. This compelling memoir covers Ratushinskaya's independent attitudes from her childhood in Odessa until she arrived in London during 1986, having survived her experience in Soviet labor camps. Most of the memoir covers her dissident years in Kiev and Odessa with her husband before her arrest.

Ratushinskaya, Irina. *Grey Is the Color of Hope*. New York: Knopf, 1988. 0-394-57140-1, 355p. On her twenty-ninth birthday in 1983, Ratushinskaya received a seven-year prison sentence. The memoir covers details (including the ways that the women tried to retain vestiges of civility in prison through ritual) of the three and one-half years that she served in a labor camp before human rights groups pressured the Soviet government to release her.

Rodgers, Dick. *Irina*. 1987. Batavia, IL: Lion, 1987. 0-7459-1367-9, 180p. After hearing about Ratushinskaya, Rodgers decided to help. As a physician and priest, he chose to live in a cell that re-created her prison conditions and called world attention to her exile. He writes about his own experience and his pleasure at meeting her.

RÉCAMIER, JEANNE (1777–1849)
Intellectual   **France**

Madame de Récamier was the hostess of a French salon. Born Françoise Julie Adélaïde Bernard on December 4, 1777, into a Lyons banker's family, she was educated at a convent. When fifteen, she went to Paris, and the next year, she married a wealthy, elderly banker. Her beauty and charm attracted many other admirers, and she became hostess of a fashionable salon for both political and literary figures. Her Royalist friends displeased Napoleon, and he exiled her in 1805. She went to Geneva to stay with **Madame de Staël** and then to Rome and

Naples. She returned to Paris after the Battle of Waterloo in 1815 and continued her salon, Châteaubriand became one of her best friends, and David painted a portrait of her in 1800 that hangs in the Louvre.

BIBLIOGRAPHY

Levaillant, Maurice. *Passionate Exiles: Madame de Staël and Madame Récamier.* Trans. Malcolm Barnes. North Stratford, NH: Ayer, 1977. 0-8369-8086-7, 354p. Levaillant details the friendship of Madame de Staël and Madame Récamier based on papers either still unpublished or rare and little known. Although well documented, its casual tone belies the anguish of the two exiles.

Récamier, Jeanne F. *Memoirs and Correspondence of Madame Récamier.* 1867. New York: AMS, 1975. 0-404-56808-4, 408p. Récamier's memoirs are isolated reminiscences of people with whom she socialized and of the times during which she lived. Unedited, they are difficult to follow.

REDPATH, ANNE (1895–1965)

Artist   Scotland

Anne Redpath was an oil and watercolor painter. Born in Galashiels, Borders, Scotland, on March 29, 1895, she was the daughter of a tweed designer. She left home to study at Edinburgh Art College, and from 1919 to 1934, lived in France. As one of Scotland's most important modern artists, her paintings show richness of color and vigorous technique. Among the honors she received were member of the Society of Scottish Artists, member of the Royal Society of British Artists, member of the Royal Institute of Oil Painters, academician of the Royal Scottish Artists, academician of the Royal West of England Academy, and associate of the Royal Society of Painters in Watercolours. Edinburgh University gave her an honorary degree, and in 1955, she became an Officer of the British Empire.

BIBLIOGRAPHY

Bruce, George. *Anne Redpath.* Edinburgh: Edinburgh University Press, 1974. 0-85224-243-3, 81p. During a series of interviews with Redpath for television, Bruce saw many of her paintings at her home before she sent them to competitions. His brief overview of her life and her work with photographs is a personal critique without documentation.

REIBEY, MARY (1777–1855)

Businesswoman   England

Mary Reibey was an Australian businesswoman who traded widely in Australia and the Pacific. Born Mary Haydock in Bury, Lancashire, on May 12, 1777, she became an orphan while still a child, and her grandmother raised her. In 1790, she was transported to Australia for a seven-year sentence after horse stealing while disguised as a boy. She succeeded in hiding her identity as a girl for four months even while in prison. In 1792, she arrived in Sydney and became a nursemaid. Two years later, she married Thomas Reibey, an Irishman working for the East India Company, and while her husband traded, Reibey managed a hotel and their seven children. She also ran the business while he was at sea and continued it after he died in 1811. She increased the business and became a leader of Sydney's society, and Lancashire honored her achievements when she returned in 1820. In the late 1820s, she began to concentrate on her city properties in Sydney and to become a philanthropist and religious worker. After her retirement, her three sons became prosperous merchants.

BIBLIOGRAPHY

Irvine, Nance. *Mary Reibey-Molly Incognita: A Biography of Mary Reibey, 1777 to 1855, And Her World.* New South Wales, Australia: Library of Australian History, 1982. 0-90812-046-X, 161p. Although the organization of this biography is disjointed, it is a carefully documented disclosure of the psychological and physical distance that Reibey traveled from being a convicted thief to wealthy businesswoman.

REITSCH, HANNA (1912–1979)

Aviator   Germany

Hanna Reitsch was a test pilot for the Luftwaffe during World War II. Born on March 29, 1912, to an eye specialist, she received a good education. Taking her patriotic and religious beliefs from her parents, she added a love of flying, which gave her renown during the Third Reich as a test pilot. After the war, someone accused her of anti-Semitism, and she gained a controversial reputation when she sued. The toil of this and other problems wore her down, but she continued to break aviation records by becoming the woman who had flown the farthest in a glider.

BIBLIOGRAPHY

Lomax, Judy. *Hanna Reitsch: Flying for the Fatherland.* London: J. Murray, 1990. 0-7195-4571-4, 244p. Using interviews, documents, letters, photographs, and excerpts from Reitsch's autobiographical books, Lomax has created a balanced biography that is documented, readable, and well written.

Reitsch, Hanna. *The Sky My Kingdom: Memoirs of the Famous German World War II Test-Pilot.* 1955. Presidio, CA: Presidio, 1991. 1-85367-093-6, 222p. In her autobiography, Reitsch reveals her love of flying and her hope that flying will somehow unify humans in a common goal.

RHONDDA, MARGARET (1883–1958)

Writer and Activist   Wales

Margaret Mackworth, viscountess of Rhondda, had a strong commitment to equality and social justice. Margaret Haig Thomas was born on June 12, 1883, as the only child of a South Wales industrialist. She was educated privately in London and St. Andrews before spending three social seasons in London. She then went to Somerville College, Oxford, for one year before marrying Humphrey Mackworth. She protested with the Women's Social and Political Union and was imprisoned. She also went on a hunger strike. Then she joined her father's business. She sailed on the *Lusitania* for the United States in 1916, but after the Germans sank the ship, she was rescued. In 1918, she succeeded to the viscountcy and received royal permission to attend the House of Lords. In 1920, she began editing a weekly review called *Time and Tide*. Its circulation reached forty thousand and was regarded as one of the leading journals of opinion in the 1930s and 1940s. Her deep commitment to equality and social justice was a dominant force between the wars. A flood destroyed her personal papers after her death, leaving a dearth of information about her life.

BIBLIOGRAPHY

Eoff, Shirley M. *Viscountess Rhondda: Equalitarian.* Columbus: Ohio State
University Press, 1991. 0-8142-0539-9, 185p. Eoff's intent in a readable,
well-researched biography is to illuminate Mackworth's struggle for equal
rights and social justice in modern Britain, with her feminist activity as the
central issue.

Mackworth, Margaret Haig Thomas, Viscountess Rhondda. *Notes on the Way.*
1937. Freeport, NY: Books for Libraries, 1968. No ISBN, 220p. Mackworth records her reactions to places and people in a straightforward, entertaining style revealing her character and personality.

RHYS, JEAN (1894–1979)

Writer   Dominican Republic and England

Jean Rhys was a novelist. Born Gwen Williams in Roseau, Dominica, on August
24, 1894, as the daughter of a doctor, she attended the Convent of the Faithful
Virgin before going to England in 1910. After attendance at two other schools,
she settled at the Royal Academy of Dramatic Art in London, but her father's
death after only one term obliged her to join a touring theater company to earn
her living. In 1919, she married a Dutch poet and translator, and they lived in
Vienna, Budapest, and, finally Paris, where she began writing with the help of
her mentor, Ford Madox Ford. Her first four novels dealt with women whom
men had betrayed. They were *Quartet* (1928), *Left Bank* (1927), *After Leaving
Mr. Mackenzie* (1930), and *Good Morning Midnight* (1939). She also worked
during this period as a fashion model, translator, and tutor. In 1934, she returned to England after a divorce and lived in retirement in Cornwall for
nearly thirty years. In 1966, she published her best-known novel, which won
three awards, *Wide Sargasso Sea*, a "prequel" to **Charlotte Brontë's** *Jane Eyre*.

BIBLIOGRAPHY

Angier, Carole. *Jean Rhys: Life and Work.* Boston: Little, Brown, 1991. 0-316-
04263-3, 762p. Angier knew Rhys in her old age, and her scholarly and
balanced biography is sensitive to both the heights of her career and the
depths of her real life as she considers that Rhys' life and work may have
become interdependent.

O'Connor, Teresa F. *Jean Rhys: The West Indian Novels.* New York: New York
University Press, 1986. 0-8147-6164-X, 247p. O'Connor's well-documented, critical, but Freudian biography combines the facets of Rhys's fiction with her colonial upbringing as a female in a land of blacks, a place
that she loved but that was indifferent to her.

Rhys, Jean. *Letters: 1931–1966.* New York: Viking Penguin, 1995. Paper, 0-
14-018906-8, 320p. Letters included here addressed to her daughter and
to friends show her seriousness as a writer and her character and personality between 1931 and 1966, the years when she struggled with writer's
block.

Rhys, Jean. *Smile Please: An Unfinished Autobiography.* New York: Penguin,
1981. 0-14-018405-8, 173p. In her autobiography, Rhys refused to include any conversation that she could not remember completely, but she
died before finishing the text.

RICHARDSON, HENRY HANDEL (1870–1946)
Writer   Australia

Henry Handel Richardson (the pseudonym for Ethel Florence Lindesay Robertson) was one of Australia's best novelists. She was born in Melbourne, Victoria, on January 3, 1870, to an Irish doctor who had emigrated during the 1850 gold rush. Her father died when she was nine, and her mother supported the family as a postmistress while Robertson attended the Presbyterian Ladies' College in Melborne. Her mother saved enough money to send her to the Leipzig Conservatoire to study piano, where she learned about German Romantic literature and the works of Nietzsche and Freud. After living in Strasbourg with her professor husband, she wrote her first novel, *Maurice Guest*, which treated homosexuality openly. It was published after they moved to London, where her husband became the first professor of Germanic and Scandinavian languages at London University. She concentrated on her writing, and in 1912, returned to Australia to research her trilogy about life in the gold fields, *The Fortunes of Richard Mahony* (1929), based on her father's life. She published a collection of stories during the 1930s and another novel. Her description of her youth, *Myself When Young* (1948), appeared after her death. Although her subject matter remains difficult to categorize, she is best described as an Anglo-Australian writer. She won the Australian gold medal for literature in 1930 and was nominated for the Nobel Prize.

BIBLIOGRAPHY
Buckley, Vincent. *Henry Handel Richardson*. New York: Oxford University Press, 1970. 0-19-550030-X, 48p. Buckley presents a brief biographical introduction and overview of Richardson's life and work.

Clark, Axel. *Henry Handel Richardson: Fiction in the Making*. Brookvale, New South Wales: Simon and Schuster Australia, 1990. 0-7318-0138-5, 297p. This recommended, readable, researched, and documented biography tells the story of Richardson's youth and her parents' marriage, which were the historical bases of her three major novels, *Maurice Guest, The Getting of Wisdom,* and *The Fortunes of Richard Mahony.*

Elliott, William D. *Henry Handel Richardson*. Boston: Twayne, 1975. 0-8057-6217-5, 174p. Elliott's critical study posits that Richardson was the first Australian, realistic novelist to develop a multidimensional single character in an extended work of fiction with her own life forming the basis of the fiction.

Green, Dorothy. *Ulysses Bound: Henry Handel Richardson and Her Fiction.* Boston: Allen and Unwin, 1986. Paper, 0-86861-809-8, 616p. Green's scholarly approach to Richardson and her work is carefully researched and documented, although not complete, because Richardson's executor refused Green access to some of Richardson's personal papers.

RIEFENSTAHL, LENI (1902–)
Actor and Filmmaker   Germany

Leni Riefenstahl was an actor, Germany's only female filmmaker in the 1930s, and a photographer. She was born Berta Helene Amalie Riefenstahl in Berlin on August 22, 1902, where she studied fine arts at the Berlin Academy. She received ballet training and danced in Max Reinhardt's theater company before appearing in films and formed her own company. Her direction of *Das blaue*

Licht (The Blue Light, 1932) caught Hitler's attention, and he asked her to film the Nazi rallies at Nuremberg in 1934. Her *Triumph des Willens* (Triumph of the Will, 1935) showcased Hitler and damaged her reputation, even though she was not a party member. She also filmed *Olympia* (1938), an epic documentary of the Berlin Olympic Games, which was premiered on Hitler's forty-ninth birthday. In that film she refused to remove footage on Jesse Owens, the black American gold medal winner. At the Venice International Film Festival in 1938, the film won the Grand Prize. During the war, the French interred her for four years until they decided that she was not a Nazi. With few film projects after the war, Riefenstahl became a still photographer for European magazines and, in the 1970s, published several photographic studies of Africa.

BIBLIOGRAPHY

Infield, Glenn B. *Leni Riefenstahl: The Fallen Film Goddess.* New York: Crowell, 1976. 0-690-01167-9, 278p. Infield shows Riefenstahl's close association with the Nazis and thinks that she was probably politically motivated during her career, although his documentation is sparse and questionable, and his text is biased against her.

Riefenstahl, Leni. *Leni Riefenstahl: A Memoir.* New York: St. Martin's, 1993. 0-312-09843-X, 669p. As Riefenstahl recalls her life, she seems self-absorbed and unable to identify with the awful problems in Germany during World War II. These memoirs offer her view, certainly not a balanced one, that World War II distressed her most because it delayed circulation of her movie about the Olympics.

RILEY, BRIDGET (1931–)
Artist   England

Bridget Riley, an op art artist, was the first English painter to win the major painting prize at the Venice Biennale (1968). She was born in London on April 24, 1931, and educated at Taplow and Cheltenham Ladies' College before attending Goldsmiths College of Art and the Royal College of Art. She spent time traveling in Europe, and when she returned to England, she taught part-time. In 1955, her work appeared in the Young Contemporaries exhibition. In 1962, she exhibited alone and caused a sensation with her style of manipulating overall flat patterns, originally in black and white but later in color, and using repeated shapes or undulating lines, which often created an illusion of movement, as seen in *Fall* (1963, Tate, London). Her works have been exhibited in the United States, Europe, Australia, and Japan. She has won several awards, and now her paintings hang in major museums around the world.

BIBLIOGRAPHY

De Sausmarez, Maurice. *Bridget Riley.* Greenwich, CT: New York Graphic Society, 1970. 0-8212-0396-7, 128p. This biography, the first full-length look at Riley's life and work, reveals her aesthetic and working methods based on a series of interviews. Also included are ninety illustrations demonstrating the "movement" of lines and shapes in op art.

ROBERTSON, JEANNIE (1908–1975)
Entertainer   Scotland

Jeannie Robertson was a folksinger with a huge repertoire of classic, traditional ballads and other songs. Born in Aberdeen, Grampian, she lived most of her life there. She belonged to the "traveling folk," a group of people whose music was passed down orally from generation to generation. She was unknown beyond the northeastern area of Scotland until 1953, when the Scottish folklorist Hamish Henderson discovered her powerful and magnetic singing style. Her subsequent work exerted a profound influence on the folkmusic revival because it represented an important link with the ancient folk culture of Scotland and the world. In 1968, she became a Member of the Order of the British Empire.

BIBLIOGRAPHY

Porter, James and Herschel Gower. *Jeannie Robertson; Emergent Singer, Transformative Voice.* Knoxville: University of Tennessee Press, 1995. 0-87049-904-1, 357p. In this scholarly biography of Robertson, the authors look at her life and work, with complete song texts, in its historical, ethnomusical, and ethnographical contexts.

ROBINSON, JOAN VIOLET (1903–1983)

Scholar   England

Joan Violet Robinson was one of the most influential economic theorists of her time, leading the Cambridge school in developing the macroeconomic theories of growth and distribution. She was born Joan Violet Maurice on October 31, 1903, in Camberley, Surrey, into a family of educators and physicians. She attended St. Paul's Girls' School and received a scholarship to Girton College, Cambridge, where she graduated in economics. She married an economist, and after briefly living in India, she returned to Cambridge as an assistant lecturer. While deciding to support the radical Left in her political beliefs, she continued her work at Cambridge by rising to university lecturer, reader, and then professor in 1965. Her first book, *The Economics of Imperfect Competition,* was published in 1933. Four years later, she published *Introduction to the Theory of Employment.* She then combined the ideas of Keynes and Marx in her *Essay on Marxian Economics* and followed it with *Accumulation of Capital* and later books. She thought that economics instruction should be improved, and in 1970, she published *Freedom and Necessity,* an appeal for progressive social science teaching. In 1973, she published a textbook, *Introduction to Modern Economics,* with one of her colleagues. She would not yield a point of discussion until she could clearly see all facets of it.

BIBLIOGRAPHY

Cicarelli, James. *Joan Robinson: A Bio-Bibliography.* Westport, CT: Greenwood Press, 1996. 0-313-25844-9, 179p. Cicarelli's recommended, scholarly view of Robinson includes her family background, her education in economics at Cambridge, and the changing times in which she lived to show how they strongly influenced her. Cicarelli comments that colleagues expected Robinson to win the Nobel Prize in economics in 1975, but she did not.

Turner, Marjorie Shepherd. *Joan Robinson and the Americans.* Armonk, NY: M. E. Sharpe, 1989. 0-87332-533-8, 315p. After her death, Robinson's family allowed Turner to see papers in King's College Archives, conduct formal interviews with colleagues, and correspond with them for her intellectual biography examining Robinson's triumphs and frustrations during her fifty years of economic thinking, from an American perspective.

ROSSETTI, CHRISTINA (1830–1894)

Poet   England

Christina Georgina Rossetti's poetry shows the influence of the Pre-Raphaelite artistic movement. She was born in London on December 5, 1830, the youngest child of Gabriele Rossetti, a political refugee from Naples who taught Italian, and a former governess. She received her education at home, publishing her first poetry privately when she was twelve and again at seventeen. When Rossetti was twenty, she used the name "Ellen Alleyne" for poems published in the Pre-Raphaelite Brotherhood's journal, *The Germ*. Her father became ill, and Rossetti started to teach Italian and tried to open schools in Camden Town, London, and Frome, Somerset, to support the family. She was a devout Anglican and used religious incompatibility as an excuse for breaking two engagements. Influenced by the Oxford movement, she wrote mainly religious poetry, such as *Goblin Market and Other Poems* (1862) and *The Prince's Progress* (1866). By 1873, she was ill with Grave's disease, but she continued writing with her best works the sonnets and lyric poems of the "Monna Innominata" series. She was also concerned about poverty, unemployment, and prostitution, subjects that she wrote about in several treatises.

BIBLIOGRAPHY

Battiscombe, Georgina. *Christina Rossetti, a Divided Life.* New York: Holt, Rinehart, and Winston, 1981. 0-03-059612-2, 233p. Battiscombe's scholarly biography uses previously unpublished materials to refute another biographer's claims that Rossetti's adult life was mired in an unrequited love for William Bell Scott.

Bell, Mackenzie. *Christina Rossetti: A Biographical and Critical Study.* 1898. New York: AMS Press, 1973. 0-404-08724-8, 405p. Biographical information precedes Bell's detailed analyses of Rossetti's poetry and prose for autobiographical elements. Since Rossetti did not date many of her letters, Bell had to identify pertinent internal references.

Bellas, Ralph A. *Christina Rossetti.* New York: Twayne, 1977. 0-8057-6671-5, 139p. Bellas examines Rossetti's background, major secular development, sonnets, and devotional poems in a critical look at her work.

Marsh, Jan. *Christina Rossetti: A Literary Biography.* New York: Viking, 1995. 0-670-83517-X, 624p. Using letters, diaries, and previously unavailable materials, Marsh examines both Rossetti and her poetry in a recommended biography from a partially psychological viewpoint and thinks that her verse was a response to the people and events in her life from her adolescent breakdown through her struggle to reconcile her ambition and Victorian ideals of women.

Sawtell, Margaret. *Christina Rossetti: Her Life and Religion.* 1955. Folcroft, PA: Folcroft, 1973. 0-81414-7616-0, 160p. Sawtell brings little new information about Rossetti, referring to prior biographers, but suggests that Rossetti intentionally arranged her poems out of chronological order so that readers could not easily interpret her life through them.

ROYDEN, MAUDE (1876–1956)

Activist   England

Agnes Maude Royden was a social worker, suffragette, and preacher. Born in Liverpool, Merseyside, she was the daughter of a shipowner. She studied at

Cheltenham Ladies' College and at Lady Margaret Hall, Oxford, where she read history. When she returned to Liverpool in 1899, she worked at the Victoria Women's Settlement before becoming a parish worker and a lecturer for extension classes from Oxford. She was a prominent voice in the woman suffrage movement, although more concerned with the ethical and religious aspects than the political concepts. She became an assistant preacher at the City Temple in London, and in 1920, she and others founded the Interdenominational Fellowship Services in Kensington Town Hall. In 1930, she became a Companion of Honour and received honorary degrees from the university at Glasgow in 1931 and the university at Liverpool in 1935. She organized the "Peace Army" and promoted it in the United States, Australia, New Zealand, India, China, and Britain, but she decided during World War II to renounce her pacifism. In 1944, she married Hudson Shaw, a man in his eighties, two months before his death, but they had been platonic friends for forty-three years while his wife still lived.

BIBLIOGRAPHY

Fletcher, Sheila. *Maude Royden: A Life.* Cambridge, MA: Basil Blackwell, 1989. 0-631-15422-1, 294p. Fletcher uses letters and other documents for this scholarly biography of Royden's life and the causes in which she was active, such as defying the church to become the first woman preacher.

RUSSIA, ELIZABETH of. *See* ELIZABETH of RUSSIA.

RUSSIA, SOPHIA of. *See* SOPHIA of RUSSIA.

RUTHERFORD, MARGARET (1892–1972)

Actor   England

Dame Margaret Rutherford was an actor who gained fame for her comedy roles. She was born in London on May 11, 1892, and educated in Wimbleton and Sussex. Before she began her stage career, she taught piano and elocution. She made her stage debut in 1925 at the Old Vic theater and gained fame as a character actor and comedienne. Among her best-known roles were Lady Bracknell in *The Importance of Being Earnest* (stage 1939, film 1952) and Miss Whitchurch in *The Happiest Days of Your Life* (stage 1948, film 1950). She also played Mrs. Malaprop in *The Rivals* (1966). She scored success as Agatha Christie's "Miss Marple" in a series of films beginning in 1962. She won an Academy Award for her role in *The VIPs* in 1964 and was created a Dame of the British Empire in 1967.

BIBLIOGRAPHY

Simmons, Dawn Langley. *Margaret Rutherford: A Blithe Spirit.* New York: McGraw-Hill, 1983. 0-07-057479-0, 208p. In this biased biography, Simmons tributes Rutherford for mentoring her even though Rutherford never recovered from her own family's betrayal when it pretended that her father was dead instead of telling her that he was incarcerated in a hospital for the criminally insane. Simmons also has a family secret that she reveals in the text. It is, however, a thorough and readable, popular biography of Rutherford and her career.

SACHS, NELLY (1891–1970)
Poet   Germany

Nelly Sachs won the Nobel Prize in literature in 1966 for her work as a poet
and playwright. She was born in Berlin on December 10, 1891, daughter of a
Jewish industrialist. She studied privately, reading German Romantics and mystical writers. She and her mother fled from Nazi Germany in 1940, and, with
the help of **Selma Lagerlöf**, with whom she had corresponded, settled in Stockholm. Sachs took Swedish citizenship and supported her mother and herself by
translating Swedish poetry. The rest of her family died in concentration camps,
and her distress at their plight led her to write powerful poetry about the tragedy. Her first two poetry collections were *In den Wohnungen des Todes* (1946)
and *Sternverdunkelung* (1949). Her next two works, *Und Niemand Weiss
Weiter* (1957) and *Flucht und Verwandlung* (1959), enlarged upon the themes
and universalized them. Her best-known play is *Eli: Ein Mysterienspiel vom
Leiden Israels* (Eli: A Mystery Play of the Sufferings of Israel, 1951).

BIBLIOGRAPHY
Celan, Paul, and Nelly Sachs. *Paul Celan, Nelly Sachs: Correspondence.* Ed.
    Barbara Wiedemann. New York: Sheep Meadow, 1995. 1-878818-37-6,
    112p. Sachs corresponded with Celan between 1954 to 1969 about their
    Jewish heritage and the trial of the Holocaust. Wiedemann includes a brief
    biography about Sachs.
Bahti, Timothy, and Marilyn Sibley Fries, eds. *Jewish Writers, German Litera-
    ture: The Uneasy Examples of Nelly Sachs and Walter Benjamin.* Ann Arbor:
    University of Michigan Press, 1995. 0-472-10621-X, 221p. A scholarly
    text, the essays discuss Sachs and her work in terms of her Jewish experi-
    ence.
Rappaport, Solomon. *Tribute to Nobel Prize Winners for Literature, 1966: S. J.
    Agnon, Nelly Sachs.* Johannesburg, South Africa: South African Zionist Fed-

eration, 1967. No ISBN, 14p. Rappaport's lecture includes background on Sachs and an interpretation of her work.

SACKVILLE-WEST, VITA (1892–1962)
Writer   **England**

Vita Sackville-West was a poet, novelist, and biographer. She was born Victoria Mary on March 9, 1892, at Knole, Kent, as the third daughter of the Baron Sackville. She received a private education and by eighteen had completed eight novels and five plays. In 1913, she married Harold Nicolson and went with him to Constantinople. Her closest friend and lover for a time was **Virginia Woolf**, and Woolf dedicated *Orlando* to her in 1928. Sackville-West published a book each year beginning in 1921 and won the Hawthornden Prize for her long poem *The Land* in 1926. She wrote biographies about **Joan of Arc, St. Teresa of Ávila**, and **St. Thérèse of Lisieux**. After her husband retired from government service, they created an elegant English garden at their Sissinghurst, Kent, estate, and she wrote a gardening column for many years.

BIBLIOGRAPHY

Glendinning, Victoria. *Vita: The Life of V. Sackville-West*. New York: Knopf, 1983. 0-394-52023-8, 436p. This authorized biography, realistic but sympathetic, attempts to show Sackville-West's aristocratic heritage, devotion to literature, unhappy marriage, and homosexual liaisons. James Tait Black Memorial Prize.

Nicolson, Nigel. *Portrait of a Marriage*. London: Weidenfeld and Nicolson, 1973. 0-297-76645-7, 235p. Nicolson, son of Sackville-West, thinks that his parents' infidelities made their marriage stronger.

Raitt, Suzanne. *Vita and Virginia: The Work and Friendship of V. Sackville-West and Virginia Woolf*. New York: Oxford University Press, 1993. 0-19-811249-1, 195p. Raitt looks at the relationship of Sackville-West and Woolf through gender, biography, and published works, concluding that Sackville-West's literary endeavors were less successful.

Stevens, Michael. *V. Sackville-West: A Critical Biography*. New York: Scribner's, 1974. 0-684-13677-5, 192p. Stevens used Sackville-West's unpublished papers, manuscript autobiography, poems, and prose writings as sources in his accessible biography.

SAGAN, FRANÇOISE (1935–)
Writer   **France**

Françoise Sagan is an award-winning author. Born Françoise Quoirez at Cajare in Lot on June 21, 1935, she received her education in Paris at a convent. After failing an examination following her first year at the Sorbonne when she was eighteen, she spent four weeks of the summer writing. She completed *Bonjour Tristesse* in 1954, (Good Morning Sadness), won the Prix des Critiques, and became an international, best-selling author, translated into many languages. Her next novel, in 1956, also exhibiting adolescent wisdom and precocity, was *Un Certain Sourire* (A Certain Smile). Her many later novels have been less successful. She has also written several plays, scripts, popular songs, and a ballet scenario. The mythical undercurrents of her work reflect a boredom evident in the later half of the twentieth century, loneliness, and unhappiness in love affairs.

BIBLIOGRAPHY

Miller, Judith Graves. *Françoise Sagan*. Boston: Twayne, 1988. 0-8057-8228-
1, 142p. In her short, biographical overview and feminist critique, Miller
examines the various aspects of Sagan's popularity, especially the fantasy
and the escapism fundamental to her work.

Sagan, Françoise. *Reponses: The Autobiography of Francoise Sagan*. Trans.
David Macey. Godalming, England: Black Sheep, 1979. 0-517-54224-2,
153p. The text is a selection of interviews that Sagan gave between 1954
and 1980, revealing rather balanced accounts of her personality and her
point of view.

Sagan, Françoise. *With Fondest Regards*. Trans. Christine Donougher. New
York: Dutton, 1985. 0-525-24334-8, 176p. Sagan writes about people she
has known and about herself with tributes to many and literary anecdotes
about mid-twentieth-century Paris.

SAINT BERNADETTE. *See* BERNADETTE.

SAINT BIRGITTA. *See* BIRGITTA.

SAINT CATHERINE of SIENA. *See* CATHERINE of SIENA.

SAINT CLARE of ASSISI. *See* CLARE of ASSISI.

SAINT ELIZABETH of HUNGARY. *See* ELIZABETH of
HUNGARY.

SAINT FRANCESCA XAVIER CABRINI. *See* CABRINI,
FRANCESCA XAVIER.

SAINT TERESA BENEDICTA of the CROSS. *See* STEIN, EDITH.

SAINT TERESA of ÁVILA. *See* TERESA of ÁVILA.

SAINT THÉRÈSE of LISIEUX. *See* THÉRÈSE of LISIEUX.

SAND, GEORGE (1804–1876)
Writer   France

An important and prolific writer, George Sand gained fame not only for her
work but for her lifestyle. Amandine Aurore Lucie Dupin, born on July 1,
1804, was the illegitimate daughter of Marshal de Saxe. Her grandmother, Madame Dupin, raised her for marriage and continuance of the family line.
Aurore married but, after having children, went to Paris with a man not her
husband, Jules Sandeau. Wanting to hear what was going on in the streets but
unable to walk alone as a woman, she had a man's suit of clothes made for her
and found work as a journalist for the newspaper *Le Figaro*. When Aurore prepared to publish a book under her name, her mother objected, saying that she
did not want her name on a book, so the name "George Sand" became Aurore's

pseudonym. Her first book, *Indiana*, attracted good critical reviews. She then wrote between midnight and four in the morning, turning out many novels. Although she never divorced her husband, she supported herself with money from her books and allowed him to live on the family estate. She became notorious for her series of lovers because the newspapers enjoyed printing scandalous stories, but the only lover who matched her talent was Frédéric Chopin. In 1848, she thought the new government would give women more rights, but it did not. She wore men's clothes because they gave her freedom, not because she wanted to be a man. She spent the last part of her life on her estate.

BIBLIOGRAPHY

Atwood, William G. *The Lioness and the Little One: The Liaison of George Sand and Frederic Chopin*. New York: Columbia University Press, 1980. 0-231-04942-0, 316p. Correspondence, journals, and other writings from Sand, Chopin, and their contemporaries form the basis of this biography of the affair between Sand and Chopin.

Barry, Joseph Amber. *Infamous Woman: The Life of George Sand*. Garden City, NY: Doubleday, 1977. 0-385-06830-1, 436p. Barry shows Sand as a product of her age and of her heredity in a readable biography, while emphasizing her behavior and her adventures.

Cate, Curtis. *George Sand: A Biography*. Boston: Houghton Mifflin, 1975. 0-395-19954-9, 812p. Using Sand's correspondence and her autobiography in a well-written and recommended biography, Cate re-creates the shock toward Sand and her refusal to bow to the conventions of her day.

Dickenson, Donna. *George Sand: A Brave Man, the Most Womanly Woman*. Herndon, VA: Berg, 1988. 0-85496-536-X, 190p. Dickenson examines Sand and her androgyny using current theories of the female psyche, including those of Carol Gilligan, Sandra Gilbert, Susan Gubar, and the late Michel Foucault.

Jordan, Ruth. *George Sand: A Biography*. London: Constable, 1976. 0-09-460340-5, 368p. Jordan uses Sand's correspondence, historical documents, and writing to demonstrate that Sand was a product of her times with her Romantic themes and social thinking.

Winegarten, Renee. *The Double Life of George Sand, Woman and Writer: A Critical Biography*. New York: Basic Books, 1978. 0-465-01683-9, 339p. Winegarten concludes from her research that Sand's greatness came from her decision to listen to her own thoughts of who she should be to be in harmony with herself.

SANDEL, CORA (1880–1974)

Writer   Norway

Cora Sandel was a novelist and short story writer. She was born in Christiania, now Oslo, on December 20, 1880, as Sara Fabricius in an upper-class family. She studied art before going to Paris in 1905, where she lived for fifteen years. She married a Swedish sculptor, Anders Jonsson, in 1913, and they returned to Sweden in 1921 with their four-year-old son but divorced five years later. Sandel stopped painting and began to write, under the influence of the French novelist **Colette**, so that she could support herself. She took her pen name in 1922, when she published the "Alberta Trilogy," three novels in which she traced a woman's growth to independence during her life in Norway and Paris. In her later novels and short stories, she showed concern for social realities and spoke against the Nazi occupation of Norway. She refused, however, to belong to any organized feminist group.

BIBLIOGRAPHY

Essex, Ruth. *Cora Sandel, Seeker of Truth.* New York: Peter Lang, 1995. 0-8204-2229-0, 248p. In her scholarly biography, Essex sees Sandel as one of the earliest women writers to illustrate the dangerous implications of male misinterpretation of Freudian theories.

SAUNDERS, CICELY (1918–)

Nurse   England

Dame Cicely Mary Strode Saunders founded the modern hospice movement. She was born in London on June 22, 1918, in a home with estranged parents. Saunders was extremely shy until high school, when she began to excel and became a leader. She studied at Oxford and trained at St. Thomas' Hospital Medical School and the Nightingale School of Nursing. Then she became founder (1967), medical director (1967 to 1985), and chairman (from 1985) of St. Christopher's Hospice, Sydenham. She promotes the principle of dying with dignity, maintaining that death is a natural process that sensitive nursing and effective pain control can ease, and has written and edited a number of books on her subject. She has received many awards for her pioneering work, such as the Templeton Prize in 1981 and the British Medical Association Gold Medal in 1987. She also has honorary doctorates from universities in the United States and Great Britain, including Yale, Columbia, Creighton, Marymount Manhattan College, Essex, Leicester, and London. She was given the Order of the British Empire in 1967 and became a Dame in 1980.

BIBLIOGRAPHY

Du Boulay, Shirley. *Cicely Saunders, Founder of the Modern Hospice Movement.* London: Hodder and Stoughton, 1984. 0-340-35103-9, 268p. Du Boulay's biography is straightforward, well documented, and scholarly.

SAUVÉ, JEANNE (1922–1993)

Politician and Journalist   Canada

Jeanne Sauvé was a journalist and politician. She was born in Prud'homme, Saskatchewan, on April 26, 1922, the fifth child of a father who followed a variety of businesses. She later attended school in Ottawa and Paris. She served as the national president of Jeunesse Etudiante Catholique in Montreal before marrying Maurice Sauvé in 1948 and going to London. In Paris with him in 1951, she worked as the assistant to the director of the Youth Section of the United Nations Educational, Scientific, and Cultural Organization (UNESCO). In 1952, they returned to Canada, and she began her twenty-year career as a journalist and broadcaster for several networks, eventually ascending to the directorship of Bushnell Communications and EKAC Radio in Montreal. In 1972, elected as a member of Parliament for Montreal-Ahuntsic, she served as the minister of environment and of communications and speaker of the House of Commons. In December 1983, she became the first woman to be governor general of Canada.

BIBLIOGRAPHY
Woods, Shirley E. *Her Excellency Jeanne Sauvé*. Toronto: Macmillan, 1986. 0-7715-98998, 242p. Woods gives a chronological account of Sauvé's life, establishing her credentials with a discussion of the office of governor general.

SAYERS, DOROTHY (1893–1957)

Writer   England

Dorothy Sayers was a celebrated writer of detective stories. She was born in Oxford on June 13, 1893, and studied at the Godolphin School, Salisbury. With a scholarship to Somerville College, Oxford, she received a first-class degree in medieval French. After working in advertising, translating medieval literature, and bearing an illegitimate son whom she always claimed to have adopted, she married in 1926. For extra income, she decided to write detective stories. Beginning with *Clouds of Witness* (1926), she related the adventures of her hero Lord Peter Wimsey in various, accurately observed milieus such as advertising in *Murder Must Advertise* (1933) and bell-ringing in *The Nine Tailors* (1934). Another character was independent Harriet Vane. In later life, Sayers became a leading Christian apologist in her plays, radio broadcasts, and essays.

BIBLIOGRAPHY
Brabazon, James. *Dorothy L. Sayers: A Biography*. New York: Scribner's, 1981. 0-684-16864-2, 308p. This biography of Sayers, using available material on her life, adds two unpublished, autobiographical fragments about her childhood to suggest that Sayers avoided reality in her detective writing, wanting to be remembered for her translations and intellectual pursuits.
Brunsdale, Mitzi. *Dorothy L. Sayers: Solving the Mystery of Wickedness*. Dover, NH: Berg, 1990. 0-85496-249-2 256p. In this accessible biography, Brunsdale shows Sayers in the context of her times as a worker who created ad campaigns, articles, speeches, and books that supported herself, her son, her husband, and her husband's former wife.
Dale, Alzina S. *Maker and Craftsman: The Story of Dorothy L. Sayers*. 1978. Wheaton, IL: Harold Shaw, 1992. Paper, 0-87788-523-0, 172p. Dale's undocumented biography explains Sayer's social background and says her novels are autobiographical.
Hone, Ralph E. *Dorothy L. Sayers: A Literary Biography*. Kent, OH: Kent State University Press, 1979. 0-87338-228-5, 217p. In this straightforward biography, Hone uses Sayers' published writings, unpublished letters to both friends and foes, fragments of newspaper columns, and reviews of her work in an attempt to reveal her life.
Reynolds, Barbara. *Dorothy L. Sayers: Her Life and Soul*. New York: St. Martin's, 1993. 0-312-09787-5, 416p. Reynolds, a friend of Sayers, uses letters, conversations, and passages from Sayers' work in her recommended biography with photographs, showing Sayers as a leading theorist in her early career and a religious writer in the latter half.

SCHIAPARELLI, ELSA (1890–1973)

Couturier   Italy

Elsa Schiaparelli was a fashion designer known for her integration of shocking pink and other colors in her clothes made from traditional fabrics. Born in

Rome to a professor of Oriental languages, she studied philosophy before going to the United States after World War I to become a translator and film
scriptwriter. After the failure of a marriage, she took her daughter to Paris in
1920, where she started producing her clothes in a Left Bank hotel room. She
designed and wore a black sweater knitted with a white bow, which a store in
the United States ordered, thereby starting her business in 1929. Her designs
were inventive and sensational, and she used color, especially shocking pink, in
an original way. She was the first designer to use padded shoulders in 1931,
and she also featured zippers, buttons, and outrageous hats. She returned to
the United States in 1939 and opened a salon in 1949 before she retired in
1954.

BIBLIOGRAPHY
White, Palmer. *Elsa Schiaparelli: Empress of Paris Fashion.* 1986. London: Au-
    rum, 1996. Paper, 1-85410-358-X, 224p. Photographs of Schiaparelli's
    clothes and background information about her life, risk in business, and
    subsequent success reveal fashion trends before World War II.

SCHREINER, OLIVE (1855–1920)
Writer and Activist   **South Africa**

Olive Schreiner was a theorist, novelist, and political analyst. She was born in
Wittebergen, South Africa, on March 24, 1855, as the sixth of twelve children,
to a German Methodist minister and his English wife. She was largely self-
educated, with a love of nature and meditations that turned her into a freethinker. She had wanted to become a doctor, but her lack of education prevented such study, and at fifteen, she became a governess. She began writing
her novel *The Story of an African Farm*, but when she could find no publisher,
she went to England in 1881. After loneliness and poverty, she met George
Meredith, who helped her revise and publish the novel in 1883 under the pseudonym of Ralph Iron. It was the first sustained, imaginative work in English to
come from Africa. She returned to South Africa in 1889, where she and her
husband supported woman's rights and the Boer cause. She returned to England in 1913 and became an active pacifist.

BIBLIOGRAPHY
Berkman, Joyce Avrech. *The Healing Imagination of Olive Schreiner: Beyond
    South African Colonialism.* Amherst: University of Massachusetts Press,
    1989. 0-8702-3676-8, 317p. Berkman based her researched, documented,
    and recommended scholarly, biography on four thousand letters through
    which she connected Schreiner to the social and cultural movements of her
    time.
Cronwright-Schreiner, Samuel. *The Life of Olive Schreiner.* 1924. New York:
    Haskell House, 1973. 0-8383-1461-9, 414p. Schreiner's husband wrote
    this biography four years after her death, and subsequent biographies have
    based their interpretation of her personality and behavior on it, although
    later feminist biographers do not think Cronwright-Schreiner understood
    her.
First, Ruth, and Ann Scott. *Olive Schreiner: A Biography.* 1980. New Bruns-
    wick, NJ: Rutgers University Press, 1990. 0-8135-1621-8, 383p. Through
    the letters and archives they used for their biography, First and Scott show
    Scheiner as a Victorian woman seeking sexual freedom by denying her sexu-

ality. They do not capture her personality, but they offer possible interpretations of her complex approach to life.

Horton, Susan R. *Difficult Women, Artful Lives: Olive Schreiner and Isak Dinesen, in and out of Africa.* Baltimore: Johns Hopkins University Press, 1995. 0-8018-5037-1, 312p. Although this scholarly look at two women has biographical elements, its major goal is to understand what influence South Africa played on the psyche of Olive Schreiner, a political activist who wanted to bring political and social changes for women and native South Africans.

Schoeman, Karel. *Only an Anguish to Live Here: Olive Schreiner and the Anglo-Boer War, 1899–1902.* Johannesburg: Thorold's Africana Books, 1992. 0-7981-3006-7, 239p. Schoeman says that Schreiner's bad health and martial law prohibitions kept Schreiner in an isolated village of a thousand people during the last half of the Boer War. This carefully researched and well-written biography gives insights about Schreiner's attitudes in the war.

SCHUMANN, CLARA (1819–1896)

Instrumentalist and Composer   **Germany**

Clara Schumann was a world-class pianist. She was born in Leipzig on September 13, 1819, to the composer Friedrich Wieck, who trained her. She began performing when she was eleven, drawing huge crowds, with people naming desserts after her and writing poems about her. She loved to tour outside Germany, wearing different white dresses every night. She composed twenty-three piano works, and she played one at almost all of her concerts until she married. Robert Schumann took lessons from her father and then married her in 1840, writing his own music with her in mind. During her marriage, people called her "Queen of the Piano," and her husband was "Clara Wieck's husband." She taught piano, organized all of her tours, practiced when her husband was out, nursed him through several mental breakdowns, had eight children in sixteen years, wrote letters, and supervised her household of three servants. Her best friend, Johannes Brahms, fourteen years younger, said that she inspired much of his music. After Robert died, she was thirty-seven. She performed full-time to support her family. In 1878, she became the principal piano teacher at the Frankfurt Conservatory, no longer performing because of arthritis in her fingers.

BIBLIOGRAPHY

Chissell, Joan. *Clara Schumann, a Dedicated Spirit: A Study of Her Life and Work.* New York: Taplinger, 1983. 0-8008-1624-2, 232p. Chissell's is a well-researched and well-written biography.

Litzmann, Berthold. *Clara Schumann; an Artist's Life, Based on Material Found in Diaries and Letters.* Trans. Grace E. Hadow. 1914. New York: Da Capo, 1979. Vol. 1, 0-8443-0016-0, 486p. Vol. 2, 0-8443-0017-9, 458p. Litzmann, who knew Schumann personally, uses her full diaries and frequent letters, along with the reminiscences of friends, in a thorough, carefully documented biography.

Macy, Sheryl. *Two Romantic Trios: A Sextet of Extraordinary Musicians.* Beaverton, OR: Allegro, 1991. 0-9627040-0-8, 250p. Macy, an avowed music lover, reconstructs conversations and scenes in dramatized passages during her discussion of two Romantic-era trios: Robert and Clara Schumann with Johannes Brahms, and Franz and Cosima Liszt with Richard Wagner.

Reich, Nancy B. *Clara Schumann, the Artist and the Woman*. Ithaca, NY: Cornell University Press, 1985. 0-8014-1748-1, 346p. Reich has thoroughly documented Schumann's story and written it as if it were a good novel, while covering her roles as concert pianist, editor and teacher, composer, wife, and mother.

Weissweiler, Eva, ed. *The Complete Correspondence of Clara and Robert Schumann*. Trans. Hildegard Fritsch and Ronald Crawford. Vol. 1. New York: Peter Lang, 1994. 0-8204-2444-7, 388p. Weissweiler has collected the letters that Robert Schumann and Clara Wieck Schumann wrote between 1832 and 1838. They document major events and valuable friends in their lives.

SCHUMANN, ELISABETH (1889–1952)
Opera Singer   Germany

Elisabeth Schumann was an operatic soprano and lieder singer. Born in Merseburg on June 3, 1889, she studied singing in Dresden, Berlin, and Hamburg before making her debut at the Hamburg Stadttheater in 1909. Richard Strauss heard her, brought her to the Vienna State Opera in 1919, and dedicated *Six Songs* to her. They came to the United States for a recital tour in 1921, and she was acclaimed as Sophie in *Der Rosenkavalier* in New York as well as England in 1924. Schumann's acting coupled with her voice made her an excellent choice for Mozart's roles of Susanna, Despina, and Zerlina. She sang and recorded the lieder of Schubert, Hugo Woof, and Schumann, as well as Strauss, with her second husband, Karl Alwin, as her pianist. She had to leave Austria in 1936, and she went to New York, becoming an American citizen in 1944. She taught and performed throughout the 1940s.

BIBLIOGRAPHY
Puritz, Gerd. *Elisabeth Schumann: A Biography*. Trans. Joy Puritz. London: Deutsch, 1993. 0-233-98794-0, 375p. Puritz combines details of Schumann's life from her memoirs and diaries with the personal views of colleagues and friends and his own as her son.

SCHWARTZKOPF, ELISABETH (1915–)
Opera Singer   Poland

Elisabeth Schwarzkopf was an operatic soprano. Born in Janotschin on December 9, 1915, the daughter of a classics professor, she studied in Berlin at the Hochschule für Musik, making her debut in 1938 at the Berlin Städtische Oper in *Parsifal*. After World War II, she sang in the Vienna State Opera, Covent Garden in London, La Scala in Milan, the Bayreuth Festival, and the Salzburg Festival. She first specialized in coloratura roles but changed to lyric soprano, especially in recitals of lieder. In 1975, she sang her farewell recital tour in the United States after making many recordings with her husband, Walter Legge, the artistic director of EMI records. She continued to give master classes after her retirement and recorded some of them for television.

BIBLIOGRAPHY
Jefferson, Alan. *Elisabeth Schwarzkopf*. Boston: Northeastern University Press, 1996. 1-55553-272-1, 285p. Jefferson's biography, the first on Schwarzkopf, relies on anecdotal information about her early opera and lieder ca-

reer, since neither she nor her friends would talk about her experiences as a Nazi during World War II.

SCOTLAND, MARGARET of. *See* MARGARET of SCOTLAND.

SCOTS, MARY, QUEEN of. *See* MARY, QUEEN of SCOTS.

SCOTT, ROSE (1847–1925)
Activist   **Australia**

Rose Scott gained renown for her feminist activism. She was born in Glendon, New South Wales, the eighth child in an immigrant family. As an adult, she lived in Sydney, where she founded the Womanhood Suffrage League in 1891 and worked with Dora Montefiore, a Marxist who went to England and became a militant suffragette, and **Vida Goldstein**. She spent over four decades in unpaid public work, primarily in law and policy reforms affecting women's and children's conditions. The themes of rape, seduction, illegitimacy, prostitution, marital violence, infanticide, abortion, and baby farming recurred throughout her papers and the over fifty letters per day that she wrote. She was a founder and associate of feminist causes for protective legislation about woman suffrage, citizen's rights, raising the age of consent, women prisoners, prostitution policies, women's wages and work conditions, and access to higher education. She would not marry, saying that her life was too short to waste admiring one man. She organized the League for Political Education, was president of it and of the Peace Society, and was a vocal pacifist during World War I.

BIBLIOGRAPHY
Allen, Judith. *Rose Scott: Vision and Revision in Feminism 1880–1925*. New York: Oxford University Press, 1994. ISBN 0-19-554846-9, 306p. Allen's scholarly biography is accessible as it discusses Scott's life and contribution to the history of feminism.

SCUDÉRY, MADELEINE de (1607–1701)
Writer   **France**

Madeleine de Scudéry was a novelist. She was born in Le Havre and became an orphan at the age of six. In 1639, she and her brother went to Paris, where Madame de Rambouillet accepted them into the society of her literary salon. She returned to Paris after living in Marseilles with her brother and started her own salon, which became associated with excessive refinement (*préciosité*). She and her brother began to collaborate on novels, their most famous being *Artamène, ou le grand Cyrus;* it took four years to write, and she wrote the last five volumes herself. After success in France, the work was translated into many languages. She continued to write essays, verses, and treatises on her own after her brother left Paris.

BIBLIOGRAPHY
Aronson, Nicole. *Mademoiselle de Scudéry*. Trans. Stuart R. Aronson. Boston: Twayne, 1978. 0-8057-6278-7, 178p. Aronson thinks that de Scudéry represents the literary evolution of the seventeenth century as one of the most knowledgeable women in French history. Keenly aware of literary changes,

she shifted style from heroic novels to the shorter *nouvelle* but kept her psychological approach.

McDougall, Dorothy. *Madeleine de Scudéry: Her Romantic Life and Death.* 1938. New York: B. Blom, 1972. No ISBN, 321p. McDougall's thorough biography of Mademoiselle de Scudéry discusses her life and the times in which she lived. Although it is loosely written, it is more accessible than Aronson's.

SEACOLE, MARY (1805–1881)

Nurse and Businesswoman   Jamaica

Mary Jane Seacole was a nurse and businesswoman. She was born in Kingston, Jamaica, the daughter of a free black woman and a Scottish army officer, with her education being the Creole medical arts and hotel-keeping, which her mother taught her. She married and traveled to England with her husband, but after his death, she established hotels in Kingston and in the New Granada (now Columbia and Panama) areas of Cruces, Gorgona, and Escribanos. With expertise gained from two cholera epidemics, she became an effective nurse. The British rebuffed her offer to go to the Crimea, possibly because of her color, but she paid her own way and set up the British Hotel in Balaclava, a center for both officers and soldiers, although she banned drinking and gambling. "Mother" or "Aunty" Seacole helped ease the pains of the soldiers on the battlefield. After the war ended, London newspapers told her story, and people gave money to pay her debts. She spent the rest of her life in either London or Jamaica.

BIBLIOGRAPHY

Seacole, Mary. *Wonderful Adventures of Mrs. Seacole in Many Lands.* New York: Oxford University Press, 1988. 0-19-505249-8; paper, 0-19-506672-3, 256p. Seacole tells about her life as a freeborn Jamaican who traveled and helped people by offering them rest in hotels and aid when wounded or ill.

SENESH, HANNAH (1921–1944)

Revolutionary   Hungary

Hannah Senesh sacrificed her life in the Jewish Resistance during World War II. She was born in Hungary on July 17, 1921, and as a teen, she opposed the rise of European fascism. She went to Israel at the beginning of the war, but when she heard of the plight of the Jews still under Hitler, she joined a commando unit that organized to bring Jews out of the occupied territories. She parachuted into Yugoslavia in 1944 in an attempt to help Hungarian Jews. When she reached the country, she was captured and tortured before her execution.

BIBLIOGRAPHY

Hay, Peter. *Ordinary Heroes: The Life and Death of Chana Szenes, Israel's National Heroine.* 1986. New York: Paragon House, 1989. Paper, 1557782768, 271p. Written by a Hungarian, this well-researched but undocumented biography of Szenes [sic] is a thorough look at the ordeal that she probably endured in her attempt to free Jewish citizens after she left Hungary for Israel.

Ransom, Candice F. *So Young to Die: The Story of Hannah Senesh.* New York: Scholastic, 1993. Paper, 0-685-65620-9, 152p. This biography for young adults recounts Senesh's life and her strong commitment to her ideals, based on her diary, which she started at thirteen.

Schur, Maxine. *Hannah Szenes: A Song of Light*. Philadelphia: Jewish Publication Society, 1985. 0-8276-0251-0, 104p. In a well-written biography for young adults, Schur gives a clear picture of Szenes' [*sic*] middle-class Hungarian life before her commitment to Zionism led her to Israel.

Senesh, Hannah. *Hannah Senesh, Her Life and Diary*. Intro. Abba Eban. New York: Schocken, 1972. No ISBN, 257p. Senesh's diary and some of her poems display her strong commitment to the Jewish resistance before her early death.

SÉVIGNÉ, MARIE de (1626–1696)
Writer   France

Madame de Sévigné was a letter writer whose insights expose the manners and daily life during the reign of Louis XIV. Marie de Rabutin-Chantal was born in the Place Royale, Paris, on February 5, 1626, with her grandmother the religious leader **Jeanne de Chantal**. Her father died the next year, and when she was six, her mother died. Her uncle, Christophe de Coulanges, took her to Brittany, where tutors introduced her to Latin, Italian, and Spanish literature. Her arranged marriage to the marquis de Sévigné lasted until his death in a duel seven years later. She had two children, and the three continued to live in Paris. Over fifteen hundred of her letters, most of them to her daughter, survive. Since she never considered herself an author, she expressed no theory of writing and composed no works in the literary genres popular in her lifetime. But Voltaire recommended her letters to an English friend as one of the best views available of French history.

BIBLIOGRAPHY
Boissier, Gaston. *Madame de Sévigné*. Trans. Henry Llewellyn Williams. 1887. Freeport, NY: Books for Libraries, 1972. 0-8369-6794-1, 154p. This scholarly biography, well researched and carefully documented, examines de Sévigné's letters.

Farrell, Michèle Longino. *Performing Motherhood: The Sévigné Correspondence*. Hanover, NH: University Press of New England, 1991. 0-87451-536-X, 302p. Farrell examines Madame de Sévigné's correspondence through feminist eyes in this carefully researched and documented biography. She thinks that de Sévigné's writing seemed maternal in a patriarchal society and, therefore, unthreatening to the male domain.

Mossiker, Frances. *Madame de Sévigné: A Life and Letters*. New York: Knopf, 1983. 0-394-41472-1, 538p. Mossiker uses her own translations of de Sévigné's letters in a recommended account to display de Sévigné's intelligent and humorous personality.

Ojala, Jeanne A., and William T. Ojala. *Madame de Sévigné: A Seventeenth-Century Life*. Herndon, VA: Berg, 1990. 0-85496-169-0, 221p. This biography, using de Sévigné's letters, is an introduction to Madame de Sévigné and her place in seventeenth-century France.

Williams, Charles G. S. *Madame de Sévigné*. Boston: Twayne, 1981. 0-8057-6438-0, 167p. Williams sees a rich repository of historical fragments in de Sévigné's letters, and along with others, he thinks that she would have been a great novelist had she lived in another age.

SEWELL, ANNA (1820–1878)
Writer   England

Anna Sewell was a novelist who created the famous story of Black Beauty. She was born on March 30, 1820, in Great Yarmouth, Norfolk, into a devout Quaker family and educated at a local day school. At fourteen, she fell and injured her ankles, which left her a semi-invalid, dependent on horses for mobility. With her mother, a writer, she started a Temperance Society, a library, and mothers' meetings. She taught reading, writing, and natural history at an evening institute for workingmen. Sewell may have originally intended *Black Beauty* (1877), written in her fifties, for men working with horses because of the careful directions on stabling horses, feeding them, and treating them for common ailments. She sold the story for twenty pounds, never to know of its success as one of the top ten best-sellers in the English language and as a film.

BIBLIOGRAPHY
Chitty, Susan, Lady. *The Woman Who Wrote Black Beauty: A Life of Anna Sewell*. London: Hodder and Stoughton, 1971. 0-340-12919-0, 256p. Chitty investigated Sewell's life to find out more about the woman who wrote a book that continues to attract readers more than one hundred years after she wrote it. Chitty speculates that Sewell wanted more humane treatment for animals.

SEYMOUR, LYNN (1939–)
Ballerina   Canada

Lynn Seymour has become a renowned ballerina and choreographer. She was born in Springbett, Alberta, on March 8, 1939, where her father was a dentist. She trained in Vancouver before spending two years at England's Royal Ballet School and making her debut in 1956 with the Sadler's Wells branch of the company. She is best known for her passionate interpretations of the choreography of Kenneth MacMillan and Frederick Ashton. She became the artistic director of the Bavarian State Opera from 1978 to 1981, but after that, she danced as a mature ballerina and choreographed several pieces, such as *Rashomon* (1976) and *Wolfi* (1987). She became a Dame Commander of the British Empire in 1979.

BIBLIOGRAPHY
Austin, Richard. *Lynn Seymour: An Authorised Biography*. London: Angus and Robertson, 1980. 0-207-95900-5, 224p. Austin uses letters written over fifteen years, press cuttings, photographs, and personal reminiscences in his balanced, readable biography of Seymour, enhanced with photographs from her performances.
Crickmay, Anthony, and Clement Crisp. *Lynn Seymour: A Photographic Study*. London: Studio Vista, 1980. 0-289-70953-9, 121p. The text is a short discussion of Seymour's ballet career, with many photographs of her alone and with several of her partners in a variety of roles.
Seymour, Lynn, and Paul Gardner. *Lynn, the Autobiography of Lynn Seymour*. New York: Granada, 1984. 0-246-11790-7, 358p. In this memoir, Seymour recounts her life and career. Among anecdotes, she identifies Rudolph Nureyev as the one person who helped her find balance in her life and the psychological stability to continue dancing.

SHAFIK, DORI'A (1910–1975)

Activist   Egypt

Dori'a Shafik was a feminist and political activist. Born as the third child, second daughter, on December 14, 1910, into a traditional middle-class family in Tanta and Mansura, she determined to finish her education. She attended the Sorbonne, where she obtained a doctorate before returning to Egypt to lead the feminist movement. She founded the Daughters of the Nile (Bint-E-Nil) for women to join together in their campaign to vote; five years after fifteen hundred women marched on the Egyptian Parliament, they got it. She also supported nationalists against the British during the Suez crisis. Since she was openly hostile to President Nasser, she had to stay secluded in Cairo after 1957 for her protection and that of her lawyer husband and daughters. She died after falling from the sixth floor of her apartment building.

BIBLIOGRAPHY
Nelson, Cynthia. *Doria Shafik, Egyptian Feminist: A Woman Apart.* Gainesville: University Press of Florida Press, 1996. 0-8130-1455-7, 322p. Nelson relies on Shafik's poetic and unedited memoirs to detail Shafik's struggle against the cultural, religious, and political conservative forces that denied women their individuality.

SHA'RAWI, HUDA (1879–1947)

Activist   Egypt

Huda Sha'rawi created schools for women, formed the first women's association, and represented Egyptian women abroad. She was born into the family of a wealthy and respected provincial administrator from upper Egypt in Minia and a Circassian mother. She was educated at home, where she learned Turkish and French, languages of the elite. Married unwillingly at thirteen to a much older cousin, she left him for seven years during which she began to notice the constraints among women. In 1923, she unveiled herself in a Cairo railway station to declare herself no longer part of a harem. She taught herself Arabic and created a liberal arts school for girls. She led women in demonstrations against the ruling British, established the Women's Union, and founded a journal, *Egyptian Women*, in which she published the goals of the union. She helped start the first secondary school for women and supported coeducational university classes. During the years betwen the world wars, she attended international women's conferences. In 1944, she helped with the All Arab Federation of Women, and the next year, spoke against atomic weapons.

BIBLIOGRAPHY
Sha'rawi, Huda. *Harem Years: The Memoirs of an Egyptian Feminist (1879–1924).* Trans. Margot Badran. New York: Feminist Press, 1987. 0-935312-71-4, 158p. Sha'rawi's autobiography is an intriguing look inside a culture that Western eyes rarely see.

SHEEHY-SKEFFINGTON, HANNAH (1877–1946)

Revolutionary   Ireland

Hannah Sheehy-Skeffington was a patriot and feminist. As the eldest of a member of Parliament for South Meath's six children, she was born on May 24, 1877, in Kenturk, County Cork. She received her education in Dublin, with a master's degree from the National University of Ireland. After teaching and helping found the Irish Association of Women Graduates, she married a radical, and they identified themselves as Sheehy-Skeffington. In 1908, she and Constance Markiewicz founded the militant Irish Women's Franchise League, and two years later, participated in the London suffrage marches. She protested the Home Rule Bill's exclusion of women and lost her lectureship in German at the Rathmines School of Commerce when chairwoman of the Irish Franchise League. In 1916, the British arrested her husband and executed him the next day, without a trial, for seeing one of them kill an unarmed boy. She never forgave them and petitioned President Wilson to intervene in Ireland. Advocate of socialism, Republicanism, and individual rights, constantly challenging the state and authority, she was tolerant of others when their beliefs did not infringe on others' rights. She also traveled throughout the United States to raise funds for the Irish Resistance Army.

BIBLIOGRAPHY

Levenson, Leah. *With Wooden Sword: A Portrait of Francis Sheehy-Skeffington, Militant Pacifist.* Boston: Northeastern University Press, 1983. 0-930350-42-1, 270p. Levenson's scholarly biography of Sheehy-Skeffington documents her political rebellion against the government's economic and political order, the British Empire, the Catholic Church, and capitalism.

Levenson, Leah, and Jerry H. Natterstad. *Hanna Sheehy-Skeffington, Irish Feminist.* Syracuse, NY: Syracuse University Press, 1986. 0-8156-0199-9, 227p. Of utmost importance to Sheehy-Skeffington were equality and freedom for all humans, and this biography documents her position as an intellectual and nationalist in a Catholic country.

Luddy, Maria. *Hanna Sheehy Skeffington.* Dublin: Dundalgan, 1995. 0-85221-126-0, 63p. Luddy concentrates on Sheehy-Skeffington's work against injustice after her husband's death and for the equality of women through World War II in a brief, well-documented introduction.

SHELLEY, MARY (1797–1851)

Writer   England

Mary Shelley was a novelist. She was born Mary Wollstonecraft Godwin, the daughter of William Godwin and **Mary Wollstonecraft,** on August 30, 1797. Her mother died at her birth, and she lived with a jealous stepmother who refused her formal education. She read widely, with her father's rational philosophy influencing her thought. In 1814, she eloped with Percy Bysshe Shelley to the Continent and, although disowned by her father, married him two years after Shelley's wife committed suicide. While traveling with Lord Byron and her husband in the Alps, Shelley took Byron's suggestion to write a ghost story. It became her most famous novel, *Frankenstein, or the Modern Prometheus.* Her first three children died young, and in 1822, her husband drowned. She returned to England and wrote travel books, journals, and other novels to support her fourth child, Percy. After their circumstances improved, she began to edit Shelley's poems but did not finish before her death.

BIBLIOGRAPHY

Dunn, Jane. *Moon in Eclipse: A Life of Mary Shelley.* New York: St. Martin's, 1978. 0-312-54692-0, 374p. In a straightforward biography, Dunn communicates that Shelley was brave, generous, imaginative, affectionate, and studious but also moody, distrustful, morbid, and demanding with her friends.

Gerson, Noel Bertram. *Daughter of Earth and Water; a Biography of Mary Wollstonecraft Shelley*. New York: William Morrow, 1973. No ISBN, 280p. The biography is a chronological account of Shelley's life and her marriage to Percy.

Leighton, Margaret. *Shelley's Mary; a Life of Mary Godwin Shelley*. New York: Farrar, Straus, and Giroux, 1973. 0-374-36779-5, 234p. In an accessible biography, Leighton examines Shelley's life, often unhappy, and the rebels, artists, misfits, and adventurers whom she knew.

Sunstein, Emily W. *Mary Shelley: Romance and Reality*. Boston: Little, Brown, 1989. 0-316-82246-9, 478p. Using letters and writings from Shelley's family, parents William Godwin and Mary Wollstonecraft, and husband Percy Bysshe Shelley, Sunstein pieces together Shelley's life in a definitive and recommended biography.

SHEPPARD, KATE (1848–1934)

Activist   England

Kate Sheppard was a feminist activist. Born Catherine Wilson Malcolm in Liverpool, Merseyside, on March 10, 1848, she emigrated to New Zealand in 1869, where she married a businessman. As a feminist, she decided to begin cycling and wearing clothes previously deemed unacceptable. Then she espoused equal status in marriage. She possessed a strong sense of social responsibility, allied to the belief that women should be entitled to participate fully in political affairs. In 1887 she became an officer of the Women's Christian Temperance Union, and from that position led a nationwide struggle for the enfranchisement of women. She wrote, organized lectures, and circulated petitions so that in 1893, New Zealand became the first country in the world to give women the vote. She then became the first president of the National Council of Women, aiming to place women in Parliament, and in 1909, she was named an honorary vice president of the International Council of Women. At her death, she left no direct descendants, her only son and grandchild having previously died.

BIBLIOGRAPHY

Devaliant, Judith. *Kate Sheppard: The Fight for Women's Votes in New Zealand*. New York: Penguin, 1992. 0-140-17614-4, 242p. Since Sheppard left no personal diaries and only a few personal letters, Devaliant uses her speeches and information from her second husband's descendants to show her struggle to win parliamentary franchise for women in New Zealand during the 1890s. This scholarly biography is well documented.

SHERIDAN, CLARE (1885–1970)

Sculptor and Writer   Ireland

Clare Sheridan was a sculptor, traveler, and writer. She was born Clare Consuelo Frewen on September 9, 1885, to an Irish father and an American mother who was a cousin of Sir Winston Churchill. After her education in Sussex, County Cork, Paris, and Germany and her society marriage to a landed aristocrat in 1910, people expected her to join society. But after her second daughter' death, she became a self-taught portrait sculptor and turned professional when her husband died in 1915. She visited Moscow after an invitation from the Soviet Trade Delegation in 1920, and society ostracized her when she returned to London, so she went to the United States and wrote about the experience in *Russian Diaries* (1921). She became a journalist for *New York World* and traveled to such places as Mexico, Ireland, and Smyrna before moving to Constantinople and then Algeria. Among the people she either interviewed or sculpted were Zinoviev, Kamenev, Lenin, Trotsky, Atatürk, Gandhi, and Lifar. After World War II, she settled in Galway and became a Roman Catholic, limiting herself to religious subjects.

BIBLIOGRAPHY
Leslie, Anita. *Clare Sheridan.* Garden City, NY: Doubleday, 1977. 0-385-06745-3, 318p. Leslie takes her account of Sheridan from family sources and her own memories of her aunt.

SHIKIBU, MURASAKI (973?–1025?)
Writer   Japan

Murasaki wrote the earliest extant long novel, *The Tale of the Genji*, often called the finest work in Japanese literature and one of the great books in the world. Although Murasaki lived in an era when educated women were scorned, her father allowed her to study with her brother. She did conceal her ability to read and write in Chinese, two tasks considered impossible for women to master. She married and had a daughter but became a widow after two years. As she wondered what her fate would be, she made notes for a novel. Her father arranged for her to become a lady-in-waiting for the teenage empress Shoshi; this position allowed her much time to continue writing. Shoshi found out that Murasaki knew Chinese, and in exchange for her teaching, she gave Murasaki paper (very rare), ink, and brushes. Murasaki refused to join in the court poetry contests, preferring to live quietly and behind the scenes. She even considered becoming a Buddhist nun. In *The Tale of Genji*, she depicted human emotions and changes in nature in ways that had not been seen before but that became very influential.

BIBLIOGRAPHY
Hisamatsu, Sen'ichi, et al. *Murasaki Shikibu; the Greatest Lady Writer in Japanese Literature.* Tokyo: Japanese National Commission for UNESCO, 1970. No ISBN, 424p. This work is scholarly, well documented, and researched, and, although it attempts to present her life and work, it cannot be a traditional biography because of the paucity of material available about women during the time that Shikibu lived.
Shikibu, Murasaki. *The Diary of Lady Murasaki.* Trans. Richard Bowring. New York: Penguin, 1996. Paper, 0-14-043576-X, 91p. The diary covers the years 1008-1009 when Lady Muraski served in the imperial household of Japan. It is the last of the female diaries in the Neian era to be translated and shows life in the Japanese court, plans of the Tsuchimikado mansion, and notes on dating, clothing, and court titles.

SIBLEY, ANTOINETTE (1939–)
Ballerina   England

Dame Antoinette Sibley has been a principal ballerina with the Royal Ballet in London. She was born in Bromley, Kent, on February 27, 1939, daughter of

Edward and Winifred Smith. Sibley trained with the Royal Ballet and appeared as a soloist for the first time in 1956 when, due to the star's illness, she stepped into the main role of *Swan Lake.* The performance brought her immediate fame. Her partnership with Anthony Dowell was one of complete compatibility, leading them to be dubbed "the Golden Pair." A dancer of great sensuality and beauty, her roles in Frederick Ashton's *The Dream* and Kenneth MacMillan's *Manon* are among her most celebrated. A knee injury forced her to early retirement in 1976. Ashton persuaded her to dance again five years later, and she did so to great acclaim. She was awarded Dame Commander of the British Empire for her achievement.

BIBLIOGRAPHY

Clarke, Mary. *Antoinette Sibley.* Photos, Leslie Spatt. London: Dance Books, 1981. 0-903102-64-1, 128p. This collection of photographs showing Sibley in a variety of roles contains almost no text.

Crickmay, Anthony, and Dale Harris. *Antoinette Sibley.* Brooklyn, NY: Dance Horizons, 1976. 0-8712-7089-7, 19p. This brief biography uses more photographs than text to describe Sibley's career and her ballet partners.

Dromgoole, Nicholas. *Sibley and Dowell.* Photos, Leslie Spatt. London: Collins, 1976. 0-00-211-047-4, 223p. A combination of interviews and photographs gives a personable account of Sibley's life and her career dancing with Anthony Dowell.

Newman, Barbara. *Antoinette Sibley: Reflections of a Ballerina.* London: Hutchinson, 1986. 0-09-164000-8, 220p. Newman's readable and researched biography of Sibley's life, with photographs, is a straightforward account of her development as a ballerina.

SIDDONS, SARAH (1775–1831)

Actor   England

Sarah Siddons was an actor. Born in Brecon, Powys, on July 5, 1775, as the eldest of Roger Kemble's twelve children, she became a member of her father's theater company at eighteen. She acted with William Siddons, whom she married in 1773 against her parents' wishes. She had success in the provinces but failed in London. She returned to the provinces for more experience, and in 1782, triumphed at Drury Lane in David Garrick's *The Fatal Marriage.* She became the unquestioned queen of the stage, unmatched as a tragic actor and hailed by all critics. Of her Lady Macbeth, Hazlitt said he could "smell the blood." She disliked publicity, worked hard, and was a shrewd businesswoman until her retirement in 1812. While performing, she bore seven children, with two daughters dying as infants.

BIBLIOGRAPHY

Campbell, Thomas. *Life of Mrs. Siddons.* 1839. New York: B. Blom, 1972. No ISBN, 378p. This researched, straightforward biography of Siddons is stylistically dated.

Ffrench, Yvonne. *Six Great Englishwomen: Queen Elizabeth I, Sarah Siddons, Charlotte Brontë, Florence Nightingale, Queen Victoria, Gertrude Bell.* Folcroft, PA: Folcroft Library Editions, 1976. 0841442193, 246 p. In her collective biography, Ffrench identifies Siddons as a woman who had largeness of spirit, strength of character, and courage.

Jonson, Marian. *A Troubled Grandeur: The Story of England's Great Actress, Sarah Siddons.* Boston: Little, Brown, 1972. No ISBN, 238p. For this biography, written like a novel and appropriate for young adults, Jonson uses only verifiable quotes from diaries and letters in dialogue. She consulted letters, play reviews, diaries, and reminiscences about Siddons.

Manvell, Roger. *Sarah Siddons: Portrait of an Actress*. New York: Putnam, 1971. No ISBN, 385p. Manvell's biography scrutinizes Siddon against a backdrop of her times and its expectations, with letters and documents as sources revealing an intelligent and emotional woman.

Parsons, Florence Mary. *The Incomparable Siddons*. 1909. New York: B. Blom, 1969. No ISBN, 298p. Parsons tries to find the genius who was Mrs. Siddons by summarizing her style, ideals, and methods, based on research.

SIENA, CATHERINE of. *See* CATHERINE of SIENA.

SIGNORET, SIMONE (1921–1985)

Actor   France

Simone Signoret was a successful actor. Born Simon-Henriette Charlotte Kaminker on March 25, 1921, in Wiesbaden, Germany, her French parents raised her in Paris. She left her job as a typist to become a film extra in *Le Prince Charmant* (1942) and soon graduated to leading roles. Frequently cast as a prostitute or courtesan, her warmth and sensuality found international favor in such films as *La Ronde* (1950), *Casque d'Or* (1952), and *Les Diaboliques* (1954). She won British and American Academy Awards for *Room at the Top* (1959) and gained further distinction for *Ship of Fools* (1965). She married actor Yves Montand in 1951, and she matured into one of France's most distinguished character actors, not being afraid of looking old, in films such as *Le Chat* (1971) and *Madame Rosa* (1977). Later, she wrote her autobiography and a novel.

BIBLIOGRAPHY

David, Catherine. *Simone Signoret*. Trans. Sally Sampson. Woodstock, NY: Overlook, 1993. 0-87951-491-4, 213 p. David's documented, popular biography re-creates Signoret as "Simone," the name that France had for her, in a balanced account.

Signoret, Simone. *Nostalgia Isn't What It Used to Be*. New York: Penguin, 1979. 0-14-005181-3, 464p. In this autobiography, Signoret uses a selection of anecdotes to discuss her life from her leftist political activities, to her favorite film experiences.

SITWELL, EDITH (1887–1964)

Writer and Poet   England

Dame Edith Sitwell was a poet. She was born on September 7, 1887, in Scarborough, North Yorkshire, daughter of the eccentric Sir George Sitwell. She spent a lonely childhood but discovered the French symbolists and Algernon Swinburne when she was seventeen. She contributed her poems to the *Daily Mirror*, and in 1915, began production of an annual anthology of new poetry, *Wheels*, which she continued for six years. She and her brothers Osbert and Sacheverell Sitwell became well known in London during the 1920s, and she gained fame with her musical collection *Façade* (1923), which William Walton set to music. Her poetry is notable for its technical dexterity, especially in the use of dance rhythms, and its ability to communicate sensation and emotion.

She also liked to attract attention with her odd costumes and jewelry, and, even though a critic, she was generous to other poets and artists. Sitwell received many honorary degrees and was created Dame of the British Empire in 1954. She became a Catholic in 1955, after which her works reflect a deeper religious symbolism.

BIBLIOGRAPHY

Elborn, Geoffrey. *Edith Sitwell, a Biography*. Garden City, NY: Doubleday, 1981. 0-385-13467-3, 322p. Elborn uses letters and his insights as a family friend in his straightforward biography of Sitwell.

Glendinning, Victoria. *Edith Sitwell, a Unicorn among Lions*. New York: Knopf, 1981. 0-394-50439-9, 393p. Glendinning's recommended biography, based on pieces of information about book sales, friendships, reviews and Sitwell's reaction to them, and fashion in poetry, demonstrates that Sitwell, both petty and kind, intensely cared about poetry. James Tait Black Memorial Prize and Duff Cooper Memorial Prize.

Lehmann, John. *A Nest of Tigers; the Sitwells in Their Times*. Boston: Little, Brown, 1968. No ISBN, 294p. Lehmann uses selections from the Sitwells' published works and commentary from their acquaintances to reveal their lives.

Salter, Elizabeth. *Edith Sitwell*. London: Oresko, 1979. 0-905368-50, 103p. Salter, Dame Edith's secretary from 1957 until her death, presents an intriguing, brief, pictorial biography with photographs and reproductions of paintings to capture the theatrical and eccentric Dame Edith rather than Edith Sitwell the poet.

SLESSOR, MARY (1848–1915)
Missionary   Scotland

Mary Slessor was a Presbyterian missionary who served in Nigeria. Born in Aberdeen, Grampian, on December 2, 1848, her father was a shoemaker, and she was the second of seven children. Slessor's mother, from a refined home, had wanted to be a missionary in Calabar before her marriage. Slessor worked as a mill girl in Dundee from childhood and spent her leisure time helping the church or pretending to be a schoolteacher for black children. The United Presbyterian Church accepted her as a missionary for teaching in Calabar (now Biafra), Nigeria, in 1876. Wanting to work with those who needed her the most, she chose the people of Okoyong first and then the slave-dealing Aros clan of the Ibo at Enyong Creek. She wanted to rid the tribes of abuses such as the murder of twins, human sacrifice, and drinking, while encouraging trade and the power of prayer. The natives called her "Great Mother," and the government gave her the powers of a magistrate. Mary Kingsley visited her and later wrote about her wonderful day. Before her death, Slessor expressed her concern about how much more work needed to be done where she had spent her life.

BIBLIOGRAPHY

Christian, Carol, and Gladys Plummer. *God and One Redhead: Mary Slessor of Calabar*. Grand Rapids, MI: Zondervan, 1971. No ISBN, 190p. The authors call Slessor "half saint, half hoyden" and use Livingstone's biography and articles about her in missionary magazines as a basis for their discussion.

Enock, Esther Ethelind. *The Missionary Heroine of Calabar, a Story of Mary Slessor*. London: Pickering and Inglis, 1973. 0-7208-0247-4, 96p. Enock's brief story about Slessor comes from Livingstone's autobiography and is a suitable, undocumented introduction for young adults.

Livingstone, W. P. *Mary Slessor of Calabar*. Grand Rapids, MI: Zondervan, 1984. 0-310-27451-6, 364p. Livingstone pieced together Slessor's story from her letters tracing her life as a Scottish factory girl and as a missionary first in Okoyong and then in Enyong Creek in a revealing and recommended biography.

Miller, Basil. *Mary Slessor*. Minneapolis: Bethany House, 1985. 0-87123-849-7, 144p. In this biography, Miller tells of Slessor and her intense faith in God, giving her courage to become a missionary in Africa.

Robinson, Virgil E. *Mighty Mary; the Story of Mary Slessor*. Washington, DC: Review and Herald, 1972. No ISBN, 127p. This fictional biography, based on Slessor's life, is a viable introduction to her achievements based on the research of other biographers.

SMITH, CHARLOTTE (1749–1806)
Poet and Writer   **England**

Charlotte Smith was a poet and novelist. Born Charlotte Turner on May 4, 1749, she was the eldest daughter of a wealthy country gentlemen with family connections. Her father introduced her to music and art and London society when she was twelve. Her aunt, however, disturbed at her conduct since her mother was dead, arranged an early marriage for her when she was fifteen to a man of twenty-one. For the first fifteen years of her marriage, she was either pregnant or recovering from childbirth, with four of her ten children dying before her. Her husband got into debt, and they had to reside in a debtor's prison before fleeing to Normandy. After returning to England, she translated *Manon Lescaut* but, fearful of its morality, withdrew it, but it was published without her name. Her poetry collections showed her genuine passion for nature, sympathy for the common man and woman, and social concerns. Her later novels were also on the cutting edge of the Romantic movement because they reflected the ideals of British liberals, contemporary Republican views on British reform movement issues, criticism of how the wealthy and powerful could abuse the law, and the powerlessness of women in the late eighteenth-century patriarchal society.

BIBLIOGRAPHY
Fry, Carroll Lee. *Charlotte Smith*. New York: Twayne, 1996. 0-8057-7046-1, 170p. Fry, in a scholarly but accessible view, notes that Smith was one of best-known writers of her day but lost ground in the early nineteenth century, possibly because her radical views were no longer palatable to a conservative, middle-class audience.

SMITH, STEVIE (1902–1971)
Poet   **England**

Stevie Smith was a poet and novelist. Florence Margaret Smith was born in Hull, Humberside, on September 20, 1902, but after her father deserted the family, moved to London where she attended Palmers Green and North London Collegiate School. She lived with her aunt after her mother's death and began to work in publishing. She then started to write herself, and in 1935, had her first collection of poems rejected. She wrote instead *Novel on Yellow Paper* (1936), a largely autobiographical monologue in a humorous, conversational style. Her first book of published poetry, *A Good Time Was Had by All*, helped her gradually acquired a reputation as a poet whose individuality combined wit with bitter irony. Her most famous collection is *Not Waving but Drowning* (1957). In the 1960s, Smith began reading her poetry, attending poetry festivals, and recording radio and television broadcasts. In 1969, she won the Queen's Gold Medal for Poetry.

BIBLIOGRAPHY

Barbera, Jack, and William McBrien. *Stevie, a Biography of Stevie Smith*. New York: Oxford University Press, 1987. 0-19-520549-9, 378p. In this chatty, recommended biography, the authors conclude that Smith's humor and eccentricity had roots in her mother's delicate health, her own tuberculosis, and her forced transition from wealth to impoverished gentility.

Spalding, Frances. *Stevie Smith: A Critical Biography*. New York: Norton, 1989. 0-393-02672-8, 331p. Spalding discusses Smith's life and focuses on its relationship to her work, especially her fascination with death.

SMYTH, ETHEL (1858–1944)

Composer   England

Dame Ethel Smyth was a composer and suffragette. Smyth was born in London on April 23, 1858, into a military family that tried to deter her from music. She went to Leipzig to study at the conservatory, however, and there Clara Schumann, Brahms, and Joachim encouraged her. She made her debut as a composer in England in 1890, but not until three years later with her *Mass in D* at Albert Hall did England recognize her as its first significant woman composer. Since Germans liked opera, she arranged to debut her first three operas there. After difficulties of being recognized by the English, she began supporting the suffrage movement, composing *March of the Women* (1911), which women sang throughout London. She also wrote orchestral and concerto works, although she became deaf in later life. As a writer, she published a two-volume autobiography, *Impressions That Remained* (1919), and eight other books. Among her friends were the empress Eugénie and **Virginia Woolf**. Durham University honored her with a doctorate in music, and she was made a Dame of the British Empire in 1922.

BIBLIOGRAPHY

Collis, Louise. *Impetuous Heart: The Story of Ethel Smyth*. London: W. Kimber, 1984. 0-7183-0543-4, 219p. Collis emphasizes Smyth's personal life and relationships, with limited analysis of her music.

Smyth, Ethel. *Impressions That Remained: Memoirs*. Intro. Ernest Newman and Ronald Crichton. New York: Da Capo, 1981. 0-306-76107-6, 566p. Smyth, composer, writer, feminist, and polemicist, recounts her life and the composers she knew, including **Clara Schumann**, Johannes Brahms, Edvard Grieg, and Petyor Tchaikovsky, and the times in which she lived.

Smyth, Ethel. *The Memoirs of Ethel Smyth*. Intro. Ronald Crichton. New York: Viking, 1987. 0-670-80655-2, 392p. These accessible memoirs recount not only Smyth's life and her friendships, including friendship with the empress Eugénie, but also the turbulence of the times in which she lived until 1925.

SÖDERGRAN, EDITH (1892–1923)

Poet   Sweden

Edith Södergran was a Finnish poet who wrote in Swedish as part of the Swedish-speaking minority. She was born in St. Petersburg, Russia, on April 4, 1892, and then her family moved to Karelia (Finland). But she returned to St. Petersburg, where she studied in a German school. Her first book of expressionist poems, *Dikter* (1916), inaugurated the Swedish–Finnish modernist movement. Her later verse included *Septemberlyran* (1918), *Rosenaltaret* (1919), and *Framtidens skugga* (1920). She lived in total isolation in a house on the Karelian Isthmus, which was on Soviet territory, after the revolution. Her best-known work is *Landet som icke är* (The Nonexistent Country), published posthumously in 1925.

BIBLIOGRAPHY

Broomans, Petra, Adriaan van der Hoeven, and Jytte Kronig, eds. *Edith Södergran, a Changing Image: Looking for a New Perspective on the Work of the Finnish Avant-Garde Poet*. Groningen, The Netherlands: RUG, Werkgroep Vrouwenstudies Letteren, 1993. 9-036-70348-4, 53p. The text contains the proceedings of an international symposium on Södergran with the central theme of the image of her as poet. The articles look at her and her work from the perspective of Karelian mysticism, aesthetic idealism, the development of the cultural image of the "new woman" in Europe at the beginning of the century, and a historical view of her work and its interpretation. Biographical elements occur throughout this critical and thoroughly documented collection. It also includes several photographs that she took.

Schoolfield, George C. *Edith Södergran: Modernist Poet in Finland*. Westport, CT: Greenwood Press, 1984. 0-313-24166-X, 175p. Schoolfield presents a thoroughly documented examination of Södergran's life and work, positing that none of her poetry is simple and that it has been difficult to translate. This critical biography will interest the scholarly reader.

SOMERVILLE, MARY (1780–1872)

Mathematician   Scotland

Mary Somerville was a scientific writer and mathematician. Born in Jedburgh, Borders, on December 26, 1780, to a naval officer, she was allowed to do as she wanted while she was growing up. When she was fifteen, she saw algebraic symbols and began studying algebra, Euclid, and the classics. Her husband disapproved of education for women, but after he died, Somerville studied mathematics and won a monetary prize at thirty-three for solving a problem on diaphiantine equations; with the money she bought texts. In 1812, she married a cousin who encouraged her work and introduced her to London's intellectual and scientific circles. She presented papers and published a translation of Pierre Simon Laplace's *La mécanique céleste*. After other expository works on science, the Royal Astronomical Society elected her an honorary member, and she was awarded a government pension. She supported the emancipation and education of women, and Somerville College at Oxford is named after her.

BIBLIOGRAPHY

Patterson, Elizabeth Chambers. *Mary Somerville and the Cultivation of Science, 1815–1840*. Boston: Nijhoff, 1983. 9-02472-823-1, 264p. Patterson makes extensive use of the Somerville papers and other contemporary sources to relate Somerville's life during the years she was "queen of science."

Somerville, Mary. *Personal Recollections, from Early Life to Old Age, of Mary Somerville.* Ed. Martha Somerville. 1876. New York: AMS, 1975. 0-404-56837-8, 377p. Somerville's daughter Martha says that her mother was averse to gossip, revelations of private life, and intimate correspondence. Somerville avoids them in her recollections of her scientific pursuits.

SOPHIA of HANOVER (1630–1714)
Scholar   Germany

Sophia, the electress of Hanover, was a German scholar. She was the twelfth child of Frederick V and and James I's daughter Elizabeth Stuart, born on October 14, 1630. Four years after she married Ernest Augustus, duke of Brunswick, he became elector of Hanover. He died six years later, and their son George became king of England at Anne's death. A distinguished scholar and influential patron, Sophia counted Leibniz among her close friends. She also corresponded with many other scholars. If she had not died before **Anne**, she would have become Queen of England instead of her son.

BIBLIOGRAPHY
Kroll, Maria. *Sophie, Electress of Hanover; a Personal Portrait.* London: Gollancz, 1973. 0-575-01585-3, 288p. Using Sophie's own writings and letters from friends and relatives, Kroll re-creates a personal portrait rather than political history in a thoroughly researched and readable, scholarly biography.

SOPHIA of RUSSIA (1657–1704)
Regent   Russia

Sophia was the regent of Russia for seven years between 1682 and 1689. She was born on September 27, 1657, the daughter of Tsar Alexey I Mihailovitch and his first wife, Maria Miloslavskaya. When her brother the tsar Fyodor Alexeyevich died, she instigated an uprising among the household troops (*streltsy*) who murdered the supporters of her half brother Peter (later, Peter the Great). She installed her brother Ivan V as coruler with Peter and took the regency for them. During her reign, she encouraged industry and concluded peace treaties with Poland and China but sponsored unsuccessful campaigns against the Crimean Tatars. Peter forced her into a Moscow convent and later imprisoned her when he suspected her of again inciting the *streltsy*.

BIBLIOGRAPHY
Hughes, Lindsey. *Sophia, Regent of Russia, 1657–1704: Ambitious and Daring above Her Sex.* New Haven, CT: Yale University Press, 1990. 0-300-04790-8, 328p. Hughes' readable, scholarly biography, based on a variety of sources, including unpublished material, relates Sophia's achievements and that Russian ties with Europe began with her rather than with her brother Peter, who deposed her when she lost campaigns against the Tatars and the Turks.

SPAIN, ISABELLA of. *See* ISABELLA of SPAIN.

SPARK, MURIEL (1918–)
Writer   **England**

Muriel Spark is a novelist. She was born Muriel Sarah Camberg on February 1, 1918, in Edinburgh as the daughter of a Jewish engineer and an activist mother. She attended James Gillespie's Girls' School and Heriot Watt College in Edinburgh before running away from home at eighteen to marry and move to Rhodesia. She returned to England with her son after the end of her marriage and began working as a freelance writer and editor. She edited *Poetry Review* for two years, and published critical studies of Wordsworth, **Mary Shelley**, and **Emily Brontë** and a poetry collection before winning a short story competition in 1950 in the *Observer*. She converted to Catholicism, and her work reflected an intelligent and witty Catholic view. Best known for her novels, especially *The Prime of Miss Jean Brodie* (1961, filmed 1969), she won the James Tate Black Memorial Prize for *The Mandelbaum Gate* in 1965.

BIBLIOGRAPHY
Bold, Alan Norman. *Muriel Spark*. New York: Methuen, 1986. 0-416-40360-3, 128p. In a critical analysis, Bold interprets Spark's novels in light of her own life and what she espouses.

Spark, Muriel. *Curriculum Vitae: Autobiography*. Boston: Houghton Mifflin, 1993. 0-395-65372-X, 224p. Spark tells about the first thirty-nine formative years of her life from her childhood in Edinburgh past the publication of her first novel, revealing some of the real-life situations that became the basis for her fiction.

Walker, Dorothea. *Muriel Spark*. Boston: Twayne, 1988. 0-8057-6960-9, 122p. Walker begins her academic study with a biographical preface to a critical analysis of some of Spark's novels.

SPENCE, CATHERINE (1825–1910)
Writer and Activist   **Scotland**

Catherine Spence was a writer, lecturer, preacher, government adviser, political candidate, lobbyist, propagandist, and feminist. She was born near Melrose, Borders, Scotland, on October 31, 1825, as the fifth of eight children to an optimistic banker who gambled and a practical mother who left him and emigrated to South Australia in 1839. Spence became a governess, and her book *Clare Morrison* (1854), published anonymously, was the first novel of Australian life written by a woman. She continued to write novels for the next thirty years and was a journalist and literary critic for newspapers in South Australia, Victoria, and London. She became concerned with destitute children and founded the State Children's Council in 1886. She advocated education for women, innovative textbooks, and proportional representation and spoke at the Chicago World's Fair in 1893 on charities, prisons, proportional representation, peace, and woman's rights. She also worked for international suffrage after 1894 when it became law in South Australia. She founded the Effective Voting league and ran unsuccessfully for the Federal Convention in 1897, the first woman to run for an elected political office. Among the honors she received after her death was her name attached to a scholarship and to an electoral district.

BIBLIOGRAPHY

Cooper, Janet. *Catherine Spence*. Melbourne, Australia: Oxford University Press, 1972. 0-19-550424-0, 30p. Cooper's brief biographical overview of Spence's life emphasizes her concern for self-fulfillment and for intelligent women being allowed education without chastisement.

Magarey, Susan. *Unbridling the Tongues of Women: A Biography of Catherine Helen Spence*. Sydney: Hale and Iremonger, 1985. 0-8680-6149-2, 240p. Magarey emphasizes Spence's feminism, both strengths and weaknesses, in her balanced and carefully documented biography.

Spence, Catherine Helen. *An Autobiography*. Ed. Jeanne F. Young. Adelaide: Libraries Board of South Australia, 1975. 0-7243-0052-X, 101p. Spence's thorough autobiography provides a history of Adelaide and discloses her interest in law, economics, politics, and social reform as well as literature.

STAËL, ANNE LOUISE de (1766–1817)
Intellectual   France

Madame de Staël wrote treatises and novels that began French Romanticism. Born on April 22, 1766, into a family encouraging her interests in religion, finances, literature, and politics, Anne Louise Germain Necker became well educated. But her arranged marriage to Baron de Staël-Holstein was unhappy, and she followed it with many love affairs. Before the French Revolution, she opened a salon that attracted liberals, but as the revolution progressed, she stopped sympathizing with the idealism of the movement and left Paris. In 1795, she returned and reopened her salon, which became a center for opposing Napoleon. He, in turn, exiled her from France after 1804. Ten years later, after his abdication, she returned from her family estate in Switzerland to Paris and continued to influence politics there until her death. She signed her name as Necker de Staël because she both loved her father and enjoyed the aristocratic position that her husband had given her.

BIBLIOGRAPHY

Besser, Gretchen Rous. *Germaine de Staël Revisited*. Boston: Twayne, 1994. 0-8057-8286-9, 180p. Besser notes in this readable biography that de Staël achieved prominence not as much for her fiction or her conversation as for her intelligent moral and political essays, which led Napoleon to exile her in 1804.

Herold, J. Christopher. *Mistress to an Age: A Life of Madame de Staël*. Westport, CT: Greenwood Press, 1975. 0-8371-8339-1, 500p. Herold reveals de Staël's passions in her life but has not attempted to write the definitive biography because he thinks more information about her life will be discovered.

Hogsett, Charlotte. *The Literary Existence of Germain de Staël*. Carbondale: Southern Illinois University Press, 1987. 0-8093-1387-1, 224p. Hogsett's scholarly, well-researched biography shows the feminist view of Staël [*sic*] and proves that Staël was able to establish her feminine voice more successfully in some works than others.

Staël, Madame de. *Ten Years of Exile*. Trans. Doris Beik. New York: Saturday Review, 1972. 0-8415-020-4, 248p. This text covers de Staël's life during the years Napoleon exiled her, when she had to travel through Switzerland, Germany, Austria, and Russia in her attempt to escape his conquests.

Winegarten, Renee. *Mme. de Staël*. Dover, NH: Berg, 1985. 0-907852-87-7, 133p. Winegarten's carefully researched biography is a thorough and readable overview of de Staël's life and career.

STAMPA, GASPARA (1523?–1554?)

Poet   Italy

Gaspara Stampa was possibly the greatest woman poet of the Renaissance, composing lyrics to reflect the style of the times in which she lived. Born into the noble Paduan family of a jeweler who died when she was young, Stampa took Count Collaltino di Collalto as her lover and protector, becoming a *cortigiana onesta* (honest courtesan). Her courtesan status encouraged her poetic creation of religious and love lyrics. She identified her loves in terms of religious feast days, and unlike Petrarch, whose love was a fantasy or daydream, she thought of the joy of love in the memory of its fulfillment. Although untrained, she was concerned with form, technique, decorum, and style. Her lyric poetry *rime* offers a variation of prosody, motif, and language. She developed her skill in a predominantly male culture but retained her feminine perspective. Her life itself became the male subject of literary battles, novels, dramas, and historical debate.

BIBLIOGRAPHY
Bassanese, Fiora A. *Gaspara Stampa*. Boston: Twayne, 1982. 0-8057-6501-8, 144p. In this critical analysis of Stampa and her work, Bassanese says that Stampa was probably the best woman writer of her Renaissance era but was the unique product of her times, the high Venetian Renaissance.
Jerrold, Maud. *Vittoria Colonna, with Some Account of Her Friends and Her Times*. 1906. Freeport, NY: Books for Libraries, 1969. 0-83695-153-0, 336p. Jerrold's biography of Colonna includes information about Gaspara Stampa. It is stylistically dated, but its commentary on Stampa notes that her direct treatment of theme in her sonnets is what made her original.
Warnke, Frank J. *Three Women Poets: Renaissance and Baroque: Louise Labe, Gaspara Stampa, and Sor Juana Ines De La Cruz*. Trans. Frank J. Warnke. Lewisburg, PA: Bucknell University Press, 1987. 0-8387-5089-3, 135p. In this academic and intellectually demanding, collective biography, Warnke includes an overview of Stampa's life and her work with translations of the poetry.

STANHOPE, HESTER LUCY (1776–1839)

Traveler   England

Lady Hester Lucy Stanhope was a traveler. She was the eldest daughter of Charles, the third earl of Stanhope, born on March 12, 1776. Her mother's death at the birth of her third child when Stanhope was quite young, affected her life. Her father considered Stanhope an excellent logician, although she was not formally educated. In 1803 until his death in 1806, Stanhope stayed with her uncle, William Pitt, who was then prime minister, as mistress of his household. After the death of Pitt and others who were close to her, she left England in 1810 and did not return. In 1814, after an affair with a young lover whom she refused to marry, she settled in the Middle East. Among the places she visited, with a doctor and a maid generally traveling with her, were Malta, Constantinople, Greece, Egypt, Syria, Palmyra, Tripoli, and Baalbeck. She adopted Eastern manners, dabbled in politics, and became a figurehead of a mountain community. When the English government stopped her pension, she locked herself in her house and died in poverty.

BIBLIOGRAPHY

Childs, Virginia. *Lady Hester Stanhope: Queen of the Desert.* London: Weidenfeld and Nicolson, 1990. 0-297-81017-0, 226p. By having lived as a female in both the area where Lady Stanhope grew up and in the Middle East, Childs addresses the motivations for Lady Stanhope's choices in a well-written, empathic, and balanced biography.

Leslie, Doris. *The Desert Queen.* London: Heinemann, 1972. No ISBN, 305p. Leslie uses letters and other accounts of Lady Stanhope to write a biography that she says is strictly factual but that reads like a novel.

Stanhope, Hester Lucy. *Memoirs of the Lady Hester Stanhope.* Salzburg, Austria: Universitat Salzburg, 1985. Written with her physician, Stanhope's memoir is partially his, but it reveals her eccentricities, interests, and prejudices.

Vogelsberger, Hartwig A. *The Unearthly Quest: Lady Hester Stanhope's Legacy.* Salzburg, Austria: Universitat Salzburg, 1987. No ISBN, 206p. This well-documented biography, a balanced view of Lady Stanhope, probes the complex facets of her personality.

Watney, John Basil. *Travels in Araby of Lady Hester Stanhope.* London: Gordon Cremonesi, 1975. 0-86033-005-2, 294p. Mainly documented with letters, Watney's biography of Stanhope reads like an adventure novel because Stanhope's actual experiences were the fabric of fiction.

STARK, FREYA (1893–1993)
Writer and Traveler   **France**

Dame Freya Stark was both a writer and a traveler. She was born in Paris on January 31, 1893, where her parents were studying art, and learned English, French, and Italian before she was five. One experience living with her bohemian parents was having her scalp caught in an Italian matting factory's machinery when she was twelve. For her formal education, she studied at London University. In World War I, she became a nurse on the Italian front and lived in Italy. She had begun to learn Arabic in London, and she knew the language well enough in 1928 to travel to Lebanon. Although she also visited Canada, she seemed more interested in the Middle East and visited Iraq and Iran where she worked on the *Baghdad Times.* During World War II, she contributed to British intelligence what she knew about Arabia. Among her awards are the Burton Memorial Medal for *The Valleys of the Assassins* and the Royal Geographical Society's Founder's Medal. She was honored with the Dame of the British Empire in 1972.

BIBLIOGRAPHY

Moorehead, Caroline. *Freya Stark.* New York: Viking, 1985. 0-670-80675-7, 143p. Moorehead uses Stark's autobiography, letters, and unpublished documents in this undocumented but readable introduction to Stark's life.

Ruthven, Malise. *Traveller through Time: A Photographic Journey with Freya Stark.* New York: Viking, 1986. 0-670-80183-6, 141p. Since Ruthven has consulted only Stark's writing and has done no research, he has not written a biography but a personal tribute to his godmother in which he recounts facets of her life and illustrates them with revealing photographs.

Stark, Freya. *Letters: The Furnace and the Cup, Vol. 1.* Ed. Lucy Moorehead.
Salisbury, England: Compton Russell, 1974–1982. 0-85955-012-5, 308p.
This first volume of Stark's letters covers the years from 1914 to 1930.
They show the strain of the war on someone barely twenty-one, the threat
to family happiness, illness, and gradual realization of the Muslim world,
which was to become the focus of the rest of her life.
Stark, Freya. *Letters: The Open Door, Vol. 2.* Ed. Lucy Moorehead. Salisbury,
England: Compton Russell, 1974–1982. 0-85955-021-4, 285p. The places
from which Stark wrote these letters from 1930 to 1935 included Baghdad,
the desert, Cairo, Aden, and hospitals in the Middle East and England.
Other volumes of her letters are *The Growth of Danger, 1935–39* (vol. 3),
Bridge of the Levant, 1940–43 (vol. 4), *New Worlds for Old, 1943–46* (vol.
5), *The Broken Road, 1947–52* (vol. 6), and *Some Talk of Alexander,
1925–59* (vol. 7).

STEIN, EDITH (1891–1942)

Religious   Germany

Edith Stein was a nun who converted from Judaism. Born on October 12,
1891, into a Jewish family in Breslau, she studied philosophy at Breslau and
Göttingen. In 1922, she read a biography of **Teresa of Ávila** and decided to
convert to Catholicism. She taught at a convent school in Speyer for eight
years, rising early, wearing patched clothes, and attending three masses each
day. In 1934, when Nazis banned Jews from teaching, she went into a Carmelite convent in Cologne and took the name of Sister Teresa Benedicta of the
Cross. In 1938, she was sent to Echt in The Netherlands, but the Germans invaded before she had a chance to transfer to a Swiss convent. She and an older
nun were arrested and died in Auschwitz in August 1942. The Catholic community saw her as a martyr, and Pope Paul II beatified her in May 1987 at Cologne. His move aroused controversy because people thought that someone
who had died as a Jew could not be a Christian martyr. In 1997, Pope John
Paul II elevated her to sainthood.

BIBLIOGRAPHY
Herbstrith, Waltraud. *Edith Stein, a Biography.* Trans. Bernard Bonowitz. San
Francisco: Ignatius Press, 1992. 0-89870-410-3, 207p. Herbstrith, a Carmelite, as was Stein, uses diaries, letters, oral history, and written testimonies to show Stein as a self-confident woman who worked on her
intellectual development and her spiritual life.
Koeppel, Josephine. *Edith Stein: Philosopher and Mystic.* Collegeville, MN: Liturgical Press, 1990. 0-8146-5625-0, 196p. Koeppel uses Stein's unfinished autobiography; archives of Carmelite monasteries of Cologne and
Tübingen, Germany, as well as Echt and Beek, Holland; and conversations
and letters from her family for a well-researched and readable biography.
Stein, Edith. *Self-Portrait in Letters, 1916–1942.* Washington, DC: ICS, 1993.
Paper, 0-935216-20-0 357p. Stein's letters reveal her opinions, her commentary on a variety of subjects, including her philosophical and theological research at the Carmelite cloister in Cologne, and her genuine goodness.
She wrote to over one hundred different people, including students, colleagues, and members of her cloister while waiting to be transported to
Auschwitz with other Jewish Christians.

322

STOCKS, MARY (1891–1975)
Scholar and Activist

England

Baroness Mary Stocks was a scholar, educator, and activist. She was born in London on July 25, 1891, into the intellectual family of a physician as the eldest of three children and was educated at St. Paul's Girls' School until sixteen. At nineteen, she entered the London School of Economics, graduating with a first. She took part in the "Mud March" of the suffragettes in 1907 and supported the constitutional side of the suffrage movement. In 1913, she married John Stocks, an Oxford don. She lectured in economics at the London School of Economics and at King's College for Women during World War I. In 1924, she and her husband moved to Manchester, where she lectured in the university extramural department and for the Workers' Educational Association. After her husband died in 1937, she returned to London and became the general secretary of the London Council of Social Service and the principal of Westfield College. She served on government committees and gained a national reputation by participation in radio programs called *The Brains Trust* and *Any Questions?* In 1966, she was created a Life Peeress.

BIBLIOGRAPHY

Hooper, Barbara. *Mary Stocks, 1891–1975: An Uncommonplace Life.* Atlantic Highlands, NJ: Athlone, 1996. 0-485-11507-7, 203p. Stocks requested that her personal correspondence be destroyed at her death; therefore, Hooper relies on the two volumes of Stocks' autobiography, newspaper articles discussing her various careers, and personal interviews with friends for her well-written and recommended biography.

Stocks, Mary Danvers Brinton. *My Commonplace Book.* London: Davies, 1970. 0-432-15750-6, 246p. Stocks says that she always had more given to her than she gave and that the only times she had to initiate situations were when she decided to enter the School of Economics in 1910 and to start a birthcontrol clinic in 1925.

Stocks, Mary Danvers Brinton. *Still More Commonplace.* London: Davies, 1973. 0-432-15751-4, 142p. Stocks takes anecdotes cut from her first book to make a second. In her well-written and entertaining memoirs, she talks of her love affairs, the theater, and with places in which she lived, including West Dorset, Manchester, and London.

STOPES, MARIE (1880–1958)
Scientist and Activist

Scotland

Marie Stopes was a paleobotanist and birth control advocate. She was born in Edinburgh on October 15, 1880, as the oldest daughter of a leisured scholar and his feminist wife, who supported higher education for women. Stopes and her family lived in London, and she was educated at home until she was twelve. She then attended St. George's School in Edinburgh and North London Collegiate School. At University College, London, she obtained concurrent degrees in geology, botany, and geography. In 1904, she obtained her doctorate in Munich and became the first woman to join the science faculty at Manchester University. An expert on paleobotany, she investigated coal mines and fossil plants and published scientific books on them. In 1911, she married, but, after no sexual life, she had the marriage annulled in 1916. She read widely on impotence and concentrated on a campaign for birth control and sex education. She married Humphrey V. Roe in 1918 and, with him, founded the first instructional clinic for contraception in Britain. She wrote books, *Married Love* (1918) and *Wise Parenthood* (1918), which sold millions of copies and were translated into many languages. In total, she wrote over seventy books. The medical establishment and the Catholic Church rallied against her, but she won a libel suit that lost on Appeal in the House of Lords. After World War II, she promoted birth control in Far Eastern countries.

BIBLIOGRAPHY

Hall, Ruth E. *Passionate Crusader: The Life of Marie Stopes.* New York: Harcourt Brace Jovanovich, 1977. 0-15-171288-3, 351p. Authoritative and balanced, this biography of Stopes shows her contributions to paleobotany and coal research as well as her contribution to helping women with their sexual needs as one of the first to recommend contraception within marriage.

Rose, June. *Marie Stopes and the Sexual Revolution.* Winchester, MA: Faber and Faber, 1992. 0-571-16260-6, 272p. Rose's biography is a straightforward, readable account of Stopes' complex character, using Stopes' personal papers as a source.

STORNI, ALFONSINA (1892–1938)
Poet   Switzerland

Alfonsina Storni was a feminist and a poet. She was born in Sala Capriasca, Switzerland, on May 29, 1892, and went to Argentina with her family. Her father died when she was fourteen, and she toured with a theater company in Argentina for a year before attending the Escuela Normal Mixta de Maestros Rurales in Coronda and obtaining a teacher's diploma. While teaching and writing her poetry, she was also a journalist in Argentina with a weekly newspaper column. She wrote about her ambivalent feelings toward men but included a desire for love and sexual passion in her poetry. Her book *El Dulce Daq* (The Sweet Injury, 1918) brought her popular success. She won the Premio Anual del Consejo Nacional de Mujeres for a series of poems, and her work *Languidez* won the Primer Premio Municipal and the Segundo Premio Nacional de Literatura. She held chairs of declamation at several schools but drowned herself on discovering that she was suffering from incurable cancer.

BIBLIOGRAPHY

Jones, Sonia. *Alfonsina Storni.* Boston: Twayne, 1979. 0-8057-6360-0, 149p. Jones examines Storni's poetry, prose, and plays along with the painful sacrifices she made to write as much as she did, mainly to support her son, while males whom she criticized wrote unfavorable reviews of her work.

Phillips, Rachel. *Alfonsina Storni: From Poetess to Poet.* London: Tamesis, 1975. 0-7293-0001-3, 131p. Phillips gives a feminist interpretation of Storni's writings and reports the public and critical reaction to them at publication in her carefully researched and recommended biography.

STREET, JESSIE (1889–1970)
Writer   India

Lady Jessie Mary Grey Street was a feminist and writer. She was born in Ranchi province on April 18, 1889, in Chota Nagpur, India, the oldest of three children. Her father, in the Indian civil service, often emphasized that the family descended from Alfred the Great. Educated first in England, she went to Sydney University, where she became concerned about social reform. She captained the women's hockey team and was a founding member of the University Sports Association. Before her marriage, she volunteered with the New York Protective and Probation Association for women arrested as prostitutes and at Creighton House in London. Later, she regularly attended the League of Nations Union meetings, arguing against armaments and international aggression. She served in 1920 as secretary to the National Council of Women and as president of the Feminist Club. In 1929, she was the founding president of the United Associations of Women, the main group for the feminist movement in New South Wales. She became a member of Birth Control International in 1930, and in Geneva during the same year, she was elected vice president of Equal Rights International. In 1945, she was the only woman delegate at the San Francisco conference from which evolved the United Nations. She wrote a song called "Australia Happy Isle," and, set to music by Lindley Evans, it won the Victorian sesquicentennial prize. Street's husband, Sir Kenneth Whistler Street, was lieutenant governor and chief justice of New South Wales, as was her son, Sir Laurence Whistler Street.

BIBLIOGRAPHY

Radi, Heather, ed. *Jessie Street: Documents and Essays*. Broadway, New South Wales, Australia: Women's Redress, 1990. 1-87527-403-0, 293p. This is not a traditional biography but a recommended collection of writings by and about Street cataloging her involvement in a variety of organizations and her commitment to suffrage and feminist rights.

Sekuless, Peter. *Jessie Street, a Rewarding but Unrewarded Life*. St. Lucia, Australia: University of Queensland Press, 1978. 0-7022-1227-X, 218p. Sekuless's biography, possibly crediting comments by and about Street that are incorrect, is somewhat biased; however, many of the facts remain accurate, and he discusses her work to gain equal rights for aborigines and women.

Street, Jessie M. G. *Truth or Repose*. Sydney: Australian Book Society, 1966. No ISBN, 338p. Street says very early in her memoir that she and her father disagreed about the status of Indians, who had helped to raise her. She saw them as equals; he saw them as children who had to be helped. She thinks that his attitude extended to women as well, but family wealth and social position allowed her to confidently pursue her many interests.

SUTHERLAND, JOAN (1926–)

Opera Singer   **Australia**

Dame Joan Sutherland is an operatic soprano. She was born in Sydney on November 7, 1926, and her mother taught her piano and voice when she was young. She made her public debut in a performance of Bach's *Christmas Oratorio* in 1946 and her distinguished debut in a concert performance of *Dido and Aeneas* in 1947. She won prizes that allowed her to continue her musical education at the Royal College of Music and Opera School in London. Although her first audition at Covent Garden was unsuccessful, she returned, and in 1952, she joined the Covent Garden company. Beginning in 1959, with the influence of her husband, Richard Bonynge, and her stunning success in *Lucia di Lammermoor* at Covent Garden, Sutherland specialized in coloratura roles of eighteenth- and nineteenth-century Italian operas, particularly the works of Bellini and Donizetti. She made her New York City debut in 1961 in the rarely heard *Beatrice di Tenda* by Bellini and as Lucia in the same year at La Scala in Milan. She toured widely, with her husband becoming her regular accompanist and conductor. In addition to her coloratura virtuosity and superb technique, her voice has an elegantly warm tone. Made Commander of the Order of the British Empire in 1961 and Dame Commander of the Order of the British Empire in 1979, she retired in 1990.

BIBLIOGRAPHY

Adams, Brian. *La Stupenda, a Biography of Joan Sutherland*. Melbourne: Hutchinson of Australia, 1980. 0-09-137410-3, 329p. Adams' popular biography developed from filming Sutherland at concert halls around the world for a television special. He gives a reasonably balanced account of a woman called the "voice of the century" and "La Stupenda."

Eaton, Quaintance. *Sutherland and Bonynge: An Intimate Biography*. New York: Dodd, Mead, 1987. 0-396-08945-3, 331p. Eaton's popular biography presents Sutherland and Bonynge before 1974 and follows them through a month of rehearsals and performances.

Major, Norma. *Joan Sutherland: The Authorized Biography*. Boston: Little, Brown, 1994. 0-316-54555-4, 324p. Major created the catalog of Sutherland's performances from opera house archives around the world and consulted with many of her colleagues as well as Sutherland to write this authorized, laudatory biography, showing Sutherland's deprecating nature and humor.

Sutherland, Joan. *The Joan Sutherland Album*. 1986. New York: Simon and Schuster, 1994. 0-684-19658-1, 191p. This collection of photographs shows Sutherland and her family in a variety of places and poses with identifying captions that depict her lengthy career and carefree moments.

SUTTNER, BERTHA von (1843–1914)

Writer and Activist   **Czech Republic**

Bertha von Suttner was a novelist and pacifist. She was born Bertha Felicie Sophie in Prague on June 9, 1843, daughter of Count Franz Kinsky von Chinic und Tettau, who died soon after her birth. She seemed unlikely to do much in her life, but in 1876 she married fellow novelist, Baron Arthur Gundaccar von Suttner, of whom her family disapproved. With no family financial support, she and her husband moved to Tiflis, in Russian Georgia, to teach languages. They viewed firsthand the horrors of the Russo-Turkish Wars beginning in 1877. In response, she founded the Austrian Society of Friends of Peace and wrote a book, *Die Waffen nieder!* (Lay Down Your Arms!), which became the most famous antiwar novel of its time when it was published in 1895 with its description of the suffering caused by wars between 1859 and 1871. They returned to Vienna, accepted by her family, and went to Paris to ask the baroness's former employer Alfred Nobel for donations for her recently established Austrian Peace Society. At the International Peace Congress in Budapest, Hungary, in 1896, she heard that Nobel had established his Peace Prize before his recent death. She lectured all over Europe about channeling energies of war into energies of peace, earning the nickname "Peace Bertha." In 1905, she won the Nobel Peace Prize. As she struggled with finances, the Carnegie Endowment for International Peace gave her a pension to support her while she warned against militarizing China and against using the airplane as a war weapon. She died one week before the beginning of World War I.

BIBLIOGRAPHY

Braker, Regina. *Weapons of Women Writers: Bertha Von Suttner's Die Waffen Nieder! As Political Literature in the Tradition of Harriet Beecher Stowe's Uncle Tom's Cabin.* New York: Peter Lang, 1995. 0-8204-2626-1, 155p. Braker notes in this dual scholarly biography of von Suttner and Stowe that they saw popular fiction as a way to express social, moral, and political concerns. Biographical information accompanies an interpretation of von Suttner's work.

Hamann, Brigitte. *Bertha von Suttner: A Life for Peace.* Trans. Ann Dubsky. Syracuse, NY: Syracuse University Press, 1996. 0-8156-0387-8, 416p. Hamann's readable, well-documented biography places Suttner in her times and afterward, when the devastation of World War I proved her prophecies about war's horrors to have been correct.

Lengyel, Emil. *And All Her Paths Were Peace: The Life of Bertha von Suttner.* Nashville, TN: T. Nelson, 1975. 0-8407-6450-2, 144p. In a brief introduction, Lengyel sees von Suttner as a courageous woman who willingly deserted her aristocratic background to support what she believed.

Suttner, Bertha von. *Memoirs of Bertha von Suttner; the Records of an Eventful Life.* 1910. New York: Garland, 1972. 2 vols. 0-8240-0317-9. These two volumes of von Suttner's memoirs are especially enlightening for the information they give about the cultural and social scenes at the turn of the century in Europe while also showing her intense concern for peace, her liberalism, and her international endeavors.

SUZMAN, HELEN (1917–)

Politician   South Africa

Helen Suzman is a South African politician. She was born Helen Gavronsky on November 7, 1917, in Germiston, Transvaal, the daughter of Lithuanian immigrants, and received her early education at a convent. In 1937, she married Dr. Moses Suzman. After working as a statistician for the War Supplies Board and having two daughters, she entered Witwatersrand University, graduated, and became a lecturer there in economics and economic history from 1944 to 1952. She was deeply concerned about the apartheid system erected by the National Party under Daniel Malan and stood election to Parliament in 1953 as a member of the opposition United Party. In 1959, she cofounded the Progressive Party, and as the party's only member of Parliament for several years, she gradually gained the respect of the black community as she continued to fiercely oppose apartheid, facing hostility from the white community. She demanded government facts about detentions, bannings, whippings, police brutality, and executions and damned laws controlling black housing, education, mass removals, and the breakup of families. In 1978, she received the United Nations Human Rights Award, and in 1980, the Medallion of Heroism. Her later concerns were finding the torturers and killers of activists in police custody. When she retired from Parliament in 1989, she began work at the South African Institute of Race Relations.

BIBLIOGRAPHY

Strangwayes-Booth, Joanna. *A Cricket in the Thorn Tree: Helen Suzman and the Progressive Party of South Africa.* Bloomington: Indiana University Press, 1976. 0-253-31483-6, 320p. The book is both a biography of Suzman and a history of the development of the Progressive Party in South Africa, which she represented as the lone member in the South African House of Assembly. Suzman's quiet charisma and refusal to accept white supremacy come through in the scholarly text.

Suzman, Helen. *In No Uncertain Terms: A South African Memoir.* New York: Knopf, 1993. 0-679-40985-8, 304p. Suzman's readable autobiography, recalling her years in politics, tells of the long, difficult, and finally successful battle against apartheid in South Africa and the less successful one against male chauvinism and anti-Semitism.

TAGLIONI, MARIA (1804–1884)
Ballerina   Sweden

Maria Taglioni was a ballerina known mainly for creating a new style of dancing called the Romantic school. Born on April 23, 1804, in Stockholm to a
dancer and choreographer, Taglioni then lived in Paris, where she studied with
Coulon at the Paris Opéra before her Vienna debut in 1822. She danced in
Paris at the Opéra in works that her father choreographed, such as *La Sylphide*
and the *Ballet of the Nuns*. Fans in Paris, London, and St. Petersburg idolized
her. She married the comte de Voisins in 1832, but they divorced, and she had
an illegitimate child with her Russian lover, who died soon after. She retired to
Lake Como in 1847 but returned to France eleven years later to become the
principal teacher at the Opéra. Her style changed dancing and the ponderous
clothing in which ballet dancers performed. Without her, **Pavlova, Markova,
Ulanova, Fonteyn,** and the rest might not have reached their heights.
BIBLIOGRAPHY
Hill, Lorna. *La Sylphide: The Life of Maria Taglioni*. London: Evans, 1967. No
    ISBN, 142p. Hill notes in a readable biography that discusses ballet during
    Taglioni's lifetime that Taglioni was a superb dancer and suggests that Ta-
    glioni *was* the dance.

TAILLEFERRE, GERMAINE (1892–1983)
Composer   France

Germaine Tailleferre was a pianist and composer. She was born in Park-St.-
Maur on April 19, 1892, and educated at the Paris Conservatoire, where she
won three first prizes. She achieved eminence for her work in the 1920s as a
member of *Les Six*, a group of composers reacting against Romanticism and im-
pressionism. Other members of the group were Auric, Durey, Honegger, Mil-
haud, and Poulenc. Her works include orchestral music; chamber music; a
ballet, *Le Marchand d'oiseaux* (The Bird-Seller) in 1923; a piano concerto; and

songs. When Les Six no longer interacted, she wrote fewer works, although some of her pieces demonstrated serial techniques. She lived in the United States during World War II.

BIBLIOGRAPHY

Shapiro, Robert. *Germaine Tailleferre: A Bio-Bibliography*. Westport, CT: Greenwood Press, 1994. 0-313-28642-6, 280p. Shapiro's scholarly guide introduces Tailleferre by presenting a brief biography (drawn from undocumented interviews with her family), information on her works and performances, and a discography.

TEBALDI, RENATA (1922–)

Opera Singer   Italy

Renata Tebaldi is an operatic soprano. She was born in Pesaro, Italy, on February 1, 1922, to a father who had studied cello and sometimes played in an orchestra. He deserted the family early, and Tebaldi had polio as a very young child. Her grandfather recognized her talent, but after his death, no one noticed her abilities. Her mother supported her financially as well as psychologically while Tebaldi studied at Parma Conservatory and made her debut at Rovigo in 1944. Toscanini invited her to appear at the reopening of La Scala, Milan, in 1946, and she sang there for the next eight years. She has since sung in many opera houses, toured widely, including a season in 1955 in New York, and made many recordings.

BIBLIOGRAPHY

Casanova, Carlamaria. *Renata Tebaldi: The Voice of an Angel*. 1981. Dallas, TX: Baskerville, 1995. 1-88090-940-5, 265p. Casanova includes a disc with this biography of Tebaldi so that readers will have a chance to hear the voice that she describes in the text along with Tebaldi's career and life.

Harris, Kenn. *Renata Tebaldi*. New York: Drake, 1974. 0-87749-597-1, 161p. Harris clearly admires Tebaldi and presents her in a readable biography with photographs as one of the main voices of the century, a woman of extraordinary stage presence whose artistry, charm, tact, and consideration won everyone she knew.

Seroff, Victor. *Renata Tebaldi: The Woman and the Diva*. 1961. Freeport, NY: Books for Libraries, 1970. 0-83698-048-4, 213p. When Tebaldi was twenty-four, Toscanini summoned her for an audition, and her career began. Seroff re-creates that audition in the beginning of his readable and researched biography.

TE KANAWA, KIRI (1944–)

Opera Singer   New Zealand

Dame Kiri Te Kanawa is an operatic soprano. She was born in Gisborne on March 6, 1944, with a Maori ancestry, and the couple who adopted her gave her the name of "Kiri" (Maori for bell). She was educated a Roman Catholic and won so many awards for her singing that the London Opera Centre accepted her with no audition. She made her debut with the Royal Opera Company in 1970 as a Flower Maiden in Wagner's *Parsifal*. In the next two years, she performed in Lyons, San Francisco, and Glyndebourne and made her debut in New York as Desdemona in 1974. She has appeared throughout the world and gained even more recognition when she sang at the 1981 wedding of the

Prince and Princess of Wales, televised around the globe. She was made a Dame of the British Empire in 1982. In addition to classical, she has has produced many nonclassical recordings, and in 1989 she published *Land of the Long White Cloud: Maori Myths and Legends.*

BIBLIOGRAPHY

Fingleton, David. *Kiri Te Kanawa: A Biography.* New York: Atheneum, 1983. 0-689-11345-5, 192p. This popular biography describes the development of Te Kanawa's voice and her repertoire and includes many details about her performances.

TE PUEA, HERANGI (1883–1952)

Activist   New Zealand

Herangi Te Puea was a Maori leader. She was born in Waikato as the daughter of Tahuna Herangi and Princess Tiahuia. Although her grandfather banned his people from attending public schools, she attended Mercer School, Mangere, and Parnell. After her mother died when she was fifteen, her actions caused hostility in the tribe, but when she rescued King Hahuta from stampeding horses, its members changed their attitudes. She began to speak at tribal meetings and to work to improve conditions for her tribe. A skilled organizer, she began to acquire influence within the Maori nationalist movement, Kingitanga, after 1911. She persuaded Waikato craftsmen to give their time in the 1920s to redevelop the forgotten arts and to carve meeting houses. She encouraged Maori agriculture and helped the social and cultural rehabilitation of the Maori. Her work gained her recognition as a Dame Commander of the British Empire.

BIBLIOGRAPHY

King, Michael. *Te Puea.* Auckland, New Zealand: Sceptre, 1987. Paper, 0-340-42096-0, 331p. Te Puea kept a diary from 1921 to 1952 and wrote many letters, which are the basis for this well-researched, scholarly biography, which also includes important insights about Maori traditions.

TERESA of ÁVILA (1515–1582)

Religious   Spain

Teresa of Ávila was a mystic who established convents emphasizing asceticism. Born Teresa De Cepeda y Ahumada on March 28, 1515, into a wealthy Spanish family in Ávila, she decided to enter a Carmelite convent at twenty. She had no particular goal, but after much prayer, she began to experience visions. She wanted to live with the most ascetic Carmelites, so she established her own house with the assistance of St. John of the Cross. In 1562, she opened St. Joseph's at Ávila, where daily mental prayer was integral to its spiritual life. Teresa traveled throughout Spain for the next twenty years to found seventeen more convents as she combined her religious vocation with practicality and efficiency. Among her writings are an autobiography, *The Way of Perfection,* and the mystical work *The Interior Castle.* She was canonized in 1622, with her feast day on October 15.

BIBLIOGRAPHY

Auclair, Marcelle. *Saint Teresa of Ávila.* Trans. Kathleen Pond. 1953. Petersham, MA: St. Bede's, 1988. 0-932506-67-4, 457p. To Auclair, Teresa's two fundamental characteristics were will and simplicity, and in her well-documented, scholarly biography, she reveals both the woman and the saint, without sacrificing either.

Du Boulay, Shirley. *Teresa of Ávila: Her Story: A Compelling Biography of One of the Most Remarkable Women of All Time.* Ann Arbor, MI: Servant, 1995. 0-89283-893-0, 260p. In this popular biography, using letters and autobiographical writings as a basis for the text, Du Boulay reveals Teresa as a woman whose outer world of travel, negotiation, and stress hid an inner world of working toward God.

Gross, Francis L., and Toni Perior Gross. *The Making of a Mystic: Seasons in the Life of Teresa of Ávila.* Albany: State University of New York Press, 1993. 0-7914-1411-6, 285p. Gross calls his book about Teresa a "developmental biography" because he cites popular characters from both history and fiction to shed light on her life from a psychological perspective. He sees qualities in her of coquette, housewife, banker, mystic, organizer, and solitary and thinks that she cuts across both male and female stereotypes and archetypes.

Papàsogli, Giorgio. *St. Teresa of Ávila.* Trans. Gloria Italiano Anzilotti. Boston: St. Paul Editions, 1990. 0-8198-6880-9, 427p. Papàsogli gives a balanced view of Teresa in terms of the times in which she lived and the expectations of the church in an accessible biography.

Slade, Carole. *St. Teresa of Avila: Author of a Heroic Life.* Berkeley: University of California Press, 1995. 0-520-08802-6, 204p. Slade looks at Teresa's texts through the theories of autobiography and feminism, scriptural hermeneutics, hagiography, and Inquistion studies to concentrate on the concept of the self that emerges. Slade concludes that what people generally think Teresa is saying is not what she may have meant.

TERESA of CALCUTTA (1910–1997)
Religious   **Albania**

Mother Teresa established the Missionaries of Charity, first in India and then around the world. Born as Agnes Gonxha Bojaxhiu on August 27, 1910, in Albania, she became a member of the Sodality of the Blessed Virgin Mary, the church organization that served the poor, at an early age. As a teenager, after reading letters to her church from missionaries in India, she prepared to enter the convent of the Sisters of Loreto, an Irish order of nuns with a mission in Calcutta, India. She chose the name Thérèse from St. Thérèse de Lisieux when she entered the convent. In Calcutta, Mother Teresa taught history and geography at the Loreto school for twenty years before God called her to live among the desperately poor. She studied nursing, and in 1950, she established a new religious community, which she called the Missionaries of Charity, with the approval of the Catholic Church. Twelve women formed the first order, rising at 4 A.M. to begin their sixteen-hour workday with prayers. They owned one change of clothing, ate the same food as the poor, and received no payment or gifts. In 1954, Mother Teresa started the Nirmal Hriday [Pure Heart] Home for the Dying in a building donated by the city of Calcutta, and then an orphanage, a home of the elderly, a women's and children's shelter, and a workshop for the unemployed. In 1965, she received permission to expand her programs outside India to five hundred centers in over one hundred countries. She won the Nobel Peace Prize for her work in 1979.

BIBLIOGRAPHY

Egan, Eileen, and Kathleen Egan. *Suffering into Joy: What Mother Teresa Teaches about True Joy.* Ann Arbor, MI: Servant, 1994. 0-89283-876-0, 156p. Eileen Egan spent more than thirty years traveling with Mother Teresa, and here she recounts the experience with anecdotes showing Mother Teresa's selflessness and sacrifice in her unselfish love.

Hitchens, Christopher. *The Missionary Position: The Ideology of Mother Teresa.* New York: Norton, 1995. 1-85984-929-6, 98p. A lone voice against Mother Teresa, Hitchens claims in this meager biography lacking evidence that she was a political opportunist who offered substandard medical care to the poor and a moralizer for the political Right.

Le Joly, Edward. *A Woman in Love . . . Mother Teresa.* Notre Dame, IN: Ave Maria, 1993. 0-87793-496-7, 192p. In this chatty biography, Le Joly talks about the vast number of projects in which Mother Teresa had been involved and her accomplishments, admitting that he has only good things to say.

Tully, Mark. *Mother.* New York: Weatherhill, 1992. 962-7283-11-8, 119p. Tully, a Calcutta native, uses black-and-white photographs from private albums, convents, and libraries to document Mother Teresa's work around the world with both the poor and the world leaders who have entertained her.

Zambonini, Franca. *Teresa of Calcutta: A Pencil in God's Hand.* Trans. Jordan Aumann. New York: Alba House, 1993. 0-8189-0670-7, 189p. Zambonini reports only incidents she observed while with Mother Teresa, a woman she sees as a mystic and contemplative as well as an administrator and an apostle of charity. Zambonini notes that Mother Teresa refused to eat outside the convent and slept only three hours a night.

TERRY, ELLEN (1848–1928)

Actor   England

Dame Ellen Terry was an English actor. She was born on February 27, 1848, in Coventry, West Midlands, the third child in a family of eleven children with actors for parents. She appeared on stage at eight in *A Winter's Tale* at the Princess Theatre in London. From 1862, she played in Bristol and, after a short-lived marriage to a man twenty-seven years older, she returned to the stage to earn money. After several roles and another marriage, she joined Henry Irving in 1878 as his leading lady and established her reputation as the leading Shakespearean actor in London, with her best roles as Beatrice, Portia, Desdemona, Viola, and Lady Teazle. In 1903, she went into theater management and began to tour and lecture widely. Among the playwrights who wrote for her during this time were James Barrie and Bernard Shaw. She continued to perform until 1925, the same year she was made a Dame of the British Empire.

BIBLIOGRAPHY

Auerbach, Nina. *Ellen Terry, Player in Her Time.* New York: Norton, 1987. 0-393-02398-2, 504p. Auerbach thinks in her literary critique that Terry's offstage life encompassed as many roles as her life onstage because she was child, child bride, fallen woman, mother, star, madwoman, and crone, or "Everywoman" to the Victorians.

Fecher, Constance. *Bright Star; a Portrait of Ellen Terry*. New York: Farrar, Straus, and Giroux, 1970. 0-374-30965-5, 236p. In addition to Terry's life in this well-documented and accessible biography, Fecher discusses the theater's history during Victorian times to show the cultural expectations of both performers and audiences.

Manvell, Roger. *Ellen Terry*. New York: Putnam, 1968. No ISBN, 390p. Using excerpts from unpublished diaries and letters as well as Terry's own notes on her interpretation of Lady Macbeth, Manvell presents Terry in a readable biography as an individual and as a performer in her time of history.

Prideaux, Tom. *Love or Nothing: The Life and Times of Ellen Terry*. 1975. New York: Limelight Editions, 1987. Paper, 0-87910-105-9, 288p. Prideaux interviewed members of Terry's family, people who worked with her onstage, and many previously unpublished letters to write a biography recognizing her generosity and her ability, which inspired much admiration.

Terry, Ellen, Dame. *The Story of My Life*. New York: Schocken, 1982. 0-8052-3814-X, 240p. Terry's memoir highlights her life of acting from nine to seventy-eight, with especially intriguing verbal portraits of friends, including the Pre-Raphaelites, Lewis Carroll, Alfred Lord Tennyson, G. B. Shaw, and Lillie Langry.

TETRAZZINI, LOUISA (1871–1940)
Opera Singer   Italy

Louisa Tetrazzini was a coloratura soprano. She was born on June 29, 1871, in Florence, Italy, and studied with her sister and at the Liceo Musicale. After she made her debut in 1895 in Meyerbeer's *L'Africaine*, she toured Italy, St. Petersburg, and Buenos Aires. In 1907, she made her Covent Garden debut singing Violetta in *La Traviata*, which she followed with other roles. Appearing mostly in Italian opera of the older school, one of her most notable successes was in Donizetti's *Lucia di Lammermoor*. She sang in London and in America, and in 1913, joined the Chicago Opera Company for a year. World War I interrupted her career, but she continued her concert tours until 1934, with her final performance in London. After her retirement, she taught in Milan.

BIBLIOGRAPHY

Gattey, Charles Neilson. *Luisa Tetrazzini; the Florentine Nightingale*. Portland, OR: Timber, 1995. 0-931340-87-X, 379p. In a scholarly, balanced biography, Gattey traces the career of Tetrazzini, the diva who Adelina Patti expected to succeed her, as she traveled from Italy to Russia, the United States, and the United Kingdom to perform.

Tetrazzini, Luisa. *My Life of Song*. 1921. New York: Arno, 1977. 0-405-09709-3, 328p. Tetrazzini's account is an enjoyable overview of the opera world as the twentieth century began, with personable anecdotes about jealous performers. She begins her story remembering the moment she heard that "Patti is dead. "

TEYTE, MAGGIE (1888–1976)
Opera Singer   England

Dame Maggie Teyte was an operatic soprano. Born on April 17, 1888, she later studied at the Royal College of Music in London and in Paris. Her formal oper-

atic debut was in Monte Carlo in 1907, when she performed Tyrcis in Offen-
bach's *Myriam et Daphné*. The following year, she appeared in Paris as **Mary
Garden**'s replacement as Debussy's *Mélisande*. She debuted in London in 1910
and Chicago in 1911. In 1922, she began singing a range of operas from the
classical to the romantic with the Beecham Opera Company, which later became the British National Opera Company. She, however, was mainly an interpreter of French song and made a second career recording French songs by
Debussy, Ravel, Berlioz, and others. She became a Chevalier of the Légion
d'Honneur in 1957 and a Dame of the British Empire in 1958.

BIBLIOGRAPHY

O'Connor, Garry. *The Pursuit of Perfection: A Life of Maggie Teyte*. New York:
    Atheneum, 1979. 0-689-10964-4, 327p. O'Connor, Teyte's great-nephew,
    discloses that she was independent and outspoken at an early age, with little
    patience for those who interfered with her career goals, and wanted free-
    dom before her society was willing to give it to her.

THATCHER, MARGARET (1925–)

Politician   **England**

Baroness Margaret Thatcher became the first female prime minster in England.
As the second daughter, born on October 13, 1925, she became the son her father never had, and he taught her that she could be anything that she wanted.
She followed him to town council meetings when she was ten and learned
about politics and gained knowledge about business from the family store. To
qualify for, and earn, a scholarship to Somerville College at Oxford, she
crammed four years of Latin into one. She learned debate at Oxford and became the president of the Oxford University Conservative Association in 1946.
She graduated with a degree in chemistry, but she wanted to be a lawyer. After
losing her first election, she married Denis Thatcher and began to attend law
school. While raising children, she became an expert on tax law. In 1959, she
won her next try at a Parliament seat in London's Finchley area. When Heath
was elected prime minister in 1970, she became his only female cabinet member when appointed secretary for education and science. In May 1979, she was
elected prime minister when no one else seemed able to lead the country out of
an economic collapse. Known as the "Iron Lady," she knew the importance of
free enterprise and entrepreneurship, and she began to denationalize Britain's
economy. But other unpopular policies forced her to resign in 1990. She was
created a life peer in 1992.

BIBLIOGRAPHY

Abse, Leo. *Margaret, Daughter of Beatrice: A Politician's Psycho-Biography of
    Margaret Thatcher*. North Pomfret, VT: Trafalgar Square, 1991. 0-224-
    02726-3, 288p. In Abse's psychoanalytic approach to Thatcher, he suggests
    that decisions she made as prime minister resulted from deprivations of her
    childhood. Although entertaining, this "biography" is imbalanced.
Harris, Kenneth. *Thatcher*. Boston: Little, Brown, 1988. 0-316-34837-6, 248p.
    Harris traces Thatcher's career from her childhood through her service as
    prime minister, focusing on the high points. His positive view perhaps bal-
    ances Abse's negative one.
Thatcher, Margaret. *The Downing Street Years*. New York: HarperCollins,
    1993. 0-06-017056-5, 914p. Thatcher covers her years as prime minister
    from 1979 to 1990 in this memoir. It reveals little of her personal life but

does reveal much about her government and her character, both faults and attributes.

Thatcher, Margaret. *The Path to Power*. New York: HarperCollins, 1995. 0-06-017270-3, 656p. Thatcher recalls her childhood as calm and orderly and continues with details about the rest of her life in this autobiography, but she fails to reflect on the meaning of her life.

Young, Hugo. *The Iron Lady: A Biography of Margaret Thatcher*. New York: Farrar, Straus, and Giroux, 1989. 0-374-22651-2, 570p. Young's popular biography of Thatcher is the best to review her life and career from her apprenticeship to Harold Macmillan to her position as senior statesman in the West.

THEODORA (497–548)
Empress   Byzantium

Theodora became the empress of Byzantium when she married Justinian. The daughter of Acadious, the bear keeper in the Hippodrome, she became an orphan at four. She went into the theater with her sister, and by fifteen, she was a dancer and mime known for her beauty and for her ability to make people laugh. She went with Hecebolus to North Africa as his mistress, but she returned to Byzantium and became a wool spinner. Justinian saw her and altered the law so that he could marry someone from a different class. Two years after their marriage in 525, he became the emperor and named her as empress. With her great intelligence and courage, Theodora played a major role throughout his long and distinguished reign and probably saved his throne during the Nika riots by her intervention in 532. She supported changes in legislation so that women could have the right of inheritance and wives could keep their dowry as their own property. Children also gained protection from being sold as slaves to pay their parents' debts. When brothels and pimps were outlawed in 535, she bought freedom for girls who had been sold into prostitution and looked after them. She was dedicated to her friends but merciless to her rivals. After she died of cancer, Justinian did little during his remaining seventeen years.

BIBLIOGRAPHY
Bridge, Antony. *Theodora: Portrait in a Byzantine Landscape*. Chicago: Academy, 1984. 0-89733-102-8, 194p. In this enjoyable biography, Bridge describes Theodora's abilities and the social atmosphere of the times that allowed her to succeed.

Browning, Robert. *Justinian and Theodora*. Rev. ed. New York: Thames and Hudson, 1987. 0-500-25099-5, 189p. As well as being a documented and recommended biography of Theodora and her consort, Justinian I, the text also describes Constantinople during the formation of modern Europe, summarizes theology, and comments on the silk trade.

THÉRÈSE of LISIEUX (1873–1897)
Religious   France

Thérèse Martin became a saint as a result of her work during World War I. Born on January 2, 1873, Thérèse said that when she was two, she wanted to be a nun. Her mother died of breast cancer when Thérèse was four, after having nine children in thirteen years and continuing to make lace to help support the family. In 1882, Thérèse had an attack of acute nervousness and said that a vision of the Virgin Mary cured it in 1883. On December 25, 1886, she had a religious experience that she called a conversion. She appealed to the pope in Rome during 1887 to be allowed to enter the Carmel at fifteen, a child, when the convent's leader would not admit her. Thérèse professed no extraordinary experiences and worked no wonders. One of her achievements was writing a play about Jeanne d'Arc while in the convent and acting in the lead role in 1894. She died at twenty-four of tuberculosis. Her book on the history of the soul and her work in World War I led the way for her to be canonized in thirty, instead of the requisite, fifty years.

BIBLIOGRAPHY

Furlong, Monica. *Thérèse of Lisieux*. New York: Pantheon, 1987. 0-394-53706-8, 144p. Furlong wants to show in her documented biography that Thérèse struggled to understand her relationship with God and that she paid the price, not that she was sugary or gentle or obedient.

Gaucher, Guy. *The Passion of Thérèse of Lisieux: 4 April–30 September 1897*. New York: Crossroad, 1990. 0-8245-0987-0, 269p. Using all available authentic documents, Gaucher traces Thérèse's illness in detail for the last few months of her life from 4 April to 30 September when she died of tuberculosis. He tries to analyze how she faced her death.

Hollings, Michael. *Thérèse of Lisieux*. Ann Arbor, MI: Servant, 1991. 0-89283-724-1, 62p. Hollings uses Thérèse's autobiography as the main source for his biography, but he also includes letters and last testimonies to present a woman whose simple life was an inspiration to others.

O'Connor, Patricia. *In Search of Thérèse*. Collegeville, MI: Liturgical Press, 1990. 0-8146-5596-3, 200p. O'Connor, in this documented biography, says that Thérèse realized how valuable her autobiography would be because it relayed the importance of a spiritual life.

Thérèse de Lisieux. *Story of a Soul: The Autobiography of St. Thérèse of Lisieux*. Trans. John Clarke. Washington, DC: ICS, 1996. 0-935216-58-8, 306p. Thérèse's autobiography, in which she relates anecdotes about her childhood and family, is the source for the story of her life and of her soul.

THORNDIKE, SYBIL (1882–1976)

Actor   England

Dame Sybil Thorndike was an actor and valuable member of the Old Vic Company. Born in Gainsborough, Lincolnshire, on October 24, 1882, she was the daughter of a Rochester Cathedral canon. She trained as a pianist but turned to the stage, making her debut in 1904 and touring England and the United States before joining a repertory company in Manchester, where she played for two periods in 1908 and 1911 to 1913. During this same time, she married and had three children. In 1914, she played leading roles in twelve Shakespearean plays in the Old Vic Company. In 1924, she played the title role in the first English performance of Shaw's *Saint Joan*. She remained a member of the company, playing a variety of roles through World War II. Throughout her life, she continued to play the piano, perferring Bach, and singing. She attributed her success to "argument, energy, and enthusiasm." She was made a Dame of the British Empire in 1931 and a Companion of Honor in 1970.

BIBLIOGRAPHY

Casson, John. *Lewis and Sybil: A Memoir*. London: Collins, 1972. 0-00-211488-7, 352p. This personal memoir of Sybil Thorndike Casson's son John includes many delightful anecdotes about the family, people they knew in the theater, and the times. He presents a positive mother who acted pleased with events.

Morley, Sheridan. *Sybil Thorndike: A Life in the Theatre*. London: Weidenfeld and Nicolson, 1977. 0-297-77388-7, 183p. Morley has written a balanced and recommended chronicle of Thorndike's long theatrical career, using her interviews from radio, television, and print journalists; her letters; reports of contemporary critics; and photographs as sources. Lists of stage, film, and television performances are appended to the text.

Sprigge, Elizabeth. *Sybil Thorndike Casson*. London: Gollancz, 1971. 0-575-01341-9, 348p. Thorndike requested that Sprigge write this "autobiographical" biography. It is researched and documented but based mainly on interviews with Thorndike and her husband, Louis Casson.

TILLEY, VESTA (1864–1952)

Entertainer   England

Vesta Tilley was a music hall entertainer. Matilda Alice Powles was born May 13, 1864, in Worcester, Hereford, and first appeared as "the Great Little Tilley," age four, in her father's Nottingham music hall. After touring with him wearing top hat and tails at five, she never changed her mode of costume, and after a London debut in 1874, she was a success at sixteen. She researched all of her roles so that the males she impersonated were realistic. In 1890, she married Walter de Frece but continued to perform, touring the United States and appearing at the first Royal Command Performance in 1912. She was a consummate professional who prepared for every moment on stage. Her husband was knighted in 1919 and later became a member of Parliament. Lady de Frece retired in 1920, and at her last performance, **Ellen Terry** presented her with "the People's Tribute," signed by nearly 2 million fans. Lady de Frece then spent much of her time in the South of France.

BIBLIOGRAPHY

Maitland, Sara. *Vesta Tilley*. London: Virago, 1986. 0-86068-795-3, 148p. Maitland says in her documented and well-written biography, with photographs, that Tilley gave the working-class woman hope and a new way of looking at both men and women, although Tilley would not join any political group, either for the proletariat or for women.

Sudworth, Gwynedd. *The Great Little Tilley: Vesta Tilley and Her Times: A Biography*. Luton, England: Cortney, 1984. 0-904378-30-6, 159p. Sudworth notes that Tilley was called the "Great Little Tilley," with her days in the music hall preceding and preparing the way for Marie Lloyd. The researched but undocumented biography includes background on the music hall.

TRISTAN, FLORA (1803–1844)

Activist and Writer   France

Flora Tristan was a socialist reformer. Born on April 7, 1803, as the daughter of a Peruvian colonel and a French mother, she grew up in France in poverty after her father's death. She married her employer in 1821 but left him in 1824, and a long battle over custody of their children began. Divorce was illegal in France, so she worked for an English family and then went to Peru to persuade her uncle to support her family. He refused. Eight years later, she wrote her autobiography, *Peregrinations d'une paria*, and called herself a "pariah." Her husband then attempted to murder her but failed and received a sentence of twenty-two years' hard labor. In 1834, after her return to France, she wrote feminist tracts and novels. On an extended trip to London, she studied Chartism, examined social conditions in the country, and wrote about them. By then she had formed her views on socialism and feminism, and she wrote *Union Ouvrière*, proposing a socialist international union. She wanted welfare and educational centers established, with women having rights to education and employment in humane conditions. During her lifetime, Peru banned her books, and the London press called her a bloodthirsty revolutionary and Jacobin. She had legal problems, few job opportunities, and poor pay. She faced double standards and was physically frail but refused to become a victim. While trying to publicize her ideas, she died of typhoid in Bordeaux. Workers in that city collected funds and bought and inscribed a tombstone for her reading "Liberté—Egalité—Fraternité—Solidarité."

BIBLIOGRAPHY

Cross, Maire, and Tim Gray. *Feminism of Flora Tristan*. New York: Berg, 1992. 0-85496-731-1, 192p. This academic biography examines Tristan and her feminism from biographical, literary, sociological, and ideological perspectives as the authors examine the images of women in her novel *Méphis*, her insights about conditions in London, her early utopianism, her revolutionism, and her attempt to put feminism in practice.

DeSantis, Dominique. *A Woman in Revolt: A Biography of Flora Tristan*. Trans. Elizabeth Zelvin. New York: Crown, 1976. 0-517-51878-3, 281p. DeSantis quotes from Tristan's journals, novels, and political writing to reveal Tristan's proposals for an international union of workers before Marx wrote *Das Kapital* and her advocacy for legal, educational, economic, and social equality for women.

Gattey, Charles. *Gauguin's Astonishing Grandmother: A Biography of Flora Tristan*. London: Femina, 1970. 0-85043-010-0, 223p. This documented biography of Tristan is readable and enjoyable, showing her, as Gauguin said, to be "an astonishing woman."

Strumingher, Laura. *The Odyssey of Flora Tristan*. New York: Peter Lang, 1988. 0-8204-0888-3, 162p. In a balanced and recommended biography, using information not previously available about Tristan, Strumingher thinks that Tristan used her bicultural heritage from French and Spanish parents to make herself into a strong woman.

TROLLOPE, FRANCES (1780–1863)

Writer   England

Frances Trollope was a Regency writer. She was born Frances Milton on March 10, 1780, at Stapleton, near Bristol, the daughter of a clergyman. Her mother died, and her father remarried before Milton left home. She went to London to become housekeeper for her brother and married Thomas Anthony Trollope, who failed as a lawyer and a farmer before trying to sell goods in Cincinnati, Ohio. His next investment in London also failed, and Frances Trollope began writing at the age of fifty-three to support her six children, one of them becoming the writer Anthony Trollope. She reflected on life in America in *Domestic Manners of the Americans* (1831), and it was a success. She produced forty-one books in twenty-four years and wrote a total of over one hundred during her long career. She wrote satirical novels of domestic manners in which she attacked offenses in society such as child labor, slavery, woman's rights, and workhouses. Book reviewers reviled her work, thinking that her candor was vulgar. She also traveled and wrote about Belgium, Paris, and Austria during the 1830s after one of her sons and her husband died in 1835. In 1843, she settled in Florence, Italy, with one of her sons.

BIBLIOGRAPHY

Bigland, Eileen. *The Indomitable Mrs. Trollope*. London: Barrie and Jenkins, 1970. 0-214-6524-6, 219p. In a researched biography, Bigland begins Trollope's life in 1808, when she was twenty-seven and marrying Thomas Trollope, her only prospect, and follows her life and career until her death.

Heineman, Helen. *Mrs. Trollope: The Triumphant Feminine in the Nineteenth Century*. Athens: Ohio University Press, 1979. 0-9214-0354-0, 316p. Heineman uses letters previously unavailable as additional sources in her scholarly biography of Trollope, exploring her wit and talent, which helped her use fiction as a way to attack social abuse and to show women in their complexity.

Johnston, Johanna. *The Life, Manners, and Travels of Fanny Trollope: A Biography*. New York: Hawthorn, 1978. 0-8015-2557-8, 242 p. Johnston retells the life of Fanny Trollope in an entertaining biography emphasizing her tours to America, her achievements, and her difficulties raising a family while writing.

Ransom, Teresa. *Fanny Trollope: A Remarkable Life*. New York: St. Martin's, 1995. 0-312-12618-2, 236p. As a descendant of Fanny Trollope, Ransom uses family memoirs, autobiographies, and contemporary letters to document Trollope's career and life as a loyal wife in face of provocation, a more dedicated parent than portrayed elsewhere, and as much a feminist as she could be within her times.

TURNER, ETHEL (1872?–1958)

Writer   **England**

Ethel Turner was a novelist and children's writer. She was born on January 24, 1872?, in Doncaster, South Yorkshire. Her father, a commercial traveler, died when Turner was two, and, although her mother immediately remarried, she soon parted from her new husband. Turner's birthdate has been unclear since her mother altered her year of birth so that she could get fare concessions for her and her sister on their journey to Australia. Turner was probably eleven when she went to Australia. She attended Paddington Public School but left high school as a result of her tumultuous childhood and began to write. With her sister, Lilian, she started a magazine and wrote the children's page, later doing the same for two other Sydney periodicals. Her first book, *Seven Little Australians*, published in 1894, was an immediate success and has been in print ever since publication. As a story about real children in a Sydney suburb, it is now a classic of Australian literature. She published a sequel in the following year and continued to write many juvenile books, short stories, and verse. She also collaborated with her daughter Jean on several books and editing a newspaper column.

BIBLIOGRAPHY

Turner, Ethel Sybil. *The Diaries of Ethel Turner*. Comp. Philippa Poole. Ed. Peita Royle. New York: Ure Smith, 1979. 0-7254-0519-8, 288p. Turner's granddaughter, after being asked to speak and write about her grandmother, decided to edit her diaries and add photographs. Many of the entries catalog Turner's activities, and therefore, present her daily life and the times in which she lived.

Yarwood, A. T. *From a Chair in the Sun: The Life of Ethel Turner*. Ringwood, Victoria, Australia: Viking, 1994. 0-670-83717-2, 391p. Yarwood's balanced, documented, and readable biography recounts Turner's life beginning in England and in Australia, where her mother immigrated.

TUSSAUD, MARIE (1761–1850)

Artist   Switzerland

Madame Tussaud modeled figures of famous people in wax. She was born on December 1, 1761, in Strasbourg as Marie Grosholtz and, as a young girl, was apprenticed to her uncle in Paris. After his death, she inherited his wax museums. During the revolution, she waited at the guillotine to make death masks of the severed heads and was imprisoned. After her release, she married a French soldier, François Tussaud. She separated from him in 1800 and moved to London with her two children. She toured Britain with her life-sized wax figures of heroes and rogues before setting up a permanent exhibition in 1835. This display burned but reopened in another London location and still contains wax works that she created of **Marie Antoinette**, Napoleon, and Sir Walter Scott.

BIBLIOGRAPHY

Chapman, Pauline. *The French Revolution: As Seen by Madame Tussaud, Witness Extraordinary*. London: Quiller, 1989. 1-870948-14-9, 193p. Chapman presents Marie Grosholtz's unique account of the French Revolution, during which she created wax effigies of some of the key participants.

Leslie, Anita, and Pauline Chapman. *Madame Tussaud, Waxworker Extraordinary*. London: Hutchinson, 1978. 0-09-133810-7, 216p. Extensive research in both English and French archives as well as Tussaud's letters and memoirs form the basis for this biography of Tussaud, but she was careful not to exert her own opinions, and the authors have not been able to express them.

TZ'U-HSI (1834–1908)

Empress   China

Tz'u-Hsi, Xiaogin or Hsiao-ch'en, who became the Empress Dowager, was the Chinese consort of the Xianfeng emperor. Born in Beijing on November 29, 1834, with the family name Yehonala, her father was a government service clerk and later a provincial administrator. She was selected in 1851 as a low-ranking concubine of Hs'en Feng, but she bore the Xianfeng emperor his only son and worked as his secretary, where she learned about the administration of the state. Her son succeeded at the age of five as the T'ung Chih emperor, and she became the Empress Dowager, requiring that all decrees bear her seal. She, her late husband's chief wife, and his brother suppressed the Taiping rebellion in the South, the Nien rebellion in the North, and the Moslem revolt in Yunnan. They also began to Westernize China with schools of foreign language, customs departments, and military reform while she made money from selling posts and promotions. When her son died in 1875, she flouted the succession laws of the imperial clan to ensure the succession of another minor, aged three, as the Guangxu emperor and continued her control. In 1900, she took China into war against the combined treaty powers in support of the Boxer movement. She had to flee but returned after 1901, ended foot-binding, allowed intermarriage of Chinese and Manchu, and opened state schools to women. She was also a calligrapher and arts patron.

BIBLIOGRAPHY

Carl, Katherine Augusta. *With the Empress Dowager of China*. 1905. New York: Methuen, 1986. Paper, 0-7103-0218-5, 306p.   Katherine Augusta Carl, painter of the empress's portrait, was the only Westerner to ever live as a member of the Chinese court. Her full and authentic record of the Forbidden City in the last days of imperial China has a stilted style, but she became friends with Tz'u-Hsi while painting four portraits of her.

Hussey, Harry. *Venerable Ancestor; The Life and Times of Tz'u Hsi, 1835–1908, Empress of China*. Drawings Shirley Wang. 1949. Westport, CT: Greenwood Press, 1970. 0-8371-4430-2, 354p. Hussey, after visiting Peking and all its splendors, researched the life of Tz'u Hsi and found that many saw her as a warm, intelligent woman instead of the hard, cruel, and scheming ruler so often described. His scholarly biography is well written and recommended.

Seagrave, Sterling, and Peggy Seagrave. *Dragon Lady: The Life and Legend of the Last Empress of China*. New York: Knopf, 1992. 0-679-40230-6, 601p. After investigating the tales surrounding Tz'u-Hsi, the authors think that she was misrepresented by three Englishmen who distorted their reports about her.

Warner, Marina. *The Dragon Empress: Life and Times of Tz'u-Hsi, Empress Dowager of China, 1835-1908*. 1972. New York: Atheneum, 1986. Paper, 0-689-70714-2, 247p. In a readable and seemingly reliable account of life in China at the end of the nineteenth century with photographs, Warner's biography of Tz'u-Hsi describes her vanity, desire for power, love of beauty, cruelty, and legacy.

Wu, Yung. *The Flight of an Empress*. Trans. Ida Pruitt. 1936. Westport, CT: Hyperion, 1973. 0-88355-098-9, 222p. Wu served in the magistracy of Huai-lai, a city north of Peking, when the Empress Dowager escaped during the Boxer rebellion. He gained her favor, and the text re-creates the circumstances of their relationship.

𝔘

UKRAINKA, LESYA (1871–1913)
Poet and Playwright   Ukraine

Lesya Ukrainka was a poetess and playwright. Born Larisa Petrovna Kosach-Kvitka on February 13, 1871, she was the second child and first daughter in her family. She became a member of the Ukrainian modernist movement in poetry and combined characteristic Ukrainian national features with a universal flair. As a young person, she was diagnosed with the incurable disease of tuberculosis of her bones. Her lyrics and dramatic poems were published as *Na krylakh pisnya* (1893), *Nevilnychi pisni* (1895), and *Lisova pisnya* (1912).

BIBLIOGRAPHY
Bida, Konstantyn. *Lesya Ukrainka; Life and Work*. Trans. Vera Rich. Toronto: University of Toronto Press, 1968. No ISBN, 259p. Bida discusses the family, the social and cultural environment in which Ukrainka matured, and some of the external factors that influenced her talent and subject matter. This is a short and readable biography with the full text of one of Ukrainka's plays.

Shakhovs'kyi, Semen. *Lesya Ukrainka: A Biographical Sketch*. Trans. Anatole Bilenko and Victor Ruzhitsky. Kiev, Ukraine: Dnipro, 1975. No ISBN, 118p. This biography, with the pedestrian style and tone of Soviet propaganda published during the Soviet regime, recognizes Ukrainka as a poet who fought against oppression.

ULANOVA, GALINA (1910–)
Ballerina   Russia

Galina Ulanova is a ballerina. She was born in St. Petersburg on January 8, 1910, as the daughter of a dancer and stage director father and a stage mechanic mother, both working for the Mariinsky Theater. She studied with her mother and made her debut at the Kirov Theater at eighteen. Her first performance of *Giselle* became the model for contemporary interpretation. In

1944, she joined the Bolshoi Ballet and the next year performed in Vienna. The Moscow State Ballet Company made several films with her. After her final performance in 1962, she became ballet mistress at the Kirov and was honored as People's Artist of the USSR. Other awards were the Leningrad Defense Medal, the Medal of Labor Valor during World War II, the State Prize four times, the Lenin Prize, the Italian Biotti Prize, corresponding Member of the German Academy of Arts, and the World Peace Council Certificate of Merit.

BIBLIOGRAPHY

Kahn, Albert E. *Days with Ulanova*. North Stratford, NH: Ayer, 1980. 0-8369-9297-0, 91p. Kahn tries to show Ulanova's single-minded devotion to her work in this pictorial biography, photographed during one of Ulanova's last ballet seasons.

Ilupina, Anna. *Ballerina, the Life and Work of Galina Ulanova*. Philadelphia: Provident, 1965. No ISBN, 94p. Ilupina was a friend of Ulanova, and this short, laudatory biography, with photographs, discusses her talent and recounts her achievements.

UNDERHILL, EVELYN (1875–1941)

Mystic   England

Evelyn Underhill was an Anglican religious mystic and poet. She was born on December 6, 1875, in Wolverhampton in a barrister's family and studied at King's College, London. In 1907, she married a childhood friend, and the same year, she made her final conversion to Christianity. She began to study mystics and wrote *Mysticism* (1911), which became the standard work on describing religious experience. She became lecturer on the philosophy of religion at Manchester College, Oxford, led religious retreats, and was a religious counselor. In 1927, she became a fellow of King's College. Although she had worked for the government during World War I, she became a pacifist in 1939 and wrote *The Church and War* in 1940. During her career, she wrote several other spiritual books, volumes of verse, and four novels.

BIBLIOGRAPHY

Armstrong, Christopher. *Evelyn Underhill: Eighteen Seventy-Five to Nineteen Forty-One: An Introduction to Her Life and Writing*. Grand Rapids, MI: Eerdmans, 1976. 0-8028-3474-4, 303p. Armstrong, using previously unpublished sources for a well-written biography, looks closely at Underhill's writings to show why she returned to organized religion after looking at other choices for her spiritual life.

Brame, Grace Adolphsen, ed. *The Ways of the Spirit*. New York: Crossroad, 1990. 0-8 245-1008-9, 247p. Brame includes four of Underhill's unpublished "retreats" (addresses) with her discussion of Underhill's concerns for holiness through prayer and inner transformation and her unique position as one of the first women in the Church of England's spiritual leadership.

Greene, Dana. *Evelyn Underhill: Artist of the Infinite Life*. New York: Crossroad, 1990. 0-8245-1006-2, 179p. New archival source material and a combination of feminist, psychological, and spiritual theory allow Greene to examine Underhill's struggle with pacifism, spiritual direction, and search for self through mysticism in a recommended biography.

Underhill, Evelyn. *Fragments from an Inner Life: The Notebooks of Evelyn Underhill*. Ed. Dana Greene. Harrisburg, PA: Morehouse, 1993. 0-8192-1600-3, 131p. In her notebooks, called *Green* and *Flowered*, Underhill records her unsystematic and private thoughts, which reveal doubts, failings, obstacles to growth, and the gradual development of her own experience for the fifteen years during which she shifted from scholar of mysticism to believer in the spiritual life for ordinary people.

UNDSET, SIGRID (1882–1949)
Writer   Denmark

Sigrid Undset was awarded the Nobel Prize in literature in 1928. She was born on May 20, 1882, in Kalundborg, before her family moved to Oslo, where her father died when she was eleven. She graduated from commercial college and worked in an office for ten years. After her marriage, she turned to writing, with her first major work as *Kristin Lavransdatter* (1920–1922), a fourteenth-century trilogy in which she presented a concern for fulfillment in women. She became a Catholic in 1924, which influenced her later work, including a four-volume series, *Olav Audunssön* (1925–1927), set in the thirteenth century. Her other works have contemporary settings, such as *Gymadenia* (1929) and *Den trofaste hastra* (1936). All her characters live in communities where people have realistic desires and failings. Although chastened for references to sex, she responded that it was integral to life.

BIBLIOGRAPHY
Bayerschmidt, Carl Frank. *Sigrid Undset.* New York: Twayne, 1970. No ISBN, 176p. This critical and recommended biography briefly recounts Undset's life and analyzes her major novels, including *Kristin Lavransdatter* and *Olav Audunssön.*

Brunsdale, Mitzi. *Sigrid Undset, Chronicler of Norway.* New York: Berg, St. Martin's, 1988. 0-85496-027-9, 160p. Brunsdale surveys Undset's life and artistic career, showing the influences of Old Norse literature and Catholicism in a biased biography.

Dunn, Margaret. *Paradigms and Paradoxes in the Life and Letters of Sigrid Undset.* Lanham, MD: University Press of America, 1994. 0-8191-9280-5, 104p. In her scholarly and disorganized but enlightening biography of Undset, Dunn imagines Undset as a "major character in each of her novels." Details from Undset's life support Dunn's thesis.

UTTLEY, ALISON (1884–1976)
Writer   England

Alison Uttley was a scientist and children's writer. She was born near Cromford, Derbyshire, on December 17, 1884, where her parents were farmers. She attended Lea School, won tuition to Lady Manners School, Bakewell, which meant a daily, twelve-mile train journey, and won a scholarship to study physics at Manchester after correctly completing an electrical experiment when she had never seen a real electrical outlet. At Cambridge, she trained to teach. In 1930, she became a widow, and to support herself and her young son, she began writing, first publishing *The Country Child* in 1931 and following it with a series of books, mainly for children, that revealed her knowledge of the countryside. Many were in the **Beatrix Potter** tradition, featuring characters such as "Little Grey Rabbit" and "Sam Pig."

BIBLIOGRAPHY

Judd, Denis. *Alison Uttley: the Life of a Country Child, 1884–1976: The Authorised Biography*. London: M. Joseph, 1986. 0-7181-2449-9, 295p. In Uttley's authorized biography, Judd uses interviews, diaries, and documents from the Alison Uttley Literary Property Trust. It is a well-documented, balanced, recommended, and scholarly biography.

Saintsbury, Elizabeth. *The World of Alison Uttley, a Biography: The Life and Times of One of the Best Loved Country Writers of Our Century*. London: H. Baker, 1980. 0-7030-0179-5, 177p. Saintsbury recaptures details from Uttley's autobiographies in a loosely written and undocumented biography with photographs. She identifies Uttley's work as social history, showing life before modern technology usurped the quiet countryside.

Uttley, Alison. *Ambush of Young Days*. Illus. C. F. Tunnicliffe. Maidstone, England: Mann, 1974. 0-7041-0038-X, 238p. Uttley discusses a variety of topics, such as different times of day on the farm, her earliest years, tree animals, playthings, bonnets and pinafores, spring cleaning, Sundays at church and religious training, folktales read aloud, school, her village, neighbors, her schoolmaster, and her favorite season, winter.

Uttley, Alison. *Country Hoard*. Illus. C. F. Tunnicliffe. London: H. Baker, 1976. 0-7030-0098-5, 130p. Uttley recalls changes during her childhood, such as inside bathrooms and the ordinary activities of writing letters, money as an adult item, birthday celebrations, Irishmen helping harvest the hay, the barbershop, field toys, and country vocabulary.

Uttley, Alison. *Country World: Memories of Childhood*. Illus. C. F. Tunnicliffe. Boston: Faber and Faber, 1984. 0-571-13328-2, 171p. Uttley uses the persona of Susan Garland in her autobiography, beginning with her birth and ending with the first day of grammar school. She describes the farm and visiting the dentist, a treat because few could afford the luxury.

𝔘

VALADON, SUZANNE (1869–1938)

Artist   France

Suzanne Valadon was a French painter, the mother of Utrillo. She was illegitimate, born in Bessines, Haute-Vienne, on September 23, 1869. She went to
Paris with her seamstress mother and became a circus acrobat, but, after falling
off a trapeze, she started modeling for artist Puvis de Chavannes. She had his
child, whom she named "Miguel Utrillo," but never told her son his father's
identity. As a single parent, she modeled nude until twenty-eight for Renoir
and Toulouse-Lautrec, who encouraged her painting and introduced her to Degas. Degas arranged the first exhibition of her portraits, especially those of her
lover Erik Satie, and her success was instant. She added prints, still lifes, landscapes, nudes, and genre scenes as subjects for her paintings. Her female nudes
and children were innovative, disrupting the existing conventions. She painted
the harsh but true images of the working class, saying that she used the best of
what she saw and made it her own. She created nearly nine hundred paintings,
drawings, and etchings, with her work appearing in shows in France and
abroad.

BIBLIOGRAPHY

Rosinsky, Therese Diamand. *Suzanne Valadon*. New York: Universe, 1994. 0-
87663-777-2, 128p. Rosinsky tries to demythologize Valadon's life as a
self-taught artist from a lower-class social background in a balanced, documented, and recommended account, including an analysis of Valadon's
work.

Warnod, Jeanine. *Suzanne Valadon*. New York: Crown, 1981. 0-517-54499-7,
96p. Warnod discusses Valadon's life and her work in a brief biography
with accompanying photographs.

VALOIS, MARGARET of. *See* MARGARET of VALOIS.

VALOIS, NINETTE de. *See* DE VALOIS, NINETTE.

VAN PRAAGH, PEGGY (1910–1990)
Ballerina and Ballet Producer   **England**

Dame Margaret Van Praagh was a ballet dancer, teacher, and producer. Born in London on September 1, 1910, she was the daughter of a Dutch-Jewish doctor and a former governess mother. She trained with Margaret Craske before joining the Ballet **Rambert** in 1933 and then joined Sadler's Wells Ballet as dancer and teacher before becoming a producer and assistant director with **Ninette De Valois** at Sadler's Wells Theatre Ballet from 1941 to 1956. She produced many ballets for BBC television and for international companies, and in 1960, became artistic director for the Borovansky Ballet in Australia. She was founding artistic director for the Australian Ballet in 1962 for nearly fifteen years before joining the Victoria Council of the Arts and serving as guest teacher until 1982. She was made an Officer of the British Empire in 1966 and a Dame in 1979.

BIBLIOGRAPHY
Sexton, Christopher. *Peggy Van Praagh, a Life of Dance.* South Melbourne, Australia: Macmillan, 1985. 0-333-40089-5, 226p. Sexton's thorough, carefully documented biography is a straightforward look at Van Praagh's life and career and includes photographs and a list of the roles that Van Praagh created as a dancer.

VERDY, VIOLETTE (1933–)
Ballerina and Director   **France**

Violette Verdy was an award-winning dancer and ballet director. She was born Nelly Armande Guillerm in Pont-L'Abbé, Lambour, France, on December 1, 1933, daughter of Renan and Jeanne Guillerm. After making her debut with Ballets des Champs-Élysées in 1945, she appeared in films and theater as an actor and dancer. She joined Roland Petit's Ballets de Paris in 1950, later freelancing with several companies, including London Festival Ballet (1954), American Ballet Theatre (1957), and the New York City Ballet (1958 to 1977). She then became artistic director of Paris Opéra Ballet from 1977 to 1980 and artistic codirector of the Boston Ballet in 1980. Her accolades include the *Dance Magazine* award for artistic excellence, an honorary doctorate from Skidmore College, appointment to the dance advisory panel of the National Endowment for the Arts, and the French government's Order of Arts and Letters as the first performing dancer to receive the award.

BIBLIOGRAPHY
Huckenpahler, Victoria. *Ballerina: A Biography of Violette Verdy.* New York: Audience Arts, 1978. 0-82476-518-4, 244p. Huckenpahler uses correspondence, newspaper clippings, legal documents, photographs, films, and personal interviews for a carefully documented, readable, and recommended biography telling Verdy's story as well as that of the mid–twentieth-century ballet world.

Swope, Martha, and B. H. Haggin. *Violette Verdy.* Brooklyn, NY: Dance Horizons, 1975. 0-87127-074-9, 23p. A brief biographical profile with comments from people who knew Verdy prefaces photographs of her in performance and in practice.

VESTRIS, LUCIA (1797–1856)
Actor and Theater Manager   England

Lucia Vestris was an actor whose stage and management career spanned four decades from the Regency to the Victorian age. She was born Lucia Elisabetta Bartolozzi on January 3, 1797, in London as the daughter of an Italian engraver. At sixteen, she married the dancer Armand Vestris, but they separated two years later, and Vestris played burlesque in Paris. She then performed in opera, extravaganza, and legitimate comedy and was especially good in the "trouser" roles of *The Beggar's Opera*, *Giovanni in London*, and a burlesque of Mozart's *Don Giovanni*. She subsequently served as director of Covent Garden, the Olympic Theater, and the Lyceum, where she initiated a variety of reforms and set production standards. After her 1820 appearance at Drury Lane, she performed a wide range of roles. In 1830, she started collecting her fortune as the lessee of the Olympic Theatre, following it with management of Covent Garden and the Lyceum. She insisted on improvements in scenery and historically accurate costuming.

BIBLIOGRAPHY

Appleton, William Worthen. *Madame Vestris and the London Stage*. New York: Columbia University Press, 1974. 0-231-03794-5, 230p. This thoroughly researched and well-written biography of Madame Vestris recognizes her technical innovations and creative productions and includes details about theaters and theatrics.

Pearce, Charles E. *Madame Vestris and Her Times*. 1923. New York: B. Blom, 1969. No ISBN, 314p. Pearce reports Vestris's escapades offstage and her performances onstage during her career and her twenty-one years as the first woman theatrical manager, defending her against the standards of her time.

Williams, Clifford John. *Madame Vestris: A Theatrical Biography*. London: Sidgwick and Jackson, 1973. 0-283-97629-5, 240p. Firsthand accounts of Vestris in the theater, as extraordinary actor, passionate woman, and disciplined manageress, form the basis of Williams' recommended biography of her.

VICTORIA of ENGLAND (1819–1901)
Queen   England

Alexandrina Victoria was the queen of Great Britain from 1837 to 1901. She was born at Kensington Palace on May 24, 1819, the only child of George III's fourth son, Edward, duke of Kent, and Victoria Maria Louisa of Saxe-Coburg. Her father died soon after her birth, and Victoria reached eighteen before her uncle, William IV, died in 1837. Crowned at Westminster in 1838, she speedily demonstrated a clear grasp of constitutional principles, about which her uncle Leopold had instructed her in many letters. Victoria fell in love with her cousin Prince Albert of Saxe-Coburg and Gotha and married him in 1840, when both were twenty. Although poor, Albert's irreproachable sexual morality was almost unprecedented at court, and the Victorian age came to be synonymous with a great revival of public morality. The royal couple produced four sons and five daughters, with their first son, Edward, Prince of Wales, born in 1841. After Albert's death in 1861, Victoria went into lengthy seclusion but recovered to become the longest-reigning English monarch, with her son Edward VII succeeding her.

BIBLIOGRAPHY

Charlot, Monica. *Victoria: The Young Queen.* Cambridge, MA: Blackwell, 1991. 0-631-17437-0, 500p. Using letters and memoirs in the Royal Archives, Charlot examines Victoria's life to show a warm and passionate woman and policy up to the death of her husband in 1861.

Erickson, Carolly. *Her Little Majesty: Queen Victoria.* New York: Simon and Schuster, 1997. 0-684-80765-3, 304p. This well-researched, well-written, and recommended popular biography of Victoria's life reads like a novel.

Richardson, Joanna. *Victoria and Albert.* New York: Quadrangle, 1977. 0-8129-0692-6, 239p. Richardson discloses through a distillation of previously published material and photographs that Victoria thought that husbands had absolute supremacy in marriage, and she ran her household and her country based on this premise.

Thompson, Dorothy. *Queen Victoria: The Woman, the Monarchy, and the People.* New York: Pantheon, 1990. 0-394-53709-2, 167p. Thompson emphasizes in this documented and well-researched biography that Victoria changed the status of the throne and nineteenth-century British politics because she was a woman who had a different relationship to her subjects than did males who preceded her.

Woodham-Smith, Cecil. *Queen Victoria, from Her Birth to the Death of the Prince Consort.* New York: Knopf, 1972. 0-394-48245-X, 486p. Using the royal family archives, Woodham-Smith re-creates Queen Victoria's life in a definitive, readable biography.

VIGÉE-LEBRUN, ÉLISABETH (1755–1842)

Artist   France

Marie-Louise-Élisabeth Vigée-Lebrun was a painter. She was born in Paris on April 16, 1755, daughter of a pastel portrait painter. She began drawing as a child while attending convent school and taking drawing lessons from her father's friends. After her father died, she painted oil portraits to support her brother. In 1775, she married a wealthy art dealer, J.B.P. Lebrun, but she continued to paint portraits. Her portrait of **Marie Antoinette** (1779 at Versailles) led to a lasting friendship and commissions for numerous portraits of the royal family. She left Paris at the outbreak of the revolution and continued painting in Florence, Rome, and Naples. She then went to Vienna and to St. Petersburg, where she spent six years at the court of Catherine II. She visited London in 1802 and painted portraits of the Prince of Wales and Lord Byron before returning to Paris in 1805. Friendly and personable, during her life, she completed over nine hundred paintings.

BIBLIOGRAPHY

Baillio, Joseph. *Élisabeth Louise Vigée-Lebrun 1755-1842.* Seattle: University of Washington Press, 1983. 0-295-96012-4, 143p. In Baillio's catalog, prepared for the Kimbell Art Museum in Fort Worth, Texas, he balances Vigée-Lebrun's accomplishments along with the difficulties she faced. The catalog includes detailed descriptions of her paintings and background information about the subjects and the circumstances in which she painted them.

Sheriff, Mary D. *The Exceptional Woman: Élisabeth Vigée-Lebrun and the Cultural Politics of Art*. Chicago: University of Chicago Press, 1995. 0-226-75275-5, 368p. Sheriff, in her feminist interpretation, thinks that Vigée-Lebrun's exceptional talent exempted her from the traditional expectations of women during her lifetime but that since Vigée-Lebrun had no alternative feminists models, she could not fully utilize her freedom in her life or in her self-portraits.

Vigee-Lebrun, Louise-Élisabeth. *Memoirs of Madame Vigée-Lebrun*. Trans. Lionel Strachey. Intro. John Russell. New York: G. Braziller, 1989. 0-8076-1221-9, 233p. Madame Vigée Lebrun details her times and her travels with descriptions of homes, gardens, dress, and family life.

VIONNET, MADELEINE (1877–1975)
Couturier   France

Madeleine Vionnet was a fashion designer. Born June 22, 1877, in Loiret, her father, a toll inspector, raised her, and she rarely saw her mother. She wanted to be a teacher, but a neighbor hired her as a seamstress, and she became apprenticed to him at fourteen. She married at eighteen, and when her daughter died in infancy, she broke ties with her husband and family and left for England. She trained in London and opened a shop before World War I, closed it during the war, and reopened in 1919. The House of Vionnet dominated women's fashion for twenty years with its emphasis on bias cut, "handkerchief point" skirts, and soft, flowing materials. As an employer, Vionnet provided social services for her employees such as clinics and gymnasiums before closing in 1939.

BIBLIOGRAPHY
Demornex, Jacqueline. *Madeleine Vionnet*. New York: Rizzoli, 1991. 0-8478-1387-8, 305p. Vionnet's goddaughter wrote this oversize biography of Vionnet, a perfectionist who loved beauty, and includes photographs of her clothes, showing how they transformed traditional concepts by adding depth and three-dimensional structure through pleats, draping, and ruffles.

VON ARNIM, BETTINA. *See* ARNIM, BETTINA von.

VON DROSTE-HÜLSHOFF, ANNETTE. *See* DROSTE-HÜLSHOFF, ANNETTE von.

VON SUTTNER, BERTHA. *See* SUTTNER, BERTHA von.

𝖂

WAGNER, COSIMA (1837–1930)
Instrumentalist   Germany

Cosima Wagner was a talented musician and writer who dedicated herself to her husband's career. Born as the second of three children on December 24, 1837, in the union of Franz Liszt and Countess Marie D'Agoult, Francesca Gaetana Liszt had an unstable childhood. She studied in France and Berlin, where her father sent her to the Bülow family to decrease her mother's influence. Critics admired her interpretations of both Liszt and Beethoven on the piano, but her father refused to let her become a pianist. Instead, she began translating from German into French before marrying Hans von Bülow in 1857 and socializing with Richard Wagner, whom her husband idolized. Six years later, after two children, Cosima declared her love for Wagner. She had two daughters by him, Isolde and Eva, and joined him in Triebschen, near Lucerne, in 1868. After a son, Siegfried, was born, Cosima married Wagner in 1870 and spent the rest of her life keeping his diaries and recording his autobiography as he dictated it. When Wagner died in 1883, Cosima became director of the Beyreuth Festival until 1906, when her son relieved her.

BIBLIOGRAPHY

Du Moulin-Eckart, Richard. *Cosima Wagner*. Trans. Catherine Alison Phillips. Intro. George Buelow. 1930. New York: Da Capo, 1981. 2 vols. 0-306-76102-5, 892p. Du Moulin-Eckart used the well-guarded family archives, quoting from Cosima Wagner's personal papers and her diaries for his biased biography, which Cosima approved. Du Moulin-Eckart worshiped Cosima, thinking her a survivor of a middle class that tried to suffocate woman's rights.

Marek, George R. *Cosima Wagner*. New York: Harper and Row, 1981. 0-06-012704-X, 291p. Marek shows Cosima's intelligence, gifts, strengths, and weaknesses in his anecdotes and selections from unpublished letters and documents in his well-researched, popular biography.

Skelton, Geoffrey. *Richard and Cosima Wagner: Biography of a Marriage.* Boston: Houghton Mifflin, 1982. 0-395-31836-X, 319p. Skelton uses Cosima's *Diaries* and Wagner's *Brown Book* as two of his sources in this well-researched and recommended, scholarly look at her marriage and the relationship of the Wagners to Cosima's first husband, Hans von Bülow.

Wagner, Cosima. *Cosima Wagner's Diaries.* Ed. Martin Gregor-Dellin and Dietrich Mack. Trans. Geoffrey Skelton. New York: Harcourt Brace Jovanovich, 1978–1980. Vol. 1, 0-15-112635-0, 1199p. Vol. 2, 0-15-122636-9, 1200p. Volume 1 of the diaries covers the years 1869 to 1877, and volume 2 covers 1878 to 1883. They are a historical document and a daily record of life with Richard Wagner in which Cosima talks about everyday events and progresses from her feelings of guilt for her marriage to Wagner and her desertion of von Bülow, Wagner's heart disease, and their growing disillusionment with the German Empire.

WARD, MRS. HUMPHRY (1851–1920)
Writer   Australia

Mrs. Humphry Ward was a writer and leader in British educational reforms while opposing suffrage. She was born Mary Augusta Arnold on June 11, 1851, in Hobart, Tasmania, Australia, a niece of Matthew Arnold. The family returned to Britain in 1856, and she had a lonely and unhappy childhood, attending private boarding schools before continuing study at her family's home in Oxford and at the Bodelian Library, since women could not attend university classes. After her marriage to Thomas Humphry, she first contributed to the *Dictionary of Christian Biography* in 1877. As a believer in higher education for women, she helped in the founding of Oxford's Somerville College and became the secretary. In London after 1881, she published in various periodicals, such as the *Times, Macmillan's Magazine,* and *Pall Mall Gazette.* Throughout her career, she wrote twenty-five novels with religion, social concern, romance, and World War I as the focus. Although the first president of the Anti-Suffrage League, she started a settlement house in Bloomsbury, founded a play center and London's first school for crippled children, and fostered a belief in Christianity devoid of its supernatural elements and based on social good. She received an honorary doctorate from Edinburgh in 1920.

BIBLIOGRAPHY
Jones, Enid Huws. *Mrs. Humphry Ward.* New York: St. Martin's, 1973. No ISBN, 179p. Jones emphasizes how Ward's novels reflected the life and times, as she also focuses on the social good that Mrs. Ward accomplished. Jones uses letters, memoirs, and other primary sources for her readable biography.

Smith, Esther Marian Greenwell. *Mrs. Humphry Ward.* Boston: Twayne, 1980. 0-8057-6766-5, 163p. This critical biography analyzes Ward's work and shows what Ward achieved through her writing.

Sutherland, John. *Mrs. Humphry Ward: Eminent Victorian, Pre-Eminent Edwardian.* New York: Oxford, 1990. 0-19-818587-1, 370p. In a definitive, scholarly biography, documented and researched, Sutherland thinks that the two most important aspects of Mrs. Humphry Ward's life were that she was an Arnold (niece of Matthew Arnold) and that she was an "eminent Victorian" whose career peaked in the Edwardian era.

WARWICK, DAISY (1861–1933)

Activist and Writer   England

The Countess of Warwick, Daisy Greville, was a socialite, socialist, writer, and philanthropist. She was born Frances Evelyn Maynard in Mayfair, London, on December 10, 1861, to a father who was the only son and heir of the third viscount Maynard and a mother who was a descendant of Charles II and Nell Gwynn. Maynard inherited her grandfather's estates when she was four. Called Daisy at an early age, she received a private education and married Charles Greville, Lord Brooke, the heir to the earl of Warwick, in Westminster Abbey during 1881. She was beautiful, wealthy, popular, a member of the "Marlborough House Set," and a mistress of the Prince of Wales during the 1890s. After an extravagant party in 1895, socialists condemned her in their newspaper, the *Clarion*. Her subsequent discussion with the editor led her further into socialism and to contribute to charity by creating schools and workshops. She established a school at Easton, a home for disabled children at Warwick, and an agricultural college for women. In 1904, she joined the Social Democratic Federation and supported their dock strike in 1912. She continued charity work during World War I, although she opposed the war, and afterward she ran for Parliament but was defeated. When her husband died in 1923, she lost her income and supported herself by writing history, biography, and two autobiographies.

BIBLIOGRAPHY

Aronson, Theo. *The King in Love: King Edward VII's Mistresses—Lillie Langtry, Daisy Warwick, Alice Keppel, and Others.* New York: Harper and Row, 1988. 0-06-016033-0, 301p. Daisy Warwick, Lillie Langtry, and Alice Keppel were the three main mistresses of Edward VII, Prince of Wales. Aronson uses previously unpublished material in this well-documented and readable collective biography, in which he details Warwick's contributions to her community.

Blunden, Margaret. *The Countess of Warwick: A Biography.* London: Cassell, 1967. No ISBN, 356p. This well-written, documented, researched, and recommended account of Warwick's life is not an official biography, but Blunden has based it on extensive unpublished and published material in public and private hands.

Buttery, David. *Portraits of a Lady.* Studley, Warwickshire, England: Brewin Books, 1988. 0-947731-43-1, 48p. This brief biography describes Warwick's life and her shift from extravagance to socialist politics, with photographs.

WEBB, BEATRICE (1858–1943)

Writer and Activist   England

Beatrice Webb was a socialist who wrote about labor. She was born Beatrice Martha Potter on January 22, 1858, near Gloucester, the daughter of a railway magnate. Educated privately, she studied a wide range of subjects, traveled with her family, made her debut at eighteen, and became her father's business associate after her mother's death. Interested in reform, she worked as a rent collector in London and researched such situations as life on the East End dock and the sweating system, about which she gave testimony at the House of Lords. In 1891, while working on her book *The Co-Operative Movement in*

Great Britain, she met Sidney Webb, a Fabian theorist. They married the next year, and together they wrote over one hundred books, articles, and pamphlets about the labor movement and helped to found the London School of Economics. Beatrice Webb was appointed to the Royal Commission on Poor Laws in 1909, and after drafting the Minority Report, she helped to advocate a new social insurance. In 1913, she and her husband founded *The New Statesman* before he became a member of Parliament and held appointments in the early Labour governments. They visited the Soviet Union after he left office and wrote *Soviet Communism: A New Civilisation* (1935) about the experience.

BIBLIOGRAPHY

MacKenzie, Jeanne. A *Victorian Courtship: The Story of Beatrice Potter and Sidney Webb*. New York: Oxford University Press, 1979. 0-19-520166-3, 148p. MacKenzie tells the story of the Webbs' courtship, using letters that the two exchanged during the two years before their marriage. They reveal little of themselves but much about their radical views.

Muggeridge, Kitty, and Ruth Allen. *Beatrice Webb; a Life, 1858–1943*. New York: Knopf, 1968. No ISBN, 271p. Based on Webb's private journals, this balanced and entertaining biography discloses Webb's personality from her great love of the politician Joseph Chamberlain, to her marriage to Sidney and gives an overview of British economics and politics in the late nineteenth and early twentieth centuries.

Radice, Lisanne. *Beatrice and Sidney Webb: Fabian Socialists*. New York: St. Martin's, 1984. 0-312-07055-1, 342p. In this joint and comprehensive biography, Radice uses manuscript material and printed sources to show that the Webbs lacked understanding of the world outside Britain and had a misguided admiration for Soviet Russia.

Seymour-Jones, Carole. *Beatrice Webb: A Life*. Chicago: Ivan R. Dee, 1992. 1-56663-001-0, 369p. Seymour-Jones views Webb as a "woman of conflict" in a psychological examination of her tensions between family and career and her political development in a balanced, well-documented, and recommended biography.

Webb, Beatrice Potter. *My Apprenticeship*. Intro. Norman MacKenzie. New York: Cambridge University Press, 1979. 0-521-22941-3, 429p. In this autobiography, Webb wanted to write from her conscience. She had qualms about what to reveal and what to conceal concerning her family and friends, but she gives a readable account of her life from birth to her marriage to Sidney Webb from 1858 to 1892 and, in essence, describes "Victorian society."

WEIL, SIMONE (1909–1943)

Writer, Philosopher, and Activist   France

Simone Weil was a philosophical writer and mystic. She was born in Paris on February 3, 1909, to an Alsatian father and a Russian mother, both Jewish, and was educated at the Lycée Henri IV and the École Normale Superieure, one of the first women to be admitted. The philosopher Alain especially influenced her thought, along with Karl Marx, and she early became concerned about the poor. She first taught philosophy in Le Puy, but her activism led to her firing. She then taught at Bourges and St. Quentin, interspersed with periods of manual labor on farms and in factories to experience the working-class life. In 1936, she served in a nonmilitary capacity in the Republican forces in the

Spanish civil war. In 1938, she had her first mystical experience, and, although not a member of organized religion, her thought appeared in her writings. As a Jew she became hostile to Judaism and then fascinated with Catholicism. In 1942, she had to leave France, and she worked for the Free French in London before dying from tuberculosis and voluntary starvation in an attempt to identify with her compatriots suffering in France.

BIBLIOGRAPHY

Fiori, Gabriella. *Simone Weil, an Intellectual Biography*. Athens: University of Georgia Press, 1989. 0-8203-1102-2, 380p. Fiori's intellectual biography of Weil, based on oral histories of those who knew her, traces her change from political action to contemplation.

McFarland, Dorothy Tuck. *Simone Weil*. New York: F. Ungar, 1983. 0-8044-2604-X, 191p. In this biography, McFarland draws on the information in Pétrement's biography and on untranslated material to emphasize Weil's analysis of intellectual failures and errors upon which social structures are based and Weil's remedies for saving the world from disaster.

McLellan, David. *Utopian Pessimist: The Life and Thought of Simone Weil*. New York: Poseidon, 1990. 0-671-68521-x, 316p. Giving equal weight to Weil's sociophilosophical thought and her religious searchings, McLellan's biography, drawing on previous books and unpublished material, is a comprehensive look at Weil's life and ideas.

Nevin, Thomas R. *Simone Weil: Portrait of a Self-Exiled Jew*. Chapel Hill: University of North Carolina Press, 1991. 0-8078-1999-9, 478p. Nevin examines Weil's essays, notebooks, and documents (some unpublished) to understand her life and thought in this carefully researched biography. He concludes that, although she verbally denied her Jewishness, her actions revealed her as a *tzeddik*, a traditional, Jewish "just person."

Pétrement, Simone. *Simone Weil: A Life*. 1977. Trans. Raymond Rosenthal. New York: Random House, 1988. Paper, 0-8052-0862-3, 577p. Pétrement, Weil's close friend, used unpublished writings and her own remembrances to create an objective, nonjudgmental, and recommended view of Weil.

WEST, REBECCA (1892–1983)

Writer   Ireland

Dame Rebecca West was a novelist and critic. Born in County Kerry on December 21, 1892, as Cecily Isabel Fairfield to a journalist who died when she was ten, she went with her mother and siblings to Edinburgh, where she attended George Watson's Ladies College. She trained for the stage and, after acting for a short time, took her name "Rebecca West" from the character she played in Ibsen's *Rosmersholm*. In 1911, she began writing and joined the staff of the newspaper her mother had refused to let her read, *Freewoman*, before becoming a political writer for *Clarion*, a socialist paper, in 1912. She believed in suffrage and retained her independence, even during an affair begun with H. G. Wells in 1913 and the birth of a son from their union. She published books and articles in both England and the United States before marrying in 1930. With her husband, she traveled several times to the Balkans, where she gathered material for a travel book. She became interested in the area, and from her research she published a two-volume analysis of the origins of World War II and directed television broadcasts to Yugoslavia. After the war, she attended the

Nuremberg war crimes trials and published important studies based on them, *The Meaning of Treason* (1947) and *A Train of Powder* (1955). During her career, she published over twenty books and many articles in a variety of newspapers and journals. She received the Order of the British Empire in 1949 and was created Dame of the British Empire in 1959.

BIBLIOGRAPHY

Deakin, Motley F. *Rebecca West*. Boston: Twayne, 1980. 0-8057-6788-6, 183p. In this critical biography and study of West's work, Deakin reveals West's interest in feminism, literary criticism, history, and treason but concludes that fiction remained her major interest.

Glendinning, Victoria. *Rebecca West, a Life*. London: Weidenfeld and Nicolson, 1987. 0-297-79084-6, 288p. Glendinning's thesis in her well-written biography on West, a twentieth-century woman who was both an agent for change and a victim of change, is that in West's early and middle years, her male and female sides fought in both her life and her work.

Ray, Gordon Norton. *H. G. Wells and Rebecca West*. New Haven, CT: Yale University Press, 1974. 0-300-0175-3, 215p. Ray demonstrates the reality of West and Wells' relationship in carefully crafted and entertaining prose based on eight hundred letters that Wells wrote to her.

Rollyson, Carl. *Rebecca West: A Life*. New York: Scribner's, 1996. 0-684-19430-9, 544p. Although Rollyson includes many details about West's life, some from the previously restricted collection at Yale, he seems merely to be cataloging her actions of rebelling against the conventions of her time and the consequences.

Weldon, Fay. *Rebecca West*. New York: Viking, 1985. 0-670-80627-7, 107p. Weldon's personal view of Rebecca West is that of a young writer watching a woman of stature who has thought a lot about things and proved her intelligence.

WIGMAN, MARY (1886–1973)
Choreographer   Germany

Mary Wigman (Wiegmann) was a dancer, choreographer, and teacher. She was born in Hanover on November 3, 1886, and later studied dance. Her career as Germany's most famous modern dancer began after World War 1, when she toured extensively and opened a school in Dresden in 1920. She created numerous solo and group dances that typified German expressionist dancing. She danced in London in 1928 and in the United States two years later. She followed a solo career until 1942 in World War II. After the war, she started working again, first in Leipzig and then in West Berlin in 1949. Through her schools, teaching, and dramatic performances, she helped to develop European modern dance.

BIBLIOGRAPHY

Manning, Susan. *Ecstasy and the Demon: Feminism and Nationalism in the Dances of Mary Wigman*. Berkeley: University of California Press, 1993. 0-520-08193-5, 353p. Manning used both published and archival material as well as supporting illustrations to indicate that Wigman's work was nationalistic and that she accommodated her choreography to the fascist aesthetic of Nazism.

Wigman, Mary. *The Mary Wigman Book: Her Writings*. Ed. and trans. Walter Sorell. Middletown, CT: Wesleyan University Press, 1975. 0-8195-4079-X,

214p. In this reminiscence, Wigman recalls her early love of dance and the pleasure of studying it in Dresden. She also examines dance theory and the relationship of dance to cultural patterns.

WILKINSON, ELLEN (1891–1947)
Politician   England

Ellen Wilkinson was a feminist and stateswoman who was elected a member of Parliament. She was born in Manchester on October 8, 1891, the third of four children to a cottonworker. Her family was committed to the labor movement, and she became a member of the Manchester and Salford Co-Operative Society, as had her mother and grandmother before her. She attended Manchester University on a scholarship and graduated second in her class in 1913. She organized women employees and briefly supported communism. She was a member of Parliament first for Middlesborough and then for Jarrow. People called her "Red Ellen" because of her hair and her politics, while members called her "Miss Perky." She was parliamentary secretary to the Ministry of Home Security (1940) and minister of education (1945), the first woman to hold such an appointment. She traveled in the United States, India, and Germany as well as other countries to mobilize for labor, and she wrote several books about unemployment among her own constituents. She used her political power to help those discriminated against because of sex, class, creed, or color. She respected ability, but she knew that class differences were an insurmountable barrier in Parliament and often felt like an outsider because she was a woman.

BIBLIOGRAPHY
Stobaugh, Beverly Parker. *Women and Parliament, 1918–1970.* Hicksville, NY: Exposition, 1978. 0-682-49056-3, 152p. In this collective biography, Stobaugh discusses Wilkinson and her realization that class differences were insurmountable in Parliament as she worked to stop discrimination.
Vernon, Betty. *Ellen Wilkinson, 1891–1947.* London: Croom Helm, 1982. 0-85664-984-8, 254p. In her biography on Wilkinson, Vernon has researched parliamentary debates, newspapers, and periodicals and included interviews with several people who knew Wilkinson to create a balanced and recommended overview of Wilkinson's struggles to implement her policies.

WILLIAMS, BETTY (1941–)
Activist   Ireland

Betty Williams won the Nobel Peace Prize for her work to make peace in Northern Ireland. She was born on May 22, 1941, in Belfast to a Protestant father and a mother of Jewish descent. A stroke paralyzed her mother when Williams was thirteen, and she raised her sister and attended Catholic school before marrying a Protestant. When Williams lived in a Republican area of Belfast, Andersonstown, she watched a getaway car for a gunman kill three children. She started her crusade for peace by talking to everyone about its necessity. One of the first persons she met was **Mairead Corrigan**, and they worked together to unify over ten thousand people for a march to begin the peace movement. After Williams and Corrigan won the Nobel Peace Prize, they began to work on small groups within the community. She left the peace movement in 1980 after a disagreement and moved to Florida, where she remarried.

BIBLIOGRAPHY
Deutsch, Richard. *Mairead Corrigan, Betty Williams*. Trans. Jack Bernard.
    Woodbury, NY: Barron's, 1977. 0-8120-5268-4, 204p. In a balanced and
    readable biography, interviews with Corrigan and Williams show the frus-
    tration they felt and why they worked for the peace movement.
O'Donnell, Dalry. *The Peace People of Northern Ireland*. Camberwell, Victoria,
    Australia: Widescope, 1977. 0-86932-015-7, 122p. This conversational bi-
    ography of Williams and Corrigan shows how they helped the peace move-
    ment in Northern Ireland.

WILLIAMS, CICELY (1893–1993)

Physician   Jamaica

Cicely Williams was a public health doctor. She was born on December 2,
1893, in Jamaica, and, after the family returned to England, she was able to obtain her medical degree in Oxford and London during World War I because
male medical students had left school for war. She worked for the Colonial
Medical Service, spending seven years in Ghana identifying such diseases as
kwashiorkor and twelve years in Malaya. She lectured in pediatrics at the College of Medicine, Singapore, where she was the senior government specialist in
child health. In World War II, the Japanese held her prisoner. Afterward, she
returned to England to become the head of the Child Health Department at the
Institute of Social Medicine, Oxford. While working with the World Health
Organization as the head of the Maternal and Child Health Section, she disapproved of condensed milk for babies, saying that "cuddling is more important
than calories," and wanted to educate mothers and help them with family planning. She was senior lecturer in Nutrition at London University and oversaw a
training program on family planning from 1964 to 1967. She was one of the
first to receive the Order of St. Michael and St. George in the British Empire.
Other awards included honorary doctorates at the University of Maryland, the
University of Tulane, and Smith College. She was inducted into the American
Pediatric Association and American Dietetic Association and became an honorary fellow of the International Health Society and an honorary fellow of Somerville, Oxford. She was the first woman with an honorary fellowship of the
Royal Society of Medicine. She received the Victor Gollancz Award for services
to humanity and the Goldberger Award. She was always certain that her way
was best to make children happier and healthier.

BIBLIOGRAPHY
Craddock, Sally. *Retired Except on Demand: The Life of Dr. Cicely Williams*.
    Oxford, England: Green College Press, 1983. No ISBN, 198p. Although
    stylistically informal, this biography contains many anecdotes about a
    woman who was one of the best pediatricians in the world but who suffered
    the ignominy of a single woman in a social system that placed her lower
    than a married woman. Craddock said she could find no one who would
    speak ill of Williams because she proved what she said by her dedication to
    her work and to making human life better.

WILLIAMS, GRACE (1906–1977)
Composer   Wales

Grace Williams was a composer. Born on February 19, 1906, she was the daughter of a schoolteacher. After her local education, she studied at University College, Cardiff, and at the Royal College of Music, London, under Vaughn Williams until 1932. She also worked with Egon Wellesz in Vienna from 1930 to 1931. She returned to Wales in 1946 after teaching in London and producing educational programming for television. She began to concentrate on composition and saw herself as a representative of Welsh music as she wrote vocal and orchestral music, including *Penillion for Orchestra* (1955), *Ballads for Orchestra* (1968), and *Missa cambrensis* (1971). An opera, *The Parlour*, was published in 1961.

BIBLIOGRAPHY
Boyd, Malcolm. *Grace Williams*. Cardiff: University of Wales Press, 1980. Paper, 0-7083-0762-0, 98p. Boyd gives the chronological detail of Williams' life and career, but the biography is neither full nor detailed. However, it is the only published monograph available and includes technical information about her music for the scholarly reader.

WOFFINGTON, PEG (1720–1760)
Actor   Ireland

Peg (Margaret) Woffington was an actor. Born on October 18, 1720, to a journeyman bricklayer who died suddenly when she was two, Woffington and her sister helped their mother earn money by working as the babies in two baskets on each end of a tightrope walker's balance. Woffington sold items on the street and got a job onstage at ten in *The Beggar's Opera*, organized by the retired tightrope walker. She continued her career in Dublin and, after being successful, moved to London at twenty. She had a number of sexual liaisons and was renowned for her "trouser" roles, with one of her most famous being Sir Harry Wildair in *The Constant Couple*. She could not play tragedy, but her superb comedy dominated Drury Lane from 1740 to 1746, Dublin from 1747 to 1754, and Covent Garden from 1754 to 1757.

BIBLIOGRAPHY
Daly, Augustin. *Woffington: A Tribute to the Actress and the Woman*. 1891. New York: B. Blom, 1972. No ISBN, 182p. Daly's researched and documented biography draws on contemporary resources of newspapers and letters to show Woffington as people in her own time saw her.

Dunbar, Janet. *Peg Woffington and Her World*. Boston: Houghton Mifflin, 1968. No ISBN, 245p. Dunbar describes the love-hate relationship of the actor with the audience as she recounts Woffington's successes and failures on stage. A professional, Woffington always prepared her roles carefully.

WOLLSTONECRAFT, MARY (1759–1797)
Writer   England

Mary Wollstonecraft was a feminist and writer. She was born in Hoxton, near London, on April 27, 1759, to a wife-beating father. She was self-educated, and after her mother died, she started a school in Newington Green, where she met many liberal nonconformists. In 1787, she published *Thoughts on the Edu-*

cation of Daughters, and in 1792, she wrote *Vindication of the Rights of Woman*, advocating equality of the sexes in education, employment, and companionship (currently recognized as the seminal work on feminism). She was in Paris during the French Revolution, where she got the material for *History and Moral View of the Origins and Progress of the French Revolution*. She returned to Paris in 1792, married the American Gilbert Imlay, and had a daughter, Fanny. After he lost interest in their relationship, she tried twice to kill herself. When they returned to England, she joined a radical intellectual group that included Tom Paine and William Godwin, whom she married in 1797. She died of blood poisoning in London eleven days after giving birth to a daughter, **Mary (Shelley)**, who later married Percy Bysshe Shelley.

BIBLIOGRAPHY

Flexner, Eleanor. *Mary Wollstonecraft; a Biography*. New York: Coward, McCann and Geoghegan, 1972. 0-698-10447-1, 307p. Flexner uses letters, memoirs, and previous biographies to trace Wollstonecraft's life in a well-researched and documented but difficult biography.

George, Margaret. *One Woman's "Situation"; a Study of Mary Wollstonecraft*. Urbana: University of Illinois Press, 1970. 0-252-00090-0, 174p. George's scholarly study of Wollstonecraft as the first feminist who refused to accept the mores of her society uses Wollstonecraft's writings as a basis of interpretation.

Sunstein, Emily W. *A Different Face: The Life of Mary Wollstonecraft*. Boston: Little, Brown, 1975. 0-316-82245-0, 383p. Sympathetic but fair, Sunstein's recommended biography of Wollstonecraft uses letters, journals, and Wollstonecraft's writing to show a woman almost pathological as a result of the imbalances in her own family.

Tomalin, Claire. *The Life and Death of Mary Wollstonecraft*. Rev. ed. New York: Penguin, 1992. 0-14-016761-7, 379p. Well documented and illustrated, Tomalin's biography recounts the life of Wollstonecraft by balancing her desperate love with her political radicalism in the world of the 1780s and 1790s. Whitbread Award.

WOOLF, VIRGINIA (1882–1941)

Writer   **England**

Virginia Woolf was a novelist. She was born Virginia Stephen on January 25, 1882, at Hyde Park Gate in London, the daughter of Leslie Stephen. While she was still young, her mother, stepsister, and elder brother died. After her father died in 1904, she, her sister Vanessa, and two brothers lived together in a house in Bloomsbury. In 1912, she married Leonard Woolf, and after the publication of her first novel, *The Voyage Out*, in 1915, the two set up Hogarth Press. A leading member of the Bloomsbury Group, she made a major contribution to the development of the novel in such works as *Mrs. Dalloway* (1925), *To the Lighthouse* (1927), and *The Waves* (1931). These novels were noted for their impressionistic style and development of the stream-of-consciousness technique. She also wrote biographies and critical essays. Although never overtly involved in the views of feminists, her two nonfiction works, *A Room of One's Own* (1929) and *Three Guineas* (1938), discussed the constraints of women who wanted to be creative. After several bouts of mental illness, she committed suicide by drowning during World War II.

BIBLIOGRAPHY

Bell, Quentin. *Virginia Woolf: A Biography.* 1972. London: Hogarth, 1990. 0-7012-0846-5, 530p. Bell, Woolf's nephew, wrote a balanced and honest biography of her life, focusing on the less familiar incidents. The first volume covers the years to her marriage, and the second looks at her marriage and her work. James Tait Black Memorial Prize and Duff Cooper Memorial Prize.

DeSalvo, Louise A. *Virginia Woolf: The Impact of Childhood Sexual Abuse on Her Life and Work.* Boston: Beacon, 1989. 0-8070-6326-6, 372p. DeSalvo uses Woolf's own testimony in letters, memoirs, and juvenilia as well as clues in Woolf's mature fiction to support her thesis that childhood sexual abuse affected Woolf's work.

Gordon, Lyndall. *Virginia Woolf, a Writer's Life.* 1981. New York: Norton, 1993. Paper, 0-393-31061-2, 360p. Gordon's biography is complementary to Bell's because it analyzes Woolf's novels and examines her education, her mental breakdowns, and her marriage to Leonard Woolf. James Tait Black Memorial Prize.

Lee, Hermione. *Virginia Woolf.* New York: Knopf, 1997. 0-679-44707-5, 893p. Lee covers aspects of Woolf's life including her tyrannical father, possible sexual abuse by her half brothers, and her sexless marriage in a throughly researched and highly readable biography.

Rose, Phyllis. *Woman of Letters: A Life of Virginia Woolf.* 1978. San Diego: Harcourt Brace Jovanovich, 1987. Paper, 0-15-698190-4, 298p. In a balanced psychological study combining Woolf's life and her novels, Rose suggests that Woolf's suicide is not the question but how she kept her sanity for so long, since her first breakdown occurred after the death of her mother when she was fourteen.

WRIGHT, HELENA (1888–1982)

Physician   England

Helena Wright was a proponent of birth control. Born Helena Rosa Lowenfeld in Brixton, London, on March 23, 1888, her father was a Polish immigrant who built and owned the Apollo Theater, from which he became very wealthy. She received her education from the Cheltenham Ladies' College where Dorothea Beale was the principal, and rather than enter society, she decided to become a doctor. She trained at the Royal Free Hospital Medical School for Women, joined the Royal Army Medical Corps, and worked at Bethnal Green Hospital in World War I, where she met a surgeon, Henry Wright, and married him. She wanted a missionary career, and after training to become a gynecologist, she, her husband, and two sons went to Shantung Christian University from 1922 to 1927. They returned home via the Trans-Siberian Railway, and perhaps on that trip, she invented disposable diapers for her four-month-old baby. In Berlin, she was interested in the intrauterine device for birth control and, when she returned to London, helped found the national Birth Control Council and joined the International Planned Parenthood Federation. In 1930, she published a successful book, *The Sex Factor in Marriage.* She retired from clinical work in 1958, practiced privately, and trained foreign students in family planning. In 1968, when she was eighty, she published *Sex and Society.*

BIBLIOGRAPHY

Evans, Barbara. *Freedom to Choose: The Life and Work of Dr. Helena Wright, Pioneer of Contraception.* London: Bodley Head, 1984. 0-370-30504, 286p. Evans' balanced biography of Wright's life tells how her charm and knowledge finally gained the Anglican bishops' approval of contraception.

WRIGHT, JUDITH (1915–)

Poet   **Australia**

Judith Wright is a poet. She was born near Armidale, New South Wales, on May 31, 1915, where she lived on the family sheep farm, Wallamumbi. A newspaper published one of her poems when she was ten, and she attended New England Girls' School before studying at Sydney University. After school, she traveled to Europe and Britain before returning to work in educational administration in Queensland. The war interrupted her travel, but she found poetic inspiration in the Queensland mountains. She was one of the first white writers to recognize aboriginal claims, and her personal lyrics won her the Commonwealth Literary Fund Fellowship and the Grace Leven Prize. She has published literary criticism and work re-creating the impact of European immigration on the aboriginal inhabitants of New South Wales and Queensland. Among her other awards are honorary doctorates at the Universities of New England, Queensland, Sydney, the Australian National University, Griffith, and Melbourne. She won the World Prize for Poetry, the Encyclopaedia Britannica Award, and the Robert Frost Award of Fellowship of Australian Writers. In 1970, she became a fellow of the Australian Academy of the Humanities. In 1978, she was the only Australian woman in the *Penguin Book of Women Poets*, and in 1992, she won the Queen's Medal for Poetry.

Strauss, Jennifer. *Judith Wright.* New York: Oxford University Press, 1995. Paper, 0-19-553278-3, 132p. Strauss presents the life and work of Wright and introduces her in this carefully documented but brief, scholarly biography as an activist for conservation and for aboriginal rights and a representative of the intellectual, political, and psychical history of the second half of the twentieth century in Australia.

Walker, Shirley. *Vanishing Edens: Responses to Australia in the Works of Mary Gilmore, Judith Wright, and Dorothy Hewett.* Townsville, Queensland, Australia: Foundation for Australian Literary Studies, 1992. 0-8644-3432-4, 64p. Walker interprets Wright's life and her poetry and shows that the poems have a central core of ideas concerning nature, love, the imagination and language, and a constant conflict between Wright's commitment to the natural world and her revulsion about the impersonality and cruelty of all natural processes.

Wright, Judith. *The Generations of Men.* New York: HarperCollins, 1995. 1-87589-216-8, 260p. Wright discusses her poetry, her life, and the political and social causes that she espouses in this autobiography.

WU CHAO (625–705)

Empress   **China**

Wu Chao was China's only female "emperor." As the daughter of a general, Tai Zong, China's ruler, summoned her when thirteen to be his concubine. There she studied music, literature, and calligraphy. At his death, when she was twenty-four, Wu Chao was expected to go into a Bhuddist convent, but she decided that she wanted to stay at court, so she carefully wooed the crown prince, Gao Zong (Kao Tsung), when he came to visit his ailing father. When Gao's wife could not have children, she summoned Wu Chao from the convent to have his child. Instead of returning to the convent as expected, she supposedly smothered the baby, although her servants accused the empress. In the ensuing intrigue, Gao Zong declared Wu the new empress, and to keep her place secure, Wu Chao sent her servants to kill the wife and the concubine. She ruled with her husband while sitting behind screens at official meetings and instituted a secret police. She took ideas from anyone and used them to help the empire prosper. After Gao Zong died, she ruled instead of her children. During her reign of nearly fifty years, she established peace and prosperity, unified the T'ang Empire, and favored cultural achievement.

BIBLIOGRAPHY

Fitzgerald, C. P. *The Empress Wu*. Vancouver, B.C., Canada: University of British Columbia Press, 1968. Fitzgerald demonstrates that Wu was the major influence of the T'ang dynasty in an accessible, carefully documented biography.

Guisso, R.W.L. *Wu Tse-t'ien and the Politics of Legitimation in T'ang China*. Bellingham, WA: Western Washington, 1978. 0-914584-11-1, 335p. In his accessible text, Guisso scrutinizes Wu's achievements from the perspective of her times to examine her legitimation, the tension between Confucian state theory and the contradiction of a female ruler, and, based on new evidence, a reinterpretation of her policies.

𝔜

YORK, MARGARET of. *See* MARGARET of YORK.

YOURCENAR, MARGUERITE (1903–1987)
Writer   **Belgium**

Marguerite Yourcenar was a novelist and poet. She was born Marguerite de
Crayencour in Brussels on June 8, 1903; her mother died the next week. As the
daughter of a leisured scholar, she was educated at home in a wealthy and cultured household. She wrote verse, which her father privately published when
she was sixteen, and for which they created her pseudonym as an anagram of
her name. The same year, she passed her baccalaureate exams. She became a
classical scholar who traveled widely and wrote a series of distinguished novels, plays, poems, and essays. Well known in the 1930s, she lost her fortune
during World War II and emigrated to the United States, where she settled in
Maine in 1950, continuing to write in French. She published major essays during the 1950s and had several religious experiences, about which she wrote.
Her novels, many of them historical reconstructions based on classical themes,
won her international acclaim. In 1980, she became the first woman writer to
be elected to the Académie Française. Among other awards and prizes were the
Prix Fémina-Vacaresco, Prix Combat, Officer of the Légion of Honor, and the
Erasmus Prize. She was also elected to Académie Royale Belge de Langue et de
Littérature Françaises and the American Academy of Arts and Letters.

BIBLIOGRAPHY
Horn, Pierre L. *Marguerite Yourcenar*. Boston: Twayne, 1985. 0-8057-6608-1,
    121p. In Horn's scholarly examination of Yourcenar's literary career, he
    includes a short biographical sketch preceding an analysis of her work.
Savigneau, Josyane. *Marguerite Yourcenar: Inventing a Life*. Chicago: Univer-
    sity of Chicago Press, 1993. 0-226-73544-3, 584p. In a well-researched bi-
    ography using the carefully arranged papers that Yourcenar left so that she
    would not be a subject whose biographer had to use whim or total conjec-

ture about her life's story, Savigneau reports both the mundane and the arcane in Yourcenar's life which Yourcenar often invented along with her fiction.

Yourcenar, Marguerite. *Dear Departed*. Trans. Maria L. Ascher. New York: Farrar, Straus, and Giroux, 1991. 0-374-13554-1, 346p. Rather than an autobiography of her own life, Yourcenar begins at her birth and moves backward, using documents and oral tradition to show the lives of her father's and mother's families.

Yourcenar, Marguerite. *How Many Years*. Trans. Maria L. Ascher. New York: Farrar, Straus, and Giroux, 1995. 0-374-17319-2, 381p. This sequel to *Dear Departed* includes many stories of Yourcenar's father and grandfather, which make it a social and cultural history of nineteenth-century France and emphasizes the timelessness of experience.

Z

ZASULICH, VERA (1849–1919)
Revolutionary   Russia

Vera Zasulich was a revolutionary and assassin. She was born on July 27, 1849, as the youngest of an impoverished landowner's three daughters. Her father died when she was three, and she spent unhappy years with relatives. After attending boarding school in Moscow, she went to St. Petersburg at seventeen, where she joined a radical group. She was arrested in 1869 and imprisoned for five years. After her release, she took medical courses and joined the Kiev underground. In 1878, when Fyodor Trepov, the governor general of St. Petersburg, ordered a political prisoner flogged for not removing his hat, she went to the city, demanded to see him, pulled out a pistol, and assassinated him in front of observers. A jury found her "not guilty" after she announced that a person intending to hurt others should be stopped. Her sentence, in essence, approved terrorism, with Tolstoy worrying about its effect on society. Exiled twenty-seven years for her revolutionary activities, she lived lonely times abroad in Switzerland and England, where she spent time translating and writing. In 1900, she, Vladimir Ulyanov Lenin, and Plekhanov, another revolutionary, started a newspaper called *Iskra* (the Spark), in which they published articles by "El Pero" (Trotsky). When Russia lost to Japan in 1905, Nicholas allowed all political dissidents to return home. Zasulich silently returned.

BIBLIOGRAPHY
Bergman, Jay. *Vera Zasulich: A Biography*. Stanford, CA: Stanford University Press, 1983. 0-8047-1156-9, 280p. Bergman's biography, carefully researched, introduces Zasulich as one who struggled in Russia's revolutionary politics but whom younger Marxists eventually rejected.

ZETKIN, CLARA (1857–1933)
Activist   Germany

Clara Zetkin was a communist leader. She was born Clara Eissner on July 5, 1857, in Wiederau, the daughter of a village schoolteacher and his wife. Her parents encouraged her to read world literature, and she was one of the first women to study at Leipzig Teacher's College for Women. While there, she saw the poverty of the local stocking knitters, and she became a socialist, staunch feminist, and member of the Social Democratic Party. She met Ossip Zetkin, married him in 1882, and moved to Paris and Switzerland with him. In 1889, she returned to Germany as a delegate to the Second Socialist International, and in 1892, began editing the paper *Gleichheit* (Equality). In 1907, she helped found the International Socialist League, and she and **Rosa Luxemburg** were some of the few social democrats to oppose World War I. In 1917, she was one of the founders of the radical Independent Social Democratic Party (the Spartacus League) before founding the German Communist Party two years later. A strong supporter of the Russian Revolution and a friend of Lenin, she became a member of the Executive Committee of the Communist International and headed the International Women's Secretariat. Her influence in Russia waned after Lenin's death, but she served as a communist in the German Reichstag from 1920 to 1932 before her burial at the Kremlin Wall.

BIBLIOGRAPHY
Reetz, Dorothea. *Clara Zetkin as a Socialist Speaker*. New York: International, 1987. Paper, 0-7178-0649-9, 80p. Reetz's straightforward, documented biography is a readable account of the influences on Zetkin and her attempts to change the world.

ZUCCHI, VIRGINIA (1849–1930)
Ballerina   Italy

Virginia Zucchi was a ballerina whose talent critics compared to that of **Eleanora Duse**, the actor. She was born in Parma on February 10, 1849, and studied in Milan before beginning her career in 1884 by performing in small Italian theaters. She danced in Padua in 1873, and the acclaim got her an engagement at La Scala to star in Manzetti's *Rolla* in 1875 and to dance in the opera *La Gioconda* the next year. She followed these experiences with performances in Berlin, London, and St. Petersburg. She danced in Moscow and St. Petersburg for seven years, establishing the Italian influence on Russian ballet. In 1889, she appeared in Nice, Monte Carlo, and Milan. After she retired from performing, she opened a school in Monte Carlo.

BIBLIOGRAPHY
Guest, Ivor F. *The Divine Virginia: A Biography of Virginia Zucchi*. New York: Marcel Dekker, 1977. 0-685-16054-8, 206p. After careful research, Guest concludes that Zucchi was one of the great ballerinas of all times, with her ability to interpret a role and her seductive costumes bringing new fans to the ballet. Photographs show her in performance.

APPENDIX A: NOTABLE WOMEN BY DATE OF BIRTH

1503 B.C.	Hatshepsut	1446	Margaret of York
c. 1300 B.C.	Nefertiti	1451	Isabella of Spain
c. 470 B.C.	Aspasia	1480	Borgia, Lucrezia
69 B.C.	Cleopatra	1485	Catherine of Aragon
28	Berenice	1490	Colonna, Vittoria
45?	Pan Ch'ao	1492	Marguerite of Navarre
d. c. 60	Boudicca	1507	Boleyn, Anne
497	Theodora	1515	Teresa of Ávila
614?	A'isha	1516	Mary I of England
625	Wu Chao	1519	Medici, Catherine de
973?	Shikibu, Murasaki	1520	Labé, Louise
1046	Margaret of Scotland	1523?	Stampa, Gaspara
1083	Comnena, Anna	1533	Elizabeth I of England
1098	Hildegard of Bingen	1542	Mary, Queen of Scots
1101	Héloïse	1546	Franco, Veronica
1122	Eleanor of Aquitaine	1553	Margaret of Valois
1188	Blanche of Castile	1572	Chantal, Jeanne-Françoise de
1194	Clare of Assisi		
1207	Elizabeth of Hungary	1582?	Nzinga
1210	Mechtild of Magdeburg	1590	Gentileschi, Artemisia
1246	Eleanor of Castile	1594?	Peeters, Clara
1256	Gertrude of Helfta	1601	Anne of Austria
1303	Birgitta	1607	Scudéry, Madeleine de
1343	Julian of Norwich	1609	Leyster, Judith
1347	Catherine of Siena	1626	Christina
1364	De Pisan, Christine	1630	Sophia of Hanover
1364	Kempe, Margery	1634	La Fayette, Madame de
1371	Jadwiga of Poland	1635	Maintenon, Françoise de
1412	Joan of Arc	1640	Behn, Aphra
1443	Beaufort, Margaret	d. 1645	Nur Jahan

1648	Guyon, Jeanne Marie	1797	Shelley, Mary
1650	Gwyn, Eleanor	1797	Vestris, Lucia
1651	Cruz, Juana Inés de la	1801	Bremer, Fredrika
1657	Sophia of Russia	1802	Martineau, Harriet
1662	Mary II of England	1803	Moodie, Susannah
1665	Anne of England	1803	Tristan, Flora
1667	Centlivre, Susanna	1804	Ding Ling
1668	Astell, Mary	1804	Farrenc, Jeanne-Louise
1692	Lecouvreur, Adrienne	1804	Sand, George
1697	Deffand, Marie du	1805	Hensel, Fanny
1709	Elizabeth of Russia		Mendelssohn
1714	Cibber, Susannah	1805	Seacole, Mary
1717	Maria Theresa	1806	Browning, Elizabeth
1720	Woffington, Peg		Barrett
1721	Pompadour, Madame de	1807	Carpenter, Mary
1722	MacDonald, Flora	1808	Chisholm, Caroline
1729	Catherine II of Russia	1808	Malibran, Marie
1731	Macaulay, Catherine	1808	Norton, Caroline
1740	Charriere, Isabelle de	1809	Kemble, Fanny
1741	Kauffmann, Angelica	1810	Colet, Louise
1745	More, Hannah	1810	Elssler, Fanny
1749	Smith, Charlotte	1810	Gaskell, Elizabeth
1750	Herschel, Caroline	1811	Lewald, Fanny
1752	Burney, Fanny	1814	Burdett-Coutts, Angela
1753	Inchbald, Elizabeth	1814	Gómez de Avellaneda,
1755	Marie Antoinette		Gertrudis
1755	Vigée-Lebrun, Élisabeth	1815	Cameron, Julia Margaret
1759	Wollstonecraft, Mary	1815	Lovelace, Augusta Ada
1761	Jordan, Dorothy	1816	Aguilar, Grace
1761	Tussaud, Marie	1816	Brontë, Charlotte
1762	Baillie, Joanna	1817	Cerrito, Fanny
1763	Bonaparte, Josephine	1818	Brontë, Emily
1764	Radcliffe, Ann	1819	Eliot, George
1766	Macarthur, Elizabeth	1819	Schumann, Clara
1766	Staël, Anne Louise de	1819	Victoria of England
1767	Edgeworth, Maria	1820	Brontë, Anne
1775	Austen, Jane	1820	Lind, Jenny
1775	Siddons, Sarah	1820	Nightingale, Florence
1776	Stanhope, Hester Lucy	1820	Sewell, Anna
1777	Récamier, Jeanne	1821	Blackwell, Elizabeth
1777	Reibey, Mary	1821	Rachel
1778	McAuley, Catherine	1822	Bonheur, Rosa
1780	Fry, Elizabeth	1825	Castellanos, Rosario
1780	Somerville, Mary	1825	Spence, Catherine
1780	Trollope, Frances	1826	Craik, Dinah
1782	Ferrier, Susan	1826	Sévigné, Marie de
1783	Morgan, Sydney	1827	Bodichon, Barbara
1785	Arnim, Bettina von	1828	Butler, Josephine
1794	Jameson, Anna	1828	Oliphant, Margaret
1797	Droste-Hülshoff, Annette	1829	Booth, Catherine
	von	1830	Ebner-Eschenbach, Marie

1830	Michel, Louise	1858	Lagerlöf, Selma
1830	Rossetti, Christina	1858	Smyth, Ethel
1831	Beale, Dorothea	1858	Webb, Beatrice
1831	Blavatsky, Helena	1860	McMillan, Margaret
1832	Bishop, Isabella Lucy	1861	Andreas-Salomé, Lou
1834	Tz'u-Hsi	1861	Bates, Daisy (or 1863)
1835	Faithfull, Emily	1861	Melba, Nellie
1836	Anderson, Elizabeth	1861	Warwick, Daisy
	Garrett	1862	Kingsley, Mary
1836	Beeton, Isabel	1864	Claudel, Camille
1837	Castro, Rosalía de	1864	Inglis, Elsie Maud
1837	Wagner, Cosima	1864	Tilley, Vesta
1840	Jex-Blake, Sophia	1865	Braun, Lily
1841	Morisot, Berthe	1865	Cavell, Edith
1843	Jekyll, Gertrude	1865	Gilmore, Mary Jane
1843	Patti, Adelina	1866	Gonne, Maud
1843	Suttner, Bertha von	1866	Potter, Beatrix
1844	Alexandra of Denmark	1867	Curie, Marie
1844	Bernadette	1867	Kollwitz, Käthe
1844	Bernhardt, Sarah	1867	Mary, Queen to George V
1844	Cambridge, Ada	1868	Bell, Gertrude
1844	Despard, Charlotte	1868	David-Neel, Alexandra
1844	Modjeska, Helena	1868	Knipper-Chehkova, Olga
1845	Pechey-Phipson, Edith	1868	Markiewicz, Constance
1846	Greenaway, Katherine	1868	Murphy, Emily
1847	Albani, Emma	1869	Goldman, Emma
1847	Besant, Annie	1869	Goldstein, Vida
1847	Fawcett, Millicent	1869	Hodgkins, Frances
1847	Scott, Rose	1869	Lasker-Schüler, Else
1848	Lawson, Louisa	1869	Valadon, Suzanne
1848	Paterson, Emma	1870	Lloyd, Marie
1848	Sheppard, Kate	1870	Montessori, Maria
1848	Slessor, Mary	1870	Richardson, Henry
1848	Terry, Ellen		Handel
1849	Burnett, Frances Hodgson	1871	Carr, Emily
1849	Zasulich, Vera	1871	Deledda, Grazia
1849	Zucchi, Virginia	1871	Luxemburg, Rosa
1850	Cabrini, Francesca Xavier	1871	Tetrazzini, Louisa
1850	Crawford, Isabella	1871	Ukrainka, Lesya
1850	Kovalevskaya, Sofya	1872	Alexandra of Russia
1851	Pardo Bazán, Emilia	1872	Butt, Clara
1851	Ward, Mrs. Humphrey	1872	Ichiyo, Higuchi
1852	Gregory, Augusta	1872	Kollontai, Alexandra
1853	Carreño, Teresa	1872	Rathbone, Eleanor
1855	Schreiner, Olive	1872	Turner, Ethel
1857	Chaminade, Cécile	1873	Colette
1857	Hoodless, Adelaide	1873	Thérèse of Lisieux
1857	Kulascioff, Anna	1874	Armand, Inesse
1857	Pankhurst, Emmeline	1874	Atholl, Katherine
1857	Zetkin, Clara	1874	Baylis, Lilian
1858	Duse, Eleanora	1874	Garden, Mary

1874	Long, Marguerite	1886	Ottesen-Jensen, Elise
1874	Mistinguett	1886	Wigman, Mary
1874	Montgomery, Lucy Maud	1887	Boulanger, Nadia
1875	King, Jessie	1887	Sitwell, Edith
1875	Preston, Margaret Rose	1888	Akhmatova, Anna
1875	Underhill, Evelyn	1888	Baum, Vicki
1876	John, Gwen	1888	Evans, Edith
1876	Modersohn-Becker, Paula	1888	Lehmann, Lotte
1876	Royden, Maude	1888	Mansfield, Katherine
1877	Eberhardt, Isabelle	1888	Rambert, Marie
1877	Knight, Laura	1888	Teyte, Maggie
1877	Sheehy-Skeffington,	1888	Wright, Helena
	Hannah	1889	Baden-Powell, Olave
1877	Vionnet, Madeleine	1889	Dabrowska, Maria
1878	Gray, Eileen	1889	Galli-Curci, Amelita
1878	Meitner, Lise	1889	Mistral, Gabriela
1879	Franklin, Miles	1889	Popova, Liubov
1879	Gwynne-Vaughn, Helen	1889	Schumann, Elisabeth
1879	Mahler, Alma	1889	Street, Jessie
1879	Naidu, Sarojini	1890	Agustini, Delmira
1879	Sha'rawi, Huda	1890	Christie, Agatha
1880	Kenny, Elizabeth	1890	Hess, Myra
1880	Pankhurst, Christabel	1890	Macphail, Agnes
1880	Sandel, Cora	1890	Schiaparelli, Elsa
1880	Stopes, Marie	1891	Nijinska, Bronislava
1881	Farjeon, Eleanor	1891	Ocampo, Victoria
1881	Macaulay, Rose	1891	Sachs, Nelly
1881	Pavlova, Anna	1891	Stein, Edith
1882	Klein, Melanie	1891	Stocks, Mary
1882	Noether, Emmy	1891	Wilkinson, Ellen
1882	Pankhurst, Sylvia	1892	Lopokova, Lydia
1882	Thorndike, Sybil	1892	Rutherford, Margaret
1882	Undset, Sigrid	1892	Sackville-West, Vita
1882	Woolf, Virginia	1892	Södergran, Edith
1883	Adivar, Halide Edib	1892	Storni, Alfonsina
1883	Chanel, Coco	1892	Tailleferre, Germaine
1883	Hall, Radclyffe	1892	West, Rebecca
1883	Prichard, Katharine	1893	Boulanger, Lili
1883	Rhondda, Margaret	1893	Sayers, Dorothy
1883	Te Puea, Herangi	1893	Stark, Freya
1884?	Arden, Elizabeth	1893	Williams, Cicely
1884	Compton-Burnett, Ivy	1894	Rhys, Jean
1884	Deutsch, Helene	1895	Flagstad, Kirsten
1884	Hanson-Dyer, Louise	1895	Freud, Anna
1884	Uttley, Alison	1895	Parra, Teresa de la
1885	Delaunay, Sonia	1895	Redpath, Anne
1885	Dinesen, Isak	1896	Brittain, Vera
1885	Horney, Karen	1896	Cunard, Nancy
1885	Karsavina, Tamara	1896	Kennedy, Margaret
1885	Sheridan, Clare	1897	Barnard, Marjorie
1886	Karinska, Barbara	1897	Mitchison, Naomi

1898	De Valois, Ninette
1898	Fields, Gracie
1898	Lenya, Lotte
1898	Lillie, Beatrice
1898	Meir, Golda
1899	Le Gallienne, Eva
1900	Elizabeth, Queen Mother
1901	Dark, Eleanor
1901	Dietrich, Marlene
1901	Lawrence, Gertrude
1901	Lehmann, Rosamond
1902	Aylward, Gladys
1902	Cartland, Barbara
1902	Levi-Montalcini, Rita
1902	Markham, Beryl
1902	Myrdal, Alva
1902	Riefenstahl, Leni
1902	Smith, Stevie
1903	Haywood, Eliza
1903	Hepworth, Barbara
1903	Lonsdale, Kathleen
1903	Nin, Anaïs
1903	Robinson, Joan Violet
1903	Yourcenar, Marguerite
1904	Allingham, Margery
1904	Danilova, Alexandra
1904	Gonzáles, Luisa
1904	Taglioni, Maria
1905	Ashton-Warner, Sylvia
1905	Garbo, Greta
1905	Rand, Ayn
1906	Arendt, Hannah
1906	Goeppert-Mayer, Maria
1906	Lutyens, Elizabeth
1906	Williams, Grace
1907	Ashcroft, Peggy
1907	Du Maurier, Daphne
1907	Kahlo, Frida
1907	Lindgren, Astrid
1908	Beauvoir, Simone de
1908	Rankin, Annabelle
1908	Robertson, Jeannie
1909	Batten, Jean
1909	Juliana of The Netherlands
1909	Mendilow, Myriam
1909	Weil, Simone
1910	Adamson, Joy
1910	Chiang Ch'ing
1910	Markova, Alicia
1910	Shafik, Dori'a

1910	Teresa of Calcutta
1910	Ulanova, Galina
1910	Van Praagh, Peggy
1911	Bourgeois, Louise
1911	Castle, Barbara
1912	Glanville-Hicks, Peggy
1912	Henie, Sonia
1912	Reitsch, Hanna
1913	Leakey, Mary Nicol
1913	Leigh, Vivien
1913	Pym, Barbara
1914	Duras, Marguerite
1914	Jansson, Tove
1915	Bergman, Ingrid
1915	Piaf, Edith
1915	Schwartzkopf, Elisabeth
1915	Wright, Judith
1916	Ginzburg, Natalia
1917	Alonso, Alicia
1917	Gandhi, Indira
1917	Suzman, Helen
1918	Saunders, Cicely
1918	Spark, Muriel
1919	Fonteyn, Margot
1919	Lessing, Doris
1919	Murdoch, Iris
1919	Perón, Eva
1920	Franklin, Rosalind
1920	James, Phyliss Dorothy
1921	Eardley, Joan
1921	Kerr, Deborah
1921	Laforet, Carmen
1921	Senesh, Hannah
1921	Signoret, Simone
1922	Sauvé, Jeanne
1922	Tebaldi, Renata
1923	Ángeles, Victoria de los
1923	Gordimer, Nadine
1924	Alegria, Claribel
1925	First, Ruth
1925	Frame, Janet
1925	Lispector, Clarice
1925	Mercouri, Merlina
1925	Plisetskaya, Maya
1925	Thatcher, Margaret
1926	Elizabeth II of England
1926	Laurence, Margaret
1926	Matute, Ana Maria
1926	Sutherland, Joan
1927	Jhabvala, Ruth Prawler
1928	Moreau, Jeanne

1929	Chamorro, Violeta	1939	Drabble, Margaret
1929	Frank, Anne	1939	Seymour, Lynn
1930	Abakanowicz, Magdalena	1939	Sibley, Antoinette
1930	Davies, Emily	1940	Makarova, Natalia
1930	Fallaci, Oriana	1941	Bessmertnova, Natalia
1931	Riley, Bridget	1941	Williams, Betty
1933	Aquino, Corazon	1942	Aidoo, Ama Ata
1933	Baker, Janet	1942	Allende, Isabel
1933	Bowen, Elizabeth	1944	Corrigan, Mairead
1933	Caballé, Montserrat	1944	Emecheta, Buchi
1933	Verdy, Violette	1944	Te Kanawa, Kiri
1934	Goodall, Jane	1945	Du Pré, Jacqueline
1934	Loren, Sophia	1946	Aung San Suu Kyi
1934	Mandela, Winnie	1947	Devlin, Bernadette
1935	Andrews, Julie	1947	Kelly, Petra
1935	Sagan, Françoise	1951	Kain, Karen
1936	Jackson, Glenda	1953	Bhutto, Benazir
1937	Cixous, Hélène	1954	Ratushinskaya, Irina
1937	Head, Bessie	1957	Díaz, Nidia
1938	Mnouchkine, Arianne	1959	Menchú, Rigoberta
1939	Atwood, Margaret		

APPENDIX B: NOTABLE WOMEN BY COUNTRY OF BIRTH

Albania
Teresa of Calcutta

Algeria
Cixous, Hélène

Angola
Nzinga

Arabia
A'isha

Argentina
Ocampo, Victoria
Perón, Eva

Australia
Barnard, Marjorie
Dark, Eleanor
Franklin, Miles
Gilmore, Mary Jane
Glanville-Hicks, Peggy
Goldstein, Vida
Hanson-Dyer, Louise
Kenny, Elizabeth
Lawson, Louisa
Melba, Nellie
Preston, Margaret Rose
Rankin, Annabelle
Richardson, Henry Handel
Scott, Rose
Sutherland, Joan
Ward, Mrs. Humphrey
Wright, Judith

Austria
Adamson, Joy
Baum, Vicki
Ebner-Eschenbach, Marie
Elssler, Fanny
Freud, Anna
Klein, Melanie
Lenya, Lotte
Mahler, Alma
Maria Theresa
Meitner, Lise

Belgium

Peeters, Clara

Yourcenar, Marguerite

Burma

Aung San Suu Kyi

Byzantium

Comnena, Anna

Theodora

Canada

Albani, Emma

Arden, Elizabeth

Atwood, Margaret

Carr, Emily

Hoodless, Adelaide

Kain, Karen

Laurence, Margaret

Lillie, Beatrice

Macphail, Agnes

Montgomery, Lucy Maud

Murphy, Emily

Sauvé, Jeanne

Seymour, Lynn

Chile

Mistral, Gabriela

China

Chiang Ch'ing

Ding Ling

Pan Ch'ao

Tz'u-Hsi

Wu Chao

Costa Rica

Gonzáles, Luisa

Cuba

Alonso, Alicia

Gómez de Avellaneda, Gertrudis

Czech Republic

Suttner, Bertha von

Denmark

Alexandra of Denmark

Dinesen, Isak

Undset, Sigrid

Dominican Republic

Rhys, Jean

Egypt

Cleopatra

Hatshepsut

Nefertiti

Shafik, Dori'a

Sha'rawi, Huda

El Salvador

Díaz, Nidia

England

Aguilar, Grace

Allingham, Margery

Anderson, Elizabeth Garrett

Andrews, Julie

Anne of England

Ashcroft, Peggy

Astell, Mary

Austen, Jane

Aylward, Gladys

Baden-Powell, Olave

Baker, Janet

Baylis, Lilian

Beale, Dorothea

Beaufort, Margaret

Beeton, Isabel

Behn, Aphra

Bell, Gertrude

Besant, Annie

Bishop, Isabella Lucy
Blackwell, Elizabeth
Bodichon, Barbara
Boleyn, Anne
Booth, Catherine
Boudicca
Brittain, Vera
Brontë, Anne
Brontë, Charlotte
Brontë, Emily
Browning, Elizabeth Barrett
Burdett-Coutts, Angela
Burnett, Frances Hodgson
Burney, Fanny
Butler, Josephine
Butt, Clara
Cambridge, Ada
Carpenter, Mary
Cartland, Barbara
Castle, Barbara
Cavell, Edith
Centlivre, Susanna
Chisholm, Caroline
Christie, Agatha
Cibber, Susannah
Compton-Burnett, Ivy
Craik, Dinah
Cunard, Nancy
Davies, Emily
Drabble, Margaret
Du Maurier, Daphne
Du Pré, Jacqueline
Edgeworth, Maria
Eliot, George
Elizabeth I of England
Elizabeth II of England
Elizabeth, Queen Mother
Evans, Edith
Faithfull, Emily
Farjeon, Eleanor
Fawcett, Millicent
Fields, Gracie
Fonteyn, Margot
Franklin, Rosalind
Fry, Elizabeth
Gaskell, Elizabeth
Gonne, Maud
Goodall, Jane
Greenaway, Katherine
Gwyn, Eleanor
Gwynne-Vaughn, Helen

Hall, Radclyffe
Haywood, Eliza
Hepworth, Barbara
Herschel, Caroline
Hess, Myra
Inchbald, Elizabeth
Jackson, Glenda
James, Phyliss Dorothy
Jekyll, Gertrude
Jex-Blake, Sophia
Julian of Norwich
Kemble, Fanny
Kempe, Margery
Kennedy, Margaret
Kingsley, Mary
Knight, Laura
Lawrence, Gertrude
Leakey, Mary Nicol
Le Gallienne, Eva
Lehmann, Rosamond
Lloyd, Marie
Lovelace, Augusta Ada
Lutyens, Elizabeth
Macarthur, Elizabeth
Macaulay, Catherine
Macaulay, Rose
Margaret of York
Markham, Beryl
Markiewicz, Constance
Markova, Alicia
Martineau, Harriet
Mary I
Mary II
Mary, Queen to George V
McMillan, Margaret
Mitchison, Naomi
Moodie, Susannah
More, Hannah
Murdoch, Iris
Nightingale, Florence
Norton, Caroline
Pankhurst, Christabel
Pankhurst, Emmeline
Pankhurst, Sylvia
Paterson, Emma
Pechey-Phipson, Edith
Potter, Beatrix
Pym, Barbara
Radcliffe, Ann
Rathbone, Eleanor
Reibey, Mary

Riley, Bridget
Robinson, Joan Violet
Rossetti, Christina
Royden, Maude
Rutherford, Margaret
Sackville-West, Vita
Saunders, Cicely
Sayers, Dorothy
Sewell, Anna
Shelley, Mary
Sheppard, Kate
Sibley, Antoinette
Siddons, Sarah
Sitwell, Edith
Smith, Charlotte
Smith, Stevie
Smyth, Ethel
Spark, Muriel
Stanhope, Hester Lucy

Stocks, Mary
Terry, Ellen
Teyte, Maggie
Thatcher, Margaret
Thorndike, Sybil
Tilley, Vesta
Trollope, Frances
Turner, Ethel
Underhill, Evelyn
Uttley, Alison
Van Praagh, Peggy
Vestris, Lucia
Victoria of Englad
Warwick, Daisy
Webb, Beatrice
Wilkinson, Ellen
Wollstonecraft, Mary
Woolf, Virginia
Wright, Helena

Fiji

Prichard, Katharine

Finland

Jansson, Tove

France

Armand, Inesse
Beauvoir, Simone de
Bernadette
Bernhardt, Sarah
Bonheur, Rosa
Boulanger, Lili
Boulanger, Nadia
Bourgeois, Louise
Chaminade, Cécile
Chanel, Coco
Chantal, Jeanne-Françoise de
Claudel, Camille
Colet, Louise
Colette
David-Neel, Alexandra
Deffand, Marie du
Eleanor of Aquitaine
Farrenc, Jeanne-Louise
Guyon, Jeanne Marie
Héloïse
Joan of Arc
Labé, Louise
La Fayette, Madame de
Lecouvreur, Adrienne
Long, Marguerite
Maintenon, Françoise de

Margaret of Valois
Marguerite of Navarre
Marie Antoinette
Michel, Louise
Mistinguett
Mnouchkine, Arianne
Moreau, Jeanne
Morisot, Berthe
Nin, Anaïs
Piaf, Edith
Pompadour, Madame de
Récamier, Jeanne
Sagan, Françoise
Sand, George
Scudéry, Madeleine de
Sévigné, Marie de
Signoret, Simone
Staël, Anne Louise de
Stark, Freya
Tailleferre, Germaine
Thérèse of Liseux
Tristan, Flora
Tussaud, Marie
Valadon, Suzanne
Verdy, Violette
Vigée-Lebrun, Élisabeth

Vionnet, Madeleine

Weil, Simone

Germany
Alexandra of Russia
Arendt, Hannah
Arnim, Bettina von
Braun, Lily
Catherine II of Russia
Deutsch, Helene
Dietrich, Marlene
Droste-Hülshoff, Annette von
Gertrude of Helfta
Hensel, Fanny Mendelssohn
Hildegard of Bingen
Horney, Karen
Jhabvala, Ruth Prawler
Kelly, Petra
Kollwitz, Käthe
Lasker-Schüler, Else

Lehmann, Lotte
Lewald, Fanny
Mechtild of Magdeburg
Modersohn-Becker, Paula
Noether, Emmy
Reitsch, Hanna
Riefenstahl, Leni
Sachs, Nelly
Schumann, Clara
Schumann, Elisabeth
Sophia of Hanover
Stein, Edith
Wagner, Cosima
Wigman, Mary
Zetkin, Clara

Ghana
Aidoo, Ama Ata

Greece
Aspasia

Mercouri, Melina

Guatemala
Menchú, Rigoberta

Hungary
Elizabeth of Hungary
Margaret of Scotland

Senesh, Hannah

India
Inglis, Elsie Maud
Cameron, Julia Margaret
Gandhi, Indira
Leigh, Vivien

Naidu, Sarojini
Nur Jahan
Street, Jessie

Indochina (Vietnam)
Duras, Marguerite

Ireland
Bates, Daisy
Bowen, Elizabeth
Corrigan, Mairead
Crawford, Isabella
De Valois, Ninette
Devlin, Bernadette
Gray, Eileen
Gregory, Augusta
Jameson, Anna

Lonsdale, Kathleen
McAuley, Catherine
Morgan, Sydney
Sheehy-Skeffington, Hannah
Sheridan, Clare
West, Rebecca
Williams, Betty
Woffington, Peg

Italy
Borgia, Lucrezia
Cabrini, Francesca Xavier
Catherine of Siena

Cerrito, Fanny
Clare of Assisi
Colonna, Vittoria

Deledda, Gracia
De Pisan, Christine
Duse, Eleanora
Fallaci, Oriana
Franco, Veronica
Galli-Curci, Amelita
Gentileschi, Artemisia
Ginzburg, Natalia
Levi-Montalcini, Rita

Loren, Sophia
Medici, Catherine de
Montessori, Maria
Schiaparelli, Elsa
Stampa, Gaspara
Tebaldi, Renata
Tetrazzini, Louisa
Zucchi, Virginia

Jamaica
Seacole, Mary

Williams, Cicely

Japan
Ichiyo, Higuchi

Shikibu, Murasaki

Lithuania
Goldman, Emma

Martinique
Bonaparte, Josephine

Mexico
Castellanos, Rosario
Cruz, Juana Inés de la

Kahlo, Frida

The Netherlands
Charriere, Isabelle de
Frank, Anne

Juliana of The Netherlands
Leyster, Judith

New Zealand
Ashton-Warner, Sylvia
Batten, Jean
Frame, Janet
Hodgkins, Frances

Mansfield, Katherine
Te Kanawa, Kiri
Te Puea, Herangi

Nicaragua
Alegria, Claribel

Chamorro, Violeta

Nigeria
Emecheta, Buchi

Norway
Flagstad, Kirsten
Henie, Sonia

Sandel, Cora

Pakistan
Bhutto, Benazir

Palestine (Israel)
Berenice

Mendilow, Myriam

Peru
Allende, Isabel

The Philippines
Aquino, Corazon

Poland
Abakanowicz, Magdalena
Curie, Marie
Dabrowska, Maria

Goeppert-Mayer, Maria
Jadwiga of Poland
Luxemburg, Rosa

Modjeska, Helena
Rambert, Marie

Rhodesia (Zimbabwe)
Lessing, Doris

Russia
Akhmatova, Anna
Andreas-Salomé, Lou
Bessmertnova, Natalia
Blavatsky, Helena
Danilova, Alexandra
Elizabeth of Russia
Karsavina, Tamara
Knipper-Chehkova, Olga
Kollontai, Alexandra
Kovalevskaya, Sofya
Kuliscioff, Anna
Lopokova, Lydia

Scotland
Atholl, Katherine
Baillie, Joanna
Despard, Charlotte
Eardley, Joan
Ferrier, Susan
Garden, Mary
Kerr, Deborah
King, Jessie
MacDonald, Flora

South Africa
First, Ruth
Gordimer, Nadine
Head, Bessie

Spain
Ángeles, Victoria de los
Anne of Austria
Blanche of Castile
Caballé, Montserrat
Castro, Rosalía de
Catherine of Aragon
Eleanor of Castile

Sweden
Bergman, Ingrid
Birgitta
Bremer, Fredrika
Christina
Garbo, Greta
Lagerlöf, Selma

Schwartzkopf, Elisabeth

Makarova, Natalia
Meir, Golda
Nijinska, Bronislava
Pavlova, Anna
Plisetskaya, Maya
Popova, Liubov
Rand, Ayn
Ratushinskaya, Irina
Sophia of Russia
Ulanova, Galina
Zasulich, Vera

Mary, Queen of Scots
Oliphant, Margaret
Redpath, Anne
Robertson, Jeannie
Slessor, Mary
Somerville, Mary
Spence, Catherine
Stopes, Marie

Mandela, Winnie
Schreiner, Olive
Suzman, Helen

Isabella of Spain
Laforet, Carmen
Malibran, Marie
Matute, Ana Maria
Pardo Bazán, Emilia
Patti, Adelina
Teresa of Ávila

Lind, Jenny
Lindgren, Astrid
Myrdal, Alva
Ottesen-Jensen, Elise
Södergran, Edith
Taglioni, Maria

Switzerland
Eberhardt, Isabelle   Rachel
Kauffmann, Angelica   Storni, Alfonsina

Turkey
Adivar, Halide Ebid

Ukraine
Delaunay, Sonia   Lispector, Clarice
Karinska, Barbara   Ukrainka, Lesya

Uruguay
Agustini, Delmira

Venezuela
Carreño, Teresa   Parra, Teresa de la

Wales
John, Gwen   Williams, Grace
Rhondda, Margaret

APPENDIX C: NOTABLE WOMEN BY TITLE, OCCUPATION, OR MAIN AREA OF INTEREST

Activist (Feminist, Political, or Social)

Adivar, Halide Edib
Aung San Suu Kyi
Beaufort, Margaret
Besant, Annie
Bodichon, Barbara
Braun, Lily
Brittain, Vera
Butler, Josephine
Corrigan, Mairead
Cunard, Nancy
Davies, Emily
Despard, Charlotte
Fawcett, Millicent
Fry, Elizabeth
Goldstein, Vida
Gonzáles, Luisa
Hoodless, Adelaide
Kuliscioff, Anna
Lawson, Louisa
Mandela, Winnie
Menchú, Rigoberta
Mendilow, Myriam
Naidu, Sarojini
Ottesen-Jensen, Elise
Pankhurst, Christabel
Pankhurst, Emmeline
Pankhurst, Sylvia
Paterson, Emma
Rhondda, Margaret
Royden, Maude
Schreiner, Olive
Scott, Rose
Shafik, Dori'a
Sha'rawi, Huda
Sheppard, Kate
Spence, Catherine
Stocks, Mary
Stopes, Marie
Street, Jessie
Suttner, Bertha von
Te Puea, Herangi
Tristan, Flora
Warwick, Daisy
Webb, Beatrice
Weil, Simone
Williams, Betty
Zetkin, Clara

Actor

Andrews, Julie
Ashcroft, Peggy
Bergman, Ingrid
Bernhardt, Sarah
Centlivre, Susanna
Cibber, Susannah
Dietrich, Marlene
Duse, Eleanora
Evans, Edith
Garbo, Greta
Gwyn, Eleanor
Henie, Sonia
Inchbald, Elizabeth
Jackson, Glenda
Jordan, Dorothy
Kemble, Fanny
Kerr, Deborah
Knipper-Chehkova, Olga

Lawrence, Gertrude
Lecouvreur, Adrienne
Le Gallienne, Eva
Leigh, Vivien
Loren, Sophia
Mercouri, Melina
Modjeska, Helena
Moreau, Jeanne
Rachel
Riefenstahl, Leni
Rutherford, Margaret
Siddons, Sarah
Signoret, Simone
Terry, Ellen
Thorndike, Sybil
Vestris, Lucia
Woffington, Peg

Anthropologist

Bates, Daisy

Kingsley, Mary

Archaeologist

Leakey, Mary Nicol

Architect

Gray, Eileen

Artist

Adamson, Joy
Bonheur, Rosa
Carr, Emily
Delaunay, Sonia
Eardley, Joan
Gentileschi, Artemisia
Greenaway, Katherine
Hodgkins, Frances
John, Gwen
Kahlo, Frida
Kauffmann, Angelica
King, Jessie
Knight, Laura

Kollwitz, Käthe
Leyster, Judith
Modersohn-Becker, Paula
Morisot, Berthe
Peeters, Clara
Popova, Liubov
Potter, Beatrix
Preston, Margaret Rose
Redpath, Anne
Riley, Bridget
Tussaud, Marie
Valadon, Suzanne
Vigée-Lebrun, Élisabeth

Aviator

Batten, Jean
Markham, Beryl

Reitsch, Hanna

Ballerina

Alonso, Alicia

Bessmertnova, Natalia

Cerrito, Fanny
Danilova, Alexandra
De Valois, Ninette
Elssler, Fanny
Fonteyn, Margot
Kain, Karen
Karsavina, Tamara
Lopokova, Lydia
Makarova, Natalia
Markova, Alicia

Pavlova, Anna
Plisetskaya, Maya
Seymour, Lynn
Sibley, Antoinette
Taglioni, Maria
Ulanova, Galina
Van Praagh, Peggy
Verdy, Violette
Zucchi, Virginia

Ballet Director

Verdy, Violette

Ballet Producer

Van Praagh, Peggy

Businesswoman

Arden, Elizabeth
Cunard, Nancy
Faithfull, Emily
Hanson-Dyer, Louise

Macarthur, Elizabeth
Reibey, Mary
Seacole, Mary

Choreographer

Cerrito, Fanny
De Valois, Ninette
Nijinska, Bronislava

Rambert, Marie
Wigman, Mary

Composer

Boulanger, Lili
Carreño, Teresa
Chaminade, Cécile
Farrenc, Jeanne-Louise
Glanville-Hicks, Peggy
Hensel, Fanny Mendelssohn

Lutyens, Elizabeth
Schumann, Clara
Smyth, Ethel
Tailleferre, Germaine
Williams, Grace

Conductor

Carreño, Teresa

Consort

A'isha
Alexandra of Denmark
Aspasia
Berenice
Elizabeth, Queen Mother

Maintenon, Françoise de
Margaret of Valois
Margaret of York
Mary, Queen to George V

Costume Designer

Karinska, Barbara

Couturier

Chanel, Coco

Schiaparelli, Elsa

Vionnet, Madeleine

Dancer. *See* **Ballerina**

Diplomat

Myrdal, Alva

Educator

Ashton-Warner, Sylvia
Beale, Dorothea
Bodichon, Barbara

Boulanger, Nadia
Carpenter, Mary
Davies, Emily

Empress

Alexandra of Russia
Bonaparte, Josephine
Elizabeth of Russia
Maria Theresa

Nur Jahan
Theodora
Tz'u-Hsi
Wu Chao

Entertainer

Fields, Gracie
Lenya, Lotte
Lillie, Beatrice
Lloyd, Marie

Mistinguett
Piaf, Edith
Robertson, Jeannie
Tilley, Vesta

Evangelist

Booth, Catherine

Filmmaker

Duras, Marguerite

Riefenstahl, Leni

Horticulturalist

Jekyll, Gertrude

Ice-Skater

Henie, Sonia

Intellectual

Cixous, Hélène
Deffand, Marie du
Héloïse
Marguerite of Navarre

Martineau, Harriet
Pompadour, Madame de
Récamier, Jeanne
Staël, Anne Louise de

Instrumentalist

Boulanger, Nadia
Carreño, Teresa
Chaminade, Cécile
Du Pré, Jacqueline
Farrenc, Jeanne-Louise
Hensel, Fanny Mendelssohn

Hess, Myra
Long, Marguerite
Mahler, Alma
Schumann, Clara
Wagner, Cosima

Journalist

Gonzáles, Luisa

Sauvé, Jeanne

Lawyer

Murphy, Emily

Pankhurst, Christabel

Martyr

Joan of Arc

Mathematician

Kovalevskaya, Sofya
Lovelace, Augusta Ada
Meitner, Lise

Noether, Emmy
Somerville, Mary

Missionary

Aylward, Gladys
Slessor, Mary

Teresa of Calcutta

Mystic

Gertrude of Helfta
Hildegard of Bingen
Julian of Norwich

Kempe, Margery
Mechtild of Magdeburg
Underhill, Evelyn

Naturalist

Adamson, Joy

Nurse

Cavell, Edith
Kenny, Elizabeth
Nightingale, Florence

Saunders, Cicely
Seacole, Mary

Opera Singer

Albani, Emma
Ángeles, Victoria de los
Baker, Janet
Butt, Clara
Caballé, Montserrat
Cibber, Susannah
Flagstad, Kirsten
Galli-Curci, Amelita
Garden, Mary
Lehmann, Lotte
Lind, Jenny

Malibran, Marie
Melba, Nellie
Patti, Adelina
Schumann, Elisabeth
Schwartzkopf, Elisabeth
Sutherland, Joan
Tebaldi, Renata
Te Kanawa, Kiri
Tetrazzini, Louisa
Teyte, Maggie

Patron

Beaufort, Margaret

Borgia, Lucrezia

Philanthropist

Baden-Powell, Olave
Burdett-Coutts, Angela

Chisholm, Caroline

Philosopher

Arendt, Hannah
Beauvoir, Simone de

Blavatsky, Helena
Weil, Simone

Photographer

Cameron, Julia Margaret

Physician

Anderson, Elizabeth Garrett
Blackwell, Elizabeth
Inglis, Elsie Maud
Jex-Blake, Sophia

Montessori, Maria
Pechey-Phipson, Edith
Williams, Cicely
Wright, Helena

Playwright

Baillie, Joanna
Behn, Aphra
Centlivre, Susanna
Gómez de Avellaneda, Gertrudis

Haywood, Eliza
Inchbald, Elizabeth
Ukrainka, Lesya

Poet

Agustini, Delmira
Akhmatova, Anna
Alegria, Claribel
Browning, Elizabeth Barrett
Castro, Rosalía de
Colet, Louise
Colonna, Vittoria
Crawford, Isabella
Cruz, Juana Inés de la
De Pisan, Christine
Droste-Hülshoff, Annette von
Franco, Veronica
Gilmore, Mary Jane
Gómez de Avellaneda, Gertrudis
Ichiyo, Higuchi

Labé, Louise
Lasker-Schüler, Else
Mistral, Gabriela
Naidu, Sarojini
Ratushinskaya, Irina
Rossetti, Christina
Sachs, Nelly
Sitwell, Edith
Smith, Charlotte
Smith, Stevie
Södergran, Edith
Stampa, Gaspara
Storni, Alfonsina
Ukrainka, Lesya
Wright, Judith

Politician

Adivar, Halide
Aquino, Corazon
Atholl, Katherine
Bhutto, Benazir
Castle, Barbara
Chamorro, Violeta

Devlin, Bernadette
Gandhi, Indira
Kelly, Petra
Macphail, Agnes
Meir, Golda
Mercouri, Melina

Perón, Eva
Rankin, Annabelle
Rathbone, Eleanor
Sauvé, Jeanne

Suzman, Helen
Thatcher, Margaret
Wilkinson, Ellen

Psychoanalyst

Andreas-Salomé, Lou
Deutsch, Helene
Freud, Anna

Horney, Karen
Klein, Melanie

Queen

Anne of Austria
Anne of England
Blanche of Castile
Boleyn, Anne
Boudicca
Catherine of Aragon
Catherine II of Russia
Christina
Cleopatra
Eleanor of Aquitaine
Elizabeth I of England
Elizabeth II of England
Hatshepsut

Isabella of Spain
Jadwiga of Poland
Juliana of The Netherlands
Margaret of Scotland
Marie Antoinette
Mary, Queen of Scots
Mary I of England
Mary II of England
Medici, Catherine de
Nefertiti
Nzinga
Victoria of England

Regent

Sophia of Russia

Anne of Austria

Religious

Bernadette
Birgitta
Cabrini, Francesca Xavier
Catherine of Siena
Chantal, Jeanne-Françoise de
Clare of Assisi

Elizabeth of Hungary
McAuley, Catherine
Stein, Edith
Teresa of Ávila
Teresa of Calcutta
Thérèse of Lisieux

Revolutionary

Armand, Inesse
Chiang Ch'ing
Díaz, Nidia
First, Ruth
Goldman, Emma
Gonne, Maud
Kollontai, Alexandra

Luxemburg, Rosa
MacDonald, Flora
Michel, Louise
Senesh, Hannah
Sheehy-Skeffington, Hannah
Zasulich, Vera

Scholar

Astell, Mary
Bell, Gertrude
Braun, Lily
Cixous, Hélène

Comnena, Anna
Cruz, Juana Inés de la
De Pisan, Christine
Héloïse

Macaulay, Catherine   Sophia of Hanover
Pan Ch'ao   Stocks, Mary
Robinson, Joan Violet

Scientist

Curie, Marie   Herschel, Caroline
Franklin, Rosalind   Levi-Montalcini, Rita
Goeppert-Mayer, Maria   Lonsdale, Kathleen
Goodall, Jane   Meitner, Lise
Gwynne-Vaughn, Helen   Stopes, Marie

Sculptor

Abakanowicz, Magdalena   Hepworth, Barbara
Bourgeois, Louise   Kollwitz, Käthe
Claudel, Camille   Sheridan, Clare

Theater Manager

Baylis, Lilian   Mnouchkine, Arianne
Le Gallienne, Eva   Vestris, Lucia

Traveler

Bishop, Isabella Lucy   Stanhope, Hester Lucy
David-Neel, Alexandra   Stark, Freya
Eberhardt, Isabelle

Writer

Adamson, Joy   Brontë, Anne
Adivar, Halide Edib   Brontë, Charlotte
Aguilar, Grace   Brontë, Emily
Aidoo, Ama Ata   Burnett, Frances Hodgson
Allende, Isabel   Burney, Fanny
Allingham, Margery   Cambridge, Ada
Andreas-Salomé, Lou   Cartland, Barbara
Arendt, Hannah   Castellanos, Rosario
Arnim, Bettina von   Charriere, Isabelle de
Ashton-Warner, Sylvia   Christie, Agatha
Astell, Mary   Colet, Louise
Atwood, Margaret   Colette
Austen, Jane   Compton-Burnett, Ivy
Barnard, Marjorie   Craik, Dinah
Bates, Daisy   Dabrowska, Maria
Baum, Vicki   Dark, Eleanor
Beauvoir, Simone de   David-Neel, Alexandra
Beeton, Isabel   Deledda, Grazia
Behn, Aphra   Dinesen, Karen
Bell, Gertrude   Ding Ling
Bishop, Isabella Lucy   Drabble, Margaret
Blavatsky, Helena   Du Maurier, Daphne
Bowen, Elizabeth   Duras, Marguerite
Bremer, Fredrika   Eberhardt, Isabelle
Brittain, Vera   Ebner-Eschenbach, Marie

Edgeworth, Maria
Eliot, George
Emecheta, Buchi
Fallaci, Oriana
Farjeon, Eleanor
Ferrier, Susan
First, Ruth
Frame, Janet
Frank, Anne
Franklin, Miles
Gaskell, Elizabeth
Ginzburg, Natalia
Gordimer, Nadine
Gregory, Augusta
Guyon, Jeanne Marie
Hall, Radclyffe
Head, Bessie
Ichiyo, Higuchi
James, Phyliss Dorothy
Jameson, Anna
Jansson, Tove
Kennedy, Margaret
La Fayette, Madame de
Laforet, Carmen
Lagerlöf, Selma
Laurence, Margaret
Lawson, Louisa
Lehmann, Rosamond
Lessing, Doris
Lewald, Fanny
Lindgren, Astrid
Lispector, Clarice
Macaulay, Rose
Mansfield, Katherine
Marguerite of Navarre
Martineau, Harriet
Matute, Ana Maria
McMillan, Margaret
Mitchison, Naomi
Montgomery, Lucy Maud
Moodie, Susannah
More, Hannah
Morgan, Sydney
Murdoch, Iris
Nin, Anaïs
Norton, Caroline

Ocampo, Victoria
Oliphant, Margaret
Pan Ch'ao
Pardo Bazán, Emilia
Parra, Teresa de la
Potter, Beatrix
Prichard, Katharine
Pym, Barbara
Radcliffe, Ann
Rand, Ayn
Rhondda, Margaret
Rhys, Jean
Richardson, Henry Handel
Sagan, Françoise
Sand, George
Sandel, Cora
Sayers, Dorothy
Schreiner, Olive
Scudéry, Madeleine de
Sévigné, Marie de
Sewell, Anna
Shelley, Mary
Sheridan, Clare
Shikibu, Murasaki
Sitwell, Edith
Smith, Charlotte
Spark, Muriel
Spence, Catherine
Stark, Freya
Street, Jessie
Suttner, Bertha von
Tristan, Flora
Trollope, Frances
Turner, Ethel
Undset, Sigrid
Uttley, Alison
Ward, Mrs. Humphrey
Warwick, Daisy
Webb, Beatrice
Weil, Simone
West, Rebecca
Wollstonecraft, Mary
Woolf, Virginia
Yourcenar, Marguerite

INDEX

About the Author

LYNDA G. ADAMSON is Professor of Literature and Chair of the Writing Department at Prince George's Community College in Maryland. She is also author of *Recreating the Past: A Guide to American and World Historical Fiction for Children and Young Adults* (Greenwood, 1994), *A Reference Guide to Historical Fiction for Children and Young Adults* (Greenwood, 1987), *Literature Connections to American History, K–6* (1998), *Literature Connections to American History, 7–12* (1998), *Literature Connections to World History, K–6* (1998), and *Literature Connections to World History, 7–12* (1998).